First in a Series of Collecting Handbooks

First in a Series of Collecting Handbooks

Published by the
National Rifle Association of America
Washington, D.C.

NRA BOOKS — Bill Askins, *Director;* Ted Bryant, *Editor;* Mike Fay, *Production Chief;*
Betty Bauser, *Art Director;* Cover photo by *Randy Lamson.*

Library of Congress Catalog Card Number 81-80476.
Published June 1981.
ISBN 0-935998-38-1
Printed in the United States of America

A Division of NRA Publications
George Martin, Executive Director

Contents:

AMERICAN HANDGUNS BY TYPE

AMERICAN HANDGUNS & THEIR MAKERS

IDENTIFICATION & DESCRIPTION

Introduction

Handguns are infinitely appealing to Americans. Tools of the frontier, precision sporting pieces of today, pistols and revolvers are assured a place in American folk lore and the contemporary scene. The *AMERICAN RIFLEMAN* has acknowledged this passion of ours for one-handed firearms by a plethora of articles over the years on every phase of their development, design and history. You will find in the following pages a fine resume of handguns in America, articles on their use, manufacture, as well as a look at the men behind the guns. From the fine flintlocks of the Revolution to the wheelguns of the Frontier, to the automatics of the Great War, there are succinct, accurate, technical, yet entertaining, treatises for your education by the leading authorities of our time.

AMERICAN HANDGUNS AND THEIR MAKERS is the first in a series of manuals that the Book Service shall produce on gun collecting and the history of firearms manufacturing. Other titles to appear in the near future will be works on American rifles and automatic pistols. A particular note of thanks to J. B. Roberts, Jr., Research Editor, and Ted Bryant, Book Editor, for their efforts in putting this book together. I believe you shall find it a valuable reference work and entertaining to boot!

Bill Askins

Bill Askins
Director
NRA Book Service

AMERICAN HANDGUNS BY TYPE

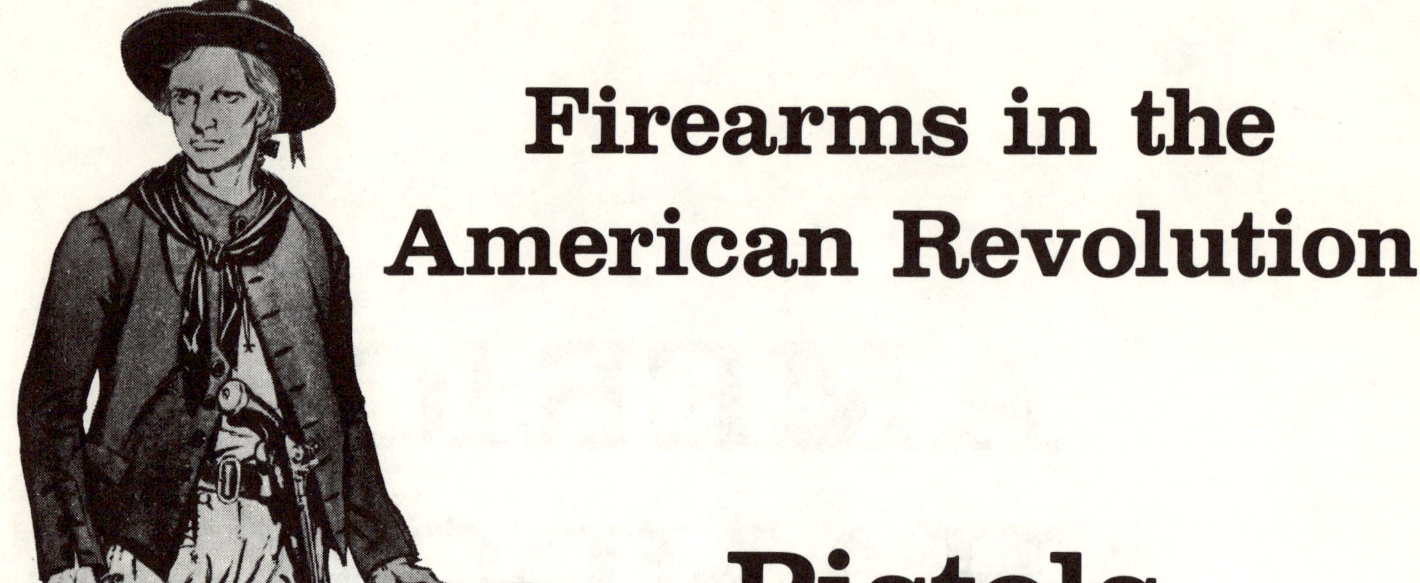

Firearms in the American Revolution

Pistols

American seaman armed with a long naval pistol, held to his waist belt by a belt hook on left side of pistol, and a straight-bladed English style cutlass. (Drawing by George C. Woodbridge.)

MANY heroic poses in 18th century illustrations include one or more pistols thrust into the waist belt or saddle holsters. In reality, however, these short weapons—being almost entirely smoothbores of limited accuracy—were seldom fired except at extremely close range. Nevertheless, they were standard armament for mounted and naval personnel, and many foot soldiers also appear to have carried them.

Most specimens of the American Revolutionary period can be considered in 4 general groupings: horseman or dragoon pistols, holster or officer types, sea service, and civilian patterns.

The usual British and German dragoon handgun prior to the U. S. War for Independence had a smoothbore barrel of at least 12″ fastened to the stock by pins (like the Brown Bess musket) and fitted with brass mountings. When England's reverses at the hands of the French and Indians in the 1750's led to creation of light infantry companies, some light dragoon units were also introduced. Included in the warrants for these new mounted troops were specifications for shorter pistols. A 10″ barrel was ordered in 1756, and a 9″ length in 1759. This 9″ version prevailed as the standard British light dragoon weapon during the American Revolution. It was generally carried in pairs in leather holsters forward of the saddle. Patterns have been found with both carbine (cal. .65) and pistol (cal. .56) bore sizes.

Most German and Dutch patterns also followed the trend toward shorter barrels as the century progressed, but still exceeded 9″ in the 1770's. It is interesting to note that many of the early long styles are discovered today with their barrels cut back to 8″ or 9″.

The French cavalry model of 1733 resembled the English dragoon pistol of the period, with a 12″ pinned barrel and brass mountings (or furniture). By 1766, however, it had become more like their muskets and acquired iron furniture, a double-strapped barrel band, plus a 9″ barrel. In 1777 a completely new styling emerged. The lock and iron rammer were held by a central brass housing which also secured the breech of a tapering 7½″ barrel. Standard bore size for French military pistols at this time was cal. .67 (muskets were cal. .69).

Pistols produced in America normally copied European styling. Walnut was the most common choice for stocks both here and abroad, while fruit woods (e.g., cherry and apple) or striped maple were also popular with local American gunsmiths.

The term holster pistols refers mainly to the type carried by infantry officers,

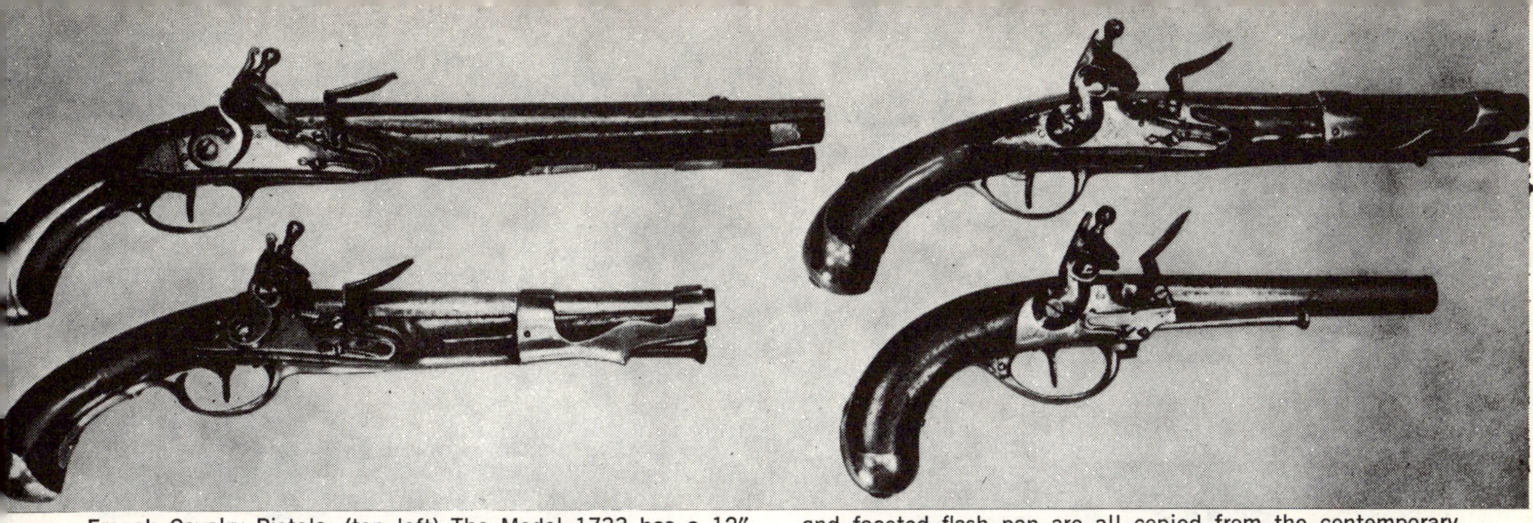

French Cavalry Pistols: (top left) The Model 1733 has a 12" pinned barrel (octagonal at the base). (Bottom left) The Model 1766 was the most common among those supplied to the colonists. The 9" barrel is secured by a double-strapped band. (The Model 1763 had a 12" barrel.) The furniture, usually iron, includes a birds-head butt cap. The trigger guard, side plate, and the flat bevel-edged lock with its reinforced cock and faceted flash pan are all copied from the contemporary musket; (top right) Model 1773 retains the previous pattern, but with a rounded lock, flash pan, and cock typical of the early 1770's. "76" on the barrel indicates proofing in 1776; (bottom right) Model 1777 introduced a radical design later copied for the U.S. North and Cheney pattern. Its barrel measures 7½". The standard French pistol bore was cal. .67.

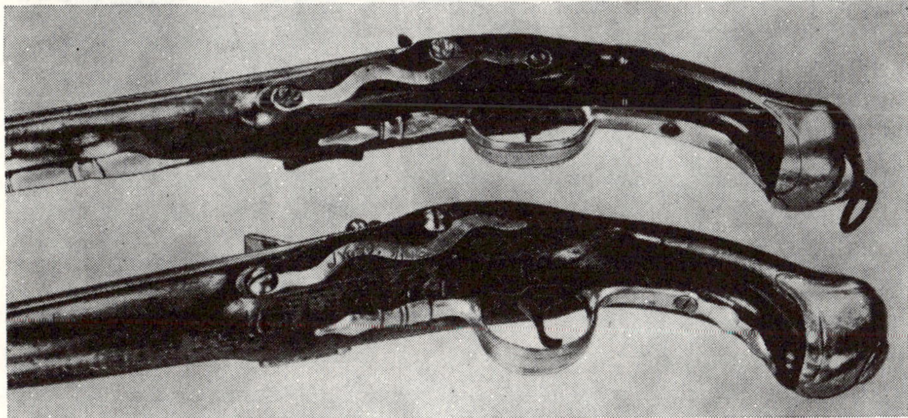

◀ Hessian Pistol Furniture: (top) c.1750-1765 mountings resemble the contemporary Prussian musket pattern—including the blunt end trigger guard and flat wavy side plate (held by 3 screws); (bottom) c.1770-1790 later model retains the earlier trigger guard, but has eliminated the rear side plate screw and butt cap sidestraps. Incised outlines have been added to the traditional raised carving on the stock.

Hessian Dragoon Pistols: c.1750-1765 long German type was used extensively in central Europe and Scandinavia. It has heavy brass furniture, a 14½" barrel (cal. .68), and raised stock carving. Total length is 22½"; the weight is 3.2 lbs. (center) c.1770-1790 German style uses a shorter barrel (11⅝"; cal. .69). It also omits the rammer channel. (bottom) c.1760-1775 variation was probably made in the Low Countries (note the flat sided butt cap). The barrel measures 12¾" (cal. .69).

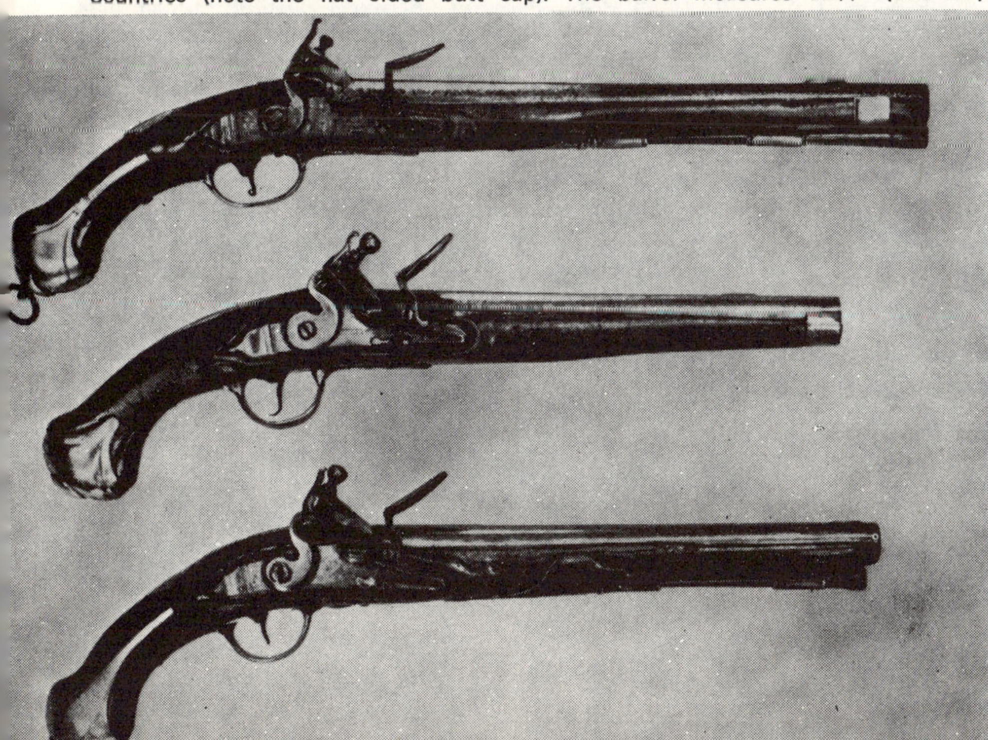

many of whom were mounted. They were usually lighter and shorter than those of the cavalry. Since handgun patterns were seldom specified for commissioned ranks, most officers had them produced by private gunsmiths who stylized the weapons (usually in pairs) for each customer. Fine metals such as silver and gold were often used in the mountings, and basic patterns generally followed the contemporary cavalry pistol. Their bore sizes varied.

An exception to the above was America's Kentucky pistol which was developed with a rifled barrel by Pennsylvania gunsmiths. Although extremely accurate as a handgun, the type was made primarily for officers and only in small numbers—probably limited by the abundant and cheaper imported European smoothbores.

The only infantry who were regularly issued pistols were the Scottish regiments. They carried a unique hand weapon of all metal construction—with either a kidney- or ramshorn-shaped butt. Although an order was issued to Scottish units on Staten Island

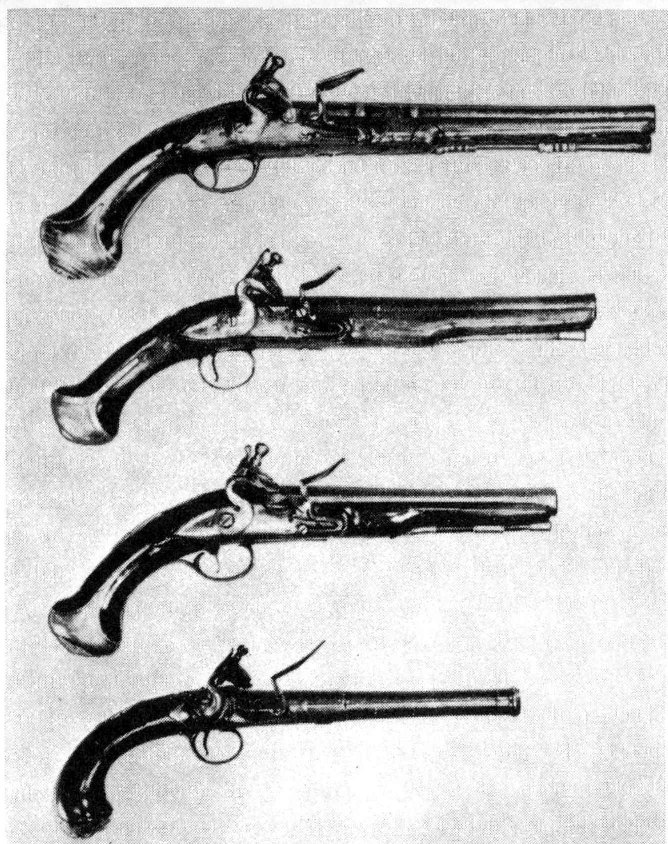

British Holster Pistols: (top) c.1720-1730 officer's silver mounted pistol includes a 10¼″ barrel (cal. .68), raised stock carving, a grotesque mask butt plate, and early ribbed rammer pipes. The lock is marked "Wilson"; (second) c.1730-1750 specimen has a shorter barrel (9″; cal. .68), brass furniture and a plain butt cap. The lock is marked "R. Farmer."; (third) c.1750-1770 hand gun mounts a 7¾″ barrel (cal. .62). Smooth pipes now hold the brass-tipped wood ramrod; (bottom) c.1750-1760 screw-barrel civilian type has a typical silver grotesque mask butt cap. The 5¾″ (cal. .58) barrel unscrews just forward of the breech housing. It is marked "TR" for the maker, T. Richards.

American Holster Pistols: (top) c.1770-1783 American made pistol lacks the balanced proportions of European models. The barrel is 7⅜″ long (cal. .56). Furniture is brass. The stock is cherry wood; (center) c.1760-1780 example combines a British lock (marked "Barbar") and butt cap (brass mask design) with a heavy walled 8″ barrel (cal. .69); (bottom) This crude specimen, c.1775-1785, copies Britain's light dragoon butt cap and trigger guard. Its 9⅛″ barrel is cal. .70.

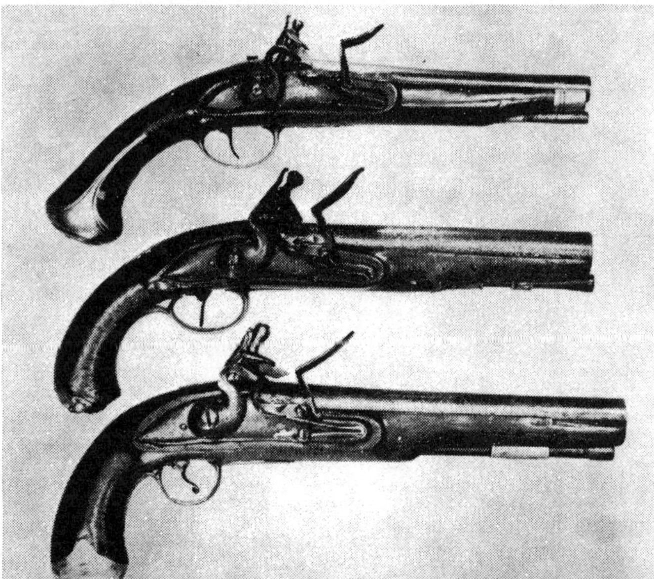

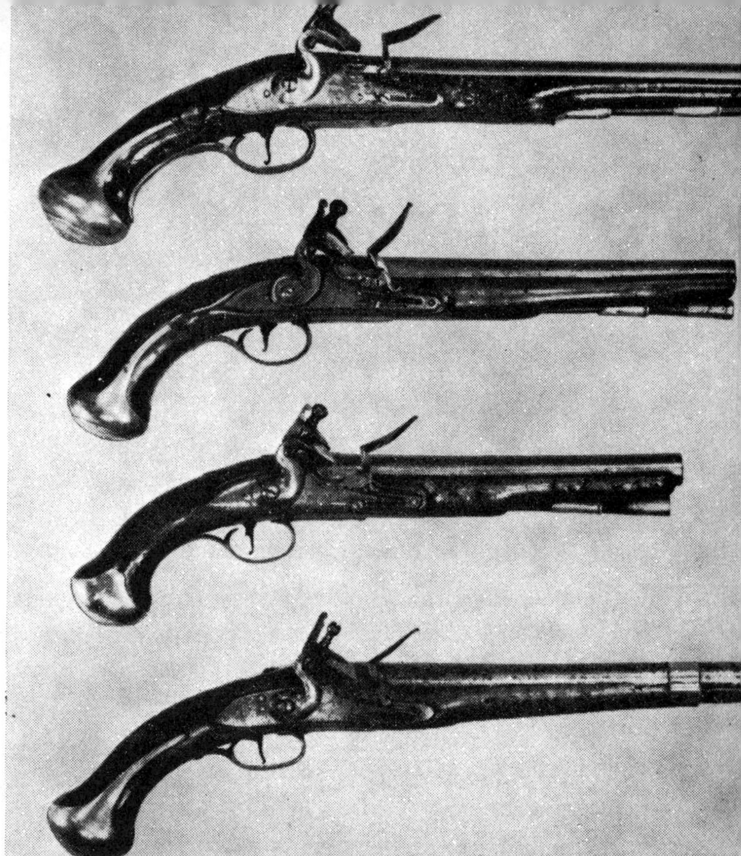

Horseman Pistols: (top) c.1730-1760 typical British dragoon pistol with a 12″ round barrel and brass 1st Model Brown Bess fittings. The lock is marked "Jordan 1744." pistol weighs 2.9 lbs.; full length is 19½″; (second) English 10″ barreled (cal. .65) light dragoon pistol, Model 1756. Note the flat lockplate and cock; (third) Britain's light dragoon pistol authorized in 1759 and used throughout the American Revolution. Barrel is 9″ (cal. .65). The butt cap's side straps have been eliminated. A new flat "S"-shaped side plate appears. The rounded lockplate is marked "Grice 1760"; (bottom) American horseman pistol c.1760-1780 mounts a salvaged British barrel (12″) on a stock which has no rammer channel. Its brass furniture copies the English dragoon pattern.

Horseman Pistol Furniture: (top) c.1759-1780 British light dragoon pistol (9″ barrel) has a brass butt cap without side straps, a flat "S" type side plate, and a pointed trigger guard; (bottom) c.1766 French cavalry model includes a side plate and trigger guard like the contemporary musket, plus a simple birds-head butt cap.

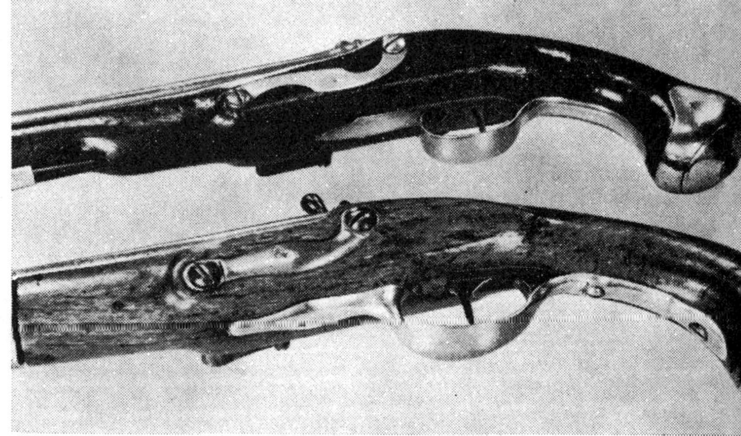

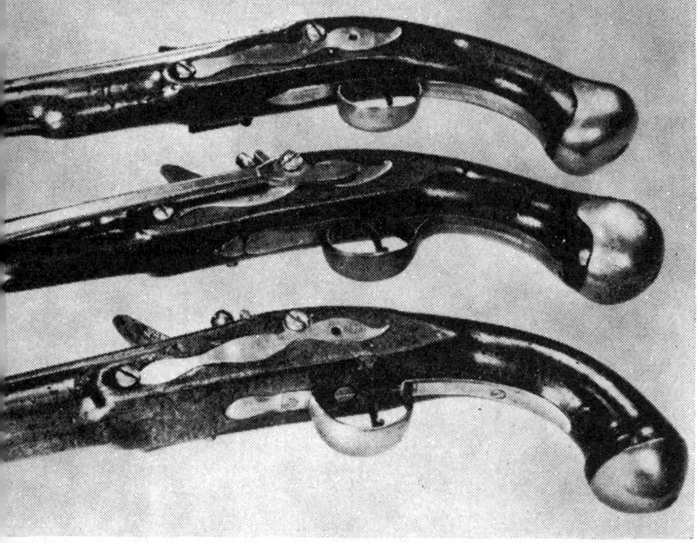

Naval Furniture: (top) c.1750-1760 British style illustrates the common pointed trigger guard and flat side plate (with a hole for the belt hook stud). All furniture is brass; (middle) c.1760-1785 English example mounts a typical belt hook and a Brown Bess pattern trigger guard; (bottom) c.1740-1750 American pistol includes colonial-made furniture with the popular naval ball tipped trigger guard.

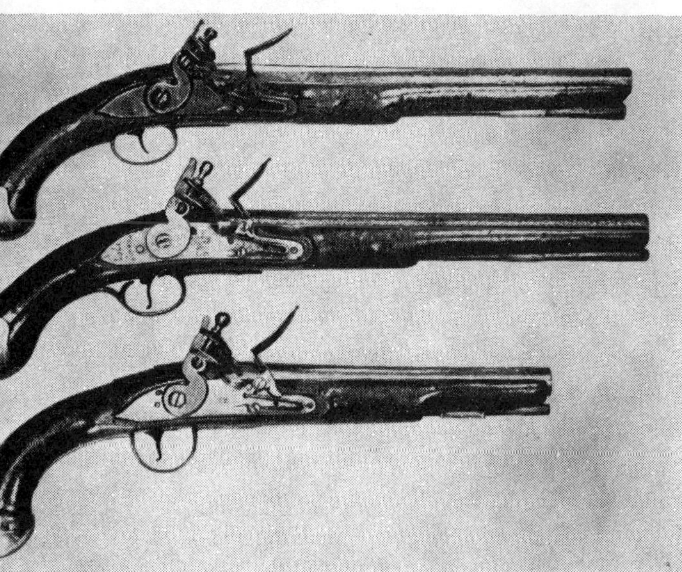

Naval Pistols: (top) c.1750-1760 British sea service pattern mounts a pinned 12" barrel (cal. .58), and a flat lock (marked "Heylin"), but omits the tailpipe and butt cap side straps. (center) This typical English style of the American Revolution continues the 12" barrel (cal. .61), brass furniture, and includes a flat naval style lock (inscribed "Vernon 1762") with a reinforced cock; (bottom) American naval hand gun c.1740-1750 uses a shortened British barrel (9") and lock (marked "I Parr") with a striped maple stock.

in 1776 to dispense with swords and pistols, there is evidence that they continued to see much action on both sides.

Pistols of England's senior service resembled early dragoon models, having 12" pinned barrels and brass furniture. Yet, like the naval muskets, they tended to be of cheap construction. Their lock was usually flat—with either a reinforced or gooseneck cock—and the majority included a long belt hook on the left side. The hole in the tail of their side plate (for the stud of the belt hook) is helpful today for quickly identifying many sea service pistols that now lack hooks.

French naval units tended to carry brass-mounted versions of the cavalry weapons previously described. The practical colonists, in turn, gathered whatever might be available.

Popular civilian pistols

It was customary for most travelers at the time to carry pistols for protection in their pockets and luggage. For this reason civilian sidearms were smaller than military styles and varied considerably in design. Because of their availability, they were also used as personal weapons by many officers.

Among the most popular was Britain's screw-barrel pattern (also called the Queen Anne or turn-off style). Its cannon-type barrel was unscrewed just forward of the lock to insert the powder and ball. Early versions had the lock on the right side, but by the 1760's most had the cock or hammer in the center of the breech housing with a reinforcing branch under the lower jaw.

In summary, the 18th century military use of pistols, as with infantry muskets, was adopted to tactics which compensated for their inaccurate smoothbore barrels. The final decision on the field came with the combatants meeting face to face in the swirling smoke where the musket bayonet could do its deadly work and the pistol couldn't miss. ■

Scottish Infantry Pistols: (top) c.1760-1795 model by John Waters of London features a kidney shaped butt (the center knob is a removable vent pick or oiler) on a stock of brass-like gunmetal. The 6⅞" barrel is cal. .57; (bottom) c.1758-1795 all-iron pattern by Isaac Bissel of Birmingham. Gun has ramshorn butt and 7⅞" (cal. .55) barrel which is marked "RHR" (Royal Highland Regt.).

The "Waters" pattern illustrates its typical plain metal stock, the traditional omission of a trigger guard, and the side hook to fit over a cross strap under the left arm; (bottom) this "Bissel" type repeats a channeled design on many components. The oval petal decoration on the butt was also common.

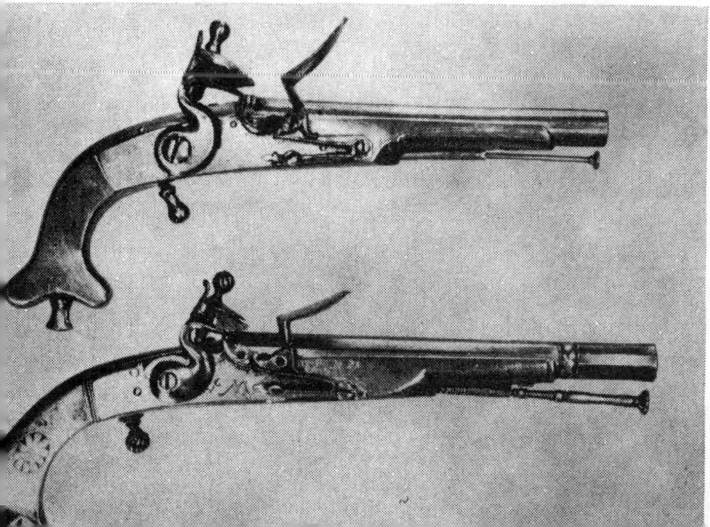

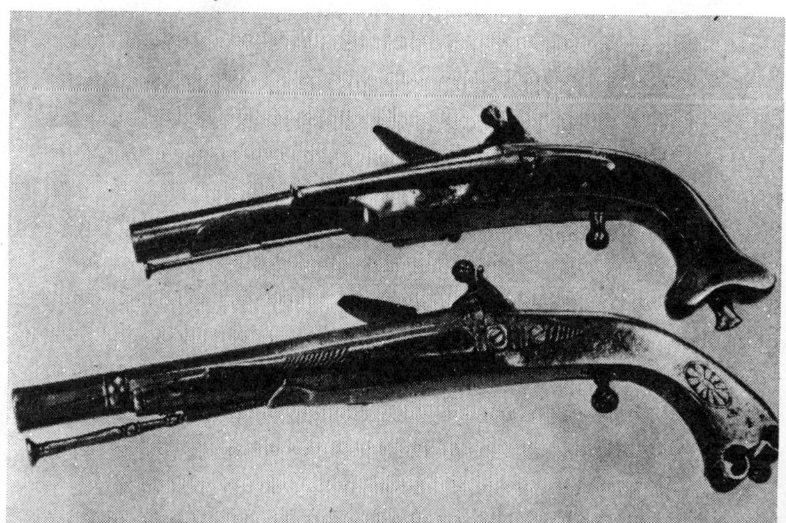

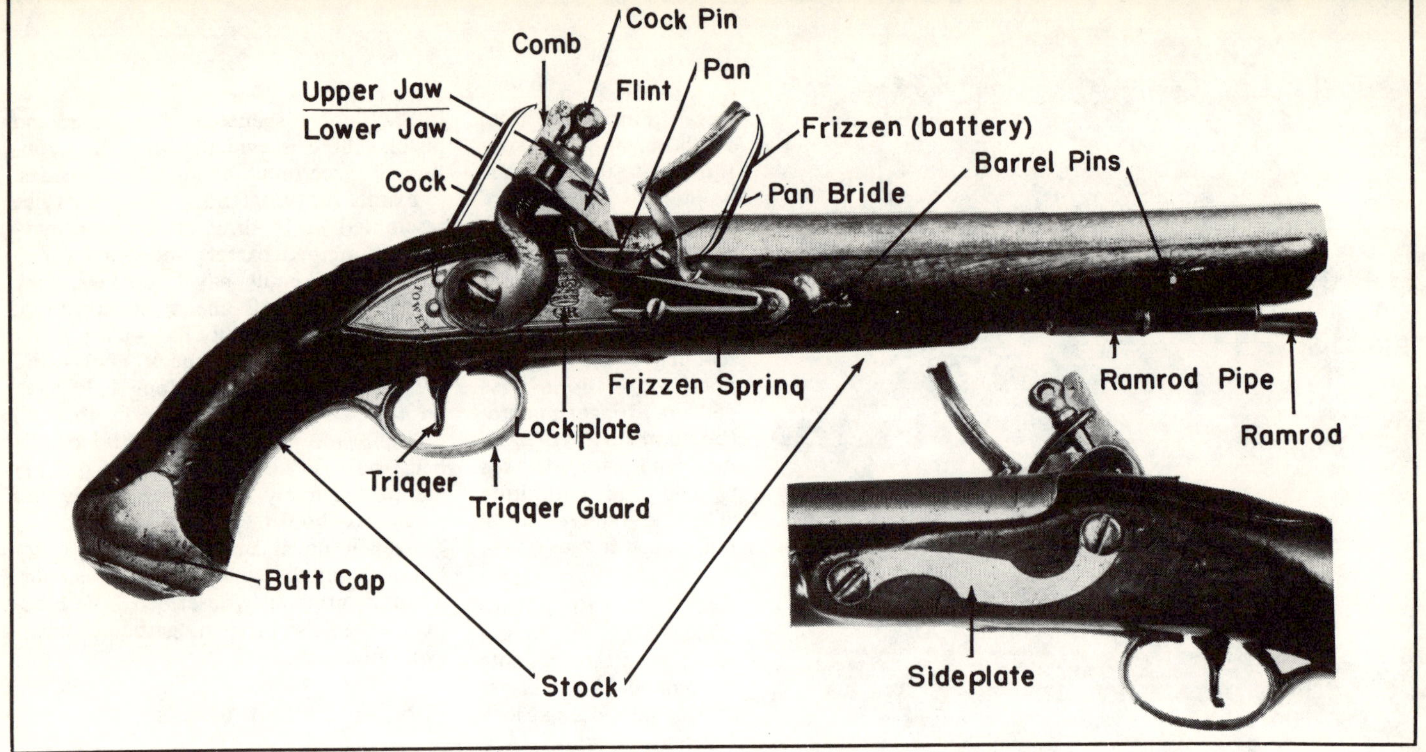

Pistols in the American Revolution

Many varied and interesting pistols were used by American and British troops

By Harold L. Peterson

THE average gun collector is inclined to think of the American Revolution in terms of muskets and rifles. He readily conjures up mental images of long lines of infantry standing shoulder to shoulder and exchanging volleys at incredibly close ranges. He pictures men in fringed hunting shirts moving silently through dense underbrush to take an unwary enemy by surprise. But he is apt to forget that the pistol was the principal firearm of a small yet important body of enlisted men.

The men who carried these pistols came from three branches of the service and included some of the most famous and colorful units of the war. There were the cavalry of both armies, the navies, and selected infantry regiments. Among these infantrymen were such renowned units as Glover's Marblehead Regiment, which was America's first amphibious team, and, also, the colorful British Highland regiments such as the Black Watch and Frazer's Highlanders.

Of all the types of pistols which these varied outfits carried during the War, the most widely used were the standard British cavalry or 'horse' pistols. These were carried not only by mounted British troops but also by a large number of Americans, for many of the Colonial arsenals had stocks of them which were quickly commandeered by local committees of safety at the outbreak of hostilities.

British used two types

The British had changed their pistol design about 1760, and both the older and newer models were used in this country. The old model British pistol had been adopted during the reign of George I (1714-1727) and used throughout the reign of George II. It was a long weapon with a 12-inch round barrel of .60 caliber. It was fastened to the walnut stock by a tang screw and two pins which passed through lugs on the under side of the barrel. At the breech was an ornamental raised band similar to that on the contemporary "Brown Bess" musket. The mounts were brass and consisted of a trigger guard, two ramrod pipes, a sideplate, a butt cap, and an escutcheon plate. The ramrod pipes resembled those on the "Brown Bess" as did the usual sideplates and escutcheon plates. Some escutcheon plates were oval, however, instead of shield-shaped, and some sideplates did not follow the standard convex-strap-with-tail pattern of the musket. The butt cap was bulbous with long projections up the sides of the grip, and the ramrod was wooden with a brass cap at the end.

The lock also was a smaller copy of the musket lock, with a goose-neck cock and a convex lockplate. On these early pistols the upper jaw of the cock had a small projection at the back which fitted into a groove in the wide comb of the cock.

The usual marks included the royal cipher (the letters "GR" under a crown), the word "TOWER", and the broad arrow denoting government ownership on the lockplate; and either London or Birmingham proofmarks on the barrel. Sometimes, however, the lockplate bore only the maker's name and the date of manufacture.

Changes on new model

The British pistol adopted about 1760 was a shorter weapon of a larger caliber. The barrel was reduced to nine inches, and the bore enlarged to .69. Other changes included removal of the escutcheon plate, the elimination of one of the ramrod pipes, the shortening of the projections on the butt cap to small lobes, and alterations in the sideplate and the lock. The sideplate was now flat instead of convex, and the tail was eliminated. The lockplate, too, was flat, and the markings on it were usually stamped instead of engraved. Finally, the cock was altered to the extent that the upper jaw was notched to fit around the comb.

In addition to the British cavalry

pistol, there was also a model for navy use. These naval pistols differed from the holster pistols in that they normally had flat reinforced cocks and were equipped with belt hooks on the reverse side. Also, even after 1760, they tended to retain the longer barrel of the George I and II types.

Highland pistols unusual

The rarest of the British pistols, however, were those carried by the enlisted men of the several Highland regiments which were sent to this country. The Highland infantry regiments were the only ones in the British army in which every private was equipped with a pistol, and these pistols were distinctive in exterior form and in mechanism.

Externally, the most striking characteristic was the fact that they were all metal, the stock being made of brass. They had no trigger guards, and the trigger itself was usually ball-shaped. The butt was often bilobate in what was known as the kidney or fishtail shape, or else it possessed two scroll-like extensions curving inward below the termination of the butt proper which gave rise to the descriptive 'ram's horn' butt appellation. In the center of the butt was a finial which could be unscrewed and used as a vent pick or oiler. The lockplate was normally cut square across the rear end, and there was no bridle from the pan to the frizzen. The ramrod was iron, and there was an iron belt hook on the left side of the stock.

Possessed odd lock

Internally, the lock mechanism was reminiscent of the earlier dog locks which had been made a hundred years before. The sear acted laterally. There was no half-cock position, and the cock was secured in the full-cock position by the end of the sear which passed through the lockplate and protruded in front of it.

The Scottish enlisted men's pistols were made in England, rather than Scotland. Many of those surviving today bear the mark of John Waters of London as well as London proofmarks. On pistols made before 1758 the engraved letters "HR" (Highland Regiment) are also often encountered. On pistols made after 1758, the letters "RHR" (Royal Highland Regiment) are more common.

Few made in America

Very few enlisted men's pistols were actually made in America during the Revolutionary War. Those that were manufactured here closely followed the 'new model' British cavalry pistol. They differed only in workmanship, the types of wood used in the stocks, and the thinness of the brass used for the mounts. The pistol illustrated above is typical. Its stock is maple instead of walnut. The brass mounts are extremely thin and flimsy, and the lock is of a type frequently found on Pennsylvania rifles of the period. Also, it possesses a front sight, which British pistols did not. This particular pistol was found in an attic in York, Pennsylvania, and was probably made somewhere nearby.

The largest manufactory of pistols in America was the Rappahannock Forge at Falmouth, Virginia. The workmanship at this establishment was of a fairly high quality, and the brass mountings were heavier and more substantial, but here also the lines of the British 'new model' pistol were followed exactly.

French pistols used

On February 6, 1778, France formally entered the War on the side of the Colonies. With this commitment the French navy and portions of the army, including selected cavalry units, entered the fray. Thus the French enlisted men's pistols appeared on the scene.

These French pistols were of three types, the army and navy models of 1763 and the Model 1776. The models of 1763 were the first to be adopted as standard by the French government. Prior to that time the selection of pistols was left to the discretion of the individual corps commanders, the only qualification being that all calibers should be the same. The new pistols, however, were manufactured in the Royal manufactories, principally at St. Étienne.

The only difference between the army and navy models of 1763 lay in the metal used for the mountings. The

Continued on page 48

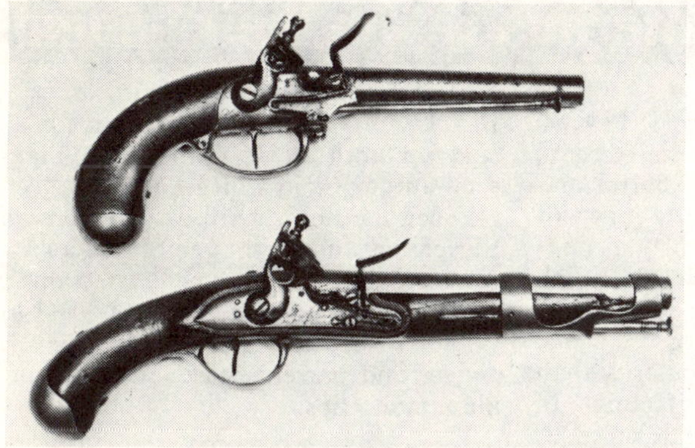
French pistol, Model 1776 (at top) and French pistol, Model 1763

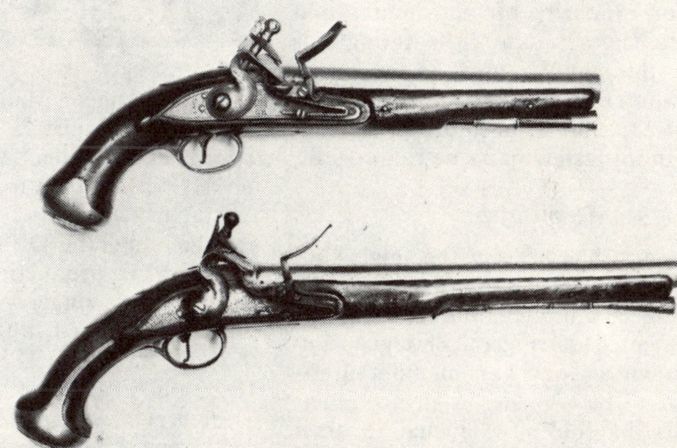
British new (at top) and old model cavalry or 'horse' pistols

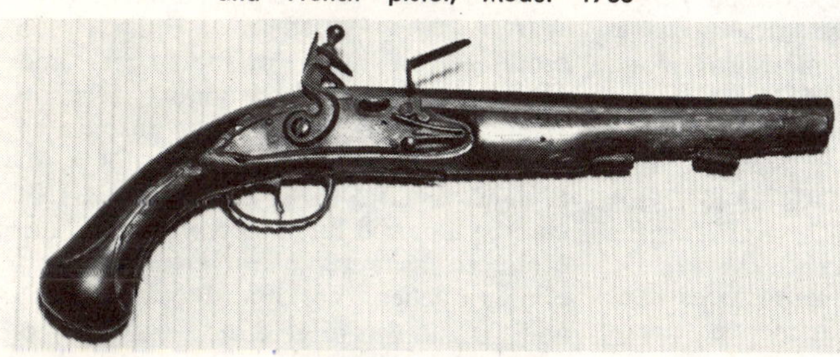
American cavalry pistol

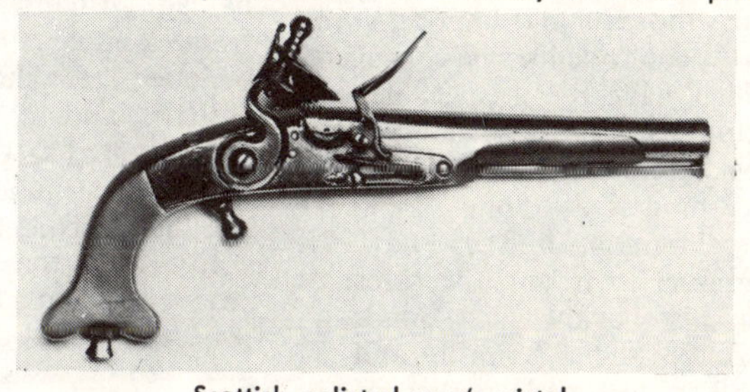
Scottish enlisted men's pistol

These .22 veterans retain their appeal in

"THE single-shot pistol is capable of greater accuracy than the repeater," was the consensus from percussion days until after the emergence of the Colt Woodsman in 1915. Then shooters began to take notice that the integral chamber-/barrel of the new semi-automatic was no different than that of the single-shot. Accuracy may have been no better, but it was good enough so that the semi-automatic soon became *the* .22 on the line. That the same gun could be used for slow-, timed- or rapid-fire matches was a decided advantage, and the .22 target pistol without a repeating action slipped from vogue. During its years of popularity, however, there were a number of American-made single-shots from which the shooter could choose. Most of them are shown on the following pages.

Today the single-shot is still made in the U.S., but primarily for the hunter and silhouette shooter, and little thought is given by the manufacturers to the casual target shooter or plinker who just might like a sleek, simple, accurate pistol that doesn't shoot faster than one can afford.

Remington

Remington has been in the single-shot pistol business since around 1860, when they produced a limited number of .17 cal. Rider patented derringers. Though primarily known as long gun manufacturers, Remington has made many popular handguns in the past, including their famous .41 over/under derringer, and today their XP-100 .221 bolt-action pistol is a popular silhouette and hunting gun.

The now-discontinued single-shot Remingtons which have the greatest general appeal to collectors are those based on the rolling block action and include the .50 cal. military models of 1865, '67 and '71 and the target versions of 1891 and 1901. The 1891 model is among the rarest of Remington pistols and was made in calibers .22, .25 and .32 rimfire and .32 center-fire. The well-made replica of the 1891 which is shown is the currently available Navy Arms .22. The same gun is also available in .357 Mag. cal.

The use of the old rolling block pistol design — when coupled with the modern materials of the Navy Arms gun — is acceptable for the powerful .357, as the action is strong. Many of the old Remingtons, in fact, will be found rebarreled for relatively modern cartridges, though conversion of an original to a magnum caliber would be foolish from a safety standpoint and criminal from that of the collector.

Stevens

Shortly after the Civil War, J. Stevens & Co., of Chicopee Falls, Mass., brought out their first .22 target pistol and called it their Old Model Pocket Rifle. It was a light-framed gun of the tip-up barrel type, with spur trigger, and followed Stevens' earlier pocket pistols in general design. The Pocket "Rifle," with 6" barrel and adjustable sights was the forerunner of several heavier target and sporting models, including the Offhand No. 35 which continued in production into World War II. Stevens' single-shot target pistols, therefore, enjoyed longer popularity than those of any other U.S. manufacturer. In 1886, the firm came to be known as J. Stevens Arms & Tool Co., and in 1916 the J. Stevens Arms Co. The Offhand *Target* No. 35 shown preceded the similarly named Offhand No. 35 and was made from about 1907 to 1916. Calibers included .22 short and long rifle, .22 W.R.F. and .25 Stevens rimfire, and barrel lengths were 6", 8" or 10". One educated estimate of the Offhand Target's production is 35,000 pieces.

In 1919, the J. Stevens Arms Co. swerved from their distinctive pistol profile and announced their Target No. 10 Pistol. Over 7000 No. 10s were made and sold up until 1933. While resembling a semi-automatic in appearance, the No. 10 retained the tip-up barrel so popular with Stevens' customers, but employed a knob-retracted internal hammer. The same 8" barreled gun was offered in a De Luxe version with browned frame, nickeled trigger and barrel release, and checkered aluminum grips.

Wurfflein

In the percussion era preceding the Civil War, Andrew Wurfflein of Philadelphia produced an array of derringers and dueling pistols of good quality. His son William followed him into the business by forming the W. Wurfflein Gun Co. of Philadelphia in 1874. After 10 years of making a varied line of firearms, William produced a target pistol greatly resembling a dueller. Workmanship was superb and the gun was offered in several calibers with .22 rimfire being the most often

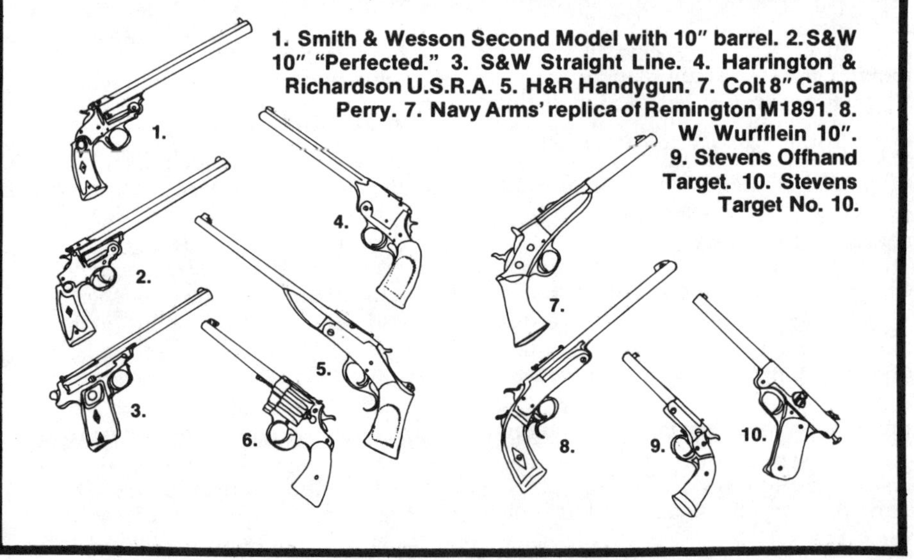

1. Smith & Wesson Second Model with 10" barrel. 2. S&W 10" "Perfected." 3. S&W Straight Line. 4. Harrington & Richardson U.S.R.A. 5. H&R Handygun. 7. Colt 8" Camp Perry. 7. Navy Arms' replica of Remington M1891. 8. W. Wurfflein 10". 9. Stevens Offhand Target. 10. Stevens Target No. 10.

TARGET PISTOLS

collections — not competitions. ★ BY PETE DICKEY

encountered. Barrel lengths ranged from 8″ to 16″, and some pistols were supplied with detachable shoulder stocks.

Most of the tip-up Wurfflein pistols were made to order and could be had with special grips and interchangeable barrels of different weights, lengths and calibers. It has been estimated that only a few hundred of the target pistols were made, and that production ceased in the 1890s, though the W. Wurfflein Gun Co. continued in operation until 1910.

Smith & Wesson

Smith & Wesson marketed four distinct single-shots, all but one being conversions for or adaptations of standard break-open revolvers. The First Model was originally offered in 1893 as a .22, .32 or .38 single-shot conversion unit for the .38 Single-Action Third Model revolver frame. 6″, 8″ or 10″ lengths were available in the three calibers, and oversized grips were developed. Later, the First Model was available only as a single-shot unit lacking a cylinder/barrel arrangement. From 1905 to 1909, the Second Model was marketed, which resembled its predecessor but lacked the cylinder recoil shield and hand and cylinder stop cuts. Most Second Model pistols were made in .22 cal. with 10″ barrel. In 1909, the Third Model, based on the .38 Perfected Double Action frame, entered its production which lasted for 24 years. The 10″ .22 Third Model is often called the Perfected Single Shot, and one variation of it, with short chamber to require finger pressure to seat the bullet into the rifling, is termed the Olympic Model. This last of the revolver-based designs is unusual in that it can be fired in double- as well as single-action style. S&W produced over 13,000 of the First, Second and Third Models. Less elegant in appearance — and less dependable in function — was the Straight Line, sold in a quantity of less than 2000 from 1924 to 1936. The name was adopted not from the "straight" semi-auto lines that the pistol emulated, but from the plunger-type hammer and trigger which slid in a straight line.

In 1912, the heyday of the single-shot target pistol, four of Smith & Wesson's Third Models are shown in use by the winning American Olympic Team in Stockholm, Sweden. Many European competitors also used the S&Ws as well as other U.S. made pistols.

Harrington & Richardson

Harrington & Richardson could claim a long history of single-shot pistol manufacture if they traced back through their previous company name Wesson & Harrington to Frank Wesson, who made brass-framed, tip-up barrel .22s as early as 1859. As matters stand, however, H&R is best known for their revolvers, and have made no single-shots since their USRA Model was dropped in World War II, after about 15 years of manufacture.

The break-open USRA, named for the United States Revolver Ass'n, was a highly successful attempt by H&R to branch out from the field of low-priced, standardized revolvers and capture the interest of serious target shooters.

H&R's other single-shot .22 was the Handygun. It was far less sophisticated than the USRA, and is best viewed as a hunting/plinking pistol. Most Handyguns were, in fact, smooth-bored and chambered for small-gauge shotshells. In this form, they are "shot pistols" and were made subject to federal regulation in 1934. Both smooth-bored and rifled Handyguns were discontinued soon after the then-new federal ruling and, having been made for only a few years, are relatively scarce in .22 cal., and scarcer still in the .32-20 version which was once offered.

Colt

Though Colt has made or marketed many action types in rifles, shotguns and handguns, their first non-revolving cylinder gun was a single-shot derringer introduced around 1870. Colt's .41 rim fire derringers continued in production until around 1910, but in 1959 a revision of their Third Model was reintroduced in .22 short cal. as a curio, and termed Deringer No. 4. In 1961, a cap and ball revolver look-alike — but actually a single-shot .22 — was developed for the nostalgia market, but now no single-shot Colt pistols are available.

The finest single-shot Colt .22 was made only from 1926 to 1941; 2525 were sold in total, including the 10″ and later 8″ barreled models. The Colt Camp Perry model was generally patterned on the conventional Colt double-action revolver frame. In profile, the d.a. revolver look was emphasized by the fluted chamber block which, with its attached barrel, swung out on the crane for loading.

In the last five years of its production, less than 500 Camp Perry models were sold. The semi-automatic pistol had established itself on the target range, and the days of the single-shot target pistol, except for highly specialized free pistols, were at an end. ■

10
9
8
7

SPUR TRIGGER

BY PETE DICKEY

Maligned by collectors typically American guns among collectors of the

IT has become convenient to categorize all single-action revolvers lacking a trigger guard as "Suicide Specials." This grisly term has been used extensively in print since Duncan McConnell wrote a brief article on the subject in the *American Rifleman,* for February, 1948.

Presumably "Suicide Special" connotes either an inexpensive tool, specifically purchased for one-time use, or an apparently sound item of hardware found to be disastrously unsound. Neither definition seems to make complete sense.

In the latter part of the 19th Century, when most spur-trigger revolvers were made and sold, there were ample supplies of single-shot handguns available at less cost than revolvers. In 1871, for instance, the Great Western Gun Works of Pittsburgh offered an Allen New Model seven-shot spur-trigger for $7.00, but Allen's single-shot derringer was only $2.85. Was the potential suicide of that day so unsure of himself that he needed a repeater? It is even less justifiable that the quality of the revolvers as a class led to the pejorative term, for Colt, Smith & Wesson, Remington, Ethan Allen, Marlin, Iver Johnson, Merwin-Hulbert, Hopkins and Allen, and Harrington and Richardson all made spur-trigger revolvers in quantity.

Apparently the lack of a trigger guard was not thought to be a hazard, as the single-action was in vogue, and inadvertently striking or pulling the trigger had no effect if the hammer was down. People understood the necessity of keeping an "empty chamber under the hammer" then as they should today.

The thought that the owner of a spur-trigger revolver was always a citizen who either wanted a simple "bureau drawer" or concealable defense gun (the lack of a trigger guard helped in the latter case) doesn't hold water either. Spur-trigger guns were sometimes supplied to police departments for holster use (the Colt New Police, sometimes called the Cop and Thug, for instance); others were offered in highly embellished finishes for presentation to dignitaries, and some were even considered for military use.

If "Suicide Special" is not used in its most general sense for *all* spur-trigger revolvers, it is often used more specifically for those guns when they: have solid rather than break-open frames, have no provision for extraction other than a detachable cylinder pin, are nickle plated, and if they are chambered for .22, .32, .38 or .41 rim-fire cartridges. In this category there are thousands of permutations of grip styles, grip materials, manufacturers, trade names, engraving patterns, barrel lengths and qualities. The majority are, in rumor and in fact, of undistinguished workmanship. Some have unrifled bores; some cast frames and barrels. Nonetheless most were, in original condition, safe for the low-powered cartridges for which they were made and were reasonably priced, to say the least. Some were of excellent quality by any standard.

In his fascinating and now standard reference on the subject "Suicide Specials" (The Stackpole Company, 1958) Donald B. Webster, Jr., delves into the subject and lists over 200 makers and brand names. Many of the actual manufacturers are familiar to us and still in business making more sophisticated wares. Some of the brand names are amusing: Pinafore, Robin Hood and Veiled Prophets; some rather impressive, Marquis of Lorne, Czar, Empress and Aristocrat; and one, at least, downright terrifying—Earthquake.

At one point these interesting little handguns were scoffed at by collectors as worthless junk. At around the time of Webster's book, things began to change, however, and today even the plainest, most common variety in very good condition will command a respectable, though quite affordable, price at gun shows. An attempt to build a "complete" collection would be impossible. A collection of representative models would be a challenge of whatever proportions the prospective collector sets for himself.

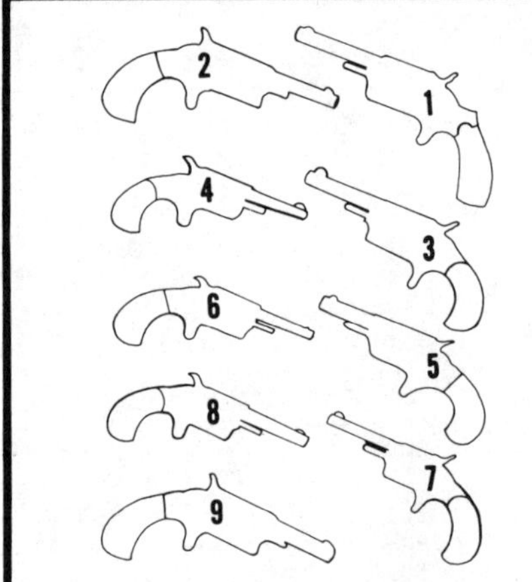

Today the spur-trigger revolver is only an interesting artifact of the past—except for Freedom Arms' Mini Revolver, a stainless steel .22 cal., five-shot, with a 1½" barrel and weight of only 4 ozs. It sells well, is beautifully made and priced accordingly ($100)—further proof that the spur-trigger revolver has many silent admirers as well as vocal detractors.

In the NRA Museum are a number of "average" spur-triggers and some particularly fine specimens which are illustrated herewith.

In the following display are nine revolvers which fit neatly into the most commonly accepted category of "Suicide Specials"—single-action, rim-fire, extraction by cylinder pin, solid-frame, spur-trigger and nickel plating. But, while they all show signs of hard use, all are in firing condition and show workmanship ranging from fair to excellent. Shown on the left hand page, from the top: 1. A Hopkins & Allen .32 Blue Jacket No. 2 with square butt, engraving, and

REVOLVERS

of years gone by, these are gaining acceptance late Twentieth Century.

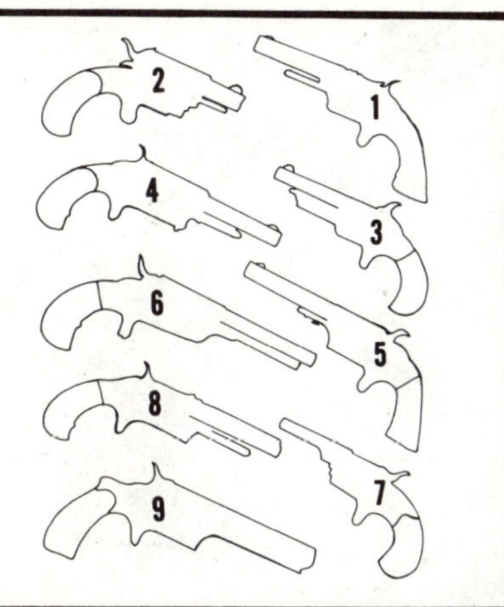

ivory grips. Donated by: W.O. Francis A. Higginson, U.S.M.C., Quantico, Va.; 2. An H&R .32, this one marked Victor No. 2 but with the same William A. Richardson patent markings as on the Aetna (see #9); 3. A Hopkins & Allen Ranger No. 2 .32. The distinctive H&A cylinder pin release is visible on the left side of the frame. Donated by B. J. McCausey of Baltimore, Md.; 4. A bone gripped Scott Arms Co. No. 3 .22. It is probable that little gun was made by Bliss & Goodyear circa 1880 in New Haven, Conn. The patent date (April 23, 1878) coincides with one in the name of William H. Bliss. This pistol, too, was donated by Mr. McCausey.; 5. This Colt New Line .32 is one of over 20,000 made between 1873 and 1884 for both rim- and center-fire cartridges. The quality is, of course, first-rate. A gift of Joe Cerbenka of Chicago, Ill.; 6. Marked only "Defender," this was an early example of a long line of similar models of the same name made by Iver Johnson between 1875 and 1895. This particular .22 was made before 1889 as in that year improved models began to use the name Defender 89; 7. Another Hopkins & Allen with the same patent markings as the Blue Jacket No. 2 (see #1 above) but this gun marked Ranger 22 Long (and so chambered) with walnut bird's-head grips. Donated by Mrs. McDaniel of Baltimore, Md.; 8. The only wording on this poorly engraved model is "Ranger 22 Long." The name "Ranger" was used by Hopkins & Allen, but it is believed this lesser quality arm was made by E. L. Dickinson of Springfield, Mass., in the 1870s. The front-of-frame cylinder pin release tends to support this theory; 9. Though simply marked Aetna No. 2, Pat May 23, 1876, this .32 with hard rubber grips was a product of Harrington & Richardson and, despite the manufacturer's decision to omit their name, is very well made.

The nine guns on the right hand page are, from the top: 1. An early Smith & Wesson that has come to be known by collectors as the Model 1 Second Issue. It was made from 1860 until 1868, in a quantity of over 115,000. Many of these little tip up revolvers and their larger .32 cal. counterparts were purchased and used by the Union officers in the Civil War. Donated by Jack Heff; 2. A Forehand & Wadsworth .41 rim-fire five-shooter with full gold plating, engraving, and ivory grips. This piece is apparently unfired, as it still retains the gold plating on the lands of the rifling. This F&W Swamp Angel was the gift of Alex Brown of Tuscon, Ariz.; 3. A beautifully made Wesson & Harrington No. 2 .22 short seven-shot revolver. This was made between 1874 and 1879 to a quantity of 15,000. Very late model revolvers are marked Harrington & Richardson. The revolver is equipped with a novel extractor which is pivoted on the cylinder pin. A gift of Eiichi Kamiya, Torrance, Calif.; 4. A brass framed Whitneyville Armory .38 rim-fire revolver known by its caliber as the Model 2½. With the Models No. 1 (.22) and 2 (.32), this gun was made to a total of about 30,000 between 1871 and 1879. Donated by Mrs. Blanche L. Spragg, Detroit, Mich.; 5. The most ornate spur-trigger in the NRA Museum collection, the Plant .30 cal. cup-primed revolver, made by Plant's Manufacturing Co., New Haven, Conn., in the mid-1860s but marked by the distributor Merwin & Bray Firearms Co., N.Y. This unique piece is replete with carved ivory grips, an engraved and stippled brass frame which is blackened to match the engraved steel barrel, and a steel cylinder etched with a game scene; 6. Made by the Bacon Arms Co. of Norwich, Conn., in the mid-1860s, this .32 cal. pocket revolver is, in essence, a smaller version of the .38 rim-fire spur-triggers with which Bacon hoped to capture the interest of the U.S. Government; 7. The official factory name for this 8-oz. .22 cal. revolver was Colt's Breech-Loading seven-shot revolving pistol. It was introduced in 1871 and some few were made with a rod ejector on the right side of the barrel. Collectors sometimes refer to the gun now as the Colt Open-Top .22; 8. In the early 1870s Marlin made at least two models of simple, solid-frame spur-triggers which they called the O.K. and the Little Joker. From 1872 to 1887 their so-called Standard Pocket Revolvers had spur-triggers also, but were more complex and appeared similar to Smith & Wesson tip up revolvers of the same period. The sample shown is marked No. 32 Standard 1875 and is of excellent workmanship. Similar revolvers were made in .22 and .38 center-fire calibers. Donated by John H. Macrae, Lake Park, Minn.; 9. Spur-triggers were favored features of many Remington handguns—single-shot military and pocket pistols, double derringers and revolvers. This Remington-Smoot New Model No. 3 revolver has a sliding rod extractor and saw-handle grip. It is in .38 rim-fire caliber but .38 center-fires of the same model are also known, as are similar guns with bird's-head grips. Some 25,000 were made between 1878 and 1888. ■

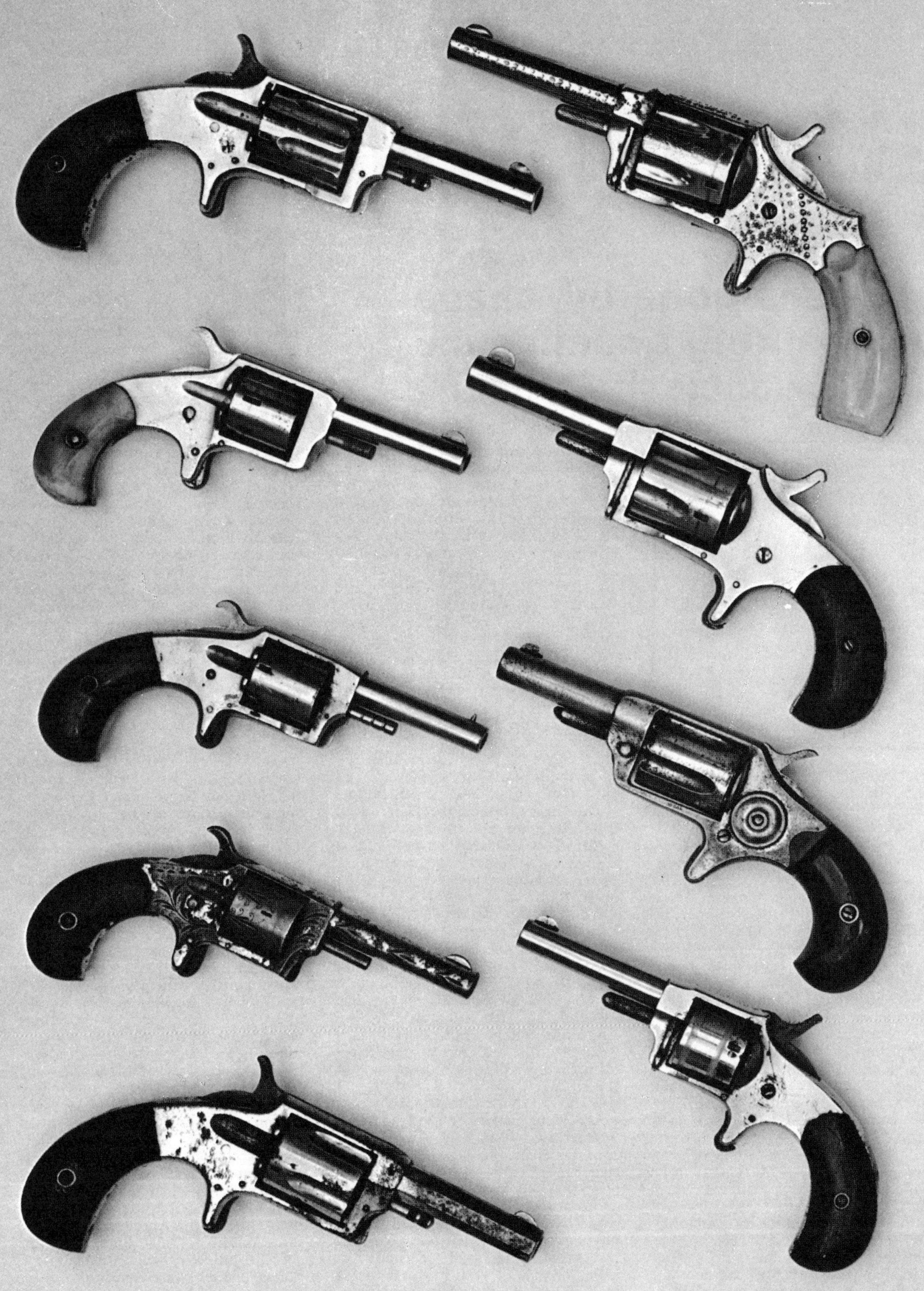

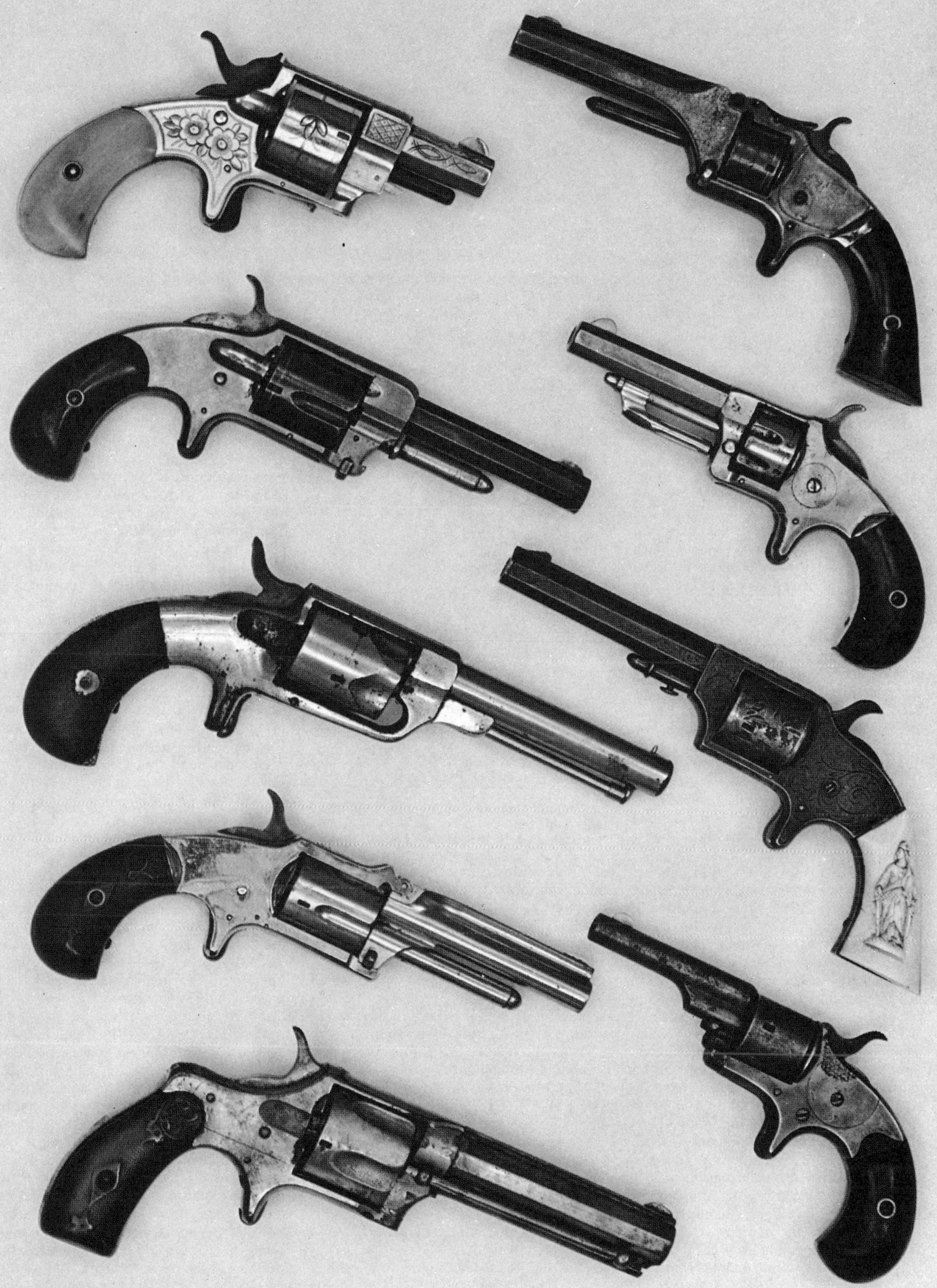

Guns For A Montana Hard work

"ED McGIVERN of Montana," read the handbills — though he came from Omaha, Nebr., and worked in Sheridan, Wyo., before moving to Great Falls, Mont. — "The Fastest Shooting in the World."

The handbill was no exaggeration. For, though McGivern looked more like a bank clerk, or maybe a sign painter, he was one of the best and best-known of America's exhibition shooters.

As an exhibition shooter, McGivern specialized in hitting aerial targets and in hitting two targets — with two revolvers — simultaneously. Photographs of McGivern performances show him using a variety of revolvers, Colt Single Actions or Officers Models and Smith & Wesson Hand Ejectors on both K- and N-size frames, to break targets held by an assistant or cut playing cards — both hand-held and thrown, edgewise, toward him — or lead discs tossed into the air in front of him.

As his shooting career progressed, so did the complexity of McGivern's act. From one gun, one aerial target, he went to two of each, firing both guns simultaneously to hit both targets. Then, switching back to a single revolver he would hit up to five airborne clay targets thrown into the air together. And, as the number of targets grew, so did the need for rapidity of fire, a challenge that must have fascinated McGivern, for he devoted most of his adult life to learning just how fast and how straight a man could shoot a handgun.

He left the results of his studies in one book, *Fast and Fancy Revolver Shooting,* published in 1938; in a number of handguns, modified to make them more accurate and faster to shoot; and in the minds of the federal, state, and local law enforcement officers, servicemen, and private citizens who studied under McGivern and learned the secrets of his success.

Though McGivern, if surviving available photographs are to be believed, used double-action revolvers for most of his exhibition shooting, he also tinkered with single-action guns and explored in depth the art of rapid shooting with them. Before he gave up single-actions — about 1936 — he tried both fanning and one- and two-handed slip shooting, turning in some impressive performances in the process. He thoroughly debunked the notion that *no one* can hit anything by fanning (holding the gun with the trigger depressed in one hand and brushing the hammer to the rear with the heel of the other hand) a single-action. McGivern regularly demonstrated his ability to put five hits on a hand-size target at ranges of 10-20 ft. in less than 1½ seconds.

McGivern's fanning guns usually show two modifications, a special hammer with a strengthened, lowered spur made by J. D. O'Meara of Lead, S. Dak., and a beefed up cylinder pin. One of his single-actions, fitted with an O'Meara hammer, also has a stop screw in the top of the backstrap to arrest rearward travel of the hammer when the full-cock position is reached. To keep the trigger from functioning, McGivern would tape it back against the trigger guard.

McGivern's fast draw experiments included work with both one and two revolvers; this pair carried butt forward and cross-drawn.

Oddly, the single-action with which McGivern did his best rapid-fire work, a series of four, five-shot targets, fan fired at a range of 10 ft., each group small enough to be covered by a hand (and two of the four by a playing card), was done with a .38 Spl. Single Action Army Colt (Serial No. 354507). Except for an uncheckered hammer spur and a wrap of tape around the trigger and guard, the gun is unaltered.

Regardless of how fast McGivern could fan a single-action, he did not use them for hitting multiple, aerial targets. For that portion of his exhibition, and for his experiments in rapidity of fire, he chose double-action revolvers.

Whereas he used both Colt and Smith & Wesson double-action guns for exhibition shooting, McGivern's speed trials were conducted almost totally with the latter company's guns. One probable reason lies in the mechanisms of the respective guns. The Colts, with their forged, V-shape mainsprings, were the darlings of the target shooters of those days. The V-spring was ideally suited to thumb cocking for timed- and rapid-fire and properly adjusted couldn't be beaten for that purpose. Smith & Wesson guns, on the other hand, used a flat leaf mainspring and a separate, coil trigger return spring. The unmodified S&W system gives a surer, more positive double-action pull, and McGivern took advantage of it.

McGivern did modify the guns he used, but not the way one might think. He began with the sights, fitting a Patridge-style front post to his guns. The post, instead of being plain, had a 0.1″ gold bead. This was the "McGivern Bead," and in the '30s both Colt and S&W offered it as an optional front sight on their adjustable-sight revolvers. The D. W. King Sight Company of San Francisco, Calif., made McGivern Bead replacement front sights for a variety of guns, both revolvers and semi-automatic pistols.

McGivern's book also covers the selection of custom grips and grip adapters available to shooters of the 1930s. It is interesting to note, that, while he tried them all, he appears — from surviving photographs — to have used only factory stocks for his exhibition shooting and for most of his record setting. The custom grips that he did use, he used for special purposes, like two-hand shooting. On pages 455-457 of *Fast and Fancy Revolver Shooting* is a description of the grips fitted to two of the revolvers illustrated here — a S&W .38 M&P Target and an S&W .44 Triple Lock. These were made by Kearsarge Woodcrafts of Warner, N.H. In addition to the carving incorporating McGivern's name into the design, the grips extend ⅜″ below the frame and include fillers ½″ deep under the trigger guard and ¼″ thick behind the top portion of the backstrap. The effect of these grips is to minimize the tendency of a gun to twist in the hand as it recoils, making it much more controllable for firing, either double- or single-action.

Marksman

Good equipment made Ed McGivern a good shot. ... made him a legend.

BY J. B. ROBERTS, JR.

McGivern's experiments with fan-fired six guns proved that the technique worked. The Colt he is using here may be revolver No. 5.

Two other McGivern guns in the NRA's collection have modifications to their trigger guards to aid trigger control or enhance accessibility. Typical of the former is a Military and Police Target .38 Spl. with 4″ barrel instead of the usual 6″. The rear of this gun's trigger guard is shrouded so that when the hammer is fully to the rear and about to fall, the trigger is inside the shroud, and its front surface is nearly flush with the edges of the shroud. In double-action use, the shooter's trigger finger contacts the shroud just before the hammer is released, allowing the shooter to pause and correct his aim prior to firing.

The other gun is a S&W .38/44 Outdoorsman modified by reshaping the front of the trigger guard to permit quicker access to the trigger. This design, executed by the late William Sukalle of Phoenix, Ariz., was McGivern's answer to those who recommended cutting away the front of a revolver's trigger guard to make the gun faster to get into action. McGivern considered cutting the trigger guard mutilation — and dangerous to boot — and did not hesitate to say so.

The Sukalle-modified Outdoorsman gives us another glimpse at McGivern's attitude toward his guns — they were tools, to be well cared for and used, within limits, according to the need at hand. Thus he gave most of his record-setting guns away. The Outdoorsman was used on Aug. 20, 1932, to fire a half-dollar size five-shot group at a range of 20 ft. in 9/20 of one second. Sukalle modified the trigger guard some time after August, 1932, and before *Fast and Fancy Revolver Shooting* was published, for the gun is illustrated as it appeared both before and after the work was done. We have the Outdoorsman and the rest of the guns and gear illustrated from McGivern's patron, Walter Groff of Philadelphia, Pa., whose wife donated her late husband's collection of McGivern artifacts to NRA.

In this day of custom revolver action jobs and special heavy barrels, guns like those that grace Police Pistol Combat firing lines, we wondered about two things. How did McGivern get the accuracy needed to reliably hit the edge of an airborne playing card? How did he get the speed to regularly fire a revolver at a cyclic rate exceeding 600 shots per minute.

We returned the original mainsprings to four of the guns: the 4″ M&P Target with its shrouded trigger guard; the record-setting Outdoorsman; a 6″ M&P Target, .38 Spl. with Kearsarge-made grips; and a commercial, 1917 DA .45 with a cylinder chambered for .45 Colt cartridges.

We began by shooting the Outdoorsman and the 1917 DA from the Ransom Rest — five six-shot groups with each gun at 25 yds. It proved little. Neither gun is exceptionally accurate; certainly not the equal of today's custom-built police combat revolver, though both are quite good by any standard. The average group size for the Outdoorsman was 2.03″; the

Continued on page 26

Editor's Note:

Ed McGivern spent his life learning how to shoot rapidly, accurately, and safely. He made his living at it. But, he was the first to discourage "playing at quick draw" or simply pulling a trigger as fast as is possible. Likewise NRA has, and does, discourage frivolous participation in this sort of handgun shooting. Quick draw, fanning, and high rates of fire are for those who are paid to be good at it, not for the sporting marksman.

Many of McGivern's record setting revolvers were marked to commemorate the event. The plaque on this Outdoorsman speaks volumes.

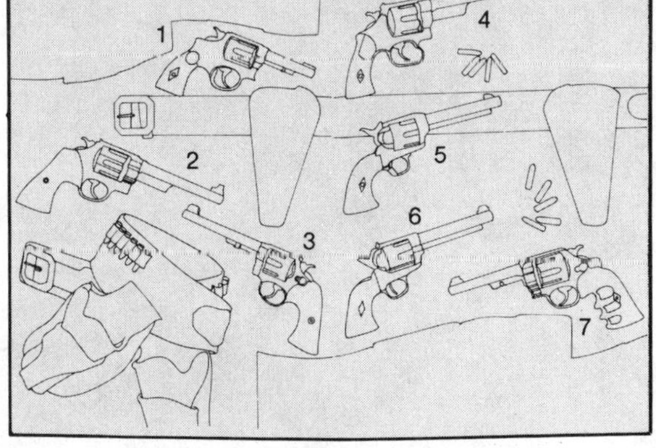

The seven revolvers that appear on the following pages are typical of the guns McGivern used as he strove to perfect the art of revolver shooting. No. 1 is an S & W 4″ Military & Police with a shrouded trigger guard to aid the shooter in trigger control. Nos. 2 & 3 have oversize grips to steady them for two-hand holding. No. 4, a .38/44 Outdoorsman, was used to set at least one record. The guard was modified in a later experiment. Nos. 5 & 6 are two of McGivern's Single Action Colts. Using No. 5 — unmodified except for the taped trigger — he set at least one record. The other Colt features a McGivern bead sight and an O'Meara hammer. No. 7, a DA .45 of 1917, sports a pair of target grips, probably for long range experiments. At one time, this gun may have had interchangeable .45 Colt and .45 ACP cylinders.

Ed McGivern
of Montana
"The

Fastest Shooting
In The World"

(L.-r.) military .38 L.C.; U.S. Ctg. blackpowder .38 Spl.; .38 Colt Spl. had flat point; early Peters .38-44 with large primer; later Peters HV lead bullet; early Rem-UMC .38-44 Special.

After 80 years of evolution, the .38 Spl. and .357 Mag. are still...

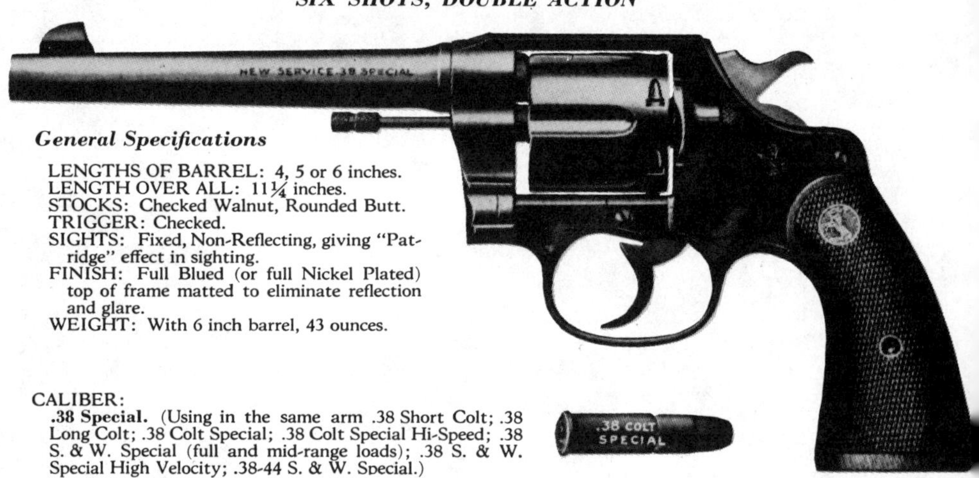

Colt New Service Revolver

CALIBER .38 SPECIAL
SIX SHOTS, DOUBLE ACTION

General Specifications

LENGTHS OF BARREL: 4, 5 or 6 inches.
LENGTH OVER ALL: 11¼ inches.
STOCKS: Checked Walnut, Rounded Butt.
TRIGGER: Checked.
SIGHTS: Fixed, Non-Reflecting, giving "Patridge" effect in sighting.
FINISH: Full Blued (or full Nickel Plated) top of frame matted to eliminate reflection and glare.
WEIGHT: With 6 inch barrel, 43 ounces.

CALIBER:
.38 Special. (Using in the same arm .38 Short Colt; .38 Long Colt; .38 Colt Special; .38 Colt Special Hi-Speed; .38 S. & W. Special (full and mid-range loads); .38 S. & W. Special High Velocity; .38-44 S. & W. Special.)

THE .38 Spl. and .357 Mag. are the most popular center-fire revolver cartridges in America. Today's wealth of good .38 and .357 guns and loads is the result of a continuing development program that began before 1900. The failure of the .38 Long Colt cartridge in combat demonstrated the need for better military ammunition and led to the development of the .38 Spl. The early shortcomings of the .38 Spl. prompted the development of more powerful loadings and stronger guns in the 1930s, which made possible the introduction of the .357 Mag. in 1935.

Since then, technology hasn't changed the actual revolver ballistics much, but years of development have brought us many new bullet weights and styles to adapt these two cartridges to almost any handgunning purpose.

The .38 S&W Spl., introduced in 1899, was intended as an improvement over the .38 Long Colt which had acquired a reputation for poor stopping power in military use. The .38 Long Colt was first loaded with an outside lubricated, heeled, 148-150-gr. round-nose bullet and 19 grs. of blackpowder, giving 770 f.p.s. in a 6" barrel. This was later changed to a hollow-base bullet of the same weight and 3 grs. of Bullseye powder producing the same nominal ballistics. The .38 Long Colt can be used in .38 Spl. handguns and was once commonly used as a lower-powered practice round, just as we now use .38 Spl. cartridges in .357 guns, but it is rarely used today.

The .38 S&W Spl. took its form from the .38 Long Colt case, lengthened by .12", to increase its capacity to 21 grs. of blackpowder. Blackpowder .38 Spl. loads were offered until about World War I, though smokeless powder ones were available as early as 1900. The long-standard charge for .38 Spl. 158-gr., lead-bullet loads is 3.6 grs. of Bullseye powder. This approximates the blackpowder velocity of 860 f.p.s. in a 6" solid test barrel, providing an obvious increase in striking energy over the woefully inadequate Colt round.

Actual revolver velocities were always less. While today's catalog numbers are lower than old ones, the ammunition is no different. The currently used 4" vented test barrels simply give a more realistic velocity figure.

Smith & Wesson coupled its introduction of the new .38 Spl. cartridge to that of the First Model .38 Hand Ejector of 1899. This revolver, now known as the Military & Police Model or Model 10, is still with us. The popular M&P or K-frame is the design model for the whole family of S&W double action revolvers.

The S&W Military and Police was popular immediately. Colt, realizing the superiority of the .38 S&W Spl. cartridge, brought out the .38 Colt Spl. cartridge in 1906. The only real difference was that the Colt round featured a flat-nose bullet that gave it somewhat better stopping power than the round-nose S&W cartridge. It was factory loaded until 1955.

The .38 Spl. was originally intended as a military cartridge, but the Army, soured on the .38 revolver after its Philippines experience, adopted the .45 Automatic Colt Pistol (ACP) in 1911. As a result, the attention of .38 revolver manufacturers drifted from the military services to police, where they found a ready market. The S&W Military & Police revolver enjoyed brisk sales, as did its Colt competitors: the Police Positive Special, introduced in 1908, and the Army Special, also introduced in 1908 and renamed the Official Police in 1928. The .38 Spl. served lawmen without challenge until about 1930, when highway patrolmen voiced a need for more powerful loads capable of penetrating automobile bodies.

The first high velocity factory loads for the .38 Spl. appeared in 1931. These cartridges were meant for use in the large frame S&Ws and Colt's New Service, Single Action, or Official Police models, not in the standard frame Military & Police Model S&W or Colt Police Positive Special. This is because these hotter loads generated higher pressures, around 20,000 copper units of pressure (c.u.p.), instead of 16,000 c.u.p. generated by standard .38 Spl. cartridges.

In the November, 1931, issue of *American Rifleman*, Phil Sharpe described S&W's new .38/44 Super Police, also known as the .38/44 Heavy Duty. "Users of the .38 Spl.", wrote Sharpe, "have asked for a heavier model. The .38/44 Super Police is built on the .44 frame but is chambered for the popular .38 Spl. cartridge. . . . For the shooter who reloads . . . the new gun will be safe with any normal overload an experimenter might develop. . . . The thickness of metal in this gun gives the writer confidence to fire standard factory proof cartridges from the hand, something no other gun has ever inspired."

The .38/44 Heavy Duty, introduced

(L.-r.) early .357s had large primer and deep seated bullet; early Rem-UMC metal point; lead bullet with exposed shoulder; post-war nickeled case; early Super-X and post-war Lubaloy.

America's Workhorse Revolvers

BY C. E. HARRIS

April 1, 1930, was a fixed-sight, 5″ barrel holster gun that weighed 40 ozs. It was also made with 4″ and 6″ barrels. Numbered in the .44 Hand Ejector series, a total of 11,111 were produced before World War II interrupted production. After the war it was reintroduced with an improved rebound-slide-actuated hammer block. Postwar guns have the letter S accompanying the serial number. In 1948, the .38/44 HD was further "improved" to incorporate the now-familiar S&W short action and remained unchanged until it was discontinued in 1966. Total postwar production was 20,604 revolvers. In 1957, when model numbers were assigned to the various S&W revolvers, the .38/44 Heavy Duty became known as the Model 20.

In the November, 1931, issue of the *American Rifleman*, Sharpe remarked, "There are no target sights available for this model, although . . . this would be highly desirable." Smith & Wesson anticipated his request and that very month introduced the .38/44 Outdoorsman with a 6½″ barrel and target sights. From 1931 until 1942, when WWII interrupted production, 4761 Outdoorsman revolvers were made. After the war, it was reintroduced with the improved hammer block, and shortly thereafter a new barrel with

Pedigree-like "Registration Numbers" graced pre-war .357 Magnums. Back then the "Magnum" was more a showpiece than a working sidearm.

Pre-war Smith & Wessons had the hammer block fitted into the side-plate, actuated by a cam on the hand.

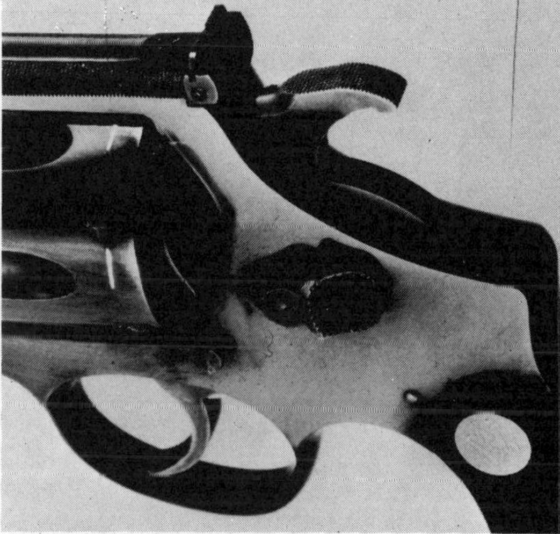

Adjustable rear sights standard on early .357 Magnums didn't have click adjustments. Hump-backed hammer was another custom option.

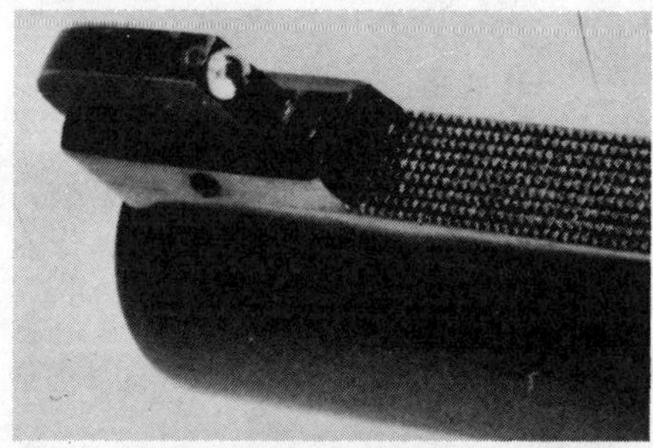

Early .357 Magnums were custom made and registered to the original owner. One of many options was this McGivern bead.

How Colt Fire Arms are Made
Colt Official Police Revolver
50 .38 CALIBRE
COLT SPECIAL
38
US
SMOKELESS
CENTRAL FIRE
UNITED STATES CARTRIDGE CO.
LOWELL, MASS.
50
Western
CENTER FIRE CARTRIDGES
Super-X
357 MAGNUM METAL PIERCING
CONICAL BULLET
Lubaloy
NICKEL PLATED CASE
HISTORICAL
TRADE FILE
COLT'S
HAND BOOK
.38 S. & W.
SPECIAL
SMOKELESS
SUPER-CLEAN
CANADIAN INDUSTRIES LIMITED

50
CENTRAL - FIRE CARTRIDGES
.38 CAL. SPECIAL S&W.
SMOKELESS
THE RHEN. WESTPH. EXPLOSIVES Co.
NUREMBERG.
GERMANY
R.W.S.
SMITH & WESSON
Manufacturers of Superior Revolvers
WINCHESTER
SUPER W SPEED
.38 SPECIAL
LEAD BULLET KOPPERKLAD
50
STAYNLESS
80th Anniversary Catalog
50 PETERS
RUSTLESS
SMOKELESS
CENTER FIRE
LEAD BULLET
FOR SMITH & WESSON, COLT AND OTHER ARMS.
.357 MAGNUM
50 CENTER FIRE
SMOKELESS CARTRIDGES
STAYNLESS
NON-MERBURIC
PETERS
HIGH VELOCITY
38 SPECIAL
HIGHWAY PATROL
110 GRAIN METAL PENETRATING BULLET
50 CENTER FIRE SMOKELESS CARTRIDGES
SMITH & WESSON

rib and micrometer rear sight was added. The new, short-throw hammer was introduced on Sept. 26, 1950, and the gun was called the .38/44 Outdoorsman Model 1950, until 1957, when it was redesignated the Model 23. Postwar production of the long-action version was 2326, and 6039 of the 1950 style were produced, bringing postwar production of the .38/44 Outdoorsman to 8365 guns. Because of their useful features and limited production, these revolvers are highly prized by collectors and shooters alike.

Describing the Outdoorsman revolver in the April, 1932, issue of the *American Rifleman*, W. D. Frazer remarked, "Many shooters have the idea that the heavier the gun, the steadier it can be held. . . . The .38/44 Outdoorsman's revolver is a target revolver in every sense of the word. . . . When the S&W company decided to chamber their .44 target revolver for the .38 Spl. cartridge, they were not content to do just that, for they knew the larger gun was capable of a much more powerful load, and they insisted on having a cartridge worthy of it. Remington soon developed a heavier load . . . stepping up the velocity to 1100 f.p.s. with 425 foot-pounds." Frazer went on to say, ". . . being most interested in the long-range possibilities of the gun and ammunition, the revolver was sighted in at 200 yds. and then 20 shots were fired . . . at the Colt's police silhouette target . . . with the gun held in both hands between the knees while the back was rested against an automobile. . . . Seventeen hits were made on the figure."

While S&W was introducing new heavy-frame .38s to handle the high-velocity loads, Colt already had several suited to the job. The Official Police on the .41 frame had been around since 1928, and the New Service was offered in .38 Spl. starting in 1930, as was the Single Action. The Officer's Model had been available in .38 Colt Spl. chambering since 1908. The Shooting Master in .38 Spl. was introduced in 1933. Once the high-velocity .38 Spl. loads came out, Colt simply changed catalog descriptions to indicate which guns were suitable for them.

These .38 Spl. high-velocity loads were developed from experiments conducted by Phil Sharpe, Elmer Keith and others. Writing in the *American Rifleman* of April, 1933, Keith suggested several handloads with cast bullets and the now long-discontinued DuPont SR-80 and #5 pistol powders. Keith experimented initially with the 172-gr. Ideal bullet #358429, but later he remarked that its heavier weight caused too great a difference in point of impact, compared to the 155- 162-gr. bullets. Thereafter, he mostly concentrated on the 155-gr. #358439 and 162-gr. #358431 bullets. After Hercules introduced #2400 powder in 1932, Keith, Sharpe and others preferred it to No. 80 in

Post-war "short-action" S&Ws have a rebound slide actuated hammer block and short throw hammer with lowered spur.

"S" accompanying serial number identifies new-style hammer block in post-war revolvers.

high-velocity handgun loads, since it permitted greater velocities with somewhat lower pressures. Hercules #2400 never was entirely satisfactory except with heavy loads, as it does not burn well with light charges. Although there are better powders for high performance handgun loads today, #2400 remained the powder of choice for such applications for many years. It wasn't until recently that newer powders such as Hercules Blue Dot or Olin W-W 296 began to replace it among the majority of magnum handgun enthusiasts.

Then, as now, the shooting industry was very cautious about handloaders exceeding recommended pressures in their attempts to gain higher velocities. What has added to the confusion over the years is that old data sources frequently list far heavier charges than are now recommended. Part of the reason for the discrepancies is that old data was seldom developed under controlled laboratory conditions where pressures and velocities could be measured accurately. Another factor is that the corrosive primers in use before about 1933 developed lower pressures than modern non-corrosive primers. F. C. Ness remarked in the September, 1933, *American Rifleman* that .38 Spl. high-velocity loads had to be reduced as much as 0.5-gr. when using the "new" non-corrosive primers with 158-gr. factory-swaged lead bullets and Unique powder. The resulting charge of 5.5 grs. agrees well with recent +P loading data for similar bullets.

In the October, 1934, *American Rifleman*, Ness cautioned against the use of heavy handloads. "This fetish for high-pressure loads is most prevalent among the handgun fraternity. The advent of Hi-Speed and High Velocity factory loads has

Colt Officer's Model was introduced in 1904 (1); the Single-Action wasn't offered in .38 Spl. until 1930 (2); the Official Police was built on the .41 DA frame (3); Colt "357" was introduced in 1954 and became the basis for the popular "Python" model introduced in 1961 (4); Colt's New Service on the .45 DA frame was offered in .38 Spl. and later in .357 Mag. (5); Smith & Wesson's .38-44 Outdoorsman used the .44 frame (6); Military & Police uses the smaller K-frame (7); the S&W .357 Magnum became the Model 27 (8); .38-44 Heavy Duty was a fixed sight service gun (9).

given it new stimulus . . . such loads develop about 20,000 lbs. pressure and are . . . decidedly not for the average revolver. . . . Our very strongest modern revolvers are the Smith & Wesson Outdoorsman and Super Police Models; the Colt Single Action, New Service (of modern manufacture) and the Shooting Master. These latter are the only revolvers adapted for the regular use of loads which develop as much as 20,000 lbs. pressure."

Handloaders of the 1930's, however, still sought more power than the .38/44 provided and persisted in wringing out all the velocity to be had from the .38 Spl. case. This set the stage for the .357 Magnum's debut in 1935.

Phil Sharpe, in his *Complete Guide to Handloading* (published in 1937), takes credit for conjuring up the idea of the .357 Mag. in concert with Douglas G. Wesson of Smith & Wesson. While on a hunting trip, Sharpe and Wesson used a variety of heavy handloads which proved very effective in a pair of Outdoorsman revolvers. Col. Wesson, however, wasn't about to undertake development of much higher pressure loads that would be dangerous in standard-frame .38 revolvers, so he sought to develop a new gun and cartridge to handle them. Various Sharpe and Keith cast bullets were tried with different powders. The factory .357 bullet resembled what is now popularly called the "Keith" form but was shorter and lighter than Keith's original design, so it could be loaded with its shoulder entirely within the .357 Mag. case. In

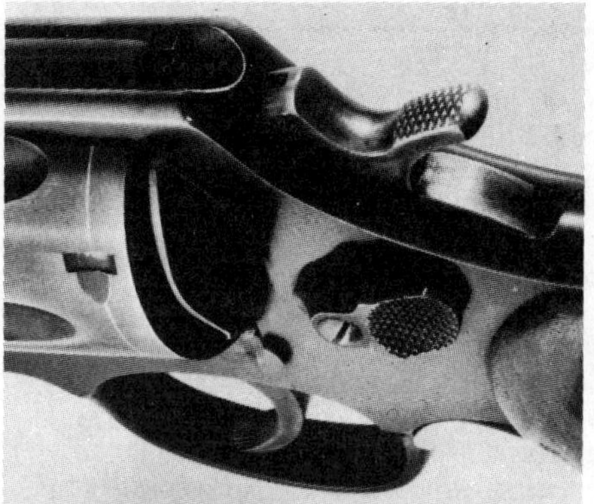

Intended primarily as a workhorse handgun, the .38-44 Heavy Duty features fixed sights, plain finish and standard hammer and trigger.

developing the bullet, Winchester rejected both Keith and Sharpe's designs, though borrowing features from both. The final result was called a "Sharpe-type" bullet in early promotional literature, though it appears both men had equal but minor roles in its design.

Before World War II, Colt revolvers for the .357 Mag. were easier to come by than the S&W model. That chambering was offered in both the New Service and Single Action revolvers starting in 1935. When the .357 Magnum Smith & Wesson revolver was introduced, it had only a limited market because it was available only as a custom revolver in barrel lengths from 3½" to 8¾".

Each S&W .357 Magnum was made to customer's specifications and stamped with a registration number in the yoke cut

ACCURACY RESULTS

Five Consecutive Five-Shot Groups At 25 Yds. From Ransom Rest

.38 Spl. Cartridge (unless noted)	Vel. @ 15' (f.p.s.)	Smallest (ins.)	Largest (ins.)	Average (ins.)	25 Shot Composite (ins.)
Smith & Wesson Model .38/44 Heavy Duty 5"					
Remington R38S4 158-gr. LRN Targetmaster	773 avg. 126 ES 28 Sd	2.31	4.26	3.10	4.26
Winchester 38S4P 150-gr. LRN +P	938 avg. 75 ES 18 Sd	1.15	3.08	2.08	3.08
Smith & Wesson Model .38/44 Outdoorsman 6½"					
Remington R38S4 158-gr. LRN Targetmaster	768 avg. 87 ES 20 Sd	1.27	2.14	1.65	2.40
Winchester 38S4P 150-gr. LRN +P	946 avg. 79 ES 14 Sd	1.03	3.21	2.05	3.21
Smith & Wesson Model .357 Magnum 6½"					
Remington R38S4 158-gr. LRN Targetmaster	757 avg. 106 ES 26 Sd	1.68	2.56	2.06	3.07
Winchester 38S4P 150-gr. LRN +P	940 avg. 37 ES 12 Sd	0.84	1.46	1.05	1.51
Winchester X3571P 158-gr. lead .357 Magnum	1254 avg. 125 ES 41 Sd	1.05	3.36	2.09	3.36

Cautions About +P Cartridges

AMMUNITION for the .38 Spl. has been loaded to two distinct pressure levels since the introduction of high velocity loads in 1931. The standard velocity .38 Spl. cartridge for many years was loaded to a maximum average pressure of 16,000 c.u.p., though recent changes in the methods of pressure measurement now permit a maximum average pressure of 17,000 c.u.p. In actual practice most standard velocity loads easily stay below this figure. High velocity, or +P loads, however, may attain up to 20,000 c.u.p. maximum average pressure.

In 1974 the Sporting Arms and Ammunition Manufacturer's Institute (SAAMI) adopted the practice of identifying ammunition loaded to the higher pressure level by a +P headstamp. This was intended to permit its identification by shooters, and thereby limit its use only to suitable firearms. With the current variety of .38 Spl. guns, shooters are often unsure of the suitability of their guns for +P loads.

S&W states that +P loads may be used in any *steel frame* revolver which has the model number stamped in the yoke cut of the frame (i.e., "10-6"), which indicates post-1957 manufacture. Therefore, +P loads may be used in the steel J-frame Models 36 or 60, or any steel K or N-frame guns, but not aluminum frame or aluminum cylinder guns such as the Airweight M&P, Airweight Chief's Special, Bodyguard or Centennial models.

Colt states that +P loads may be used in *steel* D-frame models, such as the Diamondback, Police Positive Special and Detective Special, as well as the heavier frame Official Police, Officer's Model, Trooper Mark III, etc. +P loads should not be used in the light alloy frame Cobra or Agent revolvers.

Charter Arms states that +P loads should not be used in the Undercover revolver, but should be limited to the Police Bulldog and .357 Bulldog revolvers only.

Sturm Ruger and Dan Wesson both indicate their .38 Spl. revolvers differ from their .357 Mag. models only in chambering and may be used with +P factory loads without reservation.

Experience suggests, however, that in the small steel frame revolvers, such as the S&W J-frame or Colt D-frame models, +P loads should be limited to occasional use. Owners of revolvers of other makes should refer to the manufacturer's instruction manual if any doubt exists.

Shooters must also be aware of the existence of special law enforcement loads identified by an "LE" or +P+ headstamp. These cartridges may generate pressures as much as 15% above industry +P standard and should not be used in any .38 Spl. revolver. They are intended for use in .357 Mag. guns only. These cartridges are not available in commercial channels, so the chance of your purchasing them by accident is remote. — C. E. H.

of the frame. When the gun was received and the registration card filled out, the owner received a certificate signed by either Douglas or Victor Wesson which included the owner's name, the gun serial number, barrel length, single- and double-action trigger pulls, and other options. This practice proved too costly for a revolver which then sold for $60 and was discontinued after approximately 5500 registered .357 Magnums had been produced. Production of the S&W .357 Magnum was discontinued in 1942 to allow the company to begin full wartime production. Production resumed in 1946, incorporating the improved hammer block, indicated by the letter S accompanying the serial number. All the N-frame .357 Magnums are serial numbered within the .44 Hand Ejector series. In 1948, the short action was adopted, as it was for the .38/44 HD and Outdoorsman revolvers. In 1957, the .357 Magnum was redesignated the Model 27.

Elmer Keith described the new .357 S&W Mag. revolver in the November, 1935, issue of the *American Rifleman*. Prewar guns of this type had the best of fit and finish. They were available with a variety of options: Patridge, McGivern or Call gold bead with square notch rear sight, or round notch with Paine, Sheard or Marble front sight, standard or hump-backed hammer, standard or "Magna" stocks, with or without grip adapter, etc. The hammer sides were concentrically gooved about the pivot to reduce friction with the frame, and the topstrap was checkered to reduce glare.

Neither Keith nor F. C. Ness thought much of the 8¾" long barrel. "It balances the same as a 30" Springfield International rifle and is about as handy in the field," Keith noted. Ness agreed, saying, "As to portability, it is not much of an improvement on the 44-40 carbine." The concensus of writers in the 1930s was that the 6½" barrel was best for field use, an observation which holds true today.

Colt didn't offer extra-long barrels in its .357 Mag. guns but emphasized the standard 5½" and 7½" barrel ordinarily offered in the Single Action and New Service revolvers. In 1954, it introduced the first of its medium-frame service guns for the .357 mag., using the same .41 frame that was the basis for the Officer's Model and Official Police revolvers. This adjustable sight .357 Mag. revolver was available in both 4" and 6" barrel lengths. Though it was first called simply the "Colt 357," the name was soon changed to "Trooper" after the popular, nearly identical .38 Spl. revolver. In 1955, a highly refined version of the Colt .357 was introduced with heavy-ribbed barrels in 2½", 4" and 6" lengths suitable for police service, hunting or target shooting. Since its introduction, this revolver, the Python, has become very highly regarded, and the .357 Mag. has achieved a stature unmatched by any other revolver cartridge. It also has undoubtedly contributed to the continued success of the .38 Spl., since that cartridge is commonly used in .357 guns where the full .357 Mag. load is unnecessarily powerful. Over the years, the heavy-frame 6" revolver has become the choice among hunters and target shooters, while the 4" medium-frame guns such as the S&W Model 19, Colt Python and Ruger Security Six are the standard among law enforcement officers and citizens wanting a general-purpose sidearm.

There is a popular mystique surrounding the older heavy-frame .38 Spl. and .357 Mag. S&Ws. The pre-war, long-action guns are certainly slick working and better finished than those of current manufacture, but the claims for phenomenal accuracy from old guns are mostly myth. The first real opportunity I had to explore this was when Managing Editor Joe Roberts and I test-fired some of exhibition shooter Ed McGivern's Smith & Wessons (see *American Rifleman*, August, 1980, p. 31). McGivern's revolvers were good by any standard but not exceptional. As a matter of interest, I located a 1932-vintage S&W Outdoorsman and a prewar .357 Magnum, both in nearly pristine condition, for firing tests. Later, I found a 1950 model .38/44 Heavy Duty which we shot as well. Firing each of the .38 Spl. guns with standard velocity, lead round-nose and the 150-gr. lead round-nose +P (which is the currently-produced equivalent of the original .38/44 load), we found they gave good performance, but not better than what would be expected with similar current target or service guns. The pre-war S&W .357 Magnum was fired with these and with Super-X Lubaloy ammunition similar to the original magnum loads. As might be expected, this special-order gun outshot the standard ones. It is interesting to note that while accuracy with the lead bullet .357 Mag. cartridges deteriorated as firing progressed, all 25 rounds in the 25-yd. backing target still struck in 3.36", which is useful hunting or service accuracy. Firing the gun again with jacketed soft-point ammunition brought only a modest improvement in accuracy, five consecutive 5-shot groups averaging 1.83", with the 25-round composite measuring 3.04".

Even though some of the mystique has been exploded, these are still very useful guns. The best part about our findings is that today you can buy a .38 Spl. or .357 Mag. revolver every bit as accurate as those of 40 years ago. So you, too, can enjoy the advantages of owning one of America's workhorse revolvers. ■

McGivern

Continued from page 18

largest 2.48", and the smallest 1.47". The 1917 did not do quite as well. The best group from the big .45 ran 2.58" center to center, the worst just over 4", and the average 3.6". Then we tried the guns McGivern's way — one-hand, double-action, firing five-shot groups at ranges of three to seven yards. We — *American Rifleman* Associate Technical Editor Ed Harris and I — used McGivern's guns to shoot the target, playing card-size groups, and to split the cards illustrated. Neither of us felt even tempted to try and hit a tossed card or a ¾" lead disc. Hitting a stationary playing card turned edgeways is hard enough, and Walter Groff was kind enough to leave us a selection of perforated lead wafers, shot in the air the way McGivern did it, with his collection. Nor did either of us try to dump five rounds into a 50¢ piece in ½ second. The group shown was selected from better than half-a-dozen, shot in something like a minute per group, to emulate McGivern's record. But, it's fair to note, the group was shot one-handed and double-action.

Which brings us 'round to the other side of the issue, modifications for rapid double-action firing. *There weren't any*! If anything, McGivern's guns are stiffer and more positive than factory guns bought today. His technique of shooting double-action revolvers depended on strong springs to balance the physical force involved in pulling and releasing the trigger. He got his speed from years of practice, not through any special mechanical advantage.

While he was active as an exhibition shooter and, later, after arthritis ended that career, McGivern delved deep into the practical application of his art. He studied hip (or instinct) shooting with one and two guns. He developed techniques for hitting stationary targets from moving firing points. He experimented with a nearly endless variety of holsters — from a pair that detached from a belt to the original Berns-Martin holsters we chose to illustrate. And, he taught people — private citizens like Walter Groff, law enforcement personnel from the Lewistown, Mont., police to the Federal Bureau of Investigation, and, during World War II, U.S. Servicemen — how to shoot.

He was still shooting and still teaching when he died at age 83 in December, 1957. His lessons are still startlingly simple: close attention to the fundamentals of shooting, sight alignment, sight picture, and trigger control; and practice — endless days and weeks and years of practice — make a man a marksman. And, the guns we examined and fired — guns that McGivern set records with, and which are unmodified except for sights and grips — prove that perserverance, not tricks, made him the unequalled master he was. •

Single-Shot Underhammers

A look at an unusual firearm as distinctly American as the Kentucky rifle

By HERSCHEL C. LOGAN

JUST why the unique class of arms known as 'underhammers' has, for so long, escaped the notice of serious writers on the subject of old guns is somewhat of a mystery. As distinctly American as the Deringer or the 'Kentucky' rifle, these unusual pistols, with the hammer on the underside of the barrel, are quietly but quickly on the way to becoming rare Americana. Already they are infrequent items on dealers' lists.

Fabricated for the most part in the New England states, with Massachusetts and Connecticut leading in makers (see page 30), they were also produced in later years as far west as Michigan and Minnesota. Even though of American origin, the type was adapted and made by English and Continental gunmakers.

The period of their production and popularity seems to have been from around 1835 to 1860. The assigning of this era is based on a few dated specimens, the active periods of their makers, and patent dates, where known. That they were in use at later dates is borne out by the fact that such pieces were picked up on some of the battlefields of the War between the States. From authentic sources it is certain that underhammers were used occasionally as personal side arms by soldiers on both sides of that conflict.

It appears highly probable, due to their simplicity, that the first 'understrikers' or 'undercocks', as they were often referred to at the time, were the products of individual gunsmiths working in a small way and that they were patterned after the occasional underhammer rifle then being fabricated. The products of these primitive backwoods gunshops are easy to identify—they have that peculiar handmade appearance that immediately stamps them as unique Americana. Unmarked for the most part, they are usually found with an octagon barrel not unlike that of a rifle of the time. Even the sights and inlays, where used, are mounted quite similarly to those on rifles. Truly they are splendid examples of gunsmithing ingenuity during the early days. Later they were made in considerable quantity by individuals and firms.

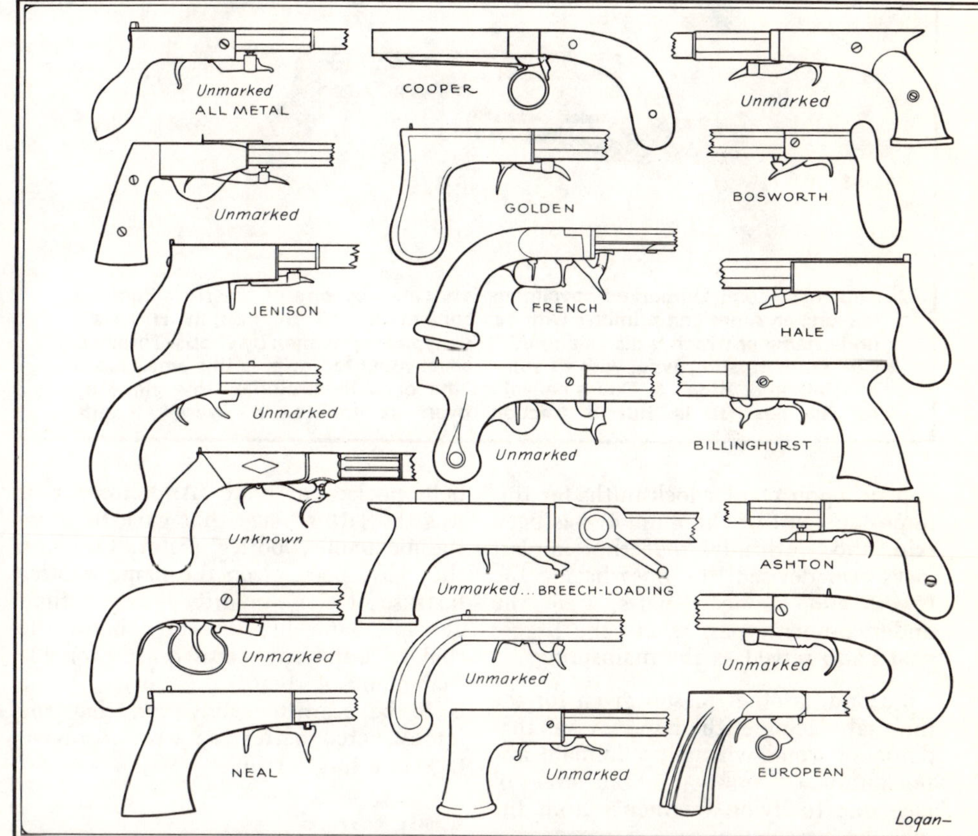

That the underhammers do not lack for variety in their grip styles is evident from this group.

The men who made them

Some of the names found on the guns are of individuals known to have been employed by larger arms manufacturers of the area. For instance, Tuller of Hale & Tuller is listed in the directories of the day as being a Superintendent and Inspector at Colt's. Peter H. Ashton (note the spelling) was a partner of Henry Aston until the firm was dissolved in 1852. It could well be that the little underhammers were the product of their home workshops during the hours away from their regular employment, or at least on their own time.

One of the first questions asked by the layman whenever an underhammer is displayed is, "Why did they put the hammer on the under side of the barrel?" Admittedly it is a fair question, to which there would appear to be three logical answers.

First, even to anyone not especially mechanically minded, it is quite obvious that the average underhammer is the personification of simplicity when compared with most arms. Its flat mainspring attached to the straight frame was housed, in a majority of the types, in the horizontal part of the grip. This simple construction permitted it to be made both easily and inexpensively. Milton Warren, an apprentice to John M. Whitesides of Abingdon, Virginia, wrote that in addition to their rifles they made a great many underhammer 'bootleg' pistols. "These," he said, "were simple things and one could be made in a day."

An important feature in relation to the manufacture of underhammers was that due to their simplicity each maker could, and did, fashion his own locks. Thus it was not necessary for him to

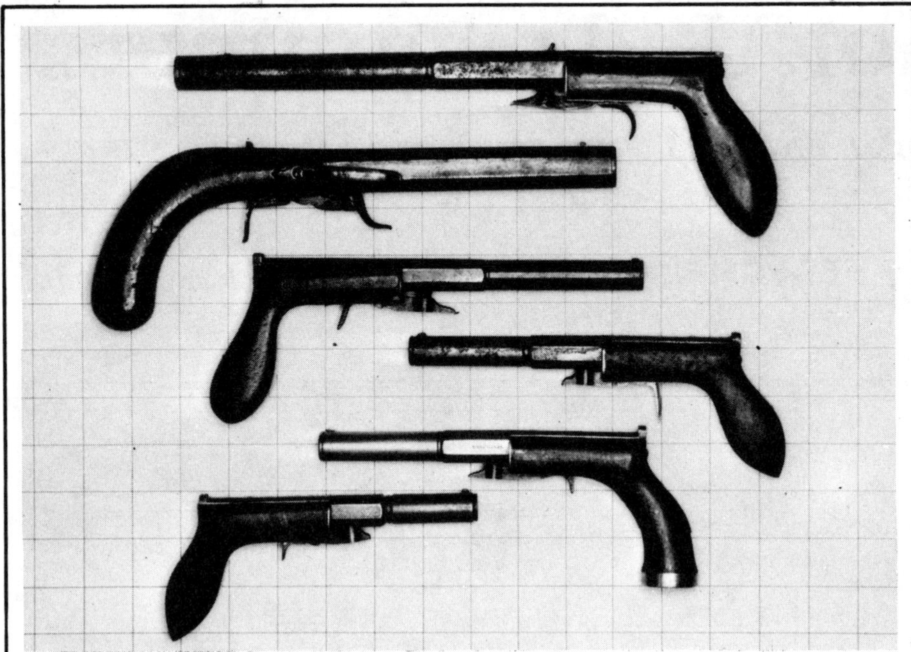

Top to bottom: Unmarked specimens fabricated by one of the New England makers; an American primitive with belt hook made by T. Bennett; the H. J. Hale underhammer which is also stamped "US"; typical specimen by Gibbs, Tiffany & Co.; an interesting type, with its round silver-mounted grip, is this small piece by Nathaniel Rider & Co.; smallest of the ones illustrated is this piece by A. Ruggles. It is but a fraction over six inches in overall length.

depend upon regular locksmiths for this important part of the gun. It has been said, and truthfully, that the simplest locks ever devised, the ones having the fewest and strongest parts, were the underhammer types, where the trigger guard also served as the mainspring.

Second, another reason given for the unusual placing of the hammer was that doing so would virtually eliminate any possibility of injury to the eyes or face due to flying fragments from the metallic percussion cap. Strange as it may seem, there were a few gunsmiths who advanced the belief that with the nipple and hammer underneath quicker fire could be achieved. Or could such belief have been merely sales talk? It belt, pocket, or boot. And, in fact, it was the latter place that gave to them the nickname 'bootleg' pistol. Or could they have been given the name bootleg because of the similarity between their general shape and that of a boot? Be that as it may, it seems quite probable that many of them were carried in the is to be admitted, however, that the unobstructed barrel top was an advantage in a target arm.

Easily carried

Third, compared with other pistols, equipped with rather cumbersome top or side hammers, the underhammers offered a convenient streamlined model. They could be carried with ease in the top of their owner's boot. However, the name bootleg alone does not denote underhammer pistols. Other single-shot pistols of the time, with conventional hammers and no wooden fore-stocks, were sometimes referred to as bootleg pistols.

Designs many and various

An examination of the illustrations accompanying this article will indicate that, with the exception of placing the hammer under the barrel, the general design of the guns themselves is as varied and individual as that found in any other class of arms of the era.

While this article will deal only with single-shots, underhammers were also made in multishot, double barrel, side-by-side, and over-and-under (two specimens of which are illustrated), and the pepperbox. The specimens illustrated in connection with this study are but representative examples of underhammer pistols. It is believed, however, that they do portray an excellent cross-section of this interesting class of arms.

Designed for protection, game, or target shooting, they were produced in a wide range of calibers, ranging from the smallbore indoor target arms to the large .50 caliber outdoor weapons. Some were rifled very nicely while others are to be found only with a smooth bore.

Target models are rare

Definitely on the rare side are the target models equipped with a bullet starter, such as the unmarked Hilliard (see page 31). William Billinghurst, one of the really fine riflemakers of his time, is also known to have produced a target model with bullet starter. And, of course, there may have been others but, if so, they are few and far between. It has been suggested that many of the fine old target models were used in the turkey shoots of the olden days.

Barrels are octagonal and round, full octagonal, or all round, in shape. They will be found in lengths varying from three to four inches on the pocket models to 18 inches, or more, for the 'buggy' type. The long-barrel jobs, carried in the buggy or wagon, were used principally for the shooting of small game or for target shooting. In either event, the gun was often rested across the free arm of the shooter.

Of tough, durable steels

On many of the earlier pieces the words "CAST STEEL" or "WARRANTED CAST STEEL" are found stamped on the barrel. In his excellent book, *The Muzzle-Loading Cap Lock Rifle*, the late Ned Roberts writes, "Cast steel for rifle barrels was not highly

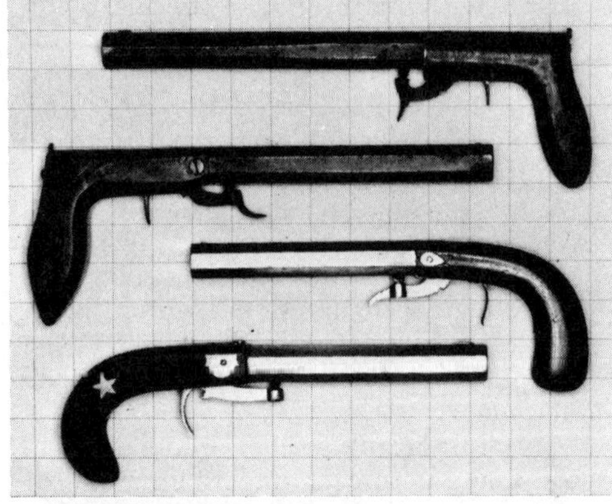

Four typically American primitives, only one of which is marked. Barrel of the double action specimen (bottom) has engraved initials J.E.W.

The American eagle stamp found on some New England pieces.

It was this convenient carrying place that gave the name "bootleg" to these early guns.

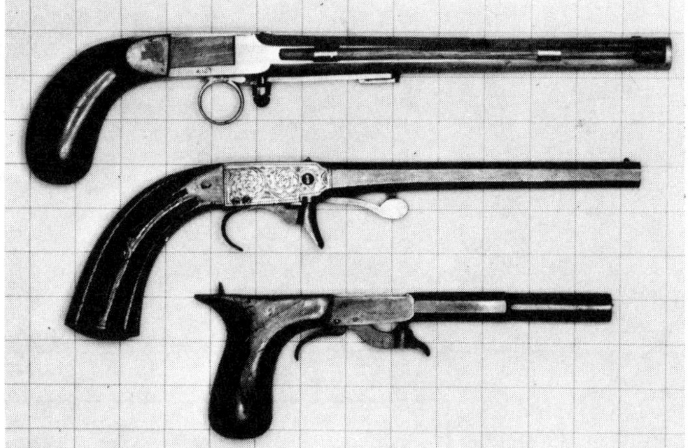

Three pieces of foreign manufacture. Top: Spanish proofmarked. The spring which serves as a hammer swings to the side for capping. Middle: Breech-loader believed to be of French origin. Bottom: Even though it closely resembles some American pieces in design, this specimen is stamped with British proofmarks.

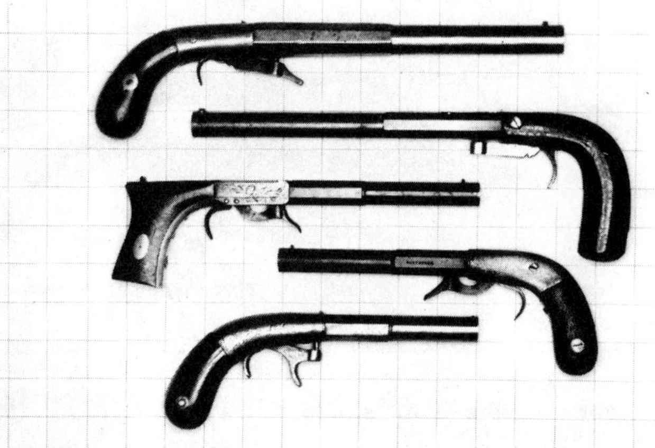

Top to bottom: This piece by S. W. Card closely resembles the Bacon (bottom); a tiny bore is the feature of this target pistol by B. A. Bailey; of Allen manufacture this piece is stamped "A. W. Spies, MISSISSIPPI POCKET RIFLE; this Allen & Thurber is of the Worcester period of production; a typical Bacon underhammer.

carbonized, gave a steel that was tough and durable and not brittle, and really was a very excellent barrel steel for muzzle-loaders." By 1840 many of the armsmakers in the United States were using the new cast steel in the making of their barrels. As time went by this identifying mark gradually disappeared as a selling feature.

Grips varied in style

Grips, insofar as shape and style were concerned, were as individualistic as the men who made them. The great majority are quite plain but occasionally specimens will be found with wire or metal inlays, lifting them out of the ordinary. Fluted grips seem to be found only on foreign-made specimens; at least most of those observed are of French or Belgian origin. On many of the New England pieces the grips are trimmed or mounted with brass or German silver. Walnut and curly maple were the principal woods used in the making of stocks. In rare cases pistols with all-metal grips, and even stag grips, may be found.

Shapes range from the rather stiff right angle, the oblique, the curved, the saw-handle, and so on to the extreme bird's-head type. Each style differs slightly, depending upon who produced it. Underhammers equipped with an extension metal or wooden stock are not unknown but they are distinctly on the scarce side, as is also the specimen illustrated (page 30) with the integral shoulder stock. One other similar piece was observed but it came more under the rifle classification with its long barrel, rather than the pistol category.

Breech-loaders rare

Breech-loading underhammers are seldom encountered. Two specimens, one of foreign manufacture, are pictured. Of small bore for indoor target shooting, the foreign piece (see page 29) required but a speck or so of powder to propel the tiny ball. The lever in front of the hammer turns a drum which permits the powder and ball to be loaded through the small hole on the right side—a simple and convenient arrangement, and one wonders why more of them were not made. It is highly probable that they were only made near the end of the underhammer period, and against the new cartridge arms they could hardly have been expected to hold their place for any great length of time. An easily removed breech plug on the Demeritt target specimen (see page 31) permits loading from the breech and also permits the finely rifled barrel to be cleaned more conveniently.

A double-action model

There is an old adage which says there are exceptions to every rule. It is proven again in this research. Amidst all the single-action underhammers there comes to light a double-action! Not that double-actions were unknown or rare in percussion arms, as witness the early pepperbox items, but they are very infrequently met with among the underhammers where the hammer is ordinarily pulled down into cocking position by hand.

Front and rear sights were of the open type except in the unusual cases where the pistols were designed only for target shooting, such as the Billinghurst. These guns were often equipped with special sights—adjustable, hooded, and even telescopic. On the other hand

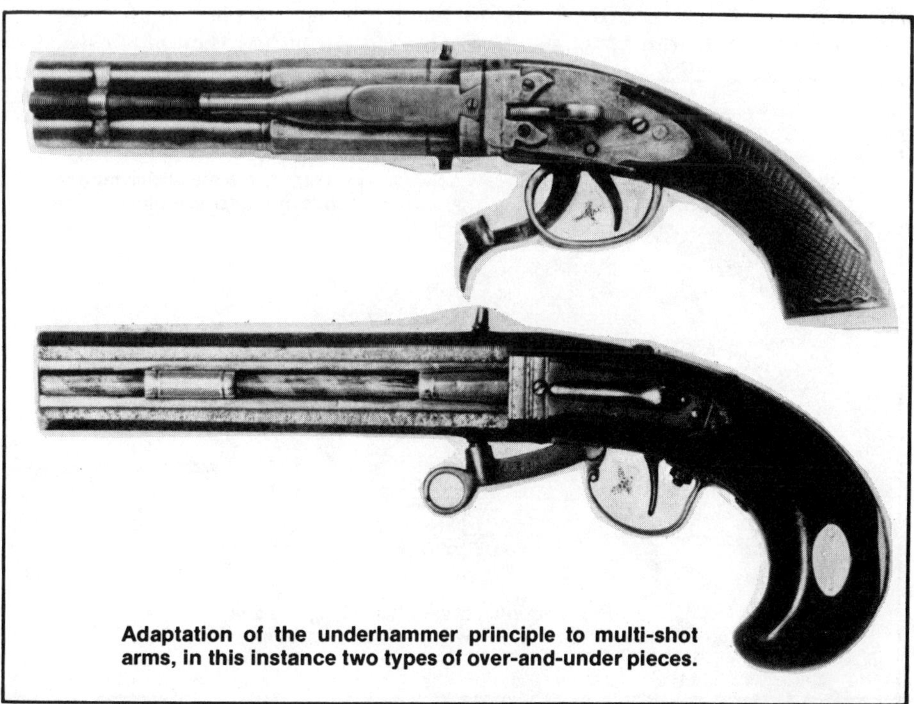

Adaptation of the underhammer principle to multi-shot arms, in this instance two types of over-and-under pieces.

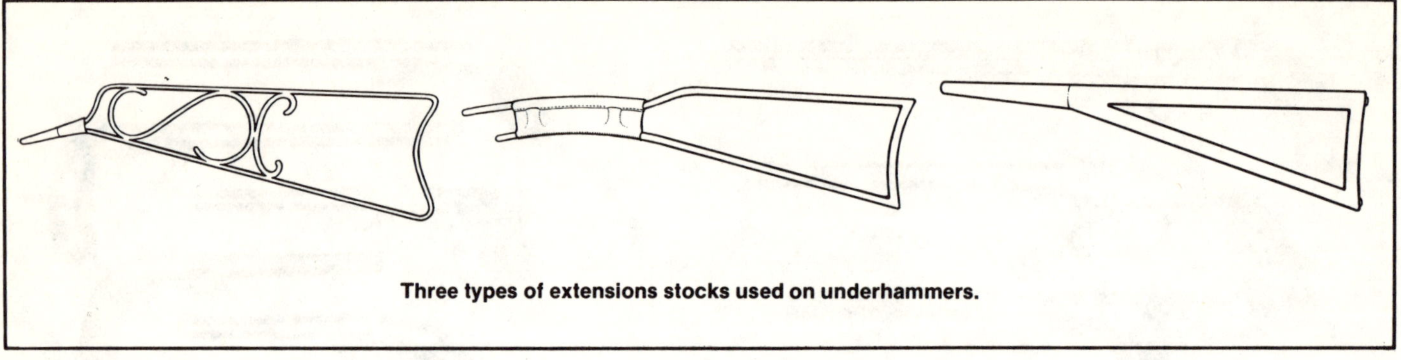

Three types of extensions stocks used on underhammers.

it is not uncommon to find specimens without sights of any kind, which would indicate that the weapon was used primarily as a defense arm and not for target or game shooting.

Trigger guards rarely seen

By far the greater number of underhammers were produced without trigger guards. In the majority of cases where a guard was employed, it also served as a mainspring. The specimen by B. C. Wood, an early riflemaker, is a splendid example of this simple but effective lock mechanism (see page 31). Sometimes the guard was slotted to permit the hammer to operate through it. Examples of both types of trigger guards are to be found among those illustrated with this article.

The rare Demeritt presents its own unique underhammer mechanism. Serving as a hammer, the trigger guard is actuated by a spring in the grip. When the guard is pushed downward, a spring fastened to it pushes an anchored pin into locked position against the back of the trigger, thus holding the hammer in cocked position. A tiny screw through the trigger makes it possible to adjust it for a feather touch in target shooting. Two other interesting underhammers which were observed, one by Cooper, employed an unusual spring arrangement. The spring is a lengthy flat type and is fastened near the muzzle on the under side of the barrel. The end which is tripped by the ring trigger serves as the hammer to detonate the cap.

Trigger design followed more or less a standard pattern. Now and then ring triggers will be found, as is evidenced by the specimens illustrated. Much more scarce are underhammers with folding triggers. They are the products of foreign manufacturers and, like the breech-loading specimens, are believed to have been of late fabrication.

Maker often unknown

While many of these interesting pistols are marked with the maker's name, there are many to be found with only the gunsmith's initials, or totally unmarked. Many of these are believed to have been the product of riflemakers who made them up for the enjoyment of it, or for a personal side arm, and did not feel it necessary to place their name thereon. (They would, I am sure, have done so had they but realized the

This H. J. Hale underhammer has integral shoulder stock.

A Pocket version of a folding-trigger underhammer.

Pen and ink sketch illustrating the simple construction of a typical underhammer.

U. S. MAKERS

Name	Place	Dates
Ethan Allen	Grafton, Mass.	1832-38
Allen & Thurber	Grafton, Mass.	1838-42
	Norwich, Conn.	1842-47
	Worcester, Mass.	1847-57
Andrus & Osborn	Canton, Conn.	circa 1860
P. H. Ashton	Middletown, Conn.	circa 1852
Wm. Ashton (W.A.)	Middletown, Conn.	circa 1854
Ashtons	Middletown, Conn.	circa 1854
J. Babcock		
Bacon & Co.	Norwich, Conn.	1852-88
G. A. Badger		1866-68
B. A. Bailey		
J. Barnes		
T. Bennett		
Wm. Billinghurst	Rochester, N.Y.	1830-80
C. Bird & Co.	Philadelphia, Pa.	
B. M. Bosworth	Lancaster Co., Pa.	
J. Brown	Freemont, N. H.	1857-70
S. W. Card		
M. Carleton & Co.		circa 1860
Case, Willard & Co.	New Hartford, Conn.	
E. Chamberlain	Southbridge, Mass.	
D. H. Colson		
J. R. Cooper	New York	circa 1849
Nelson Delaney	Reading, Pa.	1845-72
J. Demeritt	Montpelier, Vt.	
J. I. Eastman	Jaffrey, N. H.	1863-68
G. B. Fogg	Manchester, N. H.	
J. A. France	Cobbleskill, N. Y.	
W. G.		1846
Gibbs, Tiffany & Co.	Sturbridge, Mass.	1833-38
R. Golden		
E. Gray		
J. Graves	Bangor, Maine	
H. J. Hale	Bristol, Conn.	
Hale & Tuller	Hartford, Conn.	
Hall		
D. H. Hilliard	Cornish, N. H.	1860-80
J. Jenison	Southbridge, Mass.	
N. Jones		
W. W. M.		
M. Marble		
Nicanor Kendall	Windsor, Vt.	1835-43
A. D. Laws		
James Little		
Mead & Adriance		
Wm. Neal	Bangor, Maine	
S. Osborn	Canton, Conn.	
Pike	Troy, N. Y.	
Quinabaug Rifle Mfg. Co.	Southbridge, Mass.	
Charles Ramsdell	Bangor, Maine	
W. Raymond	Winona, Minn.	1864-65
Nathaniel Rider & Co.	Southbridge, Mass.	
A. Ruggles	Stafford, Conn.	
D. D. Sackett	Westfield, Mass.	
M. S. Sanderson		
Geo. V. Seaver	Vergennes, Vt.	circa 1858
Shaw & Ledoyt	Stafford, Conn.	
H. Sheets		
J. Simpson	New Britain, Conn.	
A. Smith (Importer?)	Philadelphia, Pa.	
M. Smith		
A. W. Spies (Agent)	New York, N. Y.	1820-51
C. Stuart		
E. Sutherland (Agent)	Richmond, Va.	1852-64
Tilden & Thurber		
Geo. W. Tryon	Philadelphia, Pa.	1836-66
L. B. White		
John M. Whitesides	Wolf Hills, Abingdon, Va.	
William Wingert	Detroit, Mich.	1845-67
B. C. Wood	Painted Post, N. Y.	
A. C. Wright	Fitchburg, Mass.	
J. E. W.		

FOREIGN

Name	Place	Dates
Anschutz & Sohne	Suhl	
Bentley	London	
J. B. Cessier	France	circa 1850
Day	England	circa 1832
Durs Egg	London	1785-1834
Gossett	Paris	
Ward Henfield	England	
N. S. Jesson	Bohemia	
Redferry	London	

worry these unmarked pistols would cause students of arms in later years.) Some of the New England pieces are stamped with an American eagle on the barrel strap—why, no one seems to know. The stamp appears to be identical in size and design. It could well be that it was some sort of 'guild' mark of makers working in a certain area. We can but speculate at this distant date.

A puzzle in numbers

Serial numbers, where there are any, are to be found under the barrel near the nipple or on the side of the frame under the grip. H. J. Hale has added to the mystery of markings by adding the number 140 to his guns. Even the integral stocked specimen has this same 140 in addition to the serial number. Since the pieces known are of slightly different design, it hardly refers to a model number, if indeed such were used at that early date. As if to add to the confusion two other underhammers by this maker, one stamped "H. J. Hale" and one marked "Hale & Tuller", turn up stamped "US" although none are known to have been purchased by the U. S. Government for military use!

Most authorities agree, and the record seems to bear them out, that there is no account of the Ordnance Department having purchased any underhammers. Yet, here is a specimen fully marked, and authentic. Could it have been that some department of the government other than the military purchased a few such arms with the request that they be so stamped? Or, was it, as some have suggested, merely a way of designating the gun as having been made in the U. S., the same as our "USA" stamping today, which certainly does not necessarily mean a martial arm.

In addition to those having the name and address of the maker, specimens will be encountered with the name of the agent or jobber also stamped on the gun. Three such agents were: "E. Hutchings & Co., Balt., Md."; "Rogers Bros. & Co., 52 Market St., Philad."; and "A. W. Spies", who was agent for the Ethan Allen arms from around 1835 until 1848.

Concerning the similarity in design of a few of the underhammers, it would seem that they were produced by the same firm, irrespective of the name which appears on them. It could be that they were manufactured upon order for different companies and so marked with their names. Data on the majority of makers are very meager indeed. In many cases the maker is known only by virtue of a specimen being found bearing his name, or name and address. On the other hand, enough is known regarding a few of the early makers to give a fairly accurate idea as to the actual period during which the underhammers had their beginning.

Allen & Thurber

Ethan Allen, Grafton, Massachusetts, started the manufacture of 'undercock' pistols in 1834 and continued making them for several years after his merger with Thurber, his brother-in-law, in 1838. In 1842 Allen & Thurber moved to Norwich, Connecticut, and in 1847 to Worcester, Massachusetts. The specimen illustrated is from their Worcester plant. The late Harley J. Van Cleave, who did a prodigious amount of research on the Allen arms and had access to some of Allen's day books, wrote that the Allen Pocket Rifles sold for from $4 to $4.50 per pair in 1847. The long barrel jobs brought $5.

A short, happy life

In 1833 Enoch Gibbs and Lucian Tiffany began the manufacture of pistols in a small building in Westville, a part of Southbridge, Massachusetts. Later they moved into a better structure built by David K. Porter near a dam across Hobb's Creek in Sturbridge. The place was known at the time by the name of Pistol Shop and Pond. Since specimens produced by Gibbs, Tiffany & Co., show up more frequently than do many other makes, the firm must have been quite productive during the time they were in business. In 1838 Mr. Tiffany moved from Sturbridge to Hartford and apparently the firm ceased operation soon thereafter.

The Nathaniel Rider & Co., also called the Quinabaug Rifle Mfg. Co., were others of the Southbridge armsmakers. In view of the fact that an early account mentions "the Riders were engaged at one time or another in the manufacturing of pistols", it would seem that there must have been more than one, perhaps father and sons, or brothers.

The accompanying list of makers and agents, gathered and compiled from many sources, is presented here for the first time, in the hope it will prove of real value to all who are interested in a serious study of these early arms. No such list can be final or complete. Names of other makers will, in all probability, continue to come to light here and there as the years come and go.

My special and sincere thanks to Ray C. Young, Jim Serven, Robert Abels, Jim White, Martin Retting, Maj. Hugh Smiley, Lewis Winant, the Jacob Edwards Memorial Library of Southbridge, Mass., and others who assisted in this study. —H. C. L.

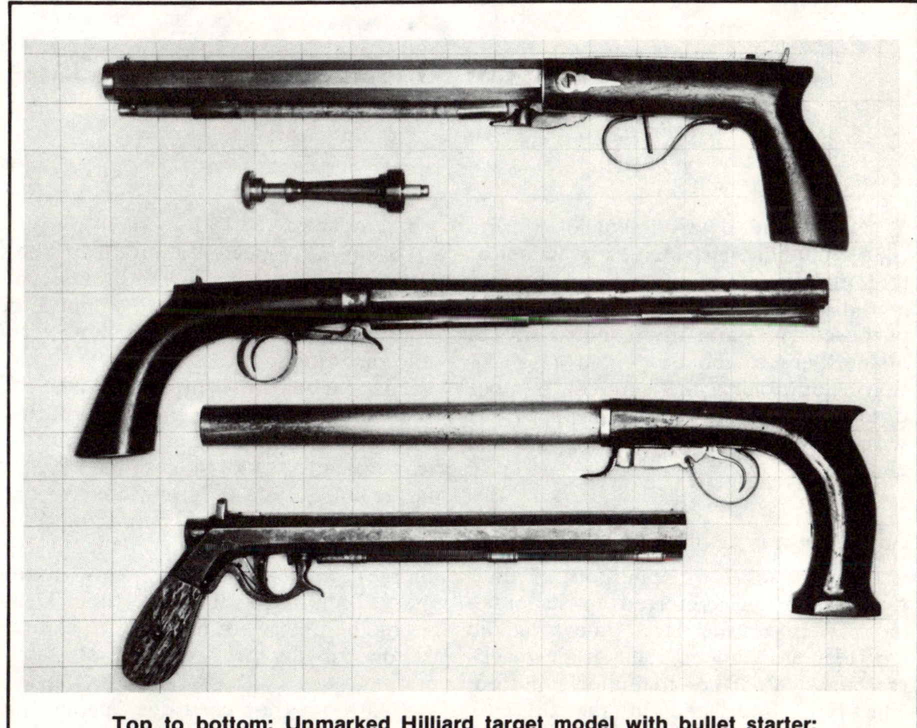

Top to bottom: Unmarked Hilliard target model with bullet starter; trigger guard is mainspring on this specimen by B. C. Wood, one of the early riflemakers; unmarked large caliber pistol on which the trigger guard serves as a mainspring; trigger guard acts as a hammer on this unique breech-loading underhammer by J. Demeritt.

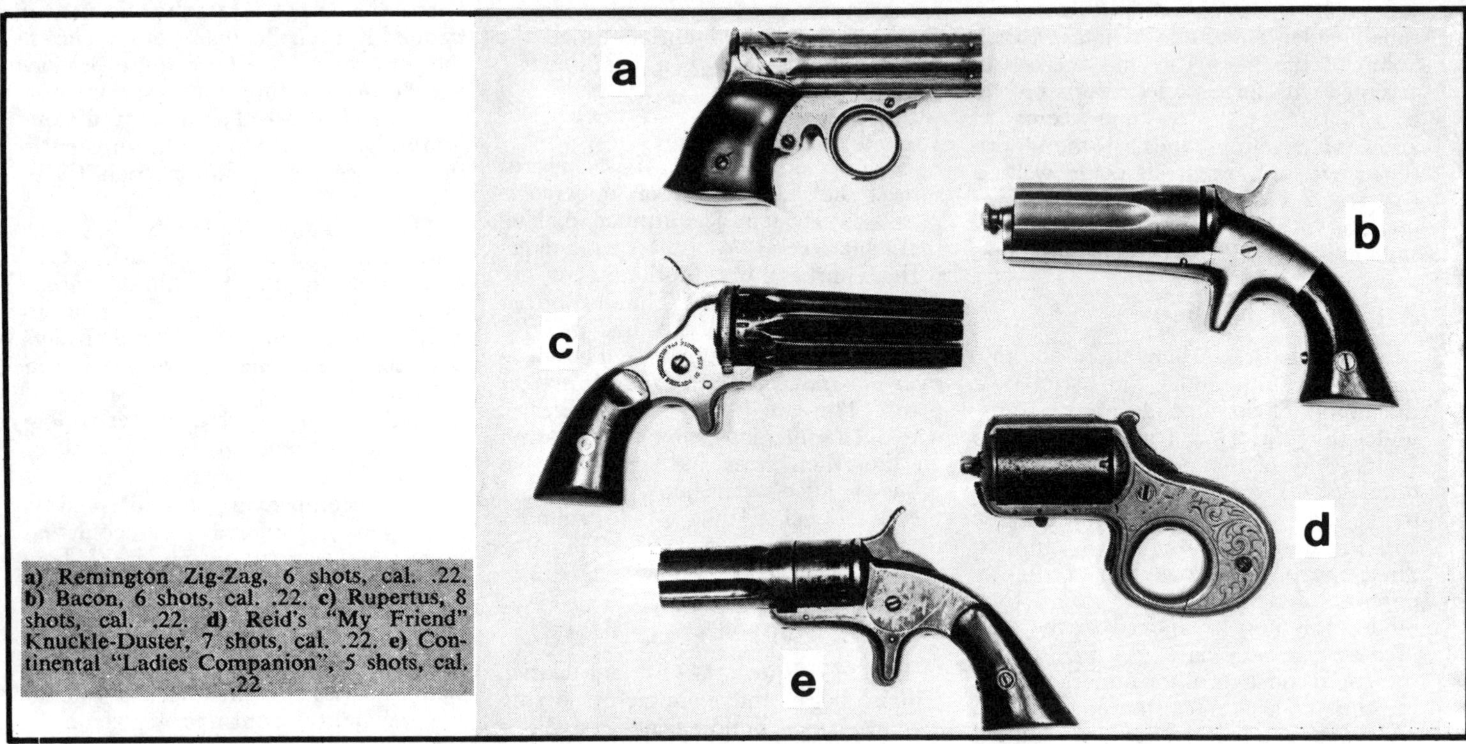

a) Remington Zig-Zag, 6 shots, cal. .22. b) Bacon, 6 shots, cal. .22. c) Rupertus, 8 shots, cal. .22. d) Reid's "My Friend" Knuckle-Duster, 7 shots, cal. .22. e) Continental "Ladies Companion", 5 shots, cal. .22

Cartridge Pepperboxes

Unusual American Revolving-Barrel Handguns

By Herschel C. Logan

WITH the development of rimfire metallic cartridges, it was logical that makers of percussion handguns—including single-shots, revolvers, dual-purpose arms, and multi-shots—should adapt them to the new fixed ammunition. Comprising the smallest number of any such group were the pepperboxes with revolving barrels having integral chambers.

Date from matchlock period

Pepperboxes, or pepperpots as they were sometimes referred to in olden days, were not a development of the cartridge era. Indeed, their origin reaches back into the matchlock period. The type flourished in the flintlock period and reached its zenith in the percussion era. Thus, it was but natural that in designing guns for the new rimfire metallic cartridges, some gunmakers should turn again to this age-old revolving firearm principle.

Considered quite ineffective by modern standards, the little pepperbox was, in its day, a respected addition to one's personal armament. It was small, compact, handy, and—of more importance—afforded its owner up to 8 shots without reloading.

The element of surprise played no small part with early multi-shot arms. It was one thing for an antagonist to be confronted with a gun having one barrel but quite a different story to find himself suddenly looking into the muzzle of a multi-barrel weapon with 6 to 8 charges and not know how many charges might go off at one time! Dealers of the time were not slow to capitalize on this feature in their sales promotion.

First of the cartridge pepperbox revolvers was the one known today as the Remington Zig-Zag. This 6-shot, double-action, cal. .22 multi-shot resembles, in general, the outward appearance of 2 other Remington stationary barrel pepperboxes, a 5-shot of cal. .22 and a 4-shot of cal. .32. The Zig-Zag has one important and unique feature not found on any of the other pepperboxes, the method of revolving the barrel group. It was this novel idea that gave it the name Zig-Zag.

Unique operation

As the ring trigger of the Zig-Zag is pushed forward, a stud within the frame moves forward in one of the straight grooves incised in the barrel group. On the rearward pull of the trigger, the stud engages one of the slanting grooves to rotate the cylinder and, at the same time, to cock the hammer. As the trigger is returned to its normal position, the hammer is tripped to fire the cartridge.

The gun was produced by E. Remington & Sons of Ilion, N.Y., under patents #21,188 and #28,461 granted to William H. Elliot on Aug. 17, 1858, and May 29, 1860. Elliot, a noted inventor, was associated with the Remingtons from 1860 to 1886.

Loading was achieved through a hole in the recoil plate. The Zig-Zag, advertised as "Elliot's Pocket Revolver", was manufactured for only a brief period in 1861-62, and only about a thousand of the guns are believed to have been made. Its limited production, plus its unusual features, make it much sought after by arms collectors.

Bacon production

Bacon Arms Co., Norwich, Conn., was the only company previously producing percussion pepperboxes to produce a revolving-barrel cartridge pepperbox. The firm appears to have enjoyed a favorable reputation and to have achieved an active business in percussion arms prior to the appearance of rimfire cartridges. That they should tool up for cartridge arms was quite understandable. Even though not in the field for too long, they did produce a varied line of cartridge arms, not the least of which was their little 6-shot pepperbox.

The Bacon was produced under a patent granted May 29, 1860. However, a perusal of patent dates does not disclose a patent on this same date and of this nature except to William H. Elliot of Remington. The gun is loaded by unscrewing the cylinder pin and removing the cylinder. The pin also serves as a ramrod for ejecting the empty cases.

Another much-sought-after pepperbox using rimfire ammunition is the 8-shot cal. .22 Rupertus. Production on this model must have been quite limited, judging by its rarity.

Jacob Rupertus of Philadelphia, Pa., secured patent #43,606 on July 19, 1864, for a single-action, sheath trigger arm with a novel breech plate. To load the gun, the hammer is pulled back to half-cock position, and the milled disk is revolved to the left. This permits opening of the loading gate contained in the breech piece, and at the same time serves as a safety in preventing the hammer from falling and accidentally firing a cartridge—a simple yet ingenious method. Whereas most other pepperboxes have the bores within the cylinder parallel to each other, the Rupertus differs in that they converge toward the muzzle. Sighting was done along the longitudinal cylinder ribs.

Dual-purpose model

Next in line was a dual-purpose arm, known today among collectors as the Knuckle-Duster. Built in a 7-shot cal. .22 revolver with a hole in the frame through which the bullet passed, it was so designed and constructed that it could be used as a pair of 'knucks' should the need arise. This oddity was the invention of James Reid of Catskill, N. Y. His patent #51,752, dated Dec. 26, 1865, provided only for the formation of a ring in the all-metal frame and a sliding safety to lock the cylinder in a position whereby the hammer rested between the chambers.

The Knuckle-Duster was produced in 3 calibers and sizes, 7-shot .22, 5-shot .32, and 5-shot .41. Of the 3, the little .22's are the most common, the .32's are not too plentiful, and the .41's seldom encountered. Even though the patent provided for a sliding safety, specimens will be found without this feature. The brass frames were engraved and usually nickel-plated.

One interesting sidelight is the name the designer and builder gave to the gun. Stamped on the left side of the frame below the cylinder are the 2 words "MY FRIEND". Some writers, in the past, have attempted to give a meaning to the words beyond that which the maker had in mind—that of a convenient pocket defense weapon which would, in time of need, prove to be a worthy companion.

One for the ladies

Last but by no means the least of the revolving-barrel cartridge pepperboxes to appear on the market was the Continental "Ladies Companion", following Reid's "My Friend" Knuckle-Duster by less than a year. Patent #57,622 for this 5-shot arm, secured by Charles A. Converse and Samuel S. Hopkins on Aug. 28, 1866, provided for a pepperbox of the Bacon type, revolving through a collar held in place by a screw through the bottom of the frame. While the patent was assigned to the Bacon Manufacturing Co., the gun was actually produced by the Contiental Arms Co. of Norwich, Conn.

Loading of the chambers is through a slot in the recoil plate on the right side. The cylinder is part round and part fluted, a feature which readily identifies this compact and diminutive "Ladies Companion".

Continental Arms Co. was active for a comparatively short time and this little gun, designed with an eye to the feminine trade, is believed to have been the only model produced. While not uncommon some years ago, the "Ladies Companion" is now difficult to find in excellent condition.

With the passing of the little pocket pepperboxes a colorful era in the development of American handguns ended. The Civil War, during which the guns had their beginning, was over, and coming into view was an era of expansion of the western frontiers, a period which demanded and received heavier types of arms.

A Warning To Collectors

Lockhart, Tex.

Editor:

I purchased a Colt 1861 factory conversion from a reputable dealer. At the time I noticed that the trigger guard was unusually thick, but thought little of it due to the exhilaration of a gun trade. Upon examining the Colt more closely at home, I discovered that both the trigger guard and backstrap were newly manufactured from aluminum. The pistol was then returned to the dealer, who promptly made good.

Valuable lessons may be drawn from this: know thoroughly the guns that are being collected; examine a great number of good specimens to get the 'feel' of a genuine piece; and, above all, study the books which have been written concerning the field of interest. Knowledge is power —particularly in gun collecting.

Do business only with reputable dealers who will stand behind what they sell. A good dealer must please his customers to remain in business, and therefore cannot afford dissatisfied ones.

By all means demand a bill of sale to protect yourself, such as the "Bill of Sale for Antique Firearms" that was designed by the NRA Gun Collectors Committee. Copies of this are available from the NRA at no charge. If the seller will not fill out this bill of sale, do not buy.

Do not knowingly aid in the alteration of firearms.

Never represent a gun for sale to be other than what it is, and never try to pass off a fake on an unsuspecting collector just because you have been stuck with it. If an altered firearm is acquired, do not be quick to accuse the seller of doing the work himself. He may have sold it in good faith.

Let *caveat emptor* be your guide.

JIMMIE HOPKINS

Colt "Pocket Model"

I have a Colt "Pocket Model" percussion revolver, cal. .31, and understand most of these were made for use in the Civil War.

Is that correct?

Answer: No. Less than a third of the total of 339,501 of these revolvers were produced during that conflict. The heaviest annual production, stimulated by the 1849 California gold rush, came in 1850 (30,000) and 1851 (31,000). Civil War production is given with other annual production and serials in *Colt's Variation of the Old Model Pocket Pistol, 1848 to 1872,* by P. L. Shumaker. This reference work shows production of this model as 26,000 in 1861, 27,000 in 1862, 25,000 in 1863 and 20,000 in 1864, with Civil War serials ranging from #197,001 to #295,000 and somewhat above. Most of those actually used in the war presumably were the personal sidearms of combatants, as the U.S. Army and Navy Colts were in .44 and .36 cals., not .31.—A.H.

Pinfire Handguns

By HERSCHEL C. LOGAN

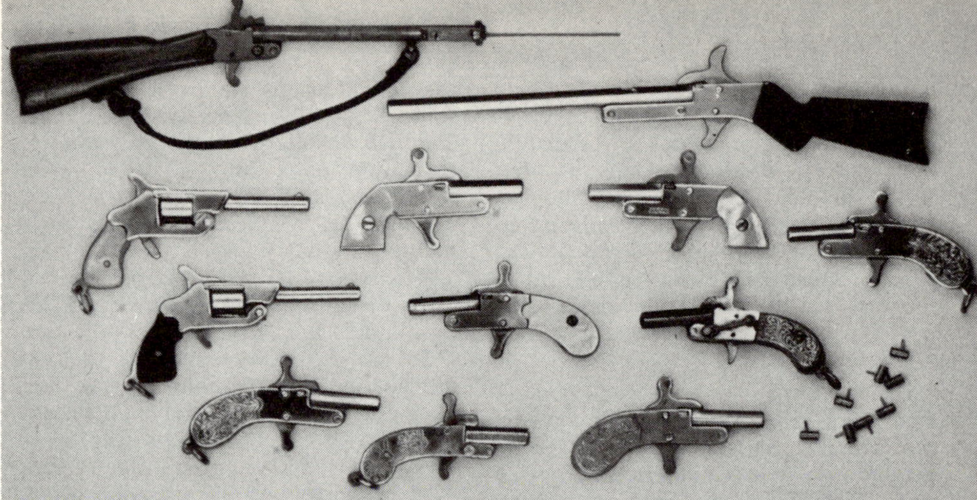

Collection of tiny blank 2 mm. pinfire watch charm pistols and 2 rifles, one of which is equipped with a bayonet.

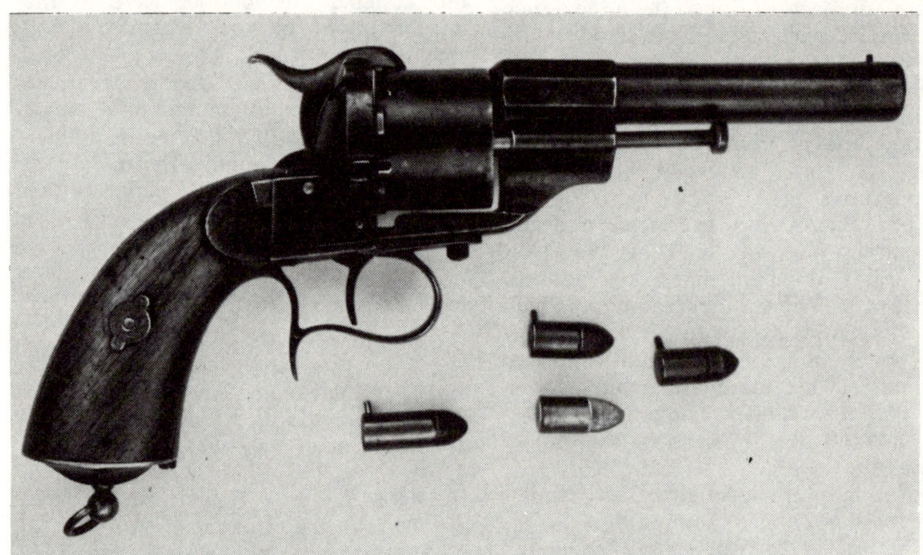

French Lefaucheux 12 mm. pinfire revolver of the type which saw service in the U. S. Civil War. Shown are both long and short cartridges used in the arm.

ALTHOUGH pinfire arms were the most common of all cartridge arms in Europe during the nineteenth century, they are still an item of curiosity to many people. The cartridge they use—with its ignition pin projecting from the side of the case—is often a curio to any but the experienced collector.

Two Frenchmen, Lefaucheux and Houllier, invented and pioneered in the development of the pinfire ignition system for firearms.

It was around 1835 that Lefaucheux of Paris invented a breakdown, breech-loading shotgun. For use in the gun he designed a cartridge not unlike the modern paper-and-metal center-fire shotgun shell, except that his had an ignition pin protruding at right angle from the case near the head. Concealed within the case was a percussion cap on which the point of the pin rested. The fall of the hammer drove the pin against the fulminate in the cap, and the resulting flame ignited the powder charge and sent the bullet, or shot, on its way.

The rather crude paper and metal cartridge used in the gun did not seal the breech effectively and this lessened the efficiency of the arm. As a result, little progress was made with the system until a few years later when Eugene G. Lefaucheux, son of the elder Lefaucheux, patented a revolver which employed an improved pinfire cartridge. It could well have been the Houllier cartridge. However, it was the younger Lefaucheux who produced the Lefaucheux arms as we know them.

Significant headway was made with the pinfire system with Houllier's French patent of 1846. This patent provided for the entire cartridge case to be made of thin copper or brass. The thin metallic case permitted obturation at the time of firing which in turn formed a gas-tight breech seal. Following discharge, the elastic metal case returned to its normal size, permitting easy extraction from the chamber. Houllier's improvement also provided for a heavy cardboard or fiber wad to be placed in the case head to hold the percussion cap and ignition pin in place. With this development, the use and acceptance of the pinfire system increased quite rapidly, so much so that it was to Europe what the rimfire system was to this country during the same period.

In contrast to the rimfire cartridges, there were reloading tools made for the pinfires. Such tools are uncommon and their effectiveness is not known.

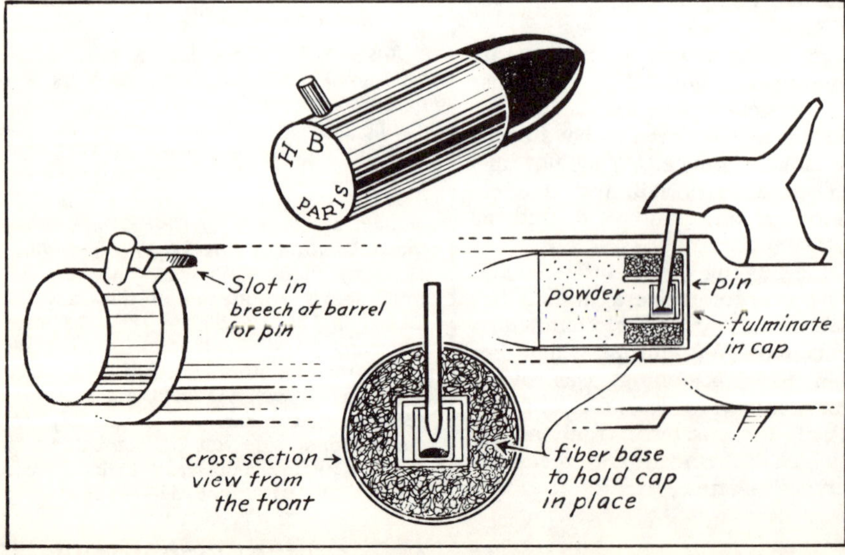

Civil War use

So advanced had the pinfire system, or "Lefaucheux system", become by 1861 that many pinfire revolvers were purchased by both sides during the American Civil War.

According to the official record of ordnance purchases by the U. S., made

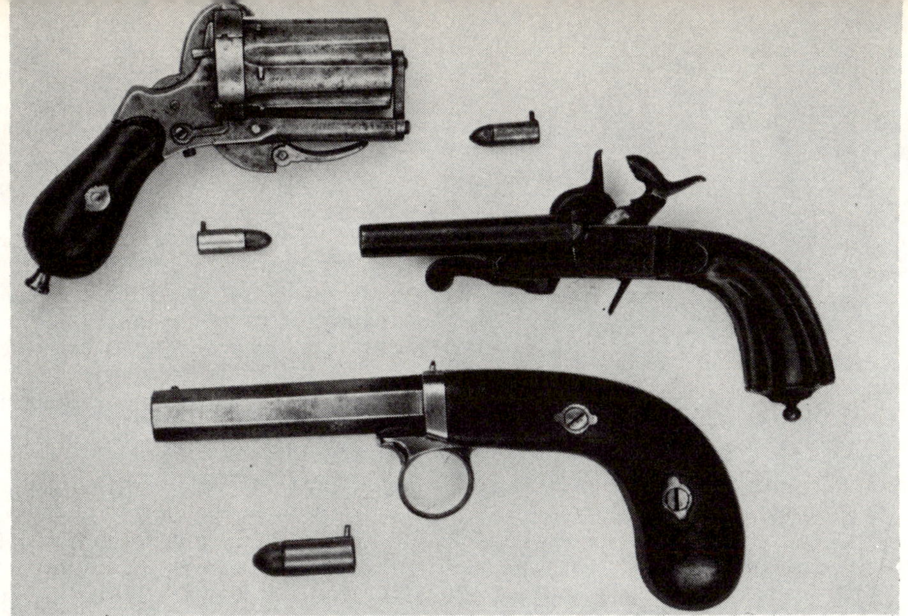

Three unusual pinfire types: (at top) Belgian 6-shot pepperbox; (center) French double-barrel pistol; and Belgian underhammer 12 mm. single-shot pistol.

by Maj. Gen. A. B. Dyer, Chief of Ordnance, USA, a total of 12,374 Lefaucheux revolvers were purchased during the war, at a cost of $167,489.99. Cartridges purchased for these guns totaled 842,880 at a cost of $17,039. The revolvers were the Model 1853, cal. 12 mm., in both single-action and double-action. The serial number range of these guns ran between approximately 25,000 and 37,000.

While the number of pinfire arms purchased by the North is known, there is no record of purchases made by the Confederacy. Many of these guns were used by enlisted men and officers alike in the South during the early years of the war, before the supply of cartridges was limited by Northern blockade.

Lefaucheux single-action revolvers have rounded grips with lanyard rings, and curved humps at the top of the grips. Finger spurs on the trigger guards give reason to believe that they were cavalry arms. Lefaucheux double-action revolvers have more pronounced humps at the top of the grips, as well as straighter grips.

With their purchase by the government during the Civil War, the Lefaucheux single-action 12 mm. revolvers are classed as secondary U.S. martial arms and are therefore of interest to collectors of martial arms.

Variety of types

From the scarce combination arm known as the Apache to the more common and simple types, pinfire arms offer a wide variety for the collector. A few of the more common types are illustrated here. As in other ignition systems, pinfire arms vary from very plain to highly ornate or profusely engraved and inlaid specimens, with ivory or pearl grips.

Pinfire handguns were made in single-shot, multi-shot, and with revolving cylinders containing from 5 to 12 or more chambers.

The Apache is an oddity with a handle designed as knucks and a folding blade extending forward from the underside of the frame. Another pinfire combination revolver resembles a pocket knife. It has a blade which folds into the handle when not in use.

Pinfire underhammer pistols were made. One pistol of Belgian manufacture is illustrated. The barrel unscrews to permit loading of the 12 mm. cartridge. The ring-trigger activates the hammer on the Mariette system.

While only toys, the tiny watch charm pinfire arms are intriguing, and a collection of them never fails to draw considerable attention. They have been made in Germany, Austria, and Japan.

Production of regular pinfire arms was centered mainly in France and Belgium, and to a lesser degree in other countries. Some pieces bearing Belgian proofmarks appear to have been produced for Lefaucheux, or at least under his patent. Belgian arms are easily identified by the familiar proofmark "ELG*" in an oval. Arms made by Lefaucheux usually carried his name, and in addition have the small letters "LF" near the serial number. Some pinfire arms carry no maker's marks.

Pinfire cartridges

Cartridges for pinfire handguns offer a wide variety for the collector. From the tiny 2 mm. watch charm pistol cartridges to the giant 15 mm., they include types by many different manufacturers in many countries. Most bear identifying headstamps, but some are totally unmarked, and can be identified only when found in a labeled box.

Both copper and brass were used for pinfire metallic cartridge cases. The 12 mm. cartridges were made in both long and short versions. Slightly varying case lengths will be found, depending on the manufacturer. Pinfire cartridges were made in 4 loads: bullet, shot, blank, and flare charge.

For the most part, the interior details of the 9 mm., 12 mm., and 15 mm. calibers are as illustrated in the sketch on page 34. On some 5 and 7 mm's., the copper or brass box holding the cap was omitted and the cap was held in place by the fiber wad only. Two unusual specimens were examined which employed lead to hold the pin in place. One used only a small amount of fulminate on the side of the case opposite the pin. The other had a percussion cap set into the lead. Neither could be reloaded. Another unmarked specimen employed a brass cup, pressed into the head, into which the percussion cap was set. Only a bit of fulminate was the detonating agent for the tiny 2 mm. blank cartridges.

Cartridges for pinfire arms were made principally in France, Belgium, Germany, Austria, Italy, England, Czechoslovakia, and Argentina.

When the need for the 12 mm. ammunition arose during the Civil War, 3 companies in this country tooled up for production and supplied cartridges for some years, even after the war.

Patents for pinfire cartridges were granted in this country, although the production on some never materialized. Christian Sharps obtained a patent for a pinfire cartridge on Apr. 15, 1862. There is a possibility that his improved cartridge may have been produced by at least one American maunfacturer. American manufacturers included the Union Metallic Cartridge Co., C. D. Leet & Co., and Ethan Allen & Co.

The list of manufacturers of pinfire ammunition given here is not intended to be a check list. It is not complete, but does give an idea of the extent this ignition system was used in Europe.

Braun & Bloem, Dusseldorf, Germany;
Cartoucherie Francaise, Paris, France;
Charles Fusnot, Brussels, Belgium;
Eley, London, England;
Gevelot, Paris, France;
Giulio Fiocchi, Lecco, Italy;
Houllier & Blanchard, Paris, France;
Keller & Co., Hirtenberg, Austria;
Kynoch & Co., Birmingham, England;
Lignose A/G, Berlin, Germany;
Pirlot Brothers, Liege, Belgium;
Sellier & Bellot, Prague, Czechoslovakia;
Societe Francaise des Munitions, Paris, France.

Although more than a 100 years have passed since the invention and perfection of the pinfire ignition system, pinfire arms and ammunition are still being used, on a limited scale, in some parts of the world. Ammunition was made and used in Europe as late as 1951. ■

Civil War Revolvers

Part 1 of 2

By C. Meade Patterson and Cuddy De Marco, Jr.

After the first United States patent for the Colt revolver was granted in 1836, other gunmakers began to design revolving handguns based on Colt's idea. It was not until 1857, however, that Colt's patent expired. One of the earlier martial-size revolvers produced was the Wesson & Leavitt .40 caliber percussion revolver, manufactured by the Massachusetts Arms Company of Chicopee Falls, Massachusetts, around 1850. Samuel Colt stopped its manufacture by means of a patent infringement suit in 1851.

Some of the first military percussion revolvers, besides Colts, were the Remington Beals revolvers, Adams-Massachusetts Arms Co. revolver, early versions of the Savage revolver, and the Starr double-action .36 and .44 caliber revolvers.

During the Mexican War the only revolver issued to United States troops was the U. S. Model 1847 revolver or Colt "Whitneyville-Walker". The famous Colt Dragoon revolvers, which were made with minor variations from the end of the Walker period (1847) until the adoption of the Colt Army revolver (1860), were nothing more than improved Walkers. These revolvers saw much hard service on our Western Frontier before, during, and after the Civil War. Of course, many Dragoons saw service in the Civil War. The United States Army still used, for the most part, smoothbore flintlock and percussion single-shot muzzle-loading pistols during the Mexican War. Even as late as the Civil War, firearms being as scarce as they were, the old 'horse pistol' was still used in limited numbers.

Many patent revolvers made

The outbreak of the Civil War in 1861 brought a great rush of inventors and promoters, who flooded the War and Navy Departments in Washington, D. C., with patented arms of all kinds. A number of patented revolvers were accepted and manufactured, but, of course, many other patented revolvers were turned down. All of the 'as issued' Civil War revolvers were manufactured in various parts of the North—mostly in New York and the New England states of Connecticut and Massachusetts, leading centers of manufacturing during the mid-19th century.

Domestic Civil War military revolvers were all percussion. Their chambers were loaded from the front of the cylinder with either combustible paper or skin cartridges containing black-powder and ball, or with loose black-powder and ball, and were fired by percussion cap. The average Civil War revolver weighs nearly three pounds. They were made in two standard calibers: .44 and .36.

It is a prevailing misconception that .36 caliber percussion revolvers were made exclusively for the Navy, and .44 caliber revolvers exclusively for the Army. Nothing could be farther from the truth! Numerous specimens of so-called "Navy" .36 caliber revolvers have Army inspectors' initials stamped in their grips, and some specimens of "Army" .44 caliber revolvers have a small Navy anchor plainly stamped on them. Civil War Army officers may have preferred .44 caliber revolvers to the so-called "Navy" .36 caliber revolvers, because they were harder hitting. Notwithstanding, battlefield relics, which are concrete evidence of "Navy" caliber revolvers being used in great land battles of the Civil War, may be seen in Civil War battlefield museums. Also widely exhibited are other .36 caliber revolvers which have been donated by members of families whose ancestors carried them in Army service.

Percussion revolvers were issued to seamen, mounted troops, and non-commissioned officers. Commissioned officers, too, were issued service revolvers, but many carried their own personal revolvers, which were sometimes even cartridge models of other manufacturers. Such personal side arms were purchased individually or presented by families, friends, or troops. Samuel Colt is well known for having presented revolvers to high-ranking officers, congressmen, governors, and other people of prominence who he considered might use their influence to his advantage.

Along with the rifle-musket, rifle, and carbine, the revolver played its part in the numerous Civil War battles. Probably no engagement throughout the entire war was fought without the percussion revolver. The Civil War really established the revolver as a military weapon.

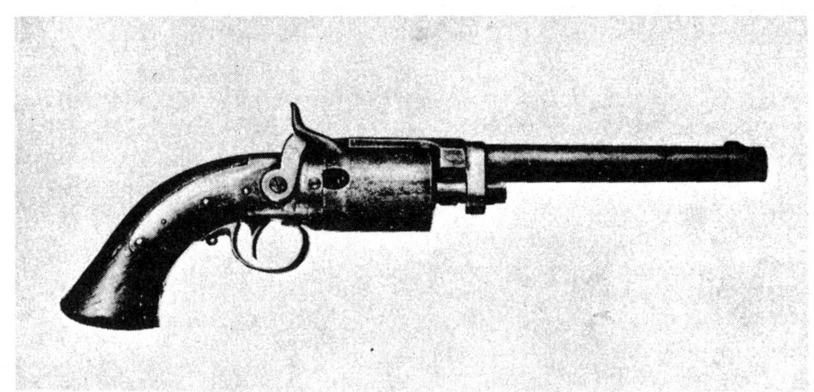

Massachusetts Arms Company Wesson & Leavitt .40 caliber percussion revolver

Many revolvers saw service

Percussion revolvers of every known caliber, model, and manufacture saw Civil War military service. Only certain American-made percussion revolvers are considered Civil War military issue or martial, and even among these government purchase of the Freeman .44 caliber revolver remains unconfirmed. Twenty different percussion revolvers make up the complete list, and of these nine are Colt and Remington models. The three military Colt revolvers include the .36 caliber revolvers of 1851 and 1861 and the .44 caliber revolver of 1860. The six military Remington models include the .36 caliber and .44 caliber single-action revolvers of each of three models, listed in order of their appearance: Beals, Model 1861 ("Old Model"), and "New Model" (1863).

Colt and Remington not only produced the greatest number of service-adopted models, but their combined total production, in sheer numbers alone, exceeded by far the total number of all other military percussion revolvers obtained by the government from all other United States revolver manufacturers as represented by the 11 other Civil War martial revolvers. In fact, the government's Civil War purchases of either the Colt Model 1860 .44 caliber revolver (128,697) or the Remington .44 caliber revolvers (115,563), which were predominantly "New Model" revolvers but may have included some earlier Model 1861 revolvers, alone exceeded the total number of revolvers purchased from all other American manufacturers.

Three Starr models and one model of each of the following manufacturers or inventors complete the list of Civil War martial percussion revolvers: Allen & Wheelock, Freeman, Joslyn, Massachusetts Arms Company, Pettengill, Rogers & Spencer, Savage, and Whitney.

To demonstrate the relative importance of certain makes and models of percussion revolvers in the Civil War, percentages of the total quantity purchased have been calculated (Table 1).

TABLE 1

Ordnance Department Purchases (April 13, 1861—April 3, 1866)

Revolver	*Quantity**	*Percentage*
Allen & Wheelock .44	198	0.1
Colt Model 1851 .36	11,696	3.1
Colt Model 1860 .44	128,697	34.5
Colt Model 1861 .36	2,363	0.6
Joslyn .44	1,100	0.3
Pettengill .44	2,001	0.5
Remington Beals .36	1,100	0.3
Remington .36	13,101	3.5
Remington .44	115,563	31.0
Rogers & Spencer .44	5,000	1.3
Savage .36	10,888	2.9
Starr .36	1,402	0.4
Starr D.A. & S.A. .44	46,052	12.3
Whitney .36	10,587	2.8
All other pistols and revolvers	24,071	6.4
	373,819	100.0

*From "Production and Purchases of Civil War Revolvers" by John F. Baenteli *(See page 10)*

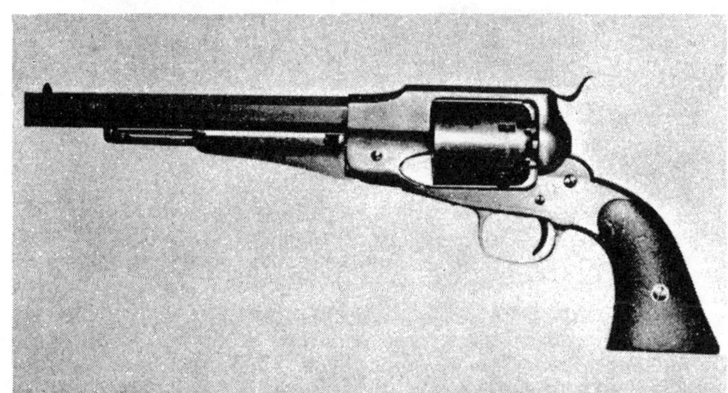

REMINGTON MODEL 1861 .44 CALIBER REVOLVER—This six-shot, single-action revolver has a total length of 13¾ inches, weighs two pounds 14 ounces, and its cylinder is two inches long. Its eight-inch octagonal barrel is mounted with a conical German silver or brass front sight. The rear sight is a groove along the topstrap. In this Remington revolver incorporating William H. Elliott's U.S. Patent 33,932 of December 17, 1861, the cylinder pin can be slid forward and the cylinder removed without lowering the loading lever. This system proved unsatisfactory because when the revolver was fired the cylinder pin would jump forward. The left walnut grip is usually stamped with inspector's initials. The cylinder does not have intermediate hammer rest notches as a rule, but there are late transitional Model 1861 Remingtons with cylinders having hammer rest notches (typical of the "New Model") showing matching serial numbers on all parts. The Model 1861 Remington revolver has this two-line address stamped on top of its barrel: "PATENTED DEC. 17, 1861." over "MANUFACTURED BY REMINGTON'S, ILION, N.Y."

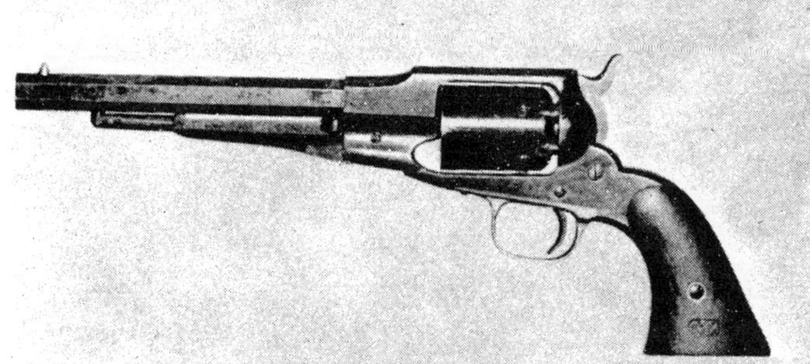

REMINGTON MODEL 1861 .36 CALIBER REVOLVER—This revolver follows the general description of the Remington Model 1861 .44 caliber except that it is .36 caliber, has a 7⅜-inch octagonal barrel with the same markings, and its frame and cylinder are slightly smaller

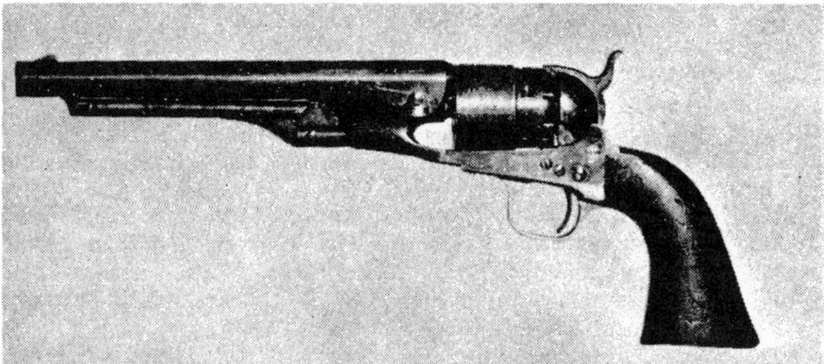

COLT MODEL 1860 .44 CALIBER REVOLVER—This well-known six-shot, single-action revolver has an eight-inch round barrel rifled with seven grooves. Some scarce early specimens, usually with fluted cylinders, have 7½-inch barrels. Total length is 14 inches, weight is two pounds 11 ounces, and cylinder length is 1-13/16 inches. This revolver has a naval engagement scene on its cylinder like the 1851 and 1861 .36 caliber models. It has a brass blade front sight and the rear sight is a notch cut in the hammer lip. It has a semi-oval brass trigger guard and iron backstrap. Recoil shield and butt of the military revolvers are notched for a detachable carbine stock, although very few were issued with one. These revolvers vary in such details as a four-screw frame model and a three-screw frame model, but this general description is typical of this revolver 'as issued' for Civil War use. Stock was walnut, oil-finished and stamped with inspectors' initials, such as "ADK" in military revolvers. The top of the barrel is stamped "—ADDRESS COL. SAM^L COLT NEW-YORK U. S. AMERICA—". Colt's Patent Fire Arms Manufacturing Company, Hartford, Connecticut, produced 200,000 of these revolvers, including the civilian model, from 1860 into 1873

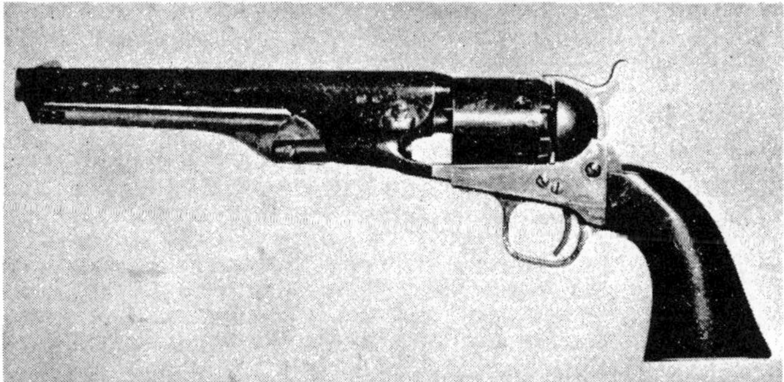

COLT MODEL 1861 .36 CALIBER REVOLVER—A six-shot, single-action revolver with the standard naval engagement on its cylinder, the Colt Model 1861 revolver was built along the same lines as the Colt Model 1860 revolver, except that it does not have a rebated cylinder, it is smaller caliber, and its 7½-inch round barrel is a half-inch shorter. It was made for both civilian and military use. Colt's Patent Fire Arms Manufacturing Company, Hartford, Connecticut, produced 38,000 of these revolvers from 1861 into 1873. The barrel markings are the same as the Colt Model 1860

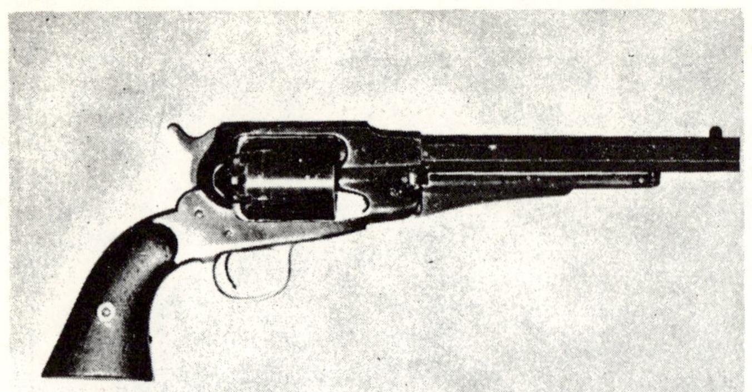

REMINGTON "NEW MODEL" .44 CALIBER REVOLVER—This famous Remington six-shot, single-action revolver has a total length of 13¾ inches, an eight-inch octagonal barrel rifled with five grooves, and weighs two pounds 14 ounces. Its barrel is mounted with either a conical German silver or brass front sight, as found on earlier military Remington models, or more commonly with a steel blade front sight. The left grip usually has an inspector's initials stamped on it, such as "BH", "GP", or "OWA". The barrel is usually stamped with the customary three-line address, "PATENTED SEPT. 14, 1858," over "E. REMINGTON & SONS, ILION, NEW YORK, U.S.A." over "NEW-MODEL", but low-serial-number barrels have a two-line marking omitting the "NEW-MODEL" designation. Although this revolver is stamped on top of its barrel "PATENTED SEPT. 14, 1858" and the Model 1861 Remington revolver is marked "PATENTED DEC. 17, 1861", the "New Model" Remington was manufactured last and not until 1863. It was the second most popular Civil War revolver. It incorporated Samuel Remington's U.S. Patent 37,921, March 17, 1863, which prevented the cylinder pin from being entirely withdrawn from the frame

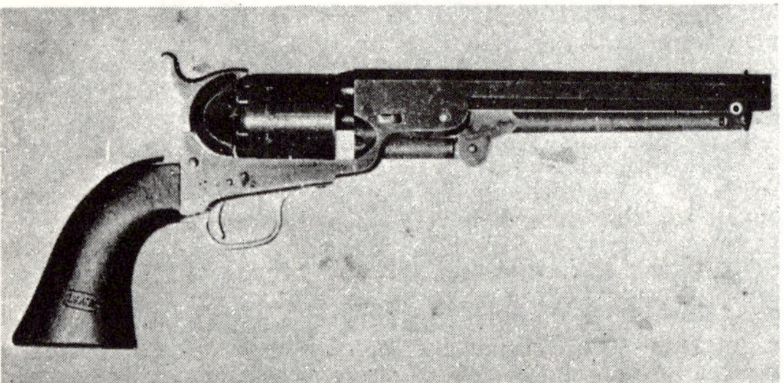

COLT MODEL 1851 .36 CALIBER REVOLVER—This six-shot, single-action Colt revolver has a 7½-inch octagonal barrel with seven grooves. Total length is 13 inches, weight is two pounds ten ounces, and cylinder is 1-11/16 inches long with the usual naval engagement scene, which is common to all Colt military-size revolvers of the Civil War period. Oiled walnut stock had inspectors' initials stamped in it and "U. S." was stamped in the left side of the frame. Those stamped "U. S. N." in the butt frame saw naval service. This revolver varies slightly in detail. The Colt Model 1851, no doubt, was the most popular .36 caliber revolver of the Civil War, because of its light weight, simplicity in loading, ease of assembly and disassembly. These guns were issued to the Army as well as the Navy, and were a popular side arm among officers. It is heresay that early in the War Confederates were willing to pay as much as $300 in gold to obtain a specimen of this much-prized weapon. "—ADDRESS COL. SAM[L] COLT NEW-YORK U. S. AMERICA—" is the most common Model 1851 .36 caliber barrel marking, but there are other markings also. Unlike the Colt Model 1860 .44 caliber, these revolvers were primarily sold to civilians. During the Civil War, 3,005 Colt 1851 revolvers were purchased by the government in four lots, and a fifth lot of 8,691 is believed to have been Colt Model 1851 revolvers. Colt's Patent Fire Arms Manufacturing Company, Hartford, Connecticut, produced 215,000 of these revolvers from 1851 through 1872

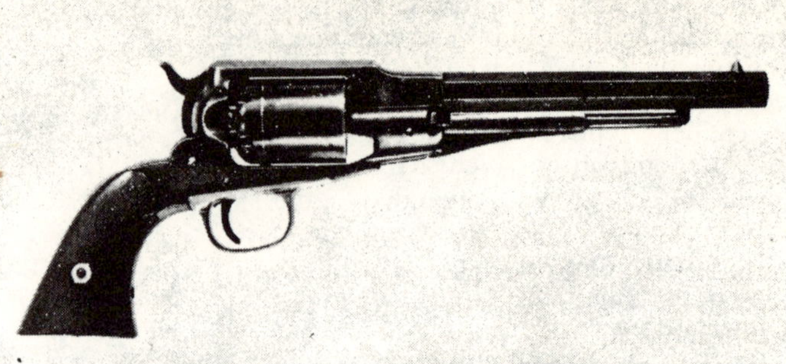

REMINGTON "NEW MODEL" .36 CALIBER REVOLVER—This model has the same general description as the Remington "New Model" .44 caliber revolver except that it is .36 caliber, has a 7⅜-inch octagonal barrel, and its frame and cylinder are slightly smaller

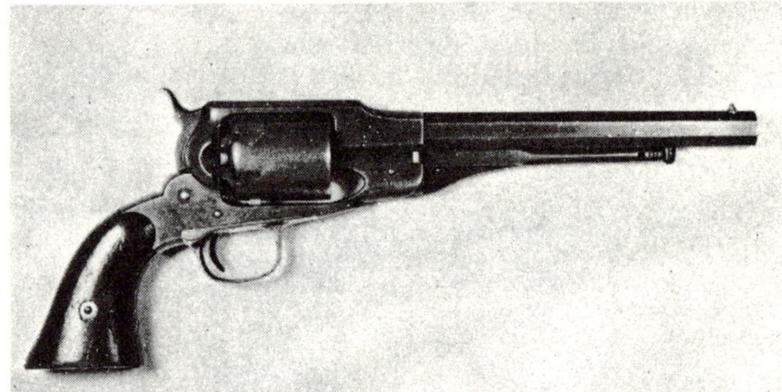

REMINGTON BEALS .44 CALIBER REVOLVER—The first of the .44 caliber percussion revolvers produced by Eliphalet Remington and Sons of Ilion, New York, was this six-shot, single-action revolver made in 1860 and 1861. It was based on Fordyce Beals' U.S. Patent 21,478 of September 14, 1858, covering the arrangement of the loading lever assembly and cylinder pin resumed in the later "New Model" series of 1863. The Beals designation for this .44 caliber revolver and its .36 caliber counterpart arose from the "BEALS' PATENT" barrel marking. This revolver measures 13¾ inches in length, has an eight-inch octagonal barrel, a two-inch cylinder, and weighs two pounds 14 ounces. It has a conical German silver or brass front sight and the rear sight is a groove along the topstrap. The very small web of its loading lever distinguishes the Beals model from the two later Remington .44 caliber percussion revolvers. Barrel threads are concealed by the frame in this model and in the low-numbered Remington Model 1861 .44 caliber revolvers. There are no intermediate hammer-rest safety notches in its cylinder nor in the cylinders of most Model 1861 revolvers

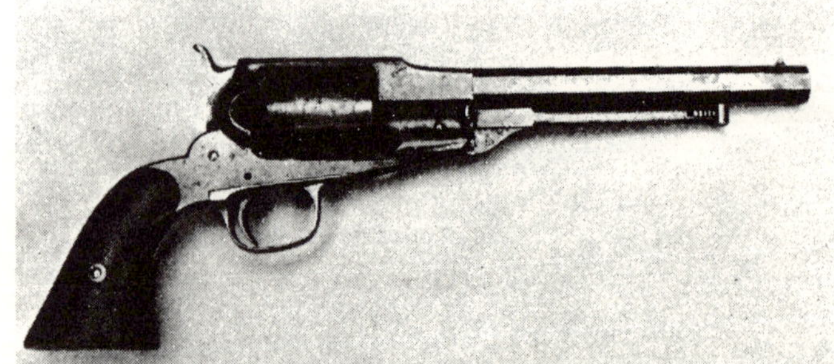

REMINGTON BEALS .36 CALIBER REVOLVER—This revolver follows the description of the Remington Beals .44 caliber revolver except that it is .36 caliber, has a 7⅜-inch octagonal barrel with the same markings, and its frame and cylinder are slightly smaller

Civil War Revolvers

Part 2 of 2

By C. Meade Patterson and Cuddy De Marco, Jr.

AMERICAN martial percussion revolvers of secondary importance in the Civil War, judging on the basis of numbers purchased, are in descending order: all model Starrs, .36 caliber Colt revolvers, .36 caliber Remington revolvers, Savage, and Whitney. If Rogers & Spencer revolvers had been delivered earlier so that they could have been issued during the Civil War, they would be included in this group of revolvers having secondary importance.

The rest of the revolvers had negligible significance. It seems perfectly reasonable to believe that a soldier might have fought through all four years of the War without ever being aware of the Pettengill, Joslyn, Allen & Wheelock, and Massachusetts Arms Company revolvers, as apparently so few of them were purchased and even a smaller number issued.

General characteristics

Most Civil War military revolvers have solid frames. Only the Colt models have open frames (no topstraps), and only the Starrs have hinged frames. All have six-shot percussion cylinders except the Joslyn and the Massachusetts Arms Company-Adams revolvers, which have five-shot cylinders. Among the martial Civil War revolvers, only the Colts and the Whitney have scenes rolled on their cylinders. Only the .36 caliber Starr and Savage revolvers have cylinders with inclined nipples. The nipples of all the other revolvers point straight back, or, in other words, are horizontal, or parallel to the cylinder axis. Except for low-serial-number Model 1860 and 1861 Colts, there are no fluted cylinders. The Colt 1860 .44 caliber revolver is the only one that has a rebated cylinder. All other cylinders are straight.

Solid or one-piece walnut stocks are found on all Colts, all Starrs, and on the Massachusetts Arms Company revolver. All other Civil War revolvers have two-piece walnut grips. Octagonal barrels predominate among Civil War revolvers. They are found on the Colt 1851 revolver, all the Remingtons, Joslyn, Massachusetts Arms Company, Pettengill, Rogers & Spencer, Savage, and Whitney. Round barrels characterize the 1860 and 1861 Colts, all the Starrs, and the Freeman. Only the Allen & Wheelock has a part-round and part-octagonal barrel. The Massachusetts Arms Company-Adams Patent .36 caliber revolver is rifled with three grooves. The Remingtons, Rogers & Spencer, Joslyn, and Savage have five-groove rifling. The Starrs, Allen & Wheelock, Freeman, and Pettengill have six grooves. All the Colts and the Whitney have seven-groove rifling.

Civil War revolvers are all single-action with the exception of the double-action .36 and .44 caliber Starrs, the Massachusetts Arms Company, and the Pettengill. Although the Savage is cocked by its cocking lever, it is still only single-action. Only the Savage and double-action Starrs have cocking levers and triggers; all the others have conventional single triggers. Most Civil War revolvers have external center hammers. However, the Joslyn has an external side hammer and the Pettengill has a concealed or internal center hammer. The loading lever assembly, including the rammer or plunger, is usually mounted under the barrel, but in the Massachusetts Arms Company revolver it is mounted on the left side of the barrel and in the Allen & Wheelock it forms the trigger guard. The cylinder pin is directly connected with the loading lever in the Rogers & Spencer, Pettengill, Savage, and Whitney revolvers.

Most Civil War revolvers no longer show any of their original factory finish. Others have been refinished or their original finish is incomplete or patchy. Table 2 indicates the character of the original factory finish of the revolvers under consideration.

A very few of these Civil War revolvers were plated all over with nickel, tin, or silver. They were exceptions. Generally at first consideration, the plated martial revolvers are regarded as having been refinished later, and probably outside the factory unless factory stampings plainly cut through the plating.

Heyday of percussion revolvers

The Civil War not only established the revolver as a vital military weapon, but it proved to be the grand heyday of the percussion revolver. Like the muzzle-loading rifle-musket and the Minié bullet, the percussion revolver's military usefulness ended shortly after the hostilities of 1861 to 1865. Small bore cartridge revolvers and pistols were already being manufactured in large numbers before the War's end. Only a short period passed before large caliber military revolvers for self-primed, metallic cartridges came into general production. Many of these Civil War military percussion revolvers were altered to fire self-contained, metallic cartridges. Enjoying the protection afforded by Rollin White's patent, Smith & Wesson led the field in producing new model cartridge revolvers of martial caliber, but Colt, Remington, and others were not far behind.

If the Civil War had been fought ten years later, providing technical progress had proceeded at the same rate, cartridge, not percussion, revolvers would have been its principal military side arm.

TABLE 2
Original Factory Finish

Model	*Frame*	*Cylinder*	*Barrel*	*Hammer*	*Loading Lever*
Allen & Wheelock .44	B	B	B	C	C
Colt Model 1851 .36	C	B	B	C	C
Colt Model 1861 .36	C	B	B	C	C
Colt Model 1860 .44	C	B	B	C	C
Freeman .44	B	B	B	C	B
Joslyn .44	B	B	B	B-C	B-C
Massachusetts Arms .36	B	B	B	C	B
Pettengill .44	B	B	B		B
Remington .36*	B	B	B	C	B
Remington .44*	B	B	B	C	B
Rogers & Spencer .44	B	B	B	C	C
Savage .36	B	B	B	C	C
Starr .36	B	B	B	C	C
Starr D.A. .44	B	B	B	C	C
Starr S.A. .44	B	B	B	C	C
Whitney .36	B	B	B	C	C

B—Blued, C—Casehardened, D.A.—Double Action, S.A.—Single Action
*All three models (Beals, 1861, and New Model)

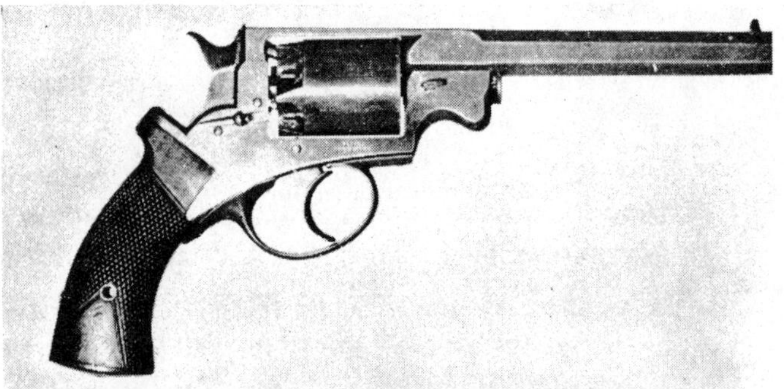

MASSACHUSETTS ARMS COMPANY-ADAMS .36 CALIBER REVOLVER—The design for this five-shot, double-action revolver with a six-inch octagonal barrel rifled with three grooves was imported from England. It has a total length of 11½ inches, weight of two pounds nine ounces, and its cylinder measures 1-15/16 inches long. It has a steel blade front sight and a V-notch rear sight in the frame. Adams revolvers were made first in England and then America. This revolver, as made by the Massachusetts Arms Company of Chicopee Falls, Massachusetts, for U. S. military use, is stamped with government inspectors' initials in script in its checkered stock. "WAT" (William A. Thornton) is stamped in the right side, and "LCA" in the left side. The top of its frame is stamped in three lines "MANUFACTURED BY" over "MASS. ARMS CO." over "CHICOPEE FALLS", the left side of the frame is stamped "ADAMS PATENT" over "MAY 3D 1853", the right side of the frame "PATENT" over "JUNE 3, 1856", and the loading lever is stamped "KERR'S PATENT" over "APRIL 14, 1857". During the Civil War, 1,049 Adams 'self-cocking' revolvers, both English and those made by the Massachusetts Arms Company at Chicopee Falls, Massachusetts, were purchased by the government

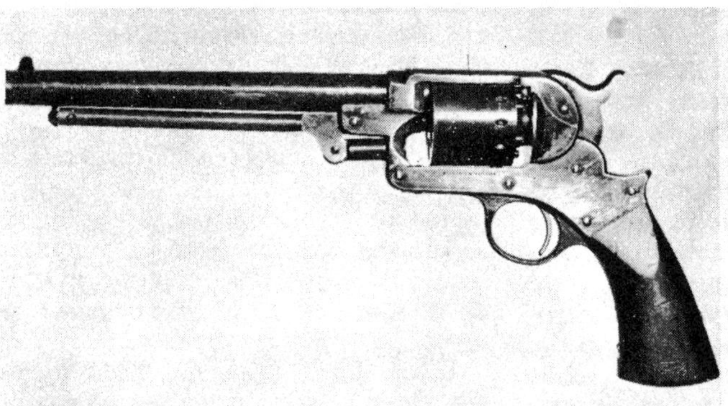

STARR SINGLE-ACTION .44 CALIBER REVOLVER—This six-shot, single-action revolver has an eight-inch round barrel rifled with six grooves, a cylinder 1⅞ inches long, weighs three pounds, has a total length of 13¾ inches. Its cylinder is removed in the same manner as in the double-action Starrs. Walnut stock of those used in military service was oil-finished and stamped with inspectors' initials. It is stamped on the right side of its frame "STARR'S PATENT JAN. 15, 1856." and on the left side of its frame "STARR. ARMS. Co. NEW. YORK."

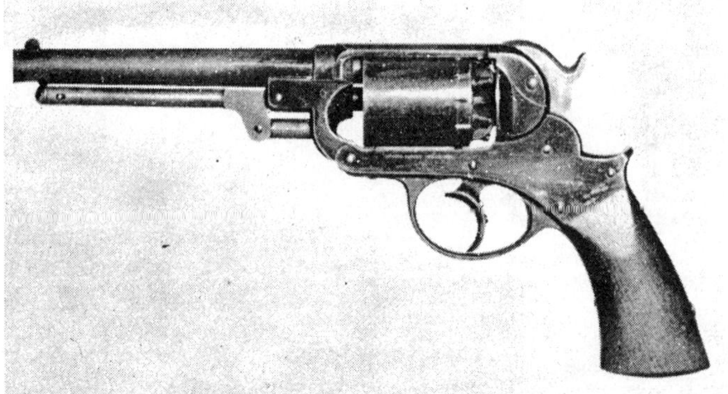

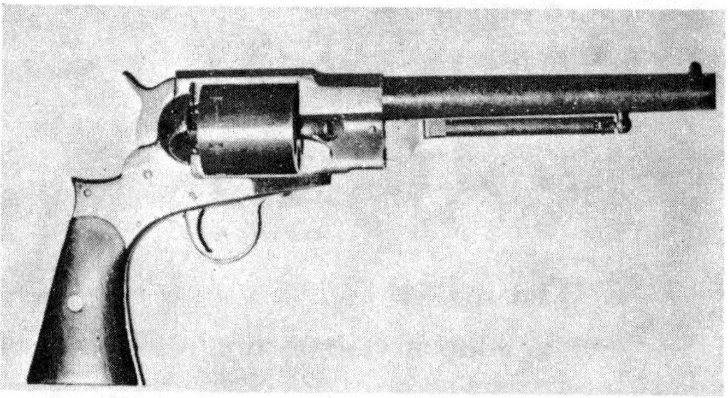

FREEMAN .44 CALIBER REVOLVER—This six-shot, single-action revolver has a 7½-inch round barrel rifled with six grooves. Cylinder is 1⅞ inches long, total length is 12½ inches, and weight is two pounds 12 ounces. It has a steel blade front sight and the rear sight is a groove in the topstrap. The cylinder and two-part cylinder pin are removed by pushing forward a slide on the right side of the frame in front of the cylinder. Grips are oil-finished and varnished. Topstrap is stamped "FREEMAN'S PAT. DECR 9, 1862" and "HOARD'S ARMORY, WATERTOWN, N.Y." in two lines on opposite sides of the rear sight groove. This revolver was patented by Austin T. Freeman of Binghamton, New York, U.S. Patent 37,091, December 9, 1862. It was manufactured by C. B. Hoard at Watertown, New York. Rogers, Spencer & Company purchased Freeman's patent. There is no known government record of any of these revolvers being purchased, although Hoard's Armory manufactured 12,800 .58 caliber rifle-muskets on contract during the Civil War. Serial numbers to over 1700 have been noted

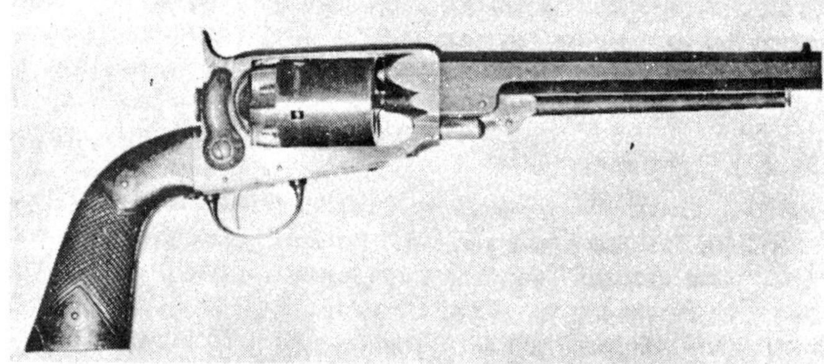

JOSLYN .44 CALIBER REVOLVER—A five-shot, single-action, side-hammer revolver, the Joslyn has an eight-inch octagonal barrel rifled with five grooves. Total length is 14⅜ inches, cylinder is 2-3/16 inches long, and weight is about three pounds. It has a steel blade front sight, and the rear sight is a groove in its frame. It has coarsely checkered, oil-finished walnut grips. No Joslyn revolver has been observed with inspectors' initials stamped in its grips. Some Joslyn revolvers show a Navy anchor stamped in the butt frame or in the underside of the barrel. The two-line barrel marking is "B.F. JOSLYN" over "PATD MAY 4TH 1858". Joslyn revolvers vary in hammer detail and some specimens have oval iron buttcaps. The side-hammer and cylinder pin, which is withdrawn to the rear, make the Joslyn resemble Colt's Model 1855 (Root) pocket revolvers. This revolver was patented by Benjamin F. Joslyn of Worcester, Massachusetts, May 4, 1858, U. S. Patent 20,160. It was manufactured by Joslyn Fire Arms Company, Stonington, Connecticut, and by W. C. Freeman at Worcester, Massachusetts. Serial numbers to 3000 have been noted

◀ STARR DOUBLE-ACTION .36 CALIBER REVOLVER—The Starr six-shot, double-action revolver weighs three pounds three ounces, barrel is six inches long, cylinder is 2¼ inches long, and total length is 12 inches. This double-action revolver is similar in all respects to the Starr double-action .44 caliber with the exception of caliber, ⅜-inch longer cylinder, streamlined curve at front of frame, and its nipples which are inclined outwards slightly, instead of straight back. Inspectors' initials are stamped in the oil-finished stock of a few. "STARR. ARMS. Co. NEW. YORK.", is stamped on the right side of the frame, and "STARR'S PATENT JAN. 15. 1856." on the left side. Serial numbers of these revolvers range from 1 to 3000

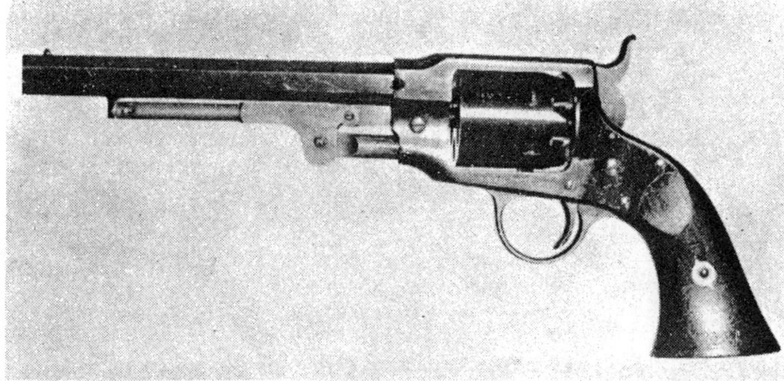

ROGERS & SPENCER .44 CALIBER REVOLVER—This late Civil War period six-shot, single-action revolver has a 7½-inch octagonal barrel rifled with five grooves. Total length is 13¾ inches, cylinder is two inches long, and weight is three pounds. It has a conical German silver or brass front sight, exactly like the Pettengill, and its rear sight is a groove along the topstrap. Its characteristic bell-shaped grips are oil-finished and the inspector's initials, "RPB" (Robert P. Barry), are always stamped in the left grip. The trigger was burnished bright. It is stamped in the topstrap on opposite sides of the rear sight groove "ROGERS & SPENCER" and "UTICA, N. Y." This was the last weapon developed in the Freeman-Pettengill-Rogers & Spencer series. If the Pettengill and Rogers & Spencer .44 caliber revolvers are placed side by side, the barrels and loading levers appear practically identical. This revolver was an intended improvement on A. T. Freeman's patent purchased by Rogers, Spencer & Company. The lot of Rogers & Spencer revolvers was manufactured by Rogers, Spencer & Company at Willow Vale, New York, seven miles south of Utica and delivered between January 30 and September 26, 1865, too late for use. It is believed that practically the entire lot was later bought out of arsenal storage, the reason so many Rogers & Spencers, as well as Remingtons, Starrs, and other Civil War revolvers are found in nearly new condition today

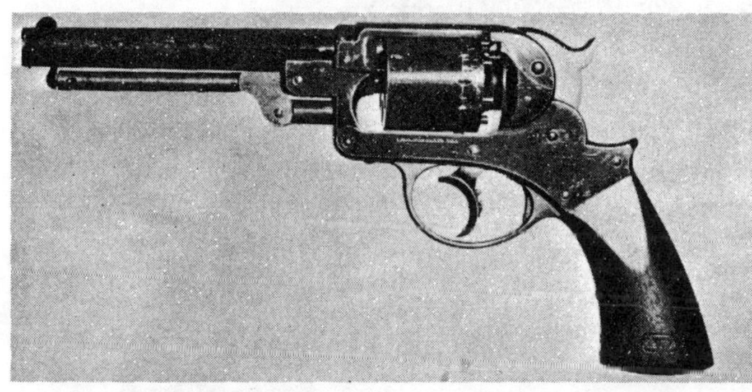

STARR DOUBLE-ACTION .44 CALIBER REVOLVER—One of the earliest American double-action revolvers, this six-shot revolver has a six-inch round barrel rifled with six grooves. Over-all length is 11⅝ inches, weight is two pounds 12 ounces, and cylinder is 1⅞ inches long. These revolvers have a steel blade front sight dovetailed into the barrel. A V-notch cut into the hammer lip serves as a rear sight. The Starr revolver is provided with a knurled screw on the right side of the frame which, when removed, allows the barrel to tip downwards on its hinged frame so that the cylinder can be removed. Starr revolvers were invented by Eben Townsend Starr of New York City, grandson of Nathan Starr and son of Nathan Starr, Jr., famous U. S. swordmakers and riflemakers of Middletown, Connecticut. This model is marked on the right side of its frame "STARR'S PATENT JAN. 15. 1856.", and on the left side "STARR. ARMS. Co. NEW. YORK." The patent date refers to E. T. Starr's U. S. Patent 14,118 for a self-cocking percussion pepperbox. His U. S. Patent 30,843, December 4, 1860, was for his double-action revolver. Starr firearms were made at Yonkers, Binghamton, and Morrisania, New York, from 1858 to 1867. The New York City address referred to the Starr Arms Company store and office at 267 Broadway. Starr double-action .44 caliber revolvers, with serial numbers from 1 to about 23,000, were manufactured first, and Starr single-action .44 caliber revolvers, with serial numbers from about 23,000 to about 54,000, last

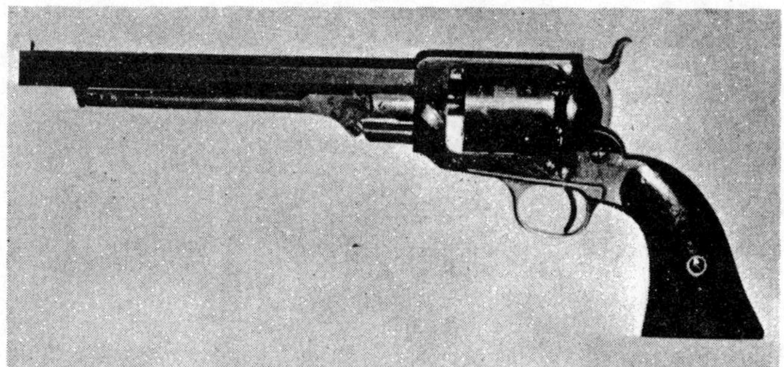

WHITNEY .36 CALIBER REVOLVER—This six-shot, single-action revolver has a 7⅝-inch octagonal barrel rifled with seven grooves. Total length is 13⅛ inches. It is similar in frame and barrel construction to the Remington. It weighs two pounds seven ounces. It has a narrow brass post front sight, a V-notch rear sight cut into the topstrap, and another U-shaped rear sight cut into the hammer lip. Its walnut grips were oil-finished and stamped with inspectors' initials sometimes when used in the U. S. armed services. Some Whitney revolvers have a small Navy anchor stamped on butt frame or on barrel; others have the state militia marks "N.J." stamped on their frames and barrels. Early specimens have a Joslyn-type, ball-latch for the loading lever and later specimens have a regular Colt revolver latch. Top of the barrel is stamped "E.WHITNEY" over "N. HAVEN" in two lines. The cylinder is stamped "WHITNEYVILLE" in a ribbon across a shield, and a combined American and British coat of arms flanked by an eagle and a lion. In low-serial-number Whitney revolvers, this cylinder design is repeated twice, but in later revolvers it appears only once combined with a naval scene. This revolver was manufactured at Whitneyville Armory (Whitney Arms Company), two miles north of New Haven, Connecticut, by Eli Whitney, Jr., son of the famous inventor of the cotton gin. Serial numbers run to about 30,000

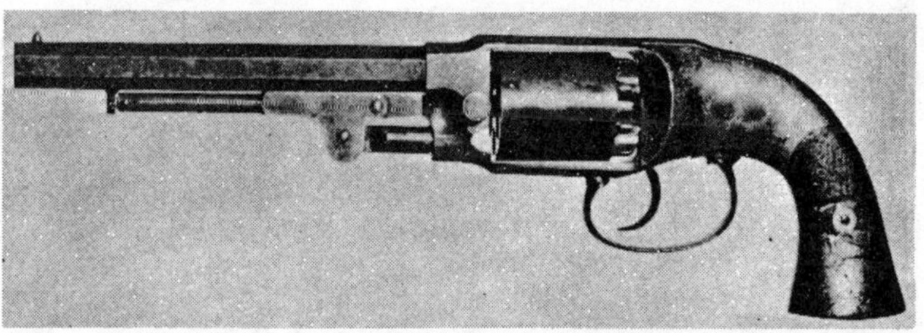

PETTENGILL .44 CALIBER REVOLVER—This unusual six-shot, self-cocking only, 'hammerless' revolver has a 7½-inch octagonal barrel rifled with six grooves. Over-all length is 14 inches, cylinder length is 2¼ inches, and weight is about three pounds. It has a conical brass front sight and its rear sight is a groove in the topstrap of the frame. Oil-finished walnut grips of military revolvers carry inspectors' initials. The L-shaped hammer is concealed within its frame. Pulling the trigger revolves the cylinder, fires the revolver, and cocks the hammer for the next shot. Specimens with casehardened frames and loading levers have been seen. This is the only martial revolver of the Civil War made with an internal hammer. Owing to its delicate mechanism, this revolver proved a failure in the field and was soon discarded. Low-serial-number Pettengills are stamped on top of their frames in two lines on each side of the rear sight groove "PETTENGILLS", "PATENT 1856", and "RAYMOND & ROBITAILLE", "PATENTED 1858". High-serial-number Pettengills are stamped on top of their frames in two lines on each side of the rear sight groove "PETTENGILLS", "PATENT 1856" and "PAT^{D} JULY 22 1856", "& JULY 27 1858". The underside of the frame of the Pettengill is stamped in two lines "PATENTED" over "NOV. 4, 1862". Its pepperbox-like mechanism was patented by C. S. Pettengill of New Haven, Connecticut, U. S. Patent 15,388, July 22, 1856, improved by Edward A. Raymond and Charles Robitaille of Brooklyn, New York, U. S. Patent 21,054, July 27, 1858, and Henry S. Rogers of Willow Vale, New York, U. S. Patent 36,861, November 4, 1862. This weapon was manufactured by Rogers, Spencer & Company at Willow Vale, New York, before the Rogers & Spencer revolver was produced. Many of the Pettengill arms delivered to the government during the Civil War were issued to the Army of the Mississippi under General William S. Rosecrans. Pettengill .44 caliber revolver serial numbers noted range from about 1600 to 4600

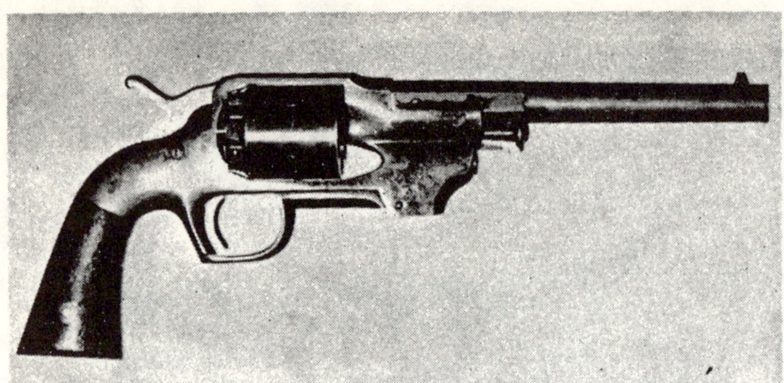

ALLEN & WHEELOCK .44 CALIBER REVOLVER—This six-shot, single-action percussion revolver has a 7½-inch part-round, part-octagonal barrel rifled with six grooves. Its total length is 13¼ inches, its cylinder is 1-15/16 inches long, and it weighs two pounds 13 ounces. A slot cut into the hammer lip serves as the rear sight. A triangular brass front sight is dovetailed in the barrel at the muzzle. The combination trigger guard and loading lever is released by means of a spring catch in the angle of the trigger guard. The plunger and loading lever operate as a rack and pinion. Its walnut grips were varnished. It is stamped on the left side of its barrel in two lines "ALLEN & WHEELOCK, WORCESTER, MASS. U. S." over "ALLEN'S PT'S. JAN. 13. DEC. 15. 1857. SEPT. 7. 1858". These revolvers never have inspectors' initials stamped in their grips. Ethan Allen patented this revolver under three patents: U. S. Patent 16,367 of January 13, 1857; U. S. Patent 18,836 of December 15, 1857; and U. S. Patent 21,400 of September 7, 1858. It was manufactured by Allen & Wheelock, Worcester, Massachusetts. About 600 were made, judging from known serial numbers

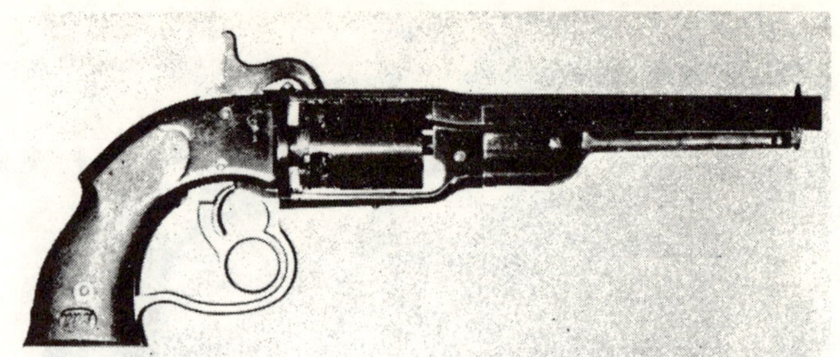

SAVAGE .36 CALIBER REVOLVER—This six-shot, single-action revolver has a 7⅛-inch octagonal barrel rifled with five grooves, a total length of 14¼ inches, a cylinder and rotating recoil shield 2-3/16 inches long, and weighs three pounds seven ounces. It has a brass cone front sight, and a round-base, V-notch rear sight set into the top of the frame under its offset hammer. It has oil-finished walnut grips sometimes stamped with inspectors' initials. This revolver has an enormous trigger guard containing a ring cocking lever and a trigger. The cocking lever cocks the hammer, and rotates the cylinder after drawing it backwards away from the barrel, and the trigger releases the hammer to fire the revolver. Releasing the ring cocking lever wedges the cylinder against the barrel in a gastight union. These revolvers were manufactured early in the War. Some are stamped "WAT" on the right grip. Barrels are stamped in three lines "SAVAGE R.F.A. CO. MIDDLETOWN-C^T", over "H. S. NORTH PATENTED JUNE 17 1856", over "JANUARY 18 1859. MAY 15, 1860". This revolver was patented by Henry S. North and Edward Savage of Middletown, Connecticut, and the dates refer to U. S. Patents 15,444, 22,666 and 28,331. The patentees formed the Savage Revolving Fire Arms Company in 1860

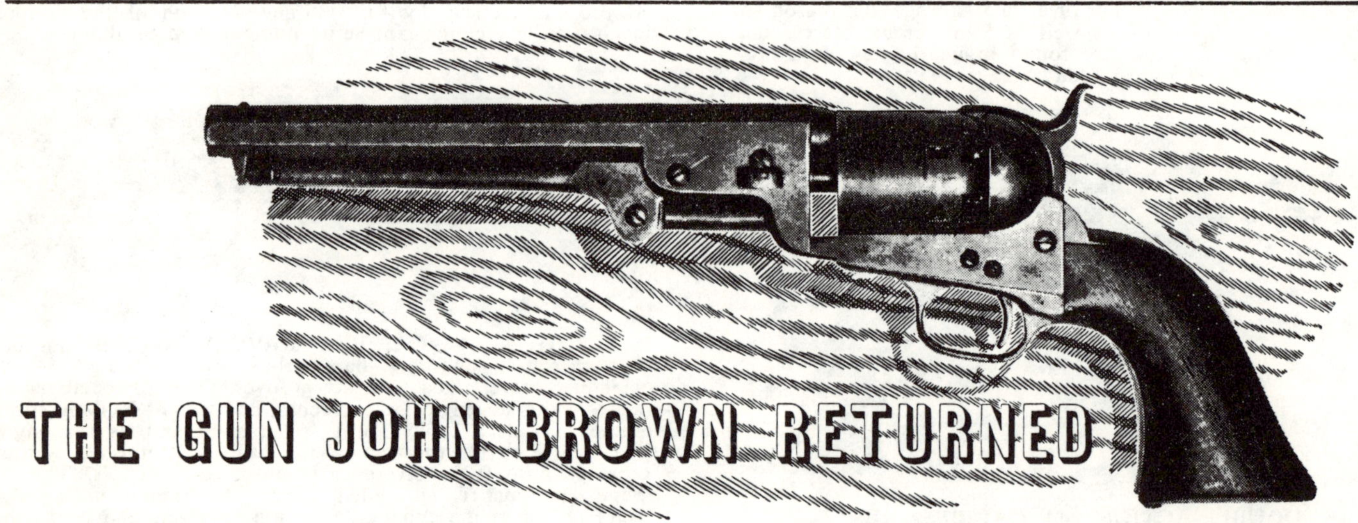

THE GUN JOHN BROWN RETURNED

The story behind this Navy Colt revolver lifts it above the ordinary

By Herschel C. Logan

AMONG the old arms in the collection of the Kansas State Historical Society there is one of more than usual interest. Not that the gun itself is extremely rare or that it is different from any other Colt Navy revolver of that period. What lifts it out of the ordinary and sets it apart is the story surrounding it.

In 1856, May 24 to be exact, John Brown, the self-styled leader of the 'free-state' settlers in Kansas, led what later became known as the Pottawatomie Massacre. This raid was in retaliation for previous depredations inflicted upon the early free-state settlers by border ruffians from neighboring states. Whatever may be said for or against the method, it did have a wholesome and sobering influence upon those who looked upon the early-day Kansas homesteaders as easy prey. It served notice that these stalwart pioneers could and would stand up and fight for what they believed to be right, cost what it would.

One man who placed his stamp of approval upon Brown's action was William F. M. Arny. This somewhat odd, though likable and well-known man was intensely interested in the free-state cause in Kansas. A member of the Leavenworth Constitutional Convention, and later elected to the first State Legislature, he previously had devoted considerable time to the raising of money in the East with which to bring in more settlers to the young territory. It was while engaged in this work that he became an admirer of John Brown, having been introduced to

Continued on page 46

Production and Purchases of

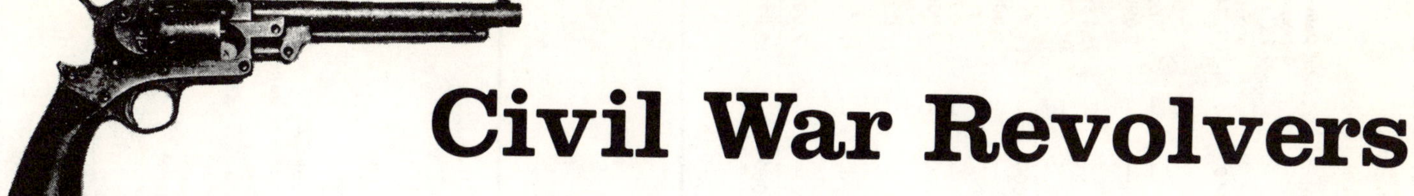

Starr single-action .44 caliber

Civil War Revolvers

By JOHN F. BAENTELI

One of the problems facing collectors of United States military revolvers of the Civil War period is to learn which revolvers were bought by the United States Government for issue to the various armed forces during that conflict. In other words, of all the revolvers manufactured during the Civil War period, which ones are properly classified as United States military revolvers?

For purposes of this discussion a military revolver is defined as any revolver purchased by or manufactured under contract for the United States Government for test purposes or for issue to the naval, military, or other armed forces. This definition thus excludes any revolvers purchased privately by any individual member of such forces.

When consulting the more readily available sources of information which are considered authoritative, one is confronted with conflicting data of various kinds.

To give but one example, Colonel Arcadi Gluckman, USA (Ret'd), in his excellent book *United States Martial Pistols and Revolvers,* does not discuss the LeFaucheaux revolver. Yet, on page six of the March 1942 issue of *The Gun Report,* item 216, Mr. Dexter advertises the LeFaucheaux as "the most rare Civil War revolver". This revolver is listed on page 74 of the second edition of Mr. Satterlee's *Catalog of Firearms* but there is no mention that it is a Civil War revolver.

The fact is that the United States Government bought 11,833 LeFaucheaux revolvers between April 13, 1861, and April 3, 1866. Therefore, this is definitely a Civil War revolver and, as will be shown later, this quantity is far larger than several other of the more commonly known Civil War revolvers, thus casting doubt on its rarity.

Moreover, when one examines sources of original information* one finds a considerable variation from the commonly held ideas about these revolvers. Diligent study of several reports published by the government a few years after the Civil War has yielded some highly interesting and significant material about the revolvers used during that conflict. This material has been very carefully analyzed and is presented in Table I in answer to the question raised in the first paragraph of this discussion.

Although much of this material is known to and has been used by advanced students and collectors, it is believed that Table I is the first attempt to carefully analyze this material and publish it completely and in easily available form.

One of the most important points brought out by Table I is that all Civil War United States military revolvers should be classified into two major groups:

1. Revolvers manufactured for the United States Government under contract.
2. Revolvers purchased by the United States Government on the open market from any source.

According to the letter of transmittal accompanying the information from which Table I was prepared, this information was intended to be a complete list of, among other things, small arms purchased since April 13, 1861. Therefore, it is assumed to be a complete list of all United States Civil War revolvers. The letter of transmittal is quoted, in part, as follows:

> Ordnance Office, War Department,
> Washington, January 11, 1868.
>
> Sir: I have the honor to transmit, herewith, the information from this bureau called for by the resolution of the House of Representatives of March 15, 1867, which is in these words:
>
> '*Resolved,* That the President be requested to inform this house what amount of money has been paid by the government since April 13, 1861, for cannon, ordnance, projectiles, and small-arms by the War and Navy Departments respectively: to whom the same was paid, and at what dates, also at what time the contracts were made under which such articles were furnished, with copies thereof . . . . '
>
> The information thus called for . . . . is contained in the 'Statement of purchases by the ordnance department, United States army, since April 13, 1861, of cannon, ordnance, projectiles, and small-arms, etc.,' and in the nineteen packages of copies of contracts and orders given for said purchases; which copies are arranged in alphabetical and chronological order.
>
> * * * * *
>
> C. A. DANA
> Assistant Secretary of War.

It is, of course, well known that certain single-shot martial pistols were manufactured for the United States Government under contract. It is less well known but equally true that certain Civil War revolvers were also manufactured for the government under contract.

Although these contract revolvers are listed in Table I

---

* "Answer to House Resolution dated Mar. 15th 1867, viz: Purchases by the Ordnance Department, U.S.A. since April 13, 1861 of Cannon, Ordnance, Projectiles and Small Arms . . .", 233 pages, January 11, 1868. Original material supplied by the author has been checked against the above hand-written Ordnance Department ledger in the National Archives, Washington, D. C. by C. Meade Patterson.

The itemized listing of Table 1 contains a number of vague descriptive terms as they were written into the original 1868 Ordnance Department record. Inadequate descriptions, such as "Navy pistols" or "revolver pistols", defy classification and render a precise and complete summary impossible. This also accounts for discrepancies between these and previously published figures.

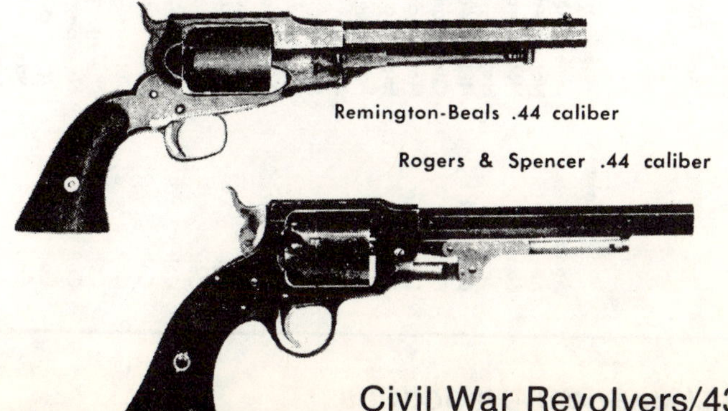

Remington-Beals .44 caliber

Rogers & Spencer .44 caliber

TABLE I
REVOLVERS AND PISTOLS BOUGHT BY THE UNITED STATES GOVERNMENT BETWEEN APRIL 13, 1861, AND APRIL 3, 1866

Make	Model	*Open Market Purchases*	*Purchases Under Contracts*	*Total*
Adams	Self-cocking	1,049	—	1,049
Allen	Not stated	198	—	198
Bacon	Not stated	2	—	2
Beals	Navy	1,100	—	1,100
Beaumont	Not stated	26	—	26
Colt	Old model army (Model 1848)	14	—	14
Colt	New model army (Model 1860)	540	1,300	1,840
Colt	Engraved army	73	—	73
Colt	Brass mounted army	350	—	350
Colt	Army	255	—	255
Colt	Old model navy (Model 1851)	2,094	—	2,094
Colt	New model navy (Model 1861)	363	2,000	2,363
Colt	Brass mounted navy	625	—	625
Colt	Navy (Model 1851 principally)	8,691	—	8,691
Colt	New model holster pistol (Model 1860)	1	95,156	95,157
Colt	4½-inch revolvers	50	—	50
Colt	4-inch revolvers	120	—	120
Colt	Colt's revolvers (Belgian)	41	—	41
Colt	Colt's revolvers	617	—	617
Colt	English navy (Model 1851)	1	—	1
Colt	New pattern dragoon (Model 1860)	—	30,700	30,700
Colt	Dragoon pistol carbine (Model 1860)	1,000	—	1,000
Colt	Navy, with stock	285	—	285
Joslyn	Army	1,100	—	1,100
Kerr's Patent	Not stated	16	—	16
LeFaucheaux	Army	52	—	52
LeFaucheaux	Not stated	11,781	—	11,781
Perrin	Not stated	550	—	550
Remington	Army	850	114,713	115,563
Remington	Navy	8,100	5,001	13,101
Remington	Pistols	1,600	—	1,600
Pettengill	Army	—	2,001	2,001
Rogers & Spencer	Army	—	5,000	5,000
Savage	Revolving pistol	888	10,000	10,888
Starr	Old model army	4,950	—	4,950
Starr	Navy	1,402	—	1,402
Starr	Army	—	41,102	41,102
Whitney	Navy	3,585	7,002	10,587
Miscellaneous	*Navy	597	—	597
Miscellaneous	Revolvers	23	—	23
Miscellaneous	Army	814	—	814
Miscellaneous	Navy	329	—	329
Miscellaneous	Revolver pistols	1,290	—	1,290
Miscellaneous	George Raphael breech-loading	912	—	912
Miscellaneous	**Navy	365	—	365
Miscellaneous	Cavalry pistols	346	—	346
Miscellaneous	Horse pistols	200	—	200
Miscellaneous	French revolvers	68	—	68
Miscellaneous	Beals and Colts	549	—	549
Miscellaneous	Percussion lock holster pistols	772	—	772
Miscellaneous	Signal pistols	752	—	752
Miscellaneous	U. S. Holster pistols	453	—	453
Miscellaneous	Fistol carbines	5	—	5
Totals		59,844	313,975	373,819

* May be Whitney ** May be Colt

TABLE II
CONTRACT REVOLVERS

Contractor	*1861*	*1862*	*1863*	*1864*	*1865*	*1866*	*Total Delivered Between April 13, 1861 and April 3, 1866*
Colt's Patent Fire Arms Manufacturing Co.							
New model army	1,300	—	—	—	—	—	1,300
New model navy	—	2,000	—	—	—	—	2,000
New model holster pistol	—	36,201	58,955	—	—	—	95,156
New pattern dragoon	13,200	17,500	—	—	—	—	30,700
E. Remington & Sons							
Army	—	4,902	31,808	58,003	20,000	—	114,713
Navy	—	5,001	—	—	—	—	5,001
Rogers & Spencer							
Pettengill army	—	1,500	501	—	—	—	2,001
Rogers & Spencer army	—	—	—	—	5,000	—	5,000
Savage Arms Co.							
Revolving pistol	2,000	8,000	—	—	—	—	10,000
Starr Arms Co.							
Army	—	9,900	7,200	24,002	—	—	41,102
Eli Whitney							
Navy	—	5,001	2,001	—	—	—	7,002
Totals	16,500	90,005	100,465	82,005	25,000	—	313,975

TABLE III
COLT REVOLVER CONTRACTS

Contract Date	*Quantity Ordered*	*Quantity Delivered*	*Description*	*Price Each*
May 4, 1861	500	500	New model army pistol	$25.00
May 15, 1861	1,000	800	New model army pistol	25.00
June 12, 1861	5,000	5,000	Dragoon pistols, new pattern	25.00
Sept. 17, 1861	Indefinite	25,700	Dragoon pistols, new model or pattern	25.00
		2,000	Navy pistols, new model	22.50
June 6, 1862	15,000	15,000	Holster pistols, new model	14.50
Aug. 14, 1862	30,000	30,001	Holster pistols, new model	14.00
Jan. 30, 1863	30,000	30,000	Holster pistols, new model	14.00
May 25, 1863	20,000	20,000	Holster pistols, new model	14.00
Nov. 14, 1863	155	155	Holster pistols, new model, without bullet molds	13.73
Total		127,156	Holster pistols, new model	
Total		2,000	Navy pistols, new model	

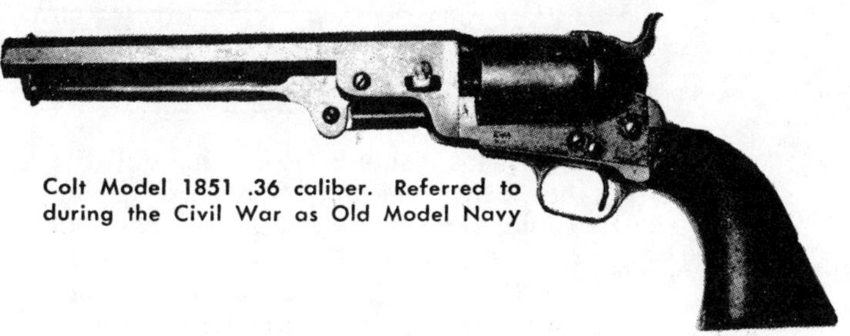
Colt Model 1851 .36 caliber. Referred to during the Civil War as Old Model Navy

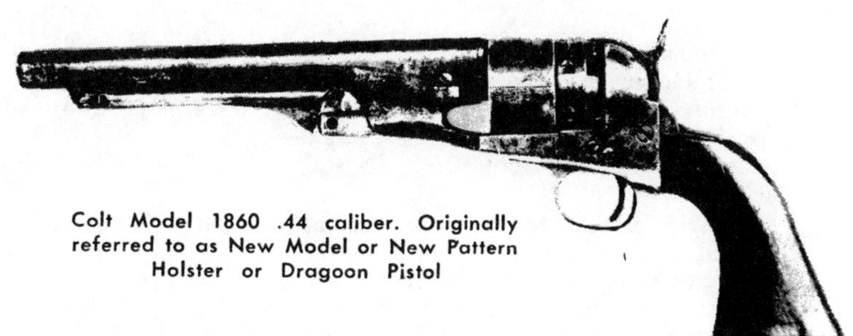
Colt Model 1860 .44 caliber. Originally referred to as New Model or New Pattern Holster or Dragoon Pistol

they are listed again in Table II in order to make clear just which ones are involved and the years in which they were delivered.

It is seen that most of the Civil War revolvers were supplied by six contractors. However, three contractors, Colt, Remington, and Starr, together furnished over 85 percent of all the revolvers purchased by the government during the Civil War.

In view of the interest of collectors and shooters in the Colt .44 caliber Army Model of 1860, Table III has been compiled showing the quantities delivered under various contracts with the United States Government. The names used in the government report from which this table was prepared have been used in the table. Variations of three names are used, "New model army pistol", "New pattern dragoon pistol", and "New model holster pistol". We may safely assume that all of these names refer to the Army Model of 1860 because production of the large, heavy Dragoon had been discontinued by 1861 in favor of the new and lighter weapon.

Table III includes a column showing the cumulative total deliveries under contract of the Army Model of 1860 to the government amounting to 127,156 revolvers. After completion of military deliveries on November 10, 1863, this revolver continued to be manufactured for civilian use. Total production reached 200,000 in 1873.

An indication of the rarity of shoulder stocks for the Colt Model 1860 revolver is revealed by Table I, which shows the delivery of March 1, 1862, of 1,000 "Dragoon pistol carbines, new model" at a price of $31.00 each. The price of the "pistol" at that time was $25.00, thus making the price of the stock $6.00.

Table III shows that only 2,000 "Navy Pistols, new model" (Model 1861), were purchased under contract with the Colt Patent Fire Arms Manufacturing Company. One thousand were delivered February 17, 1862, and 1,000 were delivered April 2, 1862, all at a price of $22.50 each. Three hundred and sixty-three were acquired through open market purchases as follows:

Aug. 29, 1861			
Joseph C. Grubb & Co., Phila.	110	@	$23.25 ea.
Sept. 2, 1861			
" " " " "	97	@	23.25 ea.
Nov. 5, 1861			
" " " " "	100	@	23.00 ea.
Jan. 26, 1863			
Colts Patent Fire Arms Co.	56	@	15.00
	363		

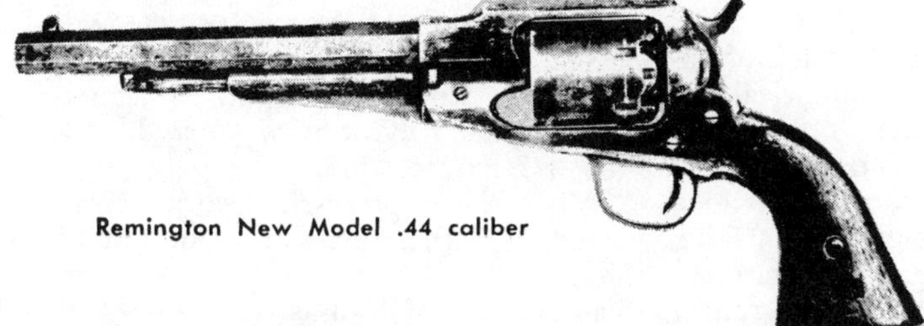
Remington New Model .44 caliber

In 1873 the total production of the Navy Model of 1861 reached 38,000. We have seen that out of this number 2,363 were purchased by the government. How many of this group of 2,363 revolvers have survived is not known but it is undoubtedly small enough to make this one of the scarce U. S. martial revolvers.

Several of the contracts with Colt for the manufacture of revolvers during the Civil War are reproduced verbatim:

(Telegram)

Ordnance Office, Washington, May 4, 1861.

Samuel Colt, Hartford, Connecticut:

Deliver the five hundred pistols to Major Thornton at New York arsenal. For further orders, wait mail.

J. W. Ripley,
Lieutenant Colonel of Ordnance

Ordnance Office, Washington, May 15, 1861.

Sir: Enclosed you will find the order requested in yours of the 13th instant. In answer to Mr. Hartley's letter, of same date, I have to state that Major Hagner, now at Hazardville, will be directed to inspect the five hundred pistols you have ready. Make another five hundred as soon as you can, and Major Hagner will inspect the thousand or as many of them as you may have ready.

Respectfully, &c.,

James W. Ripley,
Lieutenant Colonel of Ordnance

Samuel Colt, Esq., Hartford, Connecticut

Ordnance Office, Washington, June 12, 1861.

Sir: Please furnish this department, as soon as possible, with five thousand Colt's revolver pistols, of the latest pattern. The pistols are to undergo inspection, and the price will be the same as allowed for the same kind of pistols recently furnished by you.

James W. Ripley,
Lieutenant Colonel of Ordnance.

Samuel Colt, Esq., Hartford, Connecticut.

(Telegram)

Ordnance Office, Washington. September 17, 1861.

Samuel Colt, Hartford, Connecticut:

Deliver weekly, until further orders, as many of your pistols, holsters, new pattern, as you can make.

James W. Ripley,
Brigadier General

The remaining four contracts are long and formal documents and therefore are not reproduced.

The second group of revolvers, that is, the group that was purchased from dealers and other sources, is an interesting one and contains several little known specimens. These are two of the purchase orders.

ORDERS PLACED WITH A. GODILLOT

Ordnance Office, No. 55 White Street,
New York, December 19, 1861.

Sir: In compliance with instructions from Chief of Ordnance, I request that you will deliver to United States Ordnance Department, 1,000 French revolvers, like sample deposited with me, with ordnance office seal attached.

The said pistols to be furnished as stipulated in your proposal to the Assistant Secretary of War, dated December 16, 1861 and at the price therein stated.

Upon arrival of the arms in New York notice is to be given to this office, and permission will thereupon be furnished to you to receive free of duty from the Custom-house the cases which you are to deliver there for inspection at this office.

All not equal to sample in every particular affecting their value or service will be rejected, to be returned by you to the custom-house for payment of duties or for exportation.

Very respectfully, your obedient servant,
P. V. Hagner
Major of Ordnance.

Mr. A. Godillot, Paris.

Ordnance Office, No. 55 White Street,
New York, December 20, 1861.

Sir: Please furnish United States ordnance department with 2,000 Lefaucheaux revolvers, with fifty cartridges each, at $17, delivered here for inspection free of duty; also 1,500 French model rifle muskets, calibre .69, with 18-inch bayonets, with appendages, delivered here for inspection, free of duty, at $15 each.

The whole to be delivered with the least possible delay, not to exceed thirty-five days for the revolvers and a portion of the rifles; the balance as follows:
within ——— days.

Very respectfully, your obedient servant,
P. V. Hagner
Major of Ordnance

M. Alexis Godillot, New York

Deliveries against these two orders were as follows:

Jan. 6, 1862
350 revolver pistols (in bond) each $20.00
Mar. 28, 1862
100 Perrin's revolvers (in bond) each 20.00
336 French model rifled muskets (in bond) each 15.00
May 31, 1862
1,164 French model rifled muskets (in bond) each 14.62¾
100 Perrin's revolvers (in bond) each 20.00
1,500 Lefaucheux revolvers (in bond) each 17.00

These figures show that A. Godillot fell considerably short of filling his orders for he delivered only 550 Perrin revolvers against an order for 1,000, and 1,500 Lefaucheaux revolvers against an order for 2,000.

Table I includes one revolver that seems to be unknown as a United States military revolver. This is the Beaumont or English Beaumont-Adams which was "supplied impartially to both sides" during the Civil War, according to J. N. George in *English Pistols and Revolvers.*

Perhaps it should be pointed out that the Joslyn .44 and Starr .36 caliber revolvers cannot be classified as contract arms even though they were bought directly from the manufacturers. They are not mentioned in the contracts with these manufacturers and they are clearly listed as purchases, because the government report clearly labels each acquisition of arms as 'contract' or 'purchase'.

So far as is known the revolvers purchased from George Raphael are not stamped with the maker's name. For want of a better name they are known as Raphael's. This statement applies only to the 912 revolvers bought from him in 1861. The available information did not show the relationship, if any, between these revolvers and the 138 "LeFoucheux" revolvers bought from him on May 8, 1862.

LeFaucheaux spelling

Attention is called to the variation in spelling the name "LeFaucheaux" Nevertheless, it would seem that this is the correct spelling. However, this point as well as numerous others, awaits clearing up by further research on the part of students who have access to original and authoritative sources of information.

continued from page 42

Brown by one Thaddeus Hyatt, an eastern friend of the noted abolitionist.

While yet a young man Arny was on intimate terms with many of the leading men of that time. It is said that he was a favorite with Abraham Lincoln. In 1862 he moved to the territory of New Mexico where for a while he served as Indian Agent to the Navajos. Later, President Lincoln appointed him Secretary of the Territory. He also served as Territorial Governor for a short period of time. Arny is perhaps best known for his managing of the drought problems of 1860. During this time he was most active in handling millions of pounds of food and thousands of dollars for the relief of the stricken.

It was some time after the Pottawatomie incident that William Arny presented the revolver to Capt. John Brown in recognition of his service to the free-state cause. The gun is the regular issue of the Colt percussion Navy Model with the engraved cylinder marked "ENGAGED 16 MAY 1843" and the octagon barrel stamped "ADDRESS SAM'L COLT NEW YORK CITY." Serial number is 51010.

For some two years Brown carried the revolver. In fact, it might have been with him on the ill-fated raid upon Harpers Ferry had it not been for his ingrained honesty. Even though he

was of an eccentric nature, which oftentimes bordered upon the fanatical, he was a stickler for principles. Thus, when he learned that his friend Arny's admiration for him had cooled due to a disapproval of the tactics that he, Brown, was pursuing, he reasoned there was but one thing to do—return the gift, and return it he did. Shortly afterwards he embarked upon the raid at Harpers Ferry, an act which was to culminate in the execution for treason of this zealous man who felt that he had a divine commission to destroy slavery by violent means.

In 1879 while on a visit to Topeka, Kansas, Mr. Arny presented the John Brown revolver to the State Historical Society. It was his wish that the historic piece should stay in the state in which so many of Brown's activities occurred. There it rests today in a case among other mementoes of John Brown. Close by is a copy of the last message the noted abolitionist wrote only an hour or so before his death. It reads as follows:

"Charlestown, Va.
2nd December, 1859

"I, John Brown am now quite *certain* that the crimes of this *guilty land* will never be purged *away;* but with blood, I had as I now think; vainly, flattered myself that without *very much* bloodshed it might be done."

With these prophetic words there passed from the American scene one of the most controversial figures ever to tread the soil of Kansas.

An early Transition Model of the Confederate Le Mat revolver, upper rifled barrel of cal. .42 and lower shotgun barrel of cal. .60

The Confederate Le Mat Revolver

By HERSCHEL C. LOGAN

ONE of the most colorful—certainly the most unusual—of Confederate arms is the Le Mat revolver, produced in France under contract for the Confederacy. They were smuggled into the South by blockade-running ships. Few arms carried a more lethal potential than did this 9-shot revolver, with its extra shotgun barrel.

On Oct. 21, 1856, Dr. Jean Alexandre Francois Le Mat, a physician of French extraction living in New Orleans, secured U. S. patent #15925. Reduced to a few words his application provided for "A revolver having an upper and an under barrel, the lower one going back to the recoil shield and serving as an axle upon which the cylinder revolves. The chambers of the cylinder fire through the top barrel. The nose of the hammer being adjustable, the one hammer fires both bullets of the chambers through the top barrel and also the charge of shot or buckshot from the lower gun barrel."

'Grapeshot' revolver

Dr. Le Mat, with Col. P. G. T. Beauregard as partner, endeavored to get the "Grapeshot Revolver" (a name given to it at the time) adopted by the U. S. Army. Gen. Sterling Price appointed a Board of Officers, and in 1859 the Le Mat revolver was highly recommended, but it was never adopted. Beauregard sold his interest in the revolver to C. Girard, and when the South seceded he resigned from the U. S. Army and became a general in the Confederate Army. It was he who led the firing on Fort Sumter on Apr. 12, 1861.

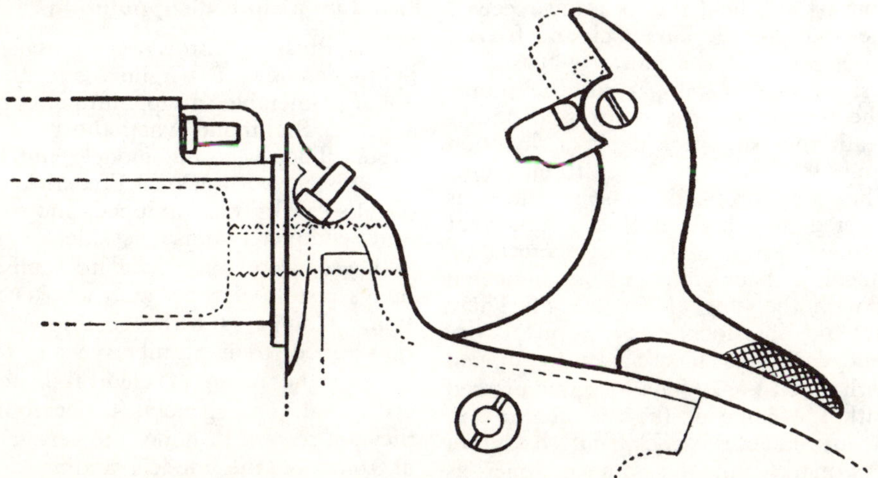

Pen sketch illustrating the operation of the unique hammer on the Le Mat revolver. The movable nose of the hammer is pictured in firing position for the shotgun barrel. Dotted lines show position for firing the charges in the chambers of the cylinder

After the outbreak of hostilities, Le Mat, concerned with questionable wartime production in this country and with a signed contract in his pocket, went to France aboard the English mail ship *Trent*. He narrowly escaped capture when the vessel was stopped and searched by officers of a Federal gun boat. Once in France Col. Le Mat—he had been an honorary colonel on staff of the Governor of Louisiana—lost no time in arranging with the firm of C. Girard & Co. of Paris for the production of his unique revolver. His first contract with the Confederacy called for 5000 arms. The actual production of his percussion arms, however, is believed to have been slightly more than half that number.

The Confederate Ordnance Dept.'s Manual of 1862 has this to say in the chapter on small arms then in use in the Army:

"GRAPESHOT PISTOL—This pistol is manufactured by M. Le Mat of Paris. It has a cylinder which revolves, containing nine chambers, a rifled barrel and a smooth-bore barrel. The latter receives a charge of eleven buckshot, and is fired by a slight change in the hammer. Some are in our service."

The personal side arm of Gen. J. E. B. Stuart was one of Le Mat's revolvers. Other noted officers carrying Le Mats included Gen. Beauregard and Gen. Patton Anderson.

By 1864, according to Col. Payne's record book, now in the Confederate Museum at Richmond, Le Mat revolvers were coming through with regularity on blockade-running steamers.

As for the gun itself, here one encounters some confusion as to variations. During the more or less short period of production, the Le Mats underwent several changes, some major and some minor. Three distinct models emerge, First Model, Transition Model, and Second Model.

The First Model has a partly octagonal and partly round barrel, spur trigger guard, swivel lanyard ring in butt, and loading lever or rammer on the right side of the barrel.

On the Transition Model the loading lever was switched to the left side of the barrel, and an octagonal barrel replaced the partly octagonal and partly round barrel.

As finally produced in the Second Model the spur was dropped from the trigger guard, and the swivel in the butt gave way to a solid plate with a hole for the ring.

The generally accepted serial number range for the 3 models is as follows:

First Model	1 to 450
Transition Model	450 to 950
Second Model	950 to 2500

Variations will be encountered among the 3 models.

Barrel markings encountered appear in this order:

First Model	LeMat's Patent Col. LeMat's Patent Col. LeMat Bte. s.g.d.g. Paris
Transition Model	Col. LeMat's Patent Col. LeMat Bte. s.g.d.g. Paris
Second Model	Col. LeMat Bte. s.g.d.g. Paris Syst. LeMat Bte. s.g.d.g. Paris Systeme LeMat Bte. s.g.d.g. Paris SYSTme LeMat Bte. s.g.d.g. Paris LeMat & Girard's Patent, London

Guns with the last marking and Birmingham proofmarks are believed to have been made under contract for the CSA Navy.

Caliber and bore varied, but for the most part the cylinder chambers were of cal. .42 and the smoothbore barrel of cal. .60, or about 20-ga. A very few were made in a smaller size, approximately cal. .36 for the rifled barrel and cal. .50 for the smoothbore.

Parts breakage

Principal weaknesses of the Le Mats were the loading lever and the small movable tip of the hammer, which turned down to fire the shotgun barrel. If it broke off, the gun was all but useless. Many of the weapons will be found without loading levers. Whether these were broken off or removed by owners for better holster carrying, is not known.

Post-war production of Le Mat pinfire revolvers has no connection with the Confederacy. Only the percussion models can lay claim to being primary Confederate arms. ■

PISTOLS OF THE AMERICAN REVOLUTION

Continued from page 7

army (cavalry) pistol was mounted in iron; the navy in brass. Otherwise both had a round barrel nine inches long and of .67 caliber. The barrel was attached to the walnut stock by a tang screw and a long double band at the muzzle. This band was held in position by a retaining spring on the obverse side. The stock was long and relatively straight with a hardly noticeable swell at the butt. The butt cap fitted the butt closely and possessed a single short extension up the back of the grip. The sideplate resembled that on the contemporary musket. The ramrod was iron with a button head and decorative turnings just below it. The lock was similar to that on the 1763 infantry musket, with a flat reinforced cock and an iron pan filed with flat faces. As the years passed, however, the lock was modified more or less in keeping with the changes in the infantry musket. The cock became convex, and the pan changed from the faceted design to a rounded shape. Yet, even in the navy model the pan remained iron.

New model quite different

In 1776, the French adopted a second model which was first manufactured and marked in 1777. The new model differed considerably from its predecessor and, indeed, resembled no other contemporary pistol. The .69 caliber barrel was 7½ inches long. It was round and tapered gradually toward the muzzle. It was received in a breech frame of brass which fitted around it on both sides and underneath. This housing also held the lock and received the iron ramrod. The cock and frizzen were iron, but the pan was brass and cast as an integral part of the frame. The frizzen spring was inverted underneath the pan, running in a direction opposite from the conventional one. The butt dropped sharply and was covered by a brass butt cap somewhat similar to the one on the preceding model. A back strap of iron connected it with the tang of the barrel. There was no forestock. Those pistols intended for naval use were equipped with a belt hook. The lock was marked with the name of the manufactory in an arc under the cock, and the barrel was marked in the same manner as the preceding model. Frequently there was also an inspector's mark with the date stamped in the wood of the butt.

It was this pistol which served as a model of the famous North & Cheney, the first pistol made under contract for the new United States government after the close of the Revolution.

German pistols on both sides

The German troops who served as auxiliaries to the British brought very few pistols with them. There were no German naval units, and very few mounted troops. The few German pistols there were varied considerably, depending upon which principality the unit which used them came from. Generally, however, they were brass mounted; the barrels were round, pin-fastened, and of large caliber, often about .75. Cocks were frequently convex and reinforced. The ramrods were iron and occasionally attached to the barrel by a swivel. Almost always there was the same elliptical brass front sight which was so typical of the German musket.

Interestingly, there were probably almost as many pistols of the Germanic type carried by American soldiers and sailors as by the German troops themselves. This situation arose because of American purchases of arms in Holland and Prussia.

Some made by Thone

Of these purchased pistols, those made in Holland were by far the better. Many of them were made by the same Thone of Amsterdam who supplied a large number of the muskets which also reached this country.

Prussian pistols disappointing

The Prussian pistols were purchased by the colony of Virginia, and there was considerable disappointment and anger in Richmond when the guns arrived. They were old models, not the new pistols with which Frederick the Great's cavalry was equipped, and some were completely unserviceable.

These were the standard enlisted men's pistols of the American Revolution. Compared with the muskets of the period their numbers were few. Yet, in the realm of colorful history, eye-appeal, and general collectability, they are second to none, the very rarity of some of the models adding extra zest and greater satisfaction to the collector who is fortunate enough to obtain one. ◆ ◆ ◆

FRONTIER REVOLVERS

By JOHN A KOPEC

Colt's Frontier Six Shooter revolver in cal. .44-40 featuring 7½" barrel and the Colt eagle hard-rubber grips. This specimen has the scarce combination of a three-line patent date and the rampant Colt trademark. Although a typically Western revolver, this particular gun was shipped to Colt's London agency in Sept. 12, 1890.

Remington M1875 Army Revolver was made in cals. .44 Remington, .44-40 Winchester and .45 Colt.

SAY ".44-40 frontier revolver" to the average gun collector, and his instinctive response is likely to be "Colt." Although at least five other well-recognized .44 revolvers also saw action along the early frontiers, none overcame the commanding position that Colt held in prestige and availability.

An important reason for the great popularity of the Colt Frontier Six Shooter, which was introduced in 1877, was that it was chambered for the .44-40 Winchester center-fire cartridge, the same round used in the popular Winchester Model 1873 lever-action rifle. Having a rifle and revolver chambered for the same reloadable cartridge was important to frontiersmen and ranchers, who were often far from a source of supply and had little money for ammunition.

Other makers were quick to copy this concept of a frontier-style revolver using rifle ammunition, but their revolvers never achieved the popularity of the Colt. Nonetheless, these arms made an impact on our Western frontier, as evidenced by the many frontier-style revolver variations encountered in collecting.

Colt's enjoyed a competitive advantage over other firms producing frontier-style revolvers because it was a well-established firm with a good reputation. Colt revolvers competed successfully against all other entries in the Army Ordnance trials of the early 1870's, and in 1873 the Army contracted with Colt's for 8,000 U.S. Cavalry single-action cal. .45 revolvers. The only other firm able to gain a significant U.S. Army revolver contract in those days was Smith & Wesson with its Schofield Model. While other manufacturers were not as successful as Colt's in obtaining government contracts, what they learned during U.S. Ordnance trials aided them in refining and improving their revolvers.

Remington produced several models of metallic-cartridge revolvers following the basic pattern of its New Model Army percussion revolver. Many were shipped originally with two styles of cylinders and could be fired either as percussion or as metallic-cartridge revolvers. Remington's M1875 Army single-action revolver was very successful. It was initially chambered for the .44 Remington cartridge which resembled the .44 Colt round used in Colt M1860 Army conversions. This Remington revolver was later chambered also for the .44-40 cartridge and, only rarely, in cal. .45 Colt.

In 1876, the M1875 Remington in cal. .44 was tested by the U.S. Army Ordnance Department against the Colt Single-Action Army Cavalry and S&W Schofield revolvers. These tests proved the Colt superior to the Schofield and Remington, which had difficulty in passing the rust and dust tests. The Remington was, nevertheless, a good, reliable revolver which was favored by many cowboys and lawmen. A later, somewhat improved version of the Remington called the M1890 Single Action was manufactured in small quantity and is now highly desired by collectors.

Smith & Wesson's contribution to the field of frontier revolvers was the New Model No. 3 Single Action Frontier revolver. Although most New Model No. 3 revolvers were chambered for the .44 S&W Russian cartridge, a few were specially manufactured in cal. .44-40 Winchester. Issued between 1885 and 1908, they fell in a separate serial range from 1 through 2072.

These revolvers were termed "longstrap" models because they required a longer cylinder and top strap to accomodate the .44-40 and .38-40 cartridges. Several other single-action S&W revolvers became popular because of the excellent accuracy of the .44 S&W Russian cartridge. The S&W cal. .44-40 revolver entered rather late on the scene and was a limited-production item.

An unusual and interesting extraction system was featured in Merwin, Hulbert revolvers. This company was organized as a firm of sales agents and promoters, operating in New York from about 1868 through 1891. Its unusual revolvers were manufactured by the Hopkins & Allen Mfg. Co. of Norwich, Conn.

Three basic Merwin, Hulbert & Co. designs are encountered. One was the Open-Top Frontier, a single-action revolver which did not have a top-strap over the cylinder. The second version was the .44 Russian model produced with an integral barrel top-

Only one Smith & Wesson model was actually designated as the Frontier, the New Model No. 3 in cal. .44-40. Specimen shown was factory converted to cal. .44 S&W Russian and shipped to the Japanese.

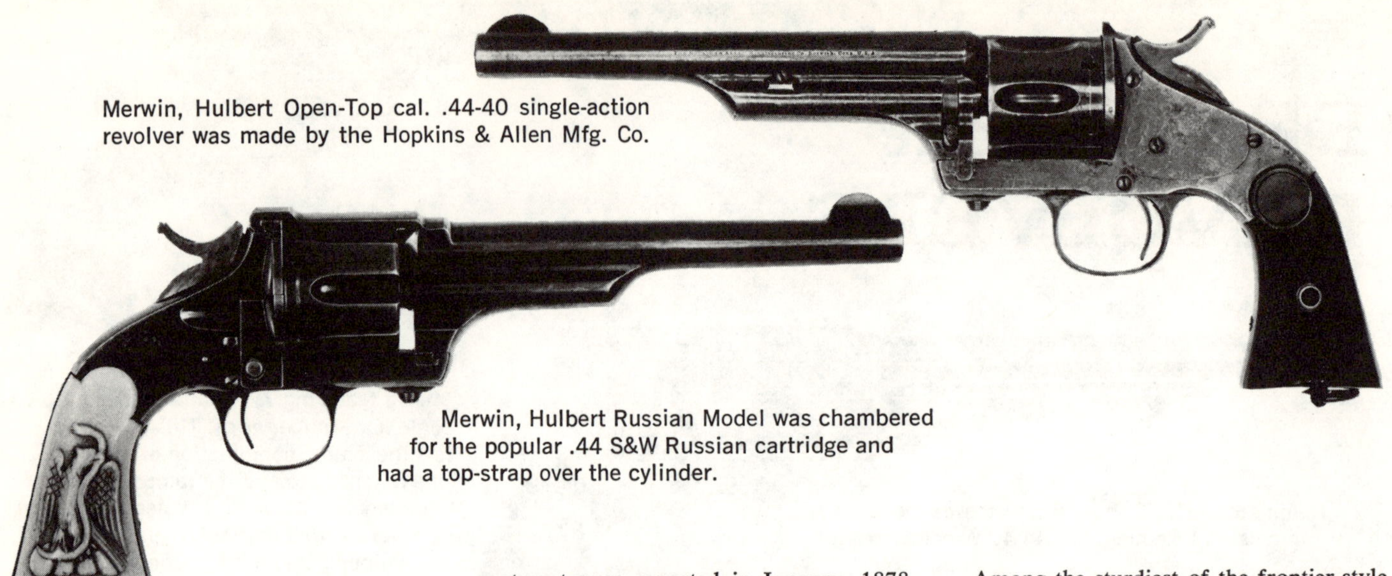

Merwin, Hulbert Open-Top cal. .44-40 single-action revolver was made by the Hopkins & Allen Mfg. Co.

Merwin, Hulbert Russian Model was chambered for the popular .44 S&W Russian cartridge and had a top-strap over the cylinder.

strap that meshed with a corresponding lug over the recoil shield. A third variant was a double-action revolver offered with choice of long or short barrels.

All these revolvers operated on the same system. After the hammer was put on half-cock, a button at the base of the frame was pushed toward the rear. This released the barrel assembly which pivoted sideways on the cylinder pin. The barrel and cylinder assembly was then pulled forward, and the cartridge cases were extracted by a circular flange integral with the recoil shield. This extraction system was very efficient, and specimens of these revolvers now encountered are usually tight-fitting and operable.

Big-bore Merwin, Hulbert revolvers were generally chambered for the .44 Merwin, Hulbert cartridge, a proprietary round with a 222-gr. bullet powered by 28-grs. of blackpowder. They were also produced in cal. .44-40 Winchester. A few chambered for the .44 S&W Russian cartridge were called the Russian Model. Only about one in 20 of these revolvers was blued, hence these are most sought after by collectors.

Tests of the Open-Top Merwin, Hulbert revolver by the U.S. Army Ordnance Department were reported in January, 1878. Although the test results on this arm proved somewhat favorable, it fell short in comparison to the Colt and did not warrant the Ordnance Board's approval. Merwin, Hulbert frontier-style revolvers are well engineered and of high quality but are generally overlooked by collectors.

The Hopkins & Allen is a little-known and seldom-encountered frontier-style revolver. Produced by Hopkins & Allen Mfg. Co. of Norwich, Conn., it was termed the XL No. 8, and was chambered for the .44 Henry rimfire cartridge. Since its manufacture was during the 1870's when the Henry cartridge was less popular than the .44-40 Winchester, this revolver was doomed to a place of little importance soon after being produced.

The XL No. 8 bore several similarities to the Merwin, Hulbert, including the shape of the grip, the loading gate, hammer profile, and contours of the trigger guard. This revolver was poorly accepted because of its delicate cartridge extraction system and only a few were produced. It is now a seldom-collected rarity.

Among the sturdiest of the frontier-style revolvers was the Forehand & Wadsworth .44-40 made by the Forehand & Wadsworth Mfg. Co., Worcester, Mass. Its general configuration is reminiscent of the Remington M1875 revolver primarily because of its peculiarly shaped ejector rod housing.

The sturdy construction of this revolver grew out of the Army trials. Improvements in it were direct results of the Ordnance Board's criticism of the first-model Forehand & Wadsworth Single Action Army revolver. Among these refinements were an improved ejector assembly and removable cylinder pin. Dating from about 1878, this revolver proved to be very reliable, but it appeared too late to compete with the well-established Colt Single-Action Army.

Many collectors now seek various makes of frontier-style revolvers. But even though more Colts in cal. .44-40 were produced than probably all other makes of frontier-style revolvers combined, the Colt Frontier Six Shooter remains one of the most desirable and sought-after revolvers for collectors. ■

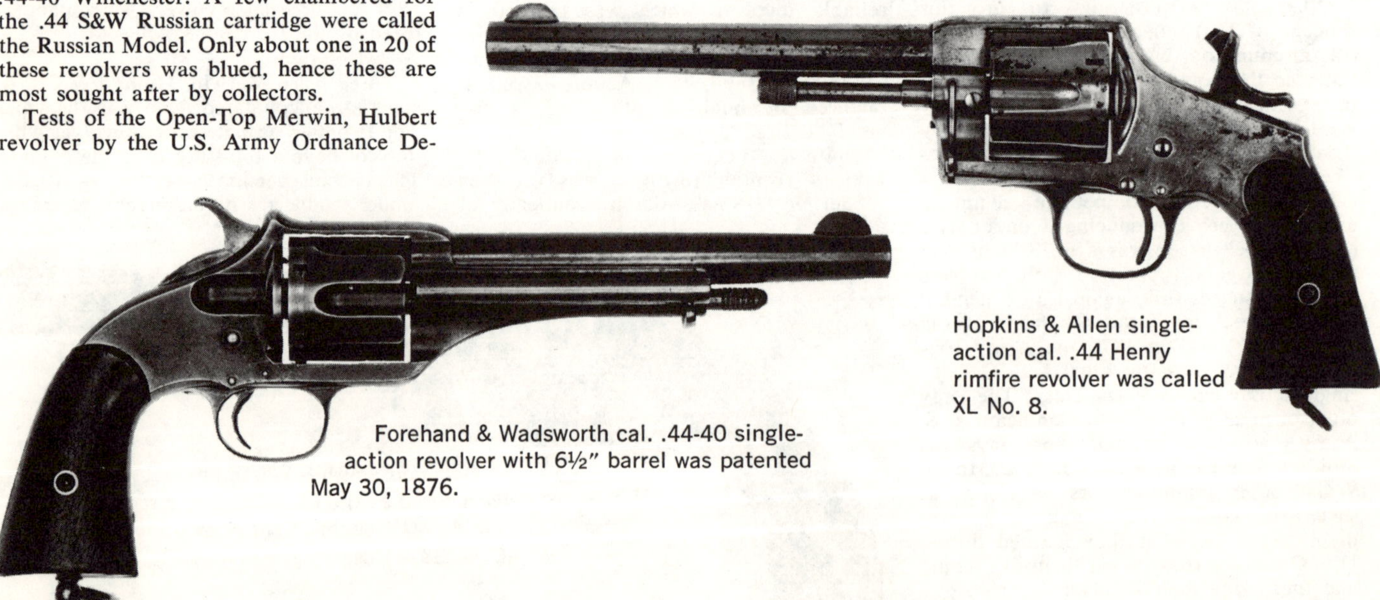

Hopkins & Allen single-action cal. .44 Henry rimfire revolver was called XL No. 8.

Forehand & Wadsworth cal. .44-40 single-action revolver with 6½" barrel was patented May 30, 1876.

AMERICAN HANDGUNS & MAKERS

Adams Percussion Revolver

Adams found that Colt patents were biggest obstacle

By PAUL S. LEDERER and BILL GAMMELL

IN its improved version, the English percussion revolver developed in the mid-19th century by London gunsmith Robert Adams represented a significant step forward in the development of effective handguns.

Of rugged construction, yet lighter than most of its competitors, the fully developed Adams revolver in final form with hammer cocking-spur offered both precise, thumb-cocked single-action shooting and rapid trigger-actuated double-action operation.

Excellent workmanship combined with other desirable qualities eventually enabled the Adams revolver to compete successfully with Samuel Colt's arms both in England and on the continent of Europe. Its success ultimately led Colt to discontinue his London operation.

An American's patent

But it was the American, not the Londoner, who got off to a flying start in the English revolver field, with an English patent (No. 6909, issued Dec. 8, 1835) covering several construction and operating features of revolving guns and pistols. Some of the details of the Colt patent are as follows: ". . . the combination of the key (cylinder bolt) and lifter (hand) with the hammer, so that backward motion of the hammer shall successively produce the unlocking, rotary motion and relocking of the cylinder. . . .", ". . . the application of the percussion tubes (nipples) in a right line with the axis of the chamber of the cylinder. . . .", ". . . the application of partitions between the percussion caps . . ." and also "the application of a (recoil) shield."

For the 14-year duration of the patent, no one else could make use of these features without a license from Colt. English multi-shot percussion firearms of this period consisted of pepperboxes and "transition" revolvers, which did not infringe on Colt's claims. They used other means of rotating and locking the cylinders, and the percussion nipples were at right angles to the bore without partitions between them.

Colt secured another English patent (No. 12,668, June 20, 1849) just before his 1835 patent expired. The new one, "Improvements in Firearms," re-patented some of the features of the earlier patent. It appears that Colt was also granted claims on "lock frame and recoil shield made in one piece," "barrel fixed to the end of the spindle (cylinder pin) and held by a key," cylinder "turned by means of a pall or key connected with the hammer," cylinder locked by "rocking lever . . . in frame . . . lever unlocked by stud attached to hammer;" also "jointed lever ramrod with . . . reciprocating motion . . . plunger parallel to the axis of the barrel."

To produce a revolver in the England of this period which did not infringe on any of Colt's patented features required an original approach. Robert Adams managed to come up with one.

On Aug. 22, 1851, Adams was granted Patent No. 13527 for "rifled, revolving and other firearms." One of his patent claims was for a method of forming the revolver frame and barrel as an integral unit. The patent specifications describe an axis rod on which the cylinder rotates and which may be withdrawn to remove the cylinder. A self-cocking lock mechanism is de-

To compete on the British market with Colt, Adams manufactured several calibers of self-cocking percussion revolvers. From top: cals. .497, .44, .388, and .339. Axis rod or cylinder pin projects from front, under barrel.

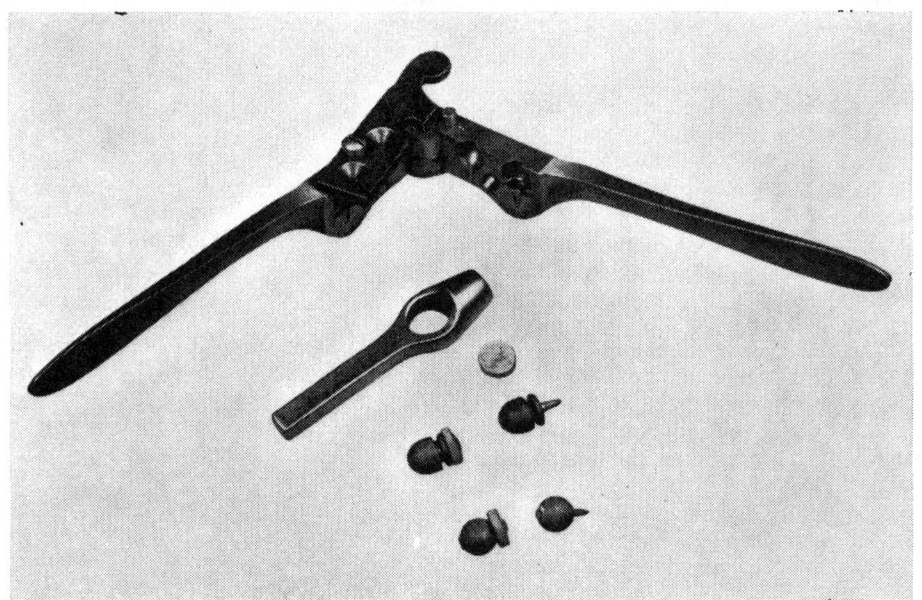

Adams bullet mold and wadcutter with wad and cast spherical and round-nose bullets used in Adams revolvers. Wads are spiked on two at left.

scribed, as is a cylinder with horizontal nipples, separated by partitions (Colt's patent protection for those 2 features ended in 1849). The cylinder is rotated by a lever connected to the trigger (*not* the hammer as in Colt's 1849 patent). A stud on the trigger engages the back of the cylinder to lock it (avoiding the use of a feature like the "rocking lever" of Colt's 1849 patent). Finally, a spring safety catch locks the hammer against accidental discharge and for capping. There is no mention of any loading lever or other kind of ramrod, nor is there a recoil shield on the frame (claimed in Colt's 1849 patent). Instead of a loading lever, Adams developed a wadded bullet which could be loaded into the chamber by finger pressure.

This revolver design, combining both old and new features, dominated the English scene until 1865. To exploit it, a partnership was formed between Robert Adams and 2 other London gunmakers, John Deane and George Deane (or John Deane, Jr.), under the name "Deane, Adams & Deane", at 30 King William St., London Bridge.

The great exhibition held in 1851 at the Crystal Palace in London gave the partners an excellent chance to publicize their revolver, and they took it. At the exhibition, the Adams revolver won a gold medal as the outstanding arm in its class, while Samuel Colt, who exhibited a large number of his revolvers, only received an Honorable Mention.

Despite this acclaim, production of the Adams revolver got underway slowly. J. Darwent of Lancashire, England, a student of these guns, says that only about 400 were produced in 1851, possibly because the patent protection was not granted until Aug. 22 of that year.

Adams revolver

The early Adams revolver is a self-cocking, 5-shot, solid-frame revolver, without loading lever. The cylinder pin, secured by a flat leaf spring on the right front of the frame, can be pulled forward to release the cylinder. The revolving mechanism is actuated by a hand pinned to the rear of the trigger which acts on a toothed ratchet on the cylinder base. When the trigger is pulled, the hand rises through a slot inside the frame, engages a ratchet, and rotates the cylinder one-fifth of a revolution. Simultaneously, a short lifter is pushed upwards against a catch in the hammer, forcing the latter upwards and backwards and compressing the mainspring until the lifter slips off the catch. With the hammer released, the mainspring forces it forward until the hammer nose strikes the end of the nipple. When the trigger is drawn back, a small extension of its back rises through the frame and presses against the partition separating the 2 lower chambers, firmly locking the cylinder in place at the time of firing. A small V-spring returns the trigger to its original position. The safety catch, a flat spring in the left side of the frame ahead of the hammer, engages a slot in the hammer when the trigger is pulled back slightly while pressure is applied to the safety. With the safety holding the hammer nose clear of the nipples, the cylinder is free to rotate for loading and capping. Any subsequent pressure on the trigger sufficient to move the hammer back slightly will disengage the safety and permit the revolver to fire.

The octagon barrel is rifled with 3 or 5 grooves and has an adjustable blade front sight. The rear sight is a V-groove in a ridge at the rear of the frame.

The slim, one-piece butt, usually of finely-checkered walnut, is attached to the frame nearly at right angles, and there is a pronounced knuckle at the juncture. The metal butt cap often has a trap for spare caps. A steel trigger guard screwed to the frame houses a small trigger. Metal parts usually have a small amount of engraving and are charcoal blued except for the cylinder, which is either bright or color case-hardened, and the hammer, which is polished bright.

Inscription

Many early Adams revolvers carry an elaborate inscription along the top barrel flat: "*Deane, Adams & Deane (Makers to H.R.H. Prince Albert) 30 King William Street, London Bridge*". Others bear the name and address of the retailer. On the right side of the frame is inscribed "*Adams Patent No. ......*", followed by a serial number and frequently an initial.

Adams revolvers were made in 3 basic sizes: 38-bore (cal. .497) with a 7½" or 8" barrel (2 lbs. 10 ozs.), often called the "Dragoon"; 54-bore (cal. .442) with a barrel about 6" long, (1 lb. 14 ozs.); and 120-bore (cal. .338) with a barrel about 4½" long. The 54-bore model is the most common. "Bore number", the English system of indicating caliber, stands for the number of round lead balls fitting the bore which together weigh 1 lb. This is also referred to as "gauge."

Adams revolvers, unlike Colts, did not have completely interchangeable parts. All major parts carry assembly numbers, and contractor's initials often appear on the frames. Since Adams revolvers were made by several different contractors they exhibit minor variations in size, shape, decoration, and finish. Many were sold in oak cases with accessories and with the maker's or retailer's label in the case lid.

Although Samuel Colt's display at the 1851 Exhibition only received an Honorable Mention, it caused a sensation nonetheless, featuring hundreds of his Navy and Dragoon revolvers, mostly of plain finish. The large number of identical guns astonished visitors unfamiliar with mass production methods. Colt exhibited his revolvers in the hope of opening a new market for them in Europe, particularly England. To avoid having to pay import duties, he decided to establish a factory in England, and the Colt-Adams rivalry was on.

Tested at Royal Arsenal

In September, 1851, both Adams and Colt revolvers were tested at the Royal Arsenal at Woolwich in the presence of both inventors. Pitted against a Colt Dragoon, the Adams Dragoon proved to be superior in speed of loading and firing, and in target penetration. It was a clear victory for Adams, but the conservative British Ordnance would not buy revolving arms of new design when rugged single-shot holster pistols were still in store. Neither maker secured government orders from the tests.

Undaunted, Colt started production in a factory at Pimlico, London, in 1853, and immediately upset English gunsmiths by using semi-skilled and even unskilled labor to produce about 600 interchangeable part revolvers per week. Mainly pocket revolvers of cal. .31, and Navy models of cal. .36, they sold well. Deane, Adams & Deane also continued to make and sell guns in the civilian market, including revolving rifles and carbines. Competition between the makers continued. The Colt's greater range and accuracy was offset by the Adams' faster rate of fire. The Adams revolver could not be jammed by small sections of exploded caps getting inside the lock, a defect to which the Colt was prone. However, its lack of a recoil shield presented a certain risk to the shooter.

A big advantage of the Colt design was the powerful lever ramrod which seated the bullet so securely on its charge as to make it virtually waterproof and relatively free from risk of chain ignition.

Adams wadded bullet

Adams could not use such a lever ramrod while Colt's 1849 patent was in force. Instead, in Nov., 1851, Robert Adams registered his design of a "wadded bullet", cast with a tang on its base. A fiber wad was fitted on the tang which was peened over to secure the bullet to the wad. The wad was slightly larger than the bullet but could be pushed into the chamber with finger pressure. The drawback was that wadded bullets tended to work forward in the chambers and jam the cylinder. Adams later patented a metallic cartridge case filled with powder and attached to the tang of his wadded bullet. They were not successful commercially because they were too hard to make.

Neither Colt nor Adams were able to snare the government contracts they sought until war clouds gathered on the horizon in 1853. A minor quarrel between Russia and France over guardianship of Palestinian holy places led to a Russian invasion of Turkish territory (Palestine was then part of Turkey). Russia quickly destroyed the Turkish fleet and threatened to overwhelm Turkey itself. Because a Russian victory would have·to put Russia astride the overland trade route to India, England entered the war on the side of the Turks in 1854.

Just before England declared war the British War Office had second thoughts about the revolver and held another trial of Colt and Adams revolvers at Woolwich. Although not wholly conclusive, test results seemed to favor the Colt. The tests, combined with the tremendous productive capacity of Colt's Pimlico plant, plus a report of revolvers being issued to the Russian Navy, led to an extensive War Department order for Colt Navy revolvers in 1854 and 1855.

Adams, meanwhile, had been developing and improving his own revolvers. The first Adams revolvers were made in holster size only, initially of 34-bore (cal. .515), later in 38-bore (cal. .497). According to J. Darwent, only about 400 were made in 1851, all in holster size. Data collected by the authors indicate that serial No. 576 is the earliest 54-bore (cal. .442) of record. No. 821 is the first in 80-bore (cal. .387) and No. 4004 the first in 120-bore (cal. .338). The 3 are believed to date from 1852.

On these early guns, the serial number on the frame and cylinder is not followed by a letter. The letter "R" after the serials indicates guns made later. Gun No. 4697R in the summary is the first specimen found with an "R".

In response to criticism, several im-

Three cal. .44 Adams revolvers illustrate design variations. Early model (at top) has small frame and trigger guard while later models have large triggers and frames.

provements were made in the Adams revolver. The butt was set less nearly at right angles to the axis of the barrel, and the small semi-circular trigger of the original revolver was replaced with a longer and less sharply curved trigger. The straight safety spring which locks the hammer was replaced by a curved one. Finally, a longer cylinder on a larger frame was introduced, capable of holding a larger powder charge. All of these changes appeared about the same time. A 38-bore gun, No. 11121R, still has the small trigger, short cylinder and straight safety spring, while a 54-bore gun, No. 12522R, has the larger trigger, long cylinder (2″, exclusive of ratchet), and curved safety spring.

Lock improved

A drawback of the earlier Adams revolvers was the relatively heavy trigger pull of their self-cocking mechanisms, which made accurate shooting difficult. To correct this, Adams took out Patent No. 2712 in Nov., 1853, for an "improvement in firearms." The improvement was a modified lock mechanism incorporating a secondary sear. One trigger pull revolved the cylinder and cocked the hammer, which was kept cocked by the secondary sear. A second trigger pull pushed against the sear, releasing the hammer and firing the gun.

Though few revolvers were made with this mechanism, the patent is interesting as a forerunner of a later development. A secondary sear to hold the hammer in cocked position was adopted by Frederick Beaumont in his famous 1855 patent for selective self-cocking or single-action fire.

During these years Adams was also improving his wadded bullets. In October 1852 he obtained a patent for a cylindrical metal powder container attached to the wadded bullet. The high cost of these cartridges led Adams to seek a cheaper design. He apparently collaborated with William Eley, who in November, 1854, patented a cartridge with a paper case attached to the wadded bullet.

Though cartridges were becoming more sophisticated, rammers were still required to seat bullets or cartridges tightly. Attempts were made to improve rammer design without infringing on Colt's 1849 patent of a jointed lever rammer with reciprocating plunger.

John Rigby of Dublin designed a one-piece rigid lever pivoted about a screw at the right front of the frame (Patent No. 1976, Sept. 11, 1854). The end of the short arm forms a plunger which enters the chamber when the long arm is pushed downward and forward from its rest position on the frame above the trigger guard.

Two months later (Dec. 15, 1854) Robert Adams took out Patent No. 2645 for further "improvements in firearms (sic) called revolvers." It described a screw to retain the cylinder axis (instead of the spring) and a sliding safety dovetailed into the right side of the frame. Pushing it forward to engage slots cut into the partitions at the back of the cylinder prevented cylinder rotation and firing.

The patent also describes a rigid lever ramrod similar to the one patented by Rigby except that the plunger is attached to the long, instead of the short, lever arm. It has been incorrectly called a "Rigby rammer," but in truth it is pure Adams. In fact, the authors have never seen a gun with a Rigby rammer.

Rammer designs

The earliest gun in our summary equipped with the Adams rammer is No. 14308R-B1024 (38-bore, a Beaumont improvement of Adams' revolver). The latest appears to be No. 36640R (a 54-bore self cocking revolver of the type known to collectors as the 1854 improved model, retailed by Reilly of London). This rammer design was not too satisfactory, as it lacked sufficient mechanical advantage to seat bullets securely.

Early in 1855, Colt's 1849 patent covering the "lever rammer" was apparently allowed to lapse. (Periodic fee payments were required in England to keep a patent valid for its legal 14-year span; non-payment caused a patent to become void). This cleared the way for gunmaker Joseph Brazier to take out a patent in April, 1855 (No. 760) for a lever-type loading lever with the plunger sliding in guides on the barrel parallel to the bore. The rammer was not a success, however, and the authors know of only a few guns (No. 30422B and 30814B) equipped with it.

Gunmaker James Kerr had better luck. He took out a patent (No. 1722, July 28, 1855) for a compound lever ramrod resting on the side of the barrel and pivoting about a screw in an extension of the barrel lug. The design was sound, and almost all later Adams revolvers were equipped with it.

In our summary, the earliest revolver equipped with the Kerr rammer is No. 14576R-B1272 (a 38-bore Beaumont-Adams). ■

Cleaning Blackpowder Guns

Portland, Oreg.

Editor:

Field cleaning of blackpowder guns is necessary for accuracy and for trouble-free use in extended shooting. This is because each shot leaves a brittle fouling on the inside of the barrel. Repeated firings cause progressive thickening of the layer and reduction of the bore diameter.

Then a blackpowder shooter usually uses a saliva-dampened swab with the ramrod to clean the bore. This is messy. Sometimes the swab comes off the ramrod and remains in the barrel, which really causes some difficulty.

The percussion revolver shooter has trouble from fouling in another way. Since he does not ram the ball down the barrel, he is often first aware that fouling is excessive when accuracy falls off.

Most of the solutions to the fouling problem require carrying a lot of cumbersome equipment when afield. But one solution is much more practical, although not widely known.

With a long arm, shoot until the gun is fouled and the balls begin to resist as they go down the bore. Then use a pure lead round ball cast considerably undersize for the rifle with 1 or 2 extra-large, pre-cut patches. Charge the rifle with a normal load of blackpowder. Ram the patched ball all the way down to the powder. Then, place a percussion cap on the nipple.

From a canteen or other convenient container, pour a little water into the barrel. Experience will teach how much. Immediately after pouring, fire the rifle. This quite nicely cleans the bore, but not the powder chamber. So routine cleaning at home is still necessary after a day's shooting. The shot must be fired immediately after pouring the water into the barrel. Otherwise, water reaches the blackpowder, spoiling it.

A rifle requires this treatment less often than a gun firing an unpatched ball. This is because the spit or grease patch used in the rifle does a fair job of cleaning the bore. This procedure is not, however, completely sufficient.

Percussion revolvers are easy to field-clean where there is a stream, lake, pond, or spring nearby. Stick the barrel of the revolver in the water as far as the front of the cylinder. Remove the barrel from the water and fire one shot.

When there is no ground water nearby, water poured from a container carried on the person can be used, but it is less handy. Of course, each loaded chamber of the cylinder must be capped with a liberal amount of automotive lubricating grease to prevent water from damaging the blackpowder. Between dips, the grease helps to reduce bore fouling. I have not found water cleaning to be necessary more often than every 25 to 30 shots, although the cylinder pin must be re-greased frequently to prevent binding.

JUDD SMITH

Adams Percussion Revolver

Complaints on Colts, Beaumont improvement turn tide for Adams

By PAUL S. LEDERER and BILL GAMMELL

CONVINCED by tests of both revolvers that the Colt Navy Model 1851 was superior to the one designed by London gunsmith Robert Adams, the British Board of Ordnance ordered between 23,500 and 30,000 Colts at the outbreak of the Crimean War in 1854.

But complaints soon trickled back from the front that the Navy Colts weren't just what the doctor ordered. Their long-range accuracy was of little use in the hand-to-hand combat which often occurred and their .36 caliber bullets lacked stopping power.

The cal. .44 Colt Dragoon had the necessary stopping power, but it was heavy—4 lbs. 2 ozs. compared with 2 lbs. 10 ozs. for the cal. .497 Adams. The Adams was deficient in long-range accuracy, but this shortcoming was soon overcome by a patent granted to a Royal Engineers Lieutenant, Frederick Blacket Edward Beaumont.

Beaumont-Adams cal. .44 percussion revolvers ended the Adams-Colt rivalry with Adams the winner.

Beaumont's patent (No. 374, Feb. 20, 1855) marked the turning point in the fortunes of the Adams revolver. It described ". . . a peculiar combination of the parts of a lock of a firearm, by which the hammer may be cocked by hand or by pulling the trigger."

Beaumont modified the Adams lock by adding a small sear with a sear spring which engaged a full cock notch in the upper part of the hammer. When the hammer was drawn back by the thumb, it was held at full cock by the sear. Slight pressure on the trigger caused the lifter (part of the self-cocking mechanism of the Adams) to press against the underside of the sear, lifting it up sufficiently to release the hammer. If, on the other hand, the trigger was pulled without first cocking the hammer, the hammer would be first raised and then released by the action of the lifter, as in the original Adams design. With the Beaumont improvement release of the hammer, coinciding with the lifter raising the sear, prevented the latter from engaging the hammer and arresting its motion. This made for a steadier "squeeze-off."

In March, 1855, British Ordnance ordered 100 Beaumont-design revolvers for trial and in July Robert Adams secured the rights for Beaumont's patent. Beaumont-Adams revolvers made by Deane, Adams & Deane during late 1855 and early 1856 were commonly fitted with the Adams rammer and did not have a half-cock position, but instead used the curved safety spring on the breech.

Tests of the Beaumont-Adams revolver conducted in late 1855 by the Board of Ordnance resulted in its adoption as the standard British Army revolver. The model chosen was the 5-shot, 54-bore (cal. .442) revolver with Kerr rammer and 5¾" barrel rifled with 3 grooves. It was superseded in 1867 by a cal. .450 center-fire revolver by John Adams, Robert Adams' brother. Initial government purchases included some 38-bore revolvers with the Adams rammer, marked "*Deane, Adams & Deane*", but probably provided by an interim company trading as "*Adams & Co*".

Subsequent government orders went to the newly formed London Armoury Co., founded by Robert Adams in partnership with James Kerr and others. This firm was chartered in Feb., 1856, following the dissolution of the Deane, Adams & Deane partnership, and was in business until Aug., 1867.

Earlier Adams revolvers also may carry the name of the retailer on the top strap rather than the actual manufacturer, who may have been J. Brazier, Hollis & Sheath, William Tranter, or others. Tranter apparently made the majority of the early Adams revolvers, whereas Deane, Adams & Deane actually manufactured very few revolvers. J. Darwent, a British firearms authority, believes the numbers on the Beaumont-Adams revolvers relate to payments of royalties—those followed by "R" for the basic Adams patent; those preceded by "B" for Beaumont payments. They also serve as serial numbers. Adams guns may be found with serial numbers followed by other letters: "Y" represents Tranters made prior to 1856, "T" for Tranter guns made after 1856. "B" represents guns made by Brazier, also "C", "P", "X" are said to stand for guns made in Birmingham by: "P" for Pryse and Redman, and "C" for Calisher and Terry and "X" for Hollis and Sheath. Finally, guns exist without initials before or after the serial number.

The London Armoury Co., known to American collectors as manufacturers of Civil War Enfield muskets, made large quantities of Adams revolvers for the British Army as well as private citizens. These guns are marked on the top strap, *"London Armoury Company," "London Armoury"*, or simply with the initials *"L.A.C."* near the proof marks on the barrel or on the right side of the barrel lug. Those initialed usually carry the name of the retailer who sold the gun.

The earliest L.A.C. Beaumont-Adams in our summary is a 54-bore percussion revolver, No. 19077R-B3663, bought by the Army and ultimately converted to cartridge; this type is called Mark I. The last one in this series is No. 36447R-B20677. Shortly after this, the initials were dropped. The last recorded number for an L.A.C. gun in our summary is 39217 (a 120-bore Beaumont-Adams in a case with a label in its top "James Kerr & Co., successors to London Armoury Company"). From the numbers observed, we believe that some 19,000 Beaumont-Adams revolvers were made by the London Armoury Co. before it ceased operations in August, 1867.

Colt's London plant closed

Adoption of the Beaumont-Adams revolver and the establishment of the London Armoury Co. diminished Colt's prospect for further British government orders. The Crimean War had ended and this, combined with Colt's expansion of his Hartford factory, made it seem unprofitable to keep his London plant going. In Dec., 1856, the plant closed. The rivalry was over. Adams had won.

With the advent of the American Civil War, the London Armoury Co. manufactured large numbers of Enfield rifle-muskets for the belligerents. Demand for revolvers declined, and it is believed that before 1863, the company ceased the manufacture of revolvers altogether. J. Darwent believes that Beaumont-Adams revolvers were made by Birmingham subcontractors exclusively as early as 1859.

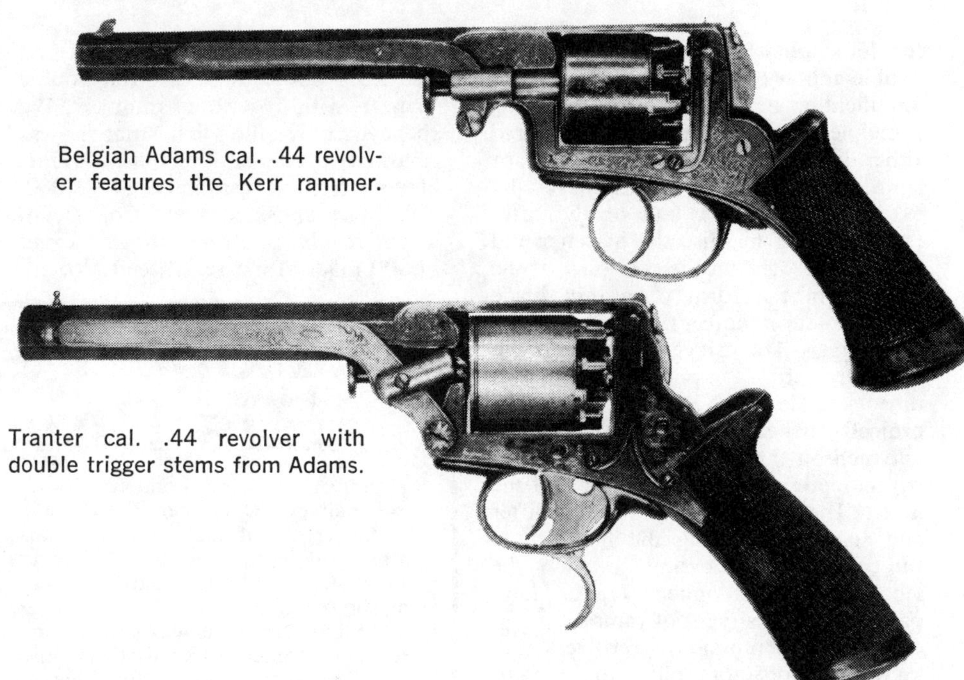

Belgian Adams cal. .44 revolver features the Kerr rammer.

Tranter cal. .44 revolver with double trigger stems from Adams.

Many Adams revolvers made by Birmingham gunsmiths have no makers' marks but they carry Birmingham proof marks, and generally have 5-groove rifling, as compared to the 3-groove rifling found in London Armoury Co. revolvers. Birmingham-made Adams revolvers sometimes have a single serial number without an initial preceding or following it. Our summary shows such guns with Nos. 30111 to 30709 and Nos. 40573 to 41235. No less than 8 guns are cited in the latter range.

(The Confederate Museum in Richmond, Va., has a cased 54-bore Beaumont-Adams revolver of this vintage, serial No. 40573 with case, handle engraved *"General Stonewall Jackson —from Robt. Adams"*. Also, a collector has a cased 120-bore Beaumont-Adams, serial No. B 16625-32299R, with case escutcheon inscribed *"Presented to Raphael Semmes by Royal Navy Club."* Semmes was Captain of the C.S.S. Alabama, built in England.)

Our summary ends with 3 high-serial Beaumont-Adams revolvers, Nos. 22683-38490, 60133P (Pryse & Redman), and 100076C (Calisher & Terry). We believe numbers do not necessarily indicate time sequence; rather, we feel that numbers were assigned to manufacturers in blocks and that numbers in a given block were not always used up. From the distribution of numbers, we feel that numbers up to about 42,000 indicate guns actually made—one serial number, one gun. But we think that only a few hundred were made in the 60,000 serial bracket and a like number near 100,000. One could also reasonably surmise that a few guns were made with serial numbers around the 70,000, 80,000, and 90,000 marks.

Fairly early in this period, Adams sought to expand the market for his revolvers by having them manufactured abroad under license. On May 3, 1853, he received U.S. Patent No. 9694 for his basic solid-frame revolver mechanism and, 4 years later, James Kerr was granted U.S. Patent No. 17,044 for his "improved rammer for many-chambered breech firearms". Shortly thereafter, the Massachusetts Arms Co. of Chicopee Falls, Mass., began making 2 models of the Beaumont-Adams revolver with the Kerr rammer. Frequently marked "Made for Adams Revolving Arms Company, N.Y.," they were made in cal. .36 with a 6" barrel and cal. .31 with a 3¼" barrel; both sizes were 5-shot models.

Massachusetts Arms Co. Adams revolvers are scarce. Highest serial number observed for the cal. .36 is No. 609; for the cal. .31 it is No. 4003. This suggests that about 3000 of the smaller and less than 1000 of the larger were made.

Revolvers of Adams design were also made in Belgium. One example, a cal. .44 five-shot revolver, it is identical to the English-made Adams save for its 6½" barrel and slightly less steep butt. The gun is marked: *"Manufactured by A. Francotte Licensed by R. Adams & Co., London,"* and the cylinder carries the Liege proof mark. The serial number of this specimen is relatively high—15817.

Still another sub-species of Adams revolver was manufactured by W. Tranter. Early Tranter revolvers were produced under the original patent of 1851. On Jan. 28, 1853, Tranter took out Patent No. 212 for a double-action system which, by a slight modification of the Adams self-cocking principle, enabled the gun to be fired either with the self-cocking motion or from full-cock. This was achieved by extending the lower end of the lifter (which serves to raise the hammer and which is pivoted on the rear part of the trigger) in the form of a thin blade which enters a slot cut in the center of the trigger. The trigger is extended in the form of a spur which passes through a slot in the trigger guard and projects beneath. A second trigger (pivoted on the same screw as the spur trigger) presses on the lower end of the lifter. The latter thus serves as lifter and sear, first raising the hammer to full-cock, then releasing it when the second trigger is pulled. Tranter later patented various types of rammers.

Adams percussion revolvers as known to collectors fall into 7 major categories, as follows:

1. Model of 1851/2—The early self-cocking revolvers with short cylinders, small frame, straight safety spring, small trigger, no rammer. About 12,000 made; last serial seen No. 11 121R.

2. Unimproved model of 1854—A self-cocking model with long cylinder, large frame, curved safety spring, large trigger, no rammer. About 2,000 made; first serial observed No. 12 522R; last serial observed No. 15387R.

3a. Semi-improved model of 1854—Self-cocking model with long cylinder, large frame, curved safety spring, also sliding safety on right, large trigger, and thumbscrew cylinder pin retainer, (Rigby) rammer.

3b. Fully improved model of 1854—All the features of 3a. above plus Rigby (Adams) rammer. About 2,000 made in both models; first serial seen No. 18730R; last serial seen No. 36640R.

4. Beaumont-Adams Model of 1855—Double-action revolvers with long cylinder, large frame, sliding safety, spring safety Adams (Rigby) rammer, but half cock bent. About 4,000 made; first serial seen No. 14 308R-B1024; last serial seen No. 20 793R-B5260.

5. Beaumont-Adams 1856 model—Double-action revolvers with long cylinder, large frame, sliding safety, Kerr rammer, London Armoury Co. marking. About 19,000 made; first serial seen No. 19077R-B3663; last serial seen No. 37807-22000.

6. Birmingham-proofed Beaumont-Adams revolvers—Long cylinder, large frame, sliding safety, Kerr rammer. Less than 3000 made; first serial seen No. 30111, last serial seen No. 41235.

7. Other revolvers made under Adams Patent include:

(a). Tranter *"Adams"* revolvers. At least 5 types with or without double trigger, with or without rammers. We believe only the first model was marked *"Adams"* on the frame. Number made estimated at 23,000.

(b). Massachusetts Arms Co., Beaumont revolvers, Kerr rammer. About 4,000 made. First serial seen No. 46, last serial seen No. 4003.

(c). Belgian Adams revolvers, self-cocking and Beaumont types, various rammers.

We believe that a total of about 16,000 Adams self-cocking models and roughly 25,000 Beaumont-Adams double-action revolvers were manufactured in England between 1851 and 1867. ■

Robert Adams & His Day In Court

GLOOM shrouded London's Guildhall one December day in 1859 as the cream of the city's gunsmiths assembled in the ancient building to sit as the Quarterly Court of Gunmakers Company.

Though Christmas was just past, no seasonal banter escaped their lips. They waited solemnly for charges they knew would be levelled against one of the most renowned of their fellows.

Presiding over the Court, Edward P. Bond, the Company's Master, read out the motion they dreaded to hear:

That "Mr. Robert Adams of King William St. be prosecuted for selling a gun to Mr. Gellatly, the barrel of which had not been duly proved."

It was unthinkable and scandalous that a member of the Gunmakers Company should have sold a gun which did not bear any proof mark. Nor was Robert Adams any run-of-the-mill journeyman, but an internationally-known master of the gunsmith's craft. His patented double-action revolver had proved that.

The gunsmiths knew well the unsettling details behind the Company Master's motion. This was the era of volunteer regiments, when patriotic British tradesmen and professionals devoted their free time to mastering the military arts for the sake of Queen and Country. A certain Mr. Gellatly, member of the Victoria Rifle Volunteers, a London-based regiment, had purchased an Adams muzzle-loader on the recommendation of a volunteer who also owned one.

During practice with ball ammunition, Gellatly's rifle had exploded. Apart from shock and powder burns, Gellatly was undamaged. His commanding officer at once rushed the ruptured rifle to the London Proof House. There it was found that the rifle had not been proved.

Learning of the calamity at the Victoria's range, Adams dashed out to the regiment's barracks, grabbed 20 or 30 rifles which bore his name and submitted them to the London Proof House. All passed the requisite tests, and he returned them to the barracks. He then wrote to Gellatly, congratulated him on his lucky escape.

Adams himself was not so lucky. His faulty rifle had blackened the good name of the Gunmakers Company to which he belonged, and the prosecution went forward. In a "never again" mood, the Gunmakers Company ran free tests on all the Victoria's rifles and warned the commanding officers of the 168 Volunteer Regiments against the dangers of unproved firearms. They also ran newspaper advertisements informing the public of the Gellatly affair and urging one and all to inspect their firearms for proof marks.

Under the malevolent gaze of the Lord Mayor of London, the hapless Adams pleaded guilty to charges before the Court at Mansion House, Jan. 30, 1860. In his defense, Adams's barrister brought out the fact that the Gellatly rifle had been fired at least 60 times before sale.

It further developed that Gellatly was not entirely blameless. He had loaded his rifle with 2 bullets and 2 powder charges ". . . which had subjected the barrel to as much explosive pressure as 3 or 4 ordinary charges. This had caused the barrel to burst. . . ."

But Adams's furtive trip to the barracks and his attempts to pin blame for the unproved gun on a foreman swung Court opinion against him. Summing up, the Lord Mayor advised that ". . . he would be failing in his duty if he inflicted a lower penalty than £10 and that for the future Adams had better look after the proving of his guns personally, as well as look after his foreman, or other accidents might happen with a more serious issue. . . ."

As a final indignity, the gunsmith who held a Royal Warrant as "Gunmaker to His Royal Highness Prince Albert" had to pay court costs of £2 2s.

Whether or not Mr. Gellatly desisted from his 2 balls, 2 charges practice is not known. But history records no further sullying of Robert Adams's name. ■

BACON ARMS

By HERSCHEL C. LOGAN

FIREARMS produced by the Bacon firm offer a diversified field for the collector. The line includes both percussion and cartridge arms, numerous interesting specimens of underhammer and regular type including single-shots, pepperboxes, and revolvers.

The firm of Bacon & Company, Norwich, Connecticut, was established in 1852 by Thomas K. Bacon. Among percussion arms manufactured by this company were an underhammer pistol, a single-shot ring-trigger pistol, and a six-shot underhammer pepperbox revolver.

Little is known of the history of the company during those early years. From available data it would appear that the original name was not used for long after the founding of the company, before it was changed to Bacon Manufacturing Company.

Frances Caulkins' *History of Norwich, Connecticut* (1874) had this to say of the new company:

"The Bacon Manufacturing Co. next made its appearance in the city, adding a considerable number of mechanics to the population. The pistols of this company were the only fire-arms made in Norwich when the war commenced; but mechanical enterprise soon took a sudden turn in that direction."

The third, and final, change appears to have been made in 1858, at least the name Bacon Arms Company seems to stem from this date, according to the City Directories of Norwich.

A booklet entitled *Norwich, Connecticut,* published in 1888 by the Norwich Board of Trade, has this comment:

"The manufacture of pistols was first commenced under the name of Bacon Arms Co. in 1858, by Thos. K. Bacon. A few years afterwards it was made a joint stock company, the business was enlarged, and for a long time did a successful business. For the last two or three years the company has given up the manufacture of pistols, and are making a breech-loading, single-barrel gun, with reduced help from what they previously employed.

"Capital stock	$40,000
Number of hands employed	20
Number of guns made in a year	2,400
Amount annually paid for labor	$10,000"

The Bacon Arms Company ceased operation in 1888, and in 1890 upon the death of Amos E. Cobb, one of the partners in the firm (and later receiver for the company), the tools and fixtures were sold to George W. Cilley, an experienced designer and toolmaker of Norwich. Cilley also assumed the unfinished contracts for the single-barrel shotguns of that company. On February 26, 1892, the new firm was incorporated as The Crescent Fire Arms Company. Officers were H. H. Gallup, president; George W. Cilley, vice president and general manager; E. R. Thompson, secretary and treasurer; and F. A. Foster, superintendent. This firm continued until 1930, when the name was changed to Crescent-Davis Arms Corporation. City Directories make no mention of this firm after 1931.

So much for the background of the company. Let us now turn to the arms produced by the three Bacon companies, starting first with the original company.

BACON & COMPANY

Three types of percussion arms are known to have been produced under this name. Typical of the underhammers then in vogue is the Bacon specimen of .34 caliber (Fig. 1a). Its four-inch round and octagonal barrel is stamped "Bacon & Co. Norwich, C.T. Cast Steel". Its iron frame is nicely engraved, as is also the backstrap.

Perhaps the most unusual of the three is the single-shot pistol of .36 caliber. Employing a center-hung hammer, it is easily identified by its unique ring trigger (Fig. 1b). The round and octagonal barrel, which incidentally unscrews to load, is marked the same as the underhammer. Iron frame and backstrap are engraved.

The six-shot pepperbox is believed to

HERSCHEL C. LOGAN *of Salina, Kans., is author-illustrator of two books on firearms and ammunition, "From Hand Cannon to Automatic" and "Cartridges".*

Figure 1: "Bacon & Co." marked arms: **a)** single shot percussion underhammer pistol; **b)** single-shot percussion ring-trigger pistol.

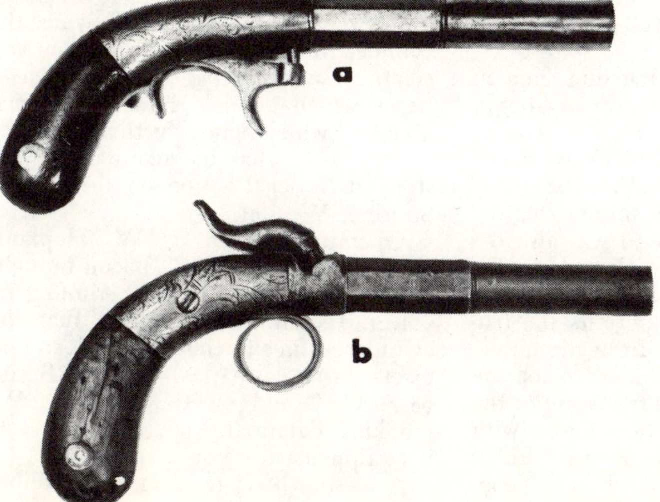

Figure 2: Six shot .31 caliber percussion underhammer pepperbox marked "Bacon & Co., Norwich, C-T" on the cylinder.

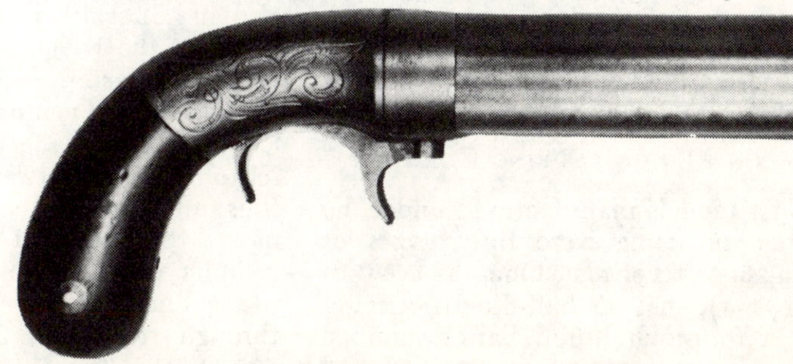

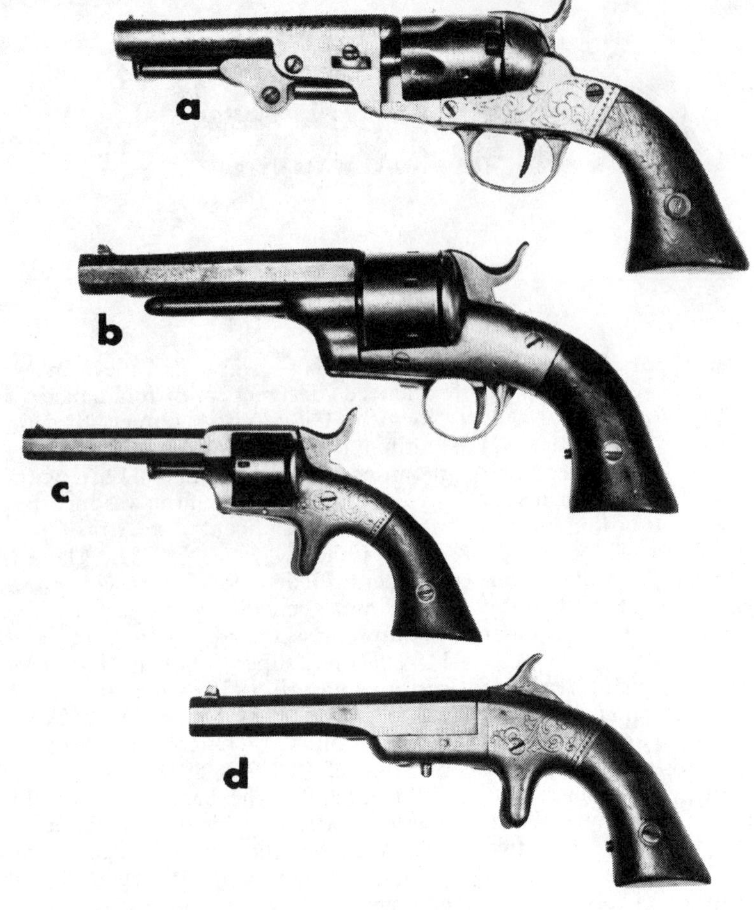

Figure 3: Bacon Manufacturing Company arms: **a)** five shot .31 caliber percussion revolver; **b)** six shot .32 caliber rimfire revolver, unmarked; **c)** seven shot .22 caliber rimfire revolver; **d)** single shot .32 caliber rimfire pistol.

Figure 5: Classical engraving design found on many Bacon arms.

Figure 4: Bacon Manufacturing Company Navy six shot revolver of .38 caliber rimfire. Barrel stamped "Bacon Mfg. Co. Norwich, Conn."

be the only multishot production of Bacon & Company (Fig. 2). Its cylinder-barrel is revolved by cocking the hammer. Stamped on the cylinder are the words "Bacon & Co. Norwich, C-T Cast Steel". Iron frame is engraved. Even though such pieces may be found unmarked, they are easily identified by the distinctive underhammer.

Bacon Manufacturing Company

First models manufactured under the change of name were three types of percussion revolvers. One, a five-shot (Fig. 3a), has a half-fluted cylinder and a four-inch round barrel stamped "Bacon Mfg. Co. Norwich, Conn." Other barrel lengths may be encountered. Its iron frame is engraved.

A similar model was made using an octagonal barrel and a straight cylinder. In appearance it is not unlike the 1849 Colt Pocket model.

The third model in the percussion series is distinguished by a spur trigger and a strap over the cylinder. Caliber is .31 and the barrel length four inches.

Following these percussion models Bacon Manufacturing Company began the manufacture of their cartridge types. One of the first to be produced was a .32 caliber rimfire (Fig. 3b), made also in .22 caliber. Its unique feature was that the trigger guard was also the means of fastening the barrel to the cylinder pin. Turning the guard to the left and unscrewing it permits the barrel to be pulled forward from the frame, thus allowing the cylinder to be removed for loading. The removing of the cylinder was all right, but not so with the cylinder itself, which was drilled through from end to end. This conflicted with the Smith & Wesson-held Rollin White patent of the same feature. Manufacture of it seems to have been discontinued in 1863. Specimens are found both with and without the maker's name.

Another model which may have run afoul of the Rollin White patent is the small, nicely designed, seven-shot revolver of .22 caliber (Fig. 3c). Its cylinder pin is removable, allowing the cylinder to be taken out for loading and ejecting shells. This is among Bacon items which do not show up too frequently, which lends further credence to the belief that its manufacture was stopped by legal action on the part of Smith & Wesson.

Operating under C. W. Hopkins' patent of May 27, 1862, Bacon brought out a six-shot .32 caliber rimfire revolver. Its unusual feature is that the cylinder swings to the right to load and eject. Barrel is marked on top "Bacon Mfg. Co." and on the side "C. W. Hopkins Patented May 27, 1862". It is equipped with a spur trigger.

A six-shot Navy revolver of .38 caliber

Continued on page 70

BROWNING'S FIRST PISTOL

By ROBERT N. SEARS
Associate Technical Editor
THE AMERICAN RIFLEMAN

So successful were John M. Browning's blowback and recoil-operated semi-automatic pistols that they have obscured the fact that the great designer's first hand gun was gas operated.

Browning entered the self loading arms field in 1889 with a lever-action rifle modified so it would be operated by gases trapped at the muzzle as the bullet emerged.

A similarly-operated machine gun followed in 1890, and two years later he developed a machine gun powered by gas tapped off through a hole in the barrel wall. With each shot an operating lever swung to and fro in an arc under the barrel. This became the Colt 1895 "potato digger" machine gun, so nicknamed probably because the lever threw chunks of turf into the air when the gun was fired with the muzzle too close to the ground.

Browning's first pistol used the same principle of operation, although the gas port and lever were on top of, rather than under, the barrel. It was demonstrated in Hartford, Conn., on July 3, 1895. Colt's Vice President, John H. Hall, and patent attorney Carl J. Ehbets, fired the pistol and were favorably impressed. A verbal agreement was reached giving Colt exclusive manufacturing rights, and a patent was applied for on September 14.

The pistol's outward appearance seems conventional to us today, but when it was made there was nothing else like it. Weighing nearly 34 ozs. and 8.59″ long, it feeds from a seven-round detachable magazine in the grip and is fired by an exposed hammer with half-cock safety. Of .352″ bore diameter, the barrel is made integral with the receiver and is chambered for a cartridge very similar to the .38 Colt Automatic.

A reciprocating breechbolt is operated through a connecting rod by a lever pivoted at the top of the receiver. With a loaded magazine in the grip, the pistol is charged by grasping the front of the lever between the thumb and forefinger and swinging the lever upward and rearward. This unlocks the action and moves the breechbolt to the rear, compressing the action spring and cocking the hammer. Releasing the lever allows the action spring which is enclosed in a brass tube under the connecting rod to return the breechbolt to its forward position, feeding a cartridge from the magazine into the chamber and locking the toggle action.

Pulling the trigger starts the firing cycle. As the bullet travels down the 5.91″ barrel, it passes a gas port located 4″ forward of the breechbolt face. Gas escaping through this port throws the lever upward and rearward in the same arc as when the pistol is charged by hand.

After the bullet has left the barrel, the toggle is thus opened and the action unlocked. Rearward travel of the breechbolt extracts the fired cartridge case and ejects it out the right side of the receiver. The pistol is now cocked, and the action spring returns the breechblock to its original position, chambering a fresh cartridge as it travels forward. With the lever and connecting rod pins in line, the toggle action is again locked so the thrust of the fired cartridge is transferred to the pistol's receiver. The cycle may be repeated until the magazine is emptied. The action is not held open after the last round is fired.

While the pistol's form with the action closed appears quite conventional by today's standards, the motion of the gas-operated lever does not appear so. It might seem that the momentum of the moving parts would add to the jump of the pistol when fired, but the exact opposite is true. Muzzle jump is minimized first by the low bore line inherent in the design. It is further reduced by the upward jet of gas and swing of the lever after the bullet has left the muzzle. These factors tend to compensate for, not add to, the pistol's muzzle jump.

Not only does the pistol possess favorable handling qualities, the entire design was thought out with great thoroughness. A typical example of simplicity and economy of parts is found in the magazine catch spring (d3 in Figs. 2 and 3). The lower end operates the catch, while the upper end acts as a disconnector between trigger and sear so that only one shot is fired each time the trigger is pulled. The catch spring also serves as the trigger spring.

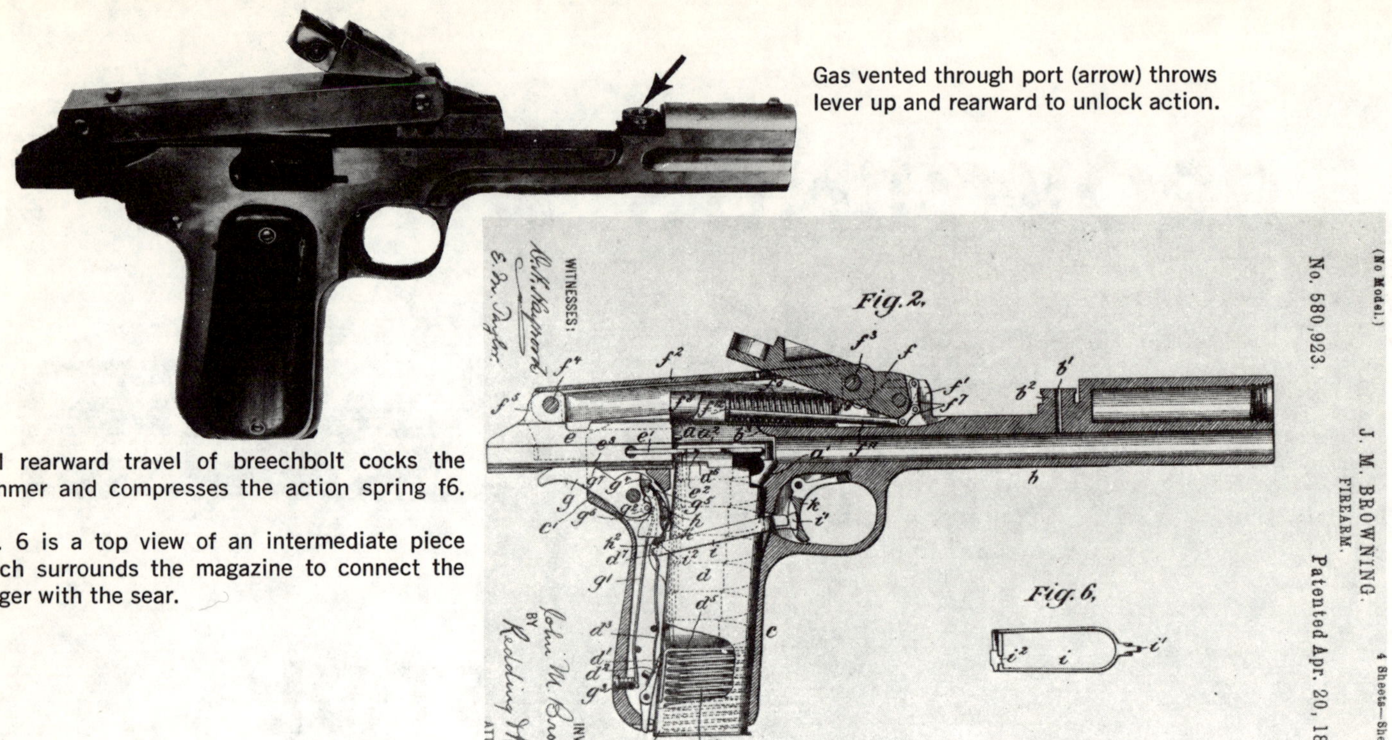

Gas vented through port (arrow) throws lever up and rearward to unlock action.

Full rearward travel of breechbolt cocks the hammer and compresses the action spring f6.

Fig. 6 is a top view of an intermediate piece which surrounds the magazine to connect the trigger with the sear.

A ½" diameter hole parallel to the bore and plugged above the muzzle lightens the pistol. That portion of the receiver above the barrel and forward of the gas port serves only to provide a mounting surface for the front sight. Apart from that function, the portion could be cut away entirely without affecting the gun's operation.

Browning's patent contains four basic claims. One covers the longitudinally movable breechbolt actuated by a gas-operated lever and connecting rod, with the breechbolt returned to battery by a spring contained within the connecting rod. The other claims concern safety features.

First of all, the pistol cannot be fired unless the action is locked. At the first upward motion of the connecting rod, an elbow lever "m" pivots rearward to block the trigger as shown in Fig. 7 of the patent drawing. As the connecting rod descends to lock the action, it swings the lower arm of the elbow lever forward allowing the trigger to be pulled.

The second safety feature prevents multiple discharges from one pull of the trigger. As the hammer falls, an intermediate piece is disconnected from the sear. The intermediate piece, "i" in the patent drawing (and now commonly known as a "trigger bow"), is reconnected with the sear "h", by allowing the trigger to move forward to its original position. The intermediate piece is shown connected with the sear in Fig. 2, and disconnected in Fig. 3. A top view of the intermediate piece which fits around the magazine is shown in Fig. 6.

The third feature considers the potential hazard to a user if any of the pivot pins

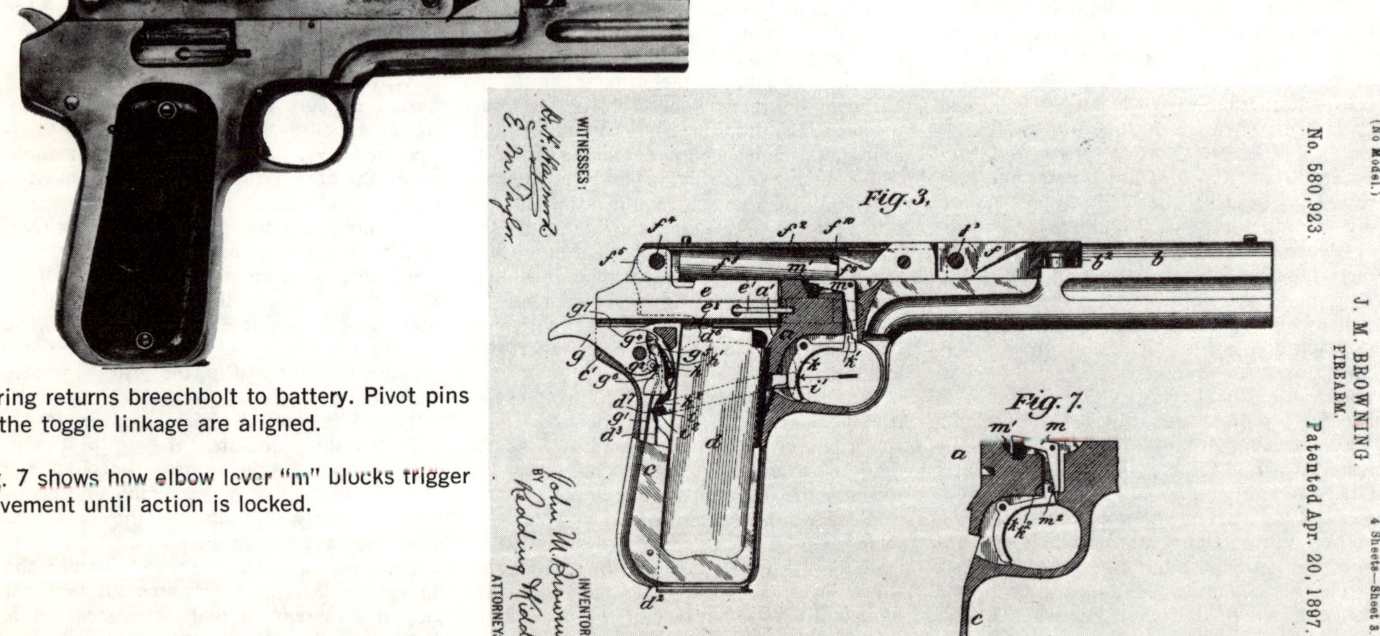

Spring returns breechbolt to battery. Pivot pins in the toggle linkage are aligned.

Fig. 7 shows how elbow lever "m" blocks trigger movement until action is locked.

in the toggle linkage fail. Should this happen, the breechbolt is kept from flying backward by the hammer, which in its rearmost position bears against the receiver to provide an effective stop. Upward movement of the breechbolt is prevented by its guides in the receiver.

By the time patent No. 580,923 was granted on his gas-operated pistol, Browning had filed claims on one blowback and two recoil-operated models, and Ehbets had filed on a very complicated blow-forward gas-operated handgun. Colt acquired the rights to Browning's designs July 24, 1896. The patent examiner seems to have gotten the whole thing straight in his mind on April 20, 1897, for he granted patents on all five designs that day.

Only one Browning gas-operated pistol was ever made. Ammunition of that time presented serious corrosion problems for gas-operated guns. The inherently cleaner operating recoil powered design covered by Browning's patent No. 580,924 was chosen as the basis for Colt's magazine handgun of 1900, the first semi-automatic pistol produced in America.

Although the gas-operated pistol was never manufactured in quantity, Browning had in his first attempt eclipsed the efforts of his contemporaries: Bergmann, Borchardt, Ehbets, Mannlicher, Mauser, Schmeisser, and Schwarzlose. All developed semi-automatic pistols during the 1890's but only Browning's designs have survived. The others compared unfavorably with Browning's designs in both compactness and reliability.

Beyond their superior mechanics, Browning's designs reflect a knowledge of the factors which made a handgun usable. The basic form for most semi-automatic handguns made since was established in his gas-operated pistol of 1895. Browning's operational principles have been copied over most of the world. To this day, 80 years later, all semi-automatic pistols produced by Colt have been based on his designs.

Browning's first pistol may be seen at the John M. Browning Armory in Ogden, Utah, where it is displayed as part of an exhibit memorializing the greatest gun designer the world has ever known. ■

Borchardt (top) and Mauser (above) pistols developed in the 1890's compared unfavorably with Browning designs in both compactness and reliability.

Repaired Tumbler

A common problem in restoring old firearms is a worn or broken tumbler. Areas most worn are the squared shank for the hammer and the boss which acts as a bearing surface in the lockplate. This latter quite often has work-hardened and partially broken loose from the tumbler and stirrup. Replacement parts are almost impossible to obtain. To fix, drill the old tumbler from the direction of the arrow with a drill approximately 1/16″ smaller in diameter than the lockplate bearing hole. Turn a new shaft from drill rod, and insert it into the drilled-out tumbler. Next, tin the tumbler hole and the shoulder portion of the new shaft with silver solder. After tinning, heat both pieces to the flow-point of the silver solder, and insert the shaft into the tumbler. After cooling, remove excess solder in a lathe or drill press, then finish by filing.—JOHN C. PALMER

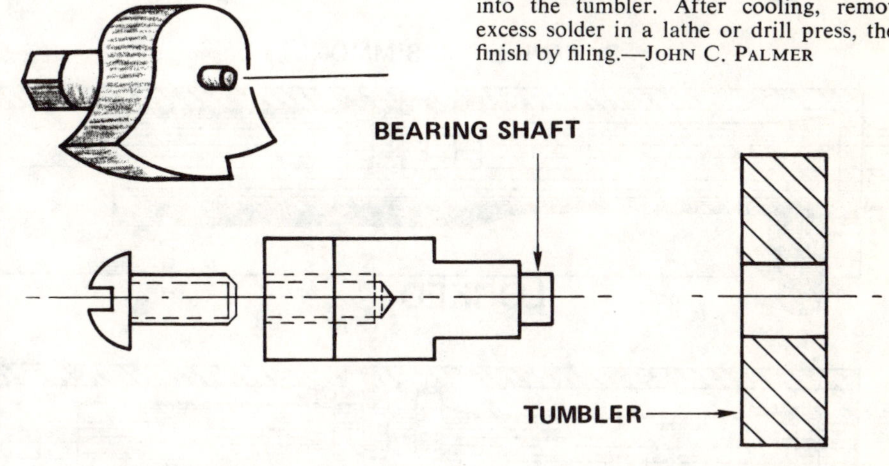

Ejection Port Loading Tool

I devised this loading tool to insert cartridges through the ejection ports of .22 rimfire rifles and pistols which do not conveniently lend themselves to single-shot loading. A .22 cartridge slides into the yoke and is held by the flat spring during insertion.—JAMES V. HARDMAN

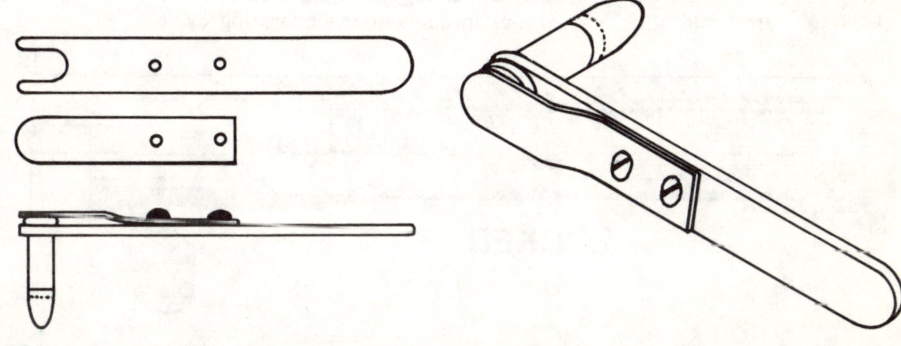

Polishing Aid

For holding pieces of abrasive cloth when polishing barrel or cylinder chambers or throats, I slot pieces of ⅛″, 5/32″, 3/16″ and ¼″ brass rod of appropriate lengths. Chuck in an electric drill, lathe, drill press, or hand drill. These are handy also for polishing insides of trigger guards and other odd shapes before bluing.

—JAMES W. FARLEY

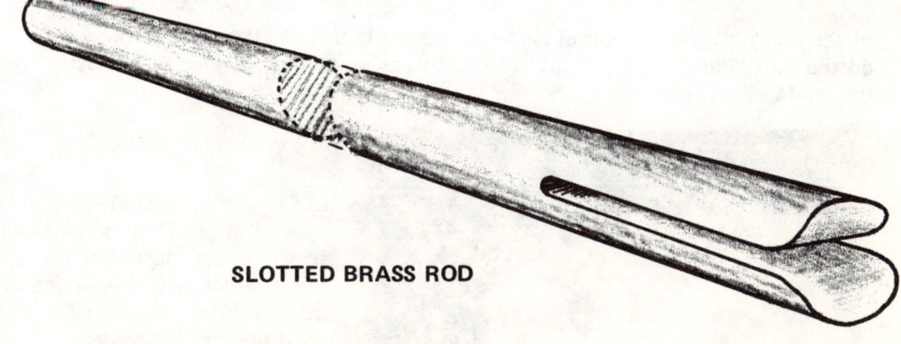

Recoil Operated Handguns By Browning

By DONALD M. SIMMONS, JR.

WHILE John M. Browning had little formal education, he had an inborn grasp of mechanics and engineering which many of today's multi-degreed designers could envy. By the time he died in 1926 his genius had touched all areas of firearms design. There are few modern arms that do not in some manner trace their antecedents to one or more of Browning's ideas. Browning always considered his recoil-operated shotgun to be his most challenging and rewarding design problem. His work with handguns, however, was no less revolutionary.

In the last years of the 19th Century, Browning conceived several methods of operating self-loading handguns. Some went no farther than the concept, but the number of designs that did become production models is awe-inspiring. In the field of successful recoil-operated automatic pistols, Browning stands almost alone.

An initial concept patented in 1897 had the barrel unlock from the slide by pivoting links mounted at the front and rear of the barrel. With this design, the barrel is parallel to the slide at all times. Colt's first automatic pistol, the Model 1900, used this principle and it was on some of that company's guns until 1927.

By 1905 when Colt produced their first

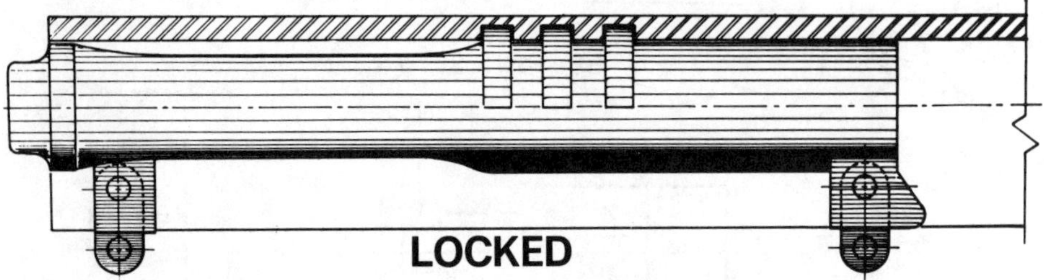

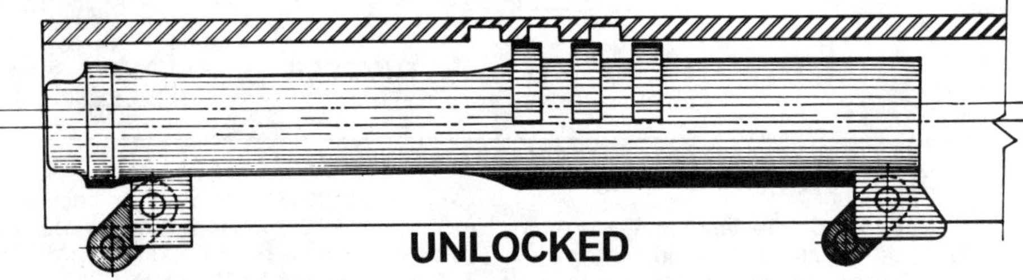

Early double link Browning design. Barrel is locked to slide above when fired. After recoiling together for a short distance, the links drop the barrel for unlocking. Barrel and slide are parallel throughout the operating cycle.

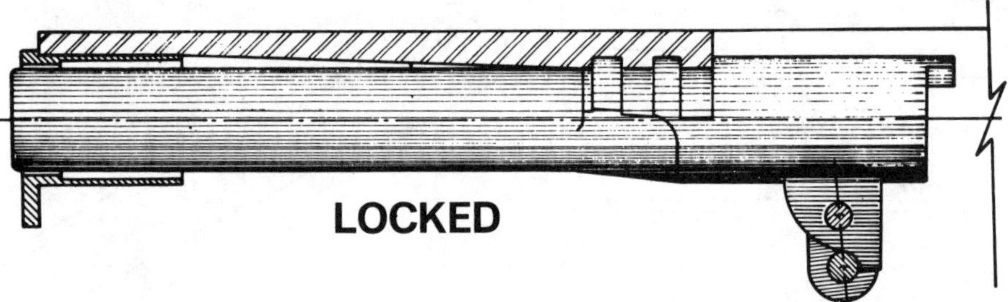

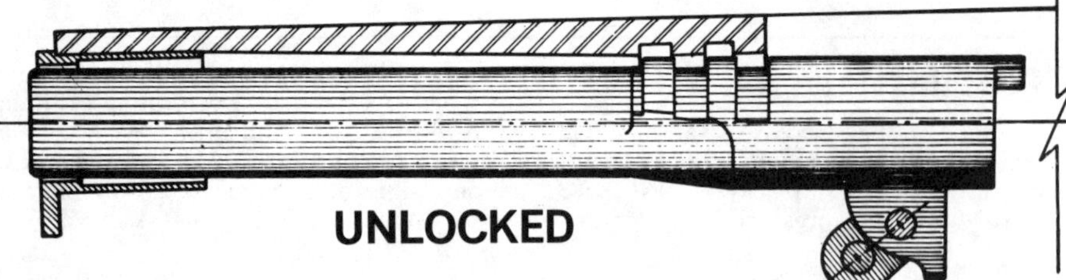

In the rear link system, rear of barrel tilts down to unlock. This system was used on the Colt Model 1911 cal. .45 pistol and has since been copied over most of the world.

Old and new commercial Colts. Model 1911 cal. .45 (above) was made in 1911. The Combat Commander (below) was made in 1970.

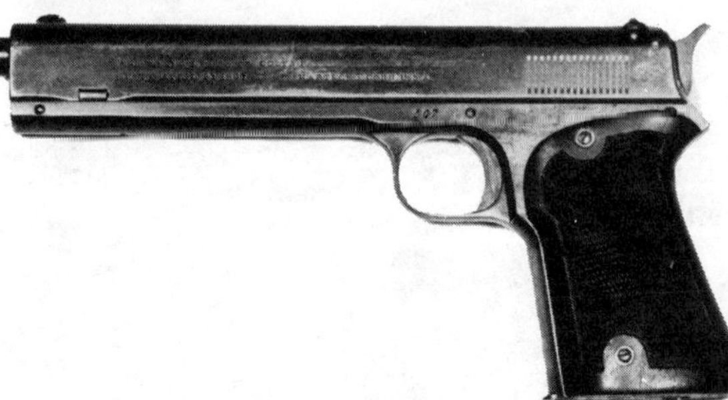

LEFT: Colt Model 1900 cal. .38 ACP pistol with special grips. This model used the double link system and was described in *Shooting and Fishing*, a predecessor of *The American Rifleman*, on April 19, 1900. RIGHT: Model 1905 Colt cal. .45 pistol also used double link system.

cal. .45 automatic pistol, Browning already had patented another design which disposed of the front link and replaced it with a loose fitting bushing. This reduced production cost and the slide could not be driven off the frame rearward under any circumstances.

With the single link, or, as it is often called, "rear link" system the barrel and slide recoil rearward approximately ¼" locked to each other. Continued rearward movement pulls the rear of the barrel downward to unlock it from the slide. After the barrel and slide are unlocked, the slide continues rearward by its own momentum to the full recoil position which ejects the fired cartridge and cocks the pistol. It is important to understand that the bullet has left the short barrel of a pistol long before the barrel unlocks. Spring pressure returns the slide, chambering a fresh cartridge and locking the action.

The best known pistol of this design is the Colt Model 1911 automatic, which became the United States sidearm during World Wars I and II, when the U.S. military used two and three-quarter million Model 1911 and 1911A1 pistols. It is still the standard U.S. service pistol. Colt's commercial production adds another four hundred thousand to the total. If no other country had used Browning's rear link system, it still would be famous for the number of guns made using this recoil operated action. But the fact is that most of the world's high power automatic pistols have used this basic principle.

Browning is the father of most of the worlds recoil-operated automatic handguns. The rear linked models shown here represent only a small part of the wealth of collectible pistols based on his design. ■

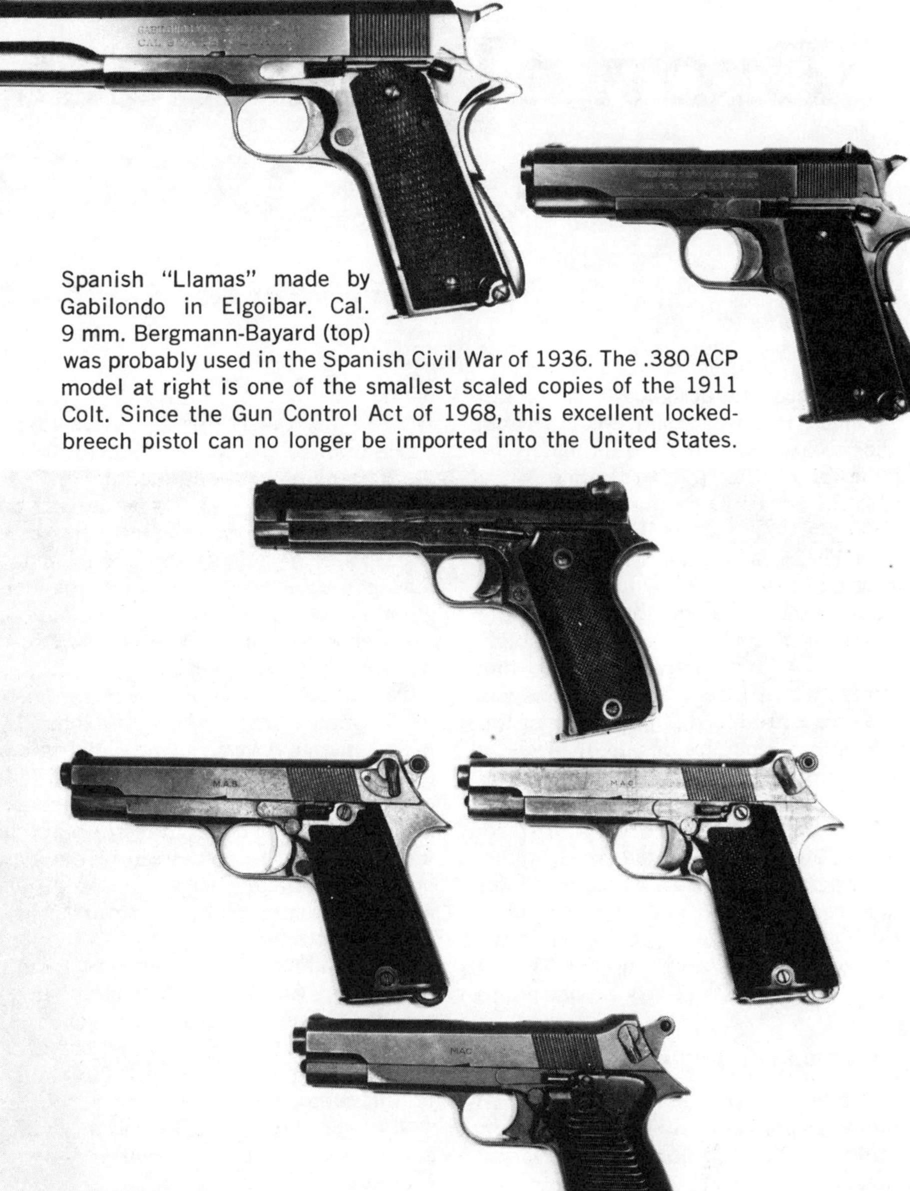

Spanish "Llamas" made by Gabilondo in Elgoibar. Cal. 9 mm. Bergmann-Bayard (top) was probably used in the Spanish Civil War of 1936. The .380 ACP model at right is one of the smallest scaled copies of the 1911 Colt. Since the Gun Control Act of 1968, this excellent locked-breech pistol can no longer be imported into the United States.

French versions. Model 1935A (top) differs from MAS and MAC 1935S pistols (center) mainly in locking lug details. Both 1935 models are chambered for the 7.65 mm. long cartridge. M1950 model (bottom) is a closer copy of the 1911 Colt. It is chambered for the 9 mm. cartridge and is the standard service pistol of France.

Argentine Army Model 1927 pistol in .45 ACP (11.25 mm.) (above) was made under license from Colt. Unlicensed "Ballester-Molina" version (below) was shipped from Argentina to England during World War II.

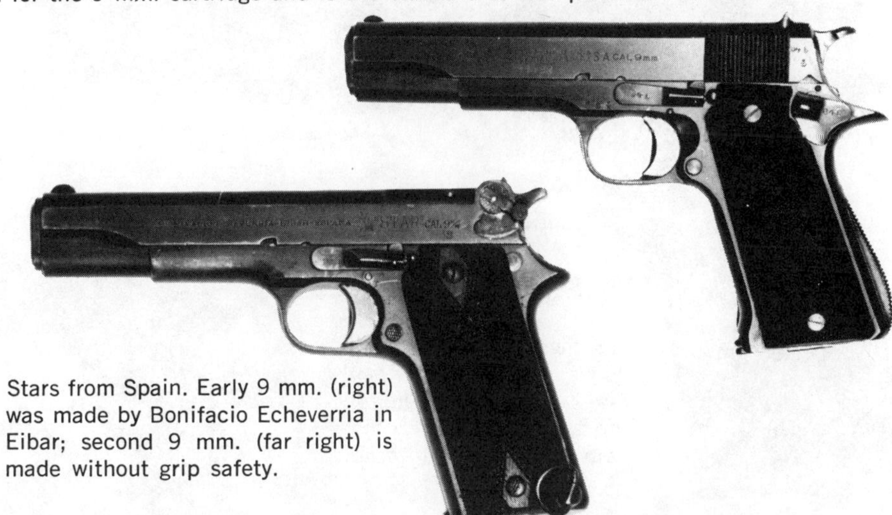

Stars from Spain. Early 9 mm. (right) was made by Bonifacio Echeverria in Eibar; second 9 mm. (far right) is made without grip safety.

Browning's Last Pistol— The Model 1935 Hi-Power

By R. BLAKE STEVENS & JACK KRCMA

THE last pistol designed by noted firearms inventor John M. Browning prior to his death in 1926 ultimately became known as the Browning Model 1935 Hi-Power. Development of this pistol began shortly after World War I.

In 1923, the French Ministry of War informed John M. Browning of its interest in obtaining a semi-automatic pistol with large magazine capacity chambered for the 9 mm. Parabellum (9 mm. Luger) cartridge. That same year Browning produced 2 prototype pistols. Operating principles of one of these pistols were eventually patented in 1927, 3 months after Browning's death. This pistol featured a locked breech, short-recoil action, and detachable magazine holding 15 cartridges. The final Model 1935 version, reduced in weight, and with magazine capacity of 13 cartridges, was adopted subsequently by the Belgian Army and other military organizations.

First made in Belgium

Production of the Model 1935 Hi-Power pistol was initiated by Fabrique Nationale d'Armes de Guerre in Herstal, Belgium.

After the fall of Belgium in 1940, some arms designers and technicians employed at the Fabrique Nationale (F.N.) plant fled to the south of France to escape the Nazi invaders. However, production of the Model 1935 pistol at the F.N. plant was continued under German supervision, and it was designated as a substitute standard German Army issue pistol. Pistols of this model made during the German occupation of Belgium, or taken over after the occupation, carry the German Waffenamt (Ordnance) acceptance stamp.

In the early 1940's, the John Inglis Co. of Toronto, Canada, was approached by the Canadian Government Department of Munitions and Supply and asked if it could produce the Model 1935 pistol. Difficulty was encountered in obtaining the necessary manufacturing drawings, but 6 hand-fitted, Belgian-made pistols were eventually obtained from China. Based on study of these pistols, dimensioned production drawings were made, toleranced for full parts interchangeability. All screw threads were changed from metric to ANF (American National Form) specifications. (Canadian production of the Model 1935 pistol was well under way before Belgian drawings and assistance became available to the Canadian Government.)

Through the Department of Munitions and Supply, contracts were let to the Inglis firm for Canadian and British Forces pattern pistols, and also for a special Chinese Nationalist model. From Inglis factory records, it has been established that a total of 151,816 Model 1935 pistols of all types were produced during the period of manufacture. The first pistol was produced in February 1944, and production ended in September 1945.

Now standard issue

The Model 1935 pistol is now standard issue for both Canadian and British Armed Forces, and existing stocks remain in use as the only source of supply. No Model 1935 pistols have been produced by the John Inglis Co. since 1945.

The Inglis Browning Model 1935 is a recoil-operated, semi-automatic pistol featuring the Browning system dropping barrel action. It is chambered for the high velocity 9 mm. Parabellum cartridge, also intended for use in submachine guns, and has a magazine capacity of 13 cartridges. Empty weight is 2 lbs. 1 oz.; loaded weight is 2 lbs. 6 ozs.

Most Inglis-made Model 1935 pistols were finished by the dull grey Parkerizing process, but some experimental and presentation pieces have been noted in bright steel color, with small parts blued. Three pistols were gold-plated. Markings were applied by machine stamping or

Experimental Inglis-made pistol with lightweight aluminum alloy frame and wood grips. Note lightening cuts at rear and midsection of slide.

Canadian Forces issue pistol showing Inglis diamond monogram on slide and style of serial number marking on barrel, slide, and frame. Note fixed rear sight and laterally adjustable front sight.

Drill purpose pistol, so marked, with component parts sectioned to expose internal mechanism. Assembled from off-standard components, these pistols were used to train armorers in assembly and lockwork.

hand engraving. (Stampings are clear and fine, while engraving is irregular and faint.) Serial numbers were engraved after the pistol was finished, and consequently show bright through the finish. A small decalcomania or transfer bearing a maple leaf in its center with the word "Canada" spelled out around its circumference in English, Chinese, and Russian, was applied to the front grip-strap. These transfers were fragile and soon wore off.

Serial numbers were factory applied, but all pistols were delivered to the Department of Munitions and Supply and distributed there. Therefore, a pistol marked as intended for the Chinese, for example, might not have been delivered to them if an order for the Canadian Army was being filled at that time.

All completed Inglis pistols were serially numbered in 3 places: on the barrel breech (number visible through ejection port); on the slide directly below the ejection port; and on the right side of the frame. These serial numbers include an alphabetical code, sometimes preceded by numbers, and usually followed by numbers. (Note: Some Inglis-made Model 1935 pistols may be found without serial numbers. These pistols were assembled from parts removed from the assembly line.)

The significance of the alphabetical codes included in the serial numbers is as follows:

Code	Meaning
T	Canadian Forces issue
CH	Chinese Nationalist Army contract
DP	"Drill Purpose", made of off-standard components and used for training in assembly, lock-work, etc.
EX,XP	Experimental and prototype

The manufacturer's legend, "BROWNING-F.N. 9MM H.P. INGLIS CANADA" appears on the left side of the slide. The only exception to this would be slides removed from the manufacturing cycle prior to marking.

A diamond about 1" long and ½" high carrying the word "INGLIS" may be present on the right side of the slide forward of the ejection port.

On some CH-numbered (Chinese) pistols, Chinese characters are present on the left side of the slide above the maker's legend. These markings translate to mean "Republic of China Government Property".

The inscription MK 1* present on the left side of the slide above the maker's legend denotes either No. 1 MK 1 or No. 2 MK 1 pistols with MK 2 parts. (See model variations.)

All Inglis-made Model 1935 pistols were fitted with inverted-V front sights. These were made in varying heights and stamped according to the table:

Sight No.	Height (ins.)
2	.125
3	.135
4	.145
5	.155
No marking	.165

Black plastic grips with checkered panels were standard, but several pistols have been noted with dull white checkered plastic grips, apparently intended for presentation purposes.

The Mauser-type, hollowed out shoulder stock for the Model 1935 pistol was designed to either clip on the butt of the pistol, or to accept the pistol as a holster. A small web belt hook was provided to clip the stock to the user's belt. Also made was an experimental model shoulder stock produced from a flat wood board, resembling the stock for the artillery model Luger pistol. This stock lacked a belt clip and could not function as a holster.

Model variations

The main variations of the Inglis-made Model 1935 pistol are with regard to model or type. These identifications are not usually marked on the pistol, and are therefore listed and explained here.

Pistol No. 1 MK 1 has a tangent rear sight adjustable from 50 to 500 meters. There is a cut in the rear grip strap to accept the Mauser-type holster stock described above. The designation "MK 1" refers to the early design of hammer, ejector, and extractor, but these parts are unmarked.

Pistol No. 1 MK 1* is basically the same as the Pistol No. 1 MK 1, but the star(*) in the designation indicates that the hammer, ejector, and extractor were modified to provide more positive action. Individual parts so modified are stamped "2" or "II".

Pistol No. 2 MK 1 has a fixed, square-notch rear sight and is without grip cut for the holster stock. Parts are of early issue and unmarked.

Pistol No. 2 MK 1* was produced with fixed, square-notch rear sight and some were made with grip cut for the holster stock. Ejector, extractor, and hammer are stamped "2" or "II" and denote manufacturing changes as outlined above under Pistol No. 1 MK 1*.

The MK 2 ejector and extractor require different tolerances in the slide, so that for practical purposes MK 1 ejectors, slides, and extractors are not interchangeable with MK 2 parts. The hammers, while modified, will interchange as long as the original hammer strut and the spring accompany the hammer. ■

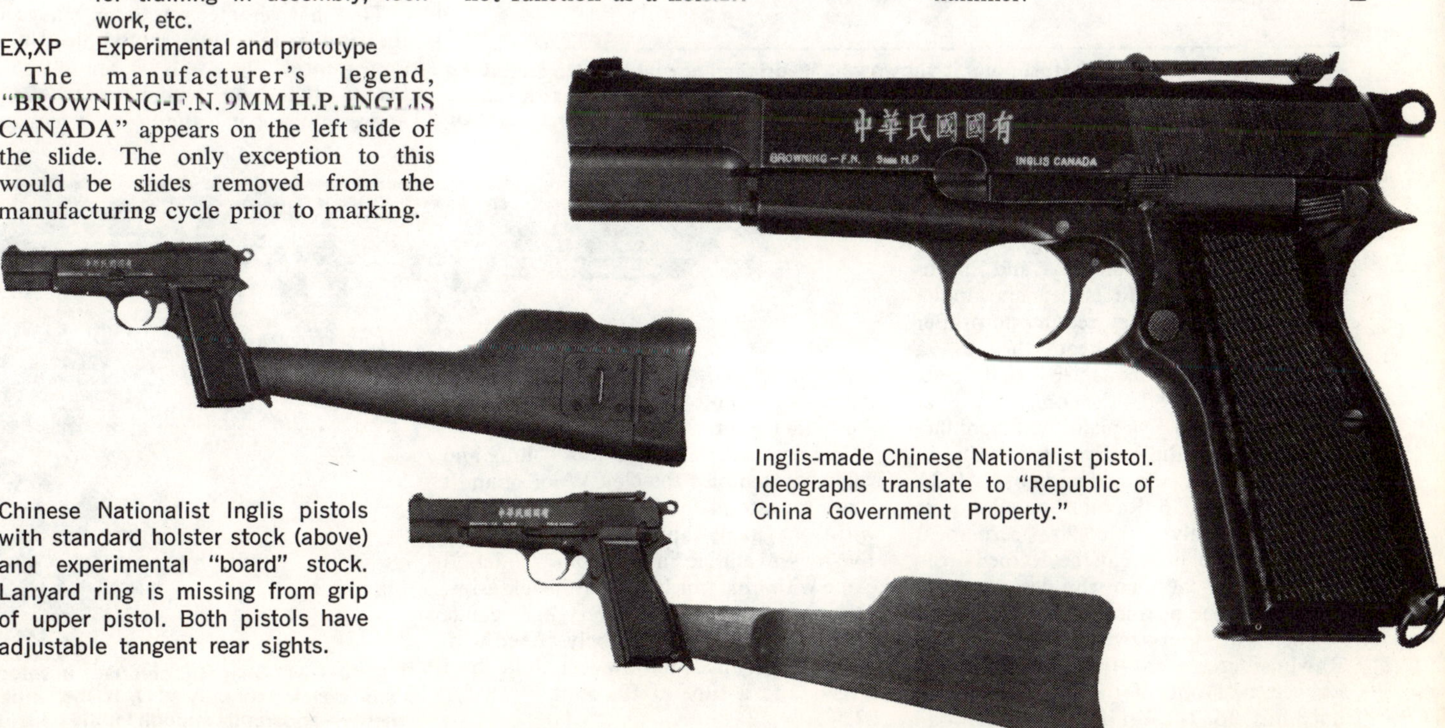

Inglis-made Chinese Nationalist pistol. Ideographs translate to "Republic of China Government Property."

Chinese Nationalist Inglis pistols with standard holster stock (above) and experimental "board" stock. Lanyard ring is missing from grip of upper pistol. Both pistols have adjustable tangent rear sights.

The Legendary Sharpshooter

"Guaranteed accurate enough to kill a house

A nickled Rawlins-made Sharpshooter is shown with its original box which also contained a loading funnel, a rubber target stamp and ink pad, a tube of shot and extra rubber bands. The bands varied in their thickness for increasing or decreasing velocities.

Most enthusiasts of the history of man and his arms are fascinated by different approaches in propelling projectiles. In line with today's energy conservation programs, the Bull's Eye and Sharpshooter pistols would be leaders among handguns because they require no primer or powder charge. Instead, they use a simple reliable mechanism that even improves with use — the common rubber band. The Bull's Eye pistol was manufactured by the Bull's Eye Pistol Co. of Rawlins, Wyo., patented on Feb. 26, 1924, and Jan. 12, 1926. Rawlins' population in 1924 was only some 200 permanent residents, and little can be learned from records as to the men who deserve credit for this unique pistol.

Through interviewing some of the Rawlins citizens of this period, it was learned that one of the inventors was a machinist for the Union Pacific Railroad who wanted to design a quiet indoor pistol that could be enjoyed in competition after the dinner hour with friends.

The original Bull's Eye was 9″ long and vaguely resembled the Colt Woodsman. It was a repeater, shooting No. 6 chilled shot with a magazine capacity of 58. The Bull's Eye was available in only one model. It came with blue finish, catalan black grips, and was stamped from a very light gauge mild steel. It was handsomely boxed with three full-shaped hollow celluloid bird targets and a tube of 100 shot — all for $2.50.

The Sharpshooter model was patented Sept. 7, 1937, and manufacturing began in Rawlins early in 1938. Though of heavier and stronger construction, it was 7¼″ long overall, or 1¾″ shorter than the Bull's Eye model. Due to this difference in length, which lessened the catapult action, the Sharpshooter did not shoot as hard as the Bull's Eye." Some octogenarians who recall the Bull's Eye believe it was hazardous in the hands of the inexperienced, and this is what influenced the change in models. In early advertising, the Bull's Eye was billed as capable of penetrating light cardboard at 20 ft. as compared to later advertising for the Sharpshooter that stressed the capability of doing in a fly at 10 paces.

The Sharpshooter was better made than the Bull's Eye and more pleasing in appearance. Early ads stated, "It is a beauty that you will have to see to appreciate as it cannot be adequately

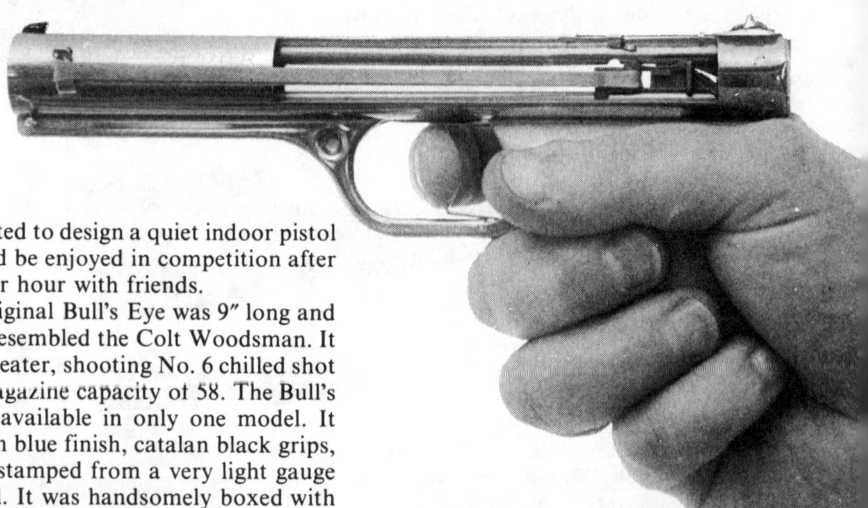

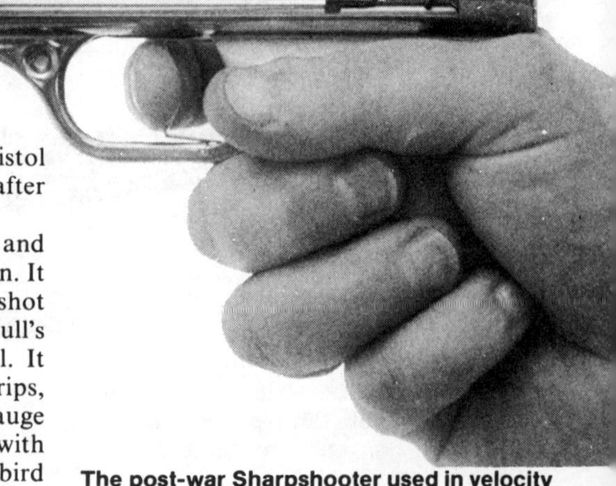

The post-war Sharpshooter used in velocity tests developed only .117 ft.-lbs. muzzle energy—apparently enough for the house fly.

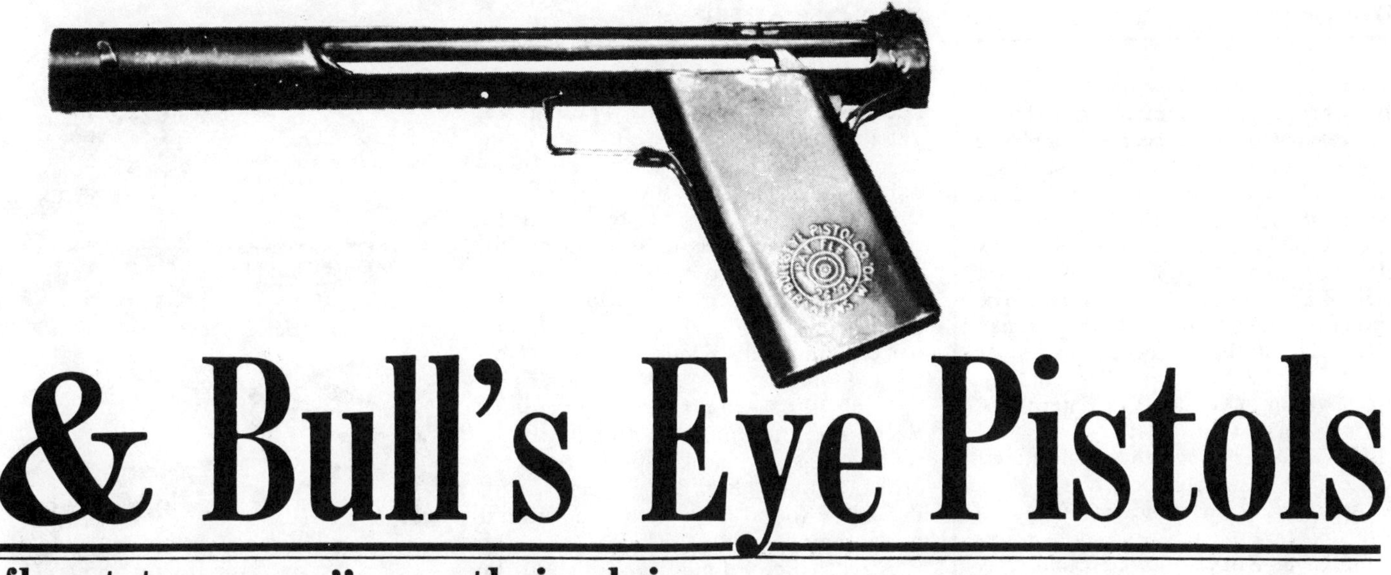

& Bull's Eye Pistols

fly at ten paces" was their claim.

BY E. DIXON LARSON

described." The handles were thicker, giving more weight and a more comfortable grip. The Sharpshooter was available in three models, and adjustable sights were standard. The nickel-finish, deluxe model with catalan ivory grips sold for $2.75. In blue finish with black catalan grips the price was $2.50, and the blued model with stamped metal grips sold for $2. Extra shot was available for one cent per 100.

The Sharpshooter pistol was highly recommended as a means of overcoming "handgun flinching." A rubber stamp target printer was furnished. The celluloid birds were omitted from some Sharpshooter sets. Instructions furnished with the pistol stressed that no change be made in the mechanical adjustments until at least 600 shots have been fired. Manufacture of the pistols ceased, temporarily, during World War II, probably due to the scarcity of materials.

The propulsion system involved in the Bull's Eye or Sharpshooter pistol is simply a rubber band connected to the slide and anchored to the stationary barrel. The mechanism is much more complex and requires manual cocking before each shot. On cocking, a single shot enters the launching chamber from the tubular magazine on top of the barrel. It is extremely interesting to observe the interaction of the mechanism as it is released and drives the shot in the launching guide through the "barrel," which is actually free space. When the shot leaves the guide, it's on its own.

Several old magazines were examined in search of ads concerning the Bull's Eye and Sharpshooter pistols. Most attested that the pistols were "Guaranteed accurate enough to kill a house fly at ten paces . . ." Currently, the little house gun is a collector's item that can be bought, fired and enjoyed on a modest budget.

Sharpshooter Stirs Fond Memories

SHARPSHOOTER pistols were discussed over the dinner table among several members and staffers at the 1978 NRA Annual Members Meetings in Salt Lake City. Everyone seemed to have fond memories of the gun, and Life Member R. L. Haygood of Sinclair, Wyo., sent a note to the *American Rifleman* on his experiences with it.

"It was in 1938 and there was never enough money, but there was an eight-year-old boy whose father wanted to buy a pistol so his son could learn to shoot. So, a Rawlins Sharpshooter was bought for $1.75. It sharpened the father's skill and taught a young boy to shoot. It is not known which of them had the most fun. It was possible to shoot at matches laid on the sidewalk and light them, and one of the favorite pastimes in the summer was to shoot flies off the woodwork, much to the mother's chagrin.

"This gun now holds the position of one of the family's treasures," Haygood said in his letter.

Ken Warner, *Gun Digest* editor and former *American Rifleman* editor,

Rubber Band Guns

claimed to have a Sharpshooter buried among his gear and eventually found it. It is nickeled with white pearlescent plastic grips, but, instead of the Rawlins, Wyo., markings, it is stamped "Bull's Eye Mfg., Co., La Jolla, Cal." The pistol, bought in the early '60s, is still in its plain white box with extra bands, a tube of shot, and a sheet of three printed 2⅛" targets. The instruction sheet is similar to that printed in Rawlins, but the address on it is neither Rawlins nor La Jolla but Bull's Eye Mfg. Co., Division of Golden Key Enterprises, Sherman Oaks, Calif. 91413.

Life Member and toy gun expert Charles W. Best volunteers that Golden Key was selling Sharpshooters as late as 1974 in several finishes with prices beginning at $10.95, but he cannot say when the firm actually ceased doing business. He traces the gun's manufacture from Rawlins to La Jolla to Lexington, Pa., in the 1940s. Then came a period of "non-manufacture" and finally the Sherman Oaks, Calif., address.

Stoeger Arms Corp. cataloged both the Bullseye and Sharpshooter in 1939 and 1940. After WW II, the Sharpshooter, complete with celluloid birds, was listed, and in 1954, the final year of inclusion, the Sharpshooter was offered not with birds but with a "spinning target."

A full-page article appeared in the December, 1925, *American Rifleman* by Julian S. Hatcher, then a major. The usually restrained Hatcher enthused about the "new" pistol which he first saw and shot at Camp Perry earlier that year. He said the Bull's Eye was invented by a Wyoming doctor, described it in detail, and commented on its accuracy. "At 10 feet it is possible to group all the shots in a quarter-inch circle. It is one of the most excellent devices for teaching marksmanship that I have ever seen." This write-up was not the end of the NRA involvement with Bull's Eye. In the December, 1930, issues of the NRA Junior Rifle Corps News, the NRA Service Company Inc., offered the Bull's Eye pistols for sale for $2.70 with an extra pound of shot.

The late M.D. "Bud" Waite, former technical editor of the *American Rifleman,* was a devotee of the Bull's Eye pistol. He ignored later production models, feeling they were inaccurate, but remarked that the early ones were indeed precision 10-ft. fly killers. Bud used to amuse himself at Camp Perry by stalking flies in the tent city which formed competitor housing in the pre-war days.

Out of curiosity, a member of the Technical Staff fired Ken Warner's later model. A 10-shot target at 15 ft. through the chronograph screens yielded a 2.35" group, an average velocity of 165 f.p.s., and energy of only .117 ft.-lbs. the common fly swatter must be overkill indeed! ■

BACON ARMS

Continued from page 60

rimfire, the invention of H. A. Briggs and Samuel S. Hopkins (January 5, 1864, No. 41117), was also produced (Fig. 4). It had a 7½-inch full octagonal barrel, and was equipped with a spur trigger. The cylinder pin extension under the barrel was used as an ejector pin. Though listed as a Navy model, it does not appear to have been officially adopted by the armed services. The barrel is marked "Bacon Mfg. Co. Norwich, Conn".

Departing from the multishots, Bacon for a time manufactured a single-shot side-swing-barrel pistol of .32 caliber rimfire (Fig. 3d). Specimens of it may be found both with and without an extractor.

A word here about the design to be found on many of the arms produced by the Bacon Manufacturing Company may not be amiss. Observation of three of the guns in Fig. 3, and the one in Fig. 4, will reveal that a similar engraving design is utilized. The pen and ink sketch in Fig. 5 shows this design in detail. A simple design, very popular with designers and engravers, it had its origin from the acanthus leaf of the Classical period. Where unencumbered by a border, it is known as a 'free design'. The added touch of the triangular border motif on the Bacon arms gives an individuality to the design.

Bacon Arms Company

Two types of arms, a pepperbox and a revolver, were manufactured under the name of Bacon Arms Company. Most unique was their six-shot .22 caliber revolving-cylinder pepperbox. The cylinder is stamped "Bacon Arms Co. Norwich, Conn". With its small size, spur trigger, and western-type grips of rosewood, it is a most attractive gun.

Next was a five-shot .32 caliber rimfire revolver with a half-fluted cylinder, spur trigger, and bird's-head grips. The round barrel is stamped "Bacon Arms Co. Norwich, CT. Cast Steel". The ejector rod is held under the barrel by a spring in the head of the cylinder pin. It is easily removable to eject the empty cases.

Unmarked Specimens

Added to the list of marked Bacon specimens there is a group of arms probably produced by them but not marked Bacon. Such a piece, a seven-shot .22 caliber revolver, is illustrated in Fig. 6c. Bearing only the name "GOVERNOR", its very shape, style, and features place it unmistakably in the Bacon camp. Others of similar design, though totally unmarked, will also be encountered.

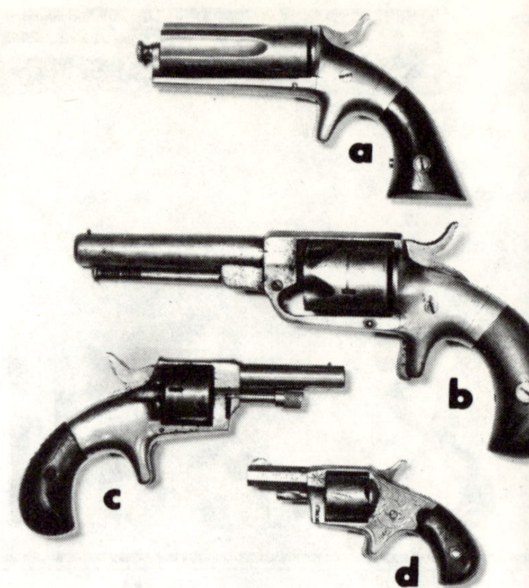

Fig. 6: Bacon Arms Company unmarked arms: a) six-shot .22 caliber pepperbox; b) five-shot .32 caliber rimfire revolver; c) "GOVERNOR" revolver seven-shot .22 caliber rimfire not marked with maker's name; d) five-shot .22 caliber revolver marked only with "GEM" and patent date

Without doubt the cutest, and most unique, of the entire group is the baby .22 caliber five-shot revolver known only as "GEM" (Fig. 6d). This smallest of American revolvers was patented by Alonzo L. Sweet of Norwich on December 10, 1878 (#210,725). According to the patent papers, one-half interest in the patent rights was assigned by him to the Bacon Arms Company. It seems reasonable that Bacon actually produced this diminutive revolver, found in both plain and engraved presentation styles.

Thus it will be seen that not only do the marked Bacon arms offer real interest, but there is a fertile field for the collector who delights to ferret out and study unmarked arms by noted makers. Often these unmarked specimens will follow the distinctive style of the Bacon arms, sometimes not. Many times the search involves the seeking out of the original patent papers, as in the case of the tiny GEM, for clues as to the manufacturer. But it is a most satisfying and rewarding feeling to have a part in the study, and dissemination of knowledge, about the great and fascinating hobby of antique arms.

While this story of Bacon may not be complete, it is hoped that it will give a more than passing picture of a once proud American arms company and an interesting array of arms which offer any enterprising collector an opportunity to "bring home the Bacon". ■

Special thanks to Miles W. Standish, Charles G. Worman, Otis Library of Norwich, Col. L. C. Jackson, Martin B. Retting, A. W. Rowe, and others who assisted with this presentation.—H.C.L.

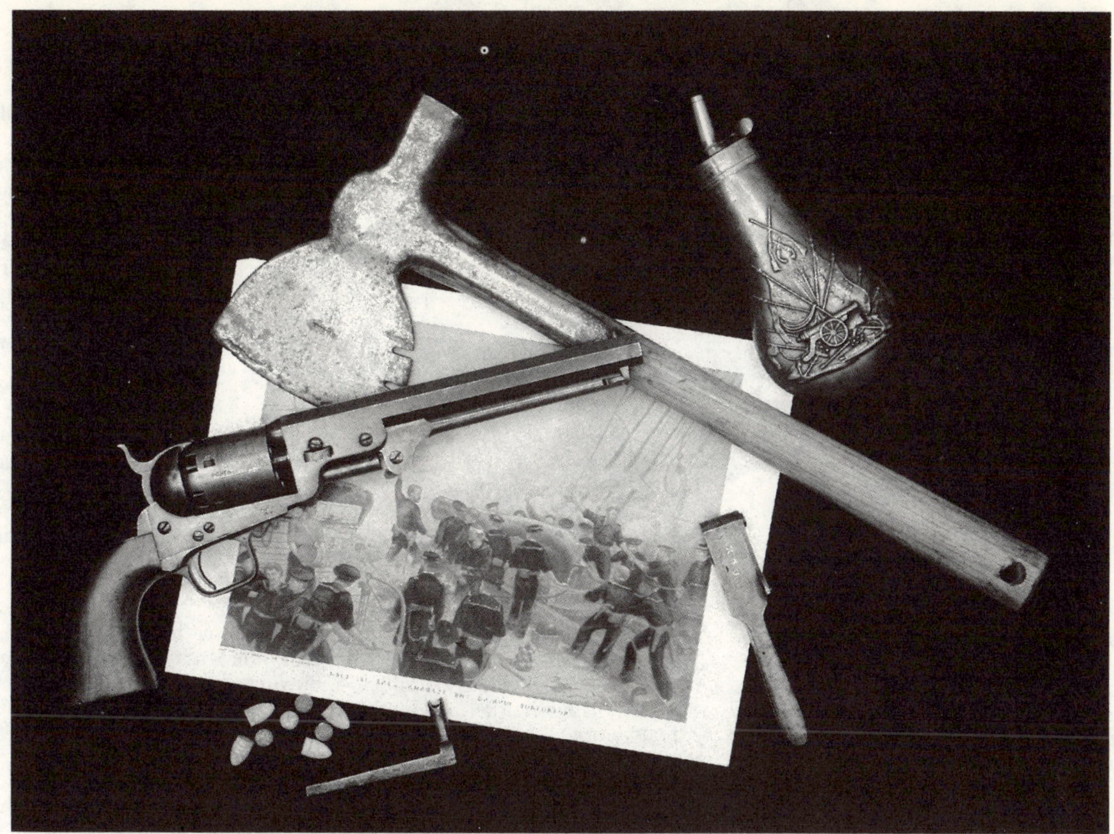

U.S. Navy issued M1851 Colt Navy-Navy revolver, with some accessories of the period, including the Ames-manufactured U.S.N. boarding axe of the Civil War era.

Sea-Going Colt Revolvers

By JOHN KOPEC

FEW collectors today realize the important naval role which was played by the Colt revolver during the 19th Century.

National Archives records indicate that the earliest Colt Paterson, five-shot, cal. .36 revolver (Holster model) was used to outfit the newly formed Texas Navy in 1839. Later, two consignments of Colt Patersons were purchased by the U.S. Navy. The first procurement of 100 revolvers was used to outfit the frigate *United States* on Dec. 28, 1841. The second purchase of 50 Paterson "pistols" was consigned to the U.S. Navy on Sept. 10, 1845. These were purchased from John Ehlers, a former Colt officer. After the Paterson, N.J., firm went into bankruptcy in 1842, Ehlers secured a quantity of incompleted Colt arms which, upon assembly, were used for this Navy purchase.

When the Colt Patent Firearms Mfg. Co. was established after the production of the famous Whitneyville-Walker, Samuel Colt capitalized on the early use of his percussion Paterson arms by the Texas Navy, and had the cylinders of all these namesake M1851 "Navy" revolvers engraved with a battle scene to commemorate an engagement between Texan and Mexican naval forces. The famous legend "Engaged 16 May 1843" was immortalized by this tribute and is found inscribed on the cylinders of all M1851 Navy revolvers.

In 1850 the now famous "Colt Navy" or Model 1851 revolver was introduced. Earliest examples were distinguished by their square-backed trigger guards. All were six-shot percussion in cal. .36 and had 7½" octagon barrels. The U.S. Navy, however, did not purchase any of these Navy revolvers until June 25, 1852, at which time two consignments, one of 50 pistols and one of 100 pistols were made. The larger shipment was sent to the Brooklyn Navy Yard to arm the frigate *Mississippi* which was then bound for the China Seas. Other orders direct from Colt followed, and because of the outbreak of the Civil War, these Colt Navy revolvers were soon to become the major side arm of the U.S. Navy.

The M1851 Colt Navy revolvers which were actually used by the U.S. Navy are known by today's collectors as the "Navy-Navy" models. These are found generally to group into two serial number classifications: the early Navy-Navies which are found in the 55500 through 62000 serial number range, and the late Navy-Navies which usually group within the 89000 through 91000 range. Both groups have one very distinguishing characteristic in that their "guards" (the trigger guards and back straps) are made of iron rather than of brass, which was then the standard. These "iron-strapped" Navy-Navy models are also interesting because their guards were not manufactured in Hartford but in Sam Colt's London factory! It is also rather strange that the Navy would prefer a rust-prone guard to a corrosion-resistant brass guard for their sea service. Most observed M1851 Navy-Navy revolvers were stamped "U.S." under the words "Colts/Patent" on their left frame panel.

Six Naval Bureau of Ordnance inspectors accepted various lots of these Colt Navy revolvers. Their method of inspec-

U.S. Navy issued Colt M1861 Navy revolver, with issue unmarked full-flap Civil War era holster, naval cartridge pouch, packet of skin cartridges and a nipple wrench.

tion and the application of their inspection marks varied considerably. The buttstraps and the butt portions of the walnut grips seemed, however, to be the predominant locations, for the standard "USN" marking, and generally the letter "I" indicating "inspected" were positioned over the initials of the Naval Ordnance inspector. The inspector's initials were usually individually separated by a star rather than a simple period, but periods or dots are sometimes encountered.

The Navy's Bureau of Ordnance method of inspection differed from that of the Army's Ordnance Department. The Army's inspectors affixed their initials into the side of the grips within a cartouche, whereas the Navy inspectors seldom used this method of identification.

It is estimated that a total of 7,151 M1851 Colt Navy-Navy revolvers were ultimately purchased by the U.S. Navy between the years 1852 and 1862. They are considered by collectors today as an important variation.

During 1861, the U.S. Navy ordered 200 M1860 Army cal. .44 Colt revolvers. But upon examination and inspection, flaws were found in their cylinders, and the entire lot was returned to Colt's to be exchanged for the "New Model" Navy revolver. Collectors today term this revolver the M1861 or "round barrel" Navy revolver. From the barrel back, these revolvers were identical to the "Old Model" or 1851 Navy, but they had a newly designed barrel and loading assembly, streamlined for its day, and patterned after the Army's M1860 revolver, (though scaled down to cal. .36). It is estimated that although the M1860 Army was considered to be an "Army" revolver, about 1,100 of these cal. .44 Colt revolvers actually were purchased by the U.S. Navy.

One of the most scarce of all collectors' Colt percussion models is this New Model or M1861 round barrel Navy revolver. Total production of this model only reached 38,843 revolvers and was comprised primarily of the civilian examples. Today, the U.S. Navy-marked examples are exceedingly rare.

It is estimated that the U.S. Navy purchased approximately 4,000 of these "N.M. Navy pistols" during the Civil War era. These revolvers differ dramatically from their M1851 counterparts in that the frames are not marked "U.S." and that their guards are made of brass rather than of iron. Butts are stamped "U.S.N.", and several recorded examples are marked with the Naval inspector's mark "P/GG" on the forward end of the cylinder between the chambers. Others have a dot in this area, and several have a cartouche with the initials "P.B." of Peter Barrett, Naval Gunner, stamped on their grips.

Although this material deals specifically with the Colt revolvers, we cannot overlook the important part played by several other arms manufacturers during the Civil War period: Remington "Old" and "New" Model revolvers, Savage Navy revolvers, and the Whitney Navy all played an important role. Several other percussion Civil War revolvers were used by the U.S. Navy to a lesser degree. Arms were at a premium and were in many cases difficult to obtain. All sources of available arms were used to secure the required revolvers.

The U.S. Navy continued to use the percussion Colts during the immediate post Civil War period. By then, paper cartridges were employed which eliminated the need for the carrying of a powder flask and lead projectiles. A specially designed, waist-belt-worn cartridge pouch held several cartridge packets where they were handy for use at a moment's notice.

During the years 1873 through 1876, about 1,000 of the outmoded percussion Colt Navy-Navy revolvers were returned to Colts to be converted to fire the then new metallic .38 Colt center-fire cartridge.

The method of conversion was patterned after the patent of C. B. Richards and William Mason. During the conversion process, Colt's fitted a new recoil "plate" and loading gate in the space formerly occupied by the percussion nipples. They also fitted a cartridge extractor while removing the percussion rammer assembly. The hammer was altered to detonate the center-fire cartridge.

Several extant examples of these Navy-Navy conversions remain in collections today. They are interesting to collectors because of variance in the markings they display and because they form a bridge between the old percussion era and the then new metallic cartridge period. One of the most significant markings found on these conversions is the "two July" patent date format which was applied by Colt's near the Colt's patent stamping on the left frame panel. The several percussion-era Naval Ordnance markings remain in prominence, together with a varied assortment of conversion-era naval inspector's marks. Newly fitted walnut grips are generally found without markings.

The Navy's entry into the 1870's was also marked by the Bureau of Ordnance tests of the Smith & Wesson (American), the Colt (Single Action Army) and the Remington (New Model Army conversion). All were chambered for these tests in the

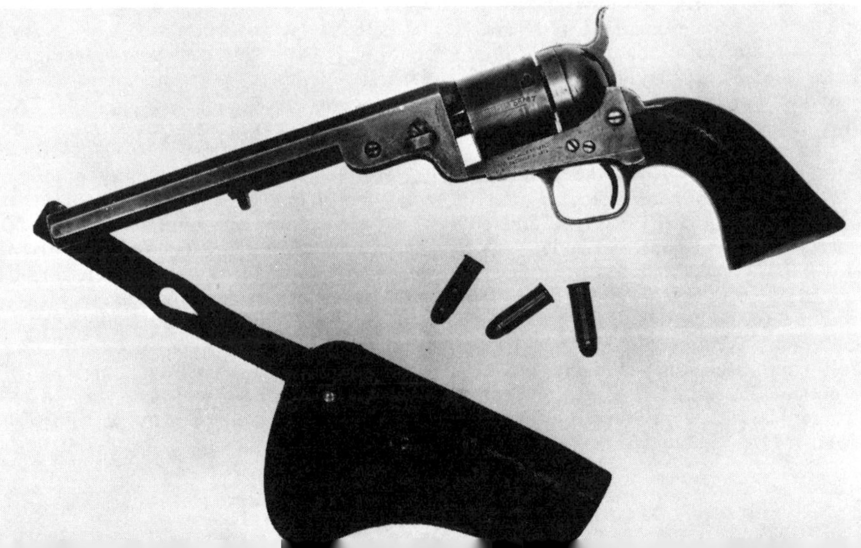

U.S. Navy issued Colt M1851 "Navy-Navy" conversion revolver. Converted in the 1870's, it was the Navy's counterpart to the U.S. Cavalry's Single Action Army revolver. The Whitney Navy skeleton holster marked "U.S.N.Y. BOSTON" fitted this converted Colt.

.44 S&W American cartridge. These tests were conducted by the Navy during April, 1873, and results of these tests are recorded in the following letter:

Rear Admiral A. L. Case, USN,
Chief of Bureau of Ordnance
Admiral:

In obedience to your order we have examined the three (3) best known revolvers adapted for the use of metallic—cartridges—viz: Smith & Wesson's—Colt's and Remington—and do report in favor of Smith & Wesson's for its cheapness, facility of loading, and excellent system of extracting the empty shells.

Seven hundred (700) rounds were fired from the Smith & Wesson's without the slightest disorder which would seem to warrant the necessary perfection of the mechanism.

We do recommend that these pistols if adopted for the Navy be nickel-plated which can be done at an additional expense of about one dollar ($1.00) per pistol.

We are, Sir, very respectfully,
Your Obt. Servants
N. N. NUEK
Commander U.S.N.
Frank Pearson
Lt. Commander U.S.N.

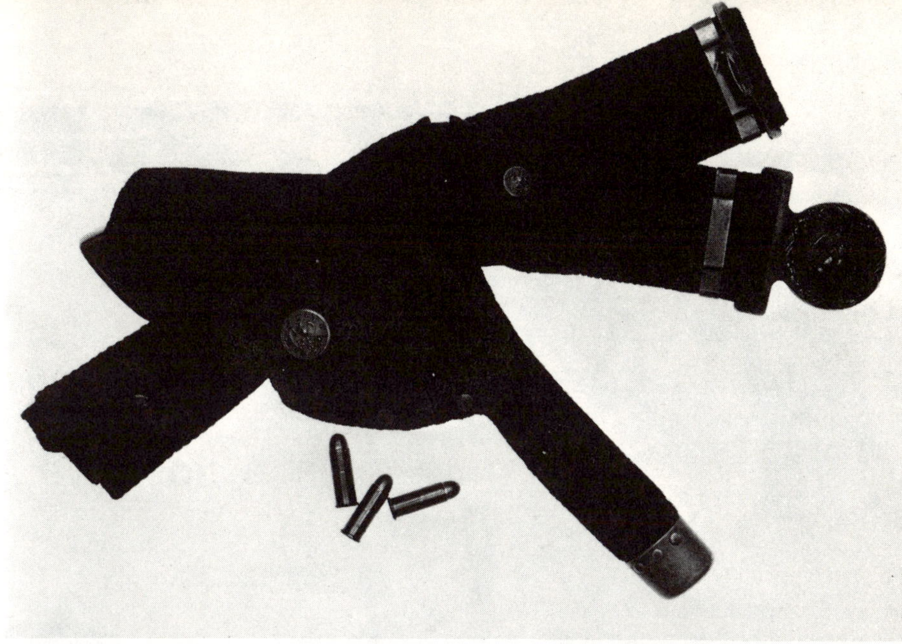

Spanish-American War period landing force naval officer's blue web belt and holster for the New Navy revolver. Belt pockets held cal. .38 Colt cartridges.

We find from the foregoing letter that the single most significant facet of the U. S. Navy Colt revolver story is the fact that the Navy declined to adopt the Colt Single Action revolver! We believe that the reasons for this were threefold: primarily, of course, because the Colt Single Action failed the initial Navy Ordnance tests. The S&W American was favored because of its simultaneous cartridge extractor system—yet, it, too, was never adapted. Secondly, military expenditure of that day favored the Cavalry as they were engaged then in fighting the Indian Wars. Lastly, the Navy, for some reason, preferred the small .38 revolver and continued to use this caliber well into this century when the cal. .45 M1909 U. S. Navy Revolver was adopted, soon to be superseded by the Colt M1911 .45 automatic.

We therefore find that the U. S. Navy continued to use its Colt M1851 and M1861 conversion revolvers throughout the entire "Indian War" period, and requisitions for spare parts for these conversions are recorded which span that entire era.

During 1889, while the U. S. Army Ordnance Department was still procuring Colt Single Action Army revolvers, the U. S. Navy officially adopted the M1889 Colt Double Action "Navy" revolver and initially purchased 5,000 of these from Colt's.

Though the M1889 was Colt's first attempt at a swing-out cylinder revolver, its adoption by the U. S. Navy was somewhat premature as the model had not sufficiently been tried in the field, and it was soon to develop serious cylinder-to-barrel alignment problems. Vast quantities of these revolvers were returned to Colt's for altering to the improved and positive cylinder locking arrangement of the later M1895 version.

Colt "swing-out" cylinder or New Navy revolver, M1895, cal. .38 Colt, with U.S.N. holster and cartridge pouch which contained two "New Cartridge Packs."

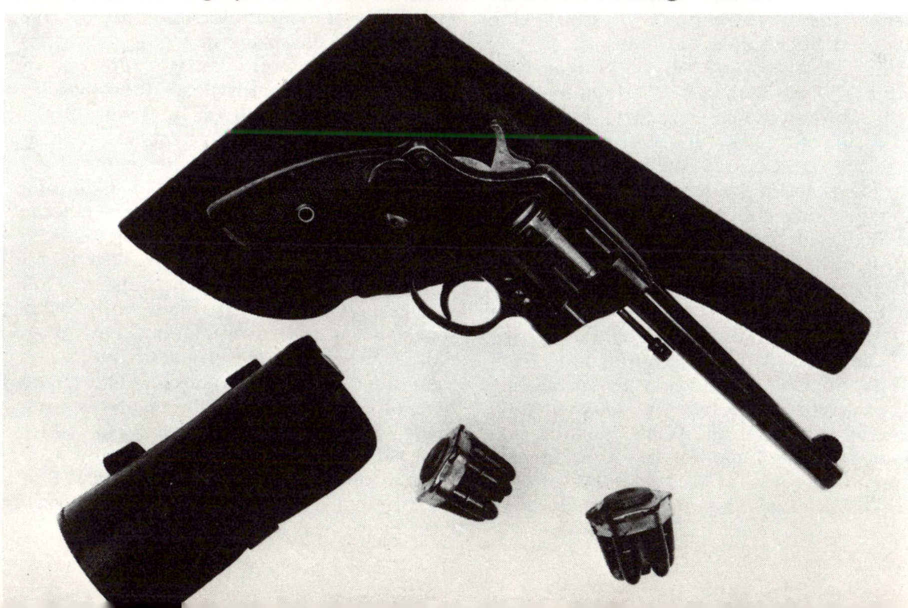

Although the M1889 was the forerunner of the modern revolver as we know it today, it had to undergo a succession of improvements before it would become a perfected revolver.

The various models into which the M1889 evolved, both Army and Navy versions, each with successive improvements, are in themselves a complete study. This model and its successive look alike models were produced well into 1907 with the ultimate total production of 272,000 revolvers. They were all characterized by their counter-clockwise revolving mechanism.

During the Spanish-American War era, the U. S. Navy adopted several of these successive models, among them being the M1889, M1892 and the M1895. They were termed "New Navy Revolvers," and all Navy versions were chambered for the .38 Colt cartridge.

As with their predecessors, Naval Bureau of Ordnance markings are found on the buttstraps of these New Navy Revolvers. These markings are usually so numerous that space in this area was at a premium.

The Navy issued its own serial numbers which were also stamped on the butts, together with the usual U.S.N., and anchor, the caliber designation (.38D.A.) and two ordnance inspector's proofing marks. Cylinders, cranes, barrels, trigger guards, and cylinder releases are found stamped with a five-pointed star bearing the letter "I" indicating full Naval Ordnance inspection of this series.

Earliest examples (M'89) had the military-style walnut grips, while the M1895 was fitted with the Colt hard rubber grips. Navy models did not have the grip lanyard as did their Army counterparts.

Though vast quantities of these revolvers remain today, a Navy example in fine condition is extremely scarce. The study of these naval arms and their numerous accompanying accoutrements is a vast and rewarding collector's experience. ■

The Walker Colt

By JOSEPH B. ROBERTS, JR.

Modern reproductions of the Whitneyville Walker revolver and its accoutrements. Flasks and combination tools were issued with each pair of military arms. The single cavity iron mold was provided on a basis of one mold for each 10 revolvers.

Legendary revolver started its maker on the road to success

MOST legends, though they have some basis in fact, grow from the admiring exaggeration of generations of storytellers. Tracing them to a single source is thus, in most cases, virtually impossible. There is one legend, however, that breaks this rule of anonymity. The brute power commonly attributed to the Colt Whitneyville-Walker revolver grew from the pen of Capt. Samuel Hamilton Walker himself.

Walker, in a letter to his brother written on October 5, 1847, stated, "They are as effective as a common rifle at 100 yds. and superior to a musket even at 200." This glowing report was passed to Walker by Col. William S. Harney, 2d Dragoons, U.S. Army. The Colonel's comment may have been based on utility as much as on ballistic equality. Even so, the 218-gr. round-nose bullet and 50-gr. powder charge that were standard for service use in the Walker Colt are prodigious for any blackpowder handgun.

When Charles T. Haven and Frank A. Belden wrote their *History of The Colt Revolver* in 1940, they described the awesome power of the Walker as greater than that of the .45 Colt, but less than that of the .357 Magnum. The authors must have based their statement on the then advertised muzzle energies of the two cartridges. It must have seemed reasonable that where the .45 Colt was concerned the Walker's powder charge would overcome the 30-gr. difference in weight of the two bullets. Similarly, they probably could not imagine any handgun producing greater energy than that advertised for the .357 Magnum. Thus did the legend of the Walker's power reach full bloom.

Today, with the reviving interest in blackpowder shooting and the availability of a shootable Walker Colt in replica form, the legend can be called to account. Just how powerful was the massive Colt?

The Walker Colt stands tall; and from the standpoint of delivering energy to a target, it handily beats the .357 Magnum. Performance data for the Walker may only be acquired by firing one of these 4½-lb., 9"-barrelled revolvers. The published figures for the .357 Magnum, however, are based on use of an 8⅜" barrel. Most .357 Magnum revolvers in use have 4" or 6" barrels, the 8⅜" Smith & Wesson being cataloged but seldom encountered.

For comparison, a replica Walker Colt and a 4" Colt Python .357 Magnum were used. Chronographed velocities for standard loadings gave six-shot averages of 977 f.p.s. for the cal. .44 Walker; 1183 f.p.s. for 158-gr. semi-wadcutter bullets in the Python. Converting velocities to energies, the Walker delivers 464 ft.-lbs., the Python, 491 ft.-lbs. But, when potential for transmitting energy is considered, the big revolver begins to stand out. Using Gen. Hatcher's scale of Relative Stopping Power, the Walker rates 80.3; the .357 Magnum, 64.5.

The .45 Colt cartridge, when fired in a 7½"-barrelled revolver is only slightly more effective than the Walker load. A six-round sample of modern .45 Colt factory ammunition fired in a 7½"-barrel Ruger Blackhawk revolver gave an average velocity of 858 f.p.s., with a corresponding energy of 417 ft.-lbs. and an R.S.P. of 81.3. Haven & Belden had it backwards.

Other blackpowder revolvers do not give such commanding performances. The Colt Dragoon load, standardized in 1858 as a 212-gr. conical bullet and 25 grs. of blackpowder, drops to an R.S.P. of 59.5. The 1860 Army revolver used a 216-gr. bullet and only 30 grs. of powder. By comparison, the .44 Special cartridge, in a 6" barrelled revolver, gives 705 f.p.s. velocity to a 246-gr. bullet, and 271 ft.-lbs. of energy. With the factory-loaded round-nose bullet the R.S.P. of the .44 Special is 57.6.

Despite their ponderous weight and imposing size, none of the Dragoon Colts equal the level of performance demonstrated by modern heavy-caliber handguns. Only the Walker is equal to the heavier, modern non-magnums and even the Walker must bow to the .41 or .44 Magnum. To make this statement does not neglect the fact that the chambers in a Dragoon cylinder will hold more than the 25 grs. of blackpowder normally loaded in military use. Indeed, most will easily accept 40 grs. and a conical bullet. That, however, is the same charge used in the commercial blackpowder load for the .45 Colt and is much inferior to the smokeless powder load presently available in that caliber.

Thus the legend of the Walker is revealed as absolute truth. The outsized Colt is every bit as big as its reputation, so big that it became its own undoing. Few originals survive. Many were destroyed when their huge cylinders ruptured. (The chambers of the later Dragoon revolvers were made with less powder capacity to reduce this hazard.) Other Walkers simply vanished. Collectors report only about 175 of the original 1100 revolvers in present-day

Revolvers used to test the Walker's legendary reputation for power were, top to bottom: Replica Arms Co. Walker Revolver, Serial No. 1027; Ruger Blackhawk, cal. .45 Colt; and 4"-barrelled Colt Python in cal. .357 magnum.

collections. Individual specimens are valued in the thousands of dollars.

In its day, this collector's prize was king of heavy caliber handguns, matching tremendous power with then nearly unknown rapidity of fire. Soon eclipsed in terms of utility, the Walker's day, in terms of ballistic supremacy as "the Big One", lasted for well over 100 years. ■

Editor's Note:

There is some doubt as to the actual powder charge intended as standard for the original Walker Colt revolver. Correspondence between Colt and Walker and the U.S. Army Ordnance Department specifies only the weight of the round ball and round-nose bullet. No mention is made of a powder charge.

A listing of U.S. small arms ammunition, prepared in 1876 and reproduced in Small Arms and Ammunition in the United States Service, *by Col. Berkeley R. Lewis, U.S.A., Ret., The Smithsonian Institution, 1956, gives the charge as 50 grs. Col. Lewis, on page 129, of the same text, says 40 grs.*

Nonetheless, the chambers of the Walker cylinder will hold 50 grs. of FFg blackpowder and a 218-gr. round-nose bullet similar in shape to the original projectile. Thus, the test firing done to gather data for this article was conducted using the 50-gr. charge.

Walker's recoil is heavy despite the revolver's 4½ lb. weight, but it is not uncomfortable. The dropping loading lever was a common failure with the original pistols and led to the use of a different latch in later Dragoons.

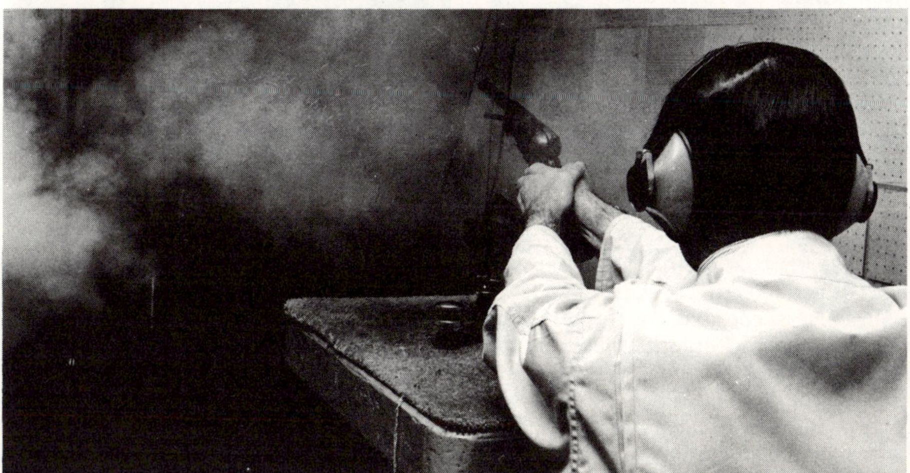

Sedgley .22 Insert

I have a portion of .22 rimfire barrel which is 5.3" long. The chamber and bore are offset and the muzzle is threaded. It is marked "R.F. Sedgley, Inc., Phila. Pa. U.S.A." What is it?

Answer: You have a .22 long rifle insert barrel for the M1911 pistol. Not much is known about just when or how many of these were produced, but they would have been a useful training device before more realistic, semi-automatic devices, such as the Colt Service Ace, became available.

The Sedgley insert barrel fits inside the standard .45 ACP barrel, locates against the chamber shoulder, and is held firmly by the muzzle nut. When assembled into the pistol, it provides a single-shot, manually-operated .22 trainer. The chamber and bore are eccentric, so the center-fire firing pin fires the cartridge, and the .45 ACP extractor can grasp the case rim. The breech of the barrel is contoured to match the barrel hood and slide, and provide extractor clearance. Each round must be inserted individually into the chamber and extracted manually by retracting the slide.

In a brief firing test, a post-World War I period Sedgley trainer fired with .22 long rifle standard velocity ammunition gave accuracy comparable to .45 ACP match hardball ammunition in the same gun, about 2½" for 10-shot groups fired from a Ransom Rest at 25 yds. The pistol was an as-issued M1911A1. Point of impact was about 3½" high at 25 yds., compared to .45 ACP service ammunition, so a sight adjustment would be required for precision shooting, though its performance is entirely adequate for its original training purpose.—C.E.H.

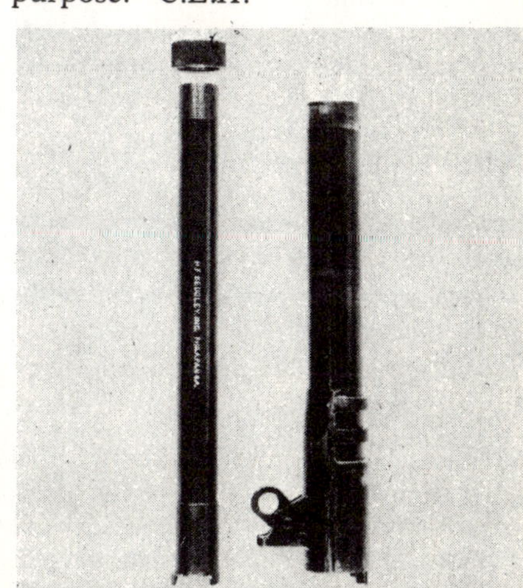

Sedgley .22 barrel for M1911 .45 was retained by nut, and used center-fire striker and extractor. The bore is offset.

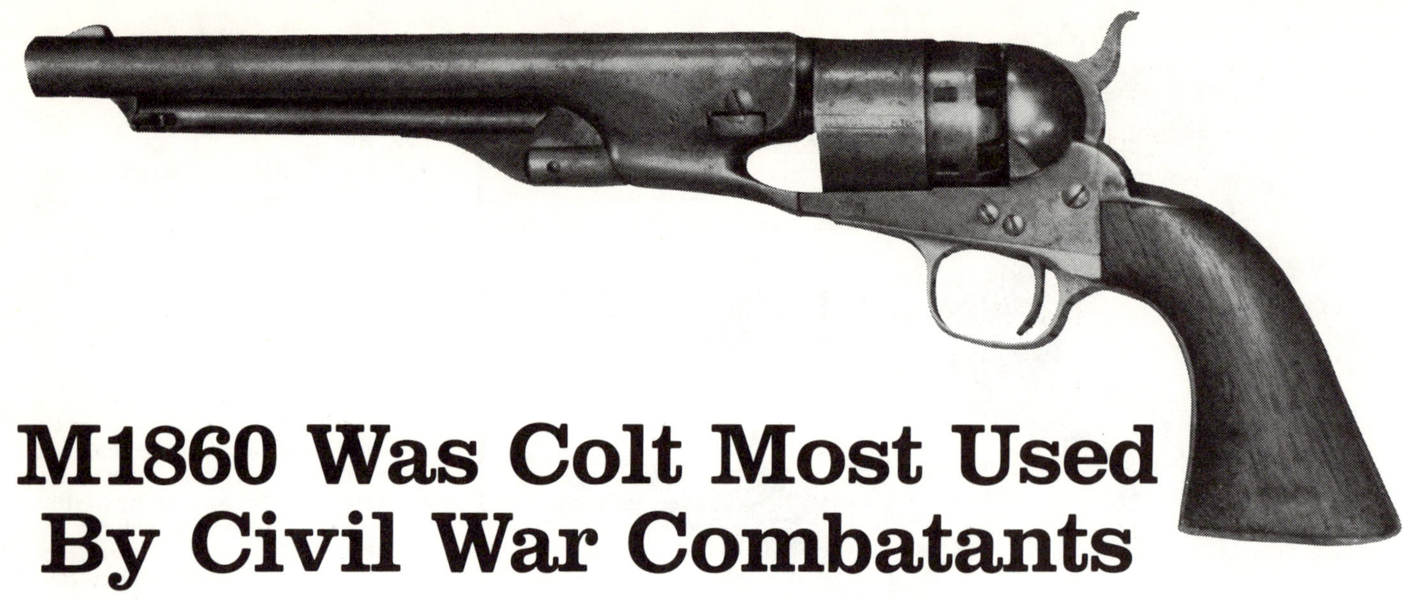

M1860 Was Colt Most Used By Civil War Combatants

By K. DALE MACDONALD

A single-action .44, it was modification of 1851 Navy Model

SAMUEL Colt's revolvers played powerful roles in a succession of conflicts during the 19th Century, including the Mexican War, the Seminole War, the Civil War, the Indian Wars and the Spanish-American War. Of these, the most destructive and tragic was the War Between The States, and the Colt that figured most prominently in that conflict was Colt's cal. .44 New Model Army, called the Model 1860.

The New Model Army was a single-action revolver like previous Colts. The hammer had to be cocked by hand each time it was fired. A notch in the lip of the hammer nose acted as a rear sight when the arm was fully cocked. To a great degree, the New Model Army was a modification of Colt's Navy Model of 1851.

The modifications comprised the following changes:

The caliber was increased from .36 to .44.

The barrel lug was thinned, lengthened, and rounded, then faired into a round barrel, which gave this Colt a streamlined look.

The loading lever plunger (rammer) was almost wholly contained within this lug, and operated on the ratchet principle by the loading lever, which had teeth on its rear portion functioning in notches in the underside of the barrel.

Space for the larger caliber was obtained by enlarging the forward 1-1/16" of the cylinder, and space for the enlarged cylinder was created by incorporating a step in the frame.

The loading cut-out was enlarged, and front and back straps were lengthened for better control of the heavier recoil. The oval trigger guard was also enlarged.

The front sight was changed to a low-profile brass blade from the Navy's conical post sight.

The bore had seven grooves with right-hand twist; later, it had seven grooves with left-hand twist.

With 8" barrel, the 1860 New Model Army was 14" long and weighed two lbs., 11 ozs. Colt had thus produced a cal. .44 six-shot arm, with 8" barrel, that weighed just one ounce more, and was one inch longer, than the cal. .36 1851 Navy. At the same time, it was a great improvement over earlier .44's. The Walker Model 1847 had weighed four lbs., 11 ozs.; the Model 1848 Dragoons had weighed four lbs., two ozs.

Grips of the new model were one-piece walnut, with an oil or varnish finish. The 1-13/16" cylinder was machine-engraved on its larger diameter with typical Colt roll engraving. The scene was a naval battle with the words "Engaged 16 May 1843" on the forward circumference of the cylinder. The words "Colt's Patent No." were followed by the last four digits of the serial number and ran fore-and-aft on the cylinder. Below this, some guns read "Patented Sept. 10th 1850" and others read "Pat. Sept. 10th 1850." The scene and engagement date referred to a confrontation between two ships of the Texas navy and seven ships of the Mexican Navy wherein the Texans put the Mexicans to flight. In the scene, Texas gunboats were chasing the Mexican gunboats.

The frame, loading lever and hammer were case-hardened while the barrel, cylinder, backstrap, trigger and screws were blued. Brass was cast into a one-piece front strap and trigger guard which was then polished. Serial numbers were stamped on the bottom of the barrel lug, the receiver, trigger guard, cylinder, backstrap, arbor pin and barrel wedge. (Of course, when all parts are original, all numbers match.)

Colt began supplying his new revolvers to the Federal Government on May 4, 1861, when the Chief of United States Ordnance, General J. W. Ripley, ordered 500 "New Pattern" pistols to be delivered to the New York Arsenal for inspection by Federal Ordnance Inspector Major William A. Thornton. Inspection either approved or rejected weapons, and this shipment of pistols was approved by Thornton who stamped his initials into the grips. All subsequent orders were likewise accepted by inspectors and marked with their stamped initials. Revolvers so

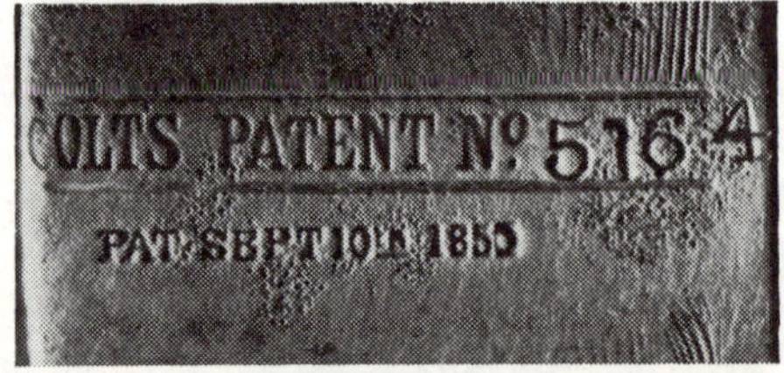

Variations of M1860 cylinder markings show differing patent designations.

Colt's ratchet loading lever activated a rammer housed in the barrel lug.

marked are genuine "martial" arms. Others sold through commercial agencies or to private individuals are called "commercial" and do not have inspector marks.

These descriptions fit the standard Model 1860, but as with most firearms production, there are variations such as barrel markings, barrel length and cylinder design.

Cylinder experiments

Before Colt put his new revolver into production, there was some experimenting with cylinders. It had been suggested that a cylinder with exterior grooves between the chambers might be an improvement. The grooves were called "flutes" and the first 6,500 (approximately) Model 1860's had full-fluted cylinders. These fluted models had barrel lengths of 7½" and 8". The 7½" barrels were standard on earlier production; the 8" barrel was later made standard.

During 1860, some 1860's were barrel-marked "Address Col. Colt Hartford Ct." Toward the end of that year, war seemed imminent, and Colt was faced with a political and moral dilemma. Hartford was a headquarters for anti-secessionist sentiment and Colt's Southern markets knew it. It was suggested that the Hartford barrel-marking might generate Southern anti-Colt sentiment, even increase the danger of personal or corporate retaliation. Thus, after about 1,500 Model 1860's had been produced, the barrel marking was changed to read "Address Col Saml Colt New York U S America." On April 16, 1861, four days after hostilities commenced, sales of Colt revolvers to Southern agents were stopped.

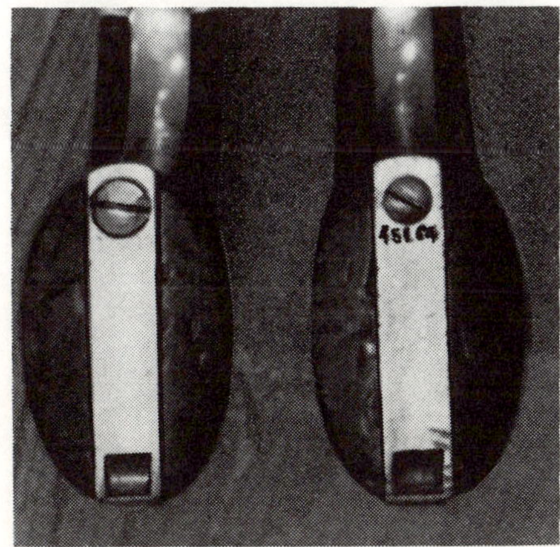

Another subtle variable in Colt Army design is the size of the butt screws.

After the change of barrel marking from the Hartford address to the New York address in 1861, both the 8" barrel and the unfluted cylinder became standard and remained so for the duration of the war.

A shoulder-stock, or as Colt himself called it, an "attachable carbine breech" was designed for the revolver to be used by the cavalry. With it attached the revolver became a "pistol-carbine", a more accurate arm for long-range shooting. The revolver and shoulder-stock combination weighed five lbs. and was 26½" long. To accommodate the stock, cuts were made in the bottom of the standing breech or recoil shield and at the bottom of the back strap. A fourth screw was inserted into the frame behind the trigger screw on both sides, and these screws or studs acted as recoil lugs. The stock could be used without them, but if recoil was severe the back strap and entire grip could be bent. The fourth screw was eliminated around serial number 30,000 to speed production and cut costs—some of the earlier Hartford and New York specimens also have been observed without them. Afterward, those pistols supplied with recoil screws were usually special orders.

In 1864, a Civilian Model 1860 was manufactured as a part of Colt's regular military production for that year—a total of 10,406 Model 1860 revolvers. The reason for this low figure was a fire on Feb. 5, 1864, which burned out the "Old Armory" and destroyed production machinery in that area. Up to the time of the fire a little more than 150,000 Model 1860's had been manufactured. The Civilian Model was manufactured in the new Armory after the fire and had serial numbers over 150,000. On the Civilian Models there was no cutout in the bottom of the recoil shield or underside of the back strap for attaching a shoulder stock.

Other variations were pistols sent out of the factory with shoulder-stocks attached and an "o" under the serial number. The stocks had the same serial number as well as the "o," which is presumed to have denoted a special order.

A few shoulder-stocks were manufactured incorporating canteens. The stocks were hollowed out, lined with tin and given a spout which came out of the point of the comb with a cap attached by a chain. These canteen-stocks were typical of the many innovations that were tried by manufacturers during the war with limited success.

Additional variations were:

- Double-stamped "Colt's Patent" on the frame.
- "Colt's Patent" stamped upside down.
- Two serial numbers on cylinder and/or frame, which indicates work or alterations done on the revolver. This was done in government arsenals and Colt's factory.
- U.S. stamped on frame, which indicates that the pistol was reissued from a government arsenal and may have mixed parts. The arsenals' ordnance men would strip the revolvers down and reassemble them with "serviceable" parts only, so one revolver might be made up of parts from two or more.
- Model 1860's which were shipped to London, England, for sale through London agents and whose barrels were stamped "Address Col Colt London" with an "L" preceding the serial numbers. These revolvers had iron back straps and trigger guards and were the "Civilian" type.

The number of Model 1860's purchased by U.S. Ordnance during the war attests to the arm's popularity. Commencing with the first order for 500 revolvers on May 4, 1861, almost 130,000 were purchased before the end of 1863. The Model 1860 also was used by the Confederates, due to the fact that Colt had sold some to his Southern agents before he ceased sales to the South. Many others were captured in battle and used against the North.

Colt charged the government an average price of $25 for the New Army revolver and $6 for a shoulder stock. These prices allowed Colt a useful profit, though they seem low by today's standards. A variety of accessories, then called "appendages", such as extra nipples, screwdrivers, nipple wrenches and bullet molds, could be had and were ordered with the 1860 Army model.

The following list of U.S. Ordnance Inspectors and the years they inspected Model 1860's will help determine whether your revolver is military issue and by whom it was inspected. In addition to these initials on the grips, the last four digits of the serial number, written in ink, will be found in the back strap groove if the grips are original to the revolver.

Inspector	Initials Used	Years
O. W. Ainsworth	O.W.A.	1831–70
George T. Balch	G.T.B.	1861–62
Peter Barrett	P.B.	1861–68
Robert Beals	R.B.	1862
A. B. Blackington	A.B.B.	1860–62
E. M. Camp	E.M.C.	1860–63
David F. Clark	D.F.C.	1861–86
James S. Dudley	J.S.D.	1861–70
Benjamin Hannis	B.H.	1861
Michael Hayes	M.H.	1860
H. L. Lathrop	H.L.L.	1862
Samuel Leonard	S.L.	1862–75
George D. Little	G.D.L.	1862–65
Chas. S. Lowell	C.S.L.	1858–61
William H. Roberts	W.H.R.	1863
John Taylor	J.T.	1861–62
William A. Thornton	W.A.T.	1861

The Model 1860 Army revolver was popular until 1873 when the cal. .45 Colt "Peacemaker" was manufactured. The serial number range can date a revolver, as follows:

Year	Serial number at beginning of year
1861	2,000
1862	25,000
1863	85,000
1864	150,000
1865	165,000

After the war, many revolvers were converted to use metallic cartridges. The first cartridge-firing kin to the solid frame "Peacemaker" in cal. .45 was an altered Model 1860 which was called the Model 1872 Open Top Frontier in cal. .44 center-fire or rimfire. Many components for this model were specially made for use with metallic cartridges, unlike other conversions which used the original cylinders and frames of the Model 1860, such as the Richards-Mason, Thuer, and Richards conversions.

Original percussion revolvers still can be found in excellent condition. Those that saw hard use range from poor condition, with badly rusted or missing parts, to good condition with all original major parts and some original finish. Barrels of some revolvers are worn down slightly near the muzzle, the result of having been carried in a holster. Other guns have minor modifications, such as having the hammer face built up or small springs and screws replaced.

Whatever condition you find them in, they are symbols of many hard-fought battles that helped bring unity and peace to a Nation, and should be cared for so that future generations of collectors can enjoy them as we do now. ■

Civil War Colts Took Some Surprising Loads

Although Civil War manuals of both conflicting armies specified the loads for the much-used Colt cal. .36 Navy and Colt cal. .44 Army percussion revolvers, it now appears from old records that the actual loads varied considerably when made up in cartridge form.

Conical bullets for the .44 Army ranged from 207 grs. to 260 grs., backed by powder charges varying from 17 to 36 grs. Those for the .36 Navy varied from a conical bullet, minimum weight of 139 grs., to a maximum of 155 grs., with charges as low as 12 to 13 grs. and as high as 21 grs.

Nearly all of these considerable variations occurred in prepared cartridges, usually encased in combustible paper, manufactured by private contractors. Few revolver cartridges appear to have been made in U.S. Government arsenals.

Union Army ordnance manuals of 1861 specify a loading of 30 grs. of powder with a .46" diameter 216-gr. conical ball in Colt Model 1860 Army revolvers and 17 grs. of powder with a .39" diameter 145-gr. conical ball in Colt Model 1851 Navy revolvers.

Considerable variation existed in cartridges prepared by private firms, as indicated by old records.

An official Confederate States publication lists 30 grs. of powder with a 250-gr. bullet for Colt's Army revolver and duplicates Union Ordnance loading for Colt Navy revolvers.

Round balls, as well as conical balls and bullets, were regularly loaded in these guns, using standard powder charges. The 81-gr. cal. .36 and the 146-gr. cal. .44 round balls were not generally made up into cartridges.

COLT ARMY

Maker	Bullet Wgt. (grs.)	Powder Wgt. (grs.)
Hazard Powder Co.	211	36
Bartholow's	260	19
Johnston & Dow	242	35
Unknown	257	17
Unknown	207	22
Hotchkiss	207	22

COLT NAVY

Maker	Bullet Wgt. (grs.)	Powder Wgt. (grs.)
Hazard Powder Co.	141	21
Bartholow's	139	14
Johnston & Dow	150	17
Unknown	155	12
Unknown	149	13

In the 1860's an average load for Colt's Army revolver was 25 grs. of powder with a 146-gr. round ball or a bullet of about 230 grs. Colt's Navy revolver loads averaged 15 grs. of powder with an 81-gr. round ball or a bullet of about 146 grs.

Correct diameter round ball and bullet molds are currently available from Lyman Gun Sight Products. Use mold #450229 casting a 155-gr. bullet for the Army revolver and mold #37583 casting a 145-gr. bullet for the Navy revolver. Round balls should be .451" diameter for the Army revolver and .375" diameter for the Navy revolver. Bullets should be sized .001" to .002" over chamber diameter and lubricated.

Loadings for Colt Army revolvers will occasionally list a 218-gr. conical ball and a 40-50 gr. powder charge. This load is intended for use in Colt Walker Model 1847 Army dragoon revolvers and should not be used in Colt Army revolvers.

—Michael Bussard

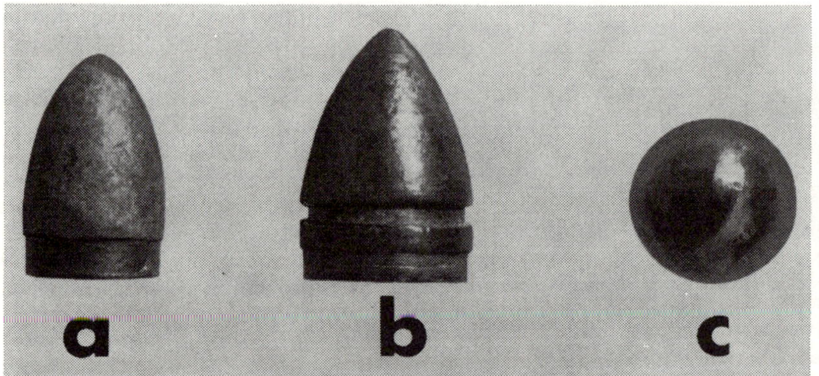

Tapered heel bullet **(a)** adopted with the Colt Navy revolver in 1851, improved accuracy. A .44 cal. bullet **(b)** with grease grooves was standardized in 1860 with adoption of the Colt Army revolver. Round balls **(c)** were fired in both guns.

Conversions of Colt Percussion Revolvers

By E. DIXON LARSON

Information on factory conversions of small-frame revolvers to fire .38 caliber cartridges

FACTORY metallic cartridge conversions of Colt small-frame percussion revolvers interest the collector because of their specialized nature. Converting these revolvers to fire cal. .38 center-fire or rimfire cartridges started in the 1870's. Colt's made the conversions to utilize leftover parts from the pocket revolvers and the cal. .36 1862 Police Model.

Major surplus parts used included frames, barrels, hammers, trigger guards, and backstraps. Only 2 types of frames were used—the Pocket revolver of Navy caliber (cal. .36) and the 1862 Police Model.

Colt's employed combinations of parts from both models. Patterns varied in shape of barrel, cylinder type (fluted or rebated), and presence or absence

Colt 1862 Police Model cal. .36 percussion revolver. Standard barrel lengths are 4½", 5½", and 6½" (shown).

Colt Pocket Model cal. .36 percussion revolver, sometimes referred to as the "1853 Pocket Model". Standard barrel lengths are 4½", 5½", and 6½".

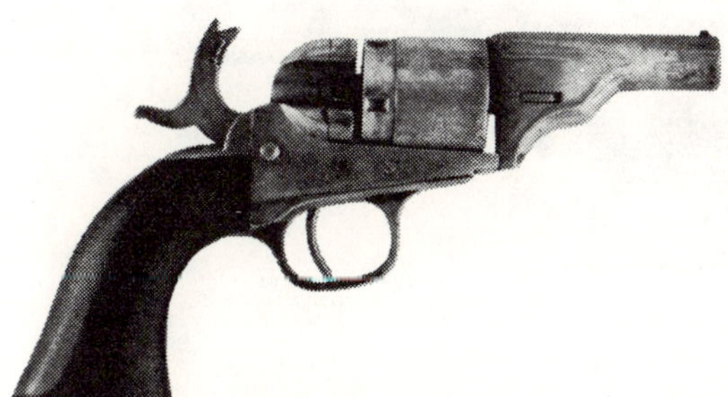

Cal. .38 center-fire conversion of Pocket revolver of Navy caliber. It is fitted with special 3½" barrel without cut-out, loading gates and ejector case. Barrel of revolver shown is 2½" long, indicating that it was shortened from 3½" length. Left side of the frame carries 1871-72 patent dates. From the number examined, it has been concluded that an equal number of rimfire and center-fire conversions were assembled.
This is an excellent example of a conversion that could almost pass for a factory original.

Cal. .38 rimfire conversion of Pocket revolver of Navy caliber revolver utilizing same barrel lengths of standard percussion models. This revolver was converted by filling in lever slot and installing loading gate with exterior loading gate spring and screw. The arm lacks an ejector case. A few revolvers of this type were made without loading gate. Rimfire conversion was predominant. One-line New York address is stamped on barrel and 1871-72 patent dates are stamped on left side of the frame of the revolver.

of ejector mechanism and loading gate. Loading gates, if fitted, had either inside or outside springs. Primary parts utilized from Model 1849 and Model 1850 percussion revolvers were trigger guards and backstraps. The original cal. .31 frame stamping was rarely altered.

All small-frame factory conversions were accomplished by installing the firing pin in the hammer nose and not by utilizing the ring-type system employed in the Richards conversion of the 1860 Army Model.

Few factory conversions of either the Pocket revolver of Navy caliber or the 1862 Police Model were made originally as percussion revolvers. Colt authorities hold that low serial numbers (up to 5 digits) indicate factory assembly as a metallic cartridge arm. Conversely, a high serial number signifies conversion of an original percussion revolver. However, many exceptions to this rule have been observed, particularly in the Pocket revolver of Navy caliber with special 3½" barrel. Converted revolvers of this pattern are found frequently with 6-digit serial numbers, an indication of substantial production.

When a percussion barrel was used, either the lever hinge slot and plunger hole in the barrel lug were plugged or just the lever hinge slot was plugged. Assembly numbers are usually found on the gate and on the frame under the trigger guard.

Cartridge conversions of Colt percussion revolvers can be separated into 3 categories: (1) Percussion revolvers returned to the factory for conversion; (2) factory conversions assembled from modified percussion parts; (3) maverick conversions made by independent gunsmiths. (Note: The Thuer cartridge conversion was intentionally omitted from this classification because of its extreme rarity.)

Revolvers illustrated in this article represent basic factory conversion types and their varieties. However, there are always interesting exceptions to Colt production models. Maverick conversions are not shown because they are not of factory origin and cannot be prototyped. They are the least desirable of all conversions although they may evidence excellent craftsmanship.

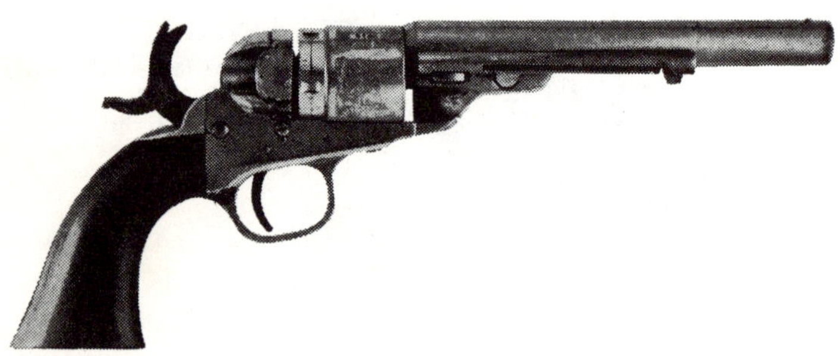

Cal. .38 center-fire conversion of Pocket revolver of Navy caliber utilizing standard barrel turned round forward of the lug. Barrel carries 2-line Hartford address and is fitted with ejector case. The lug is cut out under wedge. All revolvers of this type examined have 1871-72 patent dates on left side of frame. Arm has exterior loading gate spring and screw. Standard barrel length is 5½", but some guns observed have 6½" barrels.

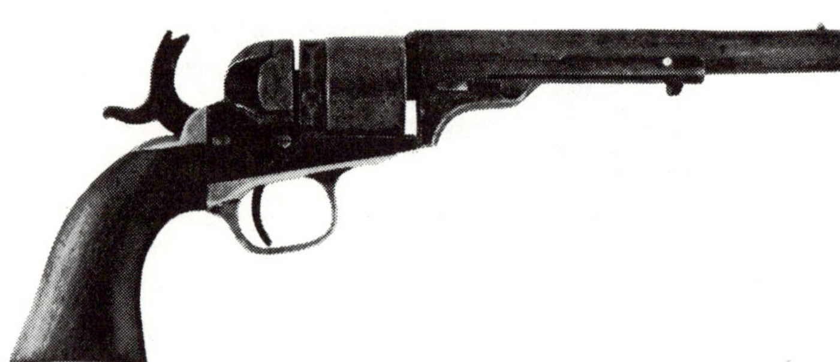

Cal. .38 center-fire conversion of Pocket revolver of Navy caliber, termed by collectors "Baby Open Top Frontier". This variation is scarce. Standard barrel length is 5½". This conversion utilizes surplus percussion parts, but is fitted with new type barrel lacking loading cut-out in lug.
Barrel carries 2-line Hartford address. Arm has exterior loading gate spring and screw.

Cal. .38 rimfire conversion of 1862 Police Model, first type, with fluted cylinder. Most conversions of this model have rebated cylinder of the Pocket revolver of Navy caliber. This cylinder was used to provide maximum strength. Revolver has Mason's ejector case on right side of barrel.
Number matching serial may be present on rear of cylinder or on crown of cylinder flute. A few pieces were observed with patent date in cylinder flute or on frame. On some, the exterior loading gate spring is retained by a screw. Standard barrel length is 4½".

Cal. .38 center-fire conversion of 1862 Police Model, second type, with rebated cylinder of the Pocket revolver of Navy caliber. Both first and second types are fitted with loading gates. The .38 rimfire conversion is most predominant in both types—about 7 to one in the series of revolvers examined. Further, only about one out of 20 revolvers have the 1871-72 patent dates stamped on the left side of the frame in place of the "Colt's Patent" marking. The majority of these revolvers have 5½" barrels. Exterior loading gate spring and screw are absent on the revolver shown. ■

Conversions of Colt Percussion Revolvers

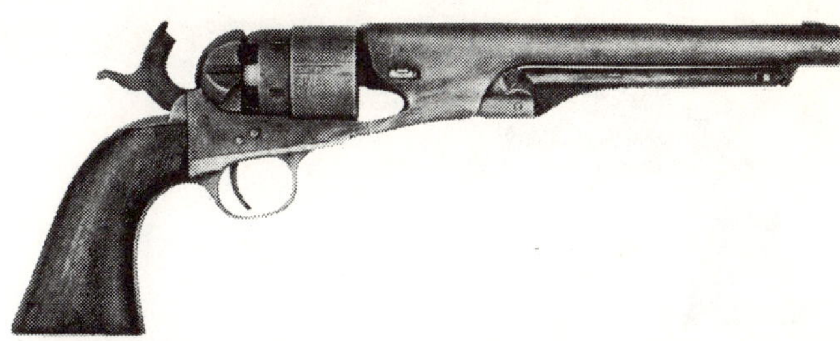

Army Model of 1860 cal. .44 percussion revolver. Rebated cylinder. Standard barrel lengths are 7½" and 8". Three-screw frame cut for shoulder stock. Most popular of all Civil War period Service revolvers. Found with 3 possible addresses, namely: "Address Col. SamL Colt-Hartford, Ct."; "Address Col. SamL Colt–New York–U.S. America"; "Address Col. SamL Colt–London".

Information on factory conversions of large-frame revolvers to fire .38 & .44 caliber cartridges

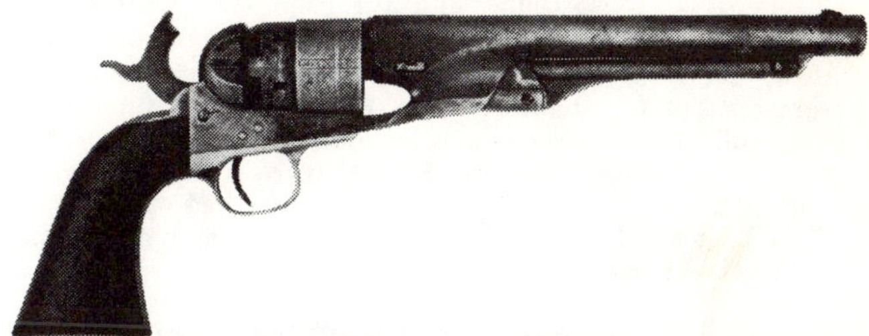

Commercial Army Model of 1860 cal. .44 percussion revolver. Rebated cylinder. Standard production model for civilian use. Three-screw frame not cut for shoulder stock. All cartridge conversions of Army Model of 1860 percussion revolvers utilized the rebated cylinder and are cal. .44 center-fire.

By E. DIXON LARSON

MANY articles and books that deal conclusively with Colt percussion and standard production models have been published, but most provide little information on Colt cartridge conversions. Since the total number of cartridge conversions was less than 10% of the total percussion revolver production, they can be classed as relatively scarce.

Until recently, converted revolvers had not achieved any great prominence. Now the interest has greatly increased and, in most instances, prices often exceed those of the original percussion models. However, many conversions offered for sale or trade are completely out of character. The majority of the 'misfits' examined were of the Army Model of 1860, but some abuse of the Navy Models has also been noted. In most cases the misrepresentation is not intentional but due to inadequate identification.

Many new Colt collectors have become interested in the conversion models. Therefore, a simple means of identification is in order. Identification seems especially necessary for the Army Model of 1860, because of the numerous combinations possible. Many pieces have been examined that were being offered as the genuine article, yet upon methodical examination proved spurious.

Conversions, unlike production percussion models, do not adhere to the rule of matching numbers. It is difficult, therefore, to identify a hybrid assembly unless some knowledge of its general appearance and features is known. With this in mind, an attempt has been made to provide a concise means of identifying cartridge conversions of the large-frame Colt percussion models, namely, the 1851-1861 Navy Model and the 1860 Army Model.

It is realized that there are exceptions to all rules where antique weapons are concerned. The pieces described here should afford the prospective conversion enthusiast a general identification of the large-frame conversions. The omission of the Thuer conversion was intentional inasmuch as few are available and in most instances they have been completely authenticated by appraisers of accepted reputation.

The Colt conversion, as stated by Charles Richards in his first patent disclosure, was designed primarily to provide an inexpensive and simple method for converting percussion revolvers (constructed for loose powder and ball) to use a flanged-head self-contained metallic cartridge loaded from the rear of the cylinder. The result proved to be a sturdy, efficient weapon. Colt's advertised these arms as "Colt's new breech loading revolver". Factory records indicate that the converted Army Model of 1860 revolver enjoyed the largest production, whereas the pocket models appear to have been the least favored; the Navy models falling in between.

The accompanying information is intended to provide the general nomenclature necessary to successfully identify Colt large-frame conversions.

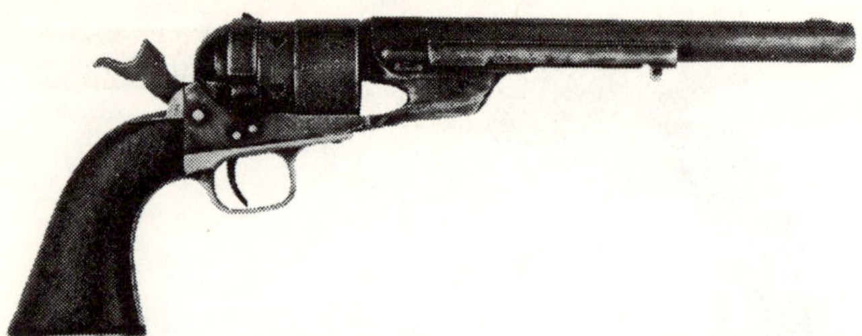

Army Model of 1860, Richards conversion, cal. .44 center-fire. Independent firing pin in conversion ring. Integral rear sight. Flat-faced hammer. Exterior gate spring attached to conversion ring. Frame not cut for shoulder stock.

General factory production of Richards conversions that were not altered from percussion models will be found with serial numbers up to 6,000. Majority (49 out of 50) will have 8″ barrels, New York address, and "Colt's Patent" marking on left side of frame. Also found with 5½″ and 7½″ barrels. About one of 75 will have patent dates instead of "Colt's Patent".

Most revolvers examined in 1 to 6,000 serial number range were not cut for shoulder stock. However, most higher numbers, indicating altered percussion models, were cut for stock. Early conversions were noted with interior gate springs and other addresses. A small number (1 in 250) had cylinders with 12 locking notches. Equal number of blued and nickel-plated revolvers was observed.

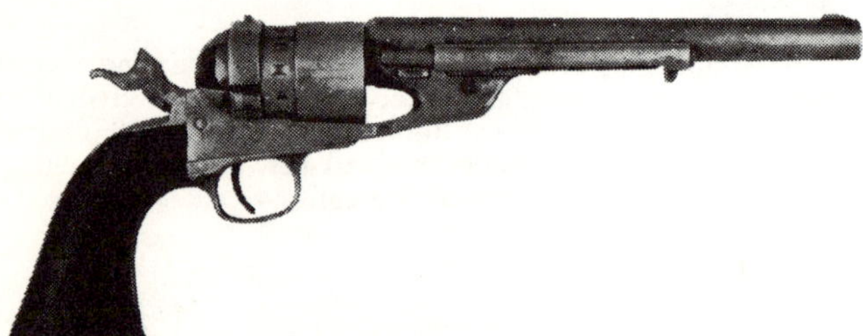

Army Model of 1860, Springfield Armory Richards conversion, cal. .44 center-fire. Only conversion of Army Model of 1860 revolver which can be called a U. S. martial arm. Marked "U. S." on left side of barrel forward of wedge. This Richards system conversion made without regard to matching parts numbers. New numbers were stamped beneath original numbers. The new numbers, usually 2 or 3 digits, were suffixed with letter "A". Colt's patent marking on left side of frame.

Springfield Armory converted approximately 1200 percussion revolvers to fire center-fire cartridge. An equal number of 6-notch and 12-notch cylinders were observed. All pieces examined were cut for shoulder stock and bore either New York or Hartford address.

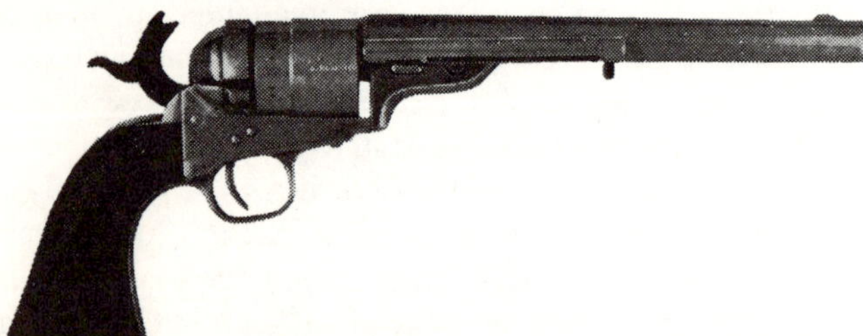

Army Model of 1860, Richards-Mason conversion, cal. .44 center-fire. No integral rear sight. Firing pin mounted in hammer nose. New-type barrel made without clearance cut out for bullet. Mason ejector case, serial number sequence up to 7,000. Assembly numbers on gate, frame, and cylinder arbor. Patent dates on left side of frame, namely: "Pat. July 25, 1871" and "Pat. July 2, 1872".

Early barrel length as shown was 8″, marked the same as percussion models. Later models have been noted with 7½″ barrel marked "Colt's Pt. F.A. Mfgr. Co., Hartford Ct. U.S.A." As this model did not involve alteration of percussion arm, production was limited. Ejector case extends to within 5/16″ of the cylinder face, an obvious difference from the Richards.

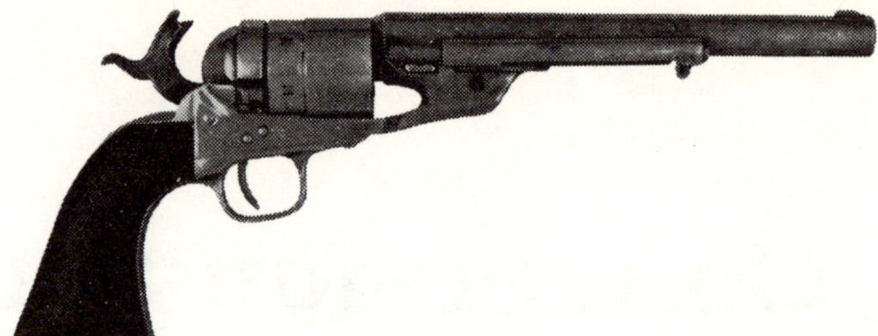

Army Model of 1860, transition conversion, cal. .44 center-fire. Sometimes referred to as Richards No. 2 conversion. Conversion has Richards-Mason type firing pin and conversion ring, with Richards-type ejector assembly mounted on 8″ percussion barrel. Pieces examined had patent dates on left side of frame and bore same addresses found on Model 1860 percussion revolver.

Almost without exception serial numbers of pieces examined were between No. 170,000 and No. 230,000. This conversion is scarce since ratio of pieces observed was as follows: 1 to every 25 Mason-Richards, and 1 to every 75 Richards.

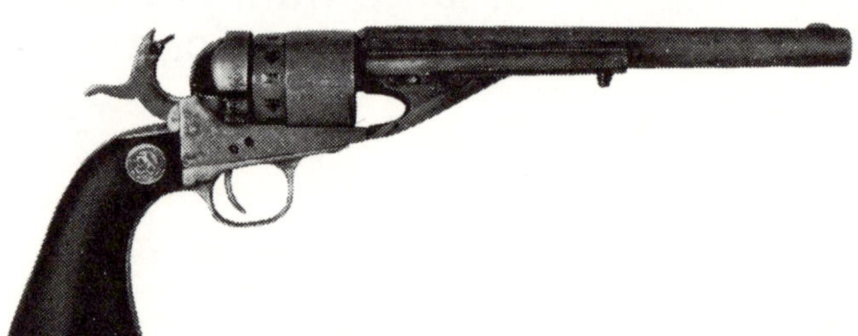

Army Model of 1860, Richards-Mason conversion, Type 1861 Navy, cal. .44 center-fire. Referred to by some authorities as "Mystery Conversion" because only 8 specimens are known. Some authorities believe this to be late factory-altered percussion arm. Serial numbers of known guns range as follows: 2 in 150,000 range, 2 in 166,000 range, 2 in 170,000 range, one in 190,000 range, and one unknown.

Conversion was made utilizing general method applied to Navy Model of 1861. Rammer hole milled and plugged, firing pin attached to hammer, no patent dates on frame. Colt's patent marking on left side of 8″ barrel, Mason-type ejector case, percussion markings, no conversion numbers, 6-notch and 12-notch cylinders, loading gate differs from Mason-Richards version. Half of guns known are engraved or have an indication of Mexican use. This has been attributed to factory special order, but model is controversial.

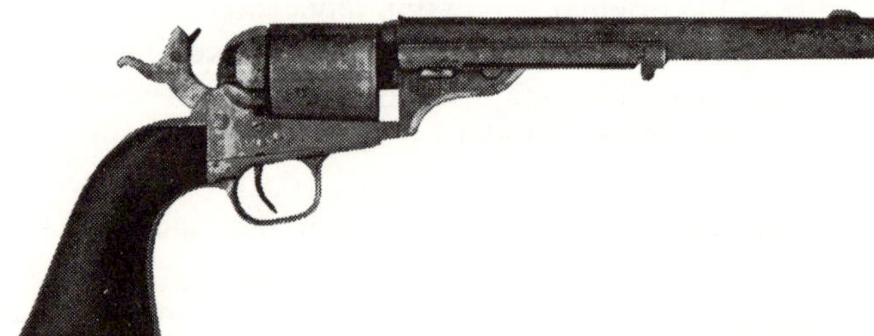

Model of 1872, cal. .44 rimfire or center-fire. Referred to by collectors as "Open Top Frontier". Shows close kinship to Richards-Mason conversion. Plain cylinder, not rebated as used on conversions, integral rear barrel sight, 7½″ and 8″ barrel lengths. Earlier model with 8″ barrel usually marked with same New York address found on percussion revolver. Later models have "Colt's Pt. F.A. Mfgr. Co. Hartford Ct." marking. Two types of gate springs, exterior and interior. Revolver shown has exterior gate spring attached to frame.

Production records indicate serial sequence up to No. 6,874. Smooth-faced loading gate is smaller than gate employed in percussion conversion.

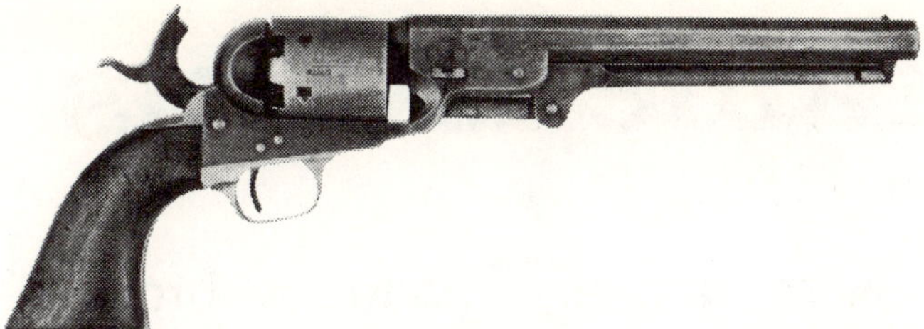

Navy Model of 1851, cal. .36 percussion revolver, 7½" barrel. Marked on barrel "Col. SamL Colt—New York—U. S. America". Typical type utilized in cartridge conversion of Navy Model of 1851 revolver.

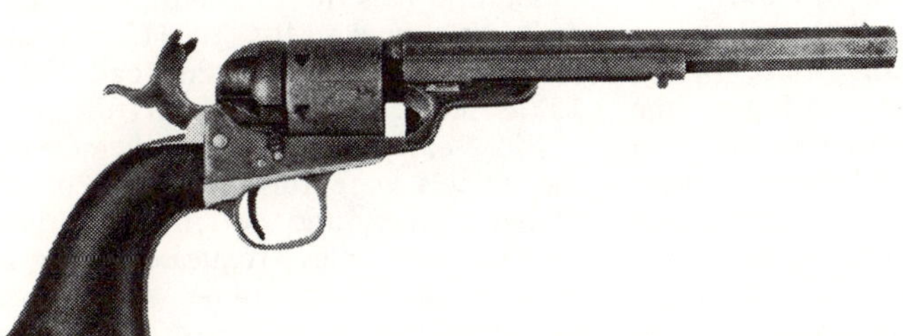

Navy Model of 1851, Richards-Mason conversion, cal. .38 rimfire or center-fire, 7½" barrel. Firing pin attached to hammer, Mason-type ejector case, cut out barrel lug, lever slot plugged, rammer hole left in frame. Revolvers with patent dates on left side of frame outnumber specimens with "Colt's Patent" marking.

Cylinder number may not match frame and barrel numbers, but close inspection of rear of cylinder adjacent to ratchet will usually reveal matching number or matching conversion number. Many percussion cylinders replaced during factory alteration. Records indicate that 2,098 Navy Model of 1851 and 1861 percussion revolvers were altered for the government. Total Navy conversion production was equivalent to 3% of percussion revolvers produced for U. S. Navy.

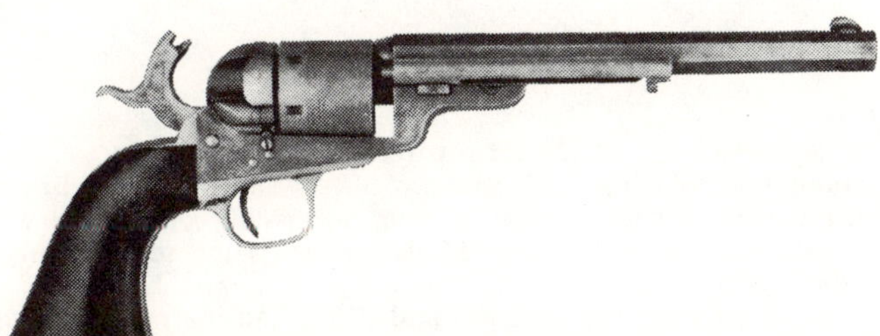

Navy Model of 1851, Richards-Mason conversion, cal. .38 center-fire. Revolver shown is typical of factory conversion never utilized as percussion arm. Characteristics similar to revolver shown above, except barrel lug not cut out. Patent dates on left side of frame, exterior gate spring on all guns examined, new unnumbered wedge without spring. Iron or brass backstraps and trigger guards will be found on all Navy conversions. Ratio of brass to iron fittings was 10 to 1. Production limited because this model was produced only as expedient to utilize stock of percussion parts. Serial numbers up to 4 digits. No cal. .38 rimfire conversions observed.

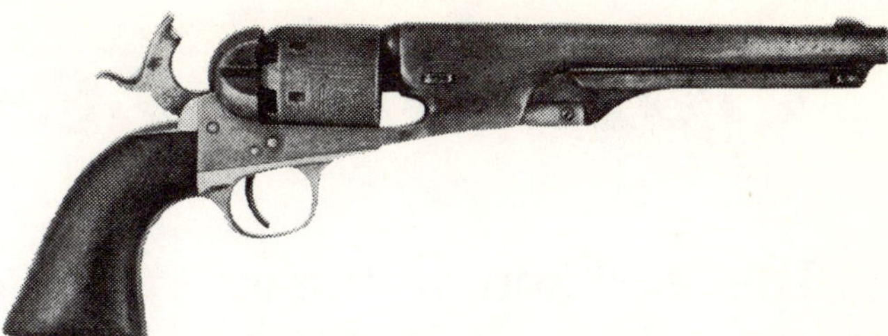

Navy Model of 1861, cal. .36 percussion revolver, 7½" round barrel. Barrel marked "Address Col. SamL Colt, New York-U. S. America". Revolver shown is typical type utilized in cartridge conversion of Navy Model of 1861 revolver.

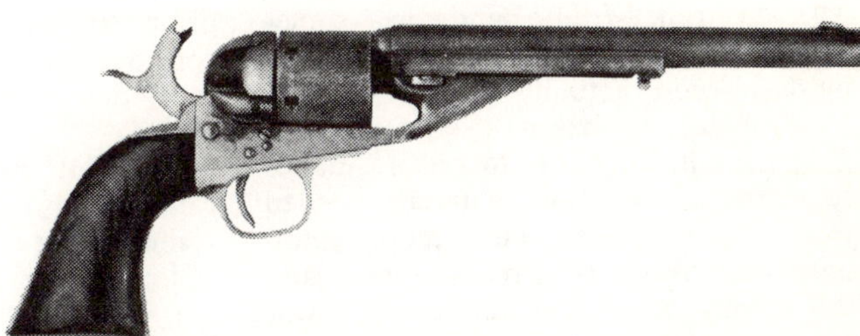

Navy Model of 1861, Richards-Mason conversion, cal. .38 rimfire or center-fire. Markings same as percussion version except for patent dates on left side of frame. Cal. .38 marking may be found on trigger guard. Most revolvers examined in cal. .38 center-fire had 4-digit serial numbers, indicating factory production rather than alteration of a percussion revolver. Exterior loading gate springs considerably outnumber interior springs. This conversion may be found with naval markings and mismatched cylinder numbers.

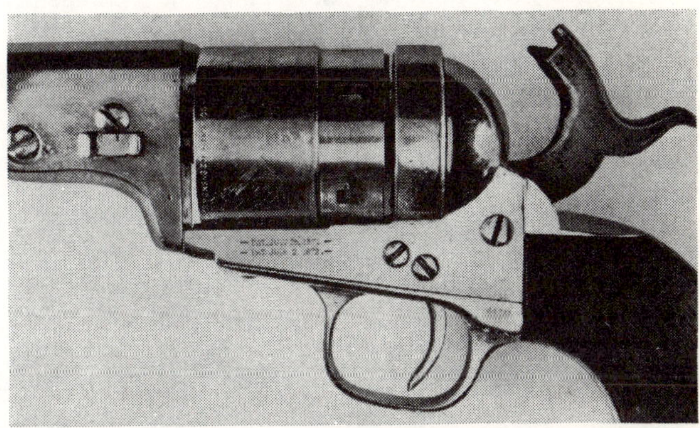

Richards-Mason patent dates, hammer, frame ring, and barrel details characteristic of Army Model of 1860 Richards-Mason cartridge conversion.

"U. S." marking found on barrels of Richards cartridge conversions altered by Springfield Armory.

Colt Bronze-Frame Models

The well-known "brass" handguns were actually made of bronze

By E. DIXON LARSON

COLT bronze-frame handguns—sometimes referred to as brass-frame models—were actually made of bronze. Undoubtedly bronze was selected by the Colt firm in an effort to reduce manufacturing costs. Raw materials needed to produce bronze were more abundant than those required for iron, and the bronze alloy, because of its lower melting temperature, was easier to produce than iron. The bronze castings were easier and less expensive to machine than iron castings, and structural strength was not an important consideration because of the small powder charges of the cartridges utilized in these models. Another advantage of using bronze was the elimination of the necessity to apply a base plating prior to nickel-plating. This gave a considerable saving since 3 out of the 5 models manufactured were nickel-plated.

The Colt bronze-frame arms can be categorized into 5 basic models: the 4-shot House Pistol, often called the "Cloverleaf"; the 5-shot House Pistol; the No. 3 single-shot Deringer; the 7-shot, cal. .22 open frame model; and the 7-shot cal. .22 solid-frame model.

Colt introduced the bronze-frame models in 1872, simultaneously with the final inventory sales of the cartridge conversions and introduction of the new single-action model. This was Colt's attempt to satisfy the demand for smaller-sized handguns and to capture the competitive market. At this time other small alloy-frame single-shot models were being manufactured by such companies as Marlin, Merwin & Bray, Allen, and Moore. An old catalog issued by James Bown & Son of Pittsburgh lists the Colt No. 3 Deringer as "Colt's Never Miss" at $12 per pair, and the 7-shot open-frame cal. .22 at $5 in half plate and $6 in full plate.

Most early advertising indicates that the models were furnished with nickle-plated frames, and not in the original bronze state unless requested. To produce such bronze-frame arms today would be extremely expensive and impractical. Some current manufacturers have simulated the old frames by alloy plating of steel or they have utilized brass alloys.

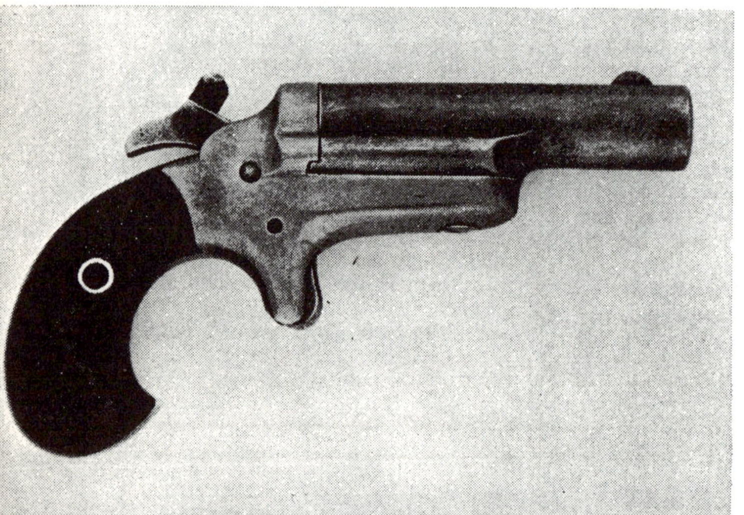

Colt Thuer Deringer, cal. .41 short rimfire. Frequently referred to by collectors as the No. 3 Model. Bronze frame, 2½" steel barrel, rosewood grips, sheath trigger, single-action. Barrel pivots to right for loading and extracting. Model shown is the third type and is more common than the other 2 variations. Essential differences are in the slant of the hammer. First type has a high-angled hammer spur and a raised boss on the frame around the pivot screw. Second type has modified high-angled hammer spur but no raised pivot screw boss. Third type, as shown, has a sloping hammer spur.

Three exceptions to the standard barrel length were observed. Markings are "COLT" in 3/16" slanted capital letters on the second and third types, and "COLT" in ⅛" block capital letters on the first type. A few were observed with the "14 Pall Mall, London" address in 2 lines on the side of the barrel. Grips may be rosewood (most common), walnut, ivory, or pearl. This model was patented in July 1870 by F. A. Thuer of the Colt Co. It can be loaded and unloaded extremely rapidly.

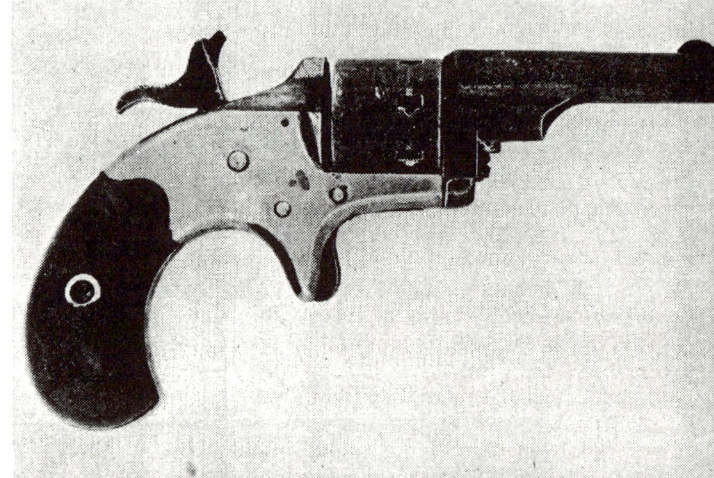

Colt Pocket cal. .22 7-shot revolver, often referred to as "open frame" or "old line" .22 model. Cal. .22 short or long, bronze frame, sheath trigger, single action, no loading gate, made with or without ejector housing. Model shown is the most common type made, without ejector housing, and will be found in round barrel lengths of 2⅜" and 2⅞". Outside cylinder locking notches, high- and low-angled hammers (low-angle shown), bird's head grips, weight 8 ozs. Many refer to the 2 types of hammer angles as first and second types, the high spur being considered the first type. High hammers were considered inconvenient and unsafe when carried in the pocket, being susceptible to catching on clothing. Detachable barrel is held in place by a pivot wedge and cylinder armor slot. Markings are in 2 lines on barrel top, "Colt's Pt. F.A. Mfg., Co." in straight capital block letters and "Hartford, Ct., U.S.A." in slanted capital block letters, and ".22 cal." stamped on left side of the frame. This was Colt's last detachable barrel model. Various combinations of nickel and blued or plain frames were observed.

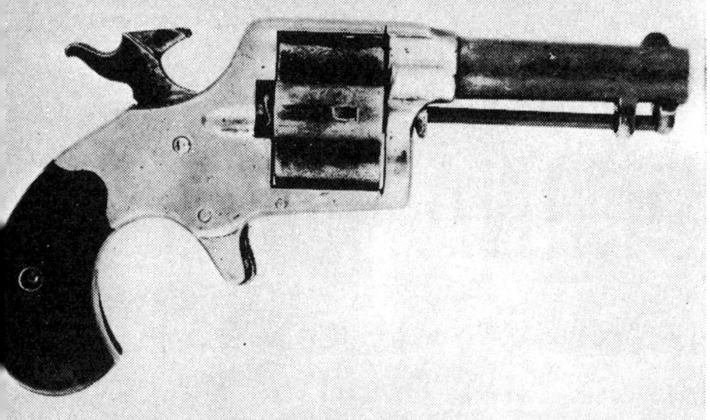

Colt House Pistol, cal. .41 rimfire, 4-shot, single-action, sheath trigger revolver commonly known as "Cloverleaf" model by collectors. One of the very few revolvers in which the cylinder rotates 90° for chamber alignment. Hand travel is critical and the design represents unusual engineering. Model shown is first-type with high-angled hammer. Second type revolver has slanting hammer spur. This was Colt's first one-piece solid-frame revolver. Integral front sight. Barrel lengths are generally accepted as 3" and 1½" octagon or round; however, the 3" models actually measure 3-15/16". The 1½" barrel models are scarce and were furnished on special order. Rosewood grips, recessed cartridge chambers, bronze frame, steel barrel, pull-rod ejector, cartridge stop (usually missing due to a high mortality rate as a result of delicate construction). Markings are "Colt's House Pistol, Hartford, Ct., U.S.A." in 2 lines on the 3" barrel length, and "COLT" on the left side of the 1½" barrel model. In the sighting groove of the bronze frame is stamped, "PAT. Sept. 19, 1871"; ".41 caliber" is stamped mid-way on frame below cylinder. Colt's first solid one-piece frame model, it was advertised as carrying a heavier ball in proportion to its weight than any other revolver.

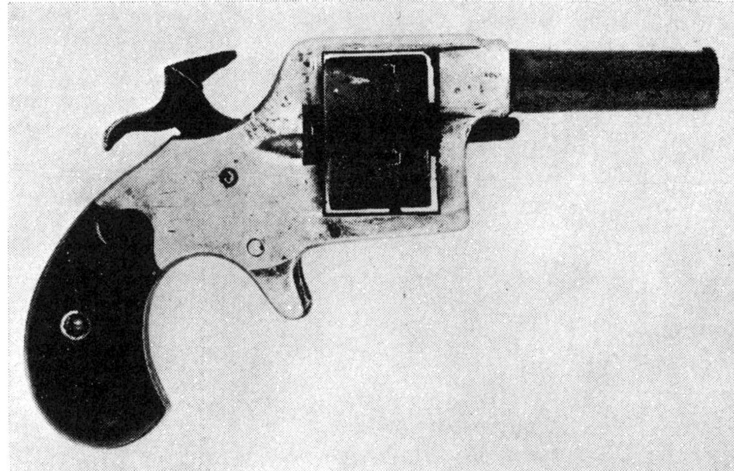

Colt House Pistol 5-shot round cylinder model with integral front sight. Bronze frame, 2⅝" round steel barrel only, sheath trigger, single action, unique integral front sight beginning at edge of muzzle, sloping hammer spur, cylinder pull pin and cartridge punch, cartridge stop. Cartridge stops were observed on only 3 House Pistols out of 76 examined. Markings are "Colt's House Pistol, Hartford, Ct., U.S.A." in 2 lines on the top of the barrel, and "Pat. Sept. 19, 1871" stamped in sighting groove. "Caliber .41" is stamped on left of frame under cylinder opening. Rosewood or walnut 2-piece grips, custom ivory or pearl. Ratio of nickeled finish to plain was 3 to 1.

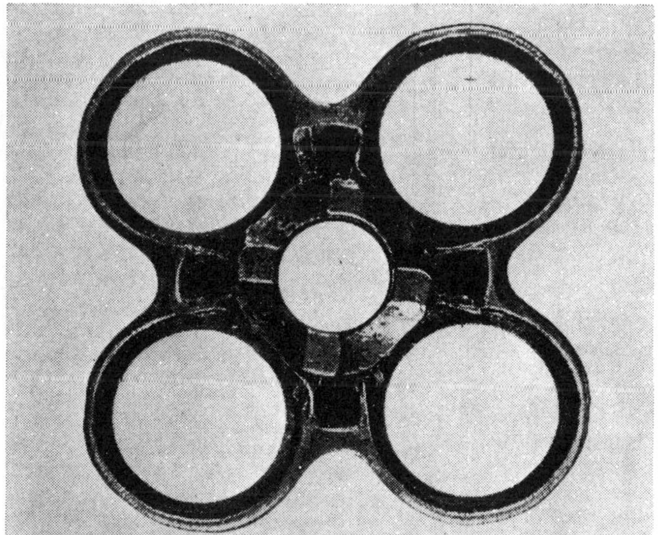

Colt House Pistol (Cloverleaf) cylinder, showing recessed chambers for cartridge heads. Such additional machining was costly and was consequently eliminated on the later 5-shot House Pistol. Note the 4 small rectangular slots on cylinder for the purpose of engaging firing pin as a safety feature.

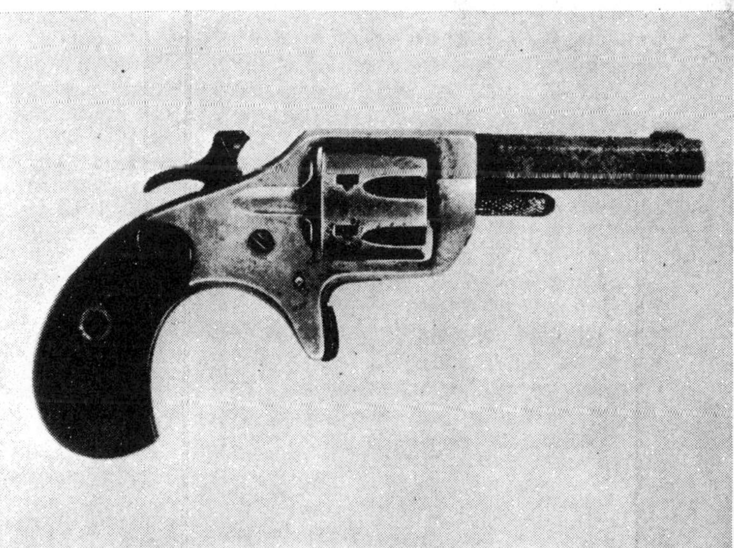

New Model cal. .22 7-shot pocket revolver. Bronze frame, sheath trigger, single action, no loading gate, pull pin ejector, introduction of long or short cylinder flutes, outside and rear cylinder locking notches (outside locking notches shown). Bird's head 2-piece walnut grips, 2¼" barrel. Barrel shape is round with flat sides. Markings will be found in 2 lines atop barrel, "Colt's Pt. F.A. Mfg. Co., Hartford, Ct. U.S.A." and "Colt New Line .22" etched on left side of barrel. Cal. 22 long or short. This was Colt's last bronze-frame model. ■

BY JOHN A. KOPEC

THE OPEN TOP .44 . . .

sire of Colt's Single Action, or was it?

Colt made Model 1872s and Richards-Mason conversions concurrently. The conversion, top, has a "two July" date, so does the 1872, center, but the 1872, bottom is marked as were percussion guns. Both the 1872s and the conversions were in .44 rimfire.

A comparison of conversion, top, and Model 1872, bottom, barrels shows their relationship. Conversion barrels are 8" long, 1872 barrels are 7½" with integral rear sight. Both use the ejector assembly for Richards-Mason guns.

THE Colt Model 1872, Open-Top, cal. .44 revolver is often called the forerunner of the Single Action. This is a misnomer. The 1872 revolver is better thought of as the last of Colt's line of percussion revolvers and cartridge-firing conversions. It is related to the Single Action only in that it was originally made to fire a self-contained metallic cartridge. All its other features are cap-and-ball.

Many collectors wonder why Colt waited until 1872 to enter the cartridge revolver market, and then with an obsolescent design chambered for an obsolescent cartridge. The Rollin White patent, after all, expired in 1869. The possible reasons are many, but for the most part they hinge on Colt's conservatism. Large caliber cartridge revolvers were largely untried in 1869, and there was no evidence that they would sell. Colt sales of percussion revolvers were still good in 1869 and 1870. Conversion, using the Richards and Richards-Mason patents, was cheaper and had the advantage of using existing tooling and parts. Colt was saving the Single Action for military contract sales.

While any or all of these reasons may have influenced Colt's decision to make a cartridge revolver, the choice of cartridge was less complex. Redesigning the Colt percussion revolver to use a rimfire cartridge was easier than using a center-fire cartridge. Then too, sales of the Henry and Winchester Model 1866 rifles, in cal. .44 rimfire provided Colt with a ready-made market.

Regardless of the reasoning, Colt limited the saleable life of the Model 1872 revolver to a very short span. Introduction, in 1873, of the vastly superior Single Action crippled U.S. sales. Most of the 7000 Model 1872s made were eventually sold in Mexico and Central America.

In studying the Model 1872, one must remember that conversion of percussion revolvers went on concurrently with production of the 1872 rimfire. Particularly where conversions of the 1860 Army revolver were concerned, the key to production changes revolved around the application of two patents.

Conversion of Model 1860 Army revolvers to cal. .44 rimfire began, probably in 1871, using the system of conversion patented on July 25, 1871, by C. B. Richards. Approximately 9000 Richards conversions of the 1860 Army were made before William Mason's modifications and improvements patented on July 2, 1872, began to be incorporated in the work. Richards conversions are, for the most part, stamped "Colts Patent," on the left side of the frame, well forward. Model 1872 revolvers, generally numbered below 1000, also carry the "Colt's Patent" marking. Some later Richards conversions, the Richards-Mason conversions, and Model 1872 revolvers generally above serial number 1000, are marked on the left side of the frame:

—PAT. JULY 25, 1871—
—PAT. JULY 2, 1872—

Returning to the theory that patent date markings hold the key to production, we find that the physical characteristics of Richards guns and Model 1872s marked "Colts Patent" are similar. Likewise Richards, Richards-Mason and Model 1872 revolvers bearing the two July dates are physically similar. Revolvers showing the old style "Colt's Patent" stampings are termed "pre-patent date" guns by today's collectors. Those showing the two July markings are known as "post-patent date" pieces.

The kinship of the Model 1872 revolver with concurrently produced conversions is further strengthened by the realization that most "conversions" are, in reality, *original metallic cartridge models*, having been manufactured expressly for use with a metallic cartridge. True, most were manufactured with existing left-over percussion parts, but as production progressed and these various parts were exhausted, newly manufactured and designed parts were substituted. The substitutions were especially adapted for use in these metallic cartridge revolvers.

It is at this juncture that we see the direct descendant relationship between the Richards and Richards-Mason Army conversions and the Model 1872 Open-Top revolver. The similarity of the newly manufactured barrels of these two models cannot be denied. Though the conversion barrel remains at the 8" length, it differs only slightly in configuration from that of the Model 1872. The main difference is the presence of the rear sight milled into the barrel of the Model 1872.

The pre-patent date relationship of

Continued

The Model 1872 cylinder, top, is special and will not interchange with the rebated Richards-Mason cylinder below. A collar on the 1872 cylinder takes up the space at the front of the gun's frame.

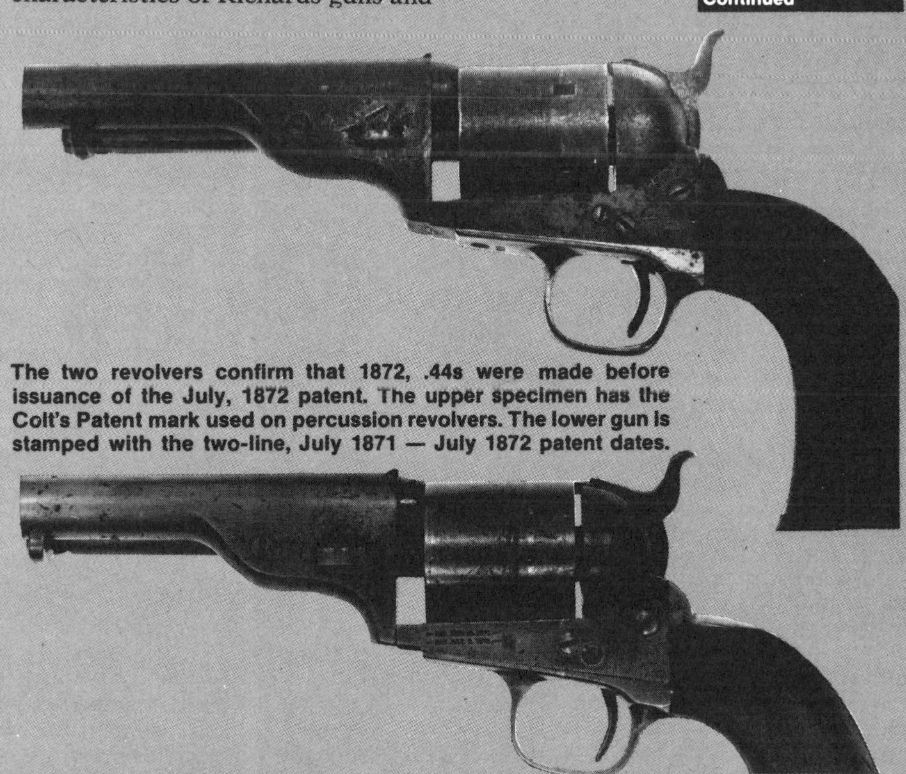

The two revolvers confirm that 1872, .44s were made before issuance of the July, 1872 patent. The upper specimen has the Colt's Patent mark used on percussion revolvers. The lower gun is stamped with the two-line, July 1871 — July 1872 patent dates.

Open Top .44

Continued from page 87

these models also is shown clearly by the employment of the loading gate spring catch on those early production examples which exhibit the "Colt's Patent" marking. This particular innovation was covered in the earlier July 25, 1871, patent of C. B. Richards. Later, after the Mason patent was granted and the patent dates stamped, we find that the internal gate locking mechanism was abandoned for the much simpler externally fastened loading gate spring used in Richards-Mason conversions. Although only a very few early examples show this internal gatespring arrangement, the fact that it was employed in some early Model 1872s helps strengthen the theory that these early examples were manufactured before the granting of the July 2, 1872, patent.

It is therefore significant to realize that an early example Model 1872 revolver which displays the old percussion era "Colt's Patent" stamping was actually manufactured before a Richards or Richards-Mason Army conversion which sports the two July dates. Yet today these conversions are generally considered to be the predecessors of the Model 1872.

Several distinct characteristics serve to distinguish the Model 1872 from its conversion counterparts. It was manufactured with a completely redesigned frame which eliminated the need for a rebated cylinder and its corresponding stepped down frame. The Model 1872 barrel, as mentioned before, was especially manufactured for this revolver, having an elongated cone section and an integral rear sight. It is also noteworthy that, although the Model 1872 had a newly designed frame which eliminated the need for the attached recoil plate of the conversions, this frame was made exactly the same length as that of the 1860 Army revolver and its conversion counterparts. This frame, longer than necessary, created a gap between the cylinder and the barrel nearly .074" greater than on the Richards-Mason conversion. The gap was compensated for by a longer barrel cone and a specially designed cylinder with a coller bushing extending forward. It may have worked well but the bushing and long cone detracted considerably from the esthetic beauty of the old percussion Model 1860 Army revolver.

The Mason patent ejector assembly used on Model 1872 revolvers, was an exact duplicate of those then being employed on the Navy and Richards-Mason Army conversions. The internal lock mechanism remained basically the same, as well as the grip fastenings to the frame. It is, however, in the grip straps proper that we find the most variance.

Earliest examples of the Model 1872 revolver are fitted with "Navy size" grip straps. These grip straps were most probably vestiges of the Model 1851 and Model 1861 Navy production. Some were made of iron, but the majority were made of brass. There are indications that the Navy-size grip was discontinued about the same time that the marking of two July dates began to be used. Beginning at, or just before, serial number 1000, Model 1872 revolvers were fitted with the longer, Army-size grip frames. These grips were possibly surplus from Model 1860 Army revolver production, as the trigger guard was of brass and the back strap was made of iron. This comb. nation of iron and brass straps has been observed into the 1600 serial number range. Thereafter, until production ended, the all-iron Army-size grips became standard, and, hence, the most common type encountered.

Few remaining revolvers show signs of anything other than hard usage. Those which come from Mexico are usually well worn. Many have had their barrels shortened, and some have even been altered to fire center-fire cartridges. Although most such alterations are very crude, an example of an expertly converted revolver which fires the .44-40 W.C.F. cartridge was recently observed.

Finish applied to the Model 1872 revolvers varied. Most were blued. Some were nickel plated. A very few have been observed which are engraved or fitted with original ivory grips.

Although some authorities choose to call this revolver the "Open-Top Frontier," the term "Frontier" was not applied to Colt revolvers until the introduction of the "Colt Frontier Six Shooter," a cal. .44-40 variant of the Single Action Army revolver, in 1877. Therefore, the term "Frontier" is better suited to handguns which are chambered for the .44-40 cartridge.

Basically, the Model 1872 rimfire revolver was a last ditch attempt by Colt to keep the old traditional Army-style revolver alive. But times were changing. New designs were being adopted by competitors, and the increased firepower that was needed of the metallic cartridge handguns demanded a revolver of solid frame construction. Though short on the production end, the Model 1872 revolver became the final link in a long successful chain of Colt percussion revolvers that began as the dream of a young seaman who carved his first wooden detachable-barreled revolver early in the 1830s. ■

Colt's .380 "Hammerless," this one of U.S. Government issue, was responsible for the CAPH headstamps by Rem.-UMC and Peters.

I have what I believe to be a standard .380 semi-automatic pistol round made by Peters. It is mysterious only because it is headstamped 380 CAPH. I assume CAP is only an anagram of the familiar A.C.P. (Automatic Colt Pistol) but what does the H represent?

Answer: The initials stand for Colt Automatic Pistol Hammerless and at one time were used by more than one manufacturer in the headstamping. The NRA's admittedly small reference collection contains one so-marked .380 by Peters and one by Remington-UMC.

The marking indicated that the cartridges were suitable for use in the once-popular Colt pistol introduced in .380 cal. in 1909. Although Colt called the pistol the "Colt Automatic Calibre .380 Hammerless," it was actually of the concealed-hammer type.

It is possible that .25 A.C.P. and/or .32 A.C.P. cartridges were also marked with the CAPH headstamp, but we have none in our collection.—P.D.

Stagecoach holdup scene on large-frame cal. .36 Colt Paterson revolvers.

First scene used by Colt on small belt and pocket Paterson revolvers. Note reverse horse head design. Few specimens with this scene still visible have survived.

Ormsby-designed scene bearing his name on Colt 1847 Walker Model and 1848 Dragoon Models 1, 2, and 3, shows mounted dragoons subduing Indians. Some believe this to be a tribute to Col. William Selby Harney for his victorious pursuit of the Seminole Indians. This has never been verified, however.

Ormsby scene on Colt 1848 Baby Dragoon cal. .31 pocket revolvers. This is another version of dragoons chasing Indians.

The stagecoach holdup scene is probably the most common and most familiar engraving to arms enthusiasts. This one is on Colt cal. .31 Pocket Models of 1848, 1849, 1850, and 1853, cal. .36 Pocket Model, and cal. .38 cartridge conversion revolvers. It is interesting to compare this scene with the holdup scene on Manhattan revolvers.

Cabin scene on Colt Root sidehammer Model 1855 cal. .28 and cal. .31 revolvers shows how well a chap might defend himself with 2 pistols, presumably Colts, against unusual odds of 6 to 1.

The Art Of Cylinder Engraving

Scenes on antique revolvers were roll-engraved

By E. DIXON LARSON

CYLINDER scenes on Colt and various other antique revolvers were roll-engraved by rotating a hardened steel die against the cylinder. Since these engravings were not very deep, they would often become partially obliterated from wear. This has resulted in many collectors requesting details of partial or faint cylinder scenes.

The sketches shown are cylinder scenes on the more popular percussion and cartridge conversion revolvers. These scenes were chiefly the work of W. L. Ormsby, a prominent New York banknote engraver of the mid 1800's. Some early Dragoon and Navy Colts as well as Metropolitan Navy Model revolvers are marked "W. L. Ormsby Sc. N.Y." The Sc. stands for Sculpsit, meaning he carved or engraved it.

Designed scenes for many arms

It is not positively known how many Colt scenes Ormsby designed. Evidence indicates that he designed scenes for Colt Walkers, Dragoons, Navy Pocket Models, Army Models, and Metropolitan Navy Models. It is not known who designed the Manhattan Navy Model cylinder scenes, which are the most intricate and delicate of all. The 5 scenes on the Manhattan are rated by students of engraved scenes as the most outstanding designed by engravers of that period.

The first Colt revolver with a cylinder scene was the earliest model, the Paterson. Sam Colt had a fertile imagination and an eye for promotion. In some instances, a scene served for advertising as well as decoration. For example, the scene on the 1855 Root Model shows a man using 2 revolvers to protect his home, wife, and child.

An original cylinder scene in good condition greatly enhances the value of an antique revolver.

Colt Deringer Variations

By HARRY C. KNODE

COLT'S Patent Fire Arms Manufacturing Co. entered the deringer field by purchasing the National Arms Co. of Brooklyn, N. Y. about 1872.

As made by Colt's, the National Deringer was offered with both metal and wood stocks in cal. .41 rimfire only.

About the time Colt's acquired the National Arms Co., Colt employee F. Alexander Thuer patented a small cal. .41 rimfire, single-shot, side-swinging-barrel pistol with an automatic ejector. The Thuer pistol was available with silver-plated frame and blued barrel, or with both barrel and frame silver-plated. Stocks were made in a choice of walnut, rosewood, ivory, or pearl.

Present collectors designate the Colt-National metal-grip and wood-grip pistols as the First Model and Second Model respectively, and the Thuer-designed pistol as the Third Model.

There are interesting variations in the 3 models of the Colt Deringers (Colt used this spelling, not Derringer), as shown in the illustrations.

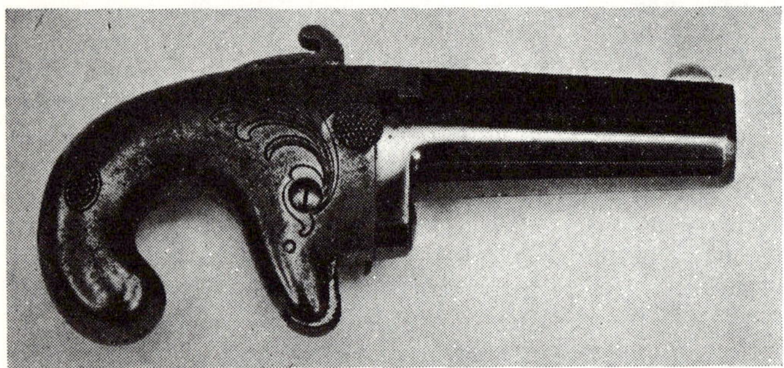

1 Colt Deringer, First Model, is of all-iron construction. There seem to be no major variations of this model, but only slight changes in the checkering in the ovals on the back and sides of the grips. The writer does have in his collection a normal First Model, serial #2290, which is stamped #2. This is believed to be apparently only an error in stamping. The serial numbers on both the barrel and grip evidently were stamped with the same die

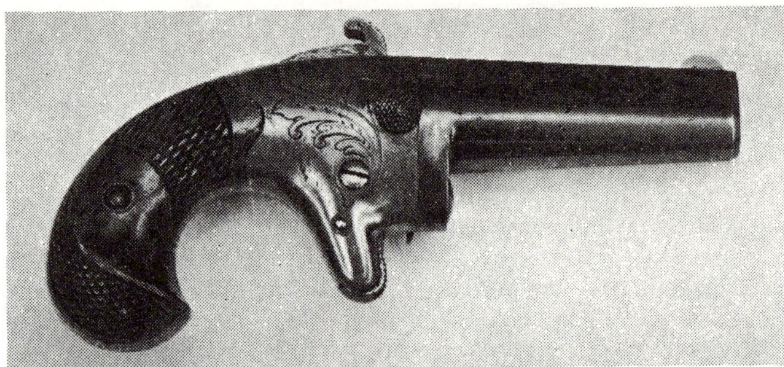

2 Colt Deringer, Second Model, is found in a few variations. Normally this model has the iron frame and barrel. In the Raymond J. Walsh collection, Hamilton, Ohio, is a #2 Deringer, serial #1515, with a brass or bronze frame and an iron barrel. Another interesting variation of the Second Model is #3642, both the frame and the barrel of which are made of German silver or similar alloy. The grips are walnut and all other features of the pistol follow the standard model. The left side of the barrel is stamped with a small circle with a dot inside and "AM. STERLING"

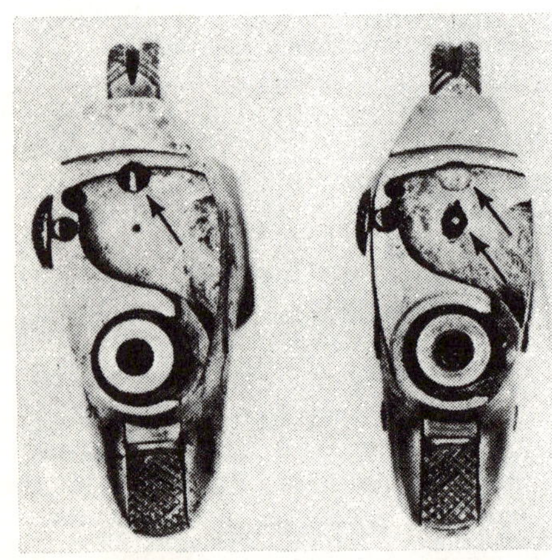

3 A variation in the Second Model, found only in English proofed pistols, is the center-fire pistol. It is my belief that the conversion to center-fire was made at the Colt factory. The recoil plate for the center-fire pistol (r.) was an alteration of the rimfire version (l.) In addition to the original hole for the rimfire firing pin at the top of the recoil shield, there is a hole in the center. John E. Parsons in his book *Henry Deringer's Pocket Pistol,* in commenting on a center-fire Second Model Colt Deringer, states that the specimen had a bushing around the firing pin hole. Specimens examined by the writer did not have a bushing

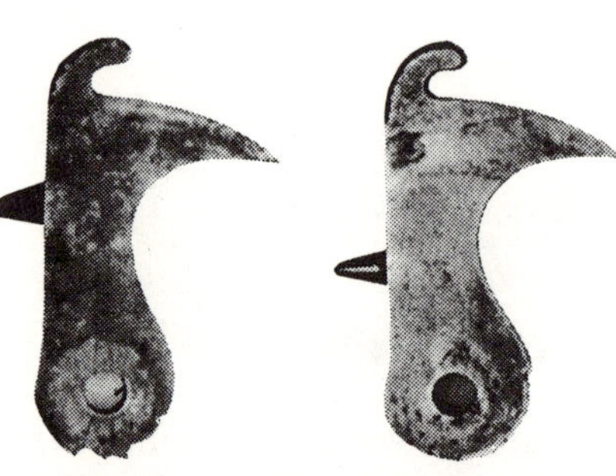

4 The most interesting feature of these center-fire deringers is the hammer. To make a center-fire hammer (r.), a regular rimfire hammer (l.) apparently was used. On the center-fire hammer, the firing pin which was integral with the rimfire hammer has been ground off and a round slug pinned on in the same manner as the firing pin of a Colt Single Action revolver. The pin apparently was machined to final shape, for rings made by the cutting tool are usually visible. On one specimen the cutting tool left spiral marks on the face of the hammer circling the base of the pin. Of the center-fire pistols with British proof marks, 5 are known presently to the writer: #7771, #8310, #8930, and # 8971 and #9014. The last 2 are a cased pair. These serial numbers tend to refute the thought that only a thousand of the pistols were made

5 The barrel signing on the Second Model Deringers is of 2 major types. The early pistols (top) carry a Maltese cross at the beginning of the signing and between the company name and the numeral 2. The later pistols carried "COLT'S PT.F.A. MFG. CO. HARTFORD CT. U.S.A. No. 2", in 2 lines with a Maltese cross before the company name and address and after the numeral 2. A specimen bearing the serial #28 has the signing as described for the early pistols except that between the Maltese cross and the numeral 2 is a small, plain cross (+)

6 The Third Models of the Colt Deringer fall into 2 major groups. The early version (top) has a reinforcing boss on the bottom of the frame where the swivel screw joins the frame and the barrel. The frame under the barrel on the later pistol (below) is much thicker due to the elimination of the boss. The hammer on the Third Model was of 2 types: The early hammer (top) was made with an upright spur and the later hammer (below) with a slanting spur

7 The early Third Model has in the grip frame a rectangular lug (top) through which the grip screw passes. Later pistols have a circular lug (below). Also, the early Third Model has a rather short, stubby bird's-head grip, and the later pistols had a longer, less curved grip. The sharper curve of the grip frame of the early version is clearly evident. My research would tend to indicate the more curved grip was used until about serial #12500. The change in the grip frame seems to have been made about the time of the hammer spur change

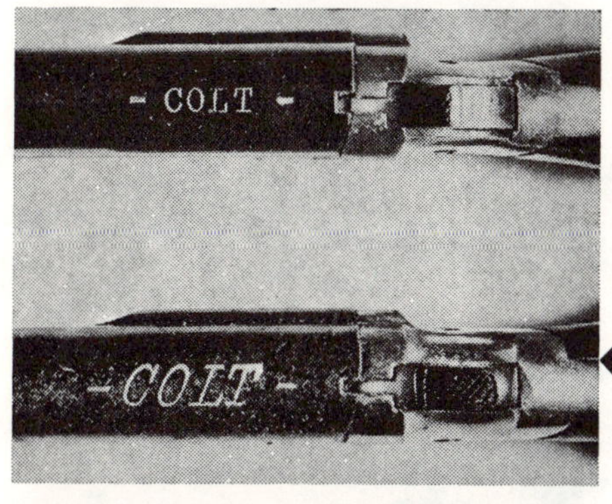

8 The barrel signing on the early Third Model was the word "COLT" in vertical letters about ⅛" high (top). Later Thuers had "COLT" in slanting letters about 3/16" high. The larger signing was continued in use for as long as Colt Deringers were produced

9 Some pistols sold in England carried the agent's name on the side of the barrels. Others carried "COLT'S FIRE ARMS CO. 14 PALL MALL LONDON" in 2 lines on the left side (l.) of the barrel. Still others had "C" and the Colt Rampant (r.) on the left side of the frame or the Colt Rampant and "14 PALL MALL" on the right

10 In the Third Model there are also a few center-fire specimens, all British proofed. In this model the alteration was made by merely slotting the recoil shield deeper (l.) and changing the hammer to strike the center of the cartridge. This hammer change was done in 2 ways, either by brazing on additional metal to the firing pin to lower the point of impact or by making a new hammer. I have 3 center-fire specimens, 2 with evident brazing ■

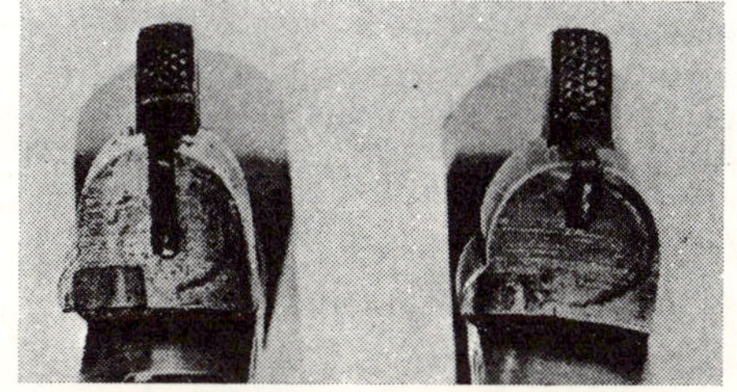

Colt .25 ACP Pistols

How many different .25 ACP pistols were made by Colt? What years were they made, and when was each type discontinued?

Colt Model 1908 .25 ACP pistol was a Browning design made from 1908 to 1941.

The Junior Colt was made by Astra and imported for Colt in both .22 and .25 cal.

Answer: There have been three models of Colt .25 ACP pistols.

The original Model 1908 (a striker-fired design) was made from 1908 until World War II, when military production took precedence. A total of 409,061 Model 1908's were made.

In 1957 the "Junior Colt" was introduced with exposed hammer. It was offered not only in .25 ACP, but also in .22 Short rimfire, and was made in Spain for Colt by Astra-Unceta y Compania, S.A. Except for markings and grips (black plastic for the Colts and white or brown plastic for most of the Astras) these Junior Colts were identical to the Astra Cub pistols which were imported concurrently. For a time, conversion units—.25 to .22 Short and vice-versa—were also sold by Colt. A total of about 67,000 Junior Colts were sold before their importation was halted by the Gun Control Act in December, 1968.

The third model Colt, in .25 ACP only, was produced between 1970 and 1973. It was made for Colt, using Astra components married to a domestically investment cast frame. It differed from the second model in markings and in the use of checkered walnut grips with Colt medallion. A total of 120,480 of the third model were produced. P.D.

THE DILEMMA OF COLT'S SINGLE ACTION

New light shed on the old problem of production variations versus serial numbers.

BY E. DIXON LARSON

THE Colt Single Action Army Revolver has long been a favorite with collectors. From 1873 until 1940 Single Actions were produced in abundant quantity, many calibers, and several important production models. Because all major parts of the Single Action are interchangeable, regardless of when they were made, specific identification can often be difficult. There is nothing more disappointing than to discover that a Single Action recently added to one's collection is in reality a spurious model.

Thus, this handy guide has been assembled for collectors of Colt Single Action revolvers. It must be remembered that there are exceptions to every rule. Reasonable overlapping of modifications to the models and strays held in inventory, make it difficult to identify a variation as having occurred during a precise span of time or within a serial number range. Many noted authorities have published volumes of information on Single Action production. Each volume seems to conflict with others chiefly with respect to changes in production. Unfortunately, some writers' conclusions were drawn from conjecture or opinion and were not necessarily predicated on matters of record. In many cases older information has been superseded by newer research. All of this is very frustrating to collectors.

Those who would travel the Colt Single Action trail must remember that there will always be new information brought to light and that most established rules have numerous exceptions. With that in mind, let's get down to specifics.

Date: Serial No.	Variation	Comments
1873/74: 1-15000	Pinched frame top.	In first 200 guns only.
	Italic barrel markings.	
	Two-line patent date.	Jul. 25, 1871/Jul. 2, 1872 on guns through about no. 25. Sept. 19, 1871/Jul. 2, 1872 thereafter.[1]
	Round ejector head.	
	Cylinder and barrel are serially numbered.	
	One piece wooden grips.	
1875: 15001-22000	Cal. .44 Rimfire introduced.	Rimfires in separate serial number range from 1-1892. Manufactured 1875-1880.
	4¾" and 5½" barrel lengths introduced.	
	Cal. .450 Boxer introduced.	
1876: 22001-33000	"Buntline Specials" made.	Serial Nos. - 28800-28830.[2]
	Cal. .476 Eley introduced.	
	Script barrel marking dropped.	About Serial No. 24000.
1877: 33001-41000	Three line patent date	Sept. 71/Jul. 72/Jan. 75 — begins about serial no. 34000.[1]
	Nickel finish available.	
1878: 41001-49000	Quantity production of cal. .44-40 "COLT FRONTIER SIX SHOOTER" began.	Cal. .44-40 revolvers have been observed in 21000 Serial No. range but appear to be refitted guns, not regular production models.
1879: 49001-53000		
1880: 53001-62000		
1881: 62001-73000	Etched "COLT FRONTIER SIX SHOOTER" marking changed to roll die.	Etched marks appear as late as Serial No. 125000-1887.
1882: 73001-85000	Sheriffs' or Storekeepers' Model: short barrel, no ejector introduced.	Serial No. 77370. Non-ejector models available in a variety of special-order barrel lengths.
	Round ejector head discontinued.	
	Eagle-motif, 2-piece hard rubber grips for non-military guns.	
1883: 85001-102000	Cal. .22 Rimfire introduced — Serial No. 95703.	Some .22 Rimfire Single Actions converted from .44 Rimfire revolvers. Serial Nos. range 1640 to 1890 — done about 1888.
1884: 102001-114000	Cals. 32-20 & .38-40 introduced.	
1885: 114001-117000	Cal. .41 Colt introduced.	
1886: 117001-118000	Cal. .38 Colt introduced.	
1887: 118001-125000	Cals. .32 Colt & .32 S&W introduced.	
1888: 125001-128000		
1889: 128001-130000		
1890: 130001-136000	Cals. .44 S&W, .380 Eley, .450 Eley, .44 Smoothbore introduced. Caliber markings stamped on barrels.	
	Change to two-line, three patent date on frame.[1]	
1891: 136001-144000	Cal. .38-44 S&W Gallery, introduced.	
	Last U.S. Cavalry order filled.	Serial No. 140361.[3]
1892: 144001-149000	Transverse cylinder pin introduced.	So-called "Smokeless powder feature".
1893: 149001-154000		
1894: 154001-159000	Bisley Model introduced.	Bisley Model cataloged from 1894 to 1912. Last Bisley shipped (No. 330184) in Nov. 1919.[4]

Sam Colt

Date: Serial No.	Variation	Comments
1895: 159001-163000		
1896: 163001-168000	Change in steel for frame and cylinder.	Another "Smokeless Powder feature".
	Eagle Motif in grips discontinued.	
1897: 168001-175000		
1898: 175001-182000	Smokeless powder advertised "standard" after Serial No. 180000.	Last Single Action production now classed as "Antique".
1899: 182001-192000		
1900: 192001-203000		
1901: 203001-220000	Factory proof-mark introduced. Front sight enlarged.	stamped on left front of trigger guard.
1902: 220001-238000	1906: 273001-288000	1910: 312001-316000
1903: 238001-250000	1907: 288001-304000	1911: 316001-321000
1904: 250001-261000	1908: 304001-308000	1912: 321001-325000
1905: 261001-273000	1909: 308001-312000	
1913: 325001-328000	Front sight enlarged.	
1914: 328001-329500		
1915: 329501-332000	Long-flute (M1878, D.A.) cylinders installed in some Single Action revolvers.	Serial No. range 33000 to 332480: incl. 2 Bisley models and 1 Sheriffs' model.
1916: 332001-335000	1925: 347301-348200	1934: 355001-355200
1917: 335001-337000	1926: 348201-349800	1935: 355201-355300
1918: 337001-337200	1927: 349801-351300	1936: 355301-355400
1919: 337201-338000	1928: 351301-352400	1937: 355401-356100
1920: 338001-341000	1929: 352401-353800	1938: 356101-356600
1921: 341001-343000	1930: 353801-354100	1939: 356601-357000
1922: 343001-344500	1931: 354101-354500	1940: 357001-357859[5,6]
1923: 344501-346500	1932: 354501-354800	
1924: 346501-347300	1933: 354801-355000	

Notes:

1. Patent date stampings on left side of frame are as follows:

1-25:	—PAT. JULY 25, 1871- —PAT. JULY 2, 1872-	34000-135000:	PAT. SEPT. 19, 1871 PAT. JULY 2, 1872 PAT. JAN. 19, 1875
26-34000:	PAT. SEPT. 19, 1871 PAT. JULY 2, 1872	135000-End:	PAT. SEPT. 19, 1871 JULY 2, 72, JAN. 19, 75

2. True "Buntline Specials" occur only in the Serial No. range 28800 to 28830. Buntlines have the flat top frame. Long Barreled standard frame revolvers were available on special order.

3. Government contract overruns refitted for civilian sale will be found in the 3000-100000 Serial No. range. They bear one or more government inspectors marks but no "U.S." stamp. All of these refitted revolvers *have* pins for 2-piece grips. Most are .44-40 cal., with 4¾" barrels.

4. Total production of Bisley Models (1894-1919) is 44,350 pieces. Total production of Flat Top Target Models is approximately 925.

5. Identification of Serial No. 357859 as last Colt Single Action made prior to World War II is from John E. Parsons' book; *The Peacemaker and its Rivals* which lists that number as the highest recorded in a pre-war shipment.

6. Approximately 300 Single Action Army revolvers were assembled from pre-war parts between 1941 and the early 1950's. Serial Numbers range from 356000 to a factory high listing of 357869. Another 75 pre-war frames were used by Colt's to refit customers' guns sent for repair.

Theodore B. Pitman

Information on one of the rarest Colt revolvers

"Buntline Special" Colt

By John S. du Mont

Possibly one of the rarest Colts from a collector's standpoint is the so-called "Buntline Special", which has a history that is fully as colorful as the gun itself.

Some of the history

Evidently Colt gave these long-barreled revolvers no particular name other than "Colt's pistol with carbine barrel and attachable stock", and collectors eventually hit upon the "Buntline Special" synonym which grew from Stuart N. Lake's fine biography, *Wyatt Earp, Frontier Marshal*.

Herein, Lake gives the account of "Ned Buntline" (Edward Z. C. Judson) presenting five of these guns to famous Western frontier marshals: Wyatt Earp, Neal Brown, Charley Bassett, Bat Masterson, and Bill Tilghman at Dodge City, Kansas, about 1876.

This is correct, insofar as it goes, but we can perhaps elaborate on this fact, and make the background a little clearer.

The year 1876 was the Centennial of American Independence, and a great exposition took place in Philadelphia as a form of celebration.

"Ned Buntline", the famous pulp writer probably best noted for his 'promotion' of "Buffalo Bill" Cody, was a visitor in Philadelphia at the time, to write up the exposition for the *New York Weekly*.

Colt arms exhibited

Displayed there were the most modern products of the time, heralding America's inventive and industrial genius. Not the least of these was a display by the Colt Patent Firearms Manufacturing Company, which included the new long-barreled pistols, first produced that year.

While Ned Buntline would like to have us believe that he was the originator of these guns, it is apparent that his first sight of them was at the Colt exhibit.

It is well to bear in mind that Buntline was not always a believer in the strict factual truth where a good story was concerned!

Technical aspects of his purchase will be discussed later, but there is no denying Buntline purchased the guns at an approximate cost of $26 each, and made the presentations where they would do the most good—for Ned.

There is absolute documented evidence of the use of one of these pistols by Wyatt Earp, and that he liked it, which was not the case with the majority of the other recipients.

Wyatt Earp told Stuart Lake that he could draw this gun just as fast as the standard shorter-barreled variety, and history confirms that this was true. Of further interest might be his statement "that the winner of a gunplay was usually the man who took his time".

Tough town of Tombstone

The "Buntline Special" soon became as famous as its owner and the hell-roaring town of Tombstone—the town 'too tough to die'.

Earp found the long barrel extremely handy in 'buffaloing' or 'pistol whipping' unruly characters in Tombstone, and there are verified accounts of this.

However, its most colorful use, also well documented, was in the O.K. Corral fight at Tombstone, indisputably one of the most famous gunfights in Western history, a history which certainly had its share of these fracases.

This 30-second encounter, which saw 17 shots fired by each side, is too well known to bear repetition here.

To my mind, there is no more stirring sight imaginable than the three Earps and "Doc" Holliday walking down Fremont Street to encounter the McLowrys and Clantons plus Billy "The Kid" Claiborne, in shoot-to-kill conflict—the title cut illustrates this.

Holliday's short shotgun

An interesting sidelight to this affair is the recent discovery of material covering the design of "Doc" Holliday's famous shotgun, which was made for him in England.

This shotgun had short sawed-off barrels, pistol-grip stock, and a swivel suspension eye for a neck cord—as illustrated. A slit was cut in Holliday's pocket whereby he could handle the gun without drawing attention to it.

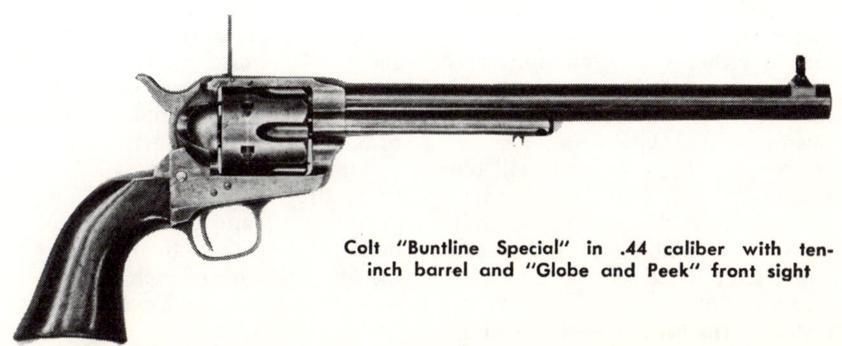

Colt "Buntline Special" in .44 caliber with ten-inch barrel and "Globe and Peek" front sight

Letters have turned up indicating that he not only designed this shotgun himself, to wear under the same overcoat he wore on the day of the O.K. Corral fight, but that he had the audacity to describe the effectiveness of the two loads of ten-gauge buckshot on his human targets.

Contrary to popular assumption, the shotgun was extensively used in Western combat, and there could have hardly been a more effective weapon in close quarters.

Well-armed referee

Wyatt Earp's "Buntline Special" continued to be his pet side arm right through his lifetime. He even wore it while refereeing the Sharkey-Fitzsimmons boxing match in San Francisco, December 2, 1896, and was fined $50 for doing so!

This famous gun (collectors please note!) met its demise when it was loaned to Wyatt by a friend carrying the U. S. mail, while in Nome, Alaska.

The mail-carrier, reaching a precarious situation requiring the immediate lightening of his small whaleboat, threw the gun overboard together with other impedimenta, and thus the "Buntline" now lies at the cold, wet bottom of the Pacific Ocean!

On the technical side

The "Buntline Special" occupied a decidedly unique position in Colt factory production. It is unlikely that Colt ever had a shorter run on any gun that was advertised as a standard item.

Factory records, by serial number, indicate that there were but 30 of these special long-barrel guns produced, and a check of the numbers on either side of this original lot, plus a check of ensuing years, confirms this.

Unlike the standard model "P", the "flat top" target models, or the few later special-order long-barrel guns, these "Buntline Specials" had a special frame with an inletted groove in the top to accommodate a folding-leaf adjustable rear sight. No other single-action Colt had a frame just like it.

Both inletted frame and folding-leaf rear sight bore a separate number, not related to either the serial number or the loading gate and frame number. The top of the frame in front of the sight was also provided with a gas port.

Finish was a high 'commercial' blue, with hammer and frame casehardened in colors, varnished walnut grips, and a variety of adjustable front sights—some of which Colt listed as the 'Globe and Peek' type.

A stock attachment screw having a large end with screw slot on one side and a small end on the other was fitted to the gun in place of the hammer screw. The hook-on portion of the stock was adapted to this peculiar screw and tightened by means of a knurled nut at the base of the butt. No groove was placed in the butt as in earlier stocked models.

Colt's records show that only 16-inch and ten-inch barrel lengths were shipped, and it is my considered opinion that only the 16-inch length was produced on the 30 guns.

Data on shipping

That these pistols were not selling 'like hot cakes' is confirmed by the shipping records.

The guns were produced in 1876, and the first shipment of four went forward on December 1, 1877. The last recorded shipment was for one gun, shipped on May 13, 1884, indicating eight years had passed since these 30 revolvers were manufactured—and there was the possibility that the factory had still not disposed of all of them.

Of the 14 revolvers shipped in this period of eight years, three are recorded as having ten-inch barrels, and the balance 16-inch. All but two were made in .45 caliber.

B. Kittredge & Company of Cincinnati, Colt's Western agent, was the largest buyer of the "Buntline Special".

The ten-inch guns were sent out on individual shipments. The first was shipped May 20, 1878, and one was made up in .44 center-fire caliber, indicating that this pistol was necessarily re-barreled and also had a new cylinder, for the ".45 cal." mark on the side of the trigger guard has been re-stamped ".44 CF" which shipping records confirm. This gun is illustrated.

Thus it would seem likely that because the "Buntline Special" was not a good seller, and because there was a definite objection to the length, the factory cut the 16-inch barrels to ten inches on order, and even changed the caliber in two cases.

The fact that three of the "Buntlines" presented by Ned were said to have been immediately cut down from the "foot" length, indicates a very positive aversion in those days to the long barrel.

Bat Masterson, one of the recipients of Buntline's gift, ordered a number of single-action guns from Colt for his own use. Of the five guns he ordered, at different times, only one had a 7½-inch barrel, and the balance of these had the 4¾-inch length, indicating a very definite preference for the short-barrel models—by a man who really used them!

To return to Ned Buntline and his five presentation pieces, there is no factory record of this shipment, indicating they were house sales or sales made directly from their display in Philadelphia.

There is no shipping record covering the one "Buntline Special" exhibited in the Colt factory museum today.

Others may have been given to Colt agents for display purposes.

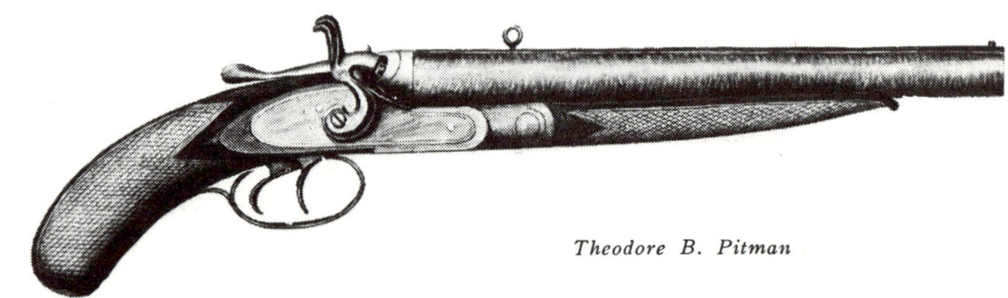
Theodore B. Pitman

"Doc" Holliday's sawed-off shotgun

In relating his life story to Lake, Wyatt Earp noted the barrel of his special Colt's single action revolver was a 'foot long'. He also stated that it was furnished with a 'walnut shoulder stock'.

Neither of these statements jibes with factory shipping records, as there is no verified record of a 12-inch barrel length being manufactured, and all shoulder stocks furnished were of the skeleton type, made of cast bronze with nickel-plated finish.

However, I still feel that Earp's statements were true.

Colt agents did special work

It is quite possible that Buntline had these guns altered, and special stocks made for them by such a dealer in Colts as Joseph Grubb & Company of Philadelphia, who was doing special work on Colts as early as 1850.

It is not generally known by collectors that Schuyler, Hartley & Graham, B. Kittredge & Company, and other Colt agents often did special work on factory guns for their customers.

Continued on page 98

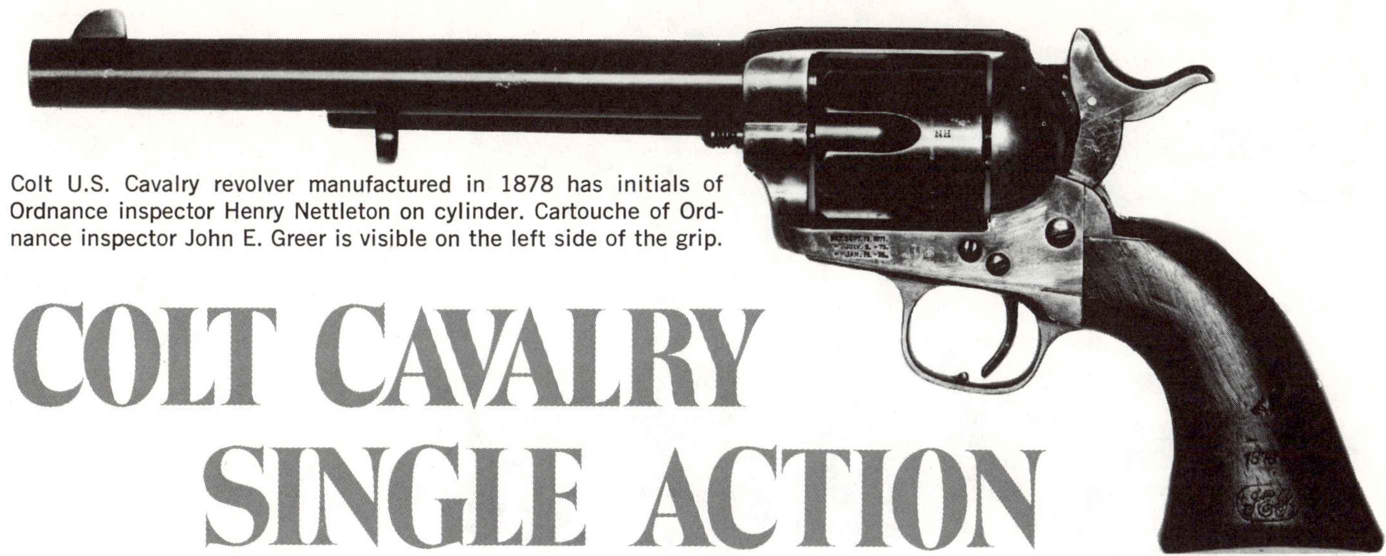

Colt U.S. Cavalry revolver manufactured in 1878 has initials of Ordnance inspector Henry Nettleton on cylinder. Cartouche of Ordnance inspector John E. Greer is visible on the left side of the grip.

COLT CAVALRY SINGLE ACTION

By JOHN A. KOPEC*

THE much-imitated 1873 Colt Single Action Army revolver probably has far more descendants today, made by at least a half-dozen manufacturers, than there are legitimate surviving specimens. Of the 37,060 U.S. Cavalry revolvers in cal. .45 with 7½" barrels produced between 1873 and 1891, it has been estimated that fewer than 10% survive. Colt collectors are constantly confronted with questions of how to verify and date these. This article on the subject is based on information on some 1200 existing specimens, and documents in the National Archives.

The original Government contract was signed on July 23, 1873, for 8,000 revolvers. This contract was later extended, and a total of 18,060 Cavalry revolvers was produced under its authority. The earliest type was manufactured through 1875 and reached the 19500 serial number range.

"Army Revolvers and Gatling Guns", published at the National Armory (Springfield) in 1875, described the method of Ordnance inspection of the various component parts of this revolver and instructed inspectors to stamp certain parts with their single initial upon acceptance. This procedure was used by four Ordnance sub-inspectors.

U.S. revolvers manufactured during 1873 and 1874 were all inspected by principal sub-inspector O. W. Ainsworth who applied his tiny letter "A" in five places on each revolver. Colt's production for the first year (1873) ran through serial number 3500 and included some 500 commercial Colt Single Actions or "Peacemakers". During 1875 three civilian principal sub-inspectors carried out this responsibility at the Colt factory. They were: A. P. Casey (C), Samuel B. Lewis (L), and an unidentified Ordnance sub-inspector who affixed his tiny initial (J) onto these same component parts. These inspector's initials on these earliest revolvers appear under the barrel near the cylinder pin head, on the periphery of the cylinder, on the backstrap behind the hammer, on the trigger guard under the serial number, and on the right hand side of the buttstock.

Early production had no Ordnance inspector's letter on the frame. Except for the first 1000, the "U.S." was stamped on these frames by Colt's before the metal was hardened. The Ordnance sub-inspector's initials were stamped in a cartouche on the lower left side of the grip. No cartouche was applied to the right side of the grip on the revolvers made through 1875.

Several distinguishing physical characteristics are found on these early specimens so admired by collectors today. First and most notable is the "script" barrel address which was used exclusively on all U.S. Cavalry revolvers through serial No. 19500. Other characteristics of these early revolvers include the "bullseye" ejector rod head, the tiny cylinder stops, the two-line early patent date stamping, and the early style ejector housing.

Beginning in 1876, a new inspection procedure for revolvers produced at the Colt factory was initiated by the Ordnance Department. This new procedure was outlined in the book "Fabrication of Small Arms", which was also designated as "Ordnance Memoranda No. 22.", and was initiated by John T. Cleveland, principal sub-inspector and Lt. David A. Lyle, Ordnance inspector. All U.S. Cavalry revolvers manufactured during 1876 and 1877 bore the cartouches of these two men on the grips.

The new inspection procedure changed most of the markings. Besides the barrels and cylinders, the frames now bore the Ordnance sub-inspector's initials in full. Trigger guards and backstraps were no longer stamped with the inspector's initial. The letters "U.S." were stamped onto the casehardened frames at final inspection. The year of manufacture was marked above the cartouche of the Ordnance inspector on the left side of the grip. There were 2,003 of these revolvers made during 1876 and 1877, with serial numbers ranging from 30693 through 35570.

Three thousand U.S. Cavalry revolvers were inspected from August through September of 1878 by Ordnance inspector Henry Nettleton, employing a combination of the two basic procedures. Nettleton not only stamped the trigger guards and backstraps during this era, reminiscent of the old inspection procedures used from 1873 through 1875, he also stamped the hammers with his "H.N." initials.

During a very short period at the outset of this series' production, we find that a temporary substitute Ordnance sub-inspector was assigned to work at the Colt plant while Henry Nettleton was ill. This Ordnance sub-inspector was E. C. Wheeler, and he used the initial "W" to pass inspected component parts. Only a few revolvers exist today with this inspector's stamp, and they are all in the 49000 serial number range. Capt. John E. Greer was the Ordnance inspector who received all these revolvers for the U.S. Government in 1878. His initials in a cartouche were located under the year marking. The serial number range for the Henry Nettleton series of Cavalry revolvers ran from 47000 through 50500.

* Supporting research by Ron Graham and C. Kenneth Moore

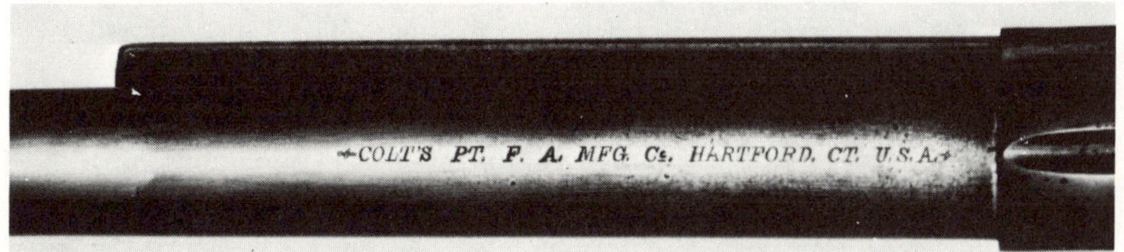

On U.S. Cavalry revolvers with serial numbers under 19500, barrel address is imprinted in slanted capital letters, as on barrel above.

Placement of initials of Ordnance sub-inspector John T. Cleveland on barrel and frame indicate that this revolver was inspected under 1876 procedure.

In 1878 series, a combination of inspection procedures was used. Inspector Henry Nettleson's initials on trigger guard and backstrap is a reversion to the earlier, pre-1876 procedure.

Revolver No. 83948 left the Colt factory Oct. 30, 1882. Initials of Ordnance sub-inspector David F. Clark are visible on the frame and barrel.

One of the largest single groups of U.S. Cavalry revolvers was produced during the years 1880 through 1887. All in this group were inspected by Ordnance sub-inspector David F. Clark. Recorded serial number ranges for this series were those revolvers found in the 41000 through 42000 and 52000 through 121000 number sequences.

The following Ordnance inspectors applied their initials in a cartouche on the left grips of these revolvers: Lt. David A. Lyle (1880), Lt. Charles C. Morrison (1880-1882), Captain John E. Greer (1882-1884), Captain Frank Heath (1884-1885), and Captain John G. Butler (1887). It was the responsibility of these Ordnance inspectors to "receive" the completed revolvers for the U.S. Government. There were 13,000 U.S. Cavalry revolvers produced under contract during the David F. Clark inspection era, making these among the most frequently found U.S. Cavalry revolvers encountered today.

The final U.S. Government contracts with the Colt factory for cavalry revolvers were signed on Nov. 12, 1889, and Sept. 19, 1890. Each was for a lot of 2,000 revolvers. The principal Ordnance sub-inspector was Rinaldo A. Carr and the Ordnance inspector was Captain Stanhope E. Blunt. Captain Blunt's initials are found in a cartouche on the left side of the grip on these revolvers. All are dated either 1890 or 1891. The serial range in which this series is found ran between 131208 and 140361, the latter number being the highest serial numbered Colt U.S. Cavalry revolver produced.

Some of these revolvers are found today in near new condition. Collectors admire these well preserved Cavalry revolvers with nearly all their original "government blue" finish and case hardening colors. While many of us would like to believe that these superb specimens survived the Indian Wars, the possibility is remote. Material researched from the National Archives indicates that these existing specimens with 7½" barrels and matching serial numbers are probably survivors of vast quantities issued to various state militias. The majority of U.S. Army-owned revolvers actually in possession of the Army and under the jurisdiction of the Ordnance Department, were recalled to the various arsenals about 1893. These were remodeled into 5½"-barreled "Artillery" revolvers between 1895 and 1903 for use during the Spanish American War. Therefore, it is believed that most true Indian War-related Colts are low serial numbered "Artillery" models modified from early Cavalry revolvers. ■

BUNTLINES

Continued from page 96

Many Colt model "P's" are noted in factory records as being shipped 'in the soft state' for engraving and finishing by the aforementioned agents.

Very possibly more guns were engraved outside the Colt factory than in it, and General Patton's famous single-action bears this out as just one noted example.

This is the only plausible explanation for the 12-inch guns, for none of these complete outfits with walnut shoulder stock has ever come to light.

Questioning surviving members of the Earp family, I found that they were all very definite on the walnut stock, but agreed that they could not recall the *exact* length of the barrel.

It is, however, probable that the presentations did have 12-inch barrels, for no one loved to be different more than Ned Buntline!

One member of the Earp family still survives who saw Wyatt's gun in Dodge City, Kansas!

The cast bronze shoulder stocks fared better as far as sales were concerned, a number being noted as shipped to the London Agency with 7½-inch standard barrels chambered for the .45 caliber "Boxer" cartridge.

At the close of operations on single-action Colts in 1940, a few of these castings were still extant, together with the original pattern, although they had never been finished.

Barrels sold at $1 per inch

In later years, Colt advertised model "P's" with extra-length barrels at "a dollar an inch" added cost. Standard guns with eight-, 8½-, nine-, 9½-, ten-, 10½-, and 14-inch barrels are recorded on individual shipments, but curiously enough—no 12-inch!

The photographs of the "Buntline Specials" accompanying this article clearly show all the salient features of these unique guns.

A word to collectors might be in order at this point. I have actually examined more spurious "Buntlines" than I have genuine. Today, five of these rare pieces are definitely known to be in existence, four of which are in private collections. There may be more, but even should all the original 30 turn up, they still could occupy, very rightfully, that particular niche in Colt history as the rarest of those famous guns. ◆◆◆

Acknowledgements
John E. Parsons, William D. McVey, John Gilchriese, Mark Dinely, Stuart N. Lake, George W. Earp, Everett M. Earp, Ray M. Earp, and the Colt's Manufacturing Company, Ron Wagner in particular.

One Rare Colt

BY JOSEPH B. ROBERTS, JR.

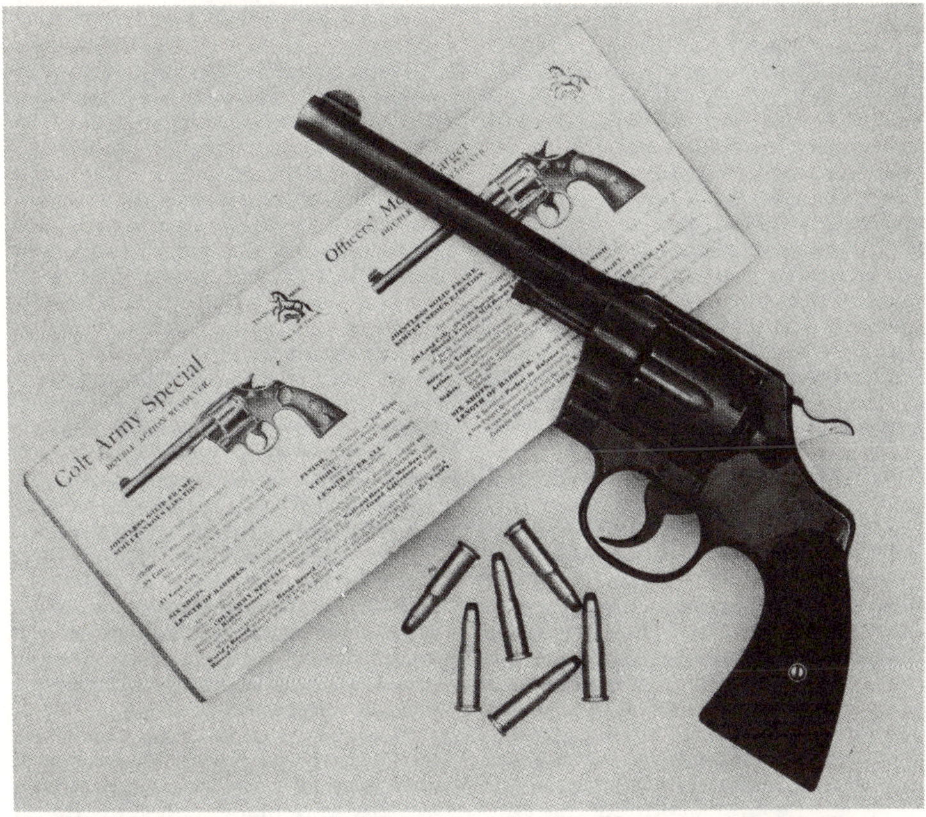

In The American Rifleman for December, 1956 James M. Triggs mentioned the possible existence of a few Colt Army Special Revolvers experimentally chambered for cal. .25-20 WCF. The revolver above, shown with a Colt catalog for 1922, is one of those few—an original .25-20 Colt.

LIMITED production firearms are always interesting. Most of these guns are commemorative or presentation pieces—many are also antique—and some are experimental. Though the commemorative and presentation guns, with their special finish and decoration, get the lion's share of admiration, experimental arms are equally admirable, and are less common. Few toolroom samples survive the rigors of product testing. Those that do, especially when the test is unsuccessful, are either destroyed or turned over to a company museum. Thus, when a factory-assembled revolver, that may well be the only survivor of such a program, turns up, it merits attention.

One such piece, a Colt Army Special revolver in the highly irregular caliber of .25-20 WCF, surfaced recently. It belongs to Petersburg, Va., gunsmith Bill Dunbar.

Is this the only one of its kind? "I like to think it is," says Dunbar. "Whenever I mention it to a Colt collector, his jaw drops a little. But, as surely as I say there aren't any others, someone will find one."

Dunbar is prudent. Colt definitely experimented with cal. .25-20 revolvers. The extent of testing and the actual number of .25-20 revolvers made is not certain. Colt's records substantiate that Dunbar's pistol, serial number 470036, is among several "open" numbers in a range that was shipped in late 1921 and early 1922. Since open numbers are those that were not shipped to a purchaser and since no record was kept of their disposition, it is fair to assume that the "several guns" cited were diverted for some special purpose. Number 470036 is undeniably a .25-20. And, it was assembled as a .25-20.

The gun's 6" barrel, for example is a product of Colt's shops. It is not relined, being bored and rifled to cal. .25. The rifling has six lands and grooves, left twist, one turn in 16"; a form peculiar to Colt handguns. Rifling dimensions are the same as those of the cal. .25 ACP Pocket Auto, leading one to believe that the same tools used to rifle barrels for the tiny pistols were used to rifle this barrel.

Even the barrel markings on this unique revolver are extraordinary. The model designation is impressed with a standard die, but the caliber marking is *hand cut engraving*. Either Colt left the caliber unmarked and the engraving was added by the gun's first owner, or so few of these revolvers were made that the factory found it cheaper to have the caliber engraved than to buy a special roll die.

Like the barrel, the cylinder was never intended to be anything but cal. .25-20. Colt, however, had to buy or make a set of chambering reamers, for they cannot be improvised. Colt may have had a set on hand. Some reports indicate that the Lightning rifle was cataloged as being available in .25-20. Historians disagree as to the number of .25-20 rifles made, but there were only a few.

Exactly how many .25-20 revolvers were made and how many have survived is an unanswerable question. It can only be said with certainty that Dunbar *has* one. How this one gun survived is easily explained. It came from the collection of Albert Foster, Jr.

Foster, one of the fortunate few for whom job and hobby are one, was an avid gun collector. He was also an employee of Colt's Firearms Division from early in the 20th Century until about 1946. For most, if not all, of those years he was manager of Colt's New York office at 20 Vesey St. A presentation Colt Officers Model, illustrated in Sutherland & Wilson's "The Book of Colt Firearms," establishes that he was at the New York office as early as 1907. Today, no one knows if Foster had any connection with any .25-20 test, but he must surely have known of it. He took the trouble to acquire Army Special revolver, number 470036, for his personal collection. He kept it until his death in March, 1948.

After Foster's death, his Army Special .25-20 was sold as part of his estate. Between 1948 and 1974 it passed through a number of dealers' and collectors' hands, finally arriving at its present owner's shop, where it was offered in trade for another unusual Colt revolver.

The Army Special is not a rare gun. Sold in .38 Special, .32-20 WCF, and .41 Long Colt calibers, the Army

Special was produced in considerable quantity between 1908 and 1926. Built on a cal. .41 frame, the Army Special represented an improvement in internal design over the New Army, New Navy, and Marine Corps models of 1892 and 1894 (note: The Marine Corps model was introduced in 1905, but is mechanically the same as earlier revolvers). Also on a medium-weight, cal. .41-size frame, these earlier service revolvers featured counter-clockwise cylinder rotation and a unique, if somewhat complicated, locking system with two locking bolts and two locking slots in each chamber.

In this system, one bolt engaged a slot near the cylinder's mid-point as the hammer was drawn to full cock. The second bolt, a lug atop the trigger, engaged a slot at the rear of the cylinder when the trigger was pulled. After issuing these revolvers, the Army found that they could be fired with the cylinder closed, but not latched shut. Beginning in 1894, at the Army's request, a safety device was installed that prevented this from happening. Earlier guns were modified to include the new device, and Colt designers began to search for an easier way to do all those jobs.

Their solution involved moving the hand from the right side of the mechanism to the left and changing cylinder rotation to clockwise. In this way, the hand will either jam an unlatched cylinder or latch it as the hammer is drawn to full cock. The paired locking bolts were discarded in favor of a single, rear-mounted bolt that engaged as the hammer was cocked, and the hand was arranged to rise slightly as the trigger was pulled, wedging the cylinder tightly between the ratchet and locking slot. First used on the heavy-frame New Service revolvers in 1897, this same system was adapted to medium-frame guns in 1908. The new medium-frame model was called the Army Special. It replaced the New Army, New Navy, and—in 1910—the Marine Corps Model. The Officer's Model, which first used the two-bolt system when it was introduced in 1904, changed to the simpler locking system and continued in production.

Army Special and Officer's Model revolvers were made until 1926, when Colt, dismayed by the Army's refusal to buy cal. .38 revolvers and enthusiastic over the same gun's acceptance by law enforcement agencies, changed the name of the Army Special to Official Police.

No mechanical changes were made at the time of the name change. In fact, the basic mechanism, with its general use of leaf springs and familiar V-shaped combination main and trigger return spring, is still used in Colt Python and Diamondback revolvers.

What do you do with a revolver that may be the sole survivor of a very small group? While mechanically perfect, Dunbar's Army Special .25-20 shows both storage wear and signs of some use. The finish on the muzzle has been worn away from carrying in a holster. Likewise, the backstrap and trigger guard are devoid of any finish, showing that the gun has been handled. A light, even drag mark in each of the cylinder locking slots shows that the gun has been fired, but not too much.

When he first acquired the gun, Dunbar fired it with factory-loaded cartridges. "I wasn't worried," he says, "about the gun's ability to handle the pressure of what were, essentially, rifle cartridges. There's plenty of metal in the cylinder, and in the barrel too. But I did have problems with cases backing out of the chambers and binding up the cylinder, just like S&W's .22 Jet, Model 53 did 15 years ago. Average velocities dropped about 500 f.p.s. in the 6" barrel as compared to the 20" barrels that Winchester put on Model 92 carbines, and I decided that shooting it wasn't worth the effort."

Dunbar still carries and fires his prized possession. But he does so only occasionally, and with due regard for the extreme scarcity of the piece. To minimize wear to the gun, only mild handloads are used now. Cal. .25-20 loading data in modern manuals are for rifles, and pressure figures are seldom given. Dunbar had to resort to the late Phil Sharpe's 1937 book on handloading for data that would identify a load as suitable for use in a medium frame revolver. His load combines the factory 86-gr. soft-point bullet, 4.5 grs. of Hercules Unique and small pistol primers in Remington cases. Accuracy with this load is very good and pressures mild. Dunbar feels that continued occasional firing of this load will give years of service with little, if any, added wear.

Bill Dunbar appreciates what he owns. Offered his choice of several exotic Colts in the trade, he selected the Army Special and turned down a Dragoon to get it.

"Colt made a lot of Dragoons, over 20,000 of these altogether," he says. "And even if I don't know how many .25-20s were made, I do know that it was doggone few."

All that considered, Bill Dunbar's Army Special revolver is a very special revolver indeed. ■

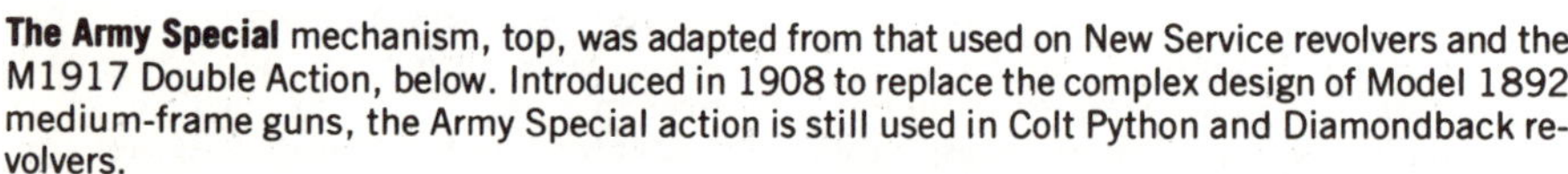

The Army Special mechanism, top, was adapted from that used on New Service revolvers and the M1917 Double Action, below. Introduced in 1908 to replace the complex design of Model 1892 medium-frame guns, the Army Special action is still used in Colt Python and Diamondback revolvers.

Close examination of the cylinder and barrel breech of this rare gun show that both the chambers and bore were originally manufactured to accommodate the .25-20 cartridge.

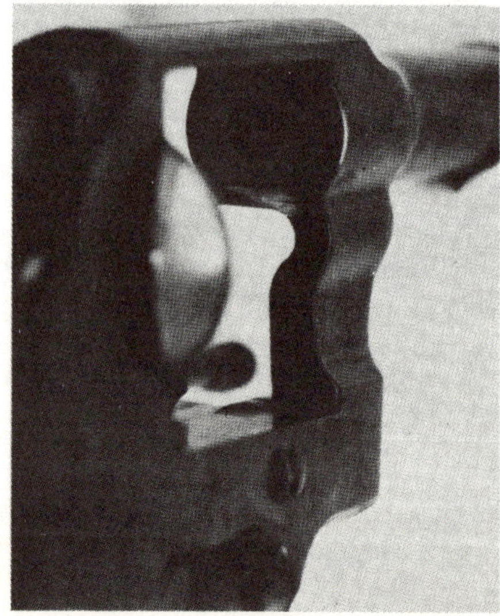

Notes on Colt 1878 Double Action

Colt Model 1878 Double Action Revolver with 7½" barrel, ejector rod, and ivory grips.

"Alaskan" or "Philippine Model" ordered by the U.S. Army in 1898 for delivery in 1902 has longer trigger and larger trigger guard than standard version.

By E. DIXON LARSON

THE Colt Model 1878 Double Action revolver offers an interesting area for Colt fanciers. This is particularly true for the starting collector. Although showing signs of increased interest, its prices have not increased proportionately with its counterpart the Colt Model 1873 Single Action Army. Quality of 1878 Double Actions available is still fairly good, and, unlike the Single Action, production was never resumed once the model was dropped.

One can always recall that certain variations of a given model were always costly, but also remember that at the same time the standard version was relatively reasonable and passed over. Most of us collectors have sat back and waited to see if our predictions materialized, and when it happened beseiged the novice with "what we could have done". The information offered in this article is intended primarily for the starting collector, but even the seasoned Colt enthusiast may find something new.

Authorities agree that the 1878 Frontier Double Action was a mechanical failure. It is prone to misfires and few gunsmiths understand the mechanism. Many pieces have been damaged because the tinkerer did not know the hammer screw has a left-hand thread. The trigger return spring cannot be made or installed by just any craftsman. If the revolver does not lock up during the cocking cycle it is best passed up as restoring proper function is quite difficult. In general, only working pieces should be considered.

Regular production calibers were .32-20, .44-40, .45 Colt, .38-40, .476 Eley. Standard barrel lengths of ejector models were 4¾", 5½", and 7½". Those without ejectors had 3", 3½", and 4" barrels.

Any other caliber or length is rare, although barrels over 7½" were available at $1.00 for each additional inch. The two-line address appears on barrel lengths up to 4¾", an important point in judging if the barrel has been cut. Barrels 5½" and longer carry the usual one-line address. An occasional Depot 14, Pall Mall, London, address will appear after the usual Hartford. The .44-40 version has "Colt Frontier Six Shooter" etched on the left side of the barrel. Serial numbers are stamped on the butt, back of the cylinder, and sometimes on the loading gate. Examples of the large framed version with serial numbers under 10000 can be considered a real find. Grips were originally two-piece checkered walnut. After 1882, two-piece hard black rubber was standard. Ivory, pearl and other materials were available on special order.

The ejectorless version has been promoted as a "Storekeeper's Model" for the past five years but this has resulted in no significant rush to buy or increased price.

A sparse few, ordered by Ben Kittredge and Company of Cincinnati, Ohio, had "Omnipotent" etched on the left side of the barrel. These are considered scarce, although as yet they do not command high prices.

A word about the military marked models, commonly termed "The Alaskan", or the "Philippine". How much service this model actually saw in the termed areas is questionable, but the United States Government did in fact contract for some 4600 in 1898 and received delivery in 1902. All were cal. .45 Colt with 6" barrels. The outstanding feature is the large trigger guard which is ¼" wider and ⅜" deeper than the standard model, and the trigger is 1⅜" long as compared to the standard length of 1". The serial number range is 43000 to 48000. Most have plain walnut grips and are stamped "RAC" on the left side of the trigger guard to signify acceptance by Army inspector, Rinaldo A. Carr.

The chart below showing years of manufacture appears in *The Book of Colt Firearms* by R. Q. Sutherland and R. L. Wilson, and elsewhere.

Year	Serial	Year	Serial
1878	1	1893	31300
1879	1450	1894	33100
1880	4000	1895	34700
1881	4500	1896	35100
1882	7450	1897	36500
1883	9500	1898	38200
1884	12200	1899	41000
1885	13700	1900	43000
1886	16100	1901	48000
1887	18100	1902	48500
1888	20900	1903	49300
1889	22300	1904	50600
1890	24600	1905	51000
1891	27200	Last No.	52180
1892	29500		

■

Large frame (left) of the first 10,000 compared with the smaller frame (right) of the following 1878 Colt revolvers.

COLT NEW LINE REVOLVERS

By E. DIXON LARSON

COLT New Line single-action sheath trigger revolvers, as with early Colt double-action models, have been somewhat neglected by collectors. However, their availability is noticeably declining and they will become more difficult to find in the future.

One model in the New Line series, the "Police and Thug", has risen noticeably in value during recent years.

The manufacture of Colt New Line revolvers began in 1873, but promotion literature of that period indicates that they were first offered to the public in 1874. William Mason's U. S. Patent No. 150,095, issued on Sept. 15, 1874, covered 6 significant features found in these small-frame metallic cartridge revolvers.

Two different methods of retaining the cylinder pin were used—a slanted screw and a spring-returned locking bar. Both methods are found in the Colt single-action Army revolver introduced contemporaneously with the New Line series: The methods of retaining the cylinder pin appear evenly distributed in both of the early and late-produced Colt New Line revolvers.

Locking the cylinder

Two systems of locking the cylinder in place were employed in New Line revolvers. Early models have the bolt locking notches milled in the outside of the cylinder and the cylinder flutes are short. Bolt locking notches of later models are milled in the rear of the cylinder and the cylinder flutes are long. The latter locking system was the better; many of the rear-locking revolvers failed to index their cylinders properly.

Loading gates have been observed only on the cal. .38 and cal. .41 models. Approximately one out of every 25 New Line revolvers in these calibers will be found with loading gates. This, of course, excludes the New Line "Police and Thug" and "New House" models which were produced from the first with loading gates. The ratio of nickel-plated to blued specimens is about 5 to 3, with the nickel finish predominating.

The revolvers illustrated are standard models that are likely to be encountered by the average collector.

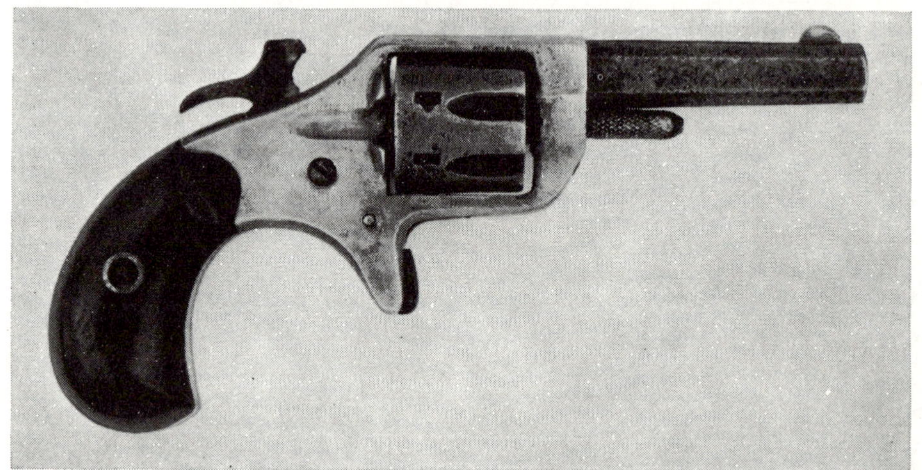

New Line cal. .22 short and long rimfire 7-shot pocket revolver, called "The Little Colt", "Rabbit's Foot", "A Joker", by arms distributors. Bronze frame without loading gate. Pull pin ejector. Shape of 2¼" barrel is distinctive—circular top and bottom with flattened sides. May have either outside or rear bolt locking notches with corresponding short or long cylinder flutes. Birdshead 2-piece walnut grips. Etched on left side "Colt New .22". Two-line marking on top of barrel is: "Colt's Pt. F.A. Mfg. Co., Hartford, Conn., U.S.A.".

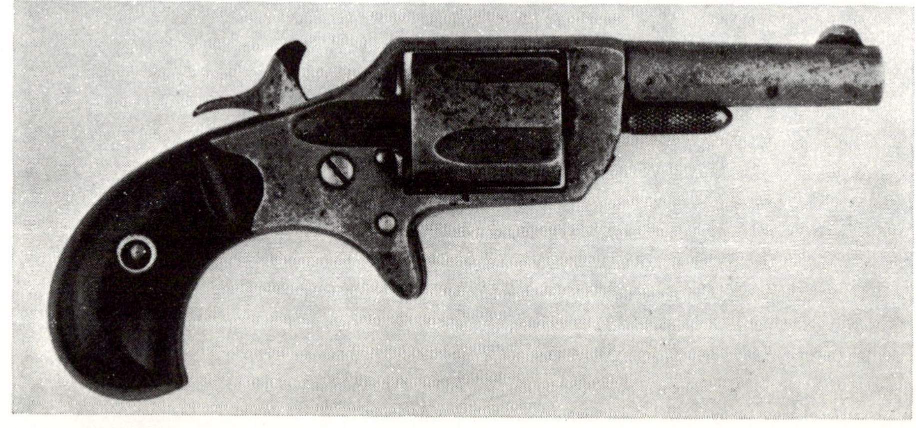

New Line cal. .30 short and long rimfire 5-shot pocket revolver, sometimes called "The Pony Colt" by arms distributors. Steel frame without loading gate. Pull pin ejector. Round 2¼" barrel, etched on left side "Colt New .30". Barrel markings same as cal. .22 revolver. May have either outside or rear bolt locking notches with corresponding short or long cylinder flutes. Birdshead 2-piece walnut grips.

New Line cal. .32 short and long Colt center-fire 5-shot pocket revolver, referred to as "The Ladies Colt" by arms distributors. Steel frame without loading gate. Pull pin ejector. May have either outside or rear bolt locking notches with corresponding short or long cylinder flutes. Round 2¼" barrel etched on left side "Colt New .32". Barrel markings same as cal. .22 revolver. Birdshead 2-piece walnut grips.

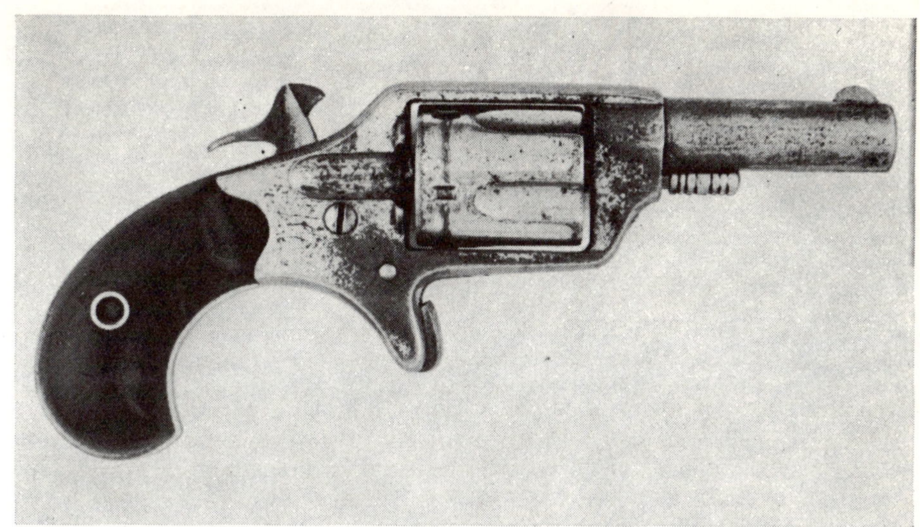

New Line cal. .38 short and long rimfire or cal. .38 short and long Colt center-fire pocket revolver, promoted as "The Pet Colt". Steel frame, furnished both with and without loading gate. Round 2¼" barrel was standard, but a few were made with 4" round barrel. Pull pin ejector. May have either outside or rear bolt locking notches with corresponding short or long cylinder flutes. Etched on left side "Colt New .38". Barrel and frame markings identical to those on cals. .30 and .32 models. Two types of cylinder pin are regularly noted in this model. Birdshead 2-piece walnut grips.

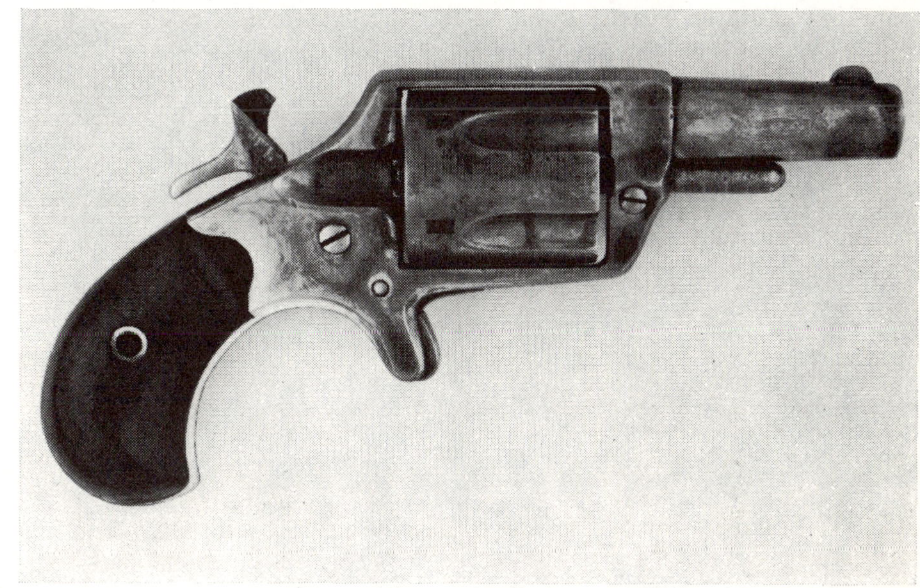

New Line cal. .41 short and long rimfire or cal. .41 short and long centerfire pocket revolver, referred to as "The Big Colt" in old catalogs. Steel frame. Furnished with and without loading gate. Round 2¼" barrel was standard, but some revolvers of this model have 4" round barrels with clearance slots to facilitate removal of cylinder pins. May have either outside or rear bolt locking notches with corresponding short or long cylinder flutes. Etched on left side "Colt New .41". Barrel and frame markings identical to those on cal. .38, except that patent date is usually found on underside of barrel. Birdshead 2-piece walnut grips. Because of its shorter cylinder, this model appears smaller than cal. .38 model.

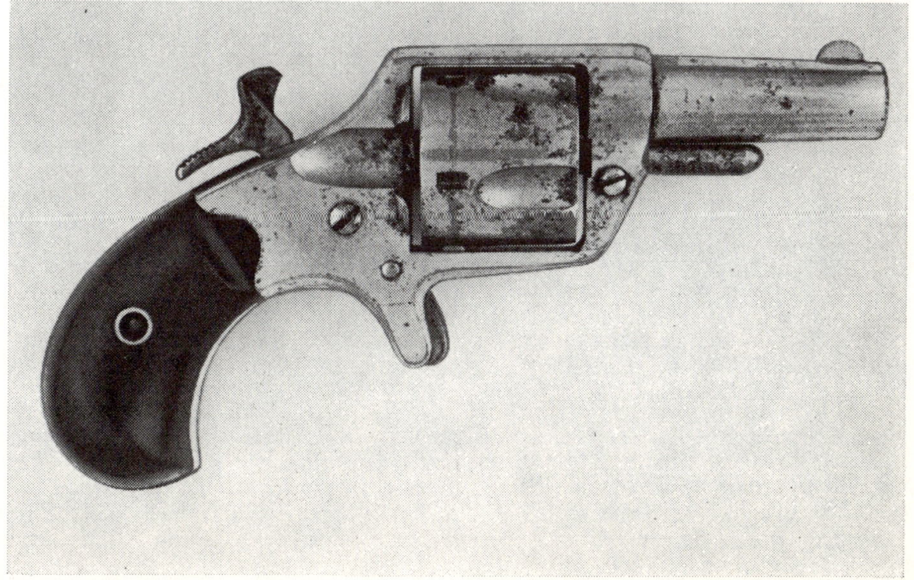

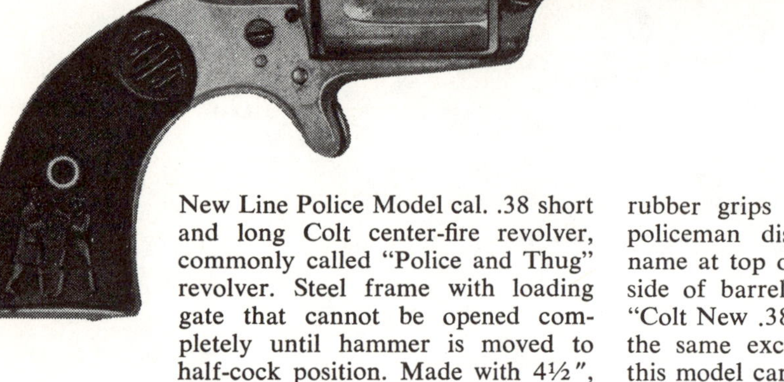

New Line Police Model cal. .38 short and long Colt center-fire revolver, commonly called "Police and Thug" revolver. Steel frame with loading gate that cannot be opened completely until hammer is moved to half-cock position. Made with 4½", 5", and 6" round barrels, with rod ejectors. Cylinder has long flutes with rear bolt locking notches. Flat, square-butt, 2-piece checkered hard rubber grips with raised figures of policeman disarming a thug. Colt name at top of grips. Etched on left side of barrel "New Police .38" or "Colt New .38". Barrel markings are the same except some revolvers of this model carry London address. At right, view of "Police and Thug" Model grip. Replicas of these grips are currently being offered by private manufacturer.

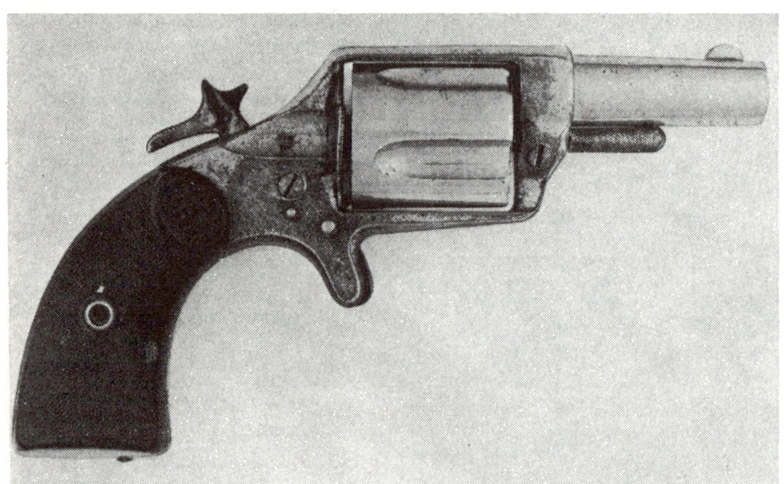

New Line House Model revolver, cal. .38 short and long center-fire or cal. .41 short and long center-fire. Cal. .32 version is very scarce. Promotional name was not applied to this model. Steel frame with loading gate. Loading gate opening mechanism catch is the same as on New Line Police Model. Cylinder has long cylinder flutes with rear bolt locking notches. There are no provisions for a side ejector. Round 2¼" barrel etched on left side "New House .38", "New House .41", "Colt House .38", or "Colt House .41". Flat, square-butt, 2-piece checkered hard rubber grips with Colt name at top. The House Model has been misrepresented as a "Police and Thug" model when fitted with figure grips. Barrel inscription identifies the House Model and figure grips will not change its identity.

Two different methods of retaining the cylinder pin were used in Colt New Line revolvers. Cylinder of revolver at left is retained in frame by slanted screw. Spring-returned locking bar performs the same function in revolver at right.

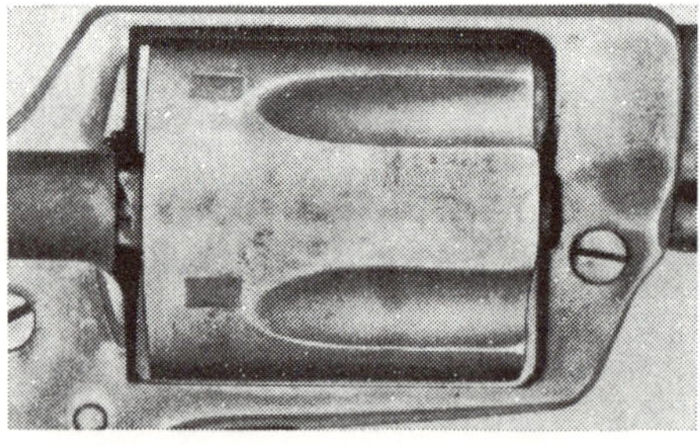

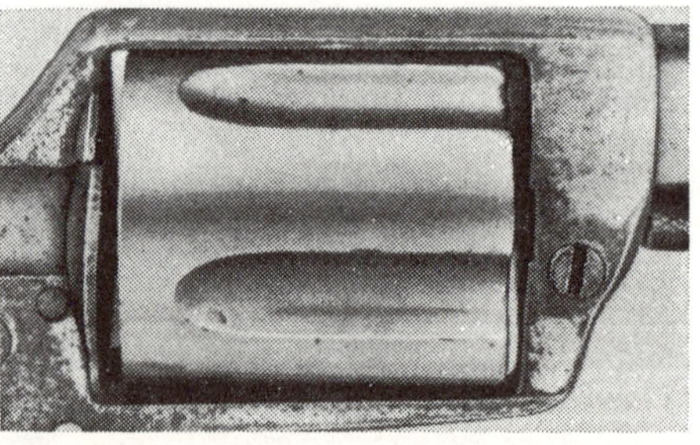

New Line revolver cylinder at top has outside bolt locking notches and short flutes, whereas lower cylinder has rear bolt locking notches and long flutes. ■

Collectors:

Don't Overlook Long-Neglected Colts

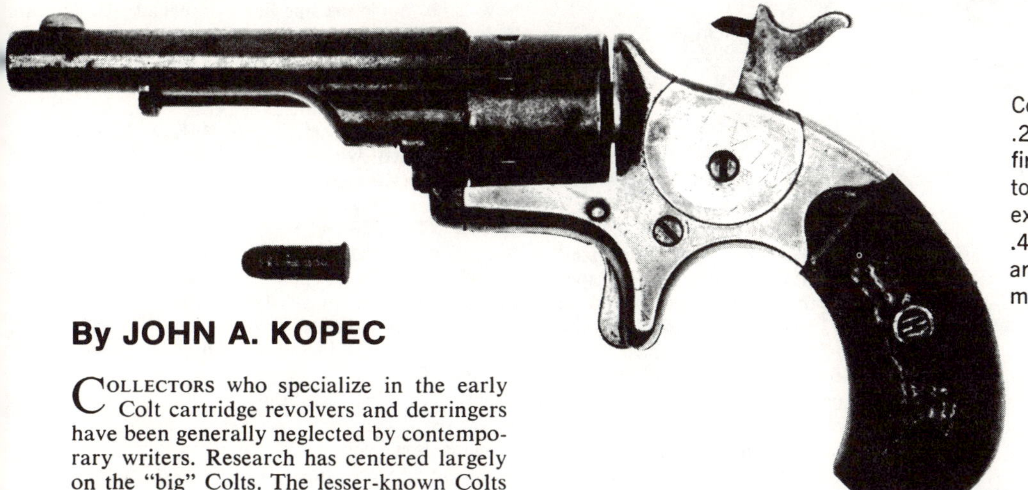

Colt open top seven-shot "Old Line" .22 rimfire (l.) has centrally located firing pin, 2⅞" barrel and integral ejector assembly. Below, early production example of Colt's No. 3 derringer, cal. .41 rimfire, 1st type, has bolster around barrel pivot screw, high hammer spur and tight grip configuration.

By JOHN A. KOPEC

COLLECTORS who specialize in the early Colt cartridge revolvers and derringers have been generally neglected by contemporary writers. Research has centered largely on the "big" Colts. The lesser-known Colts described here represent variations whose existence should be known and appreciated. None are experimental in nature, nor are they "special order" arms. The circumstances under which these small handguns were produced are:

a. Early production
b. Transitional production
c. Specialty production

Two pocket guns found in the classification we call "early production arms" are the Colt's "Old Line" cal. .22 revolver with the near round firing pin and firing pin aperture, and the first variation of the Colt's No. 3 .41 cal. derringer.

The little known cal. .22 Old Line or "open top" variation with the integral barrel ejector assembly, although generally recognized, is seldom seen in its earliest form with a round firing pin aperture and centrally located integral firing pin on its hammer. This firing pin strikes the bottom of the cal. .22 rimfire cartridge. Later examples of this model have a flat riveted or integral firing pin which strikes the cartridge rim through a slotted section in the frame. Besides having the round integral firing pin, this first style differs in that it has a shoulder under the hammer spur which acts as a stop against the frame.

Our second example of an "early production arm", the 1st model of the Colt's No. 3 cal. .41 rimfire derringer, is found with two distinct styles of barrel stamping. The earliest examples have the word "COLT" stamped in small letters on the barrel, while later examples bear the standard, larger size, slanted lettering. This earliest example of the No. 3 Colt derringer is distinctive in that it has a bolster around the barrel pivot screw head. It also shows the other characteristics associated with this series including a high hammer spur and the tight grip configuration. This tight grip configuration is easily distinguishable from the later variations as it forms a partial circle about ⅔ of the distance around a standard 25¢ piece.

Several other variations of the Colt No. 3 derringer are known, but these variations are primarily simple combinations of the high and low hammer spurs and the tight and wide grip configurations. The first variation alone has the distinction of the special bronze frame with the bolster around the barrel pivot screw.

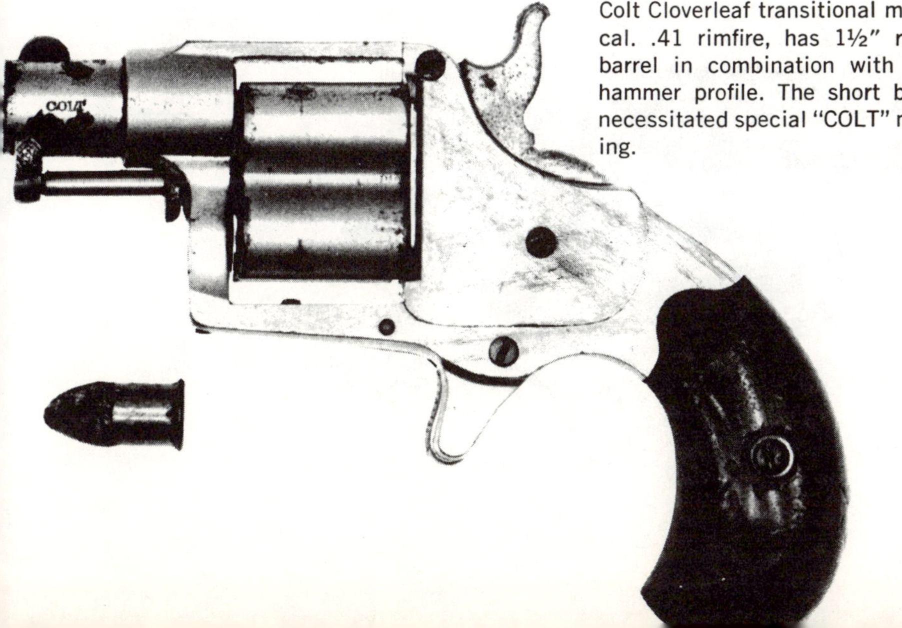

Colt Cloverleaf transitional model, cal. .41 rimfire, has 1½" round barrel in combination with high hammer profile. The short barrel necessitated special "COLT" marking.

Our transitional example is a cal. .41 Colt Cloverleaf revolver. This model is distinctive because of its four-shot "Cloverleaf" shaped cylinder. It was introduced in 1871 and production ran through 1876. Colt Cloverleaf models generally have the standard 3" round barrel. There were, however, some Cloverleaf revolvers produced

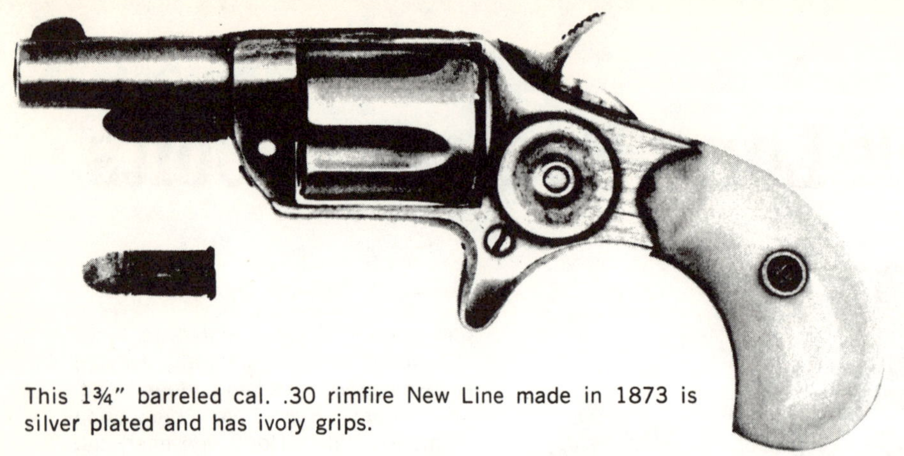

This 1¾" barreled cal. .30 rimfire New Line made in 1873 is silver plated and has ivory grips.

with 1½" octagonal or 1½" round barrels. The earlier had the 1½" octagonal barrel and the "high" hammer spur profile, while the later ones had 1½" round barrels and the "low" hammer spur profile. The transitional Cloverleaf illustrated has the combination characteristics of the short 1½" round barrel and the "high" hammer spur profile. Its serial number is 2740. The writer has observed this exact variation on only two occasions. The other such revolver, serial number 2859, is illustrated on page 185 of the book *The Wm. M. Locke Collection*. Since the change to the low hammer spur occurred during regular production at approximately serial number 2150, the writer believes that these two transitional Cloverleafs with short round barrels were made up by Colt's using "left over" high spur hammers.

Our next classification of unrecognized Colt rarities are those produced for a specialty market. Both examples are found in the "New Line" series of Colt revolvers. The cal. .30 rimfire Colt New Line revolvers were produced from 1874 through 1876. Most have the standard 2½" barrel but some were produced with a 1¾" barrel and were available through regular trade channels of the period. These 1¾" barreled variations are extremely scarce today. The example shown, serial No. 4870, is full silver plated and has ivory grips. It was manufactured in 1875. All cal. .30 "New Line" revolvers were made in the 2nd model series. That is, they had the long cylinder flutes with the cylinder locking stops at the rear of the cylinder.

The New Line revolvers afford the collector still another rare variation for a specialty market in the 4" barrel version. All examples have been within the 3rd model series, with long cylinder flutes, rear cylinder stops, and a four "screw" frame. All were either cal. .38 or cal. .41 centerfire. Two reports list a cal. .32 4" barreled New Line, but none has been observed. All 4" barreled Colt New Lines are fitted with loading gates and most have been found to have British proof marks. Our first illustration is that of a cal. .38 center-fire, 4" barreled revolver, serial No. 11800, blue finished, fitted with ivory grips. This revolver was shipped together with 80 like revolvers to Colt's London Agency on August 21, 1880. The next illustration is that of a cal. .41 center-fire, 4" barreled New Line revolver, serial No. 8050, nickel finished. It was originally shipped in a group of nine like revolvers to B. Kitterridge & Co. of Cincinnati, Ohio, on December 10, 1877.

The collecting of these early Colt cartridge revolvers and derringers can be a pleasant experience. Many combinations of calibers, sizes, finishes, styles of grips, engraved examples and cased specimens are still available at comparatively modest prices.

A fringe benefit is that a nice representative collection of these little Colts is much easier to transport for display purposes than full-sized revolvers. If I wish to transport or store my collection, it all fits into an attache case. Try that with your Dragoon models or Single-Action Armys! ■

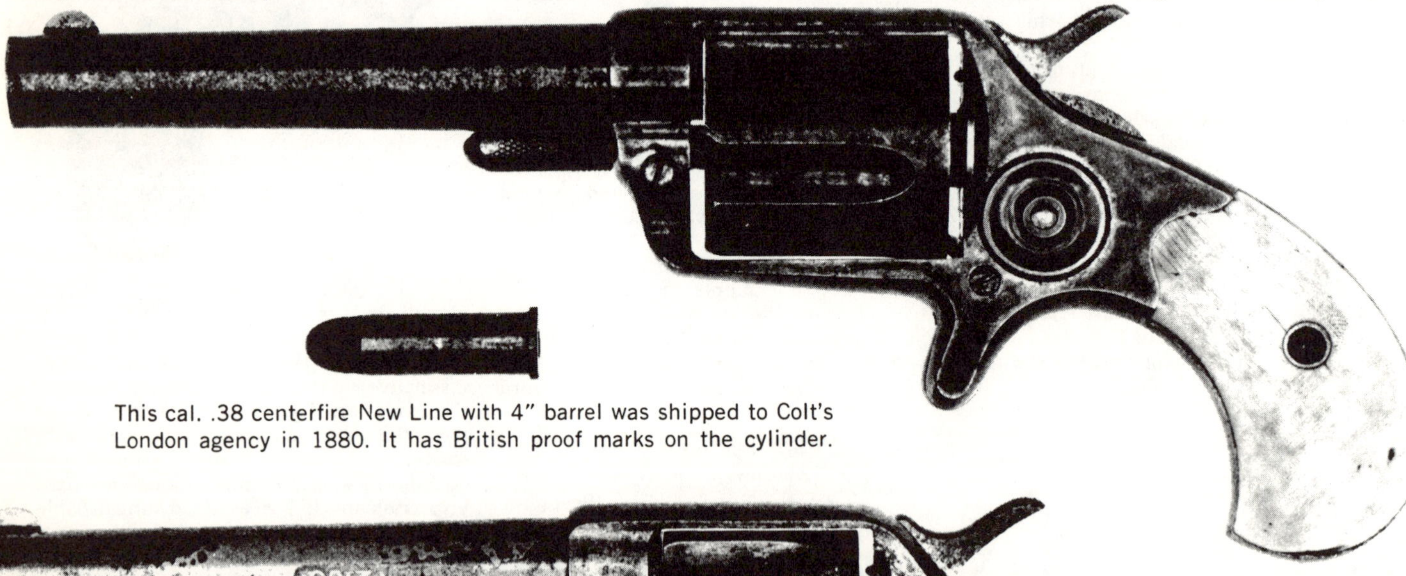

This cal. .38 centerfire New Line with 4" barrel was shipped to Colt's London agency in 1880. It has British proof marks on the cylinder.

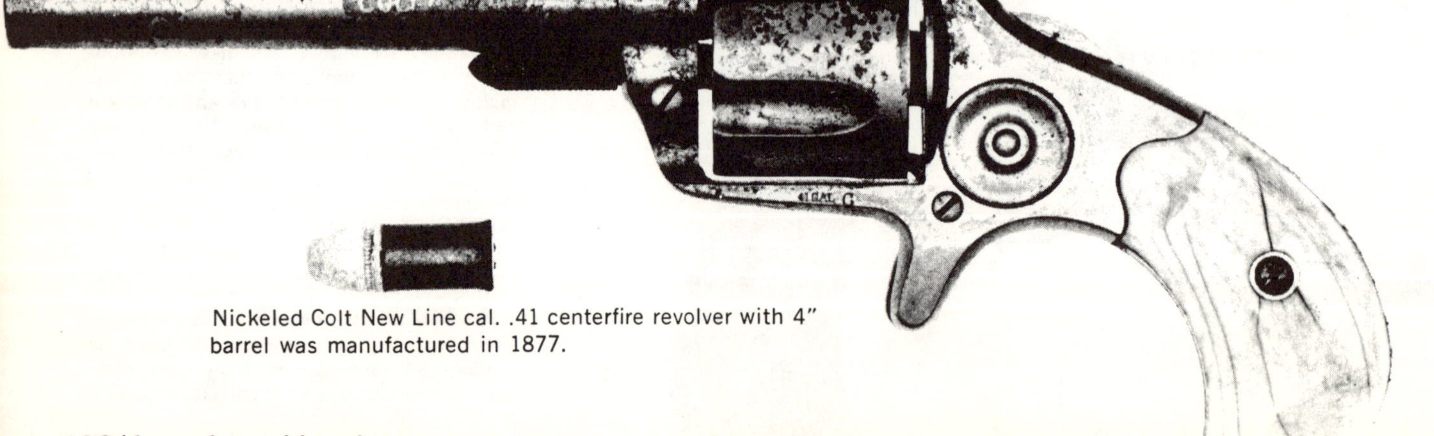

Nickeled Colt New Line cal. .41 centerfire revolver with 4" barrel was manufactured in 1877.

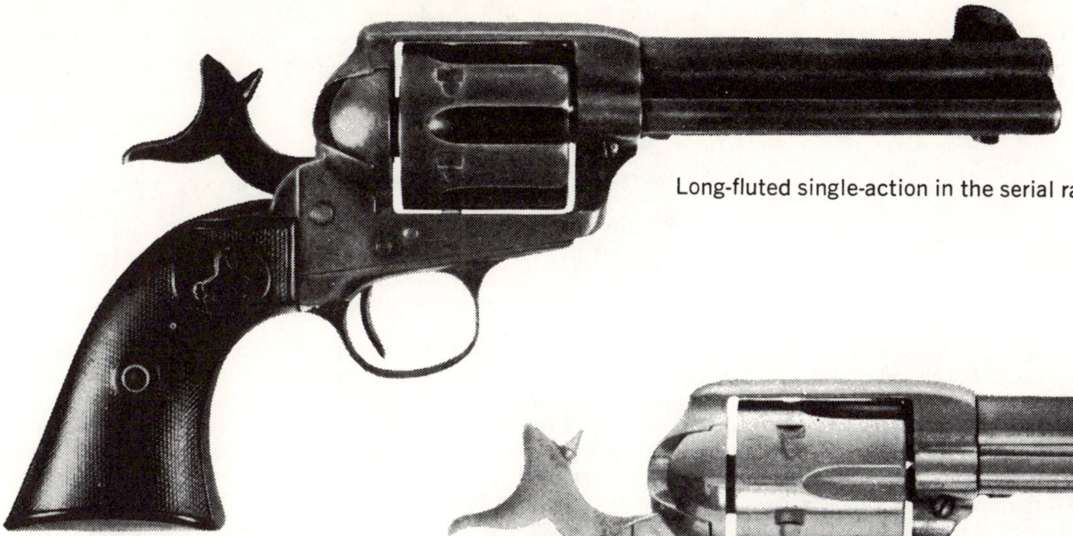

Long-fluted single-action in the serial range of 330,000.

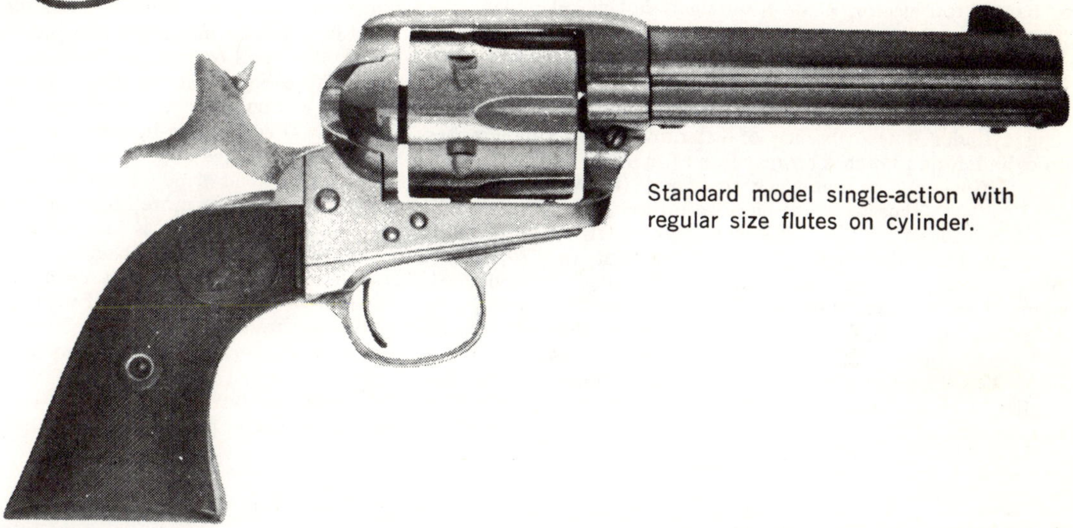

Standard model single-action with regular size flutes on cylinder.

Single-Action Colts With Long Flutes

These rare specimens are often overlooked by Colt enthusiasts

By E. DIXON LARSON

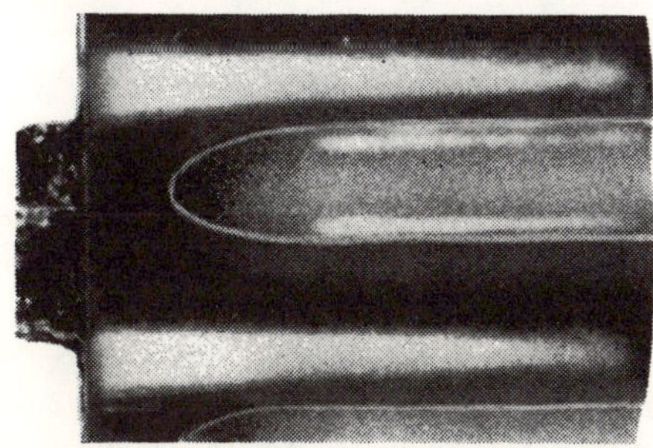

Standard double-action long-fluted cylinder of the 1878 model has locking notches on rear of cylinder.

MOST Americans, whether gun enthusiasts or not, know approximately what the Colt's Single-Action Army revolver looks like. Many, in fact, played with toy copies of it in boyhood.

There is, however, one model of this famous revolver that actually differs in appearance from the standard well-recognized version. Aside from such hair-splitting details as patent date changes, rare calibers and barrel markings, this model differs in that its cylinder flutes are 5/16" longer than the standard 1" flutes. Although readily apparent, this is often overlooked.

Based on my observations of long-fluted cylinder Colt's, it appears that about half the total production of some 1,380 of this model are owned by sportsmen or collectors who never have noticed this obvious variation from the standard model.

The long-fluted cylinder model was produced in 1915 to utilize surplus Model 1878 Double-Action Army revolver cylinders left over when that model was discontinued. The Model 1878 cylinder did not have bolt locking notches on the side or rear face, as locking was accomplished on the ratchet only. In modifying the Model 1878 cylinder for use on the Single-Action Army model, bolt locking notches were milled into the exterior surface, thereby utilizing an otherwise useless inventory of cylinders.

The prospective purchaser of a long-fluted cylinder revolver should be on guard as it is a simple task to modify a Model 1878 Double-Action cylinder to produce a spurious long-fluted cylinder. Serial numbers should be from 330,000 to 331,380 inclusive. Two revolvers have been observed slightly outside this range, but are believed to be correct. Calibers within the long-fluted series will included .45 Colt, .44-40 WCF, .41 Long Colt, .38-40 WCF, and .32-20 WCF. The caliber ratio, however, is about 5 to 1 for the .45 Colt as compared to other calibers. Barrel lengths vary, with the 4¾" length about 3 to 1 as compared to the 7½" length. Obviously, calibers other than .45 Colt in the 7½" barrel length can be considered the most scarce of the long-fluted cylinder model.

Even though few were produced, the demand for the long-fluted cylinder model has not been too great and they are still relatively available. They should prove much more valuable as Colt enthusiasts become aware of their existence. ■

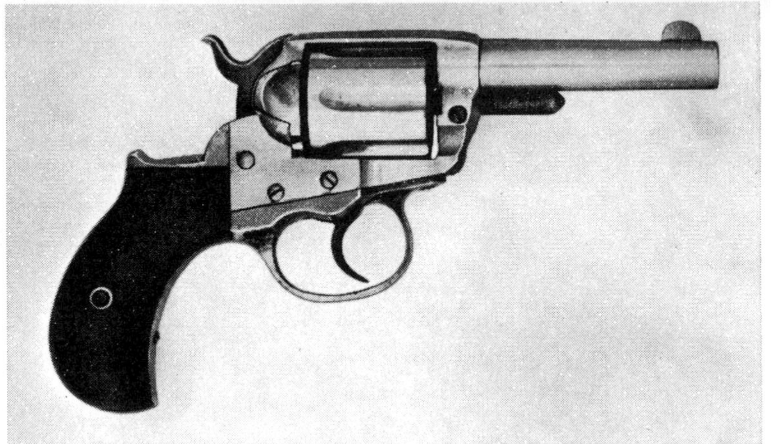

Colt Lightning 6-shot D.A. Model, cal. .38 long or short Colt, 6" barrel, rod ejector, blade front sight, full nickel plated.

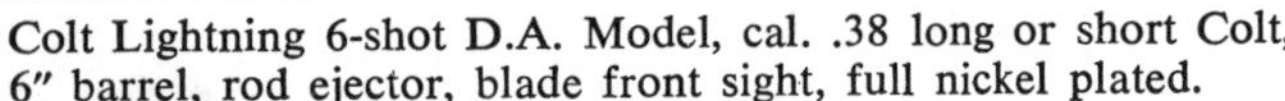

Barrel lengths with rod ejector were 4½", 5", 6", 7", and 7½" (7" and 7½" on special order only). A few revolvers of this model were chambered for .32 long and short Colt cartridges (interchangeably). Distinctive features include birdshead grip, long cylinder flutes, absence of exterior bolt locking notches on cylinder, and notches on rear face of cylinder between chambers. Grips may be one-piece rosewood (shown) or 2-piece hard rubber. Guns with one-piece rosewood grips were serially numbered under 32000. Frame markings on left side are: "Pat. Sept. 19, 1871, Pat. Sept. 15, 1874", and "Pat. Jan. 19, 1875". About 40% will be found with rampant Colt trademark stamped on left side. Markings atop barrel are: "Colt's Pt. F. A. Mfg. Co., Hartford, Ct., U.S.A." or a London address. Left side of barrel is marked "Colt D.A. .38", "Colt D.A. .41", or "Colt D.A. .32". Target models are scarce. Above nomenclature also applies to cal. .41 D.A. Thunderer Model, when furnished with rod ejector.

Colt Thunderer 6-shot D.A. Model, cal. .41 long or short Colt, 3½" barrel without rod ejector, blade front sight, full nickel plated.

Revolvers of this model without rod ejector are found with 2", 2½", 3½", 4½", and 6" barrels. This Colt revolver is sometimes referred to as Storekeepers model. Cylinder pin is distinctly different on revolvers without ejector. Knurling on head of cylinder pin facilitates withdrawal so pin can be used to punch empty cases from cylinder. Identical markings appear on cal. .38 and cal. .41 revolvers. Hard rubber birdshead grips (shown) are found at 5 to 1 ratio. One-piece rosewood grips are more highly prized by collectors. General physical characteristics such as long cylinder flutes, markings, and removable trigger guards and backstraps apply to both Thunderer and Lightning models, their only essential differences being presence or absence of rod ejector, type of cylinder pin, type of grips, and minor marking variations.

Production of cals. .32, .38, and .41 Colt D.A. revolvers began in 1878 and ceased in 1910. As a matter of interest, frame patent dates on these revolvers do not relate to double-action features, but to ejector, cylinder pin latch, and cylinder locking bolt.

Colt's Double-Action Revolvers

By E. DIXON LARSON

THEIR relative modernity may account for the lack of enthusiasm on the part of the seasoned collector for early Colt double-action revolvers. But this should be the heralding alert for the beginning collector; similar attitudes of indifference were once observed with conversions of Colt percussion models, Colt derringers, and even the Bisley model. All of these have gradually overcome their inertia in popularity and have advanced from the lower 25% of the value chart to the upper levels—all within a 10-year period or less.

Through the years, early Colt double-action revolvers, or Colt D.A.'s as they are often referred to by collectors, have suffered a high mortality rate with attendant scarcity. However, these are some of the few Colt models that are still found in attics and bureau drawers. And occasionally one is offered at a gun store. It can be assumed that interest in the development of Colt self-cocking double-action revolvers will increase in the future. Consequently, these Colt revolvers are ideal for the novice collector or for the collector who is seeking a specialized field on a moderate budget.

Colt's first introduced a double-action, self-cocking revolver in January 1877. Other manufacturers had promoted double-action handguns prior to that date, but sales were extremely slow. The Colt name was sufficient to hamper the progress of competitors, regardless of their product's principle of operation, quality or performance. The Colt name had been firmly established by previous reputation through the percussion era. In any case, the double-action principle was not new. When restrictive patents expired, Colt's recognized the sales advantages of the self-cocking arm.

The Colt double-action revolvers illustrated in this article are typical basic models and thus representative of the various early types produced.

Several of the model designations used in this article were not original with the Colt firm; they were coined and applied to the various arms by early firearms distributors. As these names are colorful and stimulating to the imagination, they have been stressed by collectors. The odd grip shape termed "birdshead" also originated in this manner.

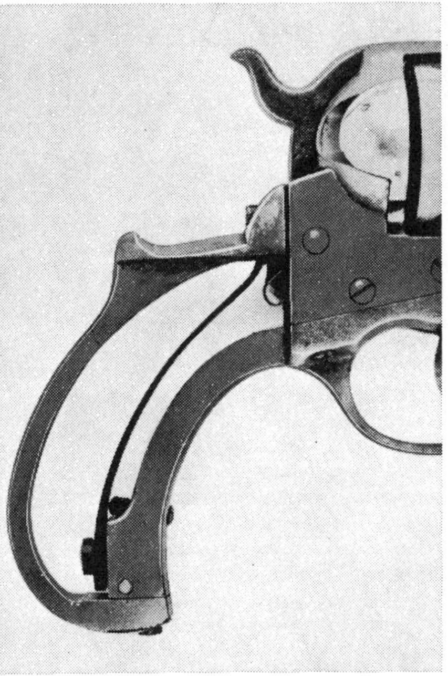

Colt Lightning and Thunderer models were last Colt revolvers with removable backstraps and trigger guards. This costly production method was superseded by one-piece frame and backstrap combination.

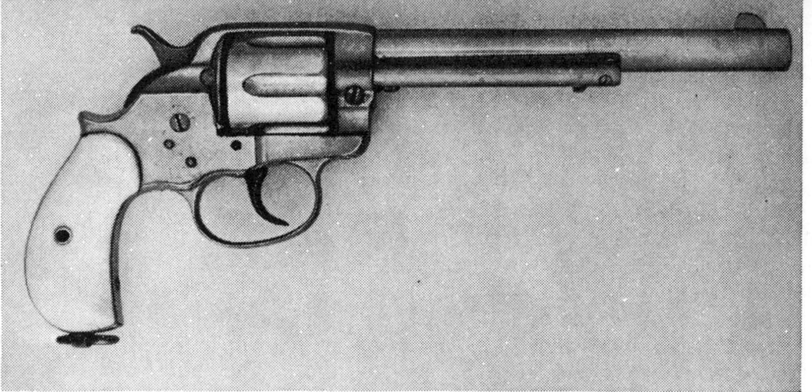

Frontier 6-shot D.A. Model, cal. .45 Colt, 7½" barrel, rod ejector, blade front sight, full nickel plated, ivory birdshead grips. Frequently referred to as Model of 1878, this revolver was offered in cals. .32-20 W.C.F., .44-40 W.C.F., .45 Colt, .450 Colt, .455 Eley, and .476 Eley.

There are no locking notches on outer surface or rear face of cylinder. Revolvers with rod ejector were made with 4¾", 5½", and 7½" barrels. Revolvers without rod ejector were furnished with 3½" and 4" barrels.

Markings atop barrel are: "Colt's Pt. F.A. Mfg. Co., Hartford, Ct., U.S.A." A few with London address were noted. Caliber marking is usually found on front left side of trigger guard. Lanyard ring on butt is standard. Trigger guard is 2" long and 1⅛" deep. Trigger extends 1" from frame. These dimensions are important as they distinguish this revolver from later Model of 1902 Army model.

Target models are scarce. Grips for this model were made of hard rubber, checkered walnut, and ivory. Grips on London-stamped revolvers were noted to be consistently larger bodied.

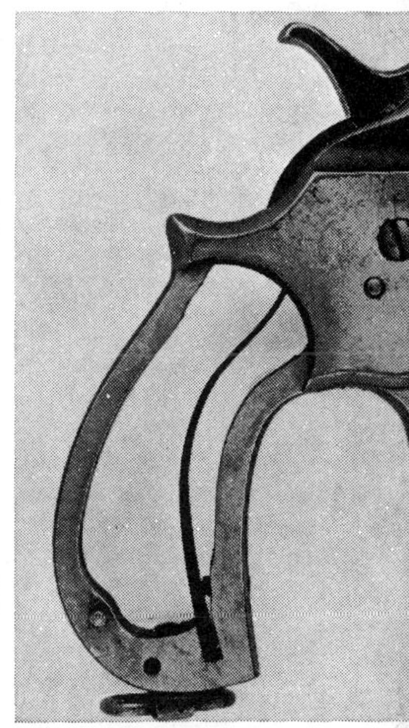

One-piece frame and backstrap construction introduced on Colt Frontier D.A. revolver.

Colt Model of 1889 6-shot D.A. revolver, cal. .38 long and short Colt, 4½" barrel, swing-out cylinder, blade front sight, blued finish, hard rubber grips. This was the first Colt swing-out cylinder model.

This square butt model retained long cylinder flutes and has no locking notches on side or rear face of cylinder. Differs from previous Colt D.A. revolvers in that cylinder rotates to left. Chambered for cal. .38 short and long Colt, and cal. .41 short and long Colt. Standard barrel lengths were 3", 4½", and 6". Barrel marked "Colt's Pt. F.A. Mfg. Co., Hartford, Ct., U.S.A., Patented Aug. 5th 1884, November 6th 1888", with either "Colt D.A. .38" or "Colt D.A. .41", on left side. Grips were predominantly hard rubber. Only cal. .38 revolvers will be found with Service markings and Inspector Rinaldo A. Carr's initials on left side of trigger guard. Model 1889 revolver was manufactured for 3 years, with production ending in 1892. This scarce model has been overlooked by collectors.

Colt Army 6-shot D.A. Model of 1902, cal. .45 Colt, 6" barrel, rod ejector, blade front sight, blued finish, hard rubber birdshead grips, lanyard ring.

Model of 1902 revolver was manufactured for Army in 6" barrel length only. As only about 5000 were produced, this model will become increasingly scarce. Serial number sequence is in 43000 to 48000 range. Initials of Army Inspector Rinaldo A. Carr are usually present on front left side of trigger guard. Model of 1902 revolver is readily distinguished from Frontier model by oversized trigger guard and longer trigger of former arm. Trigger guard of Model 1902 is 2½" long and 1½" deep, and trigger extends 1⅜" from frame. Extra large guard supposedly facilitated firing with gloved hand. ■

FROM 1897 to 1943, Colt's principal large-caliber revolver was the double-action New Service Model with solid frame and swing-out cylinder. Simple, rugged, and reliable, it was produced in many calibers for military, police, and sporting use.

There are many model variations of this revolver. Official Colt designations for these variations include New Service, New Service Target, and Shooting Master. U. S. Government designations are Model 1909 and Model 1917. Other designations such as Old Model and Improved Model are unofficial, but are used by collectors for convenience.

There are many variations of this large-caliber, double-action revolver

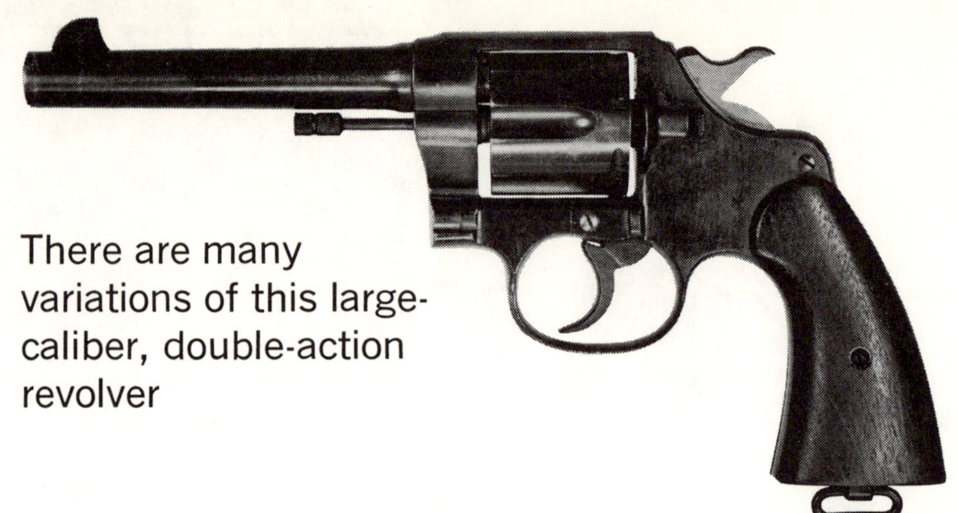

The Colt New Service

By GILBERT E. NEWTON

New Service, Old Model. Produced 1897-1905 in cals. .38-40, .44-40, .44 S&W Russian, .45 Colt, .450 Revolver, and .455 Eley. The standard barrel lengths are 4½", 5½", and 7½" revolver with 4½" barrel shown), and the grips are checkered black hard rubber with the word "COLT" in an oval at the top. A rampant colt encircled by the legend "COLT'S NEW SERVICE" is stamped on the sideplate.

While this model has a rebounding hammer, it lacks a hammer-block safety (Colt positive lock). There is a small dismounting hole through the ejector rod head, and most ejector rod heads of this model are smooth. Nickel-plated specimens have a blued hammer, trigger, screws, and lanyard swivel.

Barrels were first marked with the patent date Aug. 5, 1884. Later, the date June 5, 1900, was added.

Revolvers of this model in cals. .455 Eley and .476 Eley were used in U. S. Army handgun tests in 1904.

All variations of the New Service revolver were numbered together in the same series to over 353,000. Serial numbers on the Old Model go to about 21,000.

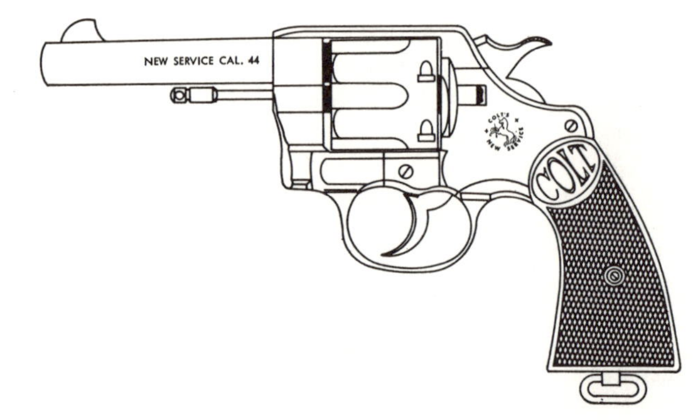

New Service Target, Old Model. Manufactured 1900-1905 in cals. .44 S&W Russian, .45 Colt, and .455 Eley. It differs from the regular version of the Old Model as follows: **(a)** Standard barrel length is 7½". **(b)** The topstrap of the frame has a flat top, and is rectangular in cross section. **(c)** A rear sight adjustable for windage is in a dovetail slot on the frame. **(d)** The front sight blade is inserted in a base permanently attached to the barrel. **(e)** The grips are hand-checkered wood. **(f)** There is no hole in the butt for a lanyard swivel. **(g)** The firing pin pivots in the hammer. (In the regular version, the firing pin is pinned rigidly in place.) **(h)** Trigger and grip straps are checkered.

Revolvers of this model in U. S. calibers have sights with adjusting screws and locking screws. Sights of cal. .455 Eley revolvers have neither adjusting screws nor locking screws. Windage is adjusted by driving the rear sight laterally, and elevation by using a higher or lower front sight blade.

Bores of cal. .455 Eley target revolvers have rounded-groove Metford style rifling (see illustration) which does not accumulate powder fouling as readily as conventional rifling.

Some cal. .455 Eley revolvers are stamped "ENGLAND" or "AUSTRALIA", or both on the bottom of the butt.

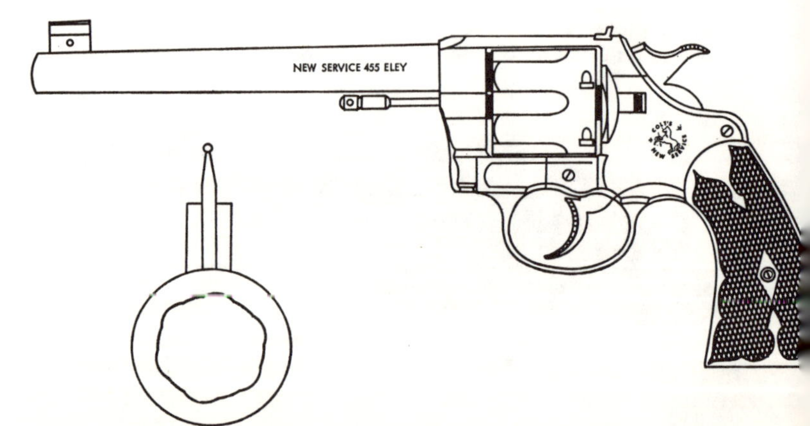

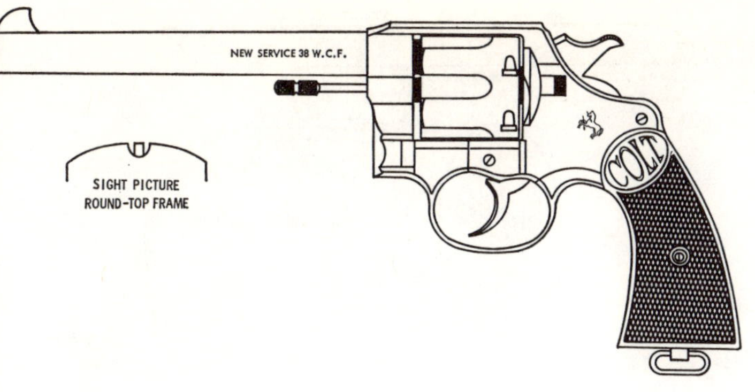

New Service, Improved Model. Introduced in 1905, this model has a number of improvements: **(a)** Hammer-block safety called Colt positive lock. **(b)** Bolt spring and hammer strut spring are coil springs, (flat springs in previous New Service models). **(c)** Rebound lever made in one piece, omitting a separate pivoted fly previously used. **(d)** Firing pin pivoted in hammer (this feature also used in New Service Target, Old Model). **(e)** Sides of trigger guard join main part of frame in a smooth contour. **(f)** Topstrap contour changed at front and rear, but U-notch rear sight retained. **(g)** Ejector rod head knurled. **(h)** Hammer spur and cylinder latch have finer checkering than on previous models. **(i)** The legend "COLT'S NEW SERVICE" omitted from sideplate. **(j)** Patent date July 4, 1905 added to legend on top of barrel.

The revolver shown is in cal. .38-40 Winchester, and has a 7½" barrel.

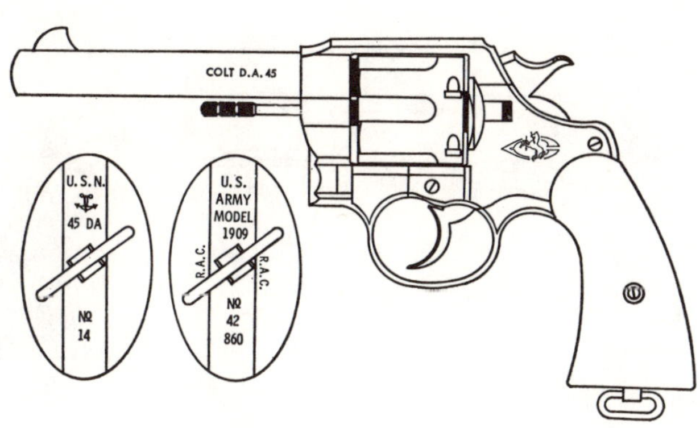

Model 1909 U. S. Army, and Model 1909 U. S. Navy— These revolvers have 5½" barrels, smooth wooden grips, and fire the .45 Colt and .45 Colt Model 1909 cartridges. (The rim of the Model 1909 cartridge is slightly larger than that of the .45 Colt to facilitate extraction.) Ejector rod heads are knurled; some have dismounting holes.

There are different markings on these revolvers. Those made for the Army bear the inspector's stamp R.A.C. (for Rinaldo A. Carr) instead of the Colt proof mark (interlocked letters VP in a triangle). They are also marked "UNITED STATES PROPERTY" on the underside of the barrel. Navy specimens have the Colt proof mark, but no inspector's marks.

A stylized "C" is on the sideplate along with the rampant Colt trademark. (Some commercial versions subsequent to the Model 1909 also have the stylized "C".) On some Model 1909's, the factory serial number differs from the military Service number on the butt.

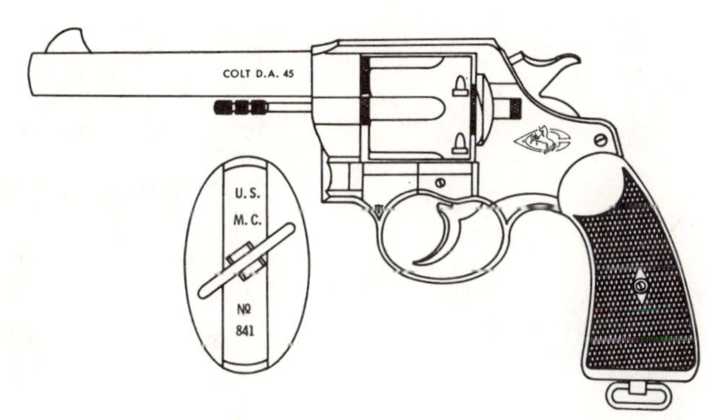

Model 1909 U. S. Marine Corps—Except for its markings, checkered grips, and slightly rounded butt, this revolver closely resembles the Model 1909 U. S. Army. Some early specimens have civilian-style hard rubber grips; later ones have wood grips checkered on the pattern of the hard rubber grips. There is a Colt proof mark on this revolver, but no inspector's marks. Unlike the Army Model, it is not marked "UNITED STATES PROPERTY", nor is it marked "Model 1909".

Most serial numbers are between 24,000 and 26,000.

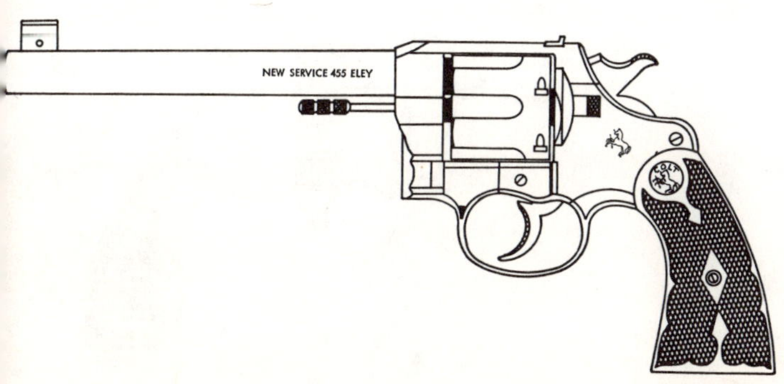

New Service Target, Improved Model—Essentially this revolver is the New Service Target Old Model, but with the 1905 improvements (see New Service, Improved Model). A typical specimen has wood grips with silver rampant colt medallions. Standard calibers are .44 S&W Special, .45 Colt, .45 Auto., and .455 Eley. There are also some revolvers of this model in cal. .44 S&W Russian (available until 1907 when the .44 S&W Special was introduced). Although listed in Colt catalogs, this model in cal. .45 Auto. is uncommon.

The cal. .455 Eley revolver shown has Metford rifling and crudely-adjustable target sights. Revolvers of this model made in the 1930's incorporate several style changes listed for the Shooting Master.

Model 1917 U. S. Army—Made during World War I, this revolver has a 5½" barrel. It bears a close resemblance to the Model 1909 U. S. Army, but fires the .45 Auto. cartridge adapted for revolver use by 3-shot semi-circular clips. Other differences between this model and the 1909 are: **(a)** The barrel of the Model 1917 is considerably tapered and has a short cylindrical section just forward of the frame. **(b)** There is no stylized "C" on the sideplate. **(c)** The Model 1917 has a rougher finish than the Model 1909. **(d)** Model 1917 has a shorter cylinder than that of the Model 1909 to give space for the 3-shot clips. The cylinder stop lug on the Model 1917 is correspondingly wider. **(e)** There is a variety of inspector's marks on the Model 1917.

Serial numbers of this revolver range from about 150,000 to approximately 300,000. Service numbers on the butts go up to about 150,000 in rough correlation to serial numbers.

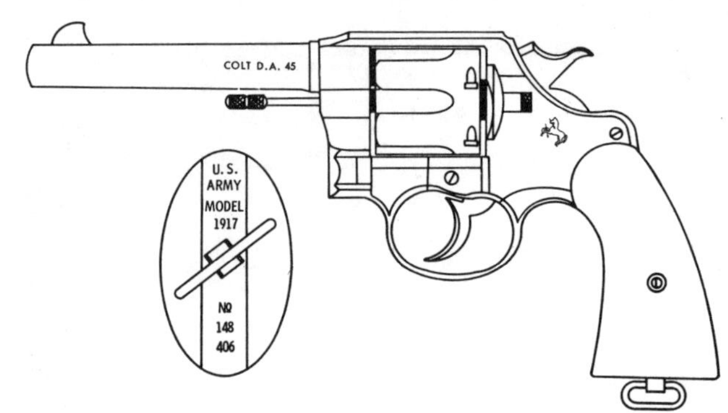

New Service, Late Model—Several minor changes made in the New Service, particularly during the 1920's, include: **(a)** Tapered barrel with contour similar to that of the Model 1917. **(b)** Checkered walnut grips with silver medallions. **(c)** Topstrap of frame partly flattened, and finished a dull gray to reduce glare. The flat portion is matted. (This topstrap change occurred about 1926 in the serial number region 325,000 to 328,000.) **(d)** Rectangular rear sight notch instead of U-notch. **(e)** Cylinder latch with rounded checkered end instead of square end that jabs the thumb during recoil. **(f)** Checkered trigger. **(g)** Patent date of Oct. 5, 1926, added to legend on top of barrel. **(h)** Front sight slightly wider than that of earlier models.

These changes occurred over a period of several years. Thus revolvers made at various times have different combinations of these features.

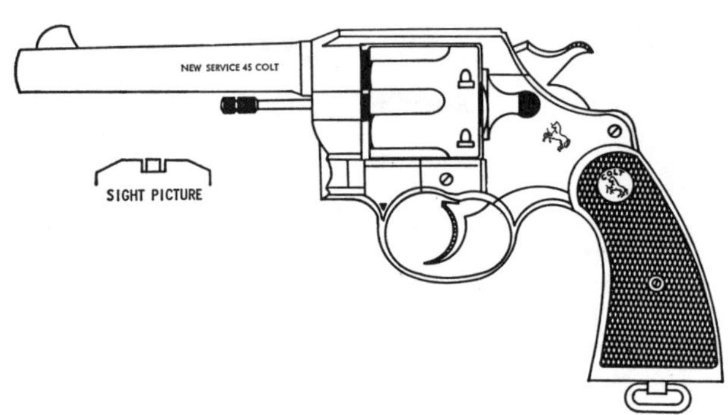

Shooting Master—Introduced in 1932, this revolver is similar in most respects to the New Service Target revolver made during the same period. The distinguishing features of each revolver are sometimes mixed in revolvers made up on special order.

Standard calibers for the Shooting Master are .38 Special, .357 Magnum, .44 S&W Special, .45 Auto., and .45 Colt. Ordinarily this revolver is encountered in .38 Special only, while the New Service Target is seldom found in any caliber under .44.

Standard barrel lengths for these revolvers are 6" for the Shooting Master, and 7½" for the New Service Target. Both models have checkered walnut grips and adjustable target sights. The butt of the Shooting Master is slightly rounded, and the grips are somewhat narrower toward the bottom than those of the New Service Target. Cylinder latches of these revolvers are alike except that the latch of the Shooting Master is smooth while that of the New Service Target is checkered.

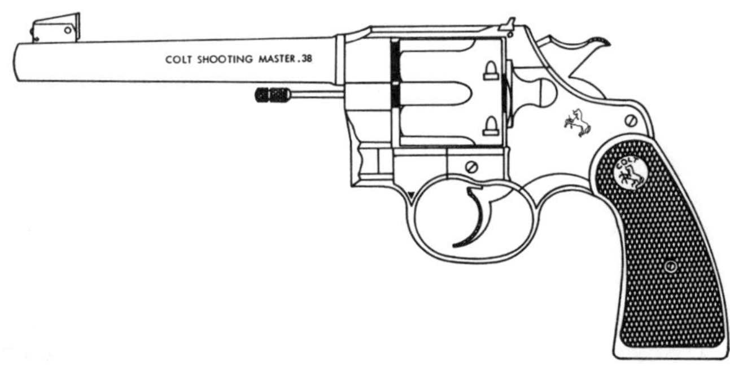

New Service .38 Special and .357 Magnum—In their standard versions, these revolvers have 4", 5", or 6" barrels, and rounded butts like that of the Shooting Master. They usually have no lanyard swivels.

The cal. .357 Magnum revolver shown has a 4" barrel, and is typical except for the unusual front sight with vertical rear face. The slanted sight base gives the effect of a ramp.

By 1940, Colt's offered the New Service, New Service Target, and Shooting Master with a choice of round or square butt. Some confusion of identifying characteristics also results from mixed features on revolvers made up on special order, and from new barrels and cylinders installed on older specimens. ■

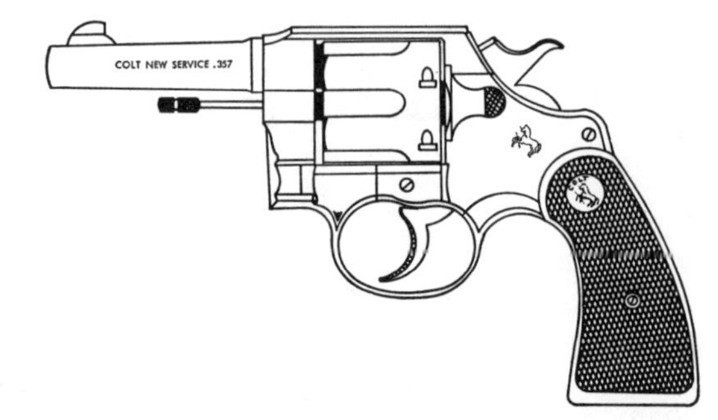

Colt New Service Revolvers

By WILLIAM M. HOUSER

GENERALLY speaking, I believe the Colt New Service is the best buy in modern collector handguns. Its many versions are appreciating rapidly and can be shot if you wish. The New Service is a rugged, dependable gun, powerful enough to save your life if a situation should arise. I have never had a New Service break, even after firing thousands of rounds.

I have built my own collection of New Service revolvers with the goal of trying to get one from the earliest series right on through its last production. While doing this, I also tried to get one of each caliber made for the U.S. market, one of each barrel length available and obtain as many model variations and different finishes as possible. For a complete collection, target models are an expensive must, but I accomplished my goal. This only required 17 different guns, which I consider the best handguns ever built by Colt.

When the Colt New Service revolver was introduced in 1898, Colt started with serial No. 1. Colt patented the name "New Service" Feb. 21, 1899; in that year 2300 guns were shipped. By 1901 and 1902, serials were only in the 6000 series. By 1903, they were up to No. 7800; 1904 to No. 9700; 1905 to No. 12600; and by 1915, due to military orders, they were beginning to take hold, serials then being in the 90000's.

By 1921 serials had jumped to No. 315000, but production leveled off. Commercial civilian production reached No. 318000 by 1923 and No. 328000 by 1928. There were 345000 by 1938 and at the end in 1943, serials were in the 355000's.

As with all good guns, you could order your New Service any way you wanted it if you didn't mind waiting until it went through the custom shop. Blue finish was standard, but nickel, silver or gold plating were available at extra cost. There were three types of engraving available, but fewer than 75 New Service revolvers were engraved at the factory, and less than 10 Shooting Masters, thus making *any* factory engraved New Service revolver exceedingly rare.

In the old model target revolvers you could only get .44 Russian and .455 Eley chamberings and the 7½" barrel was standard. In plain guns, you could get cals. .38-40, .44-40, .45 Colt, and .450, .455 and .476 Eley. The 5½" barrel was standard and other lengths were special order. Later, improved models featured the same calibers, with .44 Russian, and .44 Special, and .45 ACP added. Still later, .38 Special and .357 Magnum chamberings were offered.

At first, black hard rubber grips were standard on all guns; around 1905 deluxe hand-checkered walnut grips were standard on target models only. In 1909, you could order checkered medallion grips with any gun at extra cost, while the medallion was not present on the grips of target models until 1915. From the beginning, bone, ivory, carved or checkered ivory with medallions and mother of pearl medallion grips were available at extra cost.

In my opinion the New Service was the largest and strongest swing-out cylinder revolver ever built until S&W brought out their Model 29 in .44 Magnum. The New Service is a big gun, measuring 13" overall with 7½" barrel. It weighs 42 ozs. and

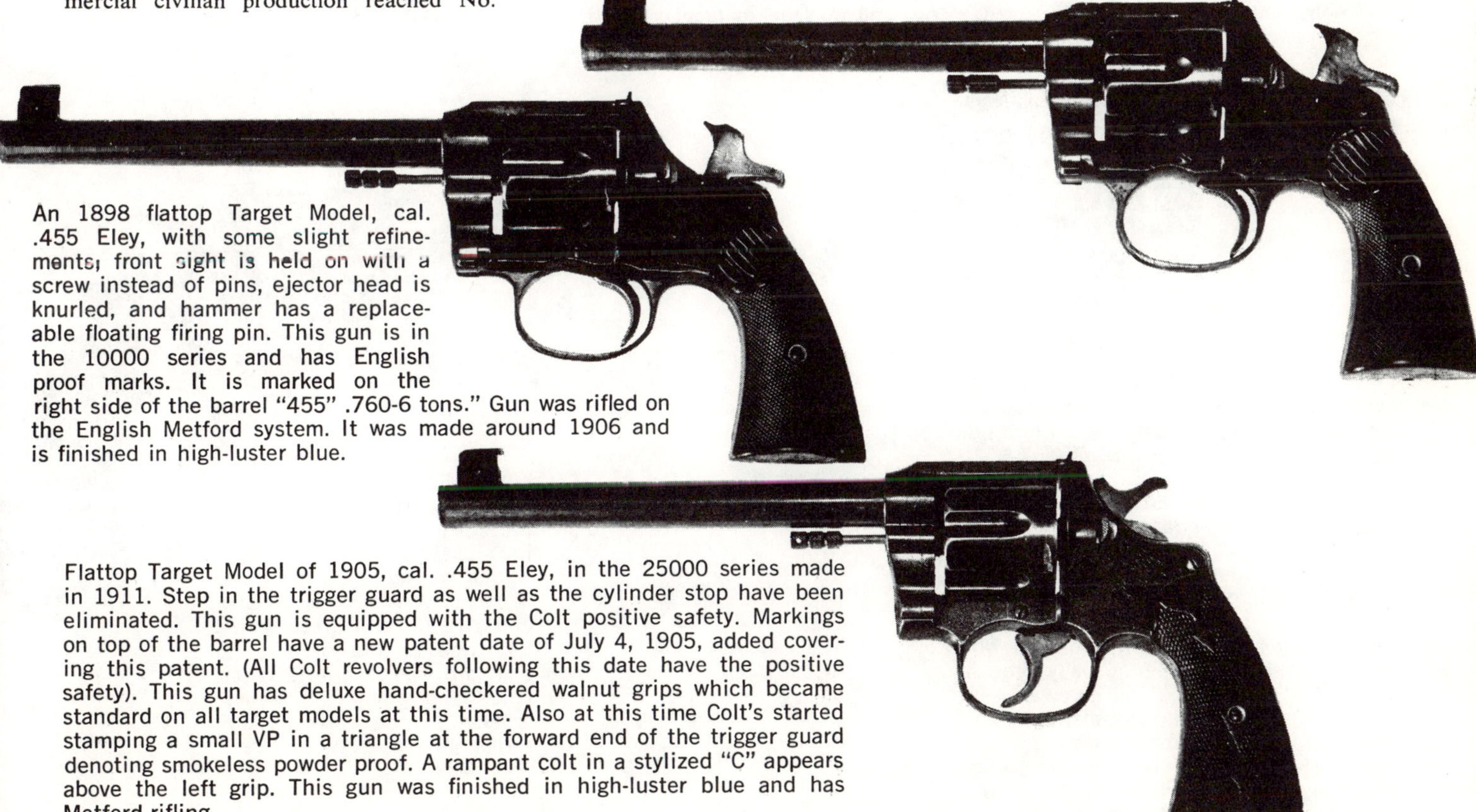

A very early 1898 type New Service flattop target model in the 6000 series, built around 1901. It is cal. .455 Eley with 7½" barrel marked on the left side "New Service .455 Eley." "Colt's New Service" is also marked in a circle above the left grip on these early guns. Barrel is marked on top with two lines "Colt's Patent Firearms Manufacturing Co. Hartford Ct. U.S.A. Pat. Aug. 5, 1884 - June 5, 1900." Gun is English-proofed. Black hard rubber grips were standard on all New Service revolvers (except military models) until the 1930's. Gun is rifled with six lands and grooves with narrow, fairly deep rifling. Ejector rod tip is smooth, and sights are quite crude, the front one being a blade double pinned to a machined slot in the barrel, while the rear sight can be tapped from side to side after loosening a tiny screw set in the top of the sight. This gun is finished in high-luster blue.

An 1898 flattop Target Model, cal. .455 Eley, with some slight refinements; front sight is held on with a screw instead of pins, ejector head is knurled, and hammer has a replaceable floating firing pin. This gun is in the 10000 series and has English proof marks. It is marked on the right side of the barrel "455" .760-6 tons." Gun was rifled on the English Metford system. It was made around 1906 and is finished in high-luster blue.

Flattop Target Model of 1905, cal. .455 Eley, in the 25000 series made in 1911. Step in the trigger guard as well as the cylinder stop have been eliminated. This gun is equipped with the Colt positive safety. Markings on top of the barrel have a new patent date of July 4, 1905, added covering this patent. (All Colt revolvers following this date have the positive safety). This gun has deluxe hand-checkered walnut grips which became standard on all target models at this time. Also at this time Colt's started stamping a small VP in a triangle at the forward end of the trigger guard denoting smokeless powder proof. A rampant colt in a stylized "C" appears above the left grip. This gun was finished in high-luster blue and has Metford rifling.

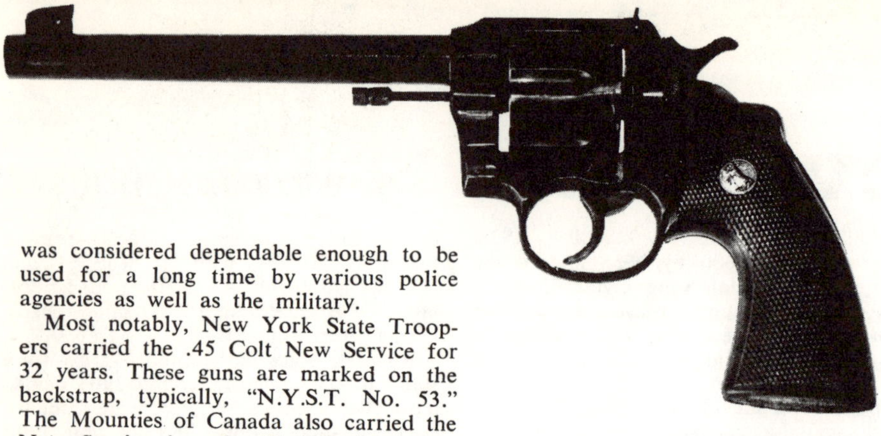

Flattop Target Model in the 50000 series made in 1913, cal. .44 Russian—.44 Special. The sights now show refinements that followed through to the end of production. The front blade is adjustable vertically by means of a small screw at the front and is locked in place by a small screw through the sight base. The rear sight is adjustable laterally by a small screw running through the frame and is locked in place with a tiny screw on top. This gun is marked on the left side of the barrel in two lines: first line "New Service Target", second "New Service Russian and S&W Special .44". This gun was factory refinished at some time as it now has dual tone blue with the sand-blasted top strap. This finish didn't come until much later. There are also a set of Roper-style grips on this gun, evidently installed when it was refinished. The Colt marking above the left grip is changed—the stylized "C" is gone and the rampant colt remained to end of production. Rifling is standard.

was considered dependable enough to be used for a long time by various police agencies as well as the military.

Most notably, New York State Troopers carried the .45 Colt New Service for 32 years. These guns are marked on the backstrap, typically, "N.Y.S.T. No. 53." The Mounties of Canada also carried the New Service in cal. .45 Colt for many years and these were marked on the backstrap either "R.C.M.P." (Royal Canadian Mounted Police) or "N.W.M.P." (North West Mounted Police). The guns carried by these law enforcement agencies were all the later improved models at time of issue.

At the beginning of World War I Colt's turned its talents to military weapons and there are few commercial New Service's in the serial range of about 100000 to 300000. When the 1917 Army model was brought out, Colt's designed a tapered barrel for it, probably because the military thought it would be stronger. After the war was over Colt's continued this type of barrel on all New Service arms.

This model is commonly called the improved model, though collectors refer to it as the 1917 type.

I have a 1921 Colt's catalog showing both standard and target models with the old-style straight barrel. They must have been using up old parts at that time. The improved model guns retained the earlier patent dates with the last one still 1905.

For some unknown reason Colt's waited until 1933 to use up some surplus 1917 Army parts and marketed a commercial 1917 Army model, marked on the left side of the barrel "Colt M1917 .45 ACP" or "Colt .45 Auto Ctg." around the 335000 serial number. These guns are very scarce and were sold with regular blue, not military finish, and had checkered medallion grips and no lanyard loop in the butt.

There were some 1917 Army revolvers re-issued at the beginning of WWII and some of these had been rebuilt and Parkerized. I have owned five of this type, but never one of the 1917 commercials.

Any New Service with a barrel length other than standard is desirable; 4", 4½", 5" and 6" lengths are the harder to find. All standard New Service and military

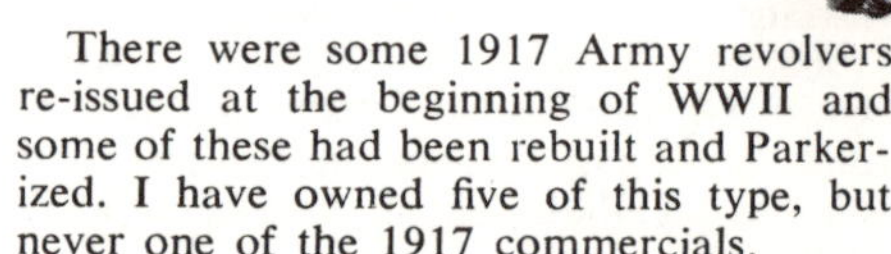

A typical New Service commercial improved type of 1917 with 7½" tapered barrel in cal. .38-40. Marked on the left side of the barrel "New Service .38 W.C.F." in very small letters. The earlier 1905 Model in this caliber is marked in larger letters. This gun, in the early 300000 series, is finished in dual-tone blue and has standard six-groove rifling.

This New Service 1898 Model is included here because of its unusual features. It is cal. .44-40 but is only marked on left side of the barrel "New Service Cal. .44." It was marked this way because at the time it was built .44-40 was the only caliber available in the standard New Service. The .44 Russian chambering was reserved for the target models. Later the 1905 and 1917 types were marked "New Service .44 W.C.F." This gun is unusual because it has an original 4½" barrel coupled with the heavy .44-40 caliber, usually ordered with the 7½" barrel. This gun was sent back to the factory and completely rebuilt including a new hammer and the later type dual-tone blue finish. The ivory grips may have been original as this gun was special ordered with the short barrel. It also has the VP mark at the front of the trigger guard.

New Service commercial improved model special-ordered in nickel plate with smooth walnut military type grips and in scarce .44 Russian-.44 Special cal., and so marked on the left side of the barrel. The standard 5½" barrel has six lands and grooves. This gun is also in the early 300000 series, made between 1921 and 1923.

models have the lanyard loop, but target models do not, nor did the commercial 1917 model.

During their years of use, New Service revolvers set quite a few records, most notable being the first perfect 100-point revolver score on Nov. 15, 1907, a world record. A New Service also fired a world record at Bisley in 1909.

One unhappy note here: Though the Shooting Master was supposed to be the best target revolver ever developed and Colt's advertised it heavily, it was kind of a dud as everyone on the line at that time still seemed to prefer the lighter Officers' Model and consequently the Shooting Master is very scarce today. These fine guns were numbered in the New Service series and mine in the early 300000's was built soon after they were introduced.

The Shooting Master came in cals. .38 Special, .357 Magnum, .44 Special and .45 ACP with 6" barrel standard. I have found the .357 Magnum and .45 ACP models to be the hard ones to locate. ■

The very scarce .38 Special Colt Shooting Master which was a special New Service target revolver with the new patent date of Oct. 25, 1926, added to the barrel markings. This was when big changes took place in the New Service. It was offered in .38 Special and .357 Magnum. Top of the frame on all standard guns was matted, the rear sight was changed from a simple "V" notch to a square notch, and machine-checkered walnut grips with Colt medallions became standard on all guns. The rounded, knurled cylinder latch was added and the front sight was modified to be wider at the bottom and tapering towards the top, with a distinct step about half way up. Target models had all these refinements and the top of the frame was sand blasted to reduce glare. This finish continued down over the rear of the frame and back strap. Up to this time all New Service revolvers had square butts except the Marine Corps Model, but from 1926 on, one could order the New Service with either round or square butt with no difference in price. Most Shooting Masters had the round butt like the one pictured, but early ones in cal. .357 Magnum came with square butt only. The gun pictured has a customized skeleton hammer with low spur and a plastic insert in the front sight. These special pieces were modified by a gunsmith named King who made a whole line of special sights and parts for both rifles and handguns. These special sights and parts were not limited to the New Service Colt but could be special ordered from the factory and installed on a gun there. The R. F. Sedgley firm was also well known for custom work on the New Service line, but their specialty was converting the New Service to .22 Hornet, etc.

Typical late model New Service revolver. This type continued to the end of production in 1943. It is a .38 Special with uncommon 5" barrel. It features 1926 patents and all the refinements mentioned earlier. This late model also has a knurled trigger. Unfortunately, this gun went to England under lend-lease at the start of World War II, and the British converted it to .38 Webley by enlarging the rear of the chambers. On the left side of the barrel where it is marked "New Service .38 Special" the word "Special" is X'd out, and it has complete British proofmarks. When these essentially new guns were shipped back to the U.S. after the war, they were thrown loose and unwrapped into big crates and thus picked up a lot of nicks and dents. This gun was made very late in production as it is in the 350000 series.

pical Army Model of 1909, arked on the left side of the rrel "Colt D.A. .45" and arked on the bottom of the tt "U.S. Army model of 1909). 22675." The Navy model of 909 is exactly the same except r the butt markings which re typically "U.S.N. (Anchor)). 29756." The Marine Corps odel of 1909 has rounded ips and typical markings on e butt would be "US-MC No. 1* 27521," the latter being e serial number of the gun. l had standard six-land 5½" rrels marked on the underde "United States Property". l have smooth walnut grips except the Marine Corps model ich has checkered grips. All re in cal. .45 Colt and fined in high lustre blue.

Typical New Service Army Model of 1917, marked on the left side of the barrel "Colt D.A. 45" and chambered for the .45 ACP cartridge. Markings on the butt of this model are "U.S. Army Model of 1917 No. 126276." It has regular smooth walnut grips and standard 5½" barrel with "United States Property" on the bottom. These guns were hurry-up pieces, blued in a crude manner without even polishing out buffing marks. Early production pieces had the chambers bored through, making the use of half-moon clips mandatory. Later the cylinders were chambered for the .45 ACP round and they could then be shot without the clips, the only drawback being the empties had to be removed one at a time.

LITTLE COLT WITH A BIG FOLLOWING

By DONALD M. SIMMONS, JR.

THE grandparent of all .25 caliber automatic pistols is John M. Browning's Vest Pocket Automatic Pistol. Browning, an American, designed this pistol in 1904 and patented it in Belgium. It was first manufactured by the Fabrique Nationale d'Armes de Guerre, in Herstal, Belgium, and it became so popular in Europe that over a million had been sold by 1912.

Colt's Patent Firearms Mfg. Co. of Hartford, Conn., had the rights to manufacture and sell the pistol in the United States, and began marketing it in 1908. It was called the "Colt Automatic Pistol Pocket Model Calibre .25 Hammerless" (it was striker fired).

The Colt .25 was called "Model N" at the factory, and it was third in quantity of Colt automatic pistols made, outdone only by the cal. .45 Model 1911-1911A1 military pistol and the cal. .32 Pocket Automatic.

The .25 ACP cartridge (known in Europe as the 6.35 mm. Browning) was developed jointly by John M. Browning and William "UMC" Thomas of the Union Metallic Cartridge Co., Bridgeport, Conn. Browning wrote to Thomas on June 16, 1904, asking for a test run of 500 cartridges of what was to become the .25 ACP round. From this development program came the universally popular .25 ACP cartridge.

Cal. .25 ACP pistols were not manufactured as extensively in the United States as they were in Europe where more than 200 models have been recorded. The only other U.S. production model was the Harrington and Richardson, introduced after Colt's brought out its model. An estimated 17,000 to 18,000 cal. .25 H&R pistols were produced from 1912 to 1915.

There are two other American .25 automatics which were actually made in Europe, but had stampings indicating domestic manufacture. The most common is F. N.'s Baby Browning which has a St. Louis, Mo., address. In the sale of the patent rights, Browning agreed that Colt's would sell only in the U.S. and Fabrique Nationale abroad, with Great Britain a common market.

The other cal. .25 automatic sometimes seen is the rare Phoenix, marketed by the Phoenix Arms Co., of Lowell, Mass., but made in Belgium.

Early issue Colt .25 ACP pistols carried only three patent dates—Aug. 25, 1896; April 20, 1897; and Dec. 22, 1903. None of these dates has much to do with the 1908 issue Colt pistol.

The 1896 patent is on a magazine pistol, not an automatic pistol and bears no resemblance to the .25 Colt. There are four 1897 patents. They launched the 1900 and 1902 Colt .38 ACP pistols and the Browning-designed 1900 .32 ACP pistol, but have no real kinship to the cal. .25 ACP pistol. The 1902 patent is the basic patent for the Colt 1903 Pocket .32 and later .380 pistols.

The Colt version of the Browning .25 caliber pocket pistol was never patented in the U.S. On Jan. 25, 1910, Browning was granted a patent on the combination safety and slide lock for the Colt .25. Interestingly the early F. N. pistols did not have a manual safety which Colt engineers apparently considered necessary. Later F. N. cal. .25 pistols looked exactly like the Colt with an added manual safety. The last patent concerning the Colt .25 pistol was issued to Colt employee G. H. Tansley on July 31, 1917, and covered the magazine safety.

Manufacture of the Colt .25 Pocket Automatic Pistol began on Oct. 30, 1908, with serial No. 1, and production continued until World War II. While manufacture of the model was not resumed after the war, a stock remained on hand until Feb. 19, 1947, and terminated with gun No. 420705, the quantity made.

Occasionally one sees a Colt .25 pistol marked "U. S. Property"; usually they are fakes. This does not rule out the possibility, however, that genuine "U. S. Property" marked Colt .25 pistols do not exist in some U.S. or foreign arsenal.

The lowest price the Colt .25 pistol sold for was $12 in a very early (1910-1911) *Sears, Roebuck & Co. Catalog.* In the 1920's and through 1934 the price was $17. There was a period in 1919 when the post World War I inflation drove the price to an alltime high of $22. From 1936 to 1942 the price was $20.50.

There is only one model of this pistol admitted by the Colt factory, but Colt literature does note the serial number at which the magazine safety was added, No. 141000. This division separates the early pistols from the later, more numerous models with magazine safety.

Early Colt .25 shipped in 1908 has patent dates 1896, 1897 and 1903 on the slide.

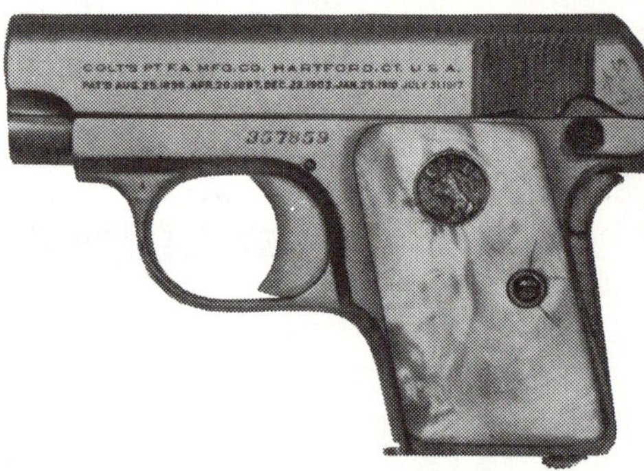

Later Colt .25, shipped in 1926, is nickel plated with early pearl medallion grips.

Baby Browning .25, made by Fabrique Nationale and marked "Browning Arms Co." was made after World War II.

Early and middle-production pistols had black rubber grips while late models had checkered walnut grips with metal medallions.

From the beginning, the Colt .25 pistol was offered with either blued or nickel plated finishes at no difference in price. Despite this, there are fewer nickel plated pistols. My guess would be about one out of every 20 or 25 was nickel plated. Early pistols had a bright blue which gave way eventually to a smoky blue finish.

Variations in slide markings are good sources of information as to the dates of manufacture. There are five different left side legends:

**COLT'S PAT. FIRE ARMS MFG. CO. HARTFORD, CONN. U.S.A.
PATENTED AUG. 25, 1896, APR. 20, 1897, DEC. 22, 1903**

This started at serial No. 1 and went at least to serial No. 559 but no further than serial No. 3744.

**COLT'S PT. F.A. MFG. CO., HARTFORD, CT. U.S.A.
PATENTED AUG. 25, 1896, APR. 20, 1897, DEC. 22, 1903**

This began at least at serial No. 3744 and went to at least serial No. 21435 but no further than serial No. 29185.

**COLT'S PT. F.A. MFG. CO., HARTFORD, CT. U.S.A.
PAT'D AUG. 25, 1896, APR. 20, 1897. DEC. 22, 1903, JAN. 25, 1910**

This type of slide marking is found from at least serial No. 29185 to at least serial No. 67235 but no further than serial No. 77330. The manual safety patent date was added.

A variation had the same copy as above, but the size of the letters was reduced from .085" high to .065" high. This small type was used until the last of the gun's production. This first small type variation started with at least serial No. 77330 up to at least serial No. 280000 but no further than serial No. 284008.

**COLT'S PT. F.A. MFG. CO. HARTFORD, CT. U.S.A.
PAT'D AUG. 25, 1896, APR. 20, 1897, DEC. 22, 1903, JAN. 25, 1910, JULY 31, 1917**

This legend includes the magazine safety patent and goes from at least serial No. 284008 until at least serial No. 402228 but undoubtedly until the terminal serial No. 420705.

The earliest right legend is:

COLT AUTOMATIC
CALIBRE 25

It has been seen from serial No. 559 but was probably used at the start of the series. The highest gun seen so marked was serial No. 41345 but could extend no further than No. 77330.

The next right side slide marking type is identical to the above, but the height of the letters was reduced from .085" to .065". This started at least at serial No. 77330 and extended to serial No. 305896 and no further than serial No. 330801.

The last type of right slide marking still has the same copy as the two variations that preceded it, one difference being the second line of the legend has no spaces at each end. The second difference is the letters are much larger, .090" high.

This type legend started with at least serial No. 330801 and lasted until at least serial No. 402228 but undoubtedly went on to terminal No. 420705.

Colt discontinued its .25 pistol because there was little demand for it just before World War II. In 1959 they began to import the Astra from Spain and called it the "Colt Junior Automatic Pistol Cal. .25". It was available with a conversion kit to make it .22 rimfire short. The ability of the Spanish Colt to shoot inexpensive .22 ammunition for practice was an excellent idea and might have given a second life to the original Colt .25. This move to an overseas source for a type of firearm that was designed in the U.S., has its irony. But more ironic is that Colt should turn to Spain for an import since Spain for years flooded the U.S. with cheap, soft-metal parades of pistols that undersold our own superior domestic guns. ■

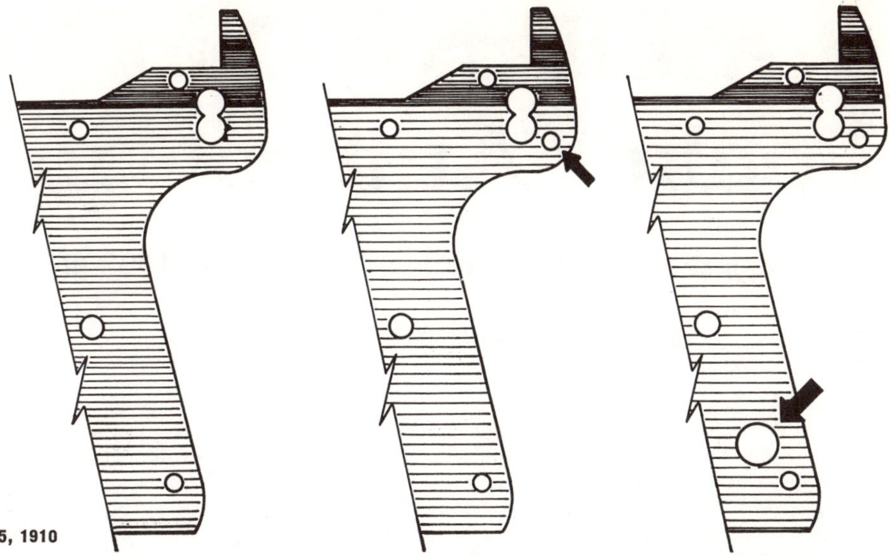

Colt made slight changes in the rear grip section of the frame. The earliest (l.) has two locating notches in the lower part of the figure eight hole for safety location. A later type (c.) has a plunger spring hole added. The third type has a spring assembly aid hole added.

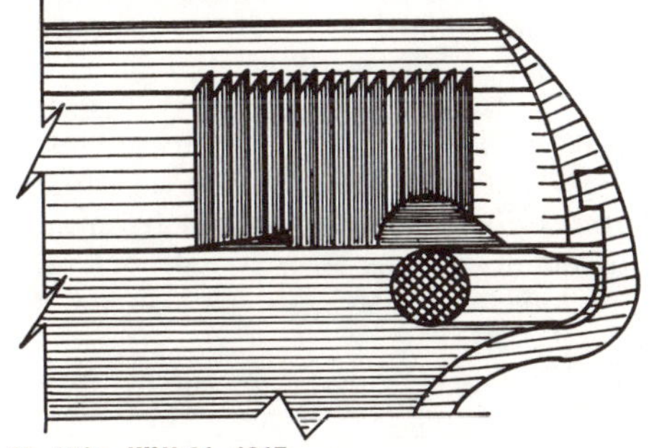

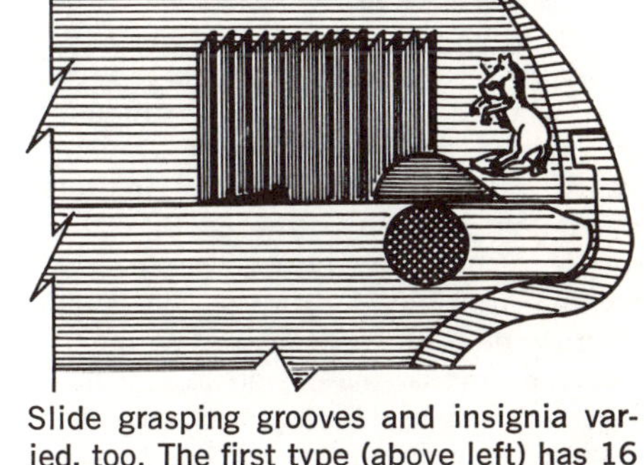

Slide grasping grooves and insignia varied, too. The first type (above left) has 16 slide grasping grooves on each side and on Colt insignia. The second (r.) has 14 grasping grooves on each side and a Colt standing on an oval. The last type (lower left) has 14 grasping grooves and a Colt standing but no oval.

The rare Phoenix .25 automatic (above) was made in Belgium. The U.S.-made Harrington & Richardson .25 A.C.P. shown below was produced in 1912.

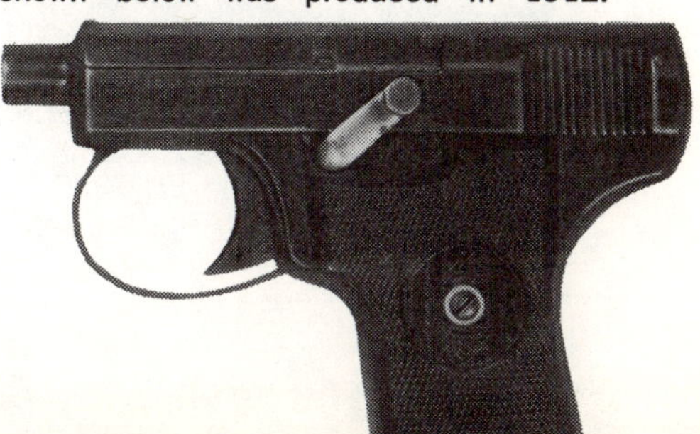

An Early Colt Pocket Automatic

The development of the so-called first model of the 1903 pistol

By DONALD M. SIMMONS, JR.

THE Colt's Patent Fire Arms Mfg. Co. terminated production of pocket automatic pistols in 1947 after producing more than 700,000 in cals. .32 ACP and .380 ACP. Of these, a total of 71,999 were of the first-model pattern. The numbering series for the first-model pistol began with No. 1 and terminated with No. 71,999. The inclusive dates of manufacture were from the summer of 1903 until 1908.

Colt initiated the manufacture of automatic pistols in the United States. They secured the John M. Browning patents and the sole rights to manufacture pistols of his design in the United States at the close of the 19th century. Browning also licensed the Belgian firm of Fabrique Nationale d'Armes de Guerre (FN), to manufacture pistols of his design in Europe. Either by accident or by arrangement, Colt made the high-power locked-breech pistols and FN made the lower powered blowback-operated pistols.

By 1902 it was obvious that the Colt locked-breech pistols were not enjoying the popularity accorded FN's blowback types. Colt had made the Model 1900, the Model 1902 Sporting, and the 1902 Military, all in cal. .38. The FN firm had made the Model 1900 pocket automatic in cal. .32 and the Model 1902/1903 Grande Modele in cal. 9 mm. Browning Long. As of late 1902, the FN firm had sold about 10 times the number of automatic pistols that had been sold by Colt.

The Colt firm apparently went to Browning with their problem, because he came up with a pared-down version of the FN Grande Modele, eliminating only the slide hold-open feature which retained the slide in full-recoil position after the last shot had been fired. This design became Colt's famous Model 1903 Pocket Automatic in cal. ".32 Rimless Smokeless", a caliber designation soon superseded by ".32 ACP" (Automatic Colt Pistol).

All first-model Model 1903 pistols had 4″ barrels and were chambered for the .32 ACP cartridge only. These 2 features distinguish this model from all subsequent models, which had barrels 3¾″ long and were made in .32 ACP and .380 ACP.

The Colt-Browning agreement provided that this pistol would be made and sold to compete with comparable revolvers. The selling price was therefore set at $15, which compared favorably with competitive revolvers made by both Colt and Smith & Wesson. The pistol was announced in the July 16, 1903, issue of *Shooting and Fishing.*

It is interesting to note that over the years the cost of pocket automatic pistols increased at a much slower rate than that of revolvers. In 1907 the price of the Colt .32 Pocket Automatic pistol was $15 compared with $14 for the Colt Police Positive revolver in cal. .38 Special. However, the same pistol in 1941 sold for $26.50 as compared with $35.50 for the same revolver. Labor costs over the years had become a larger factor in determining the selling price of handguns. The revolver has generally been more costly to manufacture than the automatic pistol because of the additional hand fitting.

The Colt Pocket Automatic is found stamped with 2 patent dates, the first being Apr. 20, 1897. This date has been assumed to apply to 4 U. S. patents issued to John M. Browning on that date. Three of these, Nos. 580,923, 580,924, and 580,925, have nothing to do with the Model 1903 pocket pistol. The last patent issued to Browning on that date, No. 580,926, does describe a blowback-operated pistol which is more like the FN Model 1900 than the Colt.

The second patent date, Dec. 22, 1903, refers to U. S. Patent No. 747,585 also granted to John M. Browning. It is a much more pertinent patent and shows a pistol very similar to the Colt Pocket Automatic. The one glaring exception is that neither the patent nor the accompanying drawings disclose a disconnector, the lack of which would have made the pistol fully automatic. I believe this was an error of omission, since from the early 1900's the fully-automatic pistol had been largely given up by designers because of the difficulty of controlling it in full-automatic fire.

Holds 9 cartridges

The Colt .32 Pocket Automatic is a blowback-operated, semi-automatic, concealed-hammer pistol. It weighs approximately 23 ozs. empty and an additional 2 ozs. with magazine loaded. The detachable magazine holds 8 cartridges, and an additional cartridge can be loaded into the chamber. The barrel is 4$\frac{1}{16}$″ long and has 6 lands and grooves with left twist. The front sight is fitted into a groove in the slide and is riveted in place. The U-notch rear sight is dovetailed to the slide. The rear sights on all pistols that I have examined are low, approximately $\frac{3}{32}$″ above the top of the slide. There is a first-model pistol in the Sidney Aberman collection with

1 Model 1900 FN Browning automatic pistol, cal. .32 ACP (Automatic Colt Pistol).

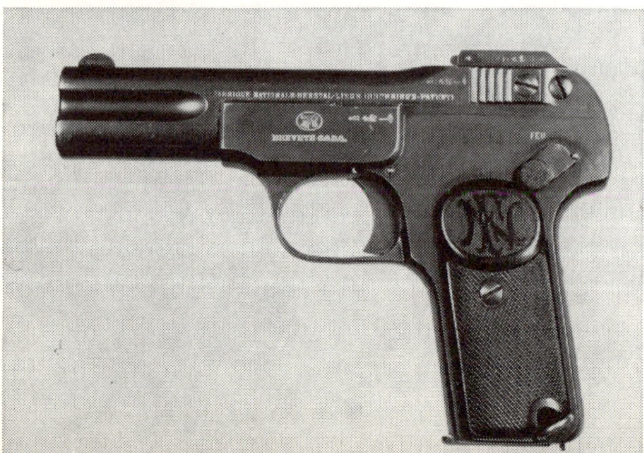

2 Model 1903 FN Browning Grande Modele automatic pistol, cal. 9 mm. Browning Long.

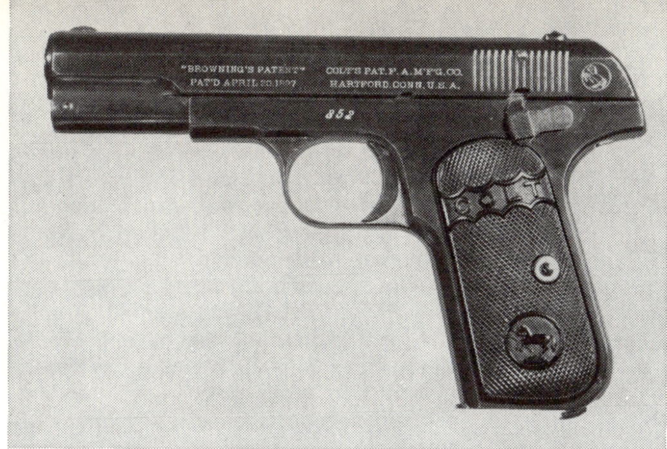

3 Left and right views of a very early first-model Model 1903 Colt Pocket Automatic pistol, No. 852. This is a rare version with single patent date, seen on guns from No. 250 to No. 8664. Not more than 11,000 first-model pistols bear this marking.

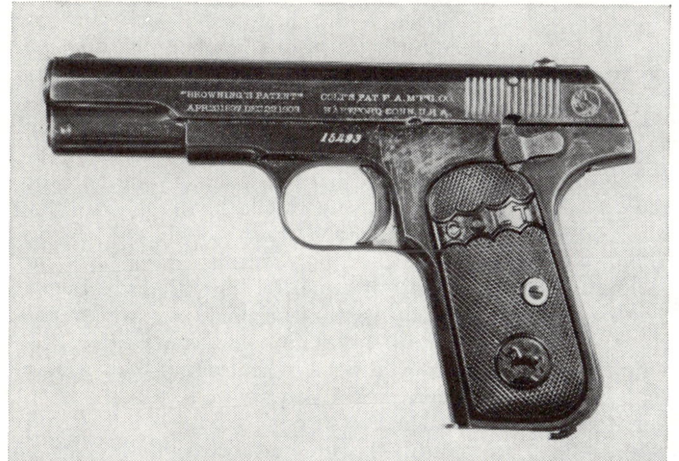

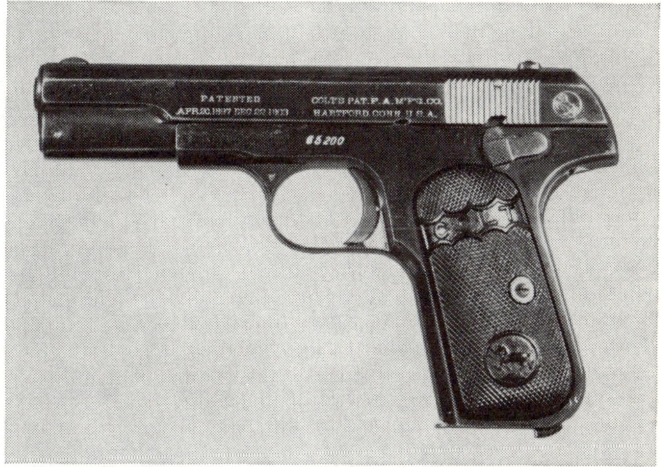

4 Early first-model Model 1903 Colt Pocket Automatic pistol (l.), Serial No. 15,493, with 2 patent dates. Second date was added after issuance of second patent on Dec. 22, 1903. This variation has been observed on guns from Nos. 11,101 to 32,189. Late first-model Model 1903 Colt Pocket Automatic pistol (r.) Serial No. 65,200. Legend carries double patent date, but word "PATENTED" has replaced "BROWNING'S PATENT" of earlier type pistol shown at left. The words "Browning's Patent" were ground off the original stamp. A second stamp using the word "Patented" in the empty space resulted in a varying depth of printing and an off-center position. This marking was seen on gun No. 40,200. A new stamp was made later to imprint the entire legend simultaneously. This marking has been seen on guns from Nos. 43,485 to 70,538.

an aperture sight ½" high. Its serial number is in the early hundreds.

These pistols have 3 safety features—(1) a disconnector which prevents more than one shot from being fired for each pull of the trigger, (2) a grip safety which must be depressed before the pistol can be fired, and (3) a manual safety on the left side of the frame. Both the manual safety and the grip safety prevent the sear disengaging the sear notch in the hammer. They also serve as cocking indicators. The grip safety protrudes from the rear of the grip when the hammer is cocked, and the manual safety will not move upward unless the hammer is cocked. (These statements apply, of course, to pistols in unaltered factory condition.)

The floorplate is attached to the sheet-metal body of the magazine by 2 pins. There are no markings of any kind to identify the magazine. It is blued a bit lighter than the pistol and its over-all finish is rougher than the finish on magazines of Colt pocket pistols manufactured at a later date.

The finish of all first-model pistols is the same. The slide and frame have a highly polished deep-blue finish. The trigger, manual safety, and barrel-bushing retaining plug have a bright mottled blue finish. Nickel finish was not offered in the first model. The hard-rubber grip pieces are also identical on all first-model pistols. The Colt name at the top is enclosed by a scalloped border. The rampant Colt insignia at the bottom is enclosed by a circle. There is a $\frac{1}{16}$" border around the entire grip. The remaining area of the grip piece is checkered.

All barrels show blue through the ejection port opening in the slide. They are not polished bright as in later models or as they are in reworked first-model pistols.

The following data furnished by the Colt firm gives the inclusive serial number range for each year that the first-model Colt Pocket Model pistol was manufactured.

Year	Serial No. Range
1903-1904	1-16,000
1904-1905	16,001-33,000
1905-1906	33,001-51,000
1906-1907	51,001-67,000
1907-1908	67,001-71,999

The readily visible differences among first-model pistols are cited in the captions to the illustrations. Some were internal. The earliest form of recoil spring had from 50 to 53 coils and an uncompressed length of about 5⅛". I found this type of closely pitched spring in guns with serial numbers up to 32,189. The later type of recoil spring is of much wider pitch having 45 coils and an uncompressed length of $5\frac{13}{16}$". It was observed in guns from Nos. 40,200 to 70,538. Both springs were wound from .040"-diameter wire.

In early 1905 the Colt firm adopted their now well-known proof mark—the interlocked letters "V" and "P" in a triangle. This was applied to guns in final inspection to show that they had been viewed and passed. The first pistol seen with this mark was No. 19,816. I did

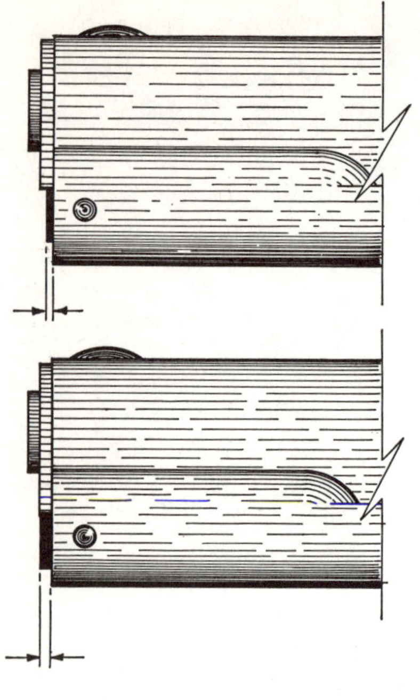

5 The barrel-bushing retaining plug on very early pistols protrudes only 1/32" as in upper sketch. This type plug has been found in guns from Nos. 250 to 8664. Plug was lengthened later by 1/32" to lie approximately flush with end of barrel bushing flange as in lower sketch. This feature has been noted in guns from Nos. 11,101 to 70,538. This was undoubtedly a modification that went to the termination of the first model since all second-model pistols have long plugs also.

not observe this marking on guns numbered between 252 and 15,493. It appears on the upper forward section of the trigger guard and is found on Colt handguns made today.

A minor variation noted on only one pistol (No. 2610) was a small dimple stamped midway of the magazine follower plate. This dimple may have been provided in order to correct a feeding difficulty encountered in early issues of this pistol.

Exciting collector item

I would estimate that approximately 50% of the first-model Colt Pocket Automatic pistols remain in use as 'working' guns. The possibility of purchasing this pistol without paying premium prices makes it an exciting collector item. Pieces in excellent condition are hard to come by because of the relatively fragile nature of the bluing applied to this model.

Reblued or refinished guns have no collector value. Beware of the example which appears original, but which has almost invisible slide markings. This almost always indicates that the gun has been buffed and skillfully reblued.

There is one form of modified pistol encountered occasionally. When first-model pistols were returned to the factory for refinishing or overhaul, the legends on both sides of the slide were sometimes restamped with the current stamps. I observed this condition on gun No. 51,386 which bore the legends found on pistols made in the 1920's.

The premium rarity among first-model pistols is the early type bearing the "Browning's Patent" marking with single date. Of more than 700,000 pocket pistols the Colt firm manufactured in cals. .32 and .380, not more than 11,000 bore this rare marking.

6 The earliest form of manual safety (see Fig. 3) was assembled into the pistol by pushing it in from left to right. It was held in place by tension of the hammer spring and the end of the safety pivot pin was visible on the right side of the frame as in upper sketch. This form of safety has been noted in guns from Nos. 250 to 2610. The safety was modified later by provision of a retaining screw in end of pivot pin as in lower sketch. This change was necessitated because the manual safety could be jarred out in firing until it would be inoperative in up or 'safe' position. This improved safety has been noted in guns from Nos. 8664 to 70,538.

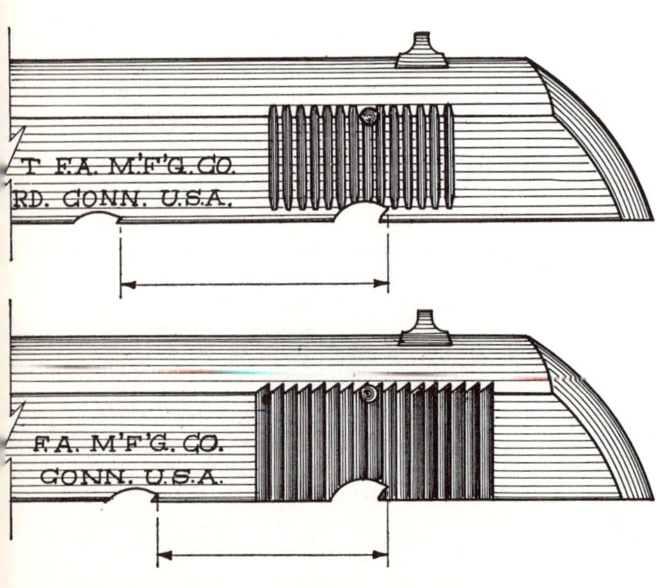

7 In early pistols the slide hold-open notch is 1-5/16" from the safety notch as in upper sketch. The position of the hold-open notch was changed later to make it 1-5/32" from the safety notch. The reason for this change is unknown. The earlier notch spacing has been seen on guns from Nos. 250 to 8664; the later spacing on guns Nos. 11,101 to 70,538. Location of notch in relation to legend letters provides quick visual check.

On early production pistols, from guns Nos. 250 to at least 19,816, the slide serrations were milled in a radius-cornered, square cross-section as in upper sketch. There were 14 serrations. See Figs. 3 and 4, left.

The slide serrations were later cut in a 17-line saw-tooth pattern as in lower sketch. See Fig. 4, right. This form of slide serration has been observed on guns from Nos. 25,157 to 70,538. ■

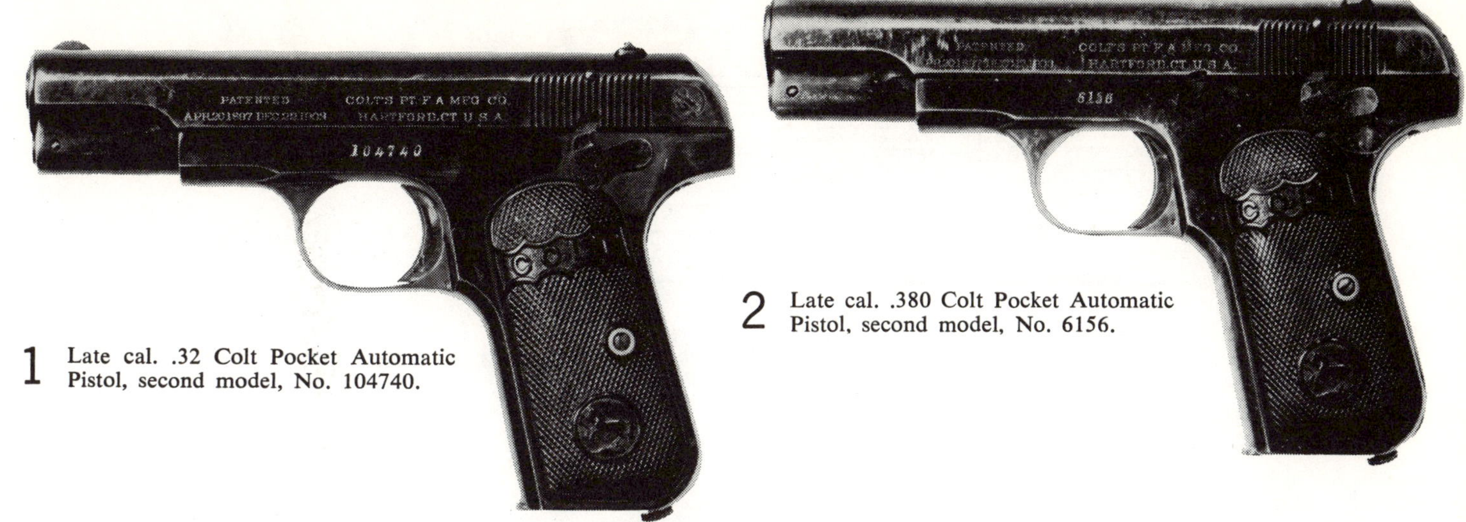

1 Late cal. .32 Colt Pocket Automatic Pistol, second model, No. 104740.

2 Late cal. .380 Colt Pocket Automatic Pistol, second model, No. 6156.

The second model

COLT POCKET AUTOMATIC PISTOL

By DONALD M. SIMMONS, JR.

THE Colt pocket automatic pistol was made from 1903 until 1947. The manufacturer lists only one model, designated "M", to cover the production of over 700,000 pistols. I divide the entire run into 4 basic models to afford collectors a way of describing types and variations.

The first model was discussed in an article appearing in THE AMERICAN RIFLEMAN in April 1964. Made in cal. .32 ACP only, this model is distinguished by having a 4″ barrel.

The second model differs from the first model in that it is shorter and was offered in 2 calibers, .32 ACP (Fig. 1) and .380 ACP (Fig. 2).

The first model pistol is 7″ long, 4⅝″ high, and 1⅛″ wide. Weight is 26 ozs. with magazine loaded. The reason for shortening this pistol is unknown.

In 1908, the over-all length of the pistol, including the barrel, was reduced ¼″. Total weight of the pistol was reduced by 1 oz.

With the advent of the second model, a new caliber, designated .380 Hammerless, was offered for the first time. The zero was added to the caliber designation to avoid confusion with the earlier .38 Automatic Colt Pistol (ACP) cartridge. According to the Remington firm, the .380 ACP cartridge was designed by John M. Browning in conjunction with William Morgan Thomas of the Union Metallic Cartridge Co. In 1912 the Union Metallic Cartridge Co. became a part of Remington Arms Co.

In November 1906, the Union Metallic Cartridge Co. received an order from John M. Browning for 1000 special automatic cartridges to be known as ".38 caliber". These cartridges were described as "straight sided—to be loaded with a 95 gr. bullet and 2.7 grs. of Bullseye powder to give a velocity of 850 feet per second." This describes the .380 ACP cartridge as made today. According to a later production order in 1908, the Union Metallic Cartridge Co. was asked to make a run of .380 CAPH (Colt Automatic Pistol Hammerless) cartridges with case length and extractor groove identical to those of the .32 ACP.

The .380 CAPH cartridge answered a need in pocket automatic pistol cartridges for greater stopping power. The .380 CAPH was considered such an improvement over existing cartridges that it was adopted by Czechoslovakia in 1922 as a Service pistol round. In 1934 the Italian Government also adopted this round. In the United States the new cartridge was quickly renamed the .380 ACP (Automatic Colt Pistol). In Europe this cartridge is designated 9 mm. Browning Short, also 9 mm. Kurz or Corto.

Manufacturing data

Second model pistols cover a very limited number of years. The cal. .32 pistol with 3¾″ barrel was first manufactured in May 1908. Production of the cal. .380 version began in September 1908. There was some earlier production of cal. .380 pistols in March 1908, but it is probable that these were prototypes or samples. Production of second model pistols ceased in either September or October of 1910. In this slightly more than 2-year period, there were 33,050 cal. .32 and 6251 cal. .380 pistols produced. Thus, as a model variation, this is the rarest general type of Colt pocket automatic pistol.

Serial number of the initial second model cal. .32 pistol was 72000; final number was 105050. Serial number of the initial second model cal. .380 pistol was No. 1; final number was 6251. This manufacturing ratio of 5 cal. .32 pistols for every cal. .380 pistol held for the entire remaining years of production.

Second model pistols have rubber grips and barrel bushings in the front of the slide like the first model. Exterior finish is a dark, high-luster blue except for the trigger, extractor, and manual safety lever, which have a bright mottled blue finish. Barrel is blued as viewed through the slide ejection port. Manual safety is retained by a screw visible in the right side of the frame. All second model guns have the screw-secured safety. This feature started in early first model guns and was discontinued early in production of the third model.

Second model variations

The first variation noted is the lack of the stamped takedown arrow and line. Found on all other Colt pocket pistols, this marking is located on the right muzzle end of the slide (Fig. 3). In first model pistols the arrow is feathered. Distance from the slide muzzle to the vertical line is ⅜″. When the slide was shortened, the arrow and line were omitted. This omission must have caused complaints, because the marking was quickly reinstated. The

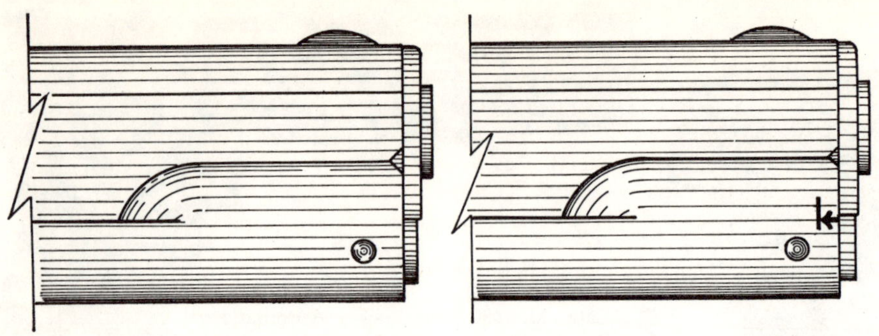

3 Early (l.) and later second model pistol slides. Early slides lack takedown arrow and line marking found on all first model pistols. Takedown marking was eventually reinstated on second model pistol slides, but arrow is unfeathered.

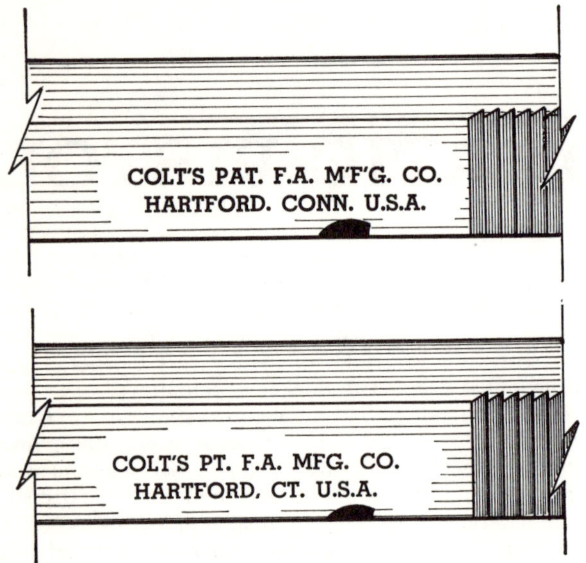

4 Early (at top) and later legends appearing on left side of cals. .32 and .380 second model pistol slides.

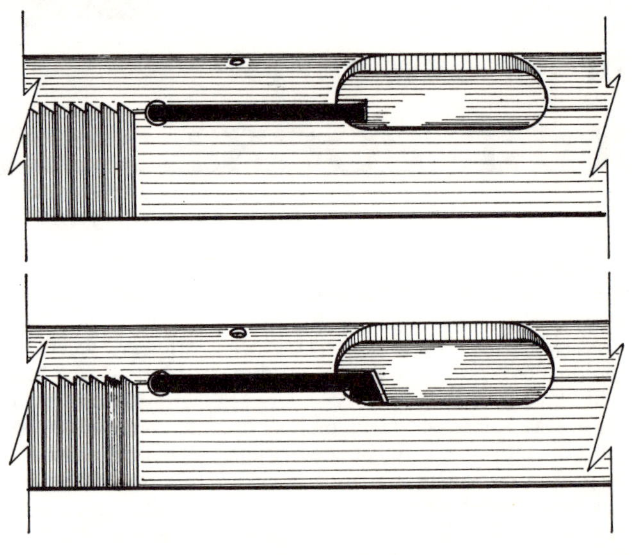

5 All first model and early second model pistols have extractors of uniform thickness as in upper pistol. Shortly after introduction of cal. .380 cartridge, extractor was thickened at front end and extractor slot in barrel widened as in lower pistol. Modified extractor was employed subsequently in cal. .32 pistols.

takedown arrow and line were absent from cal. .32 pistols Nos. 72000 through at least 74307. By serial No. 76076, a shortened, non-feathered arrow and line marking appeared, now approximately 3⁄32″ from the muzzle. Production dates of the above guns without takedown mark are from May to August 1908. All cal. .380 pistols examined had takedown marks, the earliest seen being No. 566.

The next variation noted concerns the rear left-hand slide legend (Fig. 4). Initially, the legend was the same as on late first model guns. But eventually a new stamp was used and the method of abbreviating some words was changed. These changes were:

1. The "PAT." for Patent was changed to "PT".
2. "M'F'G." for manufacturing was changed to "MFG."
3. The period after "HARTFORD" was changed to a comma.
4. The "CONN." for Connecticut was changed to "CT."

Highest numbered cal. .32 pistol seen with the original legend is No. 77723, made in October 1908. Lowest cal. .32 serial with the new legend is No. 84-599, manufactured in April 1909. Corresponding cal. .380 serial numbers are: original legend, No. 2284, December 1908; new legend No. 6156, August 1910. The latter number is undoubtedly not near the point of change; it is the lack of specimens seen that makes it difficult to authenticate changes. The legend change in cal. .380 pistols occurred after gun No. 2300 but before gun No. 2500.

The next variation observed is in the extractor (Fig. 5). All first model and early second model guns have extractors of uniform thickness as though punched from sheet metal. Following introduction of the cal. .380 cartridge, difficulty was experienced in extraction due to the case's thin rim. To overcome this, Colt's almost doubled the thickness of the extractor at the point of contact with the shell. Thickening the extractor head also necessitated a larger extractor cut in the barrel. Early extractors were .070″ thick. Later extractors were .070″ thick through the shank, but their heads were .120″ thick. First pistols to be equipped with the altered extractors were No. 95801 in February 1910 in cal. .32, and No. 4301 in November 1909 in cal. .380. This extractor change was made in cal. .32 pistols to simplify parts manufacture.

The last variation is noted only in late-production pistols in this model. On all first and most second model pistols, numbers in the serials are slanted at 75° to the horizontal. The highest numbered pistol noted with steeply slanted digits is No. 101262, made in June 1910. By pistol No. 104740, the numbers were stamped with their long axis at 85° to the horizontal. This pistol was made in September 1910.

Some writers claim that the only differences between Colt cal. .32 and cal. .380 automatic pistols are in the barrel and magazine. This is incorrect. Differences in 5 major parts between the 2 calibers prevents the interchanging of these parts between guns of different caliber.

The cal. .32 barrel bushing has an internal diameter of 7/16" compared with a diameter of 31/64" for the cal. .380 pistol. Cal. .32 and .380 barrels are naturally different in that they are bored for their respective cartridges, but outside diameters also differ. Outside diameter of the cal. .32 barrel is 27/64"; that of the cal. .380 barrel is 15/32". Both barrels have 6 lands and grooves rifled with the characteristic Colt left-hand twist.

Slide markings differ

While dimensionally identical, the slides in both calibers are different in their right side legends (Fig. 6).

Frames also differ according to caliber. The cal. .32 frame has a magazine well width of 7/16", while the thicker cal. .380 magazine requires a well width of 15/32". A cal. .32 magazine will fit the cal. .380 pistol frame, but not vice versa.

Last part that differs is the magazine (Fig. 7). These can be identified instantly by the number of vision holes in the sides. The cal. .32 magazine has 7 holes, with the lowest hole near the back edge. The cal. .380 magazine has 6 holes with lowest hole toward the front edge. Width of the cal. .32 magazine is .415"; that of cal. .380 magazine is .430". The greater diameter of the cal. .380 cartridge necessitated a wider magazine. In later models the magazine bottoms are marked with the caliber, but in second model pistols none of the cal. .32 magazines seen were marked. Most second model cal. .380 magazines are unmarked, but gun No. 6156, an exceedingly late pistol, has the single line "CALIBRE .380" inscription on the floorplate. The only "CALIBRE .32" marked magazine noted was well into the middle of third model production. Most late Colt magazines are marked "COLT" over "CAL. .32" or "CAL. .380".

Inspection marks

Inspector's marks found on second model pistols give some insight as to whether a gun has all of its original parts. All frames seen have been marked with a "3" on the inside of the recoil spring tunnel. Early second model barrels are marked "5" forward of the locking grooves. In later issued pistols, I have also seen "8" and "W" markings. If these markings are found on the barrel, they will also be found on the slide. The only outside visible marks are found on the left side of the frame on the trigger guard. Top of the trigger guard will have the characteristic "V" interlocked with a "P", all enclosed in a triangle. At the lower edge of the trigger guard will be found the final inspector's "R" stamp. If a pistol is found without "VP" or "R" marking, the question of how it got out of the factory may be asked, unless, of course, it is a prototype.

Second model pistols were offered with blue finish only. If the finish on the trigger, safety, and extractor is the same as the rest of the pistol, it has probably been refinished. However, a factory refinished pistol may be considered worthwhile by the collector. One such pistol in my collection is numbered 90493. In the refinishing process the legends on both sides were restamped to a later type and the "V" and "P" markings were removed. A final refinishing inspector at the time (1916-1917) used a "K" as his stamp on the right side of the trigger guard. Bluing and magazine of this arm are of the third model type.

Collecting

The Colt pocket automatic pistol has many variations, and just when you think you have discovered all of them, another one appears. The second model, by its rarity, is a particular instance. Of the total production, the cal. .32 second model pistol represents only 5.8% and the cal. .380 second model pistol a lowly 4.5%. To put it into related terms, the much sought-after cal. .35 Smith & Wesson automatic pistol is more common than the Colt second model cal. .380. And, there are less than 2000 cal. .380 Colt second model pistols with the thick extractor. ■

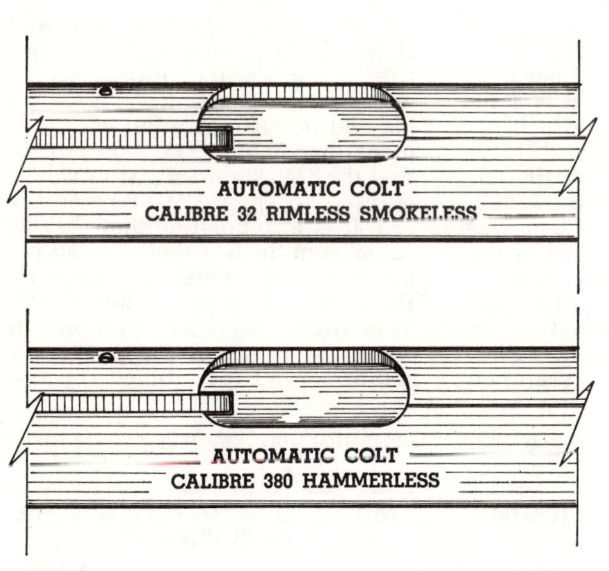

6 While dimensionally identical, slides of cals. .32 and .380 second model pistols differ in their right side legends. In later models, caliber markings were stamped on the barrels opposite ejection port. Note: Cal. .380 pistol shown has early flat extractor.

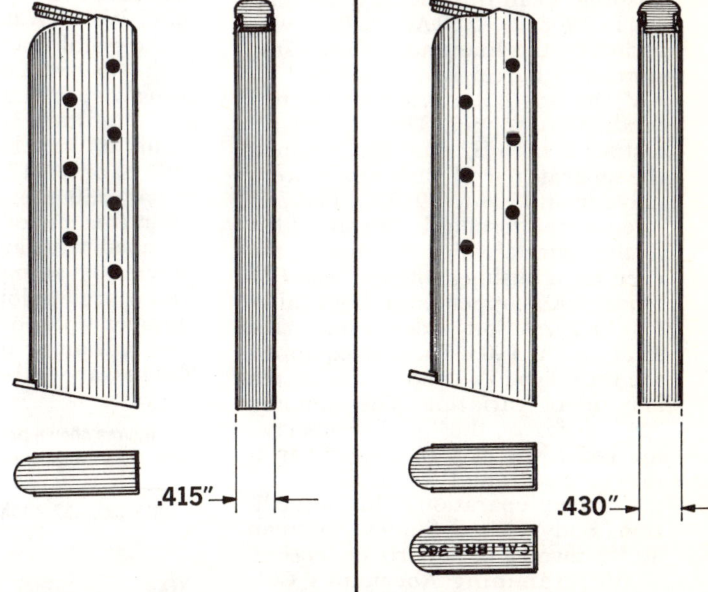

7 Magazines are readily differentiated according to caliber by number of vision holes in the sides. Cal. .32 magazine (l.) has 7 holes, with lowest hole near back edge. Wider cal. .380 magazine (r.) has 6 holes, with lowest hole towards front edge. No second model cal. .32 magazines were noted with caliber marking on floorplate. Except for late production, cal. .380 magazines lack caliber designation.

Myth Of The M-Series Colt

THE myth says, that between 1941 and 1945, Colt made approximately 200,000 cal. .32 and .380 Pocket Automatics, expressly for the United States government. The myth says, that these guns were assigned a separate serial number range from commerical production, and that it began with the number 1. The myth says that these guns all bear a prefix letter "M" stamped ahead of the serial number.

Most myths have some factual basis, but I am convinced that this one does not. The myth of the "M" series Colt is, in fact, the innocent invention of author Donald Bady.

Bady's *Colt Automatic Pistols* first appeared in 1956. It was among the earliest and most authoritative in depth studies of the production of Colt semi-automatic handguns. Its first edition devoted a full chapter to and presented much new information concerning the Model 1903 Pocket Automatic.

Unfortunately, it also gave us the myth, which was not corrected until Bady published a revised edition of *Colt Automatic Pistols,* in 1973. In the meantime, other authors accepted his erroneous theory of the "M" series as correct. So, too, did many collectors. The misinformation has been repeated since 1973, despite Bady's efforts to clear up the error.

The first Colt Model 1903 pocket .32 ACP pistols had a 4″ barrel secured to the slide by a separate barrel bushing. I call this the "Type I" pistol. In 1908, the .380 ACP caliber was added to the line and, at the same time, the barrel was shortened to 3¾″, the length it was to remain until production stopped. These "Type II" pistols, in both .32 and .380, retained the separate barrel bushing and were made from 1908 to 1910. In 1910, an integral reinforcing boss was added to the muzzle which eliminated the need for a bushing; these "Type III" Model 1903s appeared in both calibers. In 1926, Colt added a magazine safety to the 1903. Those so equipped are the "Type IV" and represent the last major variation. The rumored "M" series of the "U.S. Property" marked 1903s was an alleged variation of the "Type IV" pistols.

During preparation of his first edition, Bady visited Sidney Aberman and viewed his superb collection. While examining Aberman's Colt pocket pistols, he found a "U.S. Property" marked automatic with the serial number M 137783. I believe Bady mistakenly assumed this pistol to be a .32. Since it was of World War II vintage and since the .32s had passed serial 137000 in early 1913, he guessed that there must

BY D. M. SIMMONS

This pistol is proof that the M-series myth is only that. It is a .380, made in 1944, with no "M." An Ordnance acceptance mark is stamped behind the safety.

have been a separate military series of both .32 and .380 pistols, characterized by the "M" prefix. As he already had one in the 137000 range, he suggested that this "M" series went to as many as 200,000 pistols sold to the U.S. Government during World War II. This meant that since the last .32 was no. 572214 and the last .380 no. 138000, the total production would seem to be 572,214 plus 138,000 (plus 200,000 "M" series) or 910,214 pistols total. He also states that Colt started commercial production of these pistols again after World War II.

The pistol that started it all is still in the Aberman collection. Instead of being a special series .32, it is actually a military issue .380, which explains its serial number of 137783. This is only 217 guns from the terminal .380 gun numbered 138000. After this pistol was blued, it was stamped with an "M" ahead of the previously stamped serial number. There are undoubtedly other "M" stamped Colt pocket automatics, but they will all be in the regular series. There are also "M" stamped magazines. The stamp is the same size as the one that prefixes the serial number and is on the forward lip of the floor plate.

There are at least two possibilities as to the meaning of this "M". Since all late Colt pocket pistols were stamped "U.S. Property" and carry the ordnance acceptance stamp, there would appear to be no reason for additional indication of government ownership. Yet it is possible that the "M" stamped pistols were so marked to show "M" for Military use. It is also possible that the "M" came from the fact that the Colt pocket automatic pistol was known to the Colt factory as the Model "M". This would make an inventory delineation between the pocket automatics and their bigger brother,

The figures shown below are from Verlay's book on U.S. martial arms. Annual figures may err, but production totals are accurate.

COLT CAL. .32 POCKET MODEL AUTOMATIC PISTOL 1903

YEAR	SERIAL NUMBERS	ANNUAL PRODUCTION
1942	555000 to 557500	2500
1943	557501 to 561000	3500
1944	561001 to 568000	7000
1945	568001 to 572000	4000
		17000 total

COLT CAL. .380 POCKET MODEL AUTOMATIC PISTOL 1909 (1908)

YEAR	SERIAL NUMBERS	ANNUAL PRODUCTION
1942	134500 to 135000	500
1943	135001 to 135850	850
1944	135851 to 137800	1950
1945	137801 to 138000	200
		3500 total

the Colt Model 1911A1. Pay your money and take your choice. I doubt that Colt knows anything about the "M" stamp because it was probably added after the pistols left the factory.

Verlay, in his informative book *"United States Martial Arm Inspectors Manufacturing Dates and Serial Numbers* published in July, 1967, lists "U.S. Property" marked Colt pocket automatics. Government purchases from Colt started in 1942 with .32 ACP no. 555000 and .380 ACP no. 134500. These pistols were issed to General Officers in the caliber of their choice. They could also be requisitioned by others needing a small concealable pistol.

The history of the U.S. Property Colt pocket automatics has been explored further. The earliest .32 serial number known to me is 554447. A Colt researcher came up with the following. There were three shipments of 1,000 pocket automatics in .32 marked "U.S. Property" shipped to the Springfield Armory. The last 1,000 were marked simply as being shipped to the U.S. Government. The high serial number going to Springfield was 557591 and the high serial number of the last 1000 was 558607. In July, 1942, six more .32s were shipped to the U.S. Government with a high number of 558640. This gives a total of 3006 .32s shipped by May, 1942, which is more than Verlay's table shows for the entire year of 1942.

In 1944 or late 1943, a large quantity of the .32s was shipped by our government to the British. The English reproofed these pistols and apparently stored them, unused. They were sold back to American dealers in 1964 or 1965 in their original boxes with an extra magazine and instruction sheet, still in unfired condition. The added British proofs are a crown over BNP (Birmingham Nitro Proof), there are also the crossed lances and the barrels are additionally stamped ".32 .675" over "12 tons per." The ".675" in the barrel stamping, I believe, was supposed to be 7.65 or the metric designation. All British proofed pistols examined by me have had the ".675" mark. The dealers who sold these pistols usually matched up the serial numbers and consecutive pairs and triplets and even four in a row were available. The going price for these new condition automatics that had crossed the Atlantic Ocean twice, was $75.00. There were no .380s in these returned British proofed pistols.

Only the "U.S. Property" .32s come in two different finishes. From no. 555000 up to at least no. 560800, the guns were finished in conventional blue with the quality of polish reducing as the serial numbers advanced. By at least no. 562100, the blue finish gave way to grey Parkerizing and this more durable finish was used until the last .32 was made at serial number 572214. The .380s, while also having a deteriorated quality of polishing, are never found Parkerized.

The "U.S. Property" Colt pocket automatics have two other features distinguishing them from commercial production. All that I have examined have a square matted ramp front sight and a square profiled rear sight with square notch. These sights are exactly like those found on the Colt .45 automatic pistol Model 1911A1 and were undoubtedly requested of Colt by the military.

These "U.S. Property" pistols also differ from their commercial cousins by having revised slide serrations. The later commercial .32s and .380s have 17 slide serrations on each side of the slide. The "U.S. Property" automatics have 19 grooves each.

As late as 1963, Army Technical Manual TM 9-1005-206-14 P/ 3 "Operator Organizational and Field Maintenance Repair Parts and Tools and Equipment for Commercial Pistols" shows the "Pistols, .32 and .380 Automatic *Colt Model* "M" "and notes that no repair parts are authorized. This might lead one to believe that some of these pistols were still being issued in 1963, that they were being phased out, that there were no parts available by that date, and also that the military called them the Model "M".

Thus, I hope the myth of the separately numbered "M" series is laid to rest and that collectors who have Colt .32s and .380s with the "U.S. Property" stamp, whether "M" stamped or not, will realize the relative rarity of these interesting pistols. Rather than having one of 200,000 they have one of 20,714; or one of 17,214 .32s; or one of 3,500 .380s. If the pistol does not have British proofs it may have been issed to a General Officer of the United States Army. The highest commercial pistol would be .32 no. 554000 and .380 no. 134499.

To further refute the belief that the last Colt pocket automatics were commercial, .32 no. 571999 is a Parkerized "U.S. Property" and blued .380 number M 137925 is a "U.S. Property." These pistols are respectively 215 and 75 digits away from the known last number of 572214 (.32) and 138000 (.380). ■

Most military Colt autos were issued to General Officers. A belt and the plain, but sturdy, holster, below left, were included in the issue. Other Colts were sent to England where they were proof-fired, stored, and eventually sold back to U.S. dealers.

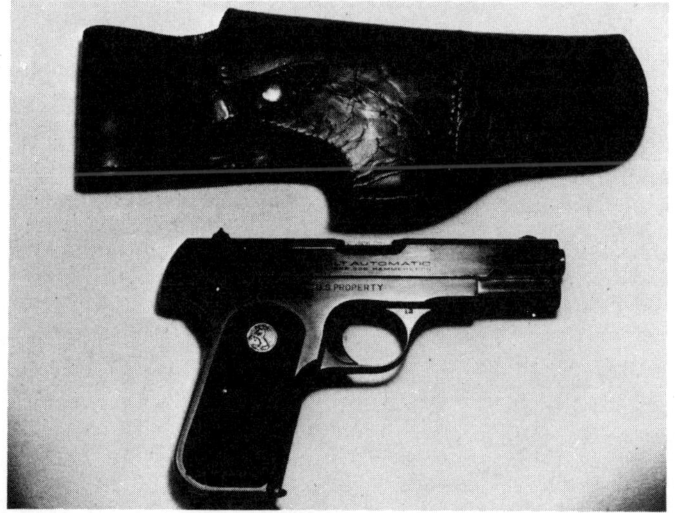

The Forgotten .45

Developed privately to meet Army needs, the M1905 pistol pioneered the .45 ACP cartridge, unlocked like a parallel rule.

Colt's Model 1905 was a hefty sidearm, built to withstand the rigors of service. A spur hammer on this specimen dates its manufacture as post 1908. The Calibre .45 Rimless Smokeless cartridge used essentially the same case as the later .45 ACP, but bullet weights differed. The former used a 200-gr. bullet; 230-gr. bullets are standard in the latter cartridge.

BY MICHAEL J. CASSITY

THE appearance, at the turn of the century, of practical semi-automatic pistols made it clear to many observers that a new era had dawned. With what now sounds forgivably naive or excessively optimistic, some advanced the notion that the semi-automatic pistol would make the revolver obsolete. To them it seemed that the revolver simply lacked the firepower, not to mention the intimidating aura, of the self-loading pistol. In 1910, a writer for the magazine *Knowledge* conveyed the supposedly revolutionary significance of the pistol with these words:

"The man armed to-day with a revolver has as much chance against an opponent with a self-loading pistol . . . as had the armies of the Dervish with their spears and swords against Kitchener's guns on the field of Omdurman. This . . . is no exaggeration."

It was, of course, an exaggeration, but it was also widely believed. Few would deny that the spirit, though not the facts, of the report was accurate. There had indeed been a revolution in modern firearms design.

In the United States, John Browning's designs of these fearsome arms quickly dominated the commercial market and soon the military as well. Basic features of Browning's design were used on various Colt, .38 cal. pistols, and in 1905 Colt introduced an automatic pistol in .45 Rimless. In its 1906 catalog, Colt boldly proclaimed this: "The Most Powerful Small Arm Ever Invented." It was the .45 Colt Automatic Pistol, Military Model, or more commonly the

M1905. And, it was this pistol that was first submitted to compete for adoption as the U.S. Army's official sidearm.

In 1911, a much-changed Colt pistol was adopted as the official U.S. service sidearm, and in that year production of the M1905 ceased. Unfortunately this short-lived pistol has been generally neglected. As an historical innovation, and as an efficient pistol in its own right, the Colt M1905 .45 cal. semi-automatic pistol deserves wider recognition.

Between 1905 and 1911, the search for mechanical improvement caused Colt to produce several variations of the M1905 pistol. Even so, during the six years in which it was commercially produced, Colt only manufactured between six and seven thousand of the pistols. At first the pistol held few surprises. Early M1905s closely resembled the .38 cal. Military and Sporting Models which preceded it. Like the .38 cal. pistols, the M1905 lacked an external safety and other more familiar features of the later 1911 service model. In fact, as Donald Bady has noted in his excellent *Colt Automatic Pistols*, no newly patented mechanisms appear to have been used in the first production models of the M1905. Its most distinctive feature was the .45 cartridge it fired.

A number of changes, however, were soon added to the pistol; these included an enlarged ejection port, occasional additions of a lanyard loop, and even attachable shoulder stocks. The most visible regular production change came in 1908 with the substitution of a new spur-type hammer for the old rounded burr hammer, a change that was incorporated in all Colt's visible hammer, semi-automatic pistols. While this is sometimes referred to as the M1908, the pistol is the same except for the hammer spur. Colt submitted a special military contract version of this pistol to the Army for its Ordnance tests from 1907 to 1911. Ultimately, after a long series of modifications, Colt's gun received top honors—government adoption.

In the process of testing and modification, this revolutionary handgun was itself revolutionized. With an external safety, a grip safety, a different slide stop, and a magazine release button, the final version of the M1911 looks markedly different and more modern than the original M1905. More important, though, and aside from the safeties, a major functional difference separated the M1911 from the M1905. The M1905 barrel was connected to the receiver by two swinging links, one at the muzzle, the other at the breech.

This tandem barrel linkage accounts for much of the potential accuracy of the M1905. The failure of the unmodified modern military .45 as a target pistol is notorious. Not without considerable refinement does the M1911A1 become a precision arm. On the other hand, when the first automatics came out some believed them so accurate and powerful that they could be sighted in at 1000 yds. While this, like the touted firepower, was an exaggeration, the accuracy of the unmodified M1905 is impressive. It shoots consistently because the barrel is attached to the receiver at both ends, and moves like a parallel rule. The paired toggle links of the M1905 cause the barrel to swing back and down in recoil, unlocking the barrel and slide. When the slide of the M1905 returns to battery, the two links guide the barrel back to virtually the same position it had assumed in the previous firing.

The safety features of the M1905 are not immediately noticeable. Indeed, upon first examination the pistol appears to lack any safety device. The manual thumb safety found on M1911 and M1911A1 pistols is not present on the M1905; nor is there a grip safety (except on some models used for military experimentation). Still the pistol has two significant safety mechanisms which enable one to carry the M1905 ready for service and, if desired, loaded with a cartridge in the chamber. First, the pistol incorporates a half-cock hammer position. That safety is not so reliable that it should be depended upon exclusively. The second safety, and the key component in this regard, is the firing pin—a type of Browning's own design. It is short enough that the hammer can rest against it without pushing the pin against the primer of a cartridge in the chamber. The hammer can even theoretically sustain a blow from the rear while in this down position with the energy being transferred to the entire breechblock instead of to the firing pin. The firing pin must receive a sharp blow from the hammer before it will strike the cartridge primer and cause ignition. Thus, according to the design, the pisto can be car-

Colt Automatic Pistol

CALIBER .45, WITH COMBINATION STOCK AND HOLSTER.

TRADE MARK

Reg. U. S. Pat. Off.

For the .45 Rimless, Smokeless Cartridge.

WEIGHT OF HOLSTER. 23 ounces.
LENGTH OF HOLSTER. 11 inches.
WEIGHT COMPLETE. 57 ounces.
LENGTH OVER ALL with Pistol attached. 19 inches.

The Automatic Pistol, caliber .45, with Combination Stock and Holster, may be quickly converted into a shoulder piece, the ammunition used being sufficiently powerful to bring down large game.

The Stock and Holster is made of extra quality black leather, well seasoned, lined with buckskin, hand-stitched over a light but strong and rigid steel frame.

The Device for attaching the Pistol to the Stock is so arranged that it is perfectly secure when in place.

For detailed description of the Pistol, see page 20.

Accidental Discharge is Absolutely Impossible with the Colt Automatic Pistol.

19

Colt, like many other makers of service pistols, advertised a combination holster and shoulder stock for the Model 1905 pistol. This cut from the 1911 Colt catalog shows the accessory used both as a holster and as a detachable stock. Stocked pistols of this type were generally unpopular due to the recoiling slide.

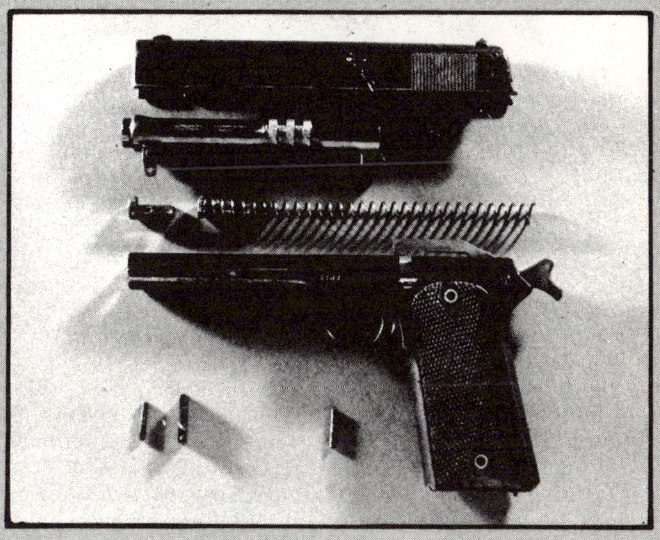
Browning's highly effective "parallel rule" locking system can be seen in this disassembled view of the Model 1905 semi-automatic pistol. Upon firing, the barrel and slide recoil together until the barrel links rotate the barrel downward, disengaging the barrel locking lugs and allowing the slide to continue to the rear.

continued on p.157

Development of the NATIONAL MATCH PISTOL

By CPT. CARL J. DAVIS, USA

Right side of a National Match pistol made up in 1962. The slide had been used on a National Match pistol made up in 1960 or 1961 and carries the number "1377" on right side just below the ejection port. The Springfield Armory acceptance stamp and National Match stamp appear on right side of the receiver.

PRIOR to 1955 there was no such thing as a U.S. National Match pistol.

As far back as the 1930's it had been recognized that the Service pistol did not possess the accuracy required in advanced target competition. Gunsmiths began refitting and 'accurizing' pistols, and soon all the better competition shooters were using something more than the pistol as issued.

During the 1953 National Matches, the first following World War II, there were no pistols available for issue in either the Small Arms Firing School or to competitors. In February 1954, Change 2 to TA 20-2 established the requirement for a Model 1911A1 National Match pistol. It was not possible to develop a Match-grade pistol for the 1954 Matches, and the Ordnance Corps furnished as-issued Service pistols for the Matches that year.

On Dec. 16, 1954, a planning conference at Springfield Armory set up a program to develop and produce the first National Match pistols. Match standards were developed for the 1955 National Match pistol, and a total of 800 M1911A1 Service pistols were rebuilt as National Match pistols for use by the Small Arms Firing School and by competitors in the 1955 Matches.

Each year since 1955, Springfield Armory has rebuilt a number of Service pistols to provide Match-grade pistols for competitors and students at the National Matches. To date, Army Service pistol assets have been rebuilt and no new receivers have been purchased.

Some National Match pistols are sold as authorized by the Director of Civilian Marksmanship (DCM). All not sold will eventually be returned to Springfield Armory for rebuild. It is unusual to find Match pistols more than 2 years old in the hands of teams that are authorized their issue. National Match pistols that are not sold will stay in the rebuild cycle until the receivers become unserviceable and are destroyed.

Only those pistols that have been sold by the DCM are available to collectors, and some models of the National Match pistol are scarce even now.

Following are the distinguishing characteristics of the National Match pistols of each year.

1955 pistol

National Match pistols produced in 1955 incorporated 4 changes to the Service pistol:

1) Checkered walnut stocks replaced the plastic Service stocks.

2) The Service barrel was replaced with a National Match barrel, Part No. NM 7267717. The barrel part number, manufacturer's identification, and pistol serial number appear on the barrel and are visible in the ejection port. The serial number was applied free-hand with individual 3/32" stamps and does not appear as a uniform row like the part number.

3) The Service pistol barrel bushing was replaced with a National Match bushing, which was designated Part No. NM 7267718. The last 4 digits of the pistol serial number are etched on the right side of the bushing, ⅛" high. The etching was done free-hand.

4) The Service pistol link was replaced with one of the so-called "mark series" links. The mark number (13, 17, or 21) is stamped on the link in 3/32" digits. The link must be removed from the barrel before the stamped mark number can be seen.

At arm's length, the 1955 National Match pistol looks like any Service pistol, only the walnut stocks giving a hint to its identity. The slide, sights, and receiver have not been modified from their Service configuration.

The pistol is identified as National Match by the "NM" and "SA" stamp appearing on right side of the receiver. Every National Match pistol which is produced at Springfield Armory is so marked and the acceptance stamps are not peculiar to any year.

1956 pistol

National Match pistols assembled at Springfield Armory for the 1956 season incorporated one external change and 2 internal changes.

The M1911A1 Service sights were replaced with ⅛" wide sights of the same height. New front blades were manufactured by investment casting, and a ⅛" wide square notch was cut in the rear Service sights.

Internally, the sear was modified to prevent interference with the disconnector by grinding a relief on the inside of the sear legs. Vertical play was removed from the 2-piece Service trigger by welding a blob on the top of the trigger, then hand-fitting each trigger to the receiver.

The 1956 National Match pistols are

easily identified by the 1/8" wide sights of Service height, and the National Match and Springfield Armory acceptance stamps on right side of the receiver.

1957 pistol

There were 2 changes in the 1957 National Match pistol, both external.

The Service-height front sight was replaced with a new 1/8" wide blade with rounded front, .295" high. New rear sights were manufactured, .395" high with a 1/8" wide square notch. A neoprene grip pad was glued to the front strap of the pistol. Serial numbering of parts and acceptance stamping of these pistols remained unchanged.

1958 pistol

The National Match pistol assembled in 1958 was provided with new sights even higher than those of 1957. The new front sight had an angular front blade 1/8" wide and .358" high with a very short top surface on the blade. The blade was filed down to meet targeting requirements, and many pistols left the Armory with blades considerably below the .358" basic height. A new rear sight was provided, with the same 1/8" wide square notch but measuring .458" high. The high sights were adopted to enable shooters to replace the fixed rear sight with any adjustable rear sight including the high Micro. All other features remained unchanged from the 1957 National Match pistol.

1959 pistol

In 1959 the National Match pistol incorporated a new barrel, Part No. NM 7790429. The major difference between this and the No. 7267717 barrel used in previous years was in the feed ramp, the 429 barrel having a wider ramp which was designed to facilitate the feeding of wadcutter ammunition. The 429 barrel has often been referred to as the "Shively barrel".

The modified Service trigger was replaced with a new National Match trigger with a plastic finger-piece and adjustable stop. All pistols were assembled with a long trigger, reproducing the original M1911 length. Triggers of the same construction but M1911A1 Service length were available through the DCM and at the National Matches, for competitive use of those who preferred the shorter length.

The neoprene grip pad of 1957 and 1958 was eliminated, and the front strap of the pistol was serrated by milling.

1960 pistol

Two forms of the National Match pistol, the standard and the "L" type, were assembled in 1960.

The slide, barrel, and barrel bushing all carried the serial number of the receiver on all pistols produced. The barrel carried the full serial number, and the bushing and slide the last 4 digits, these latter being hand-stamped with numbers 3/32" high on the right side of the slide directly below the ejection port.

The hammer was modified to insure that its safety notch could not catch on the sear nose when the trigger stop was set up tight. The modification, which was continued in all later years, appears as a flat ground on the hammer at the safety notch.

The serially numbered slide and the modified hammer distinguish the 1960 from the 1959 National Match pistol.

The so-called "L" or "lug" pistols are identified by the letter "L" stamped

HAMMER MODIFIED
TO ELIMINATE
INTERFERENCE
WITH SEAR NOSE

Hammer—1960 through 1965.

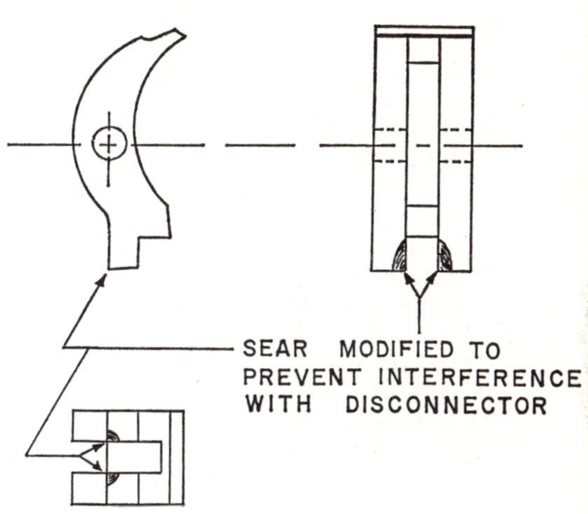

Sear—1956 through 1965.

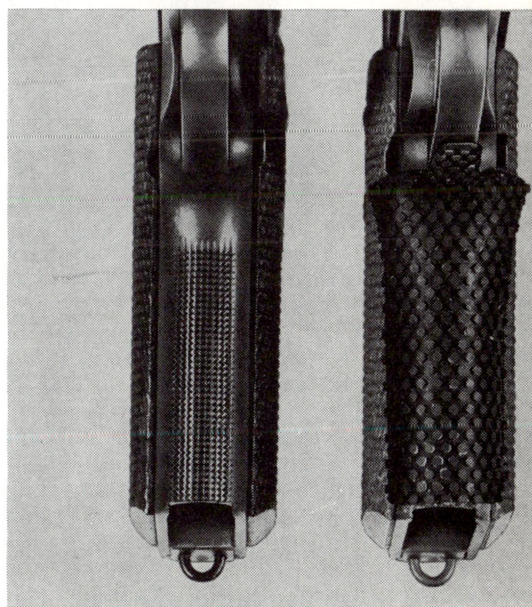

1957 and 1958 models of the National Match pistol had a neoprene grip pad glued to the front strap (right). All National Match pistols produced after 1958 were modified by milling serrations on the front strap (left).

Prior to 1968, service pistols were issued to Springfield Armory from depot stock, rebuilt into National Match pistols at Springfield, and shipped to the National Matches. Pistols that were not sold through the DCM eventually returned to depot stock for reissue to Springfield Armory and rebuild. One National Match pistol may have been rebuilt several times, each time traveling the complete cycle. In 1968, DCM sales were discontinued.

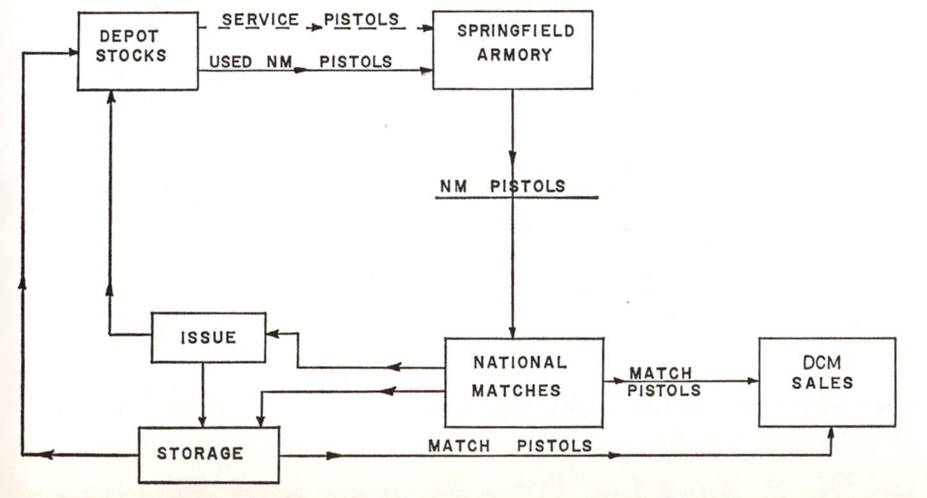

on the left side of the receiver just ahead of the slide stop pin hole. The appearance of 2 types of National Match pistol in 1960 is explained as follows.

After barrels had been ordered for the 1960 National Match pistol, it was found that accuracy could be improved by locking the barrel by means of the lug and the slide stop pin rather than by the link. During the fitting it was found that only certain barrels had sufficient material on the lug for this mode of locking. Pistols containing these barrels were fitted with Mark 13 links modified by enlarging the slide stop pin hole, so the link would be effective in unlocking the pistol but not in locking the barrel into the slide. Thus, pistols which were fitted for lug locking were identified with the "L" stamp and were highly prized by competitors during the 1960 National Matches.

Because National Match pistols are remanufactured each year it is quite possible that many produced after 1960 will have the "L" marking. A 1960 "L" pistol can be identified by the following:

1) Matched serial number on the 429 barrel, bushing, and slide.

2) Trigger with plastic finger-piece and stop screw.

3) Modified hammer.

4) The letter "L" stamped on the left side of the receiver.

5) Mark 13 link modified by enlarging the slide stop pin hole, as described.

1961 pistol

A new barrel was introduced in 1961, Part No. NM 7790313. It was manufactured with additional material on the lug to insure that every pistol would have the lug locking feature. The modified Mark 13 link continued to be used. The manufacturer's identification was moved from the top of the barrel to the right side of the barrel lug.

The plastic trigger finger-piece was replaced with a cast aluminum finger-piece. The trigger remained available in long and short lengths. Some of the 1961 pistols were provided with Micro adjustable rear sights while others were shipped with fixed rear sights. All the Micro sights installed at Springfield Armory have an Ordnance acceptance stamp (crossed cannons on a circular background) on the left side of the sight base. As in 1960, the 1961 pistols have the last 4 digits of the receiver serial number stamped on the right side of the slide.

Barrels of all 1961 and later National Match pistols were locked on the lug, and no "L" identification mark was stamped on any of these pistols after the 1960 NM Model.

A few serially numbered slides from 1960 pistols were fitted to 1961 pistols with receiver numbers which did not match; in these cases the old stamping may be found obliterated and a second number stamped on the slide.

For the most part, slides removed from the 1960 pistols were put in storage until 1962. Any pistol produced in 1962 is likely to have a serial number on the slide which does not match the receiver serial number. Stamping serial numbers on the slides was discontinued after the 1961 NM Model.

The key to identifying the 1961 National Match pistol is the 313 barrel and the modified Mark 13 link. Some 1961 pistols have Micro sights with the Ordnance stamp.

A considerable quantity of pistols produced in 1960 was returned to Springfield Armory during 1961. During rework it was found very difficult to return the slide removed from a pistol to the same receiver and still maintain some semblance of a production line. It was decided that, in the future, production slides would not reflect the serial number of the receiver.

1962 pistol

The 1962 National Match pistol was identical to the 1961 model with these 3 exceptions:

1) All pistols rebuilt in 1962 incorporated the Micro adjustable rear sight.

CHARACTERISTICS OF NATIONAL MATCH PISTOLS

Year	Rear Sight	Front Sight	Barrel	Link	Slide	Hammer	Sear	Trigger	Front Strap	Serial Numbered
1955	Service	Service	7267717	Mark Series	Service	Service	Service	Service	Service	Barrel, Bushing
1956	⅛" Service high	⅛" Service high	7267717	Mark Series	Service	Service	Modified	Service Modified	Service	Barrel, Bushing
1957	⅛"-.395	⅛"-.295	7267717	Mark Series	Service	Service	Modified	Service Modified	Neoprene	Barrel, Bushing
1958	⅛"-.458	⅛"-.358	7267717	Mark Series	Service	Service	Modified	Service Modified	Neoprene	Barrel, Bushing
1959	⅛"-.458	⅛"-.358	7790429	Mark Series	Service	Service	Modified	Plastic	Milled	Barrel, Bushing
1960	⅛"-.458	⅛"-.358	7790429	Mark Series	Service	Modified	Modified	Plastic	Milled	Barrel, Bushing, Slide
1960 "L"	⅛"-.458	⅛"-.358	7790429	Mark 13 Modified	Service	Modified	Modified	Plastic	Milled	Barrel, Bushing, Slide
1961	⅛"-.458 Micro	⅛"-.358	7790313	Mark 13 Modified	Service	Modified	Modified	Aluminum	Milled	Barrel, Bushing, Slide
1962	Micro	⅛"-.358	7790313	"S"	Service	Modified	Modified	Aluminum	Milled	Barrel, Bushing
1963	Triangle	⅛"-.358	7791414 Colt	"S"	7791435 Colt	Modified	Modified	Aluminum	Milled	Barrel, Bushing
1964	Triangle	⅛"-.358	7791414 Colt	"S"	7791435 Drake	Modified	Modified	Aluminum	Milled	Barrel, Bushing
1965	Triangle	⅛"-.358	7791414 H&R	"S"	7791435 Colt	Modified	Modified	Aluminum	Milled	Barrel, Bushing

All Pistols Have Bushing NM7267718

The Micro adjustable rear sight was installed on some National Match pistols in 1961 and on all in 1962. All these sights installed at Springfield Armory have the Ordnance acceptance stamp on left side of the sight base.

The HEG sight made by Triangle Tool was installed on all National Match pistols produced during 1963, 1964, and 1965. The government acceptance stamp, a "U.S.", appears on left side of the sight base. It may be inverted, as here.

2) A new link, which was stamped with the letter "S", replaced the modified Mark 13 link.

3) The last 4 digits of the receiver serial number do not appear on the slide.

It is remotely possible that a National Match pistol assembled in 1961 could have been rebuilt at Springfield Armory during 1962 and by chance have slide and receiver with matching serial numbers. If there is a question as to identification of such a pistol, check the link to determine if it is a 1961-modified Mark 13 link or the 1962 "S" link.

1963 pistol

The biggest change ever made in the National Match pistol occurred in 1963—the Service slide was replaced with a new National Match slide, Part No. NM 7791435. All slides for the 1963 pistol were produced by Colt and their mark appears on right side of the slide. The part number appears on the left side.

The rear sight on the 1963 pistol was of the HEG style designed by George Elliason. The HEG sights are stamped "Triangle Tool" on the right side of the base and "U.S." on the left side of the base. The "U.S." may be inverted.

A new barrel, Part No. NM 7791414, replaced the 313 barrel. The 414 barrel incorporated a new chamber giving better control of headspace and changing the chamber dimensions for the first time in over 40 years. Barrels used in 1963 were manufactured by Colt and have the manufacturer's stamp on right side of the barrel lug.

All other parts and features remained unchanged from 1962.

1964 and 1965 pistols

No design or dimensional changes were made in the National Match pistol for 1964. Slides for the 1964 pistol were produced by Drake Manufacturing Corp., and have the Drake mark on the right side of the slide and the part number on the left. Only the slide manufacture identifies a pistol of this year.

Again in 1965 the drawings and specifications for the National Match pistol remained unchanged. Slides for the 1965 pistol were manufactured by Colt as they had been in 1963. The barrels were manufactured by Harrington & Richardson, and are stamped "HR" on right side of the barrel lug.

1966 pistols

National Match pistols will again be produced at Springfield Armory for the 1966 Matches. These will be assembled to the same drawings and specifications as in 1963, 1964, and 1965 unless some last-minute change is incorporated.

How will a person be able to identify the 1966 National Match pistol? For the first time it may be impossible to determine the year in which the pistol was produced. Nevertheless, there may be a new manufacturer for one of the marked component parts that will identify the pistol as the 1966 model.

Available Springfield Armory records on National Match pistols begin with the year 1958. Quantities for 1955 and 1956 are given in the handbook on National Match rifles and pistols published by the Army Materiel Command. Following are the quantities of National Match pistols produced for the years 1955 and 1956 as given by the handbook and for 1958 and later as recorded at the Armory:

1955	800	1960	2717
1956	1250	1961	972
1957	(Records not available)	1962	3025
		1963	2418
1958	635	1964	800
1959	1065	1965	1773

The above figures for 1960 through 1964 represent an official correction of the corresponding figures in the article *The .45 National Match Pistol* in the June 1966 RIFLEMAN.

All these National Match pistols were produced by rebuild. Pistols that were not sold through the Director of Civilian Marksmanship were returned to the rebuild cycle each year, as already explained. The total number of pistols was therefore less than the total of the figures which have been listed above. ■

All National Match pistols bear the Springfield Armory acceptance stamp and the "NM" National Match stamp on right side of receiver as shown.

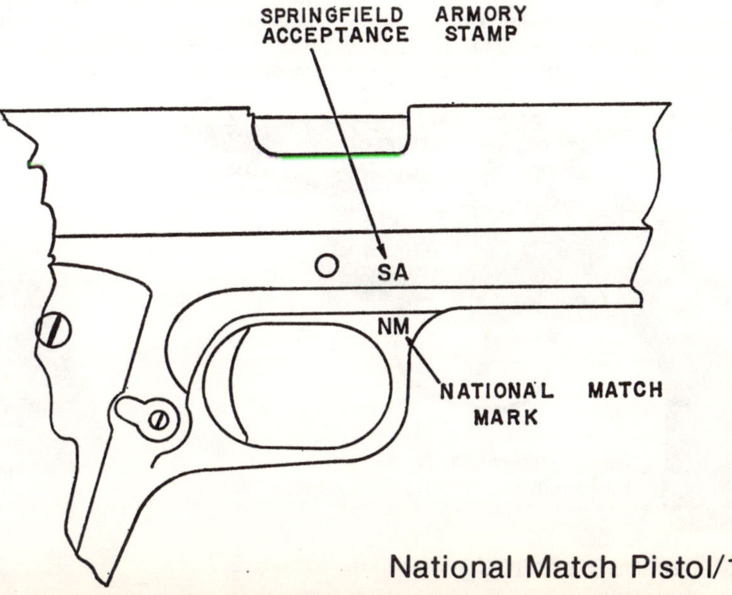

Collector Colts: Not Old But Rare

Scarcity, not antiquity, has boosted their value

By E. DIXON LARSON

To be well worth collecting, not all Colts handguns need to be antique. With every passing year or decade, more and more aging guns pass from the shooter class into the collector class. Although not yet antiques, certain Colts introduced since 1940 are disappearing from the scene and becoming even rarer than many antique arms.

Some were made in very limited quantities, fewer in fact than Colt Dragoon revolvers. Others that were produced in small numbers are simply waiting to be identified as collector pieces. Inasmuch as nearly all of these handguns are owned by shooters, use may reduce their numbers or impair their collector value. Yet a number are within the scope and budget of the average collector.

If you seek these cartridge arms, keep in mind that the 1968 Federal Gun Control Act covers all such manufactured since 1898 except for a few specially classified as curios—and that you need a Federal gun collector license in interstate transactions even for those. With that admonition, here we go.

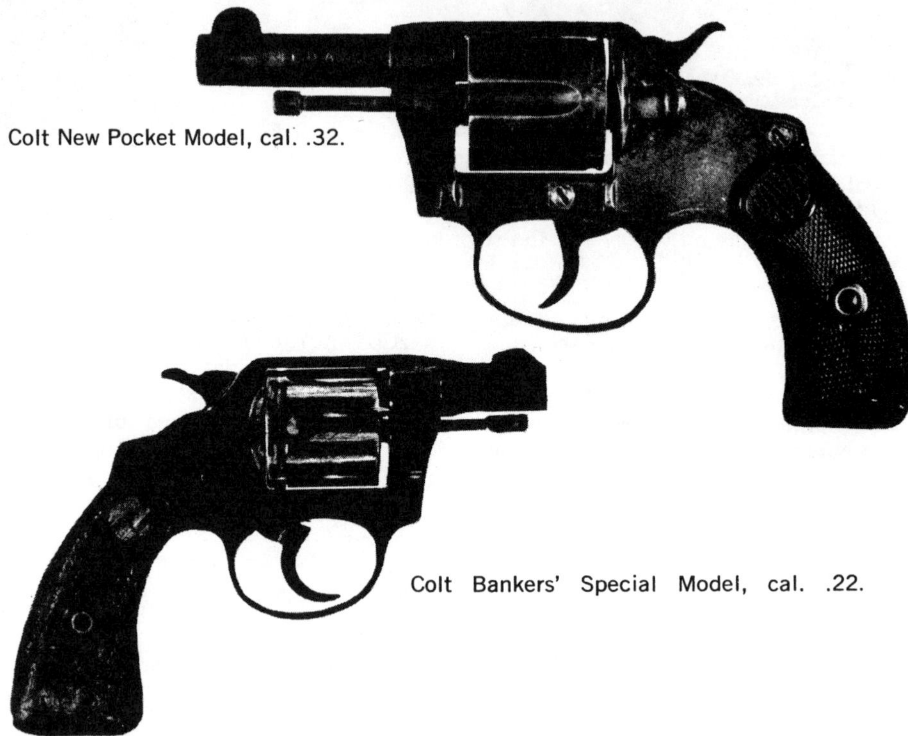

Colt New Pocket Model, cal. .32.

Colt Bankers' Special Model, cal. .22.

Perhaps the "Number One" in the field of tomorrow's rarities is the Colt Courier Model revolver, featured only in 1953-55. Most records indicate that fewer than 3,000 were made. The Courier was soon succeeded by the Agent and the Cobra. During its short-lived production the Courier was made in .22 long rifle and the .32 S&W calibers with a 3" barrel. The .22 is believed to be the rarer and more desirable of the two calibers. The collector cannot miss this one, since it is marked on the left side of the barrel "Colt Courier" and caliber. Frames are of Coltalloy, thus the weight of the .22 caliber is 19½ ounces and the .32 is 13½ ounces. They are equipped with checkered walnut, Colt medallion grips.

The "Aircrewman Model" Colt Revolver is another scarce post-1940 production model. Not over 1,200 of this model were produced—some contracts say 1,189. Because an order was issued to destroy the model, only a couple of dozen are believed to have escaped such a purge. The grips are most unusual. The Air Force silver medallion is set in the checkered walnut. Caliber is .38 Special, six-shot with the 2" barrel. The Aircrewman spans from 1951 through 1959. Model is marked on the left side, "Aircrewman", and caliber ".38 Special Ctg."

Another real find is the "Border Patrol" Model revolver, produced by Colt on special order from the U.S. Treasury Department. Approximately 400 were made. They are in .38 Special caliber, 4" heavy barrel, six-shot, closely resembling the Police Positive with a heavy barrel. The left side is clearly marked, "Colt Border Patrol" and ".38 Special—Heavy Duty." These revolvers have seen service, so it is doubtful one can be found in mint condition. Still they are a find in any condition and an enjoyable handgun in the field and on the range.

We could go back to rarities such as the 1905 Marine Double Action Colt or the Camp Perry models, but this would not serve much purpose. Most persons recognize these as rare today. After appraisal is made of models that might be found and possibly discovered, then comes the thrill of searching for them.

The "Colt Marshal" is a very scarce model. Approximately 2,500 were manufactured. This has an Official Police frame and barrel in two lengths, 4" and 2", .38 Special, six-shots. It has the rounded butt which is a slight deviation from the Official Police and is marked "Colt Marshal" on the left side of the barrel, and on the second line, ".38 Special Ctge."

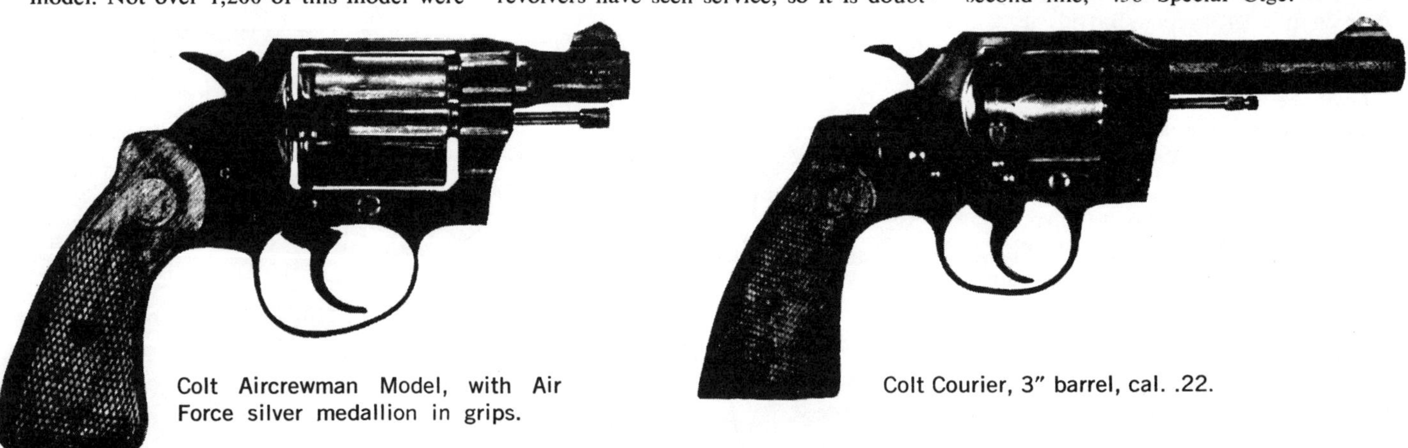

Colt Aircrewman Model, with Air Force silver medallion in grips.

Colt Courier, 3" barrel, cal. .22.

Late model Colt Single Action Army Model in discontinued cal. .38 Special, with 7½" barrel.

For the martial collector, the "Colt Commando Model Revolver" is a somewhat scarce arm, although some 50,000 were produced from 1942 to 1945. Few have been seen on the open market which indicates a low survival rate. This model is also a variation of the Official Police Model, and has the typical butt, Parkerized finish, 2", 4", and 6" barrel lengths. "Colt Commando" is marked on the left side of the barrel, and the second line reads ".38 Special." It has checkered Coltwood grips. Contrary to most records, the 2" has been seen most often.

Although they produced some 355,000 New Service Model Colts, it is worthy to mention that a good .44-40 in the 7½" barrel length is certainly a rare item and still shows up in the record after 1940.

Although the "New Model Pocket Revolver" started out in 1893 and continued through evolution as the Pocket Positive until 1940, it has never achieved any real prominence in the collecting field since there were some 160,000 produced. It is too hair splitting to separate the models and transitions. Some of the later models by numbers have a better future.

Most collectors know that the Colt "Banker's Special" has become a rarity, particularly in .22 rimfire. While at one time in the same category as the models that still might be found, a Banker's Special is not now likely to be seen in the local sporting goods store. The Banker's Special was discontinued in 1943 with a total production of some 40,000.

Of course, the old favorite and No. 1 in the collector's world is the Colt Single Action Army Model. The Single Action was discontinued in 1941 but production was resumed by popular demand in 1955. The version that has some promise is in .38 Special caliber, discontinued from the Single Action Series. This caliber will be increasingly hard to find and should escalate in value. Of the post 1940 models mentioned, this is the only one where a word of caution is needed since barrels and cylinders can be replaced and this now is a favorite model to upgrade by having it engraved. Therefore, it is advisable to verify origin of the model as a cal. .38 by obtaining a factory letter at a fee.

Colt New Service Model, the largest frame cartridge revolver the firm has manufactured, is very scarce in this 7½" barrel model cal. .44-40 W.C.F.

In the Colt automatic models, the "Colt Match Target Woodsman Model," manufactured from 1938 to 1942 is scarce because most of the 15,000 produced were enjoyed until they were discarded. This was indeed a fine arm and was designed for the most discriminating. The unique feature of this arm is its unusual barrel configuration. Made with a 6½" barrel .22 Long Rifle caliber it is marked on the left side of the barrel with a "bullseye" and the word "MATCH" above and "TARGET" below. The martial model with the extended plastic-type grips is particularly rare.

By analogy, the Colt Aircrewman can compete with the Colt Paterson or Walker by numbers and rarity. If one looks, however at the total Colt Navies as numbering over 200,000; the 1848 "Baby Dragoon" at 15,000; the 1849 Colt Pocket Model as over 340,000, and the 1860 Colt Army as 200,000, then there certainly are rarities among some of the later Colt Models currently to be discovered by today's collector who cannot afford or does not have the desire to recapture yesterday's good buys at today's prices. ■

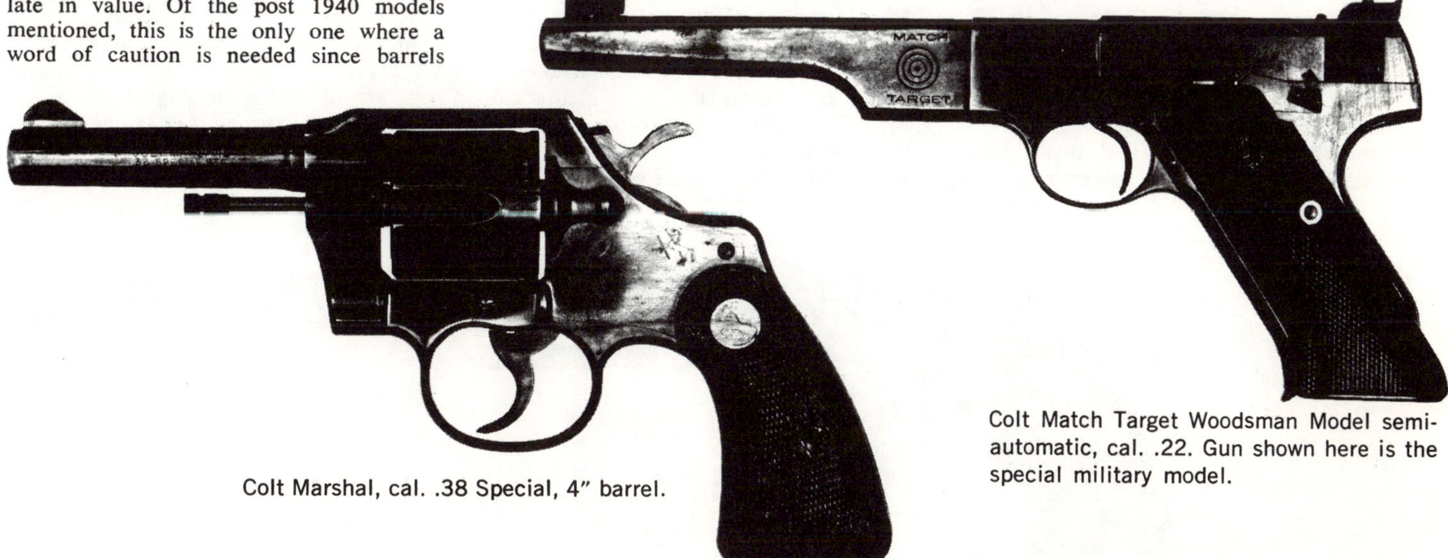

Colt Marshal, cal. .38 Special, 4" barrel.

Colt Match Target Woodsman Model semi-automatic, cal. .22. Gun shown here is the special military model.

1 Early form cal. .25 Gross revolver; 4″ octagon barrel. Brass mainframe and barrel frame are silver or tin plated; iron parts are blued. Pin extending from front of barrel frame is ejector. In use, the cylinder is inverted over the ejector pin to punch fired cases from chambers.

2 Although variations are known, barrel markings shown are typical of those found on Gross rimfire cartridge revolvers.

GROSS REVOLVERS

Information on a cartridge revolver, made in the 1860's, which has several unusual features

By THOMAS B. RENTSCHLER

ONE of the lesser lights in the history of early cartridge revolver development was the Gross Patent revolver. Made in the early 1860's, the Gross revolver had several unusual features. Little is known of its maker, and little has been written about Gross guns as an aid to identification.

Inventor and manufacturer of the Gross revolver was Henry Gross of Tiffin, Seneca County, Ohio. Born in Juniata County, Pa., on July 21, 1813, Henry Gross was the second son of Henry Gross, Sr., who came to Tiffin from Pennsylvania in 1831. The elder Gross was born in Germany in 1783 and died in Tiffin, Ohio, in 1834. In Tiffin, he carried on gunsmithing as well as watch and clock repair. As a boy, Henry Gross worked with his father in this shop and it was there that he mastered the gunsmith's trade.

To generalize, Gross revolvers were made with 7-shot bored-through cylinders and fired rimfire cartridges. Their mainframes were brass and the barrels were hinged at the top and broke at the bottom.

No classification system can be established as is possible with other guns following specific construction or appearance patterns. Yet the variations are of a minor nature, and 2 general types may be illustrated. These are shown in Figs. 1 and 3.

The earlier form, illustrated in Fig. 1, has a 4″ octagon barrel and is cal. .25. Mainframe of this revolver is a single brass casting and the barrel frame into which the barrel is screwed is also brass. There are known specimens in this caliber of the same appearance, but with iron barrel frames. Grip plates are varnished walnut. Iron parts are blued; brass parts are silver- or possibly tin-plated. Reference sources give many barrel lengths for these guns, but if measured from muzzle to the front of the cylinder, the length varies only about 1/4″ from specimen to specimen. The gun shown in Fig. 1 is marked on the upper left, top, and upper right barrel flats:

"GROSS' PATENT/1861"
"GROSS ARMS COMPANY"
"TIFFIN, OHIO."

Inscriptions on Gross revolvers are not uniform, and on some the marking reads left to right, and vice versa on others. On other Gross revolvers, only 2 of the lines are present, and not always the same 2. Typical barrel markings are illustrated in Fig. 2.

The later form of Gross revolver is illustrated in Fig. 3. It has a 6″ round cal. .30 barrel rifled with 3 narrow

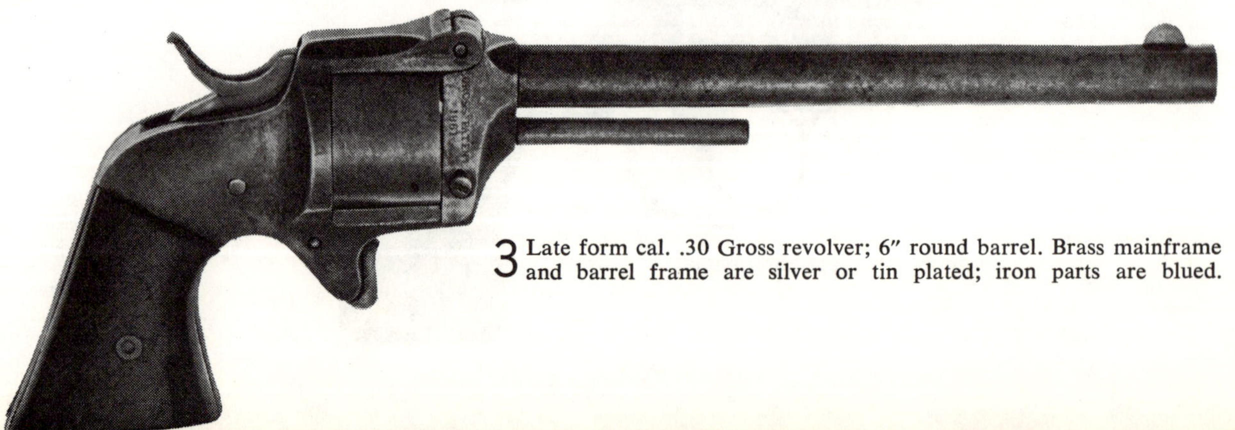

3 Late form cal. .30 Gross revolver; 6″ round barrel. Brass mainframe and barrel frame are silver or tin plated; iron parts are blued.

grooves. Length over-all is 9⅜". Mainframe is a single brass casting and is of the same size as on the earlier pattern revolver. Barrel frame is iron, but there is a specimen in this caliber with brass barrel frame. Grip plates are varnished walnut. Iron parts are blued; brass parts are silver- or tin-plated. This gun is marked on the right side of the barrel frame: "GROSS' PATENT/ 1861", and on the left side of the barrel frame, "TIFFIN, OHIO". These markings are shown in Fig. 4. One specimen seen is stamped "GROSS ARMS CO." instead of "GROSS' PATENT" and "1861". Still another specimen has stampings on opposite sides from those illustrated. And there is an unmarked specimen known.

Markings on these guns do not follow any pattern, nor do they establish the identity of specific models. Rather, these variations indicate that the revolvers were largely handmade as was typical with small, early arms manufacturers.

The revolvers discussed here were manufactured under Henry Gross' Patent No. 39,645, dated Aug. 25, 1863. Since all extant specimens are dated 1861, there is an unexplainable conflict with the 1863 patent date. No explanation is offered, and no theories are advanced. Neither are any thoughts given with regard to the fact that Gross revolvers have bored-through cylinders which must have been an infringement on the Rollin White patent held by Smith & Wesson.

1863 patent

The 1863 Gross revolver patent describes a revolving recoil plate in rear of the cylinder which was designed to prevent fired cartridge cases from binding on the rear frame, firing pin, or hand. This recoil plate is shown in Fig. 5. The slots through which the hammer strikes the cartridge also serve as cylinder catch or index notches.

Interiors of the 2 revolvers are shown in Fig. 6. Their hammers pivot on shouldered screws. Forward edges of the hammers have single notches into which the spur triggers engage when the hammers are cocked. Cocking notches are hidden by the frame. In these revolvers the hammers also serve as carriers for the hand and hand springs. Some visual differences are seen between the mechanisms of the 2 guns, but their basic operation is the same. There is an extension of brass added to the butt of the grip on the cal. .30 specimen, presumably to increase the length of the grip and thus permit employment of the same casting as was used on the cal. .25 model.

The catch mechanisms which lock the barrel to the frame are illustrated in Fig. 7. Fig. 7, left, illustrates the usual catch on cal. .25 revolvers. As the gun is being closed, a leaf spring passes through a hole at the bottom of the barrel frame and a projection on this spring snaps over the edge of the frame hole. A small pivoting lever at the front end prevents accidental release of the spring catch. Fig. 7, right illustration, shows cal. .30 model catch which is a coil-spring-backed plunger which rides vertically in a hole in the barrel frame. This plunger has a tapered projection fitting a hole in the mainframe and is raised to release the catch by means of 2 screws installed through slots in the barrel frame and screwed into each side of the plunger.

Sight variations

Both bead and leaf front sights were standard, and 2 sight mounting methods for both types of sights have been noted. In some guns the sight is fixed directly into the barrel; in others it is fastened to a flat base held in a dovetail slot in the barrel. Sights are of silver or a silver alloy. Rear sight is a notch filed in the frame at the hinge.

No pattern or sequence in the serial numbers of Gross revolvers is discernible. Many specimens examined have 3-digit numbers stamped on the butt, and sometimes, but not always, a different one or 2-digit number on the internal parts. The lower gun in Fig. 6 is an example. It has an internal number 4 with a butt number of 752.

Previous printed references to Gross rimfire revolvers list many calibers, including .22, .25, .28, .30, and .32. Because of their small bores and very narrow rifling grooves, it is difficult to measure the calibers of these revolvers with the usual tapered bore gauge. However, calibers of all revolvers studied were either .25 or .30. Measurements were taken in the cylinders and were confirmed with bore castings. My findings do not preclude the possibility of Gross revolvers being found in other calibers, but they do indicate the difficulty of identification.

Henry Gross is credited with at least 10 patents:

Number	Subject	Issue Date
12,906	Breech-loading firearm	May 22, 1855
15,072	Breech-loading firearm	June 10, 1856
25,259	Breech-loading firearm	Aug. 30, 1859
33,836	Revolver	Dec. 3, 1861
39,479	Breech-loading firearm	Aug. 11, 1863
39,645	Revolver	Aug. 25, 1863
39,646	Breech-loading firearm	Aug. 25, 1863
42,941	Breech-loading firearm	May 31, 1864
101,362	Permutation lock (safes)	March 29, 1870
177,054	Time attachments for locks	May 2, 1876

(Text continued on next page.)

4 Typical barrel frame markings on cal. .30 Gross revolver.

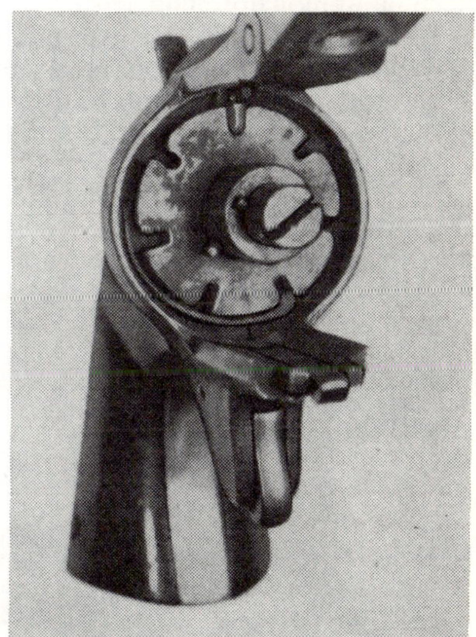

5 Notched recoil plate of Gross patent revolver revolves on arbor screwed into frame. Crosspin secures recoil plate on arbor. Key on recoil plate sleeve engages keyway in cylinder to prevent rotation of cylinder on recoil plate. Note notches in rim of recoil plate for entrance of bar firing pin.

Recoil plate and cylinder assembly is indexed by hand operating off hammer. Lug on curved leaf spring in bottom of frame engages recoil plate notch at 5 o'clock position and aligns chambers with barrel.

These patents cover a variety of mechanical innovations. For example, the first firearm patent describes a vertical turret or faucet mechanism in which the gun is loaded, capped, and the base of the paper cartridge cut, all with movement of a single lever. It is under a variation of the third patent above that Civil War Cosmopolitan rifles and carbines were manufactured by the Cosmopolitan Arms Company in Hamilton, Ohio.

The fourth patent above is for another revolver featuring a mechanism which moved the cylinder forward and backward to provide a gas seal at the barrel breech. No specimen incorporating this feature is known.

Henry Gross also was involved with Edward Gwyn in Tiffin. Gwyn founded the gas works there in 1856. Together they manufactured a breech-loading rifle of type not now specifically identified. This venture failed.

In the 1870's, Gross was with the Hall Safe and Lock Co. in Cincinnati and was highly regarded as a locksmith and trouble shooter. He traveled widely, opening and repairing safes and vaults. Henry Gross' death date and location are not known.

Henry Gross was still alive in 1880, however, when his life was summarized this way by a biographer: "If Mr. Gross' executive and financial abilities were equal to his genius, he would have been a millionaire long since."

Neither a sturdy nor exceptionally serviceable arm, the Gross revolver was a clever and unusual approach to the early cartridge revolver problem. ■

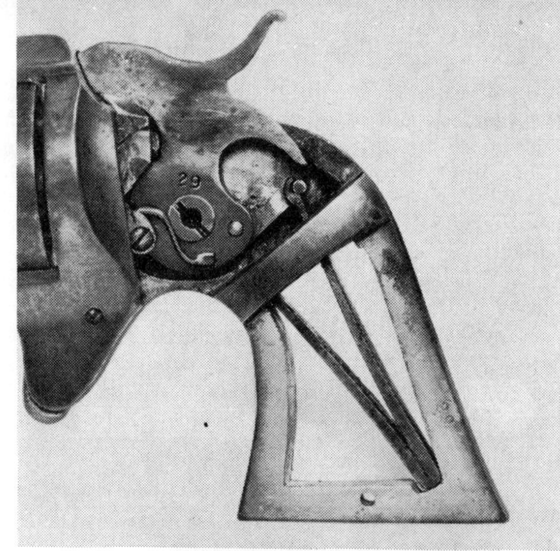

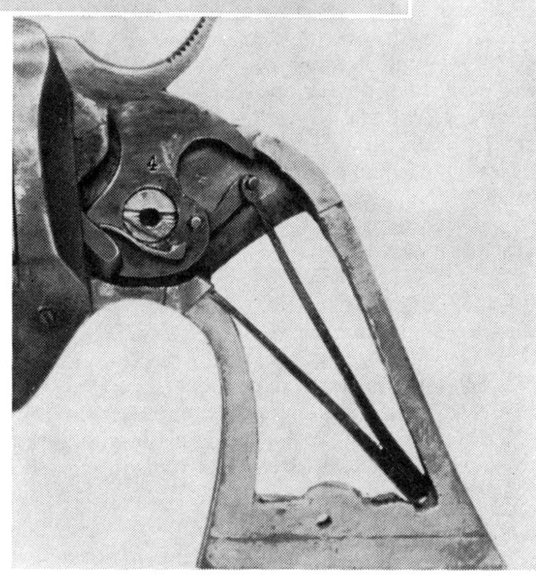

6 Lock mechanisms of cal. .25 Gross revolver (top) and cal. .30 Gross revolver (below). Extension is brazed to grip of cal. .30 revolver. Numbers stamped on hammers are probably assembly numbers applied after fitting but before hardening.

7 Frame catch mechanism of early Gross revolver (left, below) has lock spring on mainframe stud which engages barrel frame. Pivoted lever on front of barrel frame engages end of lock spring when frame is closed.

In late catch form (right), spring-loaded locking plunger in barrel frame engages locking detent in top of mainframe stud. Catch is opened by lifting plunger retaining screws extending through sides of barrel frame.

Harrington & Richardson cal. .32 pistol (r.) and cal. .25 pistol. Cal. .32 pistol weighs 22 ozs. and has 8-round magazine. Cal. .25 pistol weighs 12⅛ ozs. and has 6-round magazine. Respective barrel lengths are 3½" and 2⅛". Blued finish was standard.

H&R SELF-LOADING PISTOLS

A look at the pocket automatics made in cals. .25 and .32 by Harrington & Richardson

By DANIEL K. STERN

THE Harrington & Richardson (H&R) self-loading pocket pistols can be traced back to a series of 3 American patents obtained by William J. Whiting, superintendent for the famed English gunmaking firm of Webley & Scott (W&S). Whiting assigned his patents to W&S and that firm subsequently granted manufacturing rights to H&R during the early 1900's. H&R apparently did not obtain additional patents to cover improvements which they subsequently made in these automatic pistol designs.

The H&R cal. .25 pistol introduced in 1912 looks almost like the W&S hammer model cal. .25 pistol without, of course, the hammer. Internally, it is based almost entirely on the W&S hammerless cal. .25 pistol. In both W&S cal. .25 pistols the barrel fits inside the slide in conventional fashion, but in the H&R what appears to be the top front of the slide is actually part of the barrel.

The W&S hammerless pistol has sights; the H&R pistol does not. Also present on the W&S hammerless pistol is a removable plate which closes off the rear end of the slide. Though not found in the H&R cal. .25 pistol, this feature is employed in the H&R cal. .32 pistol.

While all other American-made pocket automatic pistols have an ejection port or a top strap over the ejection area, a feature of the second W&S patent and of the H&R cal. .25 design was to leave this area entirely open.

WEBLEY & SCOTT AUTOMATIC PISTOLS

Cal. .32 pistol.

Cal. 6.35 mm. (.25) hammerless pistol.

Cal. 6.35 mm. (.25) hammer pistol.

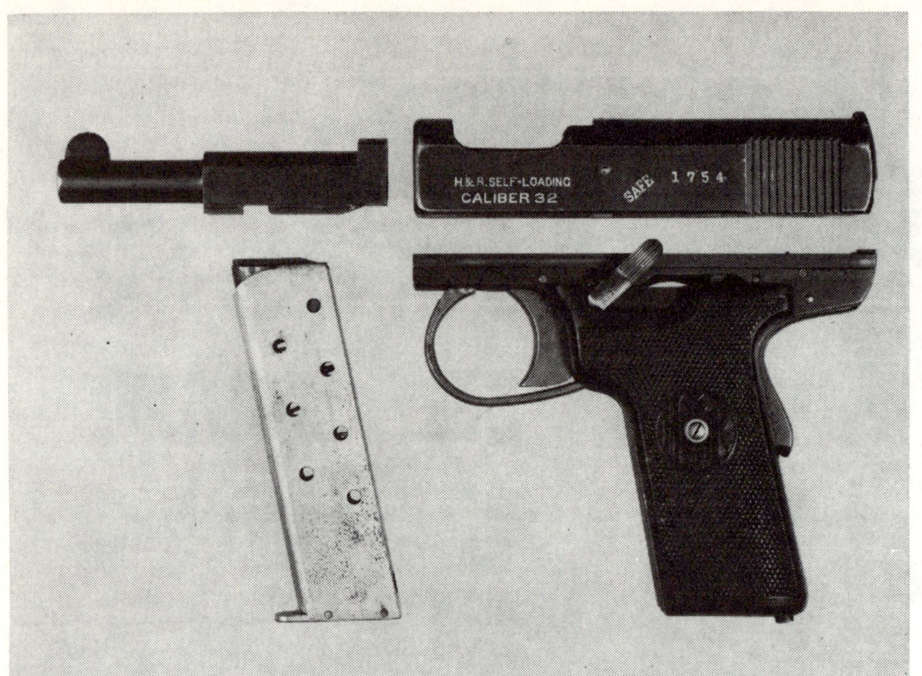

To disassemble H&R cal. .32 pistol, move safety thumbpiece downward until word "SAFE" on slide is exposed completely. Depress magazine catch button in base of grip and withdraw magazine from grip. Remove cartridges from magazine. Retract slide fully and check chamber to be sure pistol is unloaded. Replace magazine in grip, move safety thumbpiece upward to firing position (thumbpiece covers word "SAFE" on slide), and discharge lock. Withdraw magazine from grip. Move safety thumbpiece downward until word "SAFE" on slide is exposed completely. Pull trigger guard to rear and downward and at same time move barrel and slide assembly forward off frame. Reassemble in reverse. Magazine shown is common or second type.

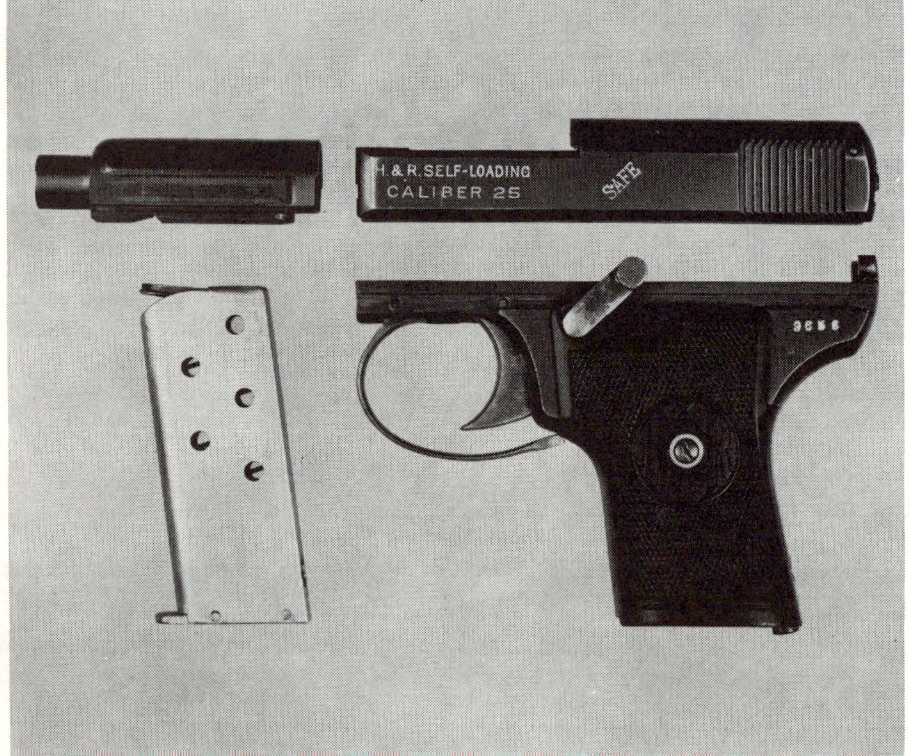

To disassemble H&R cal. .25 pistol, move safety thumbpiece downward until word "SAFE" on slide is exposed completely. Depress magazine catch button in base of grip and withdraw magazine from grip. Retract slide fully to cock hammer and at same time check chamber to be sure pistol is unloaded. Pull lower end of trigger guard loop downward until it disengages from frame. Move barrel and slide assembly forward off frame. Lift barrel from slide. Reassemble in reverse.

The manual safety on H&R cals. .25 and .32 pocket pistols works opposite to normal practice in that it is disengaged by pushing it upward instead of downward. When the safety is disengaged, the thumbpiece covers the word "SAFE" inscribed on the slide.

On both H&R pistols the magazine release button is in the bottom of the frame. Neither has a slide lock device.

Because of many thin sections, odd corners, and projections, the hard rubber grips on H&R pistols of both calibers are frequently found chipped or broken from careless handling.

While no major design changes were made during the 3-year run of the H&R cal. .25 pistol, there were 2 different issues. Early guns have blued trigger guards, but later guns have polished guards. In addition, markings were changed as shown in the illustrations of the slides. Highest serial number seen with original marking is #7658. Lowest seen with later marking is #9656.

Manufacture of the H&R cal. .25 pistol ceased in 1915. Total production was about 20,000 guns.

Cal. .32 pocket automatic

In 1916, the year after the cal. .25 pistol was discontinued, H&R introduced its cal. .32 pocket automatic pistol, or "self-loading pistol" as the company preferred to call its automatic. Like its cal. .25 predecessor, the H&R cal. .32 pocket pistol was based on W&S patents. Several W&S cal. .32 pistols were issued, but the H&R pistol follows the W&S 1913 model pistol most closely. But unlike the W&S pistol, the H&R version has a grip safety device. It is also a true hammerless or striker-fired arm, whereas the W&S pistol has an outside hammer.

Slide of the H&R pistol is about ⅛" higher than its W&S contemporary. The extra height was needed to house the counter-recoil and firing pin springs within the slide. Extractor of the H&R pistol is top-mounted within the slide and incorporates a vertical indicator pin which projects above the top of the slide when there is a cartridge in the chamber. The firing pin acts as the ejector, stopping just before the slide completes its rearward travel.

The follower in the early H&R cal. .32 magazine was flat surfaced, and the metal of the magazine body was relatively thin. Later magazines were formed from heavier metal. Upper edge of the follower was recessed about 1/32" and the top surface was given a 25° slope at the rear end. Guns fitted with magazines of original pattern are uncommon. Highest serial number seen is #2811.

The H&R cal. .32 pistol was one of

the first American-made pocket automatic pistols to have a magazine disconnector so that the gun could not be fired with magazine removed. Original grip safety is a Y-shaped device with its left arm bearing on the magazine. When the magazine is withdrawn and the grip safety released, the grip safety pulls the trigger bar downward and out of engagement with the trigger. Inserting the magazine into the frame moves the trigger bar upward so that it is aligned with the trigger when the grip safety is depressed.

This magazine disconnector system was eventually abandoned and later guns can be fired with magazine removed. The transition came fairly late in the production cycle. In the 20,000-30,000 serial number range, some specimens will be found with the disconnector and some without the disconnector.

Manual safety

Manual safety of the H&R cal. .32 pistol works the same as in the cal. .25 pistol except that the eccentric forces the trigger bar out of play instead of blocking the trigger as in the cal. .25 pistol. Sights consist of a prominent front blade brazed to the barrel, and a rear V-notch in the top of the removable slide breech plate.

Care is necessary in disassembling the slide. A small spring-loaded pin in the rear end of the slide must be depressed with a punch before the slide breech plate can be removed.

Serial numbers are found on the left rear of the slide, left side of the frame under the grip, underside of the barrel, and inside the slide. This last location shows only the last 3 digits of the serial number. Other markings are virtually identical with those of the second-issue cal. .25 pistol, except that the inscription on the right side gives the additional Nov. 9, 1909, patent date and caliber marking on left side is .32.

There were 3 issues of the cal. .32 pistol, not counting the magazine variation. First and scarcest issue has the magazine disconnector device, and the slide is scored with 12 coarse serrations in a 1" space near the rear end. Highest serial number seen is #1754.

Second issue is the same, except that there are 16 slide serrations occupying the 1" space. The serrations are shallow.

Third-issue pistols have the 16-serration slide, but lack the magazine disconnector feature.

H&R offered the cal. .32 pistol from 1916 until 1939. Total production was approximately 40,000 guns. Highest serial number seen is #34234. Its rate of sale was far slower than that achieved by the H&R cal. .25 pistol during its much shorter period of manufacture.

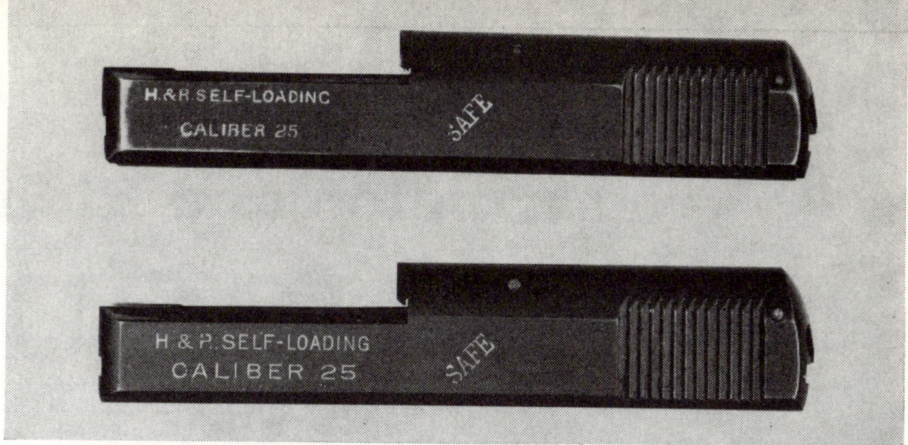

Left side view of first issue (at top) and second issue H&R cal. .25 pistol slides. Lettering on first issue slide is smaller.

Right side view of first issue (at top) and second issue H&R cal. .25 pistol slides. Lettering is larger on second issue slide and word "MASSACHUSETTS" is spelled out.

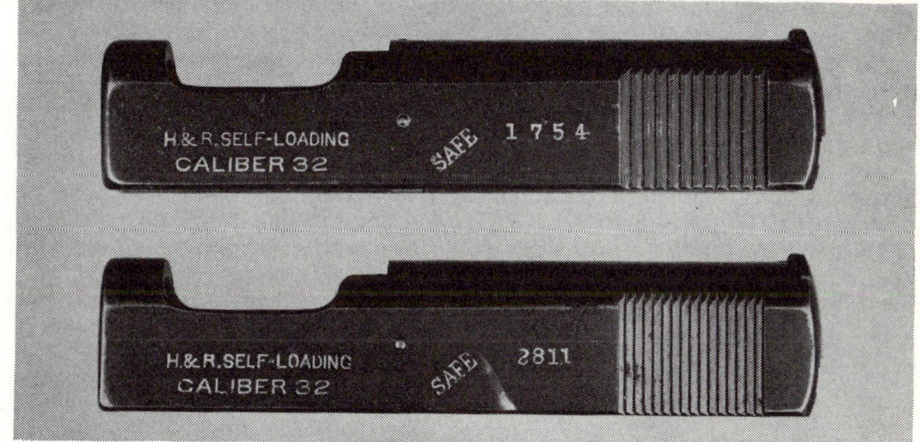

Early H&R cal. .32 pistol slide (at top) has 12 coarse serrations near rear end; later slide has 16 serrations in same 1" space.

Early H&R cal. .32 magazine (l.) with later type incorporating modified follower with recessed edge and slope at rear end. Later magazine was made stronger through use of heavier metal in body. Magazines of all H&R pistols were nickel plated. ■

Harrington and Richardson HANDGUNS

By DeWITT E. SELL

THE year 1871 is memorable in the annals of American firearms history. The National Rifle Association was formally organized during that year. In Worcester, Mass., Iver Johnson commenced operations; and Franklin Wesson formed a partnership with his nephew, Gilbert Henderson Harrington, to develop a new shell-ejecting revolver which had been invented by Harrington.

Prior to the formation of the partnership of Wesson & Harrington, Franklin Wesson (a brother of Daniel B. and Edwin) manufactured rifles and Gilbert Harrington was employed by Ballard & Fairbanks, a firm that was engaged in manufacturing revolvers.

William Augustus Richardson, a former employee of Ballard & Fairbanks, joined the new organization as plant manager. In 1874 Gilbert Harrington bought out the interest of his partner and a new firm was formed under the name of Harrington & Richardson—which trade name continues unchanged to the present day.

This article reviews, with historical background, the Harrington & Richardson line of handguns produced to World War II.

First integral ejector

By this time the Harrington revolver was proving very popular. It was the first revolver in which the cylinder could be loaded and the fired shells removed by its integral sliding ejector without removing the cylinder or detaching any component. It was manufactured until 1878.

In 1876 the company brought out another style of revolver so constructed that with a simple movement the center pin slipped out, allowing the cylinder to drop into the hand—the pin being used to eject the cartridge cases. A further perfection was a spring catch for the cylinder. Cheaper to make and to sell than the shell-ejector model, this revolver was furnished in several calibers and it proved quite popular.

In 1878, Harrington & Richardson introduced the first of their many double-action revolvers.

Periodic expansion of manufacturing quarters marked the ever-increasing demand for the firm's products. Eventually the growing popularity of H&R firearms demanded a plant that would house considerably more employees and machinery as well as allow the different departments to be placed in separate areas. By 1893 the ground was broken for the first of the buildings that would mark the permanent home of the firm. By 1894 the main building at Park Ave. and Chandler St. was completed—its equipment then being unsurpassed by any other such company in the world. A 3-story addition was added in 1900.

Export business

The firm gave considerable attention to its export business at the turn of the century and, despite competition, had notable success. By 1901 another building was erected on Chandler St. which was a replica of the first, but somewhat shorter. This gave the firm a working area of approximately 75,000 square feet, enabling it to employ some 600 people.

By 1907, more than 3,000,000 revolvers bearing the H&R trademark had been manufactured.

Neither Gilbert H. Harrington nor William A. Richardson lived to see their company reach its zenith of productivity or prosperity. Gilbert Harrington, though younger, died first, at age 52. Shortly after his funeral, William Richardson left for his summer home in New Hampshire and was at the factory but a few times following his return. Just before Thanksgiving, 1897, Richardson died at the age of 63.

The company had been incorporated in the year 1888 with G. H. Harrington as president and W. A. Richardson as treasurer. Following the death of the founders, Edwin C. Harrington, a son, was elected president. He was but 20 years old at the time. Another younger son, John W. Harrington, joined the firm somewhat later. Mrs. Mary A. Richardson became a member of the board of directors. None of the Harrington or Richardson family line is currently connected with the company, the last of the Harringtons severing his connection during the 1950's.

Trademarks

The first trademark of the firm was simply the letters H&R. On May 14, 1889, a new trademark was registered —a target with 5 shots scored on it— and this appeared on the hard rubber stocks of most H&R revolvers until rubber stocks were discontinued. The final trademark is the H&R monogram incorporating the familiar target symbol in its center.

The table at right lists 28 H&R handgun models, along with pertinent specifications, known to have been produced from the initial 'Shell-Ejector' model of 1871 up to 1941.

The following commentary will add some measure of meaning to the statistical tabulation.

The Handy Gun

The H&R Handy Gun was a unique, if somewhat controversial, arm. It resembles a single-barrel shotgun with the barrel and shoulder stock sawed off. It breaks at the breech by a lever as do the majority of single-barrel shotguns. It is perhaps best known in its .410-bore version but was made in 3 other calibers or gauges as noted. These were beautiful guns with finely checkered walnut stocks and case-hardened frames. The Handy Gun, which comes under Federal regulations, must be registered with the Alcohol and Tobacco Tax Division of the U. S. Treasury Department.

One of the most famous single-shot target pistols ever produced was H&R's

H&R Auto Ejecting Model double-action revolver, cal. .32 S&W Long

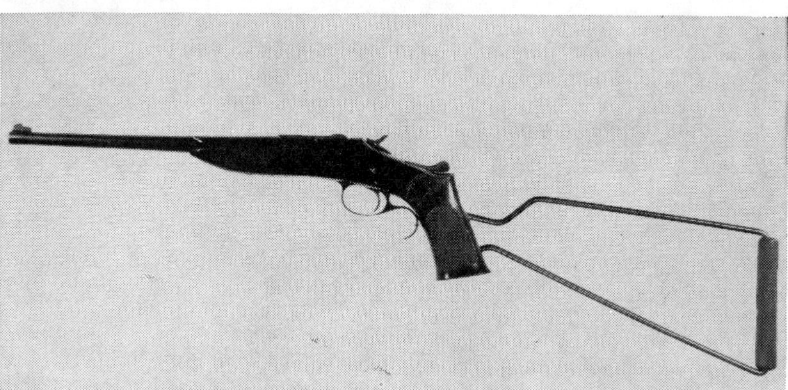

H&R Handy Gun Model single-shot pistol, cal. .22 long rifle

U.S.R.A. model. This top-break pistol was chambered for the .22 long rifle cartridge. It was the most expensive of the entire H&R line up to the time of its discontinuance (1941). Designed by Walter Roper, it incorporated a speed-action with very short hammer fall and exceptionally crisp trigger pull. Eleven one-piece stocks of varying shapes and sizes were available for this and other H&R .22 target pistols. These finely-finished one-piece interchangeable checkered walnut stocks were a distinguishing feature H&R cal. .22 handguns once possessed over other competitive makes.

The Automatic Ejecting, Premier, and Bicycle double-action top-break revolvers were made for a time in special versions known as Police models. The only difference in specifications on these models was in the hammer which had no spur to catch on the pocket but could be thumb-cocked by pulling the trigger until it reached the half-cock position.

Folding knife

The Automatic Ejecting revolver was also furnished with a folding knife beneath the barrel which, when open, extended 2″ beyond the 4″ barrel.

The H&R Hammerless double-action, top-break revolvers were made in 2 basic models as noted in the table, the principal difference being in size and weight of frame.

The American, Young America, Vest Pocket, and Bulldog revolvers were all of double-action solid-frame construction. The Vest Pocket came with a safety or spurless hammer, and such hammers could also be obtained on the American and Young America models except rimfire calibers above .22. There was no price differential as to type of hammer or finish on these models, but loading gates or special

H&R HANDGUN PRODUCTION UP TO WORLD WAR II

Model Name	*Caliber*	*Barrel (ins.)*	*No. of Shots*	*Weight (ozs.)*	*Finish*
Automatic Ejecting	.32 C.F.	3¼,4,5,6	6	16	Bl/Nk
	.38 C.F.	3¼,4,5,6	5	15	Bl/Nk
Premier	.22 R.F.	2,3,4,5,6	7	13	Bl/Nk
	.32 C.F.	2,3,4,5,6	5	12	Bl/Nk
Bicycle	.22 R.F.	2	7		Bl/Nk
	.32 C.F.	2	5		Bl/Nk
Hammerless	.22 R.F.	2,3,4,5,6	7	13	Bl/Nk
	.32 C.F.	2,3,4,5,6	5	13	Bl/Nk
Hammerless	.32 C.F.	3¼,4,5,6	6	18	Bl/Nk
	.38 C.F.	3¼,4,5,6	5	17	Bl/Nk
American	.32 C.F.	2½,4½,6	6	16	Bl/Nk
	.32 R.F.	2½	6	16	Bl/Nk
	.38 C.F.	2½,4½,6	5	15	Bl/Nk
	.38 R.F.	2½	5	15	Bl/Nk
	.44 C.F.	2½,4½,6	5	18	Bl/Nk
Young America	.22 R.F.	2,4½,6	7	8½	Bl/Nk
	.32 R.F.	2	5	9	Bl/Nk
	.32 C.F.	2,4½,6	5	9	Bl/Nk
Vest Pocket	.22 R.F.	1⅛	7	8½	Bl/Nk
	.32 C.F.	1⅛	5	9	Bl/Nk
Bulldog	.32 R.F.	2½	6		Bl/Nk
	.38 R.F.	2½	5		Bl/Nk
Model 4 (1904)	.32 C.F.	2½,4½,6	6	16	Bl/Nk
	.38 C.F.	2½,4½,6	5	16	Bl/Nk
Model 5 (1905)	.32 C.F.	2½,4½,6	5	11	Bl/Nk
Model 6 (1906)	.22 R.F.	2½,4½,6	7	10	Bl/Nk
Self-Loading	.32 ACP	3½	8	22	Blue
Self-Loading	.25 ACP	2	7	12¼	Blue
Handy Gun	.22 R.F.	12¼	1	42	Blue
	28-ga.	8,12¼	1	33-37	Blue
	.32-20	12¼	1	44	Blue
	.410 bore	8,12¼	1	33-37	Blue
U.S.R.A.	.22 R.F.	7,8,10	1	31	Blue
Sportsman D.A.	.22 R.F.	3,6	9	30	Blue
	.22 W.R.F.	3,6	7	30	Blue
Sportsman S.A.	.22 R.F.	6	9	30	Blue
Ultra Sportsman	.22 R.F.	6	9	30	Blue
Eureka Sportsman	.22 R.F.	6¼	6	32	Blue
New Defender	.22 R.F.	2,3	9	23	Blue
Target	.22 R.F.	6	7	16	Blue
.22 Special	.22 R.F.	6	9	23	Blue
	.22 W.R.F.	6	7	23	Blue
Expert	.22 R.F.	10	9	28	Blue
	.22 W.R.F.	10	7	28	Blue
Trapper	.22 R.F.	6	7	12¼	Blue
922	.22 R.F.	6	9	21¾	Blue
Hunter	.22 R.F.	10	9	26	Blue
Bobby	.32 C.F.	4	6	23	Blue
	.38 C.F.	4	5	23	Blue

H&R Young America Model double-action revolver, cal. .22 short, long, and long rifle

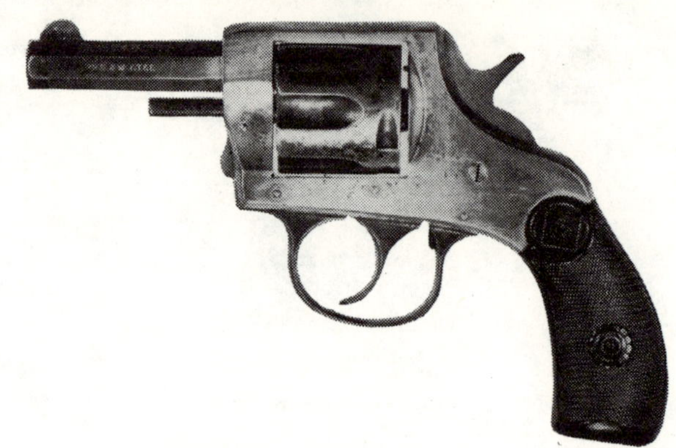

H&R Model 1904 double-action revolver, cal. .32 S&W

H&R Self-Loading pistol, cal. .32 ACP

H&R U. S. R. A. single-shot pistol, cal. .22 long rifle

stocks were supplied at added cost.

Models 4, 5, and 6 were also double-action, solid-frame revolvers and were introduced during the first decade of this century.

Two self-loading pistols

Harrington & Richardson produced but 2 commercial semi-automatic, or self-loading, pistols. These were modifications of the basic designs patented by Webley & Scott, English firearms manufacturers. H&R took out patents in 1907 and 1909 covering their refinements of these designs. These hammerless pistols operate on the blowback principle and are noteworthy for their simplified takedown system which combines the desirable features of the rigid barrel with the ease of cleaning and replacement of the removable barrel. Both models have thumb safeties. The cal. .32 model has an additional grip safety. The cal. .32 model was available up to the year 1940 but the cal. .25 model was dropped considerably earlier.

From the late 1920's on, H&R increasingly concentrated on the manufacture of target handguns.

H&R's Sportsman revolvers have been their cal. .22 target handguns over the years. They were produced in both single- and double-action models and were of top-break construction with automatic ejector and adjustable sights. The actions were hand stoned with hardened tool steel parts. Coil springs were employed throughout. All Sportsman models had the special trigger guard with finger rest spur to the rear. The Sportsman Double-Action model has enjoyed a run of more than a quarter of a century and is the only model remaining in current production. In fact, it is the only top-break revolver being produced by H&R today.

A primary refinement incorporated in the Ultra and Eureka Sportsman models was a cylinder shortened to the length of the .22 long rifle cartridge. This reduced bullet jump to the minimum before reaching the rifling. The New Defender was essentially a pocket model of the Sportsman D. A. revolver. The Target Model, .22 Special, and Expert were relatively inexpensive double-action top-break revolvers and were furnished with fixed sights in blue finish only.

The Trapper, 922, and Hunter were the least expensive revolvers of the H&R line, and were of double-action, solid-frame construction with fixed front sight in gold finish.

With the advent of high-speed cal. .22 ammunition, safety cylinders with rim counterbores were introduced for all H&R cal. .22 revolvers.

H&R developed the Bobby model in 1939 for London's some 25,000 constables, following a reversal of a long-standing policy of forbidding English policemen to carry firearms occasioned by the widespread fear of German saboteurs. This double-action top-break revolver was later offered here in both cals. .32 and .38. ■

H&R Sportsman Model single-action revolver cal. .22 long rifle

Iver Johnson Firearms

A survey of the arms produced by this old firm

By DeWITT E. SELL

IVER Johnson's Arms & Cycle Works, Inc. is only a decade away from its centennial anniversary. Of the American firearms manufacturers established following the Civil War, Iver Johnson is one of only a few that has remained in continuous production to date.

Iver Johnson and Martin Bye formed a partnership in 1871, primarily to manufacture firearms. They had acquired considerable experience and technical knowledge by association with European gunmakers and had also been employees of Ethan Allen, a gunmaker who operated at Norwich, Conn., and, later, at Worcester, Mass. They were widely recognized as expert mechanics and gunsmiths.

Their beginnings were humble, their first shop consisting of 2 small rooms in the rear of a building on Church St. in Worcester, and 3 employees.

During their first year of operation they marketed 2 muzzle-loading pistols and 2 breech-loading pistols as well as a complete line of police goods such as leg irons and handcuffs.

The drilling and reaming of pistol barrels, and inside polishing and finishing, were all done by automatic machinery. The firm of Johnson & Bye were pioneers in the use of automatic machinery in firearms manufacture. By the latter part of 1872 the business had grown to such proportions that a large 5-story building on Central St. in Worcester was purchased. Here, with more room, new machinery, and greater capacity for new business, Johnson & Bye commenced in early 1873 the manufacture of revolvers destined to make the name of Iver Johnson world-famous.

Reorganized in 1883

In 1883, Martin Bye sold his interest in the business to Iver Johnson. The firm of Johnson & Bye was dissolved and that of Iver Johnson's Arms & Cycle Works took its place. From the beginning, all Iver Johnson firearms had been marketed exclusively through the John P. Lovell Arms Co. of Boston. This policy remained in effect until 1895.

In 1891 the present location in Fitchburg, Mass., was established. The fall of 1891 saw the new armory in full operation.

The Owl's Head trade-mark, used by Iver Johnson on his products, was also his mark as a Chapter Mason. Iver Johnson died on Aug. 3, 1895, leaving an industrial legacy to be carried on by his son, Fred I. Johnson.

During the first decade of the twentieth century Iver Johnson made and sold more revolvers than anyone else in the world. In the 14-year period from 1894 to 1908, over 2,000,000 Iver Johnson Safety Automatic hammer and hammerless revolvers alone were sold. The 'Hammer the Hammer' safety feature was so widely advertised that it became virtually a household slogan. A letter postmarked at Nanterre, France, in 1908, with only "Hammer the Hammer Revolvers—Etats Unis" as the addressee, arrived with dispatch at the Iver Johnson factory.

Foreign demand became so great by 1903 that Iver Johnson found it necessary to establish a branch office in Hamburg, Germany, and subsequently in London, England. Branch offices were also maintained in San Francisco and New York for export trade. Iver Johnson's Arms & Cycle Works was truly a Goliath of the American firearms industry during this era.

During the Spanish-American War (1898), many enlisted men purchased Iver Johnson revolvers. In the Russo-Japanese War (1904-1905), thousands of Iver Johnson revolvers were carried by both sides although neither country supplied their non-commissioned soldiers with sidearms. By 1908, Iver Johnson catalogs were issued in 8 different languages.

In the early 1900's Iver Johnson revolvers were preferred by numerous law-enforcement officers throughout the United States and were issued to the mounted police of Moscow, Russia.

Following is a listing of firearms produced by the Iver Johnson firm from its inception in 1871 to early 1961.

The writer wishes to acknowledge the cooperation of Luther M. Otto, III and A. W. Guenther, respectively President and Sales Manager of Iver Johnson's Arms & Cycle Works, which made possible this article.

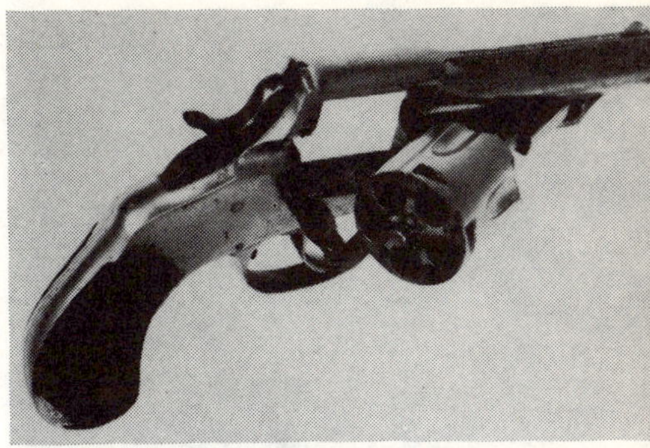

Model 1879, cal. .38 S&W, 5-shot, double-action, 3″ barrel, swing-out cylinder

(Top) Swift, cal. .38 S&W, 5-shot, double-action, 3¼″ barrel. (Lower) Swift, hammerless, cal. .38 S&W, 5-shot, double-action, 3¼″ barrel

Safety Automatic Revolver, cal. .32 S&W, 5-shot, double-action, 2″ barrel. First 'Hammer the Hammer' model

Safety Automatic Revolver, cal. .38 S&W, 5-shot, double-action, 4″ barrel, with Hi-Hold walnut grip

(Top) Safety Hammerless, cal. .32 S&W, 5-shot, double-action, 3″ barrel, with coil mainspring. (Lower) Safety Hammerless, cal. .32 S&W, 5-shot, double-action, 2″ barrel, with flat mainspring

Model 1900, cal. .38 center-fire, double-action, 5-shot

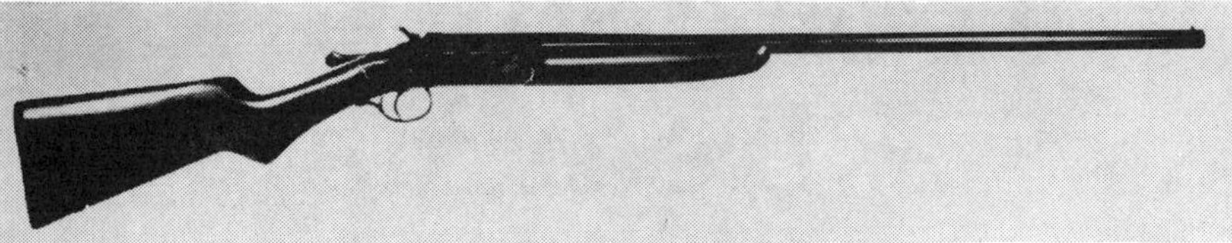

Champion shotgun

Armsworth Model 855, cal. .22 long rifle, 8-shot, single-action, 6″ barrel, adjustable sights and finger rest

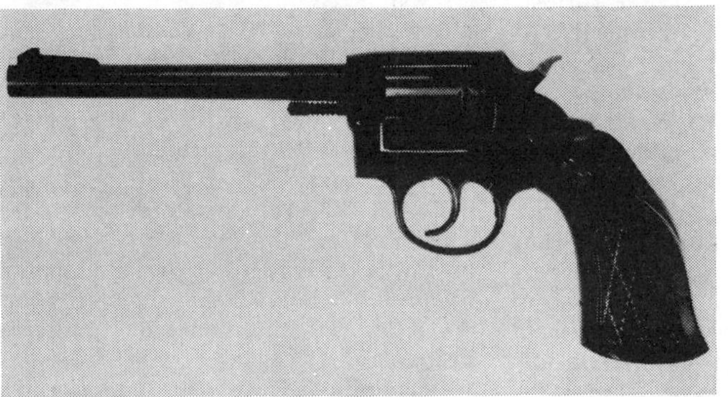

Model 55, cal. .22 long rifle, 8-shot, double-action, 6″ barrel

Production Period	Model Name and Pertinent Data
1871-1887	**Uncle Sam and Prince muzzle-loading pistols**—Approx. cal. .50; barrel lengths 2″, 3″, 4″, and 6″; nickel frame, blue barrel. Initial products of Johnson & Bye.
1871-1887	**Star Vest Pocket and Eclipse breech-loading pistols**—Single-shot; derringer type; 2¼″ barrels swinging on pivot for loading and shell extraction. First pistols of this design to employ cal. .22 and .32 rimfire cartridges.
1873-1884	**Favorite revolver**—Single-action, octagon barrel, fluted cylinder, automatic cylinder stop; cals. .22, .32, .38, and .44 short rimfire. Available with pearl or ivory grips and engraved.
1873-1887	**Tycoon revolver**—Cals. .22 short rimfire 7-shot, .32 short rimfire 5-shot, .38 rimfire 5-shot, .44 short rimfire 5-shot. Available with pearl or ivory grips and engraved.
1874-1887	**Encore and Favorite Navy revolvers**—Similar to above models except barrel is round or semi-octagon instead of octagon.
1875-1884	**Smoker revolver**—Fluted cylinder, octagon barrel, sheathed trigger, cal. .38 S&W.
1875-1895	**Defender revolver**—Single-action, 2¼″ octagon barrel, half fluted cylinder, sheathed trigger, saw-handle; cals. .22, .32 and .38 rimfire. Style of cylinder and barrels, and barrel length depended on caliber.
1878-1886	**Eagle revolver**—First Iver Johnson double-action; cals. .22, .32, .38, .44 rimfire; solid frame.
1879-1886	**Eagle revolver**—Cal. .38 S&W; 3″ barrel.
1879-1893	**Champion Side Snap single-barrel shotgun**—Hammer; 10- and 12-ga.; plain steel or twist barrels; frame and fittings nickel-plated. First single-barrel breech-loading shotgun produced with hammer set in center of frame tang.
1881-1882	**British Bull Dog revolver**—Double-action.
1882-1900	**American Bull Dog revolver**—Double-action, cals. .22, .32, and .38 rimfire and .32, .38, and .44 center-fire; 5-shot; octagon barrels of 2½″, 4½″, or 6″; nickel-plated finish only.
1883-1887	**Model 1879 double-action revolver**—Revolver with cylinder swinging to side for loading and ejecting. By throwing open a loading gate to right, cylinder could be swung out to right on arm pivoted below barrel. Then, by pressing cylinder down on base-pin, cartridges would instantly extract. Made first in cal. .38 S&W only; other calibers added later.
1885-1910	**Champion single-barrel shotgun**—Semi-hammerless, 12-ga. only.
1886-1894	**Champion Side-Snap single-barrel shotgun**—Hammerless; first single-barrel shotgun cocked by act of opening barrel for loading. Safety lever indicator prevented accidental discharge.
1886-1895	**Gem pistol**—Cal. .22 short rimfire only.
1887-1900	**Boston Bull Dog revolver**—Double-action; cals. .22 rimfire, .32 center-fire, .38 center-fire; 2½″ barrel, nickel finish only.
1890-1910	**Swift revolver**—Double-action; hammer and hammerless; cal. .38 S&W only. Barrel catch of hammer model not only held barrel to frame but rested firmly on hammer when pistol was discharged. As barrel could be opened only by pressing down on catch, it was impossible for barrel to become dislodged by detonation of cartridge.
1892-1950	**Safety Automatic Revolver**—Hammer model; cals. .32 and .38 center-fire and (1895) .22 rimfire. First revolver to employ famous 'Hammer the Hammer' safety feature.
1894-1950	**Safety Automatic Revolver**—Hammerless model; cals. .22, .32, and .38. In 1908 Safety Automatic Revolvers underwent considerable internal modification. Coil springs were used throughout and the guns were fitted with an adjustable mainspring tension bar, ball and socket mainspring plunger and hammer

contact, vanadium steel lifter, and other refinements. Available in 2″, 3″, 3¼″, 4″, 5″, and 6″ barrel lengths, blue or nickel finish, regular rubber grips, Perfect rubber grips, Western walnut grips, Hi-Hold walnut grips, pearl or ivory grips.

1900-1947 **Model 1900 revolver**—Double-action, solid frame, loading gate; cals. .22 7-shot, .32 rimfire and center-fire 5-shot, .38 center-fire 5-shot. Successor to American Bull Dog and Boston Bull Dog models.

1908-1956 **Champion Model 36 single-barrel shotgun**—12-, 16- and 20-ga. Marked "Champion Arms Co.-Fitchburg, Mass." on left side of frame. First American shotgun with barrel and lug forged in one piece.

1910-1930 **U. S. revolver**—Hammer and hammerless models; double-action; round barrel, plain cylinder, marked on frame top "U. S. Revolver Co.-Made in U.S.A." and "U.S." molded in hard rubber grips; cals. .22, .32, and .38 in hammer model and cals. .32 and .38 in hammerless model. Did not have 'Hammer the Hammer' safety.

1913-1950 **Champion Matted Top Rib single-barrel shotgun**—Hammer.

1913-1942 **Hercules double-barrel shotgun**—Hammerless, 12-ga.

1916-1957 **Champion single-barrel shotgun**—.410-ga.

1924-1942 **Hercules double-barrel shotgun**—Hammerless; 16-, 20-, and .410-ga.

1925-1942 **Model 1900 Target revolver**—Double-action; cal. .22 short, long, or long rifle rimfire 7-shot; 6″ or 9½″ octagon barrel, blue finish only, checkered walnut grips, marked on frame top "Target Model-Fitchburg, Mass., U.S.A."

1926-1931 **.22 Supershot safety hammer revolver**—Extra heavy frame, cal. .22 rimfire only, 7-shot, blue finish, 6″ barrel, Western walnut checkered grips, gold front sight and lettering, marked on left side of barrel ".22 Supershot".

Cadet Model 55-S, cal. .22 long rifle, 8-shot, double-action, 2½″ barrel

Model 56 Starter's revolver, cal. .22 blank, 8-shot, double-action

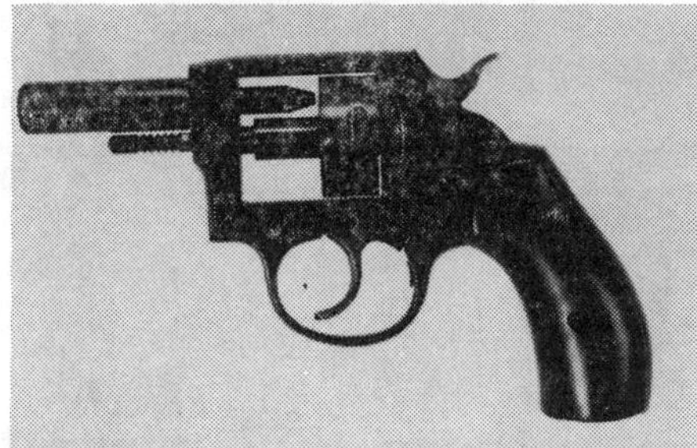

1926-1950 **Special Trap single-barrel shotgun.**

1927-1940 **Supertrap double-barrel shotgun**—Ventilated top rib, ivory sights, beavertail forearm, recoil pad, 12-ga.

1928-1948 **I. J. Self Cocking .22 Safety Rifle Model X**—Patented 'Cocked But Locked' safety feature.

1929-1946 **Model 69 I. J. Target revolver**—Double-action, extra large frame and cylinder, 9-shot, 6″ barrel with 10″ barrel designated Model 79.

1929-1949 **Model 90 .22 Supershot revolver**—Double-action, 9-shot, 6″ barrel.

1931-1957 **Model 833 Supershot Sealed Eight revolver**—Double-action, safety automatic hammer, extra heavy frame, 8-shot cal. .22 short, long, and long rifle rimfire only, 6″ barrel, scored trigger, one-piece Hi-Hold walnut grip. Designated Model 834 when furnished with adjustable finger rest, blue finish, gold lettering. Marked on left side of barrel ".22 Supershot Sealed Eight".

1931-1957 **I. J. Target Sealed Eight revolver**—Double-action extra heavy solid frame, cal. .22 rimfire only, 8-shot, counterbored chambers, blue finish, gold front sight and lettering, 6″ (Model 68) or 10″ Model 78 octagon barrel (later supplied with 4″ or 6″ round barrel), scored trigger, one-piece walnut Hi-Hold grip.

1932-1955 **I. J. Self Cocking .22 Safety Rifle Model 2-X**—Single-shot, bolt-action, full pistol grip walnut stock checkered, Patridge-type sights, rear sight adjustable, cal. .22 regular or high-speed rimfire cartridges. With adjustable aperture rear sight designated Model 2-XA.

1933-1942 **The I. J. Skeet-er double-barrel shotgun**—Hammerless, 12-, 16-, 20-, 28-, and .410-ga. Straight or full pistol grip stock, selective or non-selective single trigger or double triggers, automatic safety or independent safety.

1933-1949 **Model 84 I. J. Protector Sealed Eight revolver**—8-shot top-break similar to Supershot Sealed Eight with following exceptions: 2½″ barrel, silver lettering on barrel, fixed sights and round-butt Hi-Hold pocket-size grip. Cal. .22 rimfire only.

1938-1948 **Model 822 I. J. Champion Target Single-Action revolver**—8-shot top-break with adjustable finger rest, block trigger. Trigger and hammer highly polished. Does not have 'Hammer the Hammer' safety feature but a conventional rebounding hammer. Cal. .22 rimfire only.

1940-1947 **Model 36-T I. J. Trigger Cocking Target revolver**—Single-action, 8-shot, top-break revolver.

1955-1956 **Model 844 I. J. Supershot revolver**—Double-action, top-break, 8-shot, cal. .22 rimfire, adjustable sights, 4½″ and 6″ barrels. Last model with 'Hammer the Hammer' safety feature.

1955-1957 **Model 855 I. J. Armsworth revolver**—Single-action, top-break; 8-shot, cal. .22 rimfire; adjustable sights, adjustable finger rest, flash control cylinder, 6″ barrel.

1955- **Model 55 Target revolver**—Double-action, 8-shot, solid frame; cal. .22 rimfire; 4½″ and 6″ barrels.

1955- **Model 55-S Cadet revolver**—Double-action, 8-shot, solid frame; cal. .22 rimfire; 2½″ barrel.

1955- **Model 56 Starter's revolver**—Double-action, 8-shot, solid frame; cal. .22 rimfire blank; 2½″ barrel.

1956- **Model 57 Target revolver**—Double-action, 8-shot, solid frame, adjustable sights; cal. .22 rimfire; 2½″, 4½″, and 6″ barrels.

1958- **Trailsman 66 revolver**—Double-action, 8-shot, top-break, adjustable sights; cal. .22 rimfire; 6″ barrel.

1959- **Model 56 Starter's revolver**—Double-action, 5-shot, solid frame; cal. .32 center-fire blank; 2½″ barrel.

1959- **Trailsman 66 Snub revolver**—Double-action, 8-shot, top-break, adjustable sights; cal. .22 rimfire; 2¾″ barrel.

1960- **Trailsman 66 Snub revolver**—Double-action, 5-shot, top-break, adjustable sights; cal. .32 and .38 center-fire; 2¾″ barrel.

1961- **Model 50 Sidewinder revolver**—Double-action, 8-shot, solid frame, rod ejection, fixed sights; cal. .22 rimfire; 6″ barrel. ■

Model 57 Target, cal. .22 long rifle, 8-shot, double-action, 4½″ barrel

(Top) Model 66 Trailsman, cal. .22 long rifle, 8-shot, double-action, 6″ barrel. (Lower) Model 66 Trailsman Snub, cal. .22 long rifle, 8-shot, double-action, 2¾″ barrel

Absence of ejector and extractor permitted simple breech construction. Note fixed firing pin in percussion mechanism and rear sight notch in loading gate

Large trigger guard permitted firing with gloved hand. It extends above muzzle to form front sight

Liberator Gun

By M. D. WAITE

THE arming of partisan or other resistance forces within Nazi-occupied territories became a major problem to the Allies during World War II, especially since the production of such armament was carried out in addition to that for normal troop requirements. U. S. Army Ordnance, through its vigorous research and development program, made many significant contributions towards this little publicized effort, not the least of which was development and production of the rather unique 'Liberator' pistol.

The demand for this gun originated with the Office of Strategic Services (OSS), as that organization was vitally interested in arming resistance forces in Europe. OSS specifications called for a cheap but effective gun weighing one pound, and they wanted a million of them in a hurry!

The basic design for an effective .45 caliber single-shot pistol was soon formulated by Army Ordnance and the contract was let to the Guide Lamp Corporation, who completed tooling and production of the million guns in the record time of *thirteen weeks*. Final deliveries were made during the month of August, 1942. The ultimate cost of each unit was a little over $2.00 and the guns were constructed entirely of non-strategic materials. Each gun was individually packaged in a sturdy, paraffin-coated, cardboard box. Included were an instruction sheet, a wooden ramrod, and ten rounds of .45 ACP ammunition stored in the butt of the gun. With the exception of the 4-inch smoothbore, seamless steel tubing barrel and die-cast percussion mechanism, the gun is constructed throughout of sheet steel stampings and a few small steel pins and coil springs. The various parts are held together by a combination of folded seams, rivets, spot and acetylene welds. The net result is a very crude-looking weapon, but it was nevertheless a significant contribution towards the Allied war effort, based upon the theory that "some gun is better than none at all."

A study of the instruction sheet reveals that this is a very simple weapon to operate even though it lacks both an extractor and ejector. ◆◆◆

Firing sequence instruction sheet shows every phase of gun operation

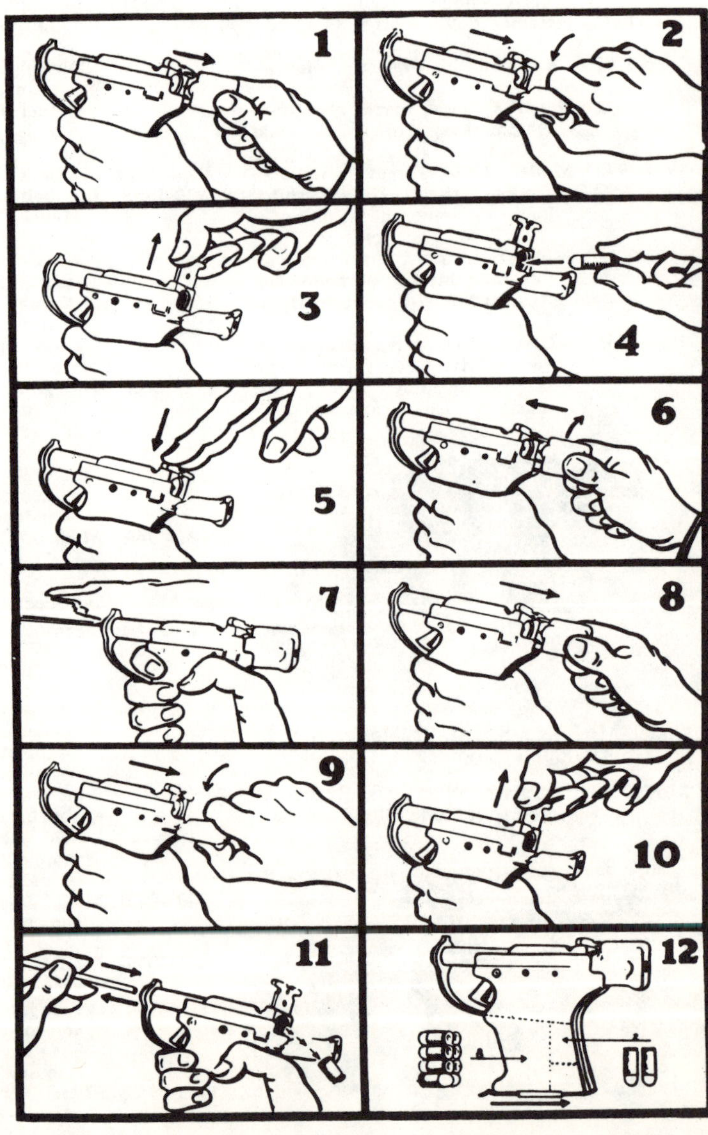

J. M. MARLIN'S HANDGUNS

By HERSCHEL C. LOGAN

TODAY the Marlin name is well known and respected in the realm of rifles and shotguns. Not so well known, however, is the line of handguns produced by Marlin prior to their entry into the long arms field. To review their interesting array of pistols and revolvers, it is necessary to turn back the pages of history to 1870.

Patented an ejector

It was on April 5 of that year that John Marlin of Hartford, Connecticut, was granted a patent (Fig. 1) for an 'improvement in cartridge ejectors'. This appears to have been Marlin's first patent, and the one which started him in the manufacturing of guns under his own name.

Born in the vicinity of Boston Neck, near the town of Windsor Locks, Hartford County, Connecticut, on May 6, 1836, John Mahlon Marlin early developed an unusual interest in guns. As a young man it seemed to him that the obvious thing to do was to seek employment in a place where he might be able to satisfy his desire for working with firearms. At that time the Colt's Patent Fire Arms Manufacturing Company of Hartford, Connecticut, was gaining world-wide renown as an arms manufacturing plant. During the Civil War they had supplied many thousands of revolvers to the War Department.

No doubt John Marlin helped to produce many of these arms, for it was at Colt's that he learned his trade as a toolmaker and gunsmith. If we are to judge by his later work, he must have been a hard worker and a devoted student, meticulous to detail, yet with a vision for the future. Later, employees of his recalled that he was an amiable boss for those who took their work seriously, but a 'terror' to slovenly and careless workmen.

It was while employed in Hartford that he conceived the idea for his basic patent and subsequently made the decision to remove to New Haven, there to begin the manufacture of arms under his own name.

According to William Dorking, an employee at Marlin's for over half a century, John Marlin's first shop was on Grand Avenue. Fire forced the removal to the corner of Collis and Water Streets. A later move was made to State Street at Hamilton where the actual production of pistols bearing the J. M. Marlin name first began.

It is believed that the earliest pistols produced by Marlin were two simple single-shot, vest pocket models. One was a tiny .22 caliber model (Fig. 2a) only four inches in length, and unmarked save for the name and address on top of the barrel. The other was the better known "OK" model (Fig. 2b), a single-shot of .22 caliber, and according to some authorities also produced in .30 and .32 calibers. The belief regarding this early manufacture is strengthened by the fact that both of these models were produced without the cartridge extractor covered by his first patent. Also, neither carries the patent date as is true of the other single-shots.

Following in rapid succession came four other single-shot pistols, foremost of which was the series of three produced under the name of "NEVER MISS" (Fig. 3). Size only is the distinguishing mark of these pistols, which were produced in .22, .32 and .41 calibers. The fourth was a large frame pistol of .38 caliber bearing the name "VICTOR" (Fig. 2c) on the top of the barrel. The reason for the larger frame for a smaller caliber than the .41 caliber "NEVER MISS" is a bit difficult to understand; unless it was designed for a pocket type rather than the vest pocket style of the then-popular .41 caliber derringers.

A single-shot known as "GEM" has often been erroneously credited to Marlin. Such a pistol was produced by Stevens, and no doubt due to its similarity to the Marlin "OK" has been thoughtlessly labeled as Marlin produced. The writer has never been able to verify, even through the factory, that this gun was ever produced by them.

John M. Marlin

While manufactured under Marlin's patent of April 5, 1870, the "XL DERRINGER" of .41 caliber was actually manufactured by Hopkins & Allen of Norwich, Connecticut, for the New York firm of Merwin & Hulbert. Early advertising of both firms illustrates this cartridge derringer, together with other models in their line.

Three general types of revolvers seem to have been produced by Marlin, in-

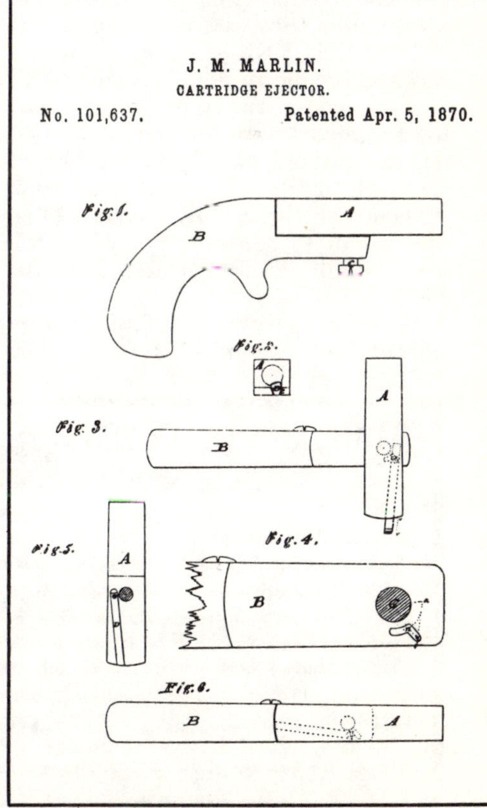

Fig. 1: Patent drawing of J. M. Marlin's cartridge ejector principle

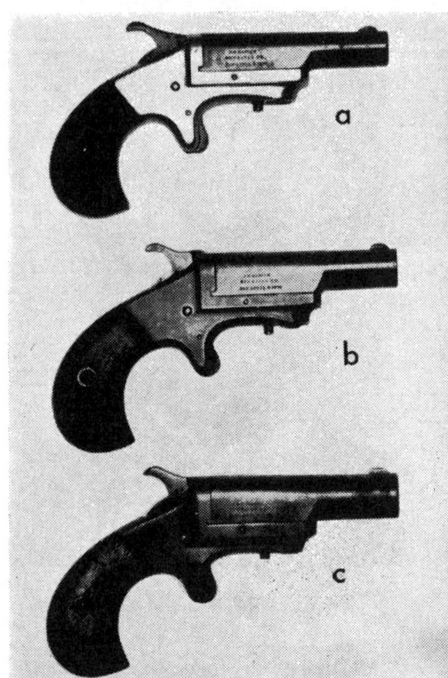

Fig. 2: (a) Tiny .22 caliber single-shot vest pocket pistol only four inches in length; **(b)** Marlin "OK" .22 caliber single-shot pistol; **(c)** Marlin "VICTOR" .38 caliber single-shot derringer

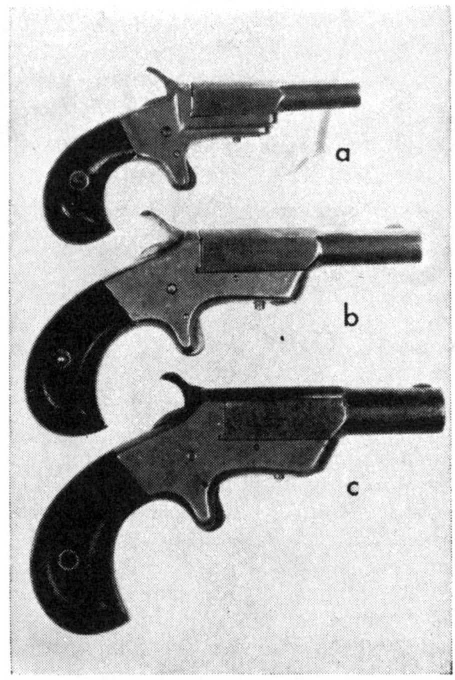

Fig. 3: The "NEVER MISS" series: **(a)** .22 caliber, **(b)** .32 caliber, **(c)** .41 caliber

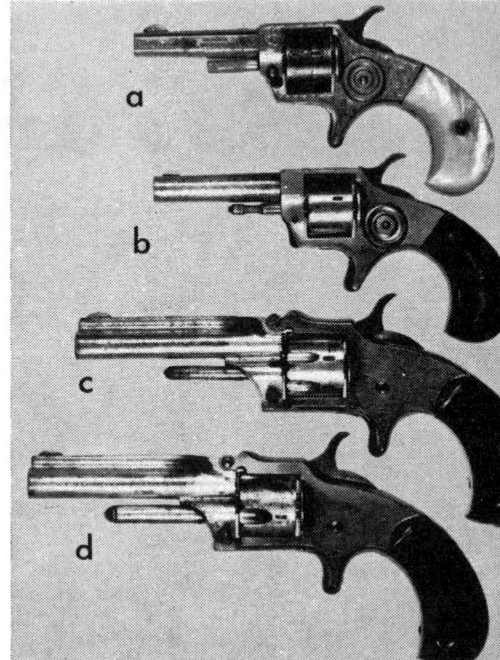

Fig. 4: (a) Presentation model of the Marlin "LITTLE JOKER"; **(b)** Marlin "OK" revolver in .22 caliber; **(c)** Marlin "XX STANDARD" .22 caliber seven-shot revolver; **(d)** Marlin "XXX STANDARD" .30 caliber five-shot revolver

cluding a solid-frame, a tip-up not unlike the early Smith & Wessons, and a top-break model.

Two versions of the solid-frame type are pictured in Fig. 4. Both are .22 caliber. The top one (Fig. 4a), in beautiful presentation style with pearl grips, is the "LITTLE JOKER". This same model was also produced in a plain style without ornamentation. In addition to having the model name on top of the barrel, the maker's name and address are stamped on the left side of the barrel. Although the little "OK" revolver (Fig. 4b) is not so generally known, it followed quite closely the design of the "LITTLE JOKER".

Along in the early '80's J. M. Marlin bought out the Standard Revolver Company which had been producing revolvers of the tip-up variety. The name Standard was kept for some time after the purchase. Advertisements for the Standard revolvers are to be found in some of the sporting goods catalogs of that time. One such ad appears in Fig. 5 and, even though no reference is made to Marlin, it will be noted that the initials "JMM" appear on the grips.

Two of the bird's-head grip type of tip-up models are also pictured. Fig. 4c is a .22 caliber, seven-shot version with the wording "XX STANDARD 1873" stamped on top of the barrel. Left side of the barrel is marked "J. M. MARLIN, NEW HAVEN, CT. USA PAT. JULY 1, 1873". A patent of this date discloses a single-action, rimfire, tip-up revolver similar to a Smith & Wesson, with a round butt and circular side-plate. Fig. 4d pictures their "XXX STANDARD 1873", five-shot in .30 caliber. These revolvers were also produced in .32 and .38 calibers. Some are marked "No. 32 STANDARD", or "38 STANDARD", with the date.

The .38 caliber tip-up revolver was produced in a model having straight rather than bird's-head grips, and with an irregular side-plate (Fig. 6). It carries the wording "38 STANDARD 1878" on top of the barrel.

Comes now one of the most unique, certainly the least known, revolver of the entire Marlin line. Its design is totally unlike any other Marlin (see Fig. 7). In general appearance it is

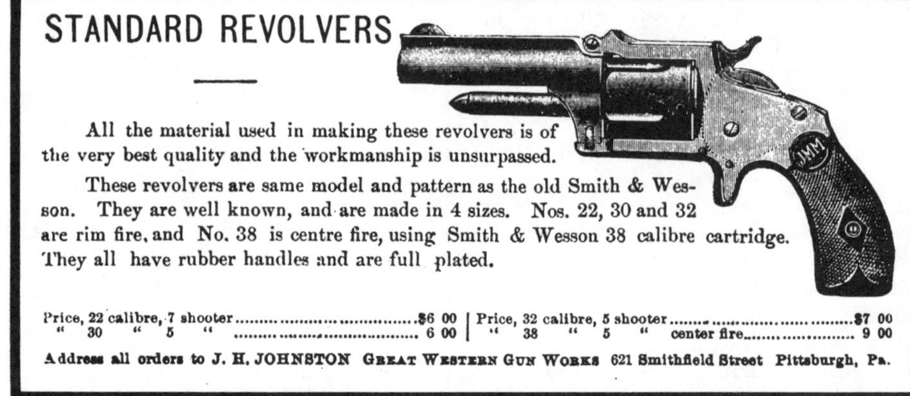

Fig. 5: "STANDARD" revolver with initials "JMM" on grip, as pictured in an advertisement

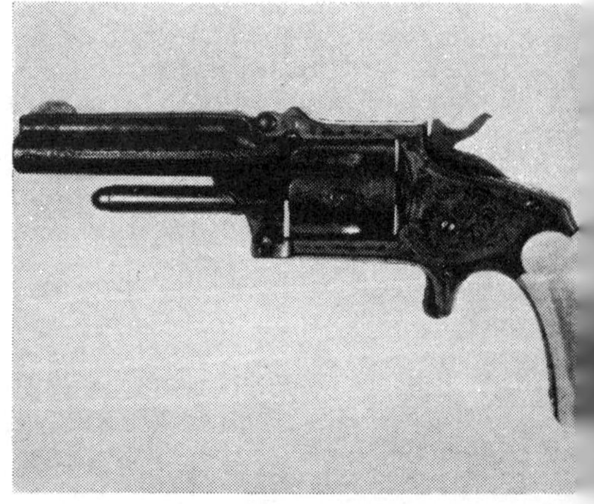

Fig. 6: Marlin "38 STANDARD" revolver of .38 caliber

not unlike some revolvers of foreign manufacture. Serial number is 2, and the caliber is .44 S&W Russian. Its rather unusual design would seem to lend credence to the belief that it was produced with an eye to a foreign market. It will be noted the cylinder swings out to the right to load. Cartridges are ejected by means of the cylinder pin, which is pulled forward to permit the release of the cylinder and then swung further over to serve as an extractor. The cylinder, which is 1-7/16 inches in length, is chambered for six center-fire cartridges. The round ribbed barrel, which carries the wording "J. M. MARLIN NEW HAVEN, CONN. USA" on the rib, is just under 5½ inches in length and is rifled with six lands and six grooves, left-hand twist. Workmanship throughout the gun is of the finest. Hammer and trigger guard are casehardened, while the rest of the gun is finished in a rich shiny blue. Grips are of nicely-checkered walnut. A lanyard ring in the butt further indicates that this double-action revolver was designed for military or constabulary use. This large revolver may be considered the enigma of the Marlin line. According to Harry Teator, Service Manager of Marlin Firearms Company, who examined this revolver, there is nothing in the present Marlin records to indicate that this gun was ever manufactured as a production item. However, it could be a tool room model.

Only one model of revolver is believed to have been manufactured by Marlin after their reorganization in 1881, when the firm name was changed from J. M. Marlin to the Marlin Firearms Company. This revolver is illustrated in their 1888 catalog as the "Marlin Double Action Revolver." It is of the top-break variety. In an obvious attempt to capitalize upon the name and popularity of Smith & Wesson it is described in the catalog in these words: "No expense or care has been spared to make this arm as near perfection as it is possible to get. The style is identical with the Smith & Wesson Revolver and in no respect whatever is it inferior."

The top-break revolver, of which a beautiful presentation specimen with pearl grips is pictured in Fig. 8, was made, according to their catalogs, in but two calibers, .32 and .38, and with but a 3¼-inch barrel length. It was still in the line, according to their catalog, in 1899. This was the model with which Marlin rang down the curtain on manufacture of handguns.

Later history of firm

John M. Marlin, founder of the firm which still bears his name, passed away at his home on George Street on July

Continued on page 154

Fig. 7: Large unique Marlin revolver of .44 S&W Russian caliber

Fig. 7a: Loading and shell extracting position of the large Marlin revolver

Fig. 8: Marlin double-action top-break .38 caliber revolver in presentation style, engraved frame and pearl grips

Barn in Chicopee Falls, Mass., in which Oscar F. Mossberg manufactured the 4-shot Novelty pistol

The 4-Shot Mossberg Pistols

By HERSCHEL C. LOGAN

THE firm of O. F. Mossberg & Sons, Inc., New Haven, Conn., is well known today for their rifles, shotguns, telescope sights, spotting scopes, and accessories. The unusually interesting background of its founder, and 2 of his early handgun productions, the 4-shots, are much less familiar. It is a typical story of American free enterprise.

O. F. Mossberg's early years

Oscar F. Mossberg was born in Sweden on Sept. 1, 1866. From early boyhood he evidenced an avid interest in things mechanical, although the genius which was to express itself in later years was developed gradually during those formative years in his home country. In addition to serving the usual apprenticeship, he also worked for a time in a small boiler shop.

Soon after his arrival in this country, young Mossberg secured a job which was to have a decided influence on the course of his life's work. His first employment was in the bicycle department of the Iver Johnson Arms & Cycle Works at Fitchburg, Mass. Noting Mossberg's mechanical ability, the management requested that he give some attention to a problem with which they were then concerned. The problem was to design some sort of a safety for their revolvers which not only would make the guns safer to carry and handle, but would give them a potent advertising feature. It was the young man, O. F. Mossberg from Sweden, who designed the famous safety feature "hammer the hammer" for which Iver Johnson revolvers became noted around the turn of the century. From then on his primary interest was to be the designing and making of arms.

In 1897 Mossberg moved to Hatfield, Mass., where he became superintendent of production at the factory of the C. S. Shattuck Arms Co. His principal work there had to do with the manufacturing of their breech-loading shotguns.

Mr. Mossberg's next, and longest, period of employment was with the J. Stevens Arms & Tool Co. of Chicopee Falls, Mass. In 1902 he entered their employ and embarked upon a career which was to culminate some 17 years later in the founding of his own company for the manufacture of arms.

As a side line while employed at Stevens, he made tape leaders and special hooks and eyes for women's clothing, and also found time to design and patent the little arm which is one of the subjects of this article. U. S. patent #837,867 for his little 4-shot Novelty pistol was secured on Dec. 4, 1906.

First guns made in spare time

Some tools Mossberg purchased from his former employer, Maj. Charles S. Shattuck, were set up in the barn back of the family home in Chicopee Falls. There, beginning in 1907, he and his 2 sons, Harold and Iver, began the manufacture of the little 4-shot pistol in their spare time. Most of the assembling was done by the boys. Both sons were still in high school, and in addition were also employed at the

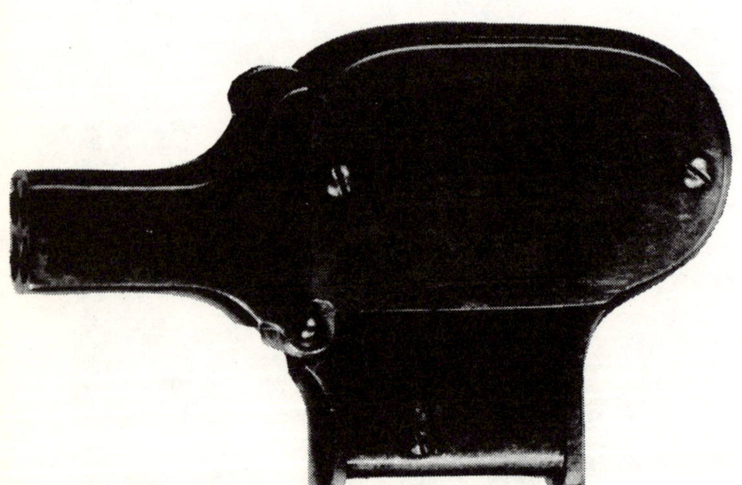

The little 4-shot Novelty pistol invented and patented by Oscar F. Mossberg. Production rights were later sold to the C. S. Shattuck Arms Co., who sold the gun under the name of Unique. Only caliber produced by Mossberg was .22

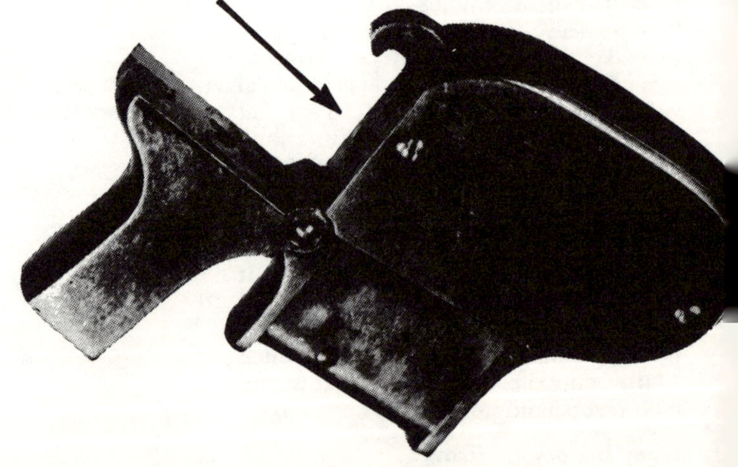

Novelty pistol with barrel group tipped down for loading. The rotating firing pin (arrow) can be seen protruding through the breechblock

First pistol to be manufactured by the newly organized firm of O. F. Mossberg & Sons was this 4-shot cal. .22 Brownie

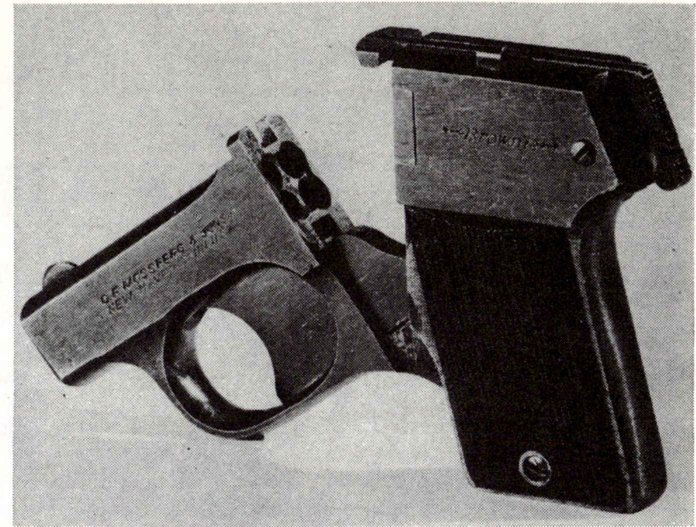

Trigger mechanism of Brownie is a part of the barrel group and tips down with it. Head of the extractor, which slides down inside the grip, is seen on the top edge of the frame

Stevens factory during summer vacations. But the hours after school, weekends, and holidays did afford time to work on the unusual guns which were destined for the South American market, a fact which possibly makes understandable their relative scarcity in this country.

With college days at Worcester Polytechnical Institute approaching and the necessity for the boys to be away, Mossberg, in 1909, sold his interest in the Novelty pistol to Maj. Shattuck, his old employer.

In 1916, Mossberg took a position with the Marlin-Rockwell Corp. of New Haven, Conn., which had acquired control of the Marlin Firearms Co. and were expanding its facilities for the development and manufacture of machine guns for the Allies. Mossberg continued with this corporation until well after the war.

Formed new firm

In 1919, Mossberg, in partnership with his 2 sons, formed the firm of O. F. Mossberg & Sons of New Haven, Conn. Their first shop was located in a small loft space on State Street. In this small and unpretentious factory was designed and developed the familiar Mossberg Brownie 4-shot pocket pistol. A patent was applied for on Aug. 28, 1919, but it was not until July 27, 1920, that patent No. 1,348,035 was granted.

The working crew at the Mossberg plant included, besides father and 2 sons, 3 other employees. The early years were a gradual overcoming of difficulties which beset the infant company. Both Harold and Iver played in an orchestra at nights to earn spending money. All money in the way of their wages went back into the business. With resolute courage, frugal living, and unbounded faith, plus the assistance of loyal friends they established the business on a solid footing.

At no time did Oscar Mossberg have a desk; a corner of the factory served as his shop. Here he designed, rebuilt, and checked manufacturing methods. From this rather rough and often cluttered work bench came many of the improvements in Mossberg guns.

Now for a brief look at the 2 subjects of this story.

The Novelty pistol

First, the Novelty pistol, as the factory refers to it. The operation of this arms oddity is best described by the inventor in his patent application, which reads in part: "This invention relates to firearms, and especially to the construction of a multiple barrel pistol, the object of the invention being to provide a pistol which by reason of its shape may be carried in the pocket without inconvenience and which may be cocked and fired by the actuation of a sliding member which moves in and out of the frame of the arm, all of the operative parts of the device being enclosed—there being no parts extending beyond the frame—."

Oscar F. Mossberg, inventor of the Novelty pistol, the Brownie pistol, and founder of O. F. Mossberg & Sons, Inc. of New Haven, Conn. Photo was made shortly before his death in 1937

As manufactured by the Mossbergs in their barn workshop this all-metal, diminutive, small-arms oddity, only 3½" over-all, carried no marking of any kind except the serial number. It was chambered for cal. .22 rimfire ammunition only. The revolving firing pin was located in the breechblock of the frame. Total production for the period between 1907 and 1909 is believed not to have exceeded 500 guns. They are therefore desirable collector items for those who prefer the unusual in American arms.

Incidentally, the author's specimen illustrated was found in a box of tools in an old hardware store in northwestern Kansas. It was thought to be some kind of tool, use unknown. That it was a gun appears not to have occurred to those who from time to time had occasion to go over the tools in the box.

After the C. S. Shattuck Arms Co. took over the manufacturing rights of the pistol, they gave it the name Unique*, and so stamped the guns along with their name and the patent date. Starting with the cal. .22 model, they added a cal. .32 of slightly differ-

Continued on page 154

* It is interesting to note that the Unique Vest Pocket Pistol was advertised in the Iver Johnson Sporting Goods Catalog (Boston) of 1915 at $4 each.

The Front-Loading Plant

By HERSCHEL C. LOGAN

IN 1859 Willard C. Ellis and John H. White of Springfield, Mass., applied for and received a patent for an 'improvement in firearms'. This patent (No. 24,726, July 12, 1859) is best explained in their own words: "The nature of our invention consists in so constructing the cylinder that the cartridge may be placed in the front end instead of the rear end, as is now the invariable method, and so constructing the cartridge as to admit of this operation."

Circumvented Rollin White patent

As will be observed from the patent drawing (Fig. 1), the cartridge is what is commonly known today as a cup-primer type. It is not known whether Ellis and White were employees of Smith & Wesson but they must have been thoroughly familiar with the Rollin White patent held by S&W. The Rollin White patent provided for a cylinder with the chambers bored through from end to end. Such a revolver, using their rimfire cartridge, had been in production by Smith & Wesson for nearly 2 years prior to the Ellis and White patent application. These men were ingenious workmen, skilled in engineering and gunsmithing as is evident from a study of the City directories of Springfield from 1846 to 1861. Both men were variously listed as armorer, machinist, pistol maker, and silver plater. Ellis was employed in 1858-61 in the James Warner pistol shop. That they were craftsmen of no small stature is verified by scrutiny of the cartridge invented by them, and the gun they fabricated to use it.

This unique cartridge, together with the specially-designed cylinder, was a definite effort to circumvent the Smith & Wesson held patent. However, nearly 4 years seems to have elapsed from the date of the first patent to the production of an arm embracing the front-loading principle. That is, if we are to judge by their next patent (No. 39,318) which was granted on July 21, 1863, and assigned to Henry Reynolds (Fig. 2), and also a subsequent patent (No. 1529) dated Aug. 25, 1863, for a front-loading cartridge (Fig. 3). This latter patent was assigned to Ebenezer H. Plant, Henry Reynolds, Amzi P. Plant, and Alfred Hotchkiss.

Just where Reynolds and Hotchkiss fitted into the picture is not known. They may have been silent partners in the Plant's Manufacturing Co., operated by the 2 Plants. Little is known of this firm. In early directories it is not listed as having been engaged in the manufacture of arms. One advertisement in the 1863 New Haven directory (Fig. 4) shows it to have been active in the making of carriage hardware.

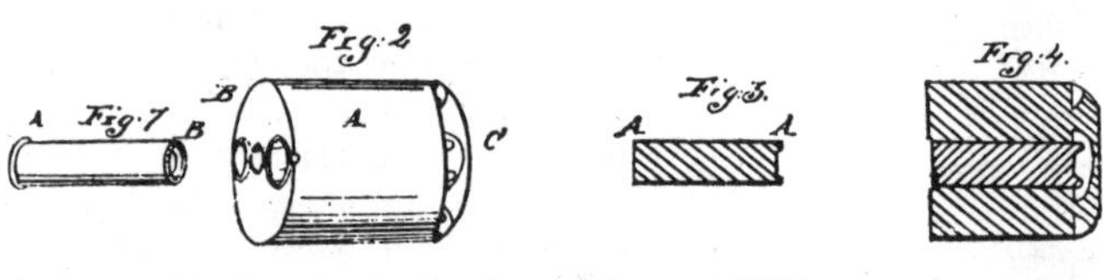

Fig. 1: Drawing from the first Ellis and White patent of July 12, 1859, for a front-loading cylinder and cartridge

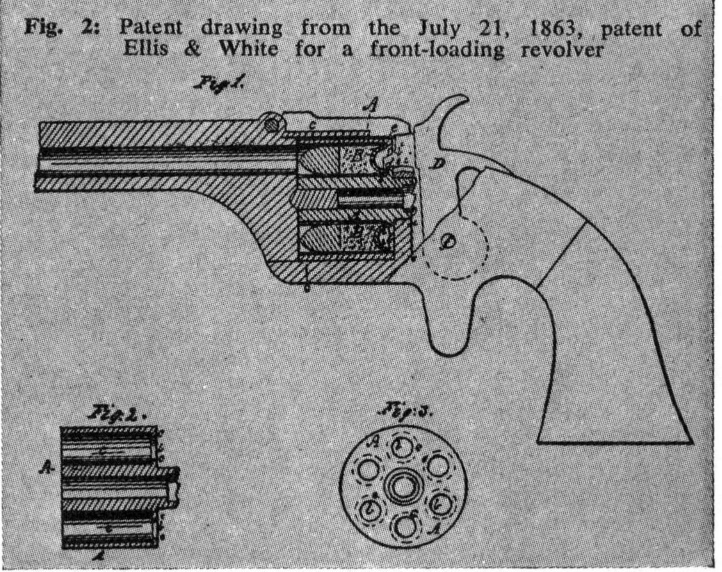

Fig. 2: Patent drawing from the July 21, 1863, patent of Ellis & White for a front-loading revolver

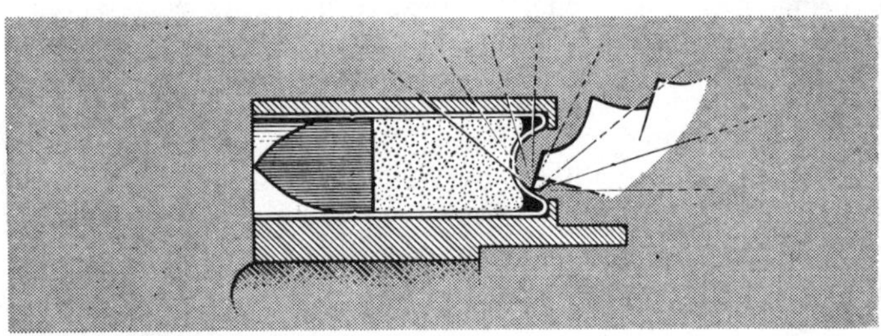

Fig. 3: Pen sketch of a longitudinal section illustrating the principle of cup-primer cartridge

Even though the principle of the front-loading, cup-primer revolver was originated by Ellis and White, the revolver never carried their names. Its name Plant came from the Plant's Manufacturing Co. which appears to have started producing these revolvers sometime in 1863.

Patent description of cartridge

Before turning to the arms produced by Plant's, it may be of interest to describe the unusual cartridge designed for their guns. A description taken directly from their patent application reads as follows: "The principal object of this invention is to provide for the loading of revolving firearms in front of the cylinder with metallic cartridges carrying their own priming; and to this

Fig. 4: Advertisement of the Plant's Manufacturing Co., from the 1863 city directory of New Haven

---

HERSCHEL C. LOGAN *of Salina, Kans., is author of 2 books on firearms history, "Cartridges" and "Hand Cannon to Automatic."*

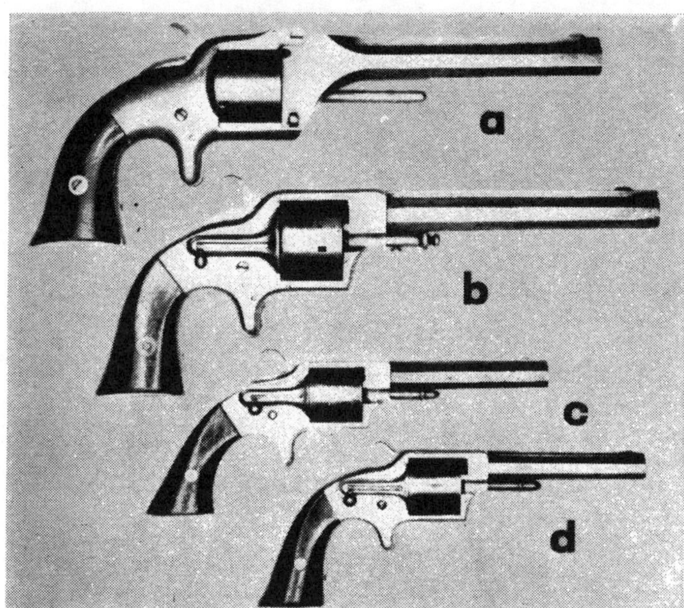

Fig. 5: (a) Early Plant .42 cal. cup-primer revolver with rounded frame and barrel that tips up to permit removal of the cylinder for loading; **(b)** Flat-sided frame Plant .42 cal. cup-primer revolver with patented extractor; **(c)** Merwin & Bray .28 cal. cup-primer revolver; **(d)** .30 cal. cup-primer revolver made by Eagle Arms Co.

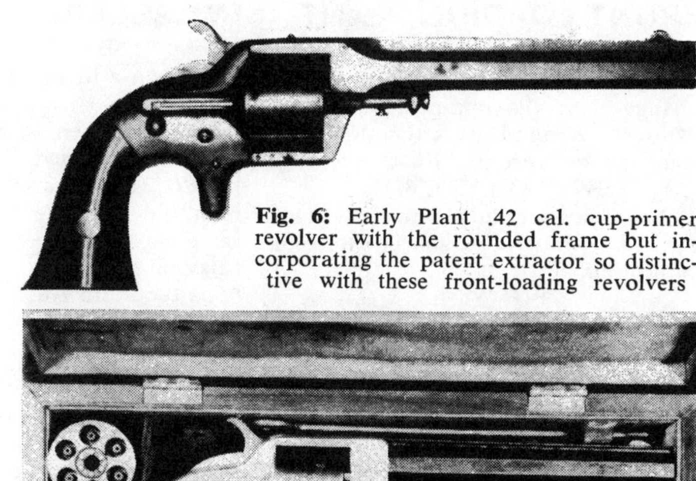

Fig. 6: Early Plant .42 cal. cup-primer revolver with the rounded frame but incorporating the patent extractor so distinctive with these front-loading revolvers

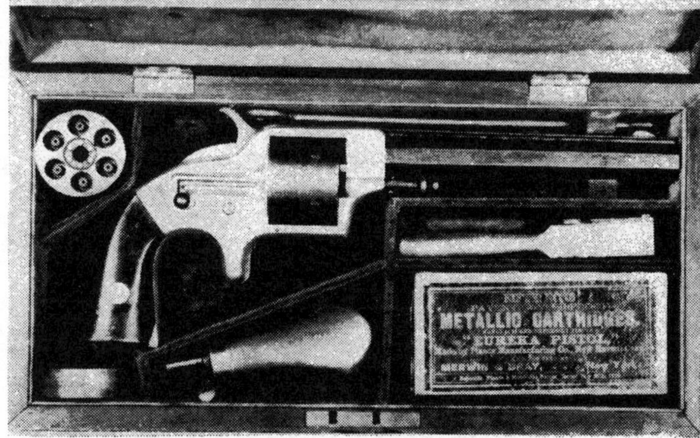

Fig. 7: A Plant .42 cal. cup-primer revolver in its case with accessories and extra percussion cylinder

end it consists in the construction of such a cartridge with a hollow flange around the rear of its metallic shell projecting backward parallel or nearly so with the length of the cartridge; and having an external circumference no greater than that of the rest of the shell; such flange to contain a fulminating priming which may be fired by the hammer of the firearm striking through a suitable opening provided in the rear of each chamber of the cylinder."

Produced in .28, .30 and .42 cals., the cup-primer cartridges were manufactured by the American Metallic Cartridge Co. (marked with a raised "A"); Phoenix Cartridge Co. (marked with a "P"), and possibly others, as specimens are found with no identifying marks.

The guns themselves followed closely the lines of the drawing in Ellis and White's patent, even to the hinged barrel. The large .42 cal. revolver (Fig. 5a) is believed to have been the first type produced by Plant's as the cylinder carries only the wording "PATENTED JULY 12, 1859", indicating that it was in production even before the second patent was applied for or secured. Such procedure was not uncommon in the early manufacture of arms.

Since the front-loading principle, while circumventing the Smith & Wesson held patent, did not actually infringe upon it, there seems to be no record that S&W sought to prevent their manufacture. The fact remains that few Plant hinged-frame revolvers are to be found. The specimen illustrated (serial number 82) is stamped "PLANT'S MFG. CO. NEW HAVEN, CT." on top of the ribbed octagon barrel, and "M & B" on the left side of the barrel in front of the cylinder. These letters refer to Merwin & Bray, the New York agents for Plant arms. In action the revolver is like the Smith & Wesson arms of the period, even to the spring in the top of the frame which serves as the cylinder lock and the barrel release button ahead of the cylinder. Altered specimens have been observed with cylinder drilled through and chambers recessed for rimfire cartridges.

Feature of solid-frame arms

On May 10, 1864, and Nov. 22, 1864, Henry Reynolds, a Springfield machinist, secured patents (No. 42688 and No. 45176) for a cartridge extractor located on the right side of the revolver frame behind the recoil shield. The ejector pin passed through the shield and chamber of the cylinder to expel the front-loaded cartridge. It is this feature on their solid-frame revolvers which identifies the Plant arms. The first arm on which this extractor mechanism is to be found appears to be a transition model between the rounded-frame tip-up and the solid-frame models. Not many of this model (Fig. 6) are known.

The era of the 1860's was still a transition period from percussion to cartridge. Some manufacturers, in an obvious effort to appeal to both markets, offered models equipped with 2 cylinders, one for cartridges and one utilizing percussion caps.

Not generally known is that the Plant's Manufacturing Co. also produced 2-cylinder sets. One such set is pictured (Fig. 7). It is cased with all accessories including cleaning rod, bullet mold, powder flask, extra percussion cylinder, and cartridge box. The nipples of the percussion cylinder are recessed

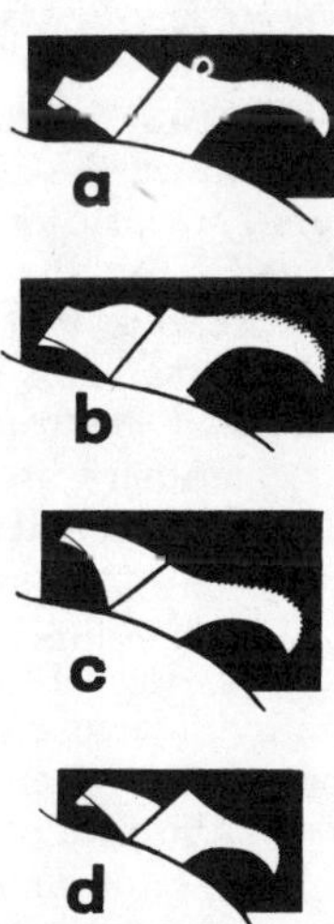

Fig. 8: (a) Hammer found on the large .42 cal. rounded-frame revolver; **(b)** Type of hammer used on the Plant revolver which also used a percussion cylinder; **(c)** Hammer on the Merwin & Bray revolver; **(d)** Hammer used on the Eagle Arms Co. revolver

FRONT LOADING PLANT

in the chambers to permit its easy exchange with the cup-primer cartridge cylinder. Around its circumference is stamped the wording "PLANT'S MFG. CO., NEW HAVEN, CT."

The following, taken from the top of the cartridge box, raises an interesting conjecture:

"FIFTY NO. 3
PATENT WATERPROOF
METALLIC CARTRIDGES.
Manufactured Expressly for the
"EUREKA PISTOL,"
Made by Plants Manufacturing Co., New Haven, Conn.
And for sale by
MERWIN & BRAY, NEW YORK.
Reynolds, Plants & Hotchkiss Patent, Issued July 12, 1859."

The pertinent question is: Was Eureka the original name for the gun that has since become known as the Plant? Perhaps in contemporary magazine ads or jobber's catalogs may be found the answer. Plant revolvers may be found marked with different names including "PLANT'S MFG. CO.", "MERWIN & BRAY", "EAGLE ARMS CO.", and "REYNOLDS, PLANT & HOTCHKISS".

Little known of these firms

Merwin & Bray were New York jobbers rather than producers of arms. The reason for those marked with this name is not known, unless it provided another trade name for the product. The Eagle Arms Co. of New York was incorporated Nov. 20, 1865, to produce the arms formerly manufactured by Plant. Records are very vague as to the reasons for Plant's agreement with Eagle Arms. In December 1866 the old Plant factory, in which the production of front-loading revolvers first started, was destroyed by fire.

From available data it seems unlikely that Eagle continued the manufacture of the revolvers for very long after the Plant's Co. faded from the scene.

It will be observed that there are slight variations in the arms bearing the different names. Fig. 8 illustrates 3 different types of hammers used, plus the dual-purpose hammer found on the gun in the cased set. The grip of the Eagle has a slightly more oblique drop to it than does the Merwin & Bray. Locking notches on the cylinder are to be found in different positions. Other minor differences may also be found.

The cup-primer ignition system was of comparatively short duration. Today, both the distinctive cartridges and the revolvers using them are little more than desirable collector items.———■

Special thanks go to James E. Serven, Glode M. Requa, Frank Wheeler, Sam Smith, and Public Library of New Haven, who helped in the preparation of this article.—H.C.L.

MOSSBERG PISTOLS

Continued from page 151

ent styling to the line. Of very limited production was a cal. .30, which the writer has seen. A cal. .25 is reported, but not verified. The Shattuck firm ceased major arms making in 1910, but did continue to make the 4-shots until around 1915 in the plant of the Bay State Screw Co., of which Maj. Shattuck and Allen W. Houghton were partners. Maj. C. S. Shattuck died on Feb. 5, 1918.

The Brownie pistol

The second pistol produced by the Mossbergs, and the first under their newly formed company, was the Brownie. This arm is described in these words in the patent papers: "My invention relates to a small firearm in which the barrel with the plural bores is stationary in the firing operation while the firing pin is revolved and its firing member, which is off the center of the pin, is caused to contact with the successive cartridges. While the invention in all its phases is not limited to a firearm of the particular type indicated, the invention lends itself more particularly to that type."

As described by the factory the Brownie "was a small, 4 barrel pocket pistol with a barrel 2½" long and was chambered to handle short, long and long rifle cartridges. It was a double-action weapon, shaped similar to an automatic pistol and broke open for loading by pressing a safety catch on the rear of the frame. It had a revolving firing pin which changed position each time the trigger was pulled. The extractor was unique, being a narrow 3" steel strip which slid into the top of the frame down to the grip. Extraction was made by breaking open the frame and pushing the shells out with this steel auxiliary extractor."

The extractor on the Novelty pistol worked in much the same manner, except that it was placed in the frame in a horizontal position instead of the vertical position as on the Brownie.

Approximately 37,000 Brownies were produced between 1919 and 1932, when the model was discontinued. Retail price at that time was $5.75 each. The finish of the guns was blue and the grips were of walnut.

Oscar F. Mossberg died on Dec. 27, 1937. But the firm which he founded today operates 2 factories producing sporting rifles and shotguns and accessories; a fitting tribute to the Swedish immigrant lad who succeeded in this land of opportunity and free enterprise. ■

My sincere thanks and appreciation to these individuals and organizations, without whose valued assistance the telling of this story would not have been possible: Dr. Harmon C. Leonard, Walter L. Pierson, Harold F. Mossberg, Mrs. Kathleen T. Doland, Frank Wheeler, O. F. Mossberg & Sons, Inc., and the Forbes Library.—H.C.L.

MARLIN HANDGUNS

Continued from page 149

1, 1901. Thus it was that both the founder and the handguns he had designed passed from the scene at virtually the same time. However, two sons, Mahlon Henry and J. Howard, were left to carry on the Marlin traditions.

The following information, taken from a catalog of the Ideal Manufacturing Company, will be found of added interest to students of the Marlin story.

"To the Trade and all my friends:

"This is to certify that I, John H. Barlow, have sold to the Marlin Firearms Co., of the city of New Haven, Conn., my entire business, the name of which is known to the general hardware and sporting goods trade throughout the country as the Ideal Manufacturing Co.

"Monday, May 16, 1910, the Marlin Firearms Co., take over all the machinery, tools, stock, fixtures and good will of the Ideal Mfg. Co. They will continue the manufacture of the well known Ideal cartridge re-loading implements for rifles, pistols and shotguns." Barlow had been a manufacturer of such items for 26 years previous to Marlin's acquisition.

In 1916 the Marlin heirs sold the plant to the Marlin-Rockwell Corporation who produced arms in sizable quantity for the Allied governments during World War I. In 1926 the firm was again reorganized, along with the purchase of the assets of Hopkins & Allen which had been absorbed previously by the Marlin-Rockwell Corporation. It resumed the name of Marlin Firearms Company, and has enjoyed uninterrupted production from that date down to the present. The Ideal Manufacturing Company was taken over by the Lyman Gun Sight Corporation effective October 1925.

Taken from the 80th Anniversary (1950) issue of the Marlin plant magazine are these meaningful words:

"When roots grow deep, the tree is strong and firm. It grows and flourishes and is welcome for the shade it provides. Such is the history of the Marlin Firearms Company, whose roots grow deep in New Haven soil. Fourscore years ago—in 1870—the Marlin Firearms Company was founded. Through three major wars, panics, booms, depressions, Marlin Firearms has taken pride in its long association with the progress of the New Haven area. One thing is certain: the roots are deep because they have been nourished by the American tradition of free enterprise."———■

Special thanks and appreciation go to the following individuals and organizations: Frank R. Horner, J. Howard Marlin, Robert Lawrence, Martin B. Retting, Charles T. Waller, Marlin Firearms Company, Free Public Library of New Haven, Frank Wheeler, Major Hugh Smiley, and others for their kind assistance in the preparation of this story.—H.C.L.

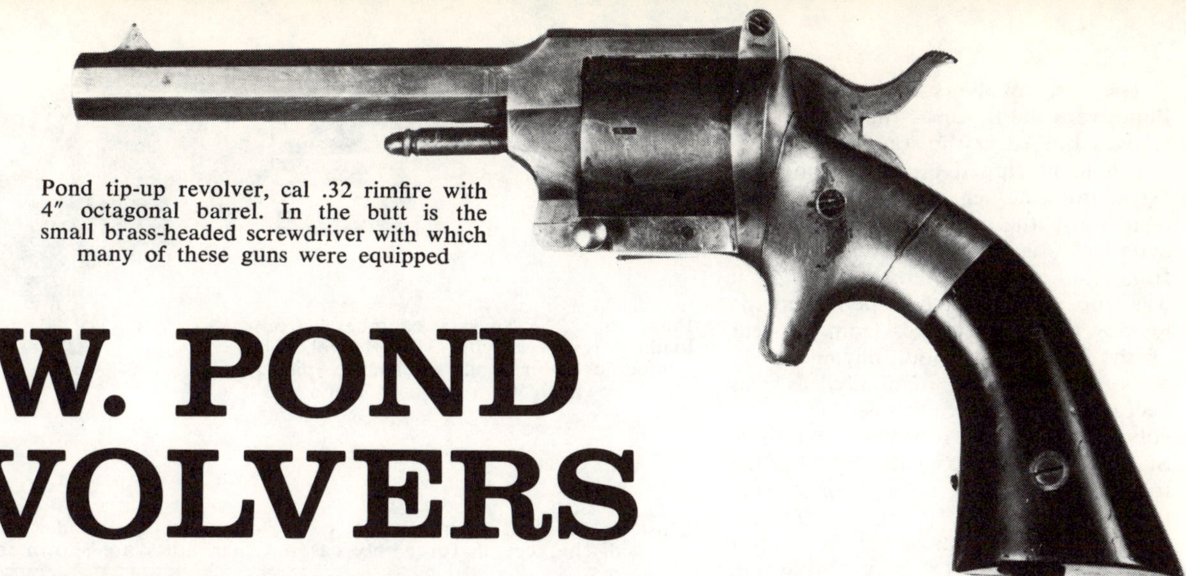

Pond tip-up revolver, cal .32 rimfire with 4″ octagonal barrel. In the butt is the small brass-headed screwdriver with which many of these guns were equipped

L. W. POND REVOLVERS

By HERSCHEL C. LOGAN

ALTHOUGH most collectors are familiar with the Pond revolvers, it is doubtful if many know the story of the man whose name they bear. Thus, a word sketch of the inventor himself may prove of interest.

Little is known of Pond

Lucius Willson Pond was born in Hubbardston, Mass., on Apr. 20, 1826. Little is known of his early life. He was educated in the Hubbardston public schools and later moved to Worcester.

At this time young Pond was serving an apprenticeship with Samuel Flagg, a prominent maker of machine tools in Worcester. Late in 1847, Pond, a fellow worker Henry Holland, and their employer organized the firm of Samuel Flagg & Co. The first location was in the Heywood Building. Later they moved to the building previously occupied by the prominent arms firm of Allen & Thurber. In 1849 a move was made to the Merrifield Building. Fire destroyed the plant in 1854, forcing the firm to set up operations on Union St. Here it remained until the completion of the Merrifield facilities.

Just prior to 1861, L. W. Pond assumed full control of the firm and the name was changed to the L. W. Pond Machine Co.

Following outbreak of the Civil War, the gun and machine shops of Worcester became a beehive of activity.

L. W. Pond, who late in 1861 had moved to the J. B. Lawrence Building at Union and Exchange Sts., was at the time engaged in the building of 20 rifled cannon of his own invention. Not then tooled up for such work, he had the work done at the shop of Goddard, Rice & Co.

Known as the Ellsworth gun, Pond's cannon was described as follows: "Breech-loading rifle-gun, four feet long, 6-inches in diameter at the breech and 3½-inches at the muzzle—with a 1½-inch bore—carrying a chilled conical ball weighing 18 ounces—which it could throw three miles. The gun weighed, carriage and all, 450 pounds and cost $350."

Following the war Pond, who had been prominent in civic affairs, continued in the manufacture of machine tools. However, the war had brought serious reverses to the company, so much so that Pond became involved in legal difficulties, having forged a number of notes. Convicted, he was sentenced to 20 years in prison. In 1882, after having served but a few years, he was pardoned by Governor Long. With the help of friends, he became active in his former business and remained so until his death in 1889.

Now a look at the handguns produced by L. W. Pond.

Produced 2 types of revolvers

Even though Pond produced but 2 different types of arms, one a tip-up revolver and the other known as a 'separate chambers' revolver, the research on them presents a curious and intriguing study. One reason is that neither of the patent dates appearing on the arms are those involving patents actually secured by L. W. Pond.

Detail of tip-up revolver showing how the frame is tipped back to permit loading of the cylinder, which is attached to the barrel assembly

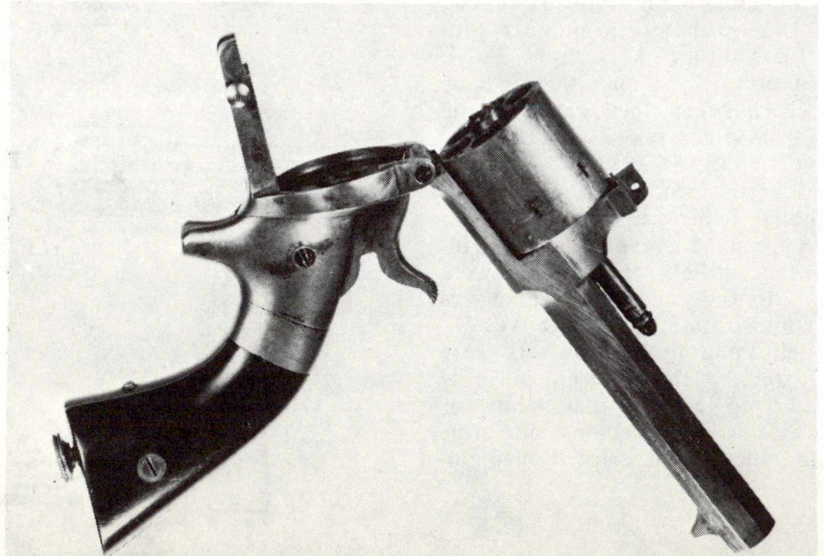

Patent on the tip-up revolver made by L. W. Pond was taken out by Abram J. Gibson

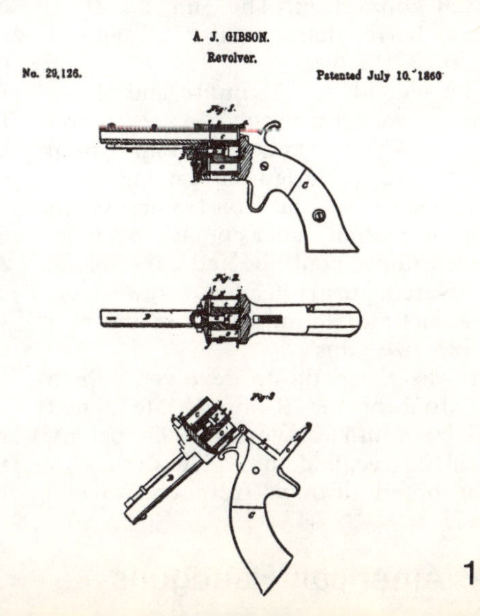

The first revolvers manufactured by Pond were the tip-ups—that is, the barrel was hinged at the top, thus permitting it to be tipped up for loading and extracting the cartridges. A notable feature of the revolver was that the cylinder was attached to the barrel frame and thus followed the barrel as it was tipped upward. This permitted the loading of the cartridges from the rear of the cylinder without having to remove the cylinder manually, as was necessary with the Smith & Wesson revolvers and some others of the time. Stamped on the top of the barrel is the following: "L. W. POND WORCESTER. MASS. PAT'D JULY 10, 1860". On this date Abram J. Gibson of Worcester took out a patent (No. 29,126) which was assigned to himself and I. P. Hale. Since the gun was produced under this patent, it is quite obvious that Pond, Gibson, and Hale reached some sort of working agreement. The Gibson revolver, illustrated on page 26, was described thus in the patent application:

"My invention relates to revolvers of that kind which have a many chambered cylinder rotating on an axis parallel with a stationery barrel.

The principal object of the invention is to provide greater facility for the loading of the chambers at the rear of the cylinder; and to this end it consists in so applying a chambered cylinder having the chambers extended through the rear, in combination with a frame opening with a hinge-joint, that when the frame is opened the cylinder remains attached to and swings with the front part of the frame."

Pond followed the Gibson patent on June 17, 1862, (No. 35,623) with a minor clarification of the frame description. This date apparently was not stamped on the guns.

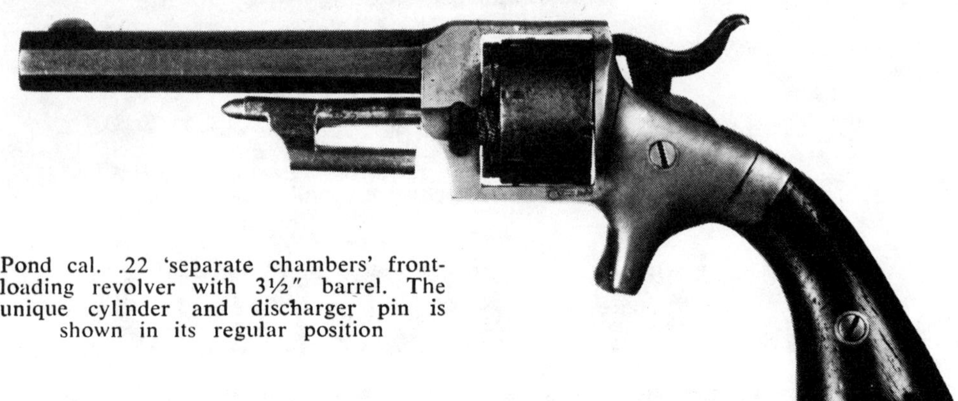

Pond cal. .22 'separate chambers' front-loading revolver with 3½" barrel. The unique cylinder and discharger pin is shown in its regular position

Close up detail of a 'lining tube' pulled out over the cylinder pin which also serves as a discharger pin for empty cases. Other tubes are shown in regular position

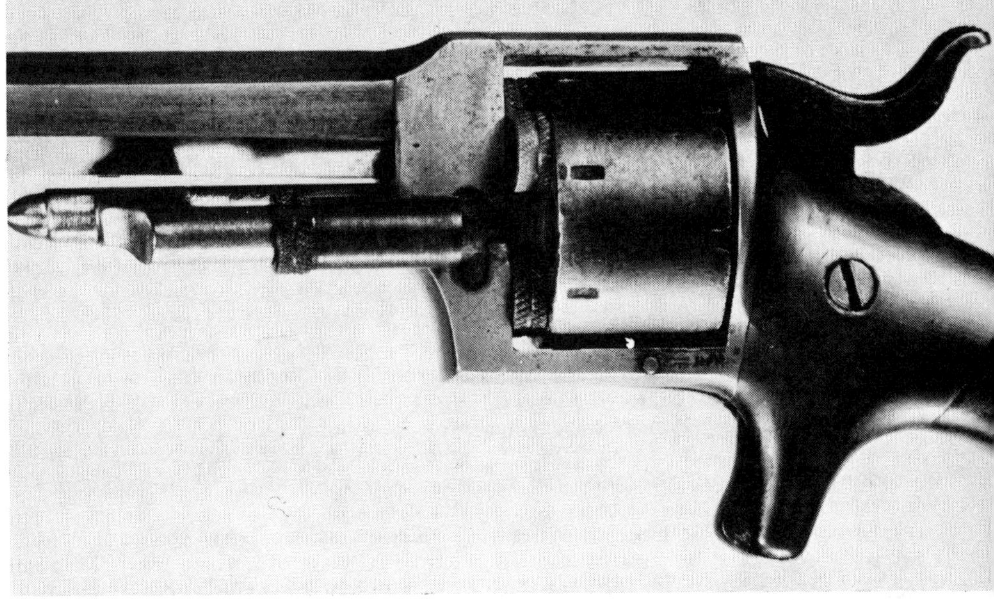

Tip-ups made in 2 calibers

Tip-up models were produced in 2 calibers. The first, a .44 rimfire, is referred to as the Pond Army Revolver though there is no record of any martial connection. The gun, a 6-shot, had a barrel length of 7¼" and a weight of 2½ lbs.

The second, a .32 rimfire and also a 6-shot, was furnished in 3 barrel lengths, 4", 5", and 6". Both tip-up models are recorded as having been made with brass and iron frames. Grips were of walnut, occasionally of rosewood. Frames could be had either blued or silvered. Brass-headed screwdrivers are sometimes to be found in the butt of both size guns.

It was these tip-up revolvers which ran afoul of the Rollin White patent held by Smith & Wesson. This patent, it will be recalled, provided for a cylinder bored through from end to end for breech-loading When Smith & Wesson, through their attorneys and the courts, moved against those firms infringing on their valuable patent, Pond, among others whose guns were held to be infringements, promptly ceased manufacture. Through court order Pond was obliged to turn over to Smith & Wesson some 4486 revolvers. These, plus a small subsequent number produced for Smith & Wesson by Pond, upon order, are the ones that will be found bearing the added stamp on the barrel—"MANUF'D FOR SMITH & WESSON PAT'D APRIL 5, 1855."

The advertisement shown on page 28, even though it pictures the early Smith & Wesson cal. .22 revolver, clearly indicates that dealers of the time were selling Moore and Pond revolvers under authorization of Smith & Wesson.

Though Pond tip-up revolvers were not adopted by the government, it is reasonable to assume that many of them were carried as personal side arms by both officers and enlisted men.

Patent for the 'separate chambers' Pond revolver was issued to Freeman W. Hood of Worcester, Mass.

F. W. HOOD.
Revolver.
No. 44,953. Patented Nov. 8, 18
Fig. 1
Fig. 2.
Fig. 3
Fig. 4
Fig. 5

Prevented from producing breech-loading revolvers, Pond set about to design a cylinder which would load from the front and yet utilize the new metallic rimfire cartridges. In conjunction with John H. Vickers of Worcester, Pond designed a cylinder which could use either rimfire cartridges or, if necessary, auxiliary chambers with nipples for percussion caps. The patent (No. 38,934) of June 16, 1863, taken out by Pond, but assigned to himself and Vickers, is described in these words:

"This invention relates to the employment in the chambers of revolving firearms of the lining-thimbles or tubes which constitute the subject-matter of a previous application made by John H. Vickers and myself; and it consists in so connecting such thimbles or tubes together at their front ends, by means of a ring or flange fitting to or against the front of the cylinder, that they can all be withdrawn from or inserted into their respective chambers at once, thereby greatly expediting the operation of loading."

Use of device not known

Whether or not such a cylinder was ever used on the Pond revolvers is not known to the writer. All observed have been of the separate-chamber variety. The gun utilizing the front-loading cylinder appears to have been patented by John H. Vickers (No. 39,869) on Sept. 8, 1863. For some reason usual patent records fail to list this patent. Authoritative sources, however, indicate that the cylinder of the gun was provided with chambers of sufficient diameter to hold 'lining-tubes'. Cartridges were loaded into the tubes, and the tubes into the chambers of the cylinder from the front. Except for a small hole to permit the nose of the hammer to contact the rim of the cartridge, the rear of the cylinder was solid—a rather novel evasion of the Smith & Wesson patent, to say the least.

Front-loading revolver

A second date, Nov. 8, 1864, which appears on the gun refers to a patent (No. 44,953) taken out by Freeman W. Hood of Worcester (see page 27). Hood explains his invention as follows:

"My invention specially belongs to that class of revolvers which have not only a series of detachable cartridge-carriers or receiving cells or tubes inserted within the rotary breech or magazine and for holding a series of cartridges, but are provided with a rammer or discharger for expelling from either of the cartridge-receiving tubes the exploded shell or remains of a discharged cartridge, the mode of effecting the expulsion of such shell from its tube being by drawing the tube out of the rotary breech or magazine and upon the rammer or discharger, so as to cause the latter to pass into the tube and force the shell from it. The United States Patent No. 39,869, granted to John H. Vickers and Lucius W. Pond, exhibits an invention of this character, and it is to such that my improvement relates, the nature of my invention consisting in the application of the shell-discharger to the center-pin or spindle of the rotary magazine or breech, so as to be movable therewith, and for the purpose or purposes as hereinafter explained; and, furthermore, my invention includes the combination and arrangement of a peculiar latching mechanism with the spindle, the discharger, and the series of cartridge-tubes, combined together and with the barrel and the rotary magazine, as hereinafter specified."

Like their predecessors, the 'separate-chamber' or front-loading Ponds, as they are known today among collectors, were made in 2 calibers. These were a .22 and a .32 rimfire. Frames were of brass, and cylinders and barrels were blued. The revolvers will be found both with and without a small brass-headed screwdriver housed in the butt of the grip.

No details are known as to the number of revolvers produced by Pond, but it is felt that the quantity was rather limited. Over the years the little separate tubes on many of the front-loading Ponds have become lost or separated from the guns. Lucky is the owner of one of these interesting guns who can show a specimen with all thimbles, or tubes, intact. ■

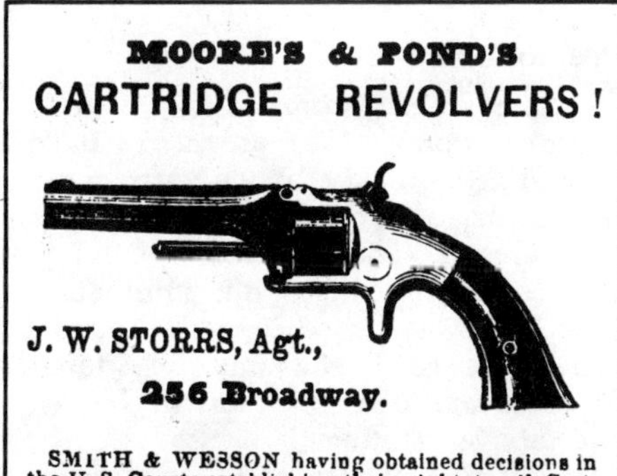

Unusual advertisement from the Apr. 11, 1863, issue of *Leslie's Weekly*. Though advertising the Moore and Pond revolvers, it pictures the early round-frame Smith & Wesson cal. .22 revolver

My sincere thanks to Clifford K. Shipton and Albert G. Waite of the American Antiquarian Society, Thurston Taylor and Mary McGrath of the Free Public Library of Worcester, and the New York Public Library for their valued assistance in the preparation of this study.—H.C.L.

The Forgotten .45

Continued from page 127

ried safely, with a cartridge in the chamber and the hammer down. The hammer needs only to be cocked manually in traditional single-action style before firing. While this is the design and intent, it should be noted that such "safety" leaves much to be desired. The safety-conscious user of the M1905 would probably be more likely to leave the chamber empty and to load a cartridge into it by pulling back and releasing the slide when use is imminent.

With the appropriate variations, dismantling the M1905 resembles the field stripping of the modern .45 automatic. *First,* remove the magazine and clear the pistol. The magazine can be withdrawn by pressing forward the magazine release lever protruding at the bottom of the butt. *Second,* press the takedown plug beneath the muzzle to the rear and tilt the weapon to the left, allowing the slide lock to fall free. Note the rear face of the lock: it is the side with the stud and the machined cut-out. The rear face rests against the forward face of the recoil spring plug. *Third,* pull the slide rearward and off the frame. *Fourth,* using a pin punch push the forward barrel locking pin from right to left. The forward barrel link assembly will be free of the frame when the punch is removed. When removing the punch, maintain pressure on the take-down plug to prevent the recoil spring from releasing and jumping away. Release the tension gradually after the punch is removed, and the forward barrel link assembly freed, and remove the take-down plug, the recoil spring plug, and the recoil spring itself. Finally, remove the rear barrel locking pin with a pin punch. The barrel is then free of the frame. To assemble the pistol, simply reverse the steps in this procedure.

From the perspective of seven decades, the M1905 appears primitive. To be sure, it does lack many of the mechanical features found on more recent arms. But it should be remembered in the light of the innovation it represented when it was introduced. By combining the mechanical advantages of the automatic pistol with the power of the cartridge that became known as the .45 ACP, this truly was "The Most Powerful Small Arm Ever Invented"—at least for a while. Moreover, with cast lead bullets to prevent excessive wear on the bore, and with an observance of the normal rules of safety supplemented by a knowledge of the particular operation of this pistol, it is possible to go back and recapture the excitement and thrill of shooting the first .45 Colt automatic pistol. ■

1 This first advertisement of the Prescott revolvers appeared in the Jan. 18, 1862, issue of *Harper's Weekly*

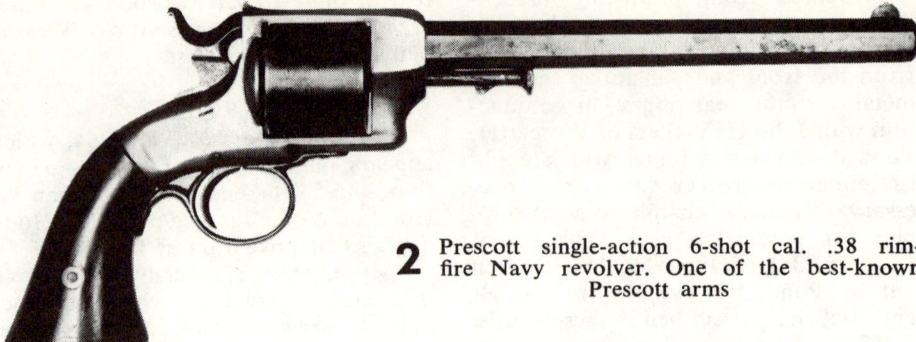

2 Prescott single-action 6-shot cal. .38 rim-fire Navy revolver. One of the best-known Prescott arms

The Revolvers of E. A. PRESCOTT

By HERSCHEL C. LOGAN

New data about a little-known maker of percussion and early cartridge revolvers

An interesting facet of arms collecting is the enjoyment of digging out little-known facts concerning guns and their makers. Take, for instance, Edwin A. Prescott. Many collectors have heard of the Prescott Navy revolver, but few know that the firm also produced other models. In this article we shall attempt to draw aside the curtain of time for a brief glimpse of the man and his guns.

Record of early employment

A Day Book of Allen & Thurber for the years 1846-48 discloses that Edwin A. Prescott was in their employ as early as Oct. 1, 1846. In fact, he moved from Norwich, Conn., to Worcester, Mass., at the same time the firm moved in 1847, and evidence indicates his continuance with them for some years afterward.

City Directories of Worcester, Mass., from 1850 to 1861 list E. A. Prescott as an 'Armorer', living at 10 Fulton St. until 1856. Later his address was given as Oak Hill. From his own testimony, given in the Rollin White-Smith & Wesson suit against Ethan Allen, it becomes apparent that he was in the employ of Allen & Thurber up to 1856, when the firm name was changed to Allen & Wheelock. The record further indicates that he continued with the newly organized company for some time thereafter.

On Oct. 2, 1860, Prescott secured U. S. patent No. 30,245 for a 'new and useful improvement in Revolver Fire-Arms'. He describes his invention in these words:

"My invention consists in a novel, simple, and effective mechanism for locking and unlocking the cylinder, whereby it is caused to be positively locked while the hammer is cocked, and while it is down and during its whole striking movement, and only unlocked at that stage of the cocking operation during which the rotary movement is required to be effected.

"It also consists in furnishing the front part of the frame with a projection extending in a rearward direction and surrounding the cylinder axis-pin in front of the cylinder, and having the part above the same pin made V-shaped and sharp-edged for the purpose of scraping off from the front of the cylinder any dirt that may result from the firing of the charges, and preventing such dirt finding its way between the cylinder and pin and clogging the operation of the cylinder."

Apparently Prescott lost no time in setting up a plant for the production of his revolvers and making arrangement for their distribution. That he was successful in both endeavors is evident from an advertisement which appeared in the Jan. 18, 1862, issue of *Harper's Weekly:*

PRESCOTT'S CARTRIDGE REVOLVERS

The 8in., or Navy Size, carries a Ball weighing 38 to the lb., and the No. 32, or 4in. Revolver, a Ball 80 to the lb. By recent experiments made in the Army, these Revolvers were pronounced the best and most effective weapons in use. For particulars call or send for a Circular to
MERWIN & BRAY, Sole Agents
No. 245 Broadway, N.Y.

Soon, however, a dark cloud arose on the horizon of his new enterprise. With the Rollin White patent for a cylinder bored through from end to end purchased and tucked away in their vault, Smith & Wesson were in no mood to tolerate any other revolvers which appeared to infringe upon the valued patent under which they had already been producing guns for some 5 years.

Prescott held out

While other companies, such as Moore, Pond, Warner, and Bacon capitulated quickly upon court action, and came to terms with Smith & Wesson, Prescott and his former employer Allen elected to hold out until an injunction was issued against them in November 1863. Not only did Smith & Wesson take over the guns on hand of the above-mentioned firms, but they actually had Moore and Pond make a quantity of revolvers for them. Such guns are easily identified by the line, "Made for Smith & Wesson by . . . (and the name of the company)" stamped on the barrel. However, such seems not to have been the case with Prescott or Allen, as arms made by them are not known with such markings.

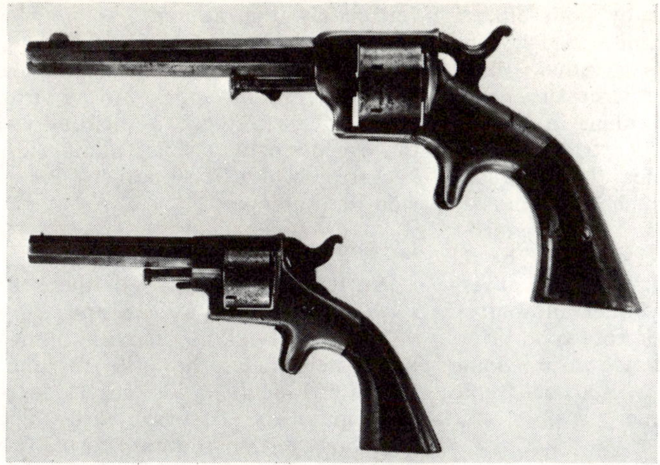

3 Two Prescott revolvers of similar style to the Prescott Navy, a 6-shot cal. .32 rimfire (top) and an unmarked 7-shot cal. .22 rimfire

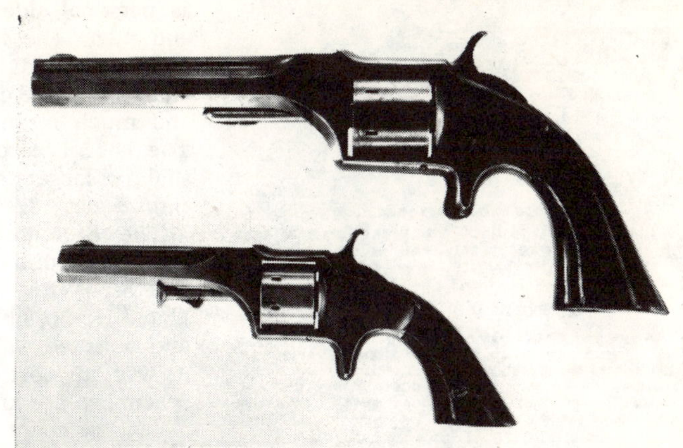

4 Following closely the lines of the early Smith & Wesson revolvers are these 2 Prescott guns, a 6-shot cal. .32 rimfire (top) and a smaller 7-shot version of cal. .22 rimfire

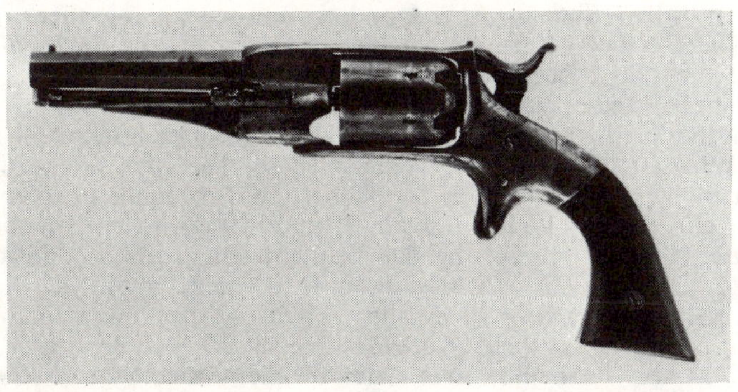

5 Generally unknown, and one of the scarcer numbers of the Prescott line, is this 6-shot cal. .31 percussion revolver

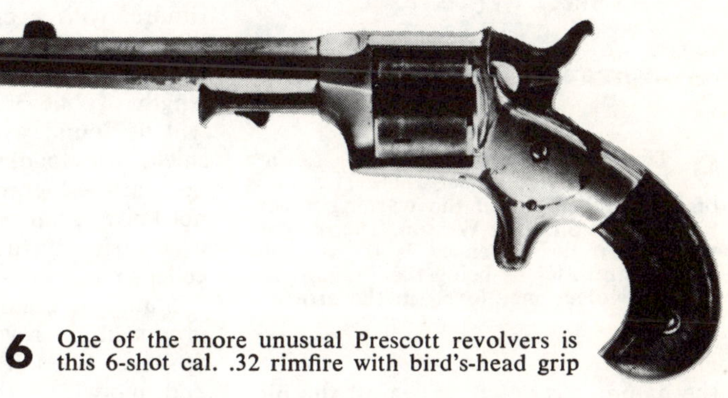

6 One of the more unusual Prescott revolvers is this 6-shot cal. .32 rimfire with bird's-head grip

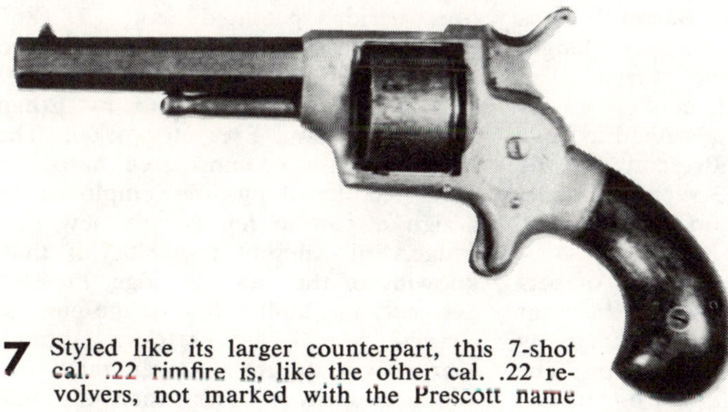

7 Styled like its larger counterpart, this 7-shot cal. .22 rimfire is, like the other cal. .22 revolvers, not marked with the Prescott name

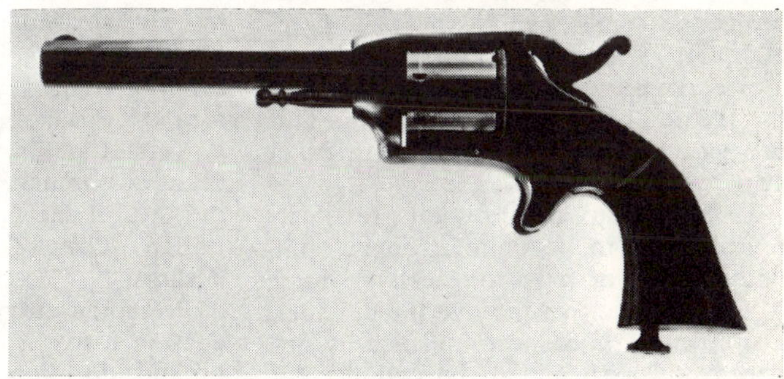

8 Though unmarked, this cal. .32 lip-fire revolver is considered by some to be of Prescott manufacture

Prescott is listed in the Directories of 1862 to 1866 as being a 'manufacturer of firearms' on Grafton St. It appears quite probable that following the court action of 1863 Prescott produced a percussion revolver in limited quantity. Specimens, both marked and unmarked, are known, though not frequently encountered. It is reported that in 1864 he considered going to Canada with Orson Hemphill to engage in the making of gun parts.

In 1867 he turned to making card setters used in carding machines for wool and cotton fibers. The arms urge was not to be denied however, and in 1872 he is again listed as a 'pistol manufacturer' at 76 Grafton St. His home was close by at 164 Grafton.

It is presumed that he moved away, or died in 1874 or early 1875, as his name disappeared from the Directories after this date.

So much for the background of Edwin A. Prescott, a man so little known that his brief gunmaking business is not even mentioned in the historical book *Industrial Worcester* by Charles G. Washburn, published in 1917 by the Davis Press of Worcester.

Prescott's patent

Turning now to the guns. Prescott's patent could apply to either percussion or cartridge revolvers, as is evidenced by one line in the application "when

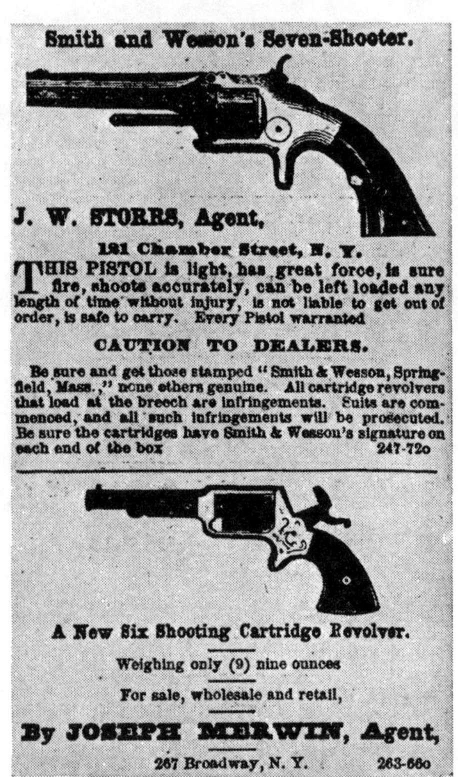

9 Two advertisements from *Leslie's Weekly* of December 1860. The top is of interest because of the warning it contained from Smith & Wesson. The revolver pictured in the lower ad is regarded by some authorities as being the Prescott lip-fire revolver mentioned in the article

the hammer is down or against the nipple." As will be seen, however, his main production was in cartridge revolvers. The writer has seen no Prescott revolvers bearing the V-shaped projection mentioned in the patent application. The guns examined do have a circular projection of brass or iron in the frame around the cylinder pin. This projection appears uncommon to other arms of the period.

Examination of Prescott revolvers reveal them to be quite strongly built, with frames of brass or steel. To load, it was necessary to remove the cylinder; a simple operation accomplished by first depressing a spring in the cylinder pin and drawing the pin toward the muzzle of the gun, thus permitting the cylinder to drop out. Also, fired cases were removed from the cylinder with the cylinder pin.

As indicated by the advertisement in *Harper's Weekly,* the first production by the factory appears to have been their cal. .38 'Navy' revolver. This was done, no doubt, with an eye for government purchases during the Civil War, then in progress. Even though the gun is called the Navy Model, there is no record of any purchases by the government. Undoubtedly, however, many of the guns were carried in the conflict as personal side arms by both officers and men. The .38 rimfire, a Prescott-created cartridge, was a rather potent charge in those days of percussion arms, and much more convenient to handle. The 1862 Prescott .38 cartridge was of slightly larger diameter than the .38 rimfire cartridge of much later years.

The Prescott Navy Model revolver could be had in 6½", 7⅛", or 8" barrel lengths. With its nickeled or silver-plated frame, blued cylinder and barrel, and polished walnut or rosewood grips, it was a most attractive arm. Some specimens are known with a steel frame instead of a brass frame.

Spur trigger revolvers

Following the lines of the Navy Model, but with a spur trigger instead of the regular trigger and guard, were 2 other revolvers, a smaller one in .32 rimfire and a still smaller version in .22 rimfire, with a circular rather than an irregular side-plate. The .32 had a barrel length of 5" and the .22 a barrel length of but 3". Some of these guns will be found with a slot in the recoil shield for loading. Whether this was done at the factory or by later owners is not known. On the specimen illustrated, it is obviously the latter, though an excellent job.

Somewhere along the line the factory produced 2 revolvers similar to the Smith & Wesson No. 2 Army and the 2nd model of their little .22 rimfire. The guns were similar only in over-all design, not in detail. Whereas the Smith & Wesson had tip-up barrels, the Prescott revolvers had solid frames and removable cylinder pins. Barrel lengths for the .32 were 6" and 5". Barrel length for the smaller .22 model was 3". The idea of producing both calibers in revolvers of similar design seemed to have been customary with Prescott, for he did this on each of his 3 separate model designs. The .32's held 6 shots, the .22's 7 shots.

Prescott's entry into the field of percussion arms appears to have been of limited duration if we may judge by the known specimens of such arms. The one illustrated in Fig. 5, is a 6-shot cal. .31 with 4" octagonal barrel, and a total length of 9". Though unmarked, it is identical to one fully marked. A removable side-plate on the left side of the brass frame is quite similar to that found on the cal. .32 rimfires.

On the scarcer side are those Prescott revolvers having bird's-head grips. These guns were also produced in both cals. .32 and .22. Whether they were made in limited quantity only is not known, but this seems likely. The workmanship and finish appears to be better than observed on the other models. Unfortunately the author has not been able to personally examine a specimen of the little 7-shot .22 with bird's-head grip. However, it appears to be virtually identical to the .32 pictured, with the exception of a small hump on the backstrap where it slopes down alongside the hammer.

.22 bears no identification

An interesting feature of these arms is that while the cal. .38 and .32 revolvers are fully marked as to maker and patent date, the little .22 model bears no identification marks except serial numbers. They are easily identified, however, as they are virtually replicas of their larger brothers. Serial numbers are quite low on most of the specimens illustrated.

Regarded by some noted collectors as being a part of the Prescott line is the lip-fire revolver illustrated in Fig. 8. And indeed the guns, for there are other known specimens, do have points of similarity with Prescott arms. An illustration of a gun similar in design is to be found in an advertisement in the December 1860 issue of *Leslie's Illustrated Weekly,* but no name is given to the gun. Could this omission of a name be due to the wording of the Smith & Wesson advertisement above it? Incidentally, the agent for this unnamed 'Cartridge Revolver' was Joseph Merwin, later of Merwin & Bray, Merwin & Hulbert, and Merwin, Hulbert & Co.

In connection with the lip-fire revolver, one facet might be observed here which could have a decided bearing on the gun. First, is that the lip-fire cartridge patented Sept. 25, 1860 (No. 30,109), only 3 months prior to the publication of the advertisement? This patent was taken out by Ethan Allen, for whom Prescott worked. The possibility must be considered that Allen requested his long-time employee to design a gun to handle his new cartridge. Still another possibility is that, knowing of the new cartridge, Prescott designed and built a few of the guns to chamber the lip-fire cartridge. Whichever it was, future research may provide the answer. Until then the gun should be classed as a possible member of the Prescott family of arms.

So passes in review another of the early American gunmakers and his revolvers—a part of the long parade of examples of Yankee ingenuity and free enterprise which have made America great. ■

My sincere thanks to the Free Public Library, Worcester, Mass., American Antiquarian Society, Worcester, Mass., New York Public Library, New York, N.Y., Samuel E. Smith, Philip F. Van Cleave, Miles Standish, Thomas J. McHugh, Jack Strassman, M.D., and others who so kindly assisted with this research.—H.C.L.

Original instruction sheet furnished with these pistols noted that percussion caps and shot were "only ammunition required". Remington made similar pistol, called Vest Pocket, in cal. .22 rimfire

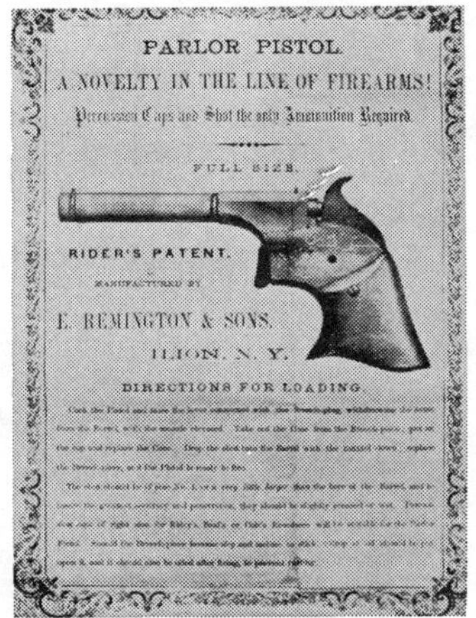
PARLOR PISTOL.

A NOVELTY IN THE LINE OF FIREARMS!

Percussion Caps and Shot the only Ammunition Required.

FULL SIZE.

RIDER'S PATENT.

MANUFACTURED BY

E. REMINGTON & SONS,

ILION, N. Y.

DIRECTIONS FOR LOADING.

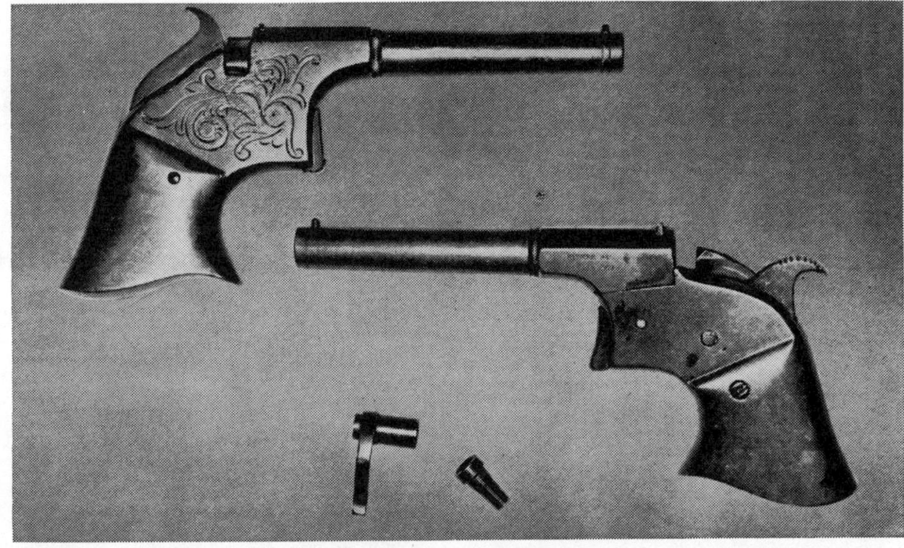
Remington Parlor Pistol is found both engraved and plain. Cap cover and cone are shown separate from lower pistol

The Remington PARLOR PISTOL

By HARRY C. KNODE

Information on a little single-shot pistol that has long been an enigma

THE little Remington single-shot percussion pistol known for many years to collectors as the Rider Single-Shot Deringer, or Remington-Rider cal. .17 Pistol, has been an enigma. Little was known as to the reason for its manufacture.

Charles Lee Karr, Jr., in his book, *Remington Handguns,* states that these pistols were made from 1860 to 1863. Although Remington made percussion arms as late as 1888, their catalogs of 1877 and 1881 did not list this pistol, but the 1877 catalog did show the similar cal. .22 Vest Pocket single-shot pistol. So, it is a likely deduction that the Remington-Rider cal. .17 pistol proved unpopular and was discontinued.

Recently, L. Dean Paisley of Wilmington, Del., obtained one of these pistols complete in its original unlabeled cardboard box with instruction sheet.

According to the instruction sheet, Remington called this the "Parlor Pistol" and indicated that it was "A Novelty In The Line of Firearms". The sheet also stated that percussion caps and lead shot were the only ammunition required. The directions for loading state, "Cock the Pistol and raise the lever connected with the Breech-plug, withdrawing the same from the Barrel, with the muzzle elevated. Take out the Cone from the Breech-piece; put on the cap and replace the Cone. Drop the shot into the Barrel with the muzzle down; replace the Breech-piece and the Pistol is ready to fire.

"The shot should be of size No. 1 or a very little larger than the bore of the Barrel, and to insure the greatest accuracy and penetration, they should be slightly greased or wet. Percussion caps of right size for Rider's, Beal's or Colt's Revolvers will be suitable for the Parlor Pistol. Should the Breech-piece become dry and inclined to stick, a drop of oil should be put on it, and it should also be oiled after firing, to prevent rusting."

These smoothbore pistols are usually

Two types of breech-piece (shown here with round ball and percussion cap) are found in Remington Parlor Pistols. Upper, with integral cone, is earlier one-piece version which was superseded by 2-piece type shown below it

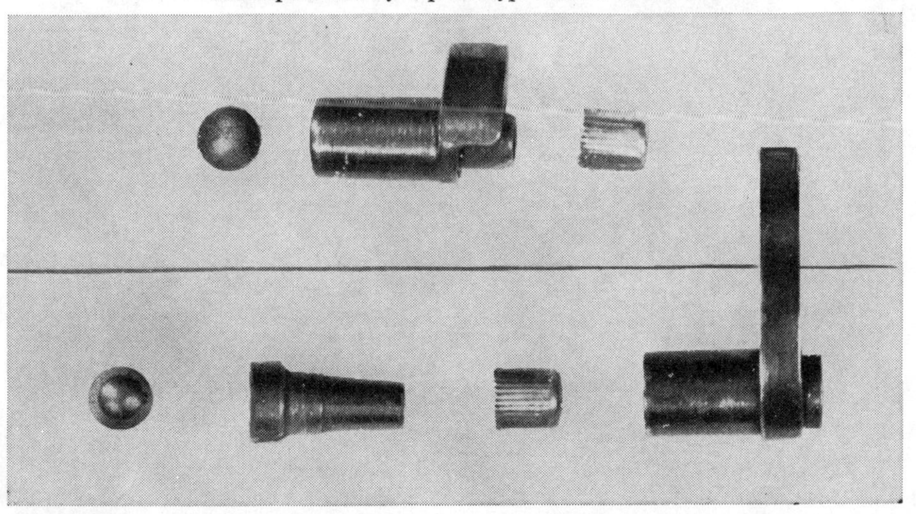

Continued on page 174

HANDGUNS BY REMINGTON

By HERSCHEL C. LOGAN

Few manufacturers have produced the variety of handguns and long arms as has this old firm

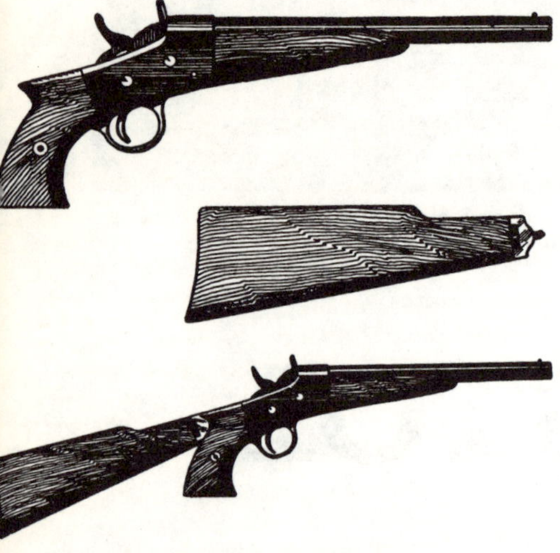

An illustration of the Remington combination shotgun taken from an early Bannerman catalog

The remodeled Remington factory in Ilion, N. Y., as it appeared in 1881

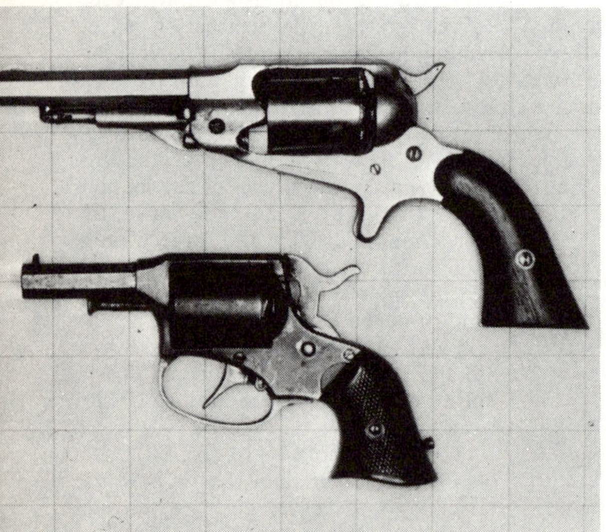

New Model Pocket Revolver (top) and Rider Pocket Revolver (below), both converted to .32 caliber rimfire

Remington multishot handguns (top to bottom): Zig-Zag Derringer, .22 caliber; Elliot's Pocket Repeater, .32 caliber; Rider Magazine Pistol, .32 caliber; Remington Double Derringer, .41 caliber.

Eliphalet Remington, father of the Remington Arms Company, Inc.

With the number of active collectors of old arms increasing yearly, there is a greater interest being expressed in 'name' collections. By this is meant building a collection of types, calibers, and models produced by one individual firm. For many years Colt arms held undisputed sway as the choice of many collectors. Today many authorities feel that Coltiana is nearing the saturation point in both popularity and demand. Thus, it is not strange that many collectors are turning to the acquisition of arms by other makers. The handguns produced by Remington, Smith & Wesson, Marlin, and others are becoming collection items of real importance.

As an oasis in the desert is to weary travelers, so are the possibilities of the Remington handgun field to the average collector. It offers all that is intriguing to those who love the old arms. Few names in American firearms history afford an older or more interesting historical background. None has the variety of totally different models in both handguns and long arms.

A humble beginning

Historically Remington is the oldest arms company in the United States, in point of continuous lineage. It was started in 1816 in a very simple manner. A conservative father's answer to his son's pleading for a rifle was that he did not propose to have a son of his spending hard-earned money for a gun which, due to the scarcity of guns in those days, was a bit on the expensive side. Eliphalet (pronounced E-life-a-let) Remington's desire for a rifle was not to be denied. If Father would not permit the buying of one—well, he'd have one if he had to make it himself. And make one is exactly what this blacksmith farm boy did!

In the family's tiny blacksmith shop at Ilion, N. Y., the 23-year-old youth forged his first gun barrel out of scrap iron. Having no method for rifling it, he walked the fifteen miles to Utica, where he enlisted the services of a gunsmith to help with the rifling. So intrigued was the gunsmith with the ingenuity displayed by the young man in forging the barrel that he not only rifled the barrel but gave him a lock and helped him adapt it to the barrel. Returning home, young Eliphalet lost no time in fashioning a stock and completing the rifle. It was a proud young man who exhibited his first gun to the interested neighbors of Ilion.

So splendidly had Eliphalet Remington fashioned his gun, and so well did it shoot, that many of the pioneering neighbors besieged Remington to make rifles for them. Ere long the elder Eliphalet was helping his gunsmith-son fashion arms for an ever-increasing list of customers. The little forge was soon outgrown as machinery was brought in, or fabricated, to aid in the production of the early rifles.

From that humble beginning emerged the vast Remington Arms Company, Inc., which for some 138 years has operated under its own name. Truly the name Remington is renowned and respected today among all who know guns. It has been, and is, an inseparable companion of American firearms development.

It is the purpose of this study to present a few of the interesting types to be found in the Remington handgun field . . . for the benefit of beginning collectors, and laymen, alike.

Beals New Pocket Revolver

It was in 1857 that the story of Remington handguns really began—with the manufacture of a small percussion revolver which employed an outside pawl for revolving the cylinder. Patented by Fordyce Beals (#15167, June 24, 1856 and #17359, May 26, 1857), its peculiarities were noted on the patent application as follows: "The nature of my invention consists in the combination and arrangement in which an arm pivot or axis is employed, passing through the hammer at its center of motion, moving or vibrating with it, it being connected at the arm to the pawl by which the cylinder is rotated, thus operating on the chambered breech or cylinder at a point remote from its center, thereby giving great force to its rotary movement, and also by this arrangement placing the working parts most liable to friction, requiring attention and frequent lubrication, in a position readily accessible."

Three models of the Beals New Pocket Revolver were produced in the years from 1857 to 1860. The second and third models were equipped with spur triggers and checkered hard-rubber, western-type grips.

The military models

Next in order was the beginning of Remington's bid for military contracts in the large caliber handgun field. Three models in .44 caliber were produced, the Beals Army Revolver, the Model 1861 Army Revolver, and the New Model Army Revolver. The familar New Model was a splendidly made weapon and proved a trustworthy military arm. Many of them found their way to frontiers of the Old West at the close of the Civil War.

The three Army models were likewise

produced in Navy models of .36 caliber, though in smaller quantities.

One of the most unusual of Remington's percussion arms, insofar as outside appearance is concerned, was the Rider Pocket Revolver. Patented by Joseph Rider (#21215, Aug. 17, 1858 and #23861, May 3, 1859), its unique mushroom type of cylinder and its rather odd outline set it apart from other revolvers of the day.

In 1860 Remington produced the first of their single-shot derringers. This tiny gun of .17 caliber utilized no powder but propelled the small ball by the detonation of a percussion cap.

Two other percussion arms should be mentioned, the New Model Pocket Revolver and the Revolving Rifle. The Pocket Model is in reality a small scale reproduction of the larger Army and Navy models, in .31 caliber and equipped with a sheathed trigger. The Revolving Rifle, produced in both .44 and .36 calibers, was but an adaptation of the revolver employing a longer barrel and shoulder stock.

While their percussion arms are interesting, it is in the cartridge arms that Remington displayed the most ingenuity, particularly in outside appearance. It is this variety in shapes and styles which appeals greatly to many collectors.

Pepperbox types

First in the distinguished line of Remington cartridge handguns was a double-action multishot gun, known among collectors as the "Zig-Zag". Patented by William H. Elliot (#21188, Aug. 17, 1858 and #28461, May 29, 1860), it is a six-shot, pepperbox-type of arm with the barrel group revolving like the cylinder of a revolver. Its unusual name came from the peculiar grooves on the barrel group near the breech end. Through the means of a stud riding in the grooves, the barrel assembly is rotated by the action of pushing the ring trigger forward. This brings the loaded chamber into line with the firing pin, which is released upon the backward motion of the trigger. Manufactured in limited quantity during 1861-62, it is the scarcest of Remington multishot arms.

Two guns of similar shape followed the "Zig-Zag", one a five-shot, round barrel group in .22 caliber, the other a four-shot, square-type barrel group in .32 caliber. On both of these Elliot Pocket Repeaters, the firing pin was made to revolve while the barrel group remained stationary, tipping down to load.

Applying Elliot's patent (#33382, Oct. 1, 1861), which provided for a hammer hung underneath and serving not only as a striker but also as a breechblock, Remington produced the first of their unique single-shot Vest Pocket Pistols. However, only on the .22 caliber model does the hammer serve as a breechblock. The .30, .32, .38, and .41 calibers were all equipped with a split breechblock, even though they did retain the general unique appearance of the smaller .22 caliber arm. Of the five calibers, the .30 is rarely encountered on dealers' lists today.

Single-shot martials

In the single-shot line, Remington next produced a martial pistol in large caliber, the .50 caliber rimfire Model 1865 Navy. The pistols supplied to the Navy on first order were equipped with sheathed triggers, making them easily distinguishable from the 1867 Model, which utilized an ordinary trigger with guard. To be entirely factual, there was in reality no 1867 Model. Most all of the 1865 Models were recalled by the Ordnance Department and a contract was made with Remington to alter them as follows:

1. Rimfire to central fire	$1.00
2. Cut off barrel and reset sight	1.00
3. Replace sheathed trigger with regular type trigger and guard	2.00
Total	$4.00

So, in fact, the 1867 Model is nothing more or less than a contract alteration job. This no doubt accounts for some of the high serial numbers to be found on the 1865 Model.

The change in design for the Model 1871 Army single-shot pistol was brought about by an Army Ordnance Board known as the "St. Louis Commission." Foremost change was the better balanced grip. It was this feature which achieved for this large caliber handgun much of the popularity which has endured to this day. Rebarreled for smaller calibers, it provides a most excellent target arm. In fact, Remington themselves produced target arms (Model 1891 and Model 1901) of this type in various smaller calibers in both rimfire and center-fire. The long life and popularity of these single-shot pistols is a splendid tribute to the ability of Remington engineers. In an early catalog Francis Bannerman Sons advertised a combination 20-gauge shotgun, with detachable stock, built along the lines of the popular single-shot Army pistol. Some years ago I saw one of these combinations in splendid condition at a leading gun collectors' meet.

Derringers and Cane guns

Two other single-shot models should be mentioned, the Elliot single-shot derringer and the Cane gun. Manufactured only in .41 caliber rimfire, the Elliot derringer followed the usual shape of other derringers of that period. Its principal difference lay in its simple construction, whereby the hammer served as a breechblock. It was based on Elliot's patent (#68292) of August 27, 1867. The Cane gun is somewhat of a hybrid. Even though it was advertised in early catalogs as a Rifle Cane, it hardly falls into either the rifle or pistol classification. Produced in both

Top to bottom: Remington .50 caliber Model 1867 Navy, .22 caliber Vest Pocket Pistol, .30 caliber Vest Pocket Pistol, .41 caliber Elliot Single-Shot Derringer, .22 caliber Rifle Cane

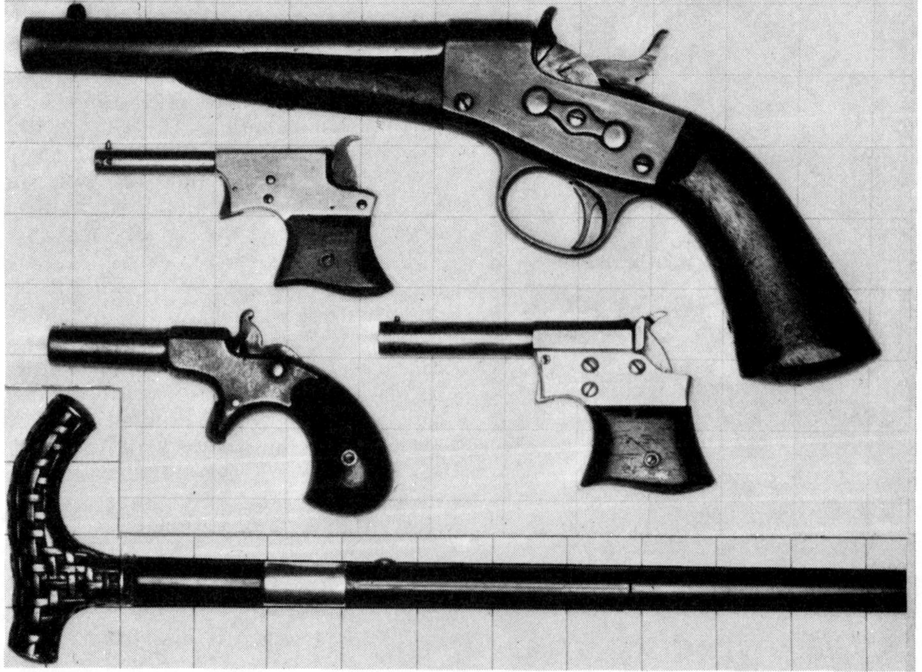

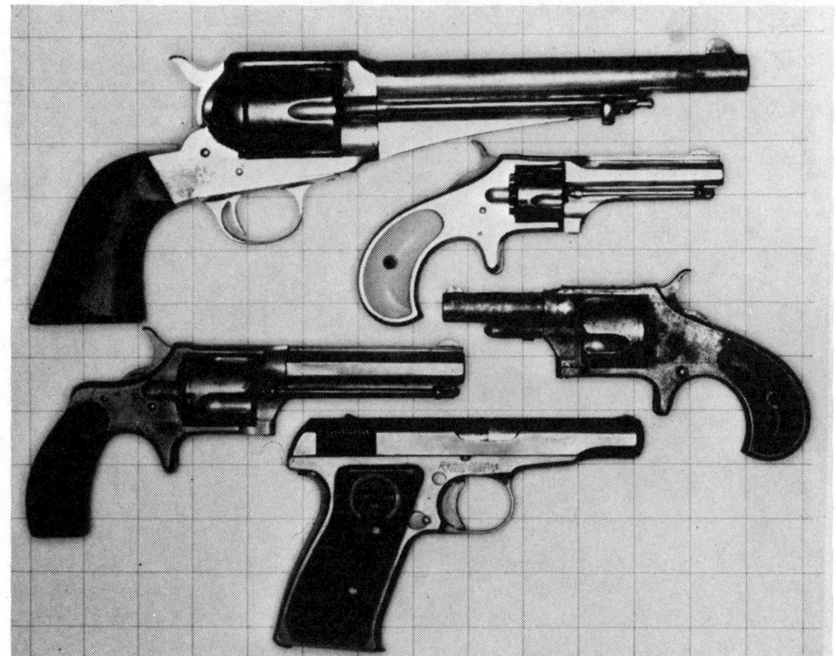

Top to bottom: Remington Model 1875 Army Revolver (civilian model) in .44-40 caliber, .30 caliber New Line Revolver No. 1, .41 caliber New Line Revolver No. 4, .38 caliber New Line Revolver No. 3, and .32 caliber Model 51 Automatic Pistol

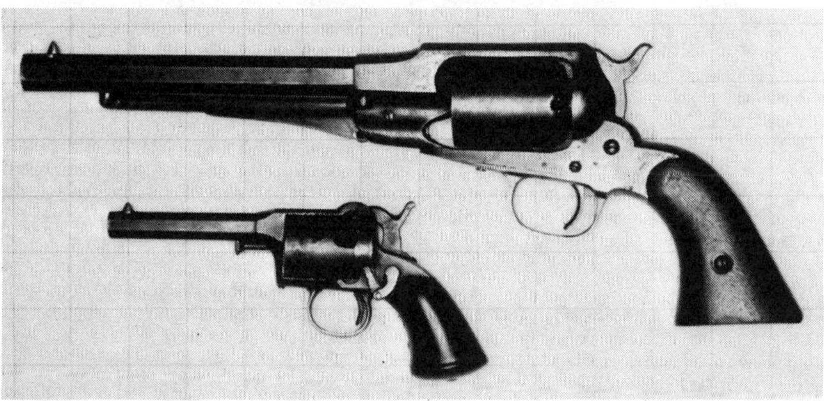

Remington's New Model Navy .36 caliber revolver (top) and the first model of Beals' .31 caliber Pocket Revolver, the first handgun produced by Remington

.22 and .32 calibers, under a patent (#19328, Feb. 9, 1858) granted to John F. Thomas and assigned to Samuel Remington, it provided an effective weapon for the gay blades of that day. It was made with two types of heads, one a curved handle and the other in the shape of a dog's head. In the accompanying illustration will be found another type of head, though this may be a replacement.

The year 1866 saw the advent of the now famous Remington Double Derringer. This potent .41 caliber rimfire arm was in production longer than any other Remington handgun. During the 69 years between 1866 and 1935, it is estimated that over 150,000 of this still-popular model were manufactured.

Another of the unusual types introduced by Remington was their single-action Rider Magazine Pistol. Patented by Joseph Rider (#118152, August 15, 1871), the arm carried its five rimfire cartridges in a tube on the underside of the barrel. Cartridges were removed from the magazine and inserted into the chamber by a downward, back-and-forward motion of the breechblock.

New Line Revolvers

Three models of the New Line Revolvers were produced, No. 1—.30 caliber, No. 2—.32 caliber, and No. 3—.38 caliber. They were manufactured under William S. Smoot's patent (#143855) of October 21, 1873. Points of difference between the three models are more or less minor, with no radical change in the general shape, though the .38 caliber (No. 3) had a totally different style grip.

A fourth model of the New Line differed considerably from the others. Produced in both .38 and .41 rimfire calibers, it was a more compact weapon with short, round (instead of octagon) barrel and minus the distinctive ejector rod of the earlier models. A .22 caliber revolver patterned after the fourth model New Line was brought out in 1878. Many of them bore the name "IROQUOIS".

One of the fine old frontier arms was the Remington Model 1875 Army. Although designated Army, authorities seem to disagree as to the extent of its use by the military services. Some specimens, however, do carry the inspector's marks usually found on military arms, but not on commercial models. It is known that the Model 1875 did undergo tests by the Ordnance Department and the results of these tests are covered in "Ordnance Notes No. 54". But, from a perusal of some of these old Ordnance reports, one gains the impression that many of the Ordnance inspectors all but had a phobia for any arm not labeled Colt, however splendid that arm may have been. In any event, the Model 1875 .44-40 caliber pistol did give a good account of itself on the western frontier, where it was much respected.

And the automatics

Last in the illustrious line of Remington handguns are the automatics. First produced in 1918, the Model 51 semi-automatic enjoyed 16 years of popularity. Manufactured under patents granted to John D. Pedersen and C. C. Loomis, it was produced in two calibers, .32 A.C.P. and .380. The arm is easily distinguished by its streamlined appearance and its form-fitting grip. Much attention was given by the factory to the style of grip and it is to the credit of Remington that many present-day manufacturers have utilized a similar style.

As an armsmaker for the government during World War I, Remington produced the regulation .45 government automatic. This was merely a contract arm and, as such, offers little to those interested mainly in arms actually designed and produced by Remington. Also manufactured during World War I was the Mark III Signal Pistol, a large single-shot pistol of 10 gauge and equipped with a nine-inch barrel.

It is hoped that this bird's-eye view of Remington handguns may stimulate and intrigue others to a greater interest in the arms produced by Remington, an old name in American arms. ◆ ◆ ◆

My personal thanks to Lt. Col. R. C. Kuhn, James E. Serven, Frank Wheeler, A. W. Rowe, Cy Karr, and others who so kindly assisted with this study.—H.C.L.

Remington 51: Still One Of The Best

By D. R. LULLING and E. R. GERBSCH

ALTHOUGH the Remington Arms Company is now noted almost exclusively for its sporting rifles and shotguns, this firm once ranked among the leading producers of handguns. This held true from the mid-1800's until 1910, when the Remington Arms Co. merged with the Union Metallic Cartridge Co.

After the merger, Remington left the handgun field to such competitors as Colt's and Smith & Wesson and concentrated on shoulder arms and ammunition. Only two Remington handguns were introduced after 1910. One of these, the Model XP-100 single-shot pistol, which appeared in 1963, is still offered. The other was the Remington Model 51 semi-automatic pistol, sold from 1918 to 1934.

As the Model 51 bids fair to become more and more of a collector item as the years pass, while it is still a serviceable sidearm some facts about it are worth noting for the future.

The Remington Model 51 is a hammerless (concealed-hammer) semi-automatic pocket pistol which was offered first in cal. .380 ACP and later .32 ACP. Total production was approximately 64,786 pistols. Most were made in cal. .380.

Very early Model 51 pistols did not have the letters PA preceding the serial number as is normal on these pistols. Although there are no records to verify the exact date production of the Model 51 was started, it was sometime in 1918. A total of 22,966 pistols were shipped by the end of 1919. Production ceased Dec. 12, 1926, but sales continued on a large scale through 1927, with 3,045 pistols being sold after 1926. Only 61 pistols were sold from 1928 to 1934.

The basic patent for the Model 51 was number 1,348,733 dated Aug. 3, 1920, and was issued to John D. Pedersen, who designed several models of Remington guns. The original application for the patent was filed July 30, 1914, and was renewed July 17, 1919. Patent No. 1,348,733 is an extensive document with 19 pages of drawings and 102 pages of text. A total of 31 patents issued on various features are attributed to the Model 51. Twenty-six patents were granted to Pedersen, three to Crawford C. Loomis, and one each to C. B. Dygert and G. H. Garrison. Many of the patents relating to the Model 51 were never utilized in final production pistols. Eight patents described features which were actually implemented in production of the Model 51:

1. Barrel attaching means: Split pin (Mar. 9, 1920—1,333,570, 1,333,571, and 1,333,572)
2. Barrel bushing for slide (Aug. 3, 1920—1,348,284)
3. Action spring bushing (June 14, 1921—1,381,291)
4. Extractor (Dec. 27, 1921—1,401,552)
5. Magazine safety (Sept. 4, 1923—1,466,749)
6. Ejector (Dec. 9, 1924—1,518,602)
7. Grip plates (Mar. 1, 1925—1,531,796)
8. Breechbolt and magazine for cal. .32 (Feb. 2, 1926—1,571,592)

Much of the Model 51's frame results from its excellent balance and specially-designed grip which positions the gun low in the hand. The grip is angled in relation to the barrel to provide a natural position of the hand and wrist, which gives the pistol excellent pointing qualities for fast and accurate shooting. Hundreds of experiments were made with hand molds to determine the correct shape, length, and pitch to provide the most nearly perfect average grip. The pistol was designed to be as flat as possible with carefully-rounded corners.

The action of the Model 51 is not a true blowback, but is actuated by cartridge set-back to give what is sometimes called hesitation action or impinging action. The barrel is fixed to the frame. However, the breechbolt is a separate movable part not locked to the slide or barrel. This is designed to slightly delay opening of the action.

During firing, the cartridge case is set back about .08″ by chamber pressure. This starts rearward movement of the breechbolt and slide. The breechbolt engages a shoulder on the frame after having traveled about 3/32″. The slide continues rearward, lifts the breechbolt out of its temporary engagement, and continues to compress the action spring. As the slide returns forward under pressure of the action spring during counter-recoil, it drops the breechbolt back into its locking recess in the frame.

Capacity of the box magazine is seven cartridges in cal. .380 ACP and eight in cal. .32 ACP. An additional cartridge may be carried safely in the chamber with the safety lever engaged. The 3¼″ barrel is rifled with seven grooves, right twist. Overall length of the pistol is 5⅝″, width

Remington Model 51 pistol was produced from 1918 to 1926. Factory stocks of the pistol were exhausted in 1934.

is .9", and weight unloaded 21 ozs. The serial number stamped on the left side of the frame has a "PA" (Pedersen's Automatic) prefix.

Sights are open Patridge fixed type with a square-notch rear and blade front. Both are integral with the top of the slide which is milled flat and matted to avoid light reflection. Made low so as not to catch on clothing, the sights are small and not picked up quickly by the eye.

Metal parts are finished dull black, the only finish recorded as being used. A pin locks the barrel to the receiver. The action spring of rectangular cross section encircles the barrel, and is positioned about ¼" back from the muzzle. There is a close fit of the barrel to the barrel bushing which is assembled permanently to the slide.

The trigger bar is a standard stirrup type that straddles the magazine. While some Model 51 pistols have good trigger pulls, most have either spongy or heavy pulls. This is one point of complaint about the pistol.

Located on the left side of the receiver behind the trigger, the magazine catch button is depressed to release the magazine. A rectangular hole in the front edge of the magazine engages the magazine catch. The magazine floorplate is not removable. Observation slots in the magazine body allow the number of cartridges to be verified. The magazine is stamped on the side near the floorplate with the caliber designation.

The extractor of the cal. .380 pistol is a formed flat spring with a claw in the front, a locking projection behind the claw, and a tail which fits into a T-slot at the rear of the breechbolt. In the cal. .32 pistol, the extractor has no spring action, but is cammed by a groove in the slide into engagement with the extraction cannelure of the cartridge. The ejector is a flat metal piece pinned to the receiver.

Made of black hard rubber, the grips are checkered and bear the circular Remington-UMC trademark. Each has a metal plate that engages undercuts in the receiver. This permits easy removal of the grips and makes grip screws unnecessary.

There are three safety devices: A grip safety, thumb-operated safety lever on the left side of the receiver, and a magazine safety. The grip safety prevents firing unless it is depressed by grasping the pistol. It also serves as a cocking indicator by extending rearward when the hammer is cocked. If the grip safety is not depressed when the slide is pulled fully to the rear, the slide is locked open automatically. This is a highly desirable feature as it permits the slide to be locked open in a safe position on shooting ranges. Depressing the grip safety releases the slide which moves forward under force of the action spring.

The safety lever can also be used to lock the slide to the rear by pulling the slide fully back and at the same time turning the lever upward to safe position. Unless the hammer is cocked, the safety lever cannot be put on safe.

Removing the magazine causes the magazine safety to block the sear and thus prevents any cartridge remaining in the chamber from being fired. This prevents accidental firing by persons who assume that the pistol is unloaded if the magazine is removed.

A contemporary Remington catalog lists as a fourth safety feature the solid breech with enclosed hammer. This construction prevents the hammer from being released by striking it against some object or dropping the pistol. The hammer can be cocked only by rearward movement of the slide.

While the Model 51 appeared only in one basic type, there were variations in slide serrations, the legend on top of the slide, and other markings. When this pistol was first marketed in 1919 by the Remington Arms-Union Metallic Cartridge Co., the top of the slide was stamped with the two-line inscription:

"THE REMINGTON ARMS UNION METALLIC CARTRIDGE CO., INC. REMINGTON ILION WKS. ILION, N.Y. U.S.A. PEDERSEN'S PATENTS PENDING."

This inscription has been observed on a specimen as late as serial no. PA45657.

In 1920, the Remington Arms-Union Metallic Cartridge Co. again reorganized and returned to the name Remington Arms Company. About that time the slide inscription was changed to read:

"REMINGTON ARMS COMPANY, INC. ILION, N.Y. USA. PEDERSEN PATENTS PAT'D MAR. 9, 20, AUG. 3, 20, JUNE 14, 21, OTHERS PENDING."

The original Model 51 pistol in cal. .380 was produced up to about serial no. 1600 (#1627 has been observed) without the words "Remington Trade Mark" on the right side of the frame. There are no caliber markings except on the magazine and no company name except on the grips and top of the slide. Each side of the slide has nine grasping serrations. These serrations are slightly rounded and fairly wide.

A change in the cal. .380 was made late in 1919, about serial no. PA23602, when the marking "Remington Trade Mark" was added on the right side of the frame. Daniel K. Stern stated in his article in the Sept., 1965, issue of *The American Rifleman,* that "This is the scarcest variation, with 5,000 to 6,000 pistols so marked."

Prior to September, 1921, Remington began production of the Model 51 in cal. .32 ACP. Early cal. .32 pistols were apparently available as a special order item and not generally marketed. The earliest cal. .32 ACP pistols appeared about serial no. PA40000. Addition of a second caliber necessitated marking the barrels with the caliber designation which can be seen at the ejection port.

Thumb safety in "safe" position locks grip safety in extended position, indicating that hammer is cocked.

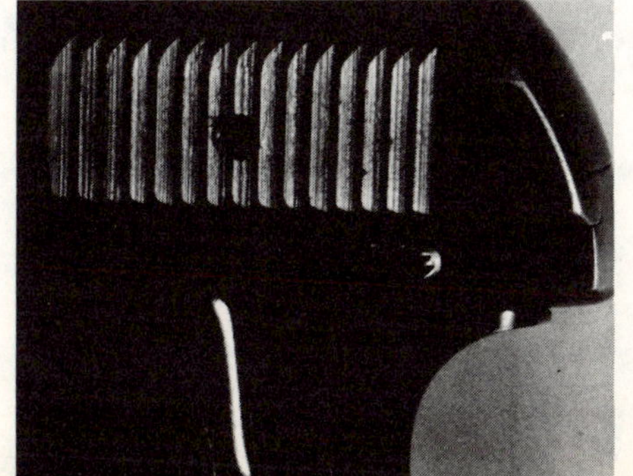

To avoid the confusion of a single set of serial numbers for the two calibers, Remington assigned a block of 20,000 numbers to the cal. .32 ACP in September, 1921. Since serial numbers of the cal. .380 ACP had already passed PA40000, the first regular cal. .32 ACP number was PA60829, for a pistol produced in September, 1921. Due to the time involved in this transition, between 100 and 400 cal. .32 pistols carry numbers below this regular range.

Initial manufacture of the cal. .32 pistol continued through pistol serial number PA70280, completed in December, 1925. Another skip in sequence of 20,000 numbers was made at that time with a final assignment of 2,127 numbers from PA-90501 through PA92627. Production of the Model 51 was terminated Dec. 12, 1926. The Remington factory refers to Model 51 cal. .380 pistols as the series of 1918 and cal. .32 pistols as the series of 1921.

Through at least serial no. PA3800, slide serrations of the cal. .380 pistol are the early slotted type with nine rounded cuts. A change to triangular slide serrations was authorized in February, 1919, but reportedly was not carried out for several years. The earliest reported specimen with such serrations bears serial no. PA39192. The last serial no. recorded in cal. .380 is PA60800 on a pistol sold Sept. 22, 1926.

Introduction of the cal. .32 pistol involved few changes from the cal. .380. The outside diameter of the barrel was unchanged, and concentric rings on the barrel starting ¼" from the muzzle in the cal. .380 were moved forward only 1/16". The face of the breechblock was altered to accept the smaller-diameter .32 ACP cartridge, the extractor hook was lengthened, and the magazine follower was redesigned. Most cal. .32 pistols have only 15-groove triangular slide serrations.

Serial number totals for both calibers of the Model 51 are greater than the actual number of pistols produced. There were 60,774 serial numbers in the cal. .380 series which probably includes a few of the early cal. .32 numbers, and 11,298 serial numbers in the two groups of the cal. .32 series. Factory quality control rejects, cutaway demonstrators, and samples account for a few of the missing numbers.

In 1925, the Model 51 could be purchased for $15.75, and was sold with a cardboard box, an instruction brochure, wiping rod, and a cleaning brush. Current market values range from $50-$125 for the .380 and $75-$150 for the scarcer cal. .32.

Although the Model 51 was last produced in 1926, it still ranks among the world's finest semi-automatic pistols in design, workmanship, and reliability. The authors feel that its sales decline was due partly to the shooting public having long identified Remington as a producer of shoulder arms, and that this resulted in a decision by the company's management to get out of the pistol business. ■

THE demand for various antique firearms waxes and wanes like the change in women's fashions. Presently, the Remington Improved Army Model revolvers of both 1875 and 1890 are on top. They disappear from gun show tables within hours of their appearance. In most cases, sale prices for the 1875 and 1890 Remingtons, compared to Colts of like condition, are higher. All considered, and from sales tabulated, the Remington Improved Army Models are in great demand.

As expected, reproductions of the 1875 made in Italy are finding their way into the marketplace, aged, and in some instances, even reworked to resemble the 1890 model. It was bound to happen, "for where there is big game, there will always be the jackals." Also, some 1875 models have been observed with the barrel web reshaped and the guns misrepresented as 1890 revolvers. In view of the activity in the marketplace, a summary of both models is in order and may be helpful to prospective buyers.

The 1875 model was produced from early 1875 through 1889 by E. Remington and Sons Company of Ilion, N.Y. Thus the 1875 Improved Army Model was stamped "E. Remington and Sons, Ilion, New York, U.S.A." on the barrel. Barrel stampings have been observed reading both toward the front sight and toward the cylinder. The 1875 model retained a web beneath the ejector housing that first appeared as a reinforcement for the rammer lever on the Remington 1858 New Model Army. Approximately 10,000 1875 models are sold outside the United States, principally to Egypt. As a total of 25,000 Improved Army Revolvers, model of 1875, were produced, this left 15,000 for distribution within the United States. During this same period, Colt produced nearly six times as many Single Action Army revolvers. Therefore, even the Remington 1875 models are not plentiful.

The 1875 Remington was produced in three calibers: the .44 Rem. cartridge which is interchangeable with ammunition for Colt Richards and Richards-Mason conversions of the 1860 Army revolver; the .44 W.C.F., or .44-40; and the .45 Gov't, which is the short .45 cal. cartridge that also fits S&W Schofield revolvers. The latter is the rarest, in a ratio of 1 to 35, to revolvers in .44-40.

Production of both models included two barrel lengths, 5½" and 7½"; both had five-groove rifling, and six-shot, 1 17/32" long, half-fluted cylinders. Serial numbers are found inside of the top strap, on the frame under the grip, and at the tip end of trigger guard. The weight of 1875 pistols is 44 ozs. The 1890 Model was produced in the .44-40 caliber only and weighs 42 ozs. Both revolvers were produced with or without lanyard rings.

The 1890 model Remington Army revolver is among the rarest of American firearms. Only 2000 were produced, considerably fewer than any other Remington pistol except the practically unknown brass frame Remington-Rider derringer. Neither of these revolvers had ever attained its rightful status in the collecting field until recently.

Production of 1875 Improved Army Revolvers ceased in 1889, at about the same time and for the same reason that production of all Remington revolvers ceased. E. Remington and Sons went bankrupt. The new Remington Arms Co. chose to return only the large-frame single-action "Army Model" to the inventory. They did so in 1890, making three changes in the old 1875 design.

Internally the gun's backstrap was strengthened by an increase in the thickness of the mainspring well. Externally, barrel markings were changed from "E. Remington and Sons" to "Remington Arms Co., Ilion, N.Y.," and the triangular web of the 1875 revolver was drastically changed in size and shape.

SCARCE ARMY

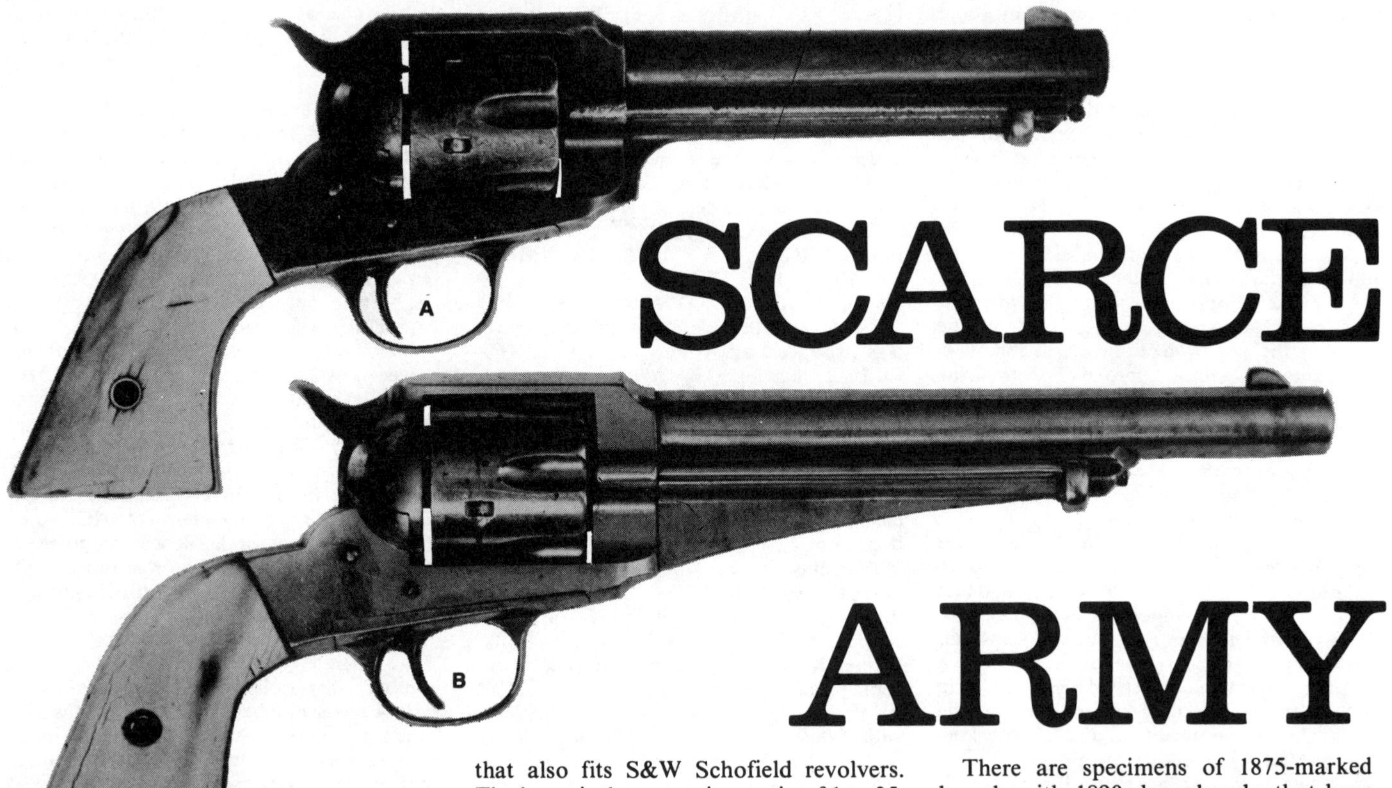

There are specimens of 1875-marked barrels with 1890-shaped webs that have been ground to the new contour. Some call them transitional models, but that is doubtful. Ground-off webs generally fail to properly match the contour of 1890 frames. The correct web/frame shape is the product of new and different forgings not interchangeable with the 1875 version and saving in both material used and, consequently, weight.

Observations of 1890 models indicates that the majority have lathe chatter marks, irregular barrel lengths, varying up to 3/16" from the standard 5½" and 7½" lengths. It is believed, from available financial records, that such an undercapitalized, newly formed company was also understaffed; and in attempting to recapture the sidearm market, the quality of the 1890 Improved Army Model was

E. Dixon Larson is a well known collector and the author of several books on antique guns and western Americana. He is shown above with two of his favorite Remington Army revolvers and two of the saddles that fill his collection of tools of the Old West.

inferior to that of the 1875 model. The 1890 was the Remington Arms Company's first and last bid to build a competitive large-caliber revolver. Hence, the 1890 New Improved Army Model, caliber .44-40 W.C.F., is a rarity in itself. By the same token, the 1875 was the only large-frame single action cartridge revolver manufactured by E. Remington and Sons. Most collectors agree that for years Colt arms have reigned supreme. However, prices and saturation appear to be causing the collectors to look elsewhere. Remington is the oldest armsmaking company in the United States. As such Remington-made arms certainly possess an interesting historical background.

A careful study will show that it is very simple to identify authentic models of either revolver. Both models should be highly regarded as collectors' arms, and from the number of 1875 models that have been remodeled in an effort to resemble later revolvers, the original 1875 models will soon be as scarce in number as the 1890 models. ■

REMINGTON MODELS

C

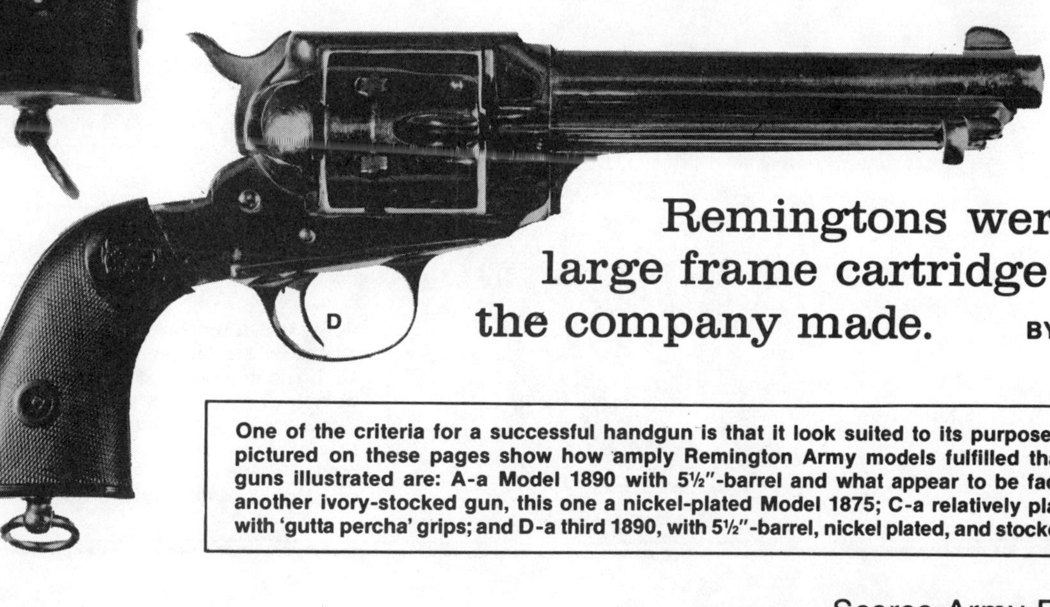

D

The 1875 and 1890 Remingtons were the only large frame cartridge revolvers the company made.

BY E. DIXON LARSON

One of the criteria for a successful handgun is that it look suited to its purpose. The four revolvers pictured on these pages show how amply Remington Army models fulfilled that requirement. The guns illustrated are: A-a Model 1890 with 5½"-barrel and what appear to be factory ivory grips; B-another ivory-stocked gun, this one a nickel-plated Model 1875; C-a relatively plain 7½" Model 1890, with 'gutta percha' grips; and D-a third 1890, with 5½"-barrel, nickel plated, and stocked with 'gutta percha.'

THE 1915

was Savage's better mousetrap, but nobody

THE Savage Model 1915 Pocket Autoloading Pistol endures as proof positive that more sophisticated is not always more saleable. An attempt to improve Savage's already popular Model 1907 autoloader, the 1915 pistol failed in the marketplace, and, instead of a commercial success, has become an elusive and desirable collectors' item.

What became the M1915 began to exist about 1912, with experimental attempts to add a grip safety to M1907 pistols. The grip safety itself derives from three U.S. patents requested by Savage designer Charles A. Nelson on Oct. 15, 1912, each of which describes a grip safety for incorporation in the M1907 design.

Each of these safeties was very complicated and, although patented, none was used in production. They received U.S. patent numbers 1,080,364 on Dec. 2, 1913, 1,082,969 on Dec. 30, 1913, and 1,085,698 on Feb. 3, 1914. In June of 1914, Nelson applied for a patent on a fourth type of grip safety. This patent, No. 1,168,024, granted Jan. 11, 1916, also covered a slide hold-open device, a simplified magazine catch (which was, in fact, used on Savage M1907s made in and after 1912) and a new, simplified sear trip. Finally, two of Nelson's fellow employees, Charles Lang and William Swartz, piggy-backing on Nelson's idea, came up with a fifth type of grip safety, which actually was used.

Purchasers of Savage's Pocket Automatics also often got a book, *It Banishes Fear*, touting the gun's value for self-defense.

What led to this desire to modify the M1907? The answer usually given is Savage's competition, but those who say this overlook two facts. The first is that until 1913 Savage had only Colt as a domestic competitor. The flood of autos from overseas was more than a decade away. Second, during those years Savage pistols were selling as well as Colts did. This fact is brought out by a comparison of pre-World War I Savage and Colt production rates.

If we allow for the fact that Savage's autos sold slowly in their first year of

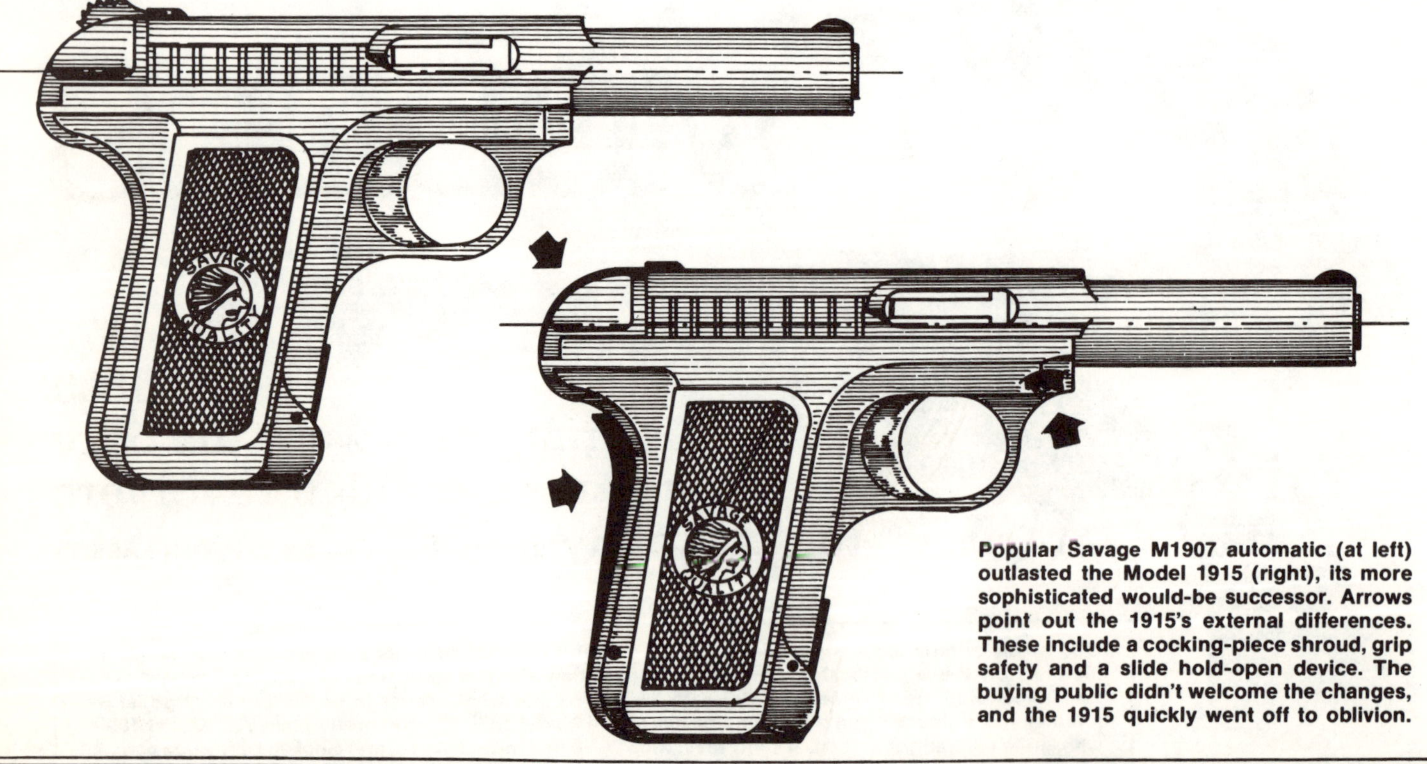

Popular Savage M1907 automatic (at left) outlasted the Model 1915 (right), its more sophisticated would-be successor. Arrows point out the 1915's external differences. These include a cocking-piece shroud, grip safety and a slide hold-open device. The buying public didn't welcome the changes, and the 1915 quickly went off to oblivion.

POCKET AUTO...

beat a path to their door.

BY DONALD M. SIMMONS

production (1908), and for their having no .380 until 1913, we can see that Colt and Savage were neck and neck in the production of pocket autos up until 1915. In early 1915 Savage, responding not only to Colt's offering of a hammerless, grip safety-equipped pocket auto but also to the introduction of a similar auto by S&W, announced their Model 1915 pistol. The M1915 Savage featured Nelson's patented sear trip and slide hold open device, the Lang and Swartz grip safety and a concealed cocking piece.

Though the changes made in the 1915 Savage appear cosmetic, they actually amounted to a major redesign of the pistol, requiring extensive changes in both production and tooling.

The concealed cocking piece for example required that the M1907's burr-headed cocking piece be removed and a shroud added to the end of the breech block and pinned in place at the bottom of the shroud.

The grip safety required milling the rear of the frame and drilling a hole at the base. The grip safety sliding lock entailed delicate machining in the area of the manual safety which had an additional cut made in its barrel. The trigger locking bar had to have its rear end machined to a flat locking surface, and, in some cases, a clearance cut had to be added to the top rearward edge of the left grip.

The addition of the hold-open device called for a notch on the right slide guide rails and extensive machining on the right trigger well in the frame. This desirable device also demanded a special magazine that had a small lip added to its follower and a notch in the magazine lips. The M1907 magazine will not operate the slide hold-open or lock in the magazine well of the M1915 without being forced.

APPROXIMATE NUMBER POCKET PISTOLS PRODUCED

	SAVAGE			COLT		
Year	.32's	.380's	Total	.32's	.380's	Total
1908	2000	—	2000	13000	2000	15000
1909	13000	—	13000	12000	2000	14000
1910	16000	—	16000	14000	3000	17000
1911	20000	—	20000	19000	3000	22000
1912	30000	—	30000	18000	3000	21000
1913	20000	4000	24000	17000	4000	21000
1914	16000	3000	19000	14000	5000	19000
1915	14000	1000	15000	21000	6000	27000

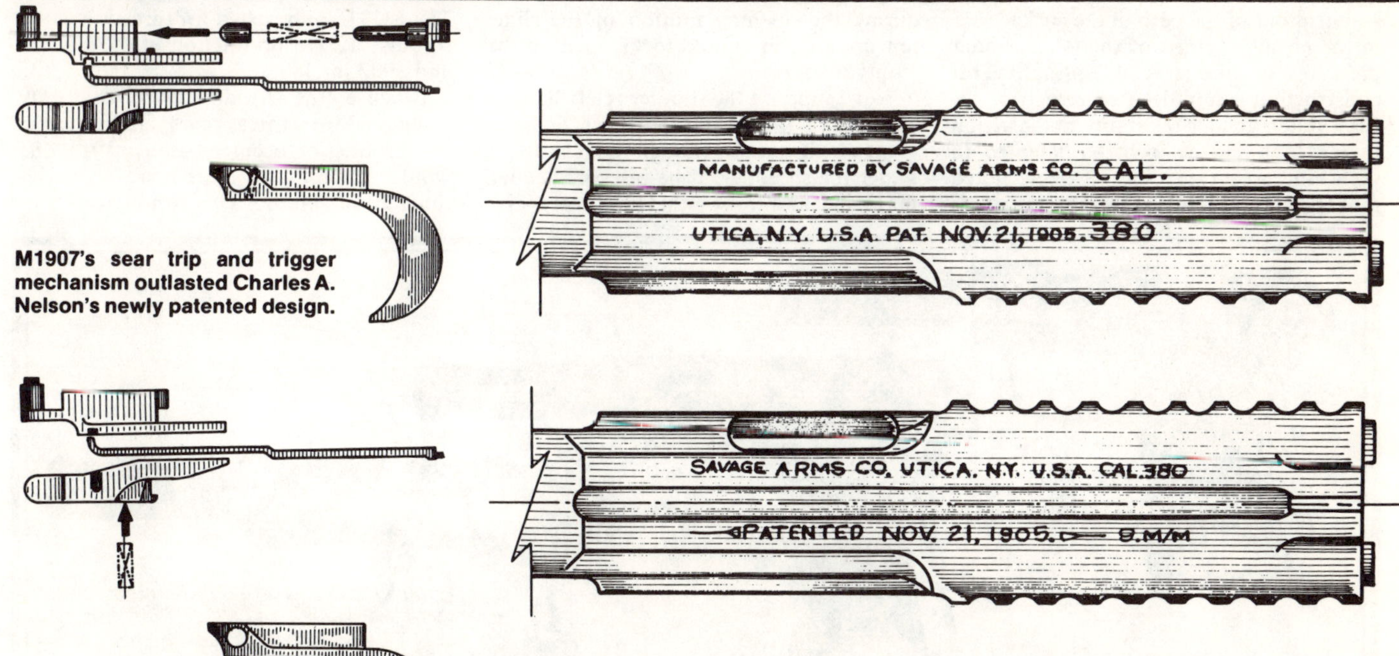

M1907's sear trip and trigger mechanism outlasted Charles A. Nelson's newly patented design.

Nelson's simplified M. 1915 sear trip was dropped quickly, maybe because of accidental firings.

Logo variations exist on M1915 .380 cal. Savage automatics. Logo at top is rarely found on M1915s, while the lower one is the common variety. The mark appearing before the word "Patented" and after "1905" is referred to as the trumpet by collectors of Savage pistols.

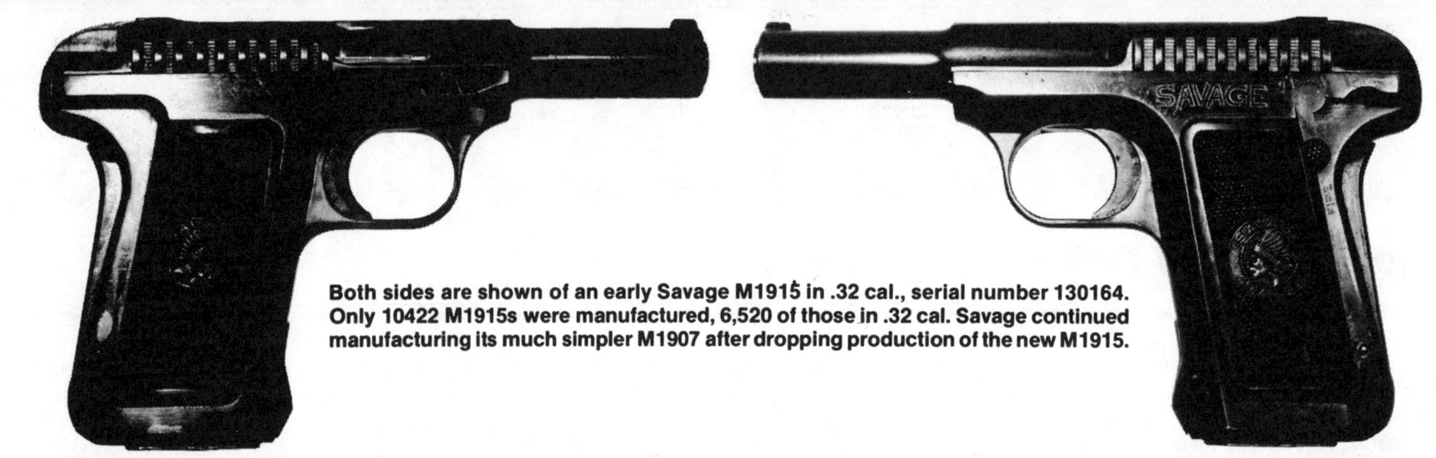

Both sides are shown of an early Savage M1915 in .32 cal., serial number 130164. Only 10422 M1915s were manufactured, 6,520 of those in .32 cal. Savage continued manufacturing its much simpler M1907 after dropping production of the new M1915.

The new type sear trip did away with a small locking toe and its spring and plunger used in M1907 pistols. During disassembly these parts had a way of flying across the room and were easily lost. The new sear trip was locked in by the forward end of the trigger bar and had no tendency to fly like its predecessor. In Nelson's patent, he describes the new sear trip's action as follows:

"For preventing double-firing in the present case the sear trip has a rigid toe which, when a pull on the trigger brings it against the vertical face of a fixed shoulder on the gun frame and this results in the discharge of the arm and is followed by the depression of the sear-trip under the wiping action of the rearward sliding breech bolt (actually the slide), snaps under the shoulder and locks down the sear-trip out of the path of the cocked sear in the ensuing return of the (slide) under pressure of the (recoil spring). This construction simplifies the sear-trip, insures much greater reliability of the action thereof and makes it better adapted to withstand wear and tear, it being noted that the elasticity of the flesh of the user's finger affords the necessary impetus to the sear-trip to cause it to catch under the shoulder."

All this sounds great and, as a disconnector during intentional firing of the pistol, it works fine. But as Daniel K. Stern, author of *Ten Shots Quick,* points out, Savage was quick to get rid of Nelson's sear trip and return almost instantly to the older 1907 type. Why? The answer lies in the possibility of an accidental firing of the pistol equipped with Nelson's sear trip. The accident requires a lot of unusual actions on the part of the shooter, but it could and possibly did happen. The stage is set when the last round of the magazine is fired. In this case the slide travels to the rear, cocks the firing pin (Savage M1915 pistols, unlike most striker-fired pistols, cock during the opening motion of the slide, not upon closing), and locks open on the empty magazine.

Now, suppose the shooter is left-handed and has his finger on the trigger, depressing it a little but not enough to lock the toe under the shoulder. If he inserts a loaded magazine and raises the hold-open arm with his right forefinger to drop the slide, the pistol might discharge. In this case, the "elasticity of the flesh of the user's finger" doesn't come into play; the sear trip engages the sear as the slide slams forward, and the gun fires. So, one of the M1915's improvements turns out to be an accident looking for a place to happen.

Potentially dangerous sear trip and all, the M1915 pistol had 10 parts not found on M1907 pistols, used seven modified M1907 parts and 15 parts that were interchangeable between models. Three parts, used in M1907 guns, were deleted from the M1915 design.

The higher production cost of the M1915, plus the fact that Savage sold it at the same price as their M1907 pistols — $15 for a .32 and $16 for a .380 — doomed the "improved" pistol to early retirement. The M1915 only lasted for three years and through a total production of 6520 in .32 and 3902 in .380.

Because the Model 1915 was only assembled for three years, and because real production occurred only in 1915, one would suspect that there were no variations in this model. This is not true.

M1915 with serial number 13004B was made in October, 1915. This doesn't equate with other guns.

This .380 was made in May, 1916, but carries lower serial number than does gun at left, 12256B.

Though not made until January, 1917, this .380 carries a serial number near gun at left, 12605B.

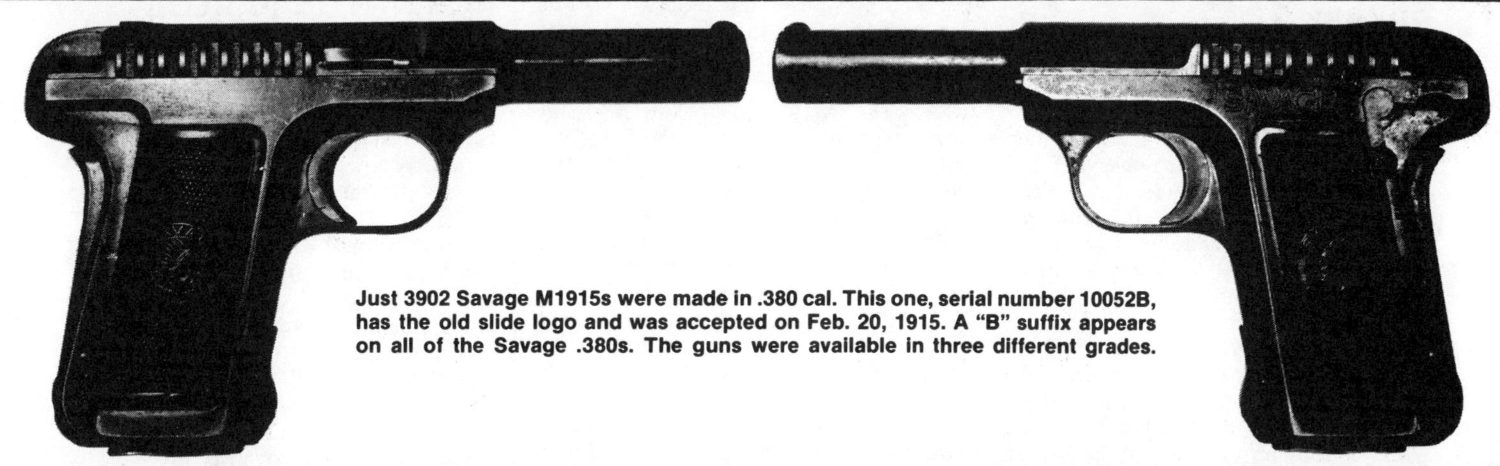

Just 3902 Savage M1915s were made in .380 cal. This one, serial number 10052B, has the old slide logo and was accepted on Feb. 20, 1915. A "B" suffix appears on all of the Savage .380s. The guns were available in three different grades.

The M1915 .380s were the first to be manufactured, and the serial number for the first pistol was 10,000B. The letter B is always added as a suffix to M1915 serial numbers on .380 cal. guns. Production of .380s began in February, 1915. The M1915 in .32 cal. was first produced in April, 1915, beginning with serial number 130,000. The slide legend on an M1907 .380 was:

MANUFACTURED BY SAVAGE ARMS CO.
CAL. .380 UTICA, N.Y. U.S.A. PAT-NOV. 21, 1905

This marking will also be found on the first few hundred .380 M1915s, making a very rare variation. I have seen two M1915 .380s, Nos. 10052B and 10111B, with these old slide markings. The legend was then changed to:

SAVAGE ARMS CO. UTICA, N.Y. U.S.A. CAL.380
—◁ PATENTED NOV. 21, 1905 ▷— 9. M/M

This marking is called the trumpet type by collectors because of the little figures in the second line which spaced it to match the upper line. This legend is found on most M1915 .380s and came into use around serial number 10400B.

The legend on the M1915 .32 was always the same:

SAVAGE ARMS CO. UTICA, N.Y. U.S.A. CAL. 32
PATENTED NOVEMBER 21, 1905 — 7.65 M-M

Most Model 1915s in either caliber will have the large stamped SAVAGE on the left hand side of the frame just above the grip piece. They will also have the words SAFE and FIRE around the manual safety. At least one M1915 .32, serial No. 134452, was made without the SAVAGE mark on the frame.

The trigger of the late M1907 Savage pistols had a small pin driven into its upper face. This pin kept the sear trip from slipping up during assembly and disassembly. The Nelson patent sear trip had no need for the pin and therefore most M1915s will be found without it. Probably because Savage had some M1907 triggers in stock, these will also be found on about one pistol in three.

Another variation found in either caliber is the installation of the 1907-type sear trip in some M1915 pistols. This has been observed on M1915 .32s, numbered 130699 and 136297 and .380s numbered 12256B and 12768B.

Still another variation which has been encountered is a Model 1915 without the loaded chamber indicator and no cuts for it on the barrel. This variation is undoubtedly due to Savage equipping the pistol with a new barrel some time after they had dropped the loaded chamber indicator. M1915 .380 number 11655B is an example of this variation.

Another variation rarely seen but worth mentioning is that some breechblocks were given a serial number to match that of the frame. This double numbering occurs on M1915 .32 number 133854 and on .380 number 22904B.

Jim Carr, author of *Savage Automatic*

Savage made ammunition for its .32 and .380 pocket pistols, as this full box of .380 ammo illustrates. Savage actually out-produced Colt in this field during two years, 1912-13. Logic dictates that the much-improved Savage M1915 would have captured the marketplace.

Savage 1915

Pistols, had a M1915 with a lanyard loop attached to its magazine somewhat like that on early Colt M1911s. Jim's pistol was a .32 number 135988. It is the only M1915 I know of so equipped and could indicate the interest of some country's military forces in these pistols.

That Savage autos were used overseas is well known. M1907s were used by both the French and the Portuguese; the French just before the introduction of the M1915, and the Portuguese just after. While no military purchase of the M1915 is known to have been made, they will occasionally be found with foreign proof marks. Three such M1915 .380s,numbers 10052B, 10390B and 11785B, are known. These three pistols were purchased from Savage by a John Rollins and Son in 1915. These are British proofed but have no military markings. The typical "crown" over "V" proof marks are found on the frame near the manual safety; on the slide over the left slide pulls near the rear sight; on the left side of the rear of the breech block; and on the barrel visible through the ejection slot above the loaded chamber indicator. On the barrel is a "crown" over "P".

Savage Arms Co. always offered various grades of their autos. The regular finish was a high-luster blue. The barrel and the loaded chamber indicator are polished and left bright. The trigger and the magazine catch are a mottled, case-hardened finish. The special grades came with pearl grips with the Savage, Indian-head medallion, and various grades of engraving were also available. These grades were called "Protector," "Monitor," and "Special." I have only seen one M1915 "Monitor" grade with pearl medallion grips. In preparing for this article, I found three M1915s in .32 cal. (132350, 134452 and 136247) which had pearl medallion grips, and one .380 (22904B). These are all rare factory variations. Savage also offered, as a "special," nickel plating. While I have seen M1907s with this finish, I have never seen an original factory nickeled M1915, but such pistols may exist.

As production of the M1915 .32s ground to a halt in 1916, there had been 6250 made. Although the serial numbers ran from 130000 to 137690, there were many blanks in the higher numbers of Savage's books. The production of the .380s lasted a year longer, but only about 400 pistols were assembled during 1916 and 1917. The total production of M1915, .380s was 3902, with the serial numbers running from 10000B to 13900B and a few before 10000B and a few after, like Jim Carr's .380 22904B, with pearl medallion grips, which was made up much later than 1917. As previously stated, the M1907 was not discontinued with the introduction of the M1915, and Savage made about 49000, M1907 .32s during the years in which the M1915 pistols were being produced. In any one of these years, M1907 .32 production exceeds the entire production of the M1915.

The M1915 should have been a successful arm, but it wasn't; and the only real reason must have been that the public didn't like it. It couldn't have been Nelson's sear trip alone. I think that the loss of the cocking piece which gave the shooter and indication of whether the pistol was cocked had a lot to do with the M1915's lack of acceptance. The public wasn't ready for a slide hold-open device in a pocket pistol and didn't appreciate this feature as we do today. The grip safety has always had its supporters and its opponents, but I for one don't feel comfortable carrying a loaded cocked pistol with its manual safety off and relying on its grip safety only.

As late as 1925-1926, we find that Von Lengerke and Detmold of New York was selling, of all things, M1915s. These must have come from some wholesaler's overstock but as an epitaph to the Model 1915, here is their description:

SAVAGE AUTOMATIC PISTOLS
THE .32 and .380 SAVAGE AUTOMATIC PISTOLS
.32 Calibre Pocket Model

"The Savage Automatic is a powerful, accurate and rapid fire pistol, which carries ten cartridges in the magazine. An extra one may be placed in the chamber, giving the arm a capacity of eleven shots. The mechanism is semi-automatic or self-loading, in which the recoil or firing the cartridge extracts and ejects the empty shell, cocks the pistol, reloading it in readiness for the next shot, to fire each of which the trigger must be pulled.

"The pistol in its new form is entirely hammerless, with the upper end of the cocking lever covered and the entire top of the breech plug enclosed, which prevents the necessity or possibility of cocking or uncocking the pistol without retracting the bolt. No. G251 — .32 Calibre Automatic — hammerless — grip safety and magazine capacity of 10 shots. Barrel 3¾ inches — weight 20¼ ounces — length overall 6½ inches. Price $19.00.

Extra Magazines each $1.00
.380 Calibre Pocket Model

"The .380 has the same mechanism as the .32 and is operated in exactly the same way. It differs only in calibre, length of pistol, length of barrel, weight, and magazine capacity. Weight 21 ounces; length overall 7 inches; length of barrel 4¼ inches. Price No. G252 $19.00. Extra magazines, each $1.00."

So ends the story of the Savage autoloading pistol Model 1915. While not a success in the market, it is a very rare and under-appreciated collector's item. ■

REMINGTON PARLOR PISTOL

Continued from page 161

found in natural bronze finish, although this one and a few others are nickel-plated. A few are engraved. Nearly all have 3" barrels, but I know of one with 4" barrel. The caliber is given as .17", but a #21 twist drill of .159" diameter will barely enter the muzzle. These pistols weigh from 4 to 4½ ozs., depending on barrel length.

The left side of the barrel is marked "RIDER'S PT. SEPT 13, 1859" on 2 lines. There are 2 types of breech-piece. The rarest and possibly the first type is the one-piece; no cover is provided to enclose the cap and the locking lever is quite short. The second type is made in 2 pieces. There is a cone to hold the cap and the cover has a longer lever. The first type was probably dropped as it would permit the cap to burst and fly.

In his book, Karr estimated that not more than 1000 of this type pistol were made. This could be true as only about 20 are now known to exist. The original selling price is unknown. It is interesting to note that Remington's 1877 catalog lists the cal. .22 Vest Pocket Pistol at $3.25 blued, $3.75 plated, and $5.75 engraved. Surely the Parlor Pistol didn't cost that much.

Frank N. Russell of Fort Lauderdale, Fla., owns a larger model of this pistol which weighs 8½ ozs. and has a 4" barrel of cal. .136" (equal to a #29 twist drill). Firing mechanism is of 2-piece type. The barrel tapers to ⅜" at the muzzle and over-all length of the pistol is 6", as against 4⅞" for the normal pistol. There is no maker's name or date on this pistol, but there is a stamping on the right barrel flat which appears to be "N. E WAI," or "WAT". ■

Larger version of Parlor Pistol owned by Frank N. Russell of Fort Lauderdale, Fla., shown with standard Remington model, does not bear usual Rider patent inscription

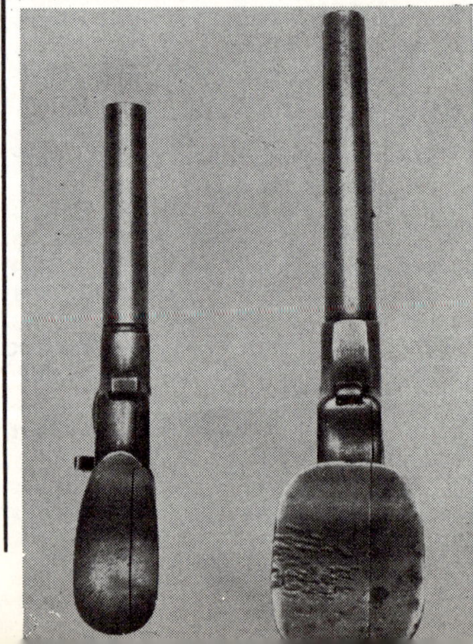

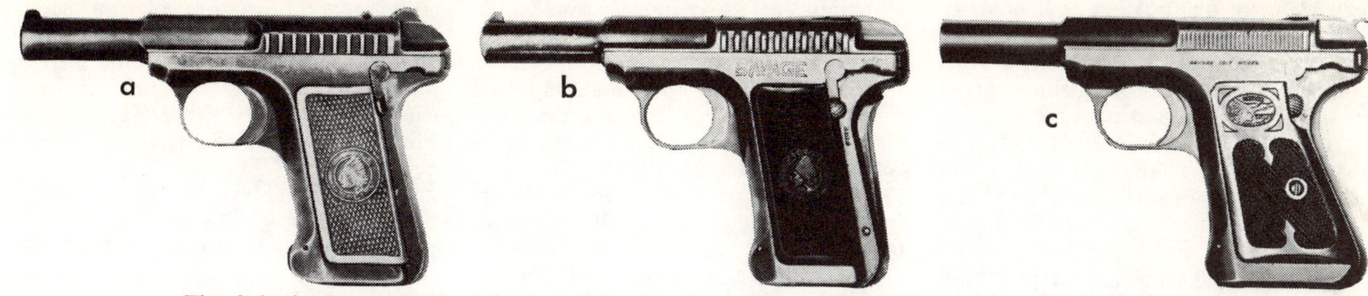

The 3 basic Savage pocket pistol models: **(a)** The original Model 1907 with pressed steel grips and small safety lever but without words "Safe" and "Fire"; **(b)** Model 1915 hammerless with grip safety and large word "Savage" on frame (this also appears on many 1907 models); **(c)** Model 1917

SAVAGE POCKET PISTOLS

Models and variations of a once popular pocket automatic

By DANIEL K. STERN

A NUMBER of years have passed since the last Savage pistol was made in 1928. Although they are not antiques, they do have an interesting history, novel operating features, considerable accuracy, excellent balance, grips which point naturally, good sights, and unusually fine trigger pull.

Many variations made

The Savage pocket pistols were produced in cals. .32 and .380, each made in 3 models, plus a number of variations due to changes in design not warranting re-designation. Through these changes can be traced the evolution of a firearm from introduction to obsolescence—in the case of the Savage pocket pistols, a span of 21 years during which more than 270,000 were sold.

More than a dozen Savage pistols are needed to cover the 3 calibers, various models, and major variations.

There has been a general lack of knowledge concerning Savage pistols. For example, the original cal. .32 model, officially designated Model 1907, is usually referred to as the Model 1910, less often as the Model 1909, and, by some, as the Model 1905, probably because it bears that patent date.

The scarce grip-safety, concealed-hammer Savage is almost always labeled a variation of the original gun, although Savage issued it as the Model 1915. Late variations of the Model 1907 are at times confused with the Model 1917.

There are obscure areas which even the company cannot clear up, due to the long period which has elapsed since production ceased and the fact that the factory moved twice in those years.

Thus, this account is constructed from available information and production records of Savage Arms Corp., their specimen pistols, those of the author and other guns examined and checked by him—all told, these were nearly 40.

Savage pocket pistols were beautifully made and finished. Their designer was Maj. Elbert Hamilton Searle, an Ordnance officer formerly stationed at Springfield Armory. The guns were produced under 2 basic patents granted to him in 1905. His locked-breech design utilized bullet thrust to delay opening of the breech.

An early Savage folder says, "The opening of its breech and the rearward escape of gas is mechanically prevented until the bullet has left the barrel".

Unsupportable conclusions

From this Savage drew rather unsupportable conclusions—that "superior accuracy and penetration are obtained" and that their gun was the only one to get "full accuracy and power out of every cartridge fired".

Nor was the advertising department content to let things rest there:

"Woodsmen . . . have on a number of occasions killed bear, mountain lion and elk. It (the Savage) has proved its accuracy at Sea Girt and Camp Perry in the hottest competition with the big military and target revolvers".

Although the big game part might well have occurred in isolated instances, the target-pistol accuracy claim is stretching things and, actually, was not needed. As noted earlier, the Savage had enough legitimate good points not to need such dubious puffing.

Another claim—and a true one—was that the Savage could fire 11 shots faster than any other pistol, to be exact in 2⅖ seconds. What was not said, of course, was that no other pistol had the magazine capacity of the Savage. All of this in a gun weighing only about 19 ozs. empty with a 6½″ over-all length. Even the 21-oz. cal. .380, which measures 7″ over-all, holds 10 rounds counting the chambered round. The Savage magazine is one of the strongest and best ever made.

Of the 5 comparable American pocket automatics, the Savage is the lightest

Cal. .25 Savage automatic pistol, commercial sale of which the company considers doubtful. Note grip safety and later versions of rear sight and slide serrations

in weight by up to 4 ozs., yet holds as many as 3 more cartridges.

Savage was the first American arms company to provide a challenge to Colt in the automatic pocket pistol field.

Indicative of their efforts to improve these pistols are the more than 30 changes made in the cal. .32 Model 1907 pistol alone, a gun which appears in no fewer than 12 variations.

Although the slide legend lists only one patent date, Searle received, in addition to the original pair, 2 later patents for minor improvements. Three more were issued to Charles A. Nelson, who invented the grip safety and other changes in the Model 1915.

Production of the first gun, the cal. .32, began on Apr. 22, 1907. It is finished in bright blue, and trigger and magazine release are case-hardened.

Serial numbers started at "1" and progressed upward. These pistols were made with a slide, or 'bolt' as Savage called it, with both front and rear sights pressed in place. Ribs and slide serrations are rounded and wider-spaced than in succeeding issues. The slide is bored to take a barrel of about .417" outside diameter with a corresponding counter-recoil spring encircling it.

On top of the slide is the 2-line legend in capital letters: "MANUFACTURED BY SAVAGE ARMS CO. UTICA, N. Y., U.S.A. PAT.-NOV. 21, 1905".

In larger letters at the end of the 2 lines is a bold: "CAL. 32".

The serial number is on underside of the frame in front of the trigger guard. Magazine release is in leading edge of grip frame and works from the top rather than customary bottom position. The idea, and a good one, is that it can be easily released by the third finger of the right, or firing hand, without having to change grip on the gun. However, this release was too ingenious and simple for people accustomed to a release operated by the left hand, a practice difficult with the Savage. Moreover, the release has to be pressed down again to allow entry of a fresh magazine.

Unconventional mainspring

The trigger is attached to a trip-lever which forces the sear up and out of its notch, allowing the cocking lever to drop as the burr-type hammer and firing-pin spring drives the striker into the cartridge. In this action there is no conventional mainspring. The firing pin is surrounded by a coil spring and joined to the rounded hammer, lower portion of which is the cocking lever.

When the pistol recoils during firing, the cocking lever is returned to position as it hits the back of the frame, readying the weapon for a second shot.

A manual safety is on left side of the frame. When turned up to 'safe' position, the safety lever brings an eccentric into play inside the frame, blocking fall of the cocking lever. Unless this lever drops, the firing pin cannot move forward to fire the cartridge.

The lever originally provided differs from the one usually seen in that it has a smaller head, is somewhat dished out, or concave, and has no knurling as do the later ones. Moreover, the words 'Safe' and 'Fire' do not appear on the frame.

The breechblock is retained by a single shoulder engaging a matching shoulder in the slide. Extractor is mounted on the right and is highly efficient, tossing empties 15 to 20 ft. to the side.

Although the trigger mechanism utilizes several pieces, it works in a straight line and is usually beautifully polished and fitted, to give a trigger pull far better than average.

Simply disassembled

One of the assets of the Savage is its extremely quick and simple takedown. With clip out, pull slide back and lock it with safety. Squeeze hammer and cocking lever, give them a quarter turn right, and out comes the whole breechblock. Barrel and slide can be pulled off by releasing safety while pulling trigger. Everything is then exposed. No screws are present in this model.

Grips, originally of steel, snap into place. Removal is not necessary or recommended. Later, hard rubber grips were standardized. These are easily broken if removed improperly.

In the original pistol, the magazine recess walls are thinner than in later models and lack the square corners commonly seen.

This, then, is the original Savage Model of 1907, a gun rarely seen today. Considerable detail has been supplied to permit explanation of later design changes.

Production of the original model was limited; probably not more than a few thousand, perhaps less. Highest serial noted is No. 867.

First to go were the steel grips, the small safety latch, and the thin-walled magazine recess. The steel grips are slippery and not as attractive as the hard rubber, which is undoubtedly why they were discarded.

The safety release was found to be too small, and the larger knurled one substituted. Also, the words "Fire" and "Safe" were added.

The thicker walls and squared ends of the magazine recess provide better protection for the magazine.

With these changes came the widely seen second variation of the Model of 1907. These were the first of many changes during the next decade, making possible even more variations than indicated here. However, the guns were all Model 1907's to Savage.

Production was brisk

Production moved at a fairly brisk pace, although it was mid-1909 before the first 10,000 pistols were finished. Production then started to pick up with

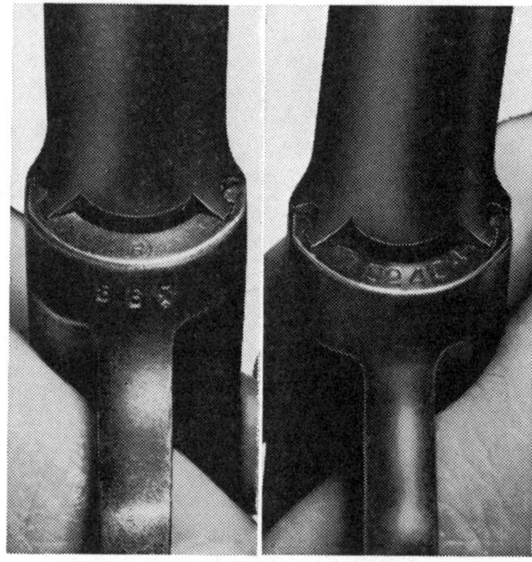

Original (l.) and later systems of marking serial number on gun. Change is believed to have been made at about #50,000

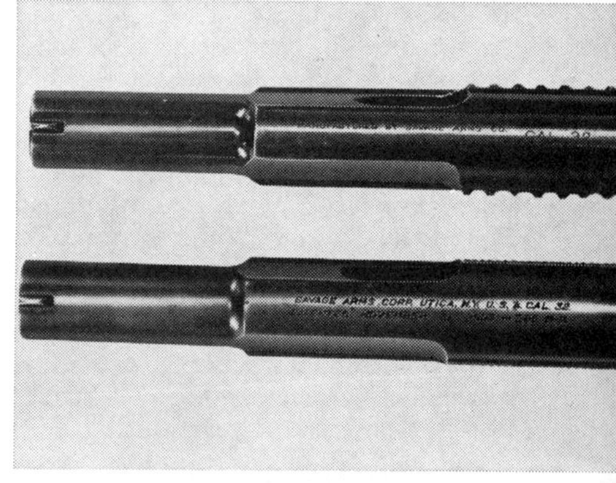

Two Savage pocket pistol slides showing variation in stamping. Early slide (at top) has original legend

serials reaching the mid-30,000's by the end of 1910. The pistol cost $15 then.

Output took a big jump in 1912 with 30,000 made that year.

At or about gun No. 50,000 Savage moved the serial number from the underside to the leading edge of the frame.

Sometime in 1912, and before gun No. 72221 left the production line, the breechblock was strengthened by addition of a rib which locked between corresponding frame ribs.

Savage meanwhile had been experimenting with a cal. .380 pistol, a caliber

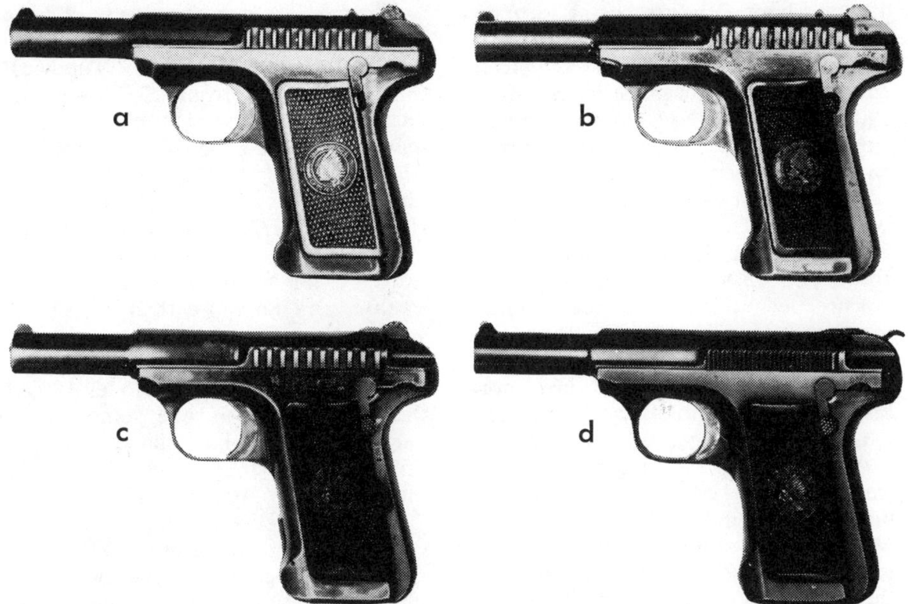

Four issues of the Savage Model 1907; **(a)** First Issue; **(b)** Second Issue with different grips, safety, and safety markings; **(c)** Eighth Issue with numbered breechblock, larger barrel, forged rear sight, and new magazine latch; **(d)** Final Issue, similar to Model 1917 except for the old type frame and grips

already produced by Colt for about 5 years. The year 1913 saw the introduction of the Savage cal. .380, and many additional changes in the cal. .32 pistol as well.

One change, quite likely made before the cal. .380 was introduced, involved the diameter of the barrels. Up to gun No. 75,000 finished barrel outside diameter is about .417″. Possibly Savage at this point decided to turn cals. .32 and .380 barrels from the same diameter stock. In any event, cal. .32 barrels were increased to an outside diameter of around .448″. Later parts lists noted: "When new barrels are required for pistols whose serial number is below 75,000, it is necessary to return pistol to factory."

But this was but one of many modifications made around the same time, or by early 1914 at the latest.

The rear sight, formerly separate, is now forged on the slide. Operation of magazine release latch is reversed to work from bottom. Fresh magazines can also be inserted without having to depress the catch. The revamped latch can still be worked by the little finger of right hand, but not as well as before.

The change does permit easier magazine removal using the left hand.

Magazine latch reversed

Originally the magazine had a single latching notch in the front side above the floorplate. A second hole is cut ¾″ above the first, permitting use of the new magazine in either old or new pistols. The original magazines do not lock when inserted in the later guns because this second hole is lacking. Eliminated from the frame at the same time is an elliptical depression on either side of the original latch.

Other changes were also made. A trigger locking bar was added, a slim strip of steel engaging the sear trip lever at one end and safety lug at the other. With the safety on, the locking bar prevents the sear trip lever from moving back to engage the sear while the eccentric blocks fall of the cocking lever.

The sear was made stronger and given a greater bearing surface where it engages the sear trip lever.

Less important are 2 slide changes. A bigger ejection port is provided and given more slope at the rear. Slide serrations, while still rounded, were altered by widening the ribs and narrowing the grooves.

At about the same time, a device known as a chamber indicator appeared. This is a strip of metal yoked around the rear of the barrel with a long arm running parallel to the barrel. At the breech end it has an inward pointing tip. Thus, with a cartridge in the chamber, running the finger over the ejection port area of the barrel indicates if the gun is loaded because the chamber indicator projects slightly.

This idea, borrowed from the Luger, was not too successful, the indicator being easily broken, and was later dropped. Late production Model 1907's do not have it. It is not a part of the extraction apparatus.

Serial numbers do not start with zero for the cal. .380. Instead they begin with No. 2000 and carry the letter B.

The cal. .380 pistol weighs a couple of ounces more, has a ½″ longer barrel and proportionally greater over-all length, but is otherwise almost identical to the cal. .32. One surface difference is the groove that runs down the slide from rear to front sight.

In early 1914 still more changes were occurring. Serials in the cal. .32's had passed 100,000, while the slower-moving cal. .380 was at about No. 6000B or a little higher. Savage cal. .380 figures are a bit confusing at this point. At any rate, more than 4000 of the cal. .380's had been made.

Now, for the first time, the word Savage begins to appear on the left side of the frame. Earliest cal. .32 seen so marked is No. 101737 while the earliest cal. .380 is 7245B. This does not mean, particularly in the latter caliber, that it could not have occurred several hundred numbers earlier.

Within a matter of days, judging by serial numbers, Savage started to number breechblocks as well as frames. Hardly had they started, when they stopped. My cal. .32 No. 102404 has such a breechblock number, but No. 101737 does not. Neither does gun No. 103384. Savage, however, has a cal. .380, No. 6332B, which has the breechblock serial, but not the word Savage, while my cal. .32 has both. It is not known by the company today just why they started or stopped these.

Not more than a week or two could have passed before Savage changed the legend stamped on the slides of both calibers from start of production.

New slide legend

The new slide legend reads: "Savage Arms Co. Utica, N.Y. U.S.A. Cal. .32/Patented November 21, 1905—7.65 m.m." All of this, including caliber, is in identically sized small capital letters but set in italic sloped type rather than Roman upright letters. Change came somewhere between No. 103384 which carries the old legend and No. 108602 which has the new one. In cal. .380, pistol No. 8573B still carries the old legend, but doubtless some made later were changed.

The rounded burr-type hammer of the Savage is difficult to cock with the thumb of the firing hand.

Recognizing this, the catalog for the summer of 1914 noted that new pistols would be supplied with rounded hammer or new spur-type cocking lever.

Savage eventually offered to install spur-type hammers on all previously issued pistols for $1.50. Thus you may see spur-type hammers on pistols with low serials, and you may see round cocking levers on guns as high—or higher—than 179,350. In neither case does it mean you have a Savage rarity. About all that can be said is that pistols with the new slide legend, spur hammers, and serial number above 110,000 are likely to be genuine. Too few cal. .380's have been seen to set a number point of reference for this caliber.

Meanwhile, Savage had been contemplating the concealed hammer, grip-safety products of Colt and Smith & Wesson and decided to offer a similar weapon. This was the Model 1915. The grip safety, based on patents of Nelson, operates off the trigger locking bar, already a part of the revamped pistol. Until the grip is squeezed, the bar prevents the sear trip from moving back and engaging the sear. The regular safety also operates as before.

Made hammerless

Rear end of the striker is made smaller and covered with a shroud, making it a hammerless weapon. Also added to the Model 1915 is a hold-open device to retain the slide back when the last shot is fired. A lever on the right side of the frame above the trigger guard can be depressed to release the slide manually when the user does not wish to reload.

Savage's 1915 Summer catalog says, "Magazines for the 1907 Model are different from those for the 1915 Hammerless". Unfortunately, this was true. The 1907 magazine is not cut away for the hold-open lever and will not seat by a good ⅛".

An additional change was made in the rear sight of the Model 1915 in which the raised portion of the slide was lengthened from about 7/32" to 9/32" and the sight groove lengthened from 3/8" to 9/16". This change will be found also in some slides of regular Model 1907's, as both were produced concurrently in cals. .32 and .380.

Savage engineers at this time were working on a cal. .25 model to complete their pocket pistol series.

Roe S. Clark, Jr., of the Savage Research and Development Div., says, "I doubt very much if the cal. .25 pistol was ever offered to the public. I have heard that less than 12 were produced."

There is no question that the cal. .25 is an extremely scarce item. The picture of the factory specimen pistol supplied by Mr. Clark shows the 1917-type slide serrations, while another pictured in W. H. B. Smith's *Book of Pistols and Revolvers* has the slide serrations of the earlier 1907-1915 models.

I believe that experimentation with the cal. .25 extended over a period of at least 2 years and that some guns got out of the factory as possible samples, perhaps to check public reaction.

The Model 1915 had only a brief life of about 2 years, being dropped on introduction of the Model 1917.

Shortly before the Model 1915 bowed out, 2 changes were made in the Model 1907. The word "Savage" was dropped from the frame as was the unsatisfactory chamber indicator.

For some reason, today obscure but possibly due to the advent of World War I, the Model 1907 continued in production with the new Model 1917.

The new pistol has the familiar flared grip to give it a bit more slope and a little racier appearance. Grips are shaped to match and are screw fastened. All hammers are spur type. On the slide legend, "CO" becomes "CORP". Finally, the bright blue of the earlier Model 1907's and 1915's is replaced by a dull blue-black and the wide-spaced, round slide serrations yielded to closely-spaced flat ones. On the left side of the frame were the words: "SAVAGE 1917 MODEL".

The final Model 1907 cal. .32 and the sixth variation of the cal. .380 matched their successors in all respects except that the old-style, straighter frame was retained along with the older type grips. In finish, hammer, legend, and slide serrations they followed the Model 1917 pattern. The Model 1907's were finally discontinued late in 1919 or early in 1920. Gun No. 226825 is the highest numbered Model 1907 I've seen. There are a great many of these cal. .32 pistols in the 200,000-210,000 range, however. Cal. .380's that were noted were in the 15,000B series. In both calibers, figures include Model 1907 pistols.

After 1920, production slowed rapidly. Anti-pistol laws were being widely enacted, and people seemed to have lost interest for firearms in general and pocket pistols in particular.

From late 1920 until production of cal. .32's ceased in 1926, only about 15,600 were made. Savage lists its last cal. .32 serial as No. 256,000 although over 14,000 of these numbers were never made, leaving total cal. .32 production at 241,920.

The cal. .380's were made until 1928, but production from the end of 1920 totaled barely over 9000. Total cal. .380 production from 1913 was only 28,104, making the cal. .380 by far the scarcer of the 2 production calibers.

The Model 1915 is the scarcest in either caliber. Savage thinks a total of about 35,000 were made in both calibers, although this writer believes it to be far fewer, possibly less than 11,000, and no more than 15,000.

Model 1907 .32's

Of the cal. .32's, the Model 1907 is the most common but some of the variations, particularly the steel-gripped original and those with numbered blocks and frames, are rare.

While there are about 8 cal. .32's to every cal. .380, the former offer many more variations and tell a more complete story than do the bigger guns. Nearly new specimens also seem to be more common.

The Model 1907 cal. .380's are the most plentiful, with the Model 1917, although more were made, seemingly harder to come by. This model was once used by the Portuguese military, so some may be in Europe.

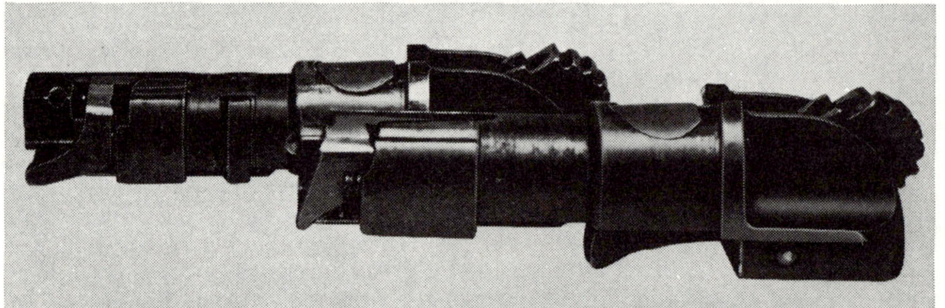

New (l.) and old breechblocks for Savage pocket pistol. Note lack of rib and smaller sear on old. New sear is better positioned and has greater bearing surface. This alteration, as can be seen, necessitated many changes in the machining of the breechblock

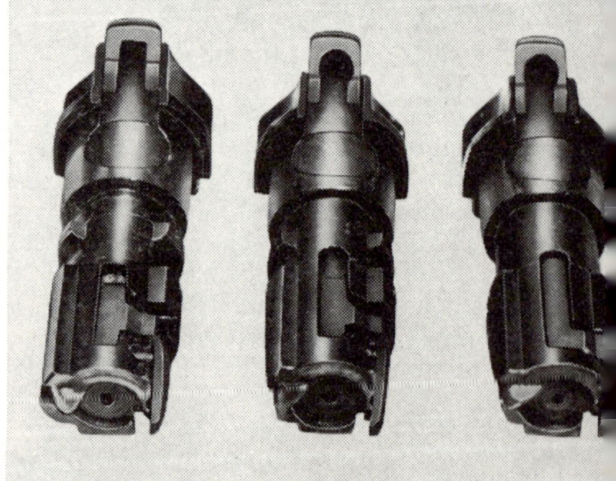

Another view of breechblocks. Old L-type sear (r.) is shown with newer types. Left front corner of final block (l.) has been altered from the center type. Constant change and improvement was characteristic of Savage pistols

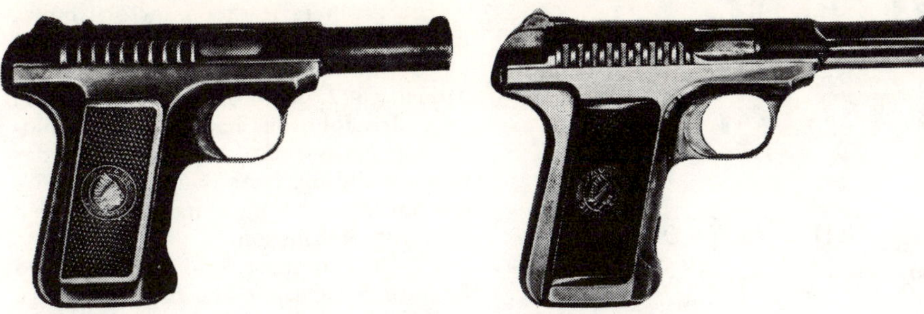

Right side of original Model 1907 (l.) and later pistol with chamber indicator shows how frame was altered and magazine latch reversed. Changes in ejection port and slide serrations can also be seen

During its existence the Savage was subjected to a number of criticisms, some relatively unfounded.

It was said to recoil more heavily than comparable guns. I have not found this to be noticeable. True, it is lighter, so a bit more recoil could be expected.

More serious is the charge that the guns would, on occasion, fire full automatic. A dirty weapon can cause this as can a weak sear spring.

However, out of the nearly 40 guns checked, some of which were fired a total of several hundred times, only one gave this trouble.

The Savage pistol cannot be carried with hammer down and chamber loaded. The striker, when uncocked, bears against the primer and a sharp blow or fall can easily fire the pistol.

Finally, Savage never got around to providing a 'magazine safety' for blocking discharge of a cartridge in the chamber when the magazine is out.

To trained shooters this is no handicap, but it may be dangerous should the gun fall into the hands of careless or inexperienced persons.

Nonetheless, the many good qualities of the Savage outweigh its shortcomings. Beautifully built, pointing naturally, and most specimens having superb trigger pulls, it has surprising accuracy.

Production of this article would not have been possible without the help of the Savage Arms Corp., and specifically O. M. Knode and Roe S. Clark, Jr., who dug through old records and checked factory samples to confirm much of the information herein.—D.K.S.

TABLE 1

MODELS 07, 15, 17
CAL. .32 PISTOL

Years	From	To	
1908-1909	1	to 10000	
1909-1910	10000	20000	
1910	20000	30000	
1910-1911	30000	40000	
1911-1912	40000	50000	
1912	50000	60000	
1912	60000	70000	
1912-1913	70000	80000	
1913	80000	90000	
1913-1914	90000	100000	
1914	100000	110000	
1914-1915	110000	120000	
1915	120000	125000	
1915	125000	130000	
1915-1916	130000	136520	
	136520	150000	(omitted)
1915-1916	150000	160000	
1916-1917	160000	170000	
1917	170000	180000	
1917-1919	180000	190000	
1919	190000	200000	
1919	200000	220000	
1919-1920	220000	230000	
1920	230000	240000	
1920-1922	240000	246020	
	246020	246620	(omitted)
1922 thru 1926	246621	256000	

Tables 1 and 2 were supplied by Savage Arms Corp. and give serial numbers and years of production by caliber. Table 3 is an attempt by this writer to recreate production volume by model and caliber. It is based on Tables 1 and 2 and on specimens known to exist.

TABLE 2

MODELS 07, 15, 17
CAL. .380 PISTOL

Years	From	To	
1913	2000	to 4000	
1913-1914	4000	6000	
1913-1914-1915	6000	8000	
1914-1915	8000	10000	
1915-1916	10000	12000	
1915-1916-1917-1919	12000	14000	
1919-1920	14000	16000	
1920	16000	20000	
1920-1921	20000	22000	
1920-1921-1922-1923	22000	24000	
1923-1924-1925	24000	25242	
	25243	26000	(omitted)
1925-1926-1927	26000	28000	
1927-1928	28000	29669	
	29670	29861	

TABLE 3

ESTIMATES OF MODEL PRODUCTION

(This table is based on production dates correlated as far as possible to known specimens. Some variation should be expected.)

Cal. .32

Model	Production
Model 1907 (all variations)	180,000
Model 1915	11,500
Model 1917	49,500

Cal. .380

Model	Production
Model 1907 (all variations)	10,000
Model of 1915	3,000
Model of 1917	14,100 ■

Revolving-Barrel Pepperboxes

Most collectors are familiar with the so-called pepperbox pistol, a multiple-shot transition arm between the single-shot pistol and the true revolver with its rotating cylinder holding the charges or cartridges. All the pepperboxes that I have seen were percussion-cap arms, but I have been told that several were manufactured for rimfire cartridges. Is there any record of such arms?

Answer: Yes. There are at least four or five makes of rimfire cartridge pepperboxes. The Bacon Arms Co., Norwich, Conn., made a six-shot .22 caliber revolving-barrel pepperbox. Continental Arms Co., also of Norwich, produced a five-shot .22 pepperbox. An eight-shot model in .22 caliber was made by the Rupertus Patent Pistol Manufacturing Co., Philadelphia, Pa. James Reid, Catskill, N.Y., manufactured his My Friend "knuckleduster" pepperboxes for .22, .32 and .41 rimfire cartridges.

Some collectors also classify the five-shot Remington Elliot .22 "zig-zag" pistol as a pepperbox.

Remington-Elliot .22 caliber "zig-zag" pistol.

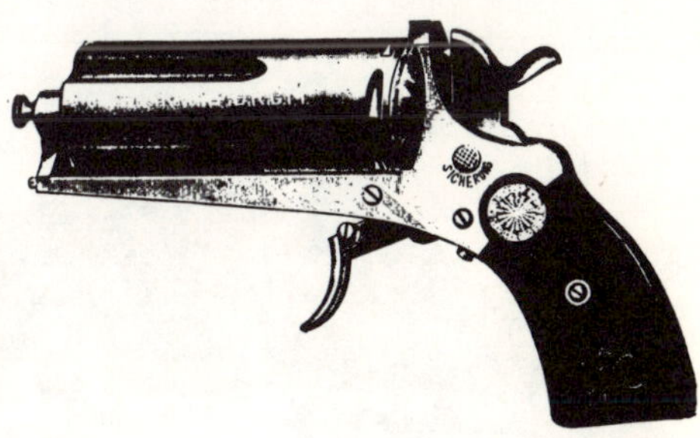

German-made pepperbox gas pistol, ca. 1912.

All of these long-obsolete handguns are pictured and described in Jack Dunlap's *American, British and Continental Pepperbox Firearms,* published in 1964.

Revolving-barrel pepperbox pistols chambered for tear gas cartridges were manufactured in Germany up to the World War I period.—A.H.

The Smith Who Wasn't With Wesson

Otis Smith worked for many famous firearms makers before he struck out on his own

By KENNETH L. COPE

OTIS Smith was one of that breed so often found in the early history of American arms making; a journeyman machinist who went from company to company in the Connecticut River Valley until he had gained enough experience to start his own business. Jenks, Ames, Colt, Sharps, Henry Aston, Charles King, Ira Johnson, Edward Savage; Otis Smith was connected with all of these makers during his lifetime.

His father, James Smith, came to America in the 1830's from Inverness, Scotland, as an attache of the British government. Apparently liking the new country, he resigned from his position and settled in Long Meadow, Mass. where he married Sabrina Jenks of the Jenks gunmaking family. Otis Smith was born Sept. 19, 1836, in Ludlow, Mass. His family moved soon afterward to Chicopee Falls, Mass., and then to Springfield, Mass. At age 17 he entered a five-year machinist apprenticeship in Springfield and, with two years left of his apprenticeship, moved to Holyoke, Mass.

After receiving his journeyman's papers in 1858, Smith took a job with the Ames firm in Chicopee Falls, Mass. Staying there only a short time, he moved to Hartford, Conn., where he worked first for Sam Colt and later for the Sharps Rifle Co. His stay in Hartford was also short as he soon moved to Bridgeport, Conn., where he worked for the Wheeler & Wilson Sewing Machine Co. His final move was made to Middletown, Conn., in 1860 to contract with Edward Savage who was making percussion revolvers for the Navy.

The portion of Middletown in which Smith lived split away from the rest of the town in 1866, becoming the town of Middlefield. Smith's factory building on the Connecticut River was located about two miles away at a place called Rockfall. This explains the confusion in recent years about just where Smith was located.

In 1862, Smith and Charles King formed a partnership to make musket locks on sub-contract. King was associated later with Smith & Wesson when they bought his 1869 patent providing for a system of simultaneous ejection for a top-break revolver. Despite persistent reports of a connection between Otis Smith and Smith & Wesson, this is the closest they ever came.

The partners leased a factory building at Rockfall which had been erected in 1845 for the manufacture of the U.S. Model 1842 pistol. Henry Aston, and later, Ira Johnson, had used the building for that purpose. Ira Johnson, owner of the building, later bought out King's interest and the partnership continued as Smith & Johnson.

In 1868, Johnson sold his interest to Edward Savage and the firm of Savage & Smith was formed. It was this firm that made the first Otis Smith revolvers.

Otis Smith received three patents in 1873, all for improvements in cartridge revolvers. The first two, both issued on Jan. 28, 1873, (Nos. 135,377 and 135,378) were for features that were never put into production. On April 15, 1873, Smith was granted patent No. 137,968 which formed the basis for his first revolvers.

The allowed claims were as follows:

1. "Combining with the hammer and cylinder a locking-lever (cylinder stop) which is raised by the hammer when drawn back, and from which the hammer escapes after the locking lever has secured the cylinder in the required position.

2. "The arrangement of a pintle within the cylinder, provided with a spring which, when free, will hold the pintle with the cylinder, combined with a bolt upon the frame, which, when the cylinder is in position, will, striking the forward end of the pintle, force that back into a seat in the frame at the rear, the bolt entering the forward end of the cylinder, the bolt and pintle forming the pivot upon which the cylinder turns."

The first feature proved very difficult to manufacture and was used on only one model. The second feature was a comparatively complicated way to hold the cylinder in a gun, but did have real advantages.

With the design thus protected, production of the first Smith revolvers began early in 1873. Although Savage & Smith were newcomers to the market, public acceptance was very good. In

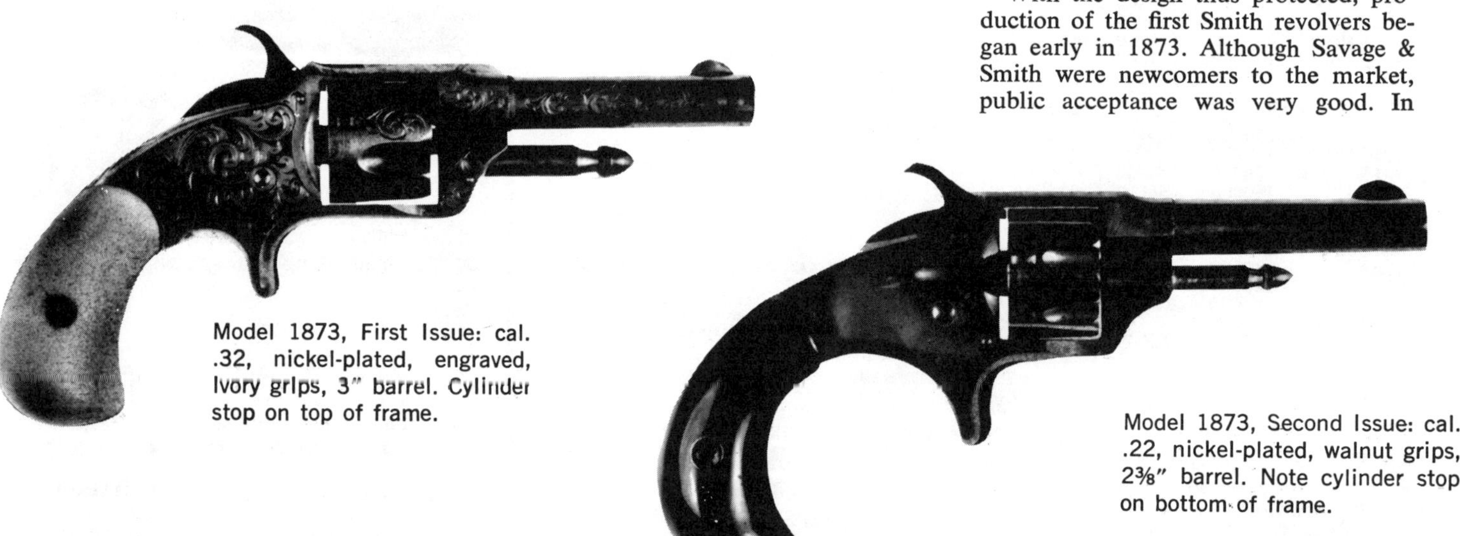

Model 1873, First Issue: cal. .32, nickel-plated, engraved, Ivory grips, 3" barrel. Cylinder stop on top of frame.

Model 1873, Second Issue: cal. .22, nickel-plated, walnut grips, 2⅜" barrel. Note cylinder stop on bottom of frame.

only six years an estimated 18,000 revolvers were sold. An unusually large number of these were finely engraved and furnished with ivory or pearl grips. Workmanship on all parts of the early revolvers was of the highest quality.

In 1879, Smith bought out Edward Savage and assumed entire control of the business. In Sept. of that year, the factory was destroyed by a fire in which Smith lost all his machinery and stock. This total loss accounts for the great difference between the early Smith revolvers and the later New Model revolvers. Forced to retool from scratch, he must have bought relatively simple machines and fixtures that were not capable of making the complex parts required for the early revolvers. The New Model revolvers were designed to be made with the minimum possible machining.

Smith installed his new machinery in rented quarters and was making revolvers again in Nov., 1880. In Dec., 1881, he bought the site of the burned out factory and erected a new, three-story, brick building. Here he continued to make revolvers and a line of hardware items such as pin vises, pliers, and wire cutters.

During the time the new factory was being built, Otis Smith's brother, John T. Smith, came to Rockfall to work for his brother. John T. Smith must have done most of the development work after his arrival, since all subsequent patents for Smith revolvers were granted in his name.

Beginning about 1884, Otis Smith began making revolvers of several types on contract for other companies. From this point on, revolvers marked with the Smith name became a smaller part of his total output.

His first important customer was the Norwich Falls Pistol Co. of Norwich, Conn., a captive shop owned entirely by Maltby, Curtiss & Co. of New York. Their production was a wide range of cheap single-action revolvers. Most of the guns were marked with trade names such as "Defiance" and "Protector". All were marketed through Maltby, Curtiss & Co. who were suppliers to the hardware trade. Surviving correspondence shows that Smith did a lively contract business with them, supplying finished guns of several types. No records exist to show the exact numbers or types, but a very large number of leftover revolvers were sold as scrap during World War II. Many were marked with Norwich Falls Pistol Co. brand names.

Smith may also have contracted directly with Maltby, Curtiss & Co. Close examination of the "Metropolitan Police" double-action revolver marked Maltby, Curtiss & Co., shows very definite Smith features. The most noticeable is the cylinder pin release which is made to appear as a hinge and thus give the gun the appearance of a top-break revolver. In this respect it is identical to the Smith New Model revolver.

In 1887, both the Norwich Falls Pistol Co. and Maltby, Curtiss & Co. went bankrupt. The latter was reorganized as Maltby, Henley & Co. and continued as a distributor of low-priced revolvers.

With their factory gone, the new company turned to Otis Smith to make the revolvers sold under the Maltby, Henley name. All Maltby, Henley & Co. revolvers examined are marked with dates of patents issued to John T. Smith and show very definite Smith construction features such as the one-piece brass barrel and frame found on some models.

As late as 1915, Smith also supplied mail order houses with two models of very cheap single-action revolvers. Made in cals. .22 and .32, they are found in many different catalogs of the period under such names as "Bull's Eye", "Royal", "Liberty" and "Champion". Retail price was as low as 90¢. None were marked with Smith's name. The only unique feature of these revolvers is a bust of George Washington found on the hard rubber grips of the cal. .22 model.

Smith remained in active control of his business until his death in 1916 at the age of 80. Revolver production stopped then, although a son-in-law continued to operate the plant, producing the hardware line. In 1923, the son-in-law sold the factory and hardware line to the M. W. Robinson Co. which continues to make many of the same items.

The following descriptions are of those revolvers marketed directly by Otis Smith. The numerous contract revolvers, while of considerable interest, are beyond the scope of this article. Much of the data comes from Otis Smith catalogs and records still in the possession of the M. W. Robinson Co. and so kindly made available by Mr. John V. C. McKinney, President. Production estimates are based on a study of serial numbers found on surviving specimens.

MODEL DESCRIPTIONS

Model 1873, First Issue:

This solid-frame, single-action revolver was the first model in production and the only one containing all features claimed in Otis Smith's April 15, 1873, patent.

Extremely complex, lock contains 18 parts including five springs. Complexity largely resulted from design of the cylinder stop which, on this model only, is located at the top of the frame. The cylinder stop is operated by a spring-loaded follower riding on a cam which extended rearward from the stop. As

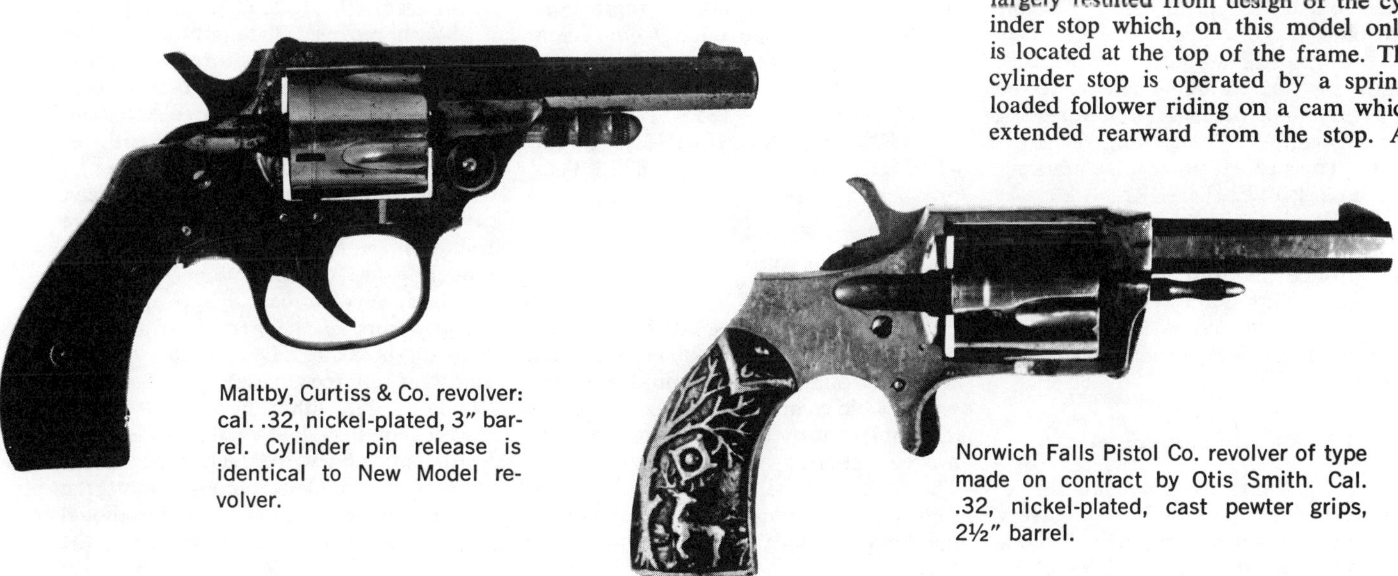

Maltby, Curtiss & Co. revolver: cal. .32, nickel-plated, 3" barrel. Cylinder pin release is identical to New Model revolver.

Norwich Falls Pistol Co. revolver of type made on contract by Otis Smith. Cal. .32, nickel-plated, cast pewter grips, 2½" barrel.

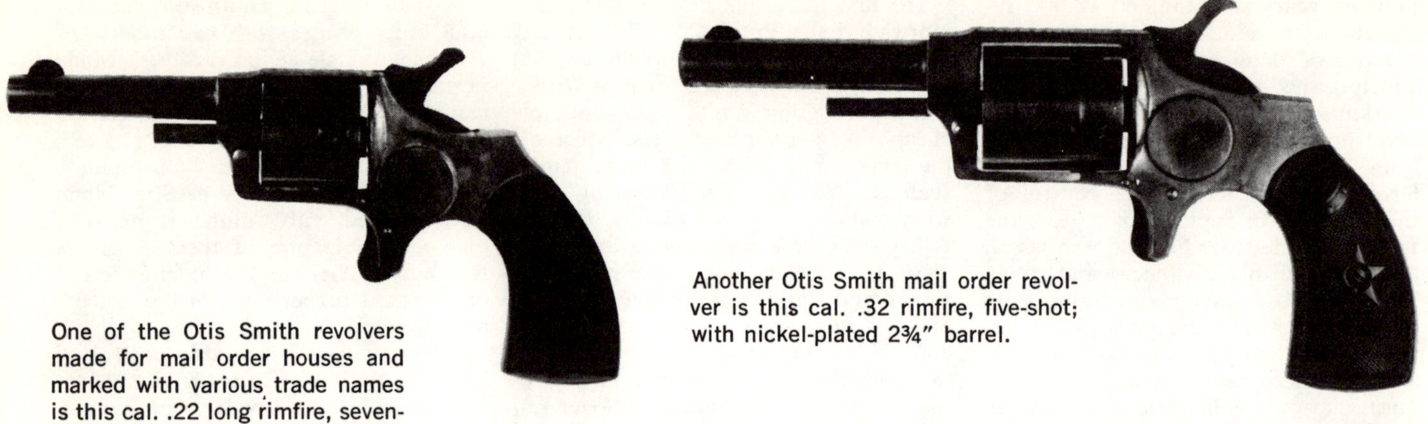

One of the Otis Smith revolvers made for mail order houses and marked with various trade names is this cal. .22 long rimfire, seven-shot, 2-5/16" barrel, nickel-plated.

Another Otis Smith mail order revolver is this cal. .32 rimfire, five-shot; with nickel-plated 2¾" barrel.

the hammer is drawn back, the follower, which extends through the right side of the hammer, forces the hardened cam downwards, thus lifting the stop out of engagement with the cylinder. When the hammer reaches its rearmost position, the follower comes off the cam, allowing the stop to be spring returned to engagement with the cylinder.

This was a unique design, but would have been difficult to manufacture as considerable extra machining and hand fitting was required compared to a more conventional design. The result, of course, was high production cost for this model.

The cylinder pin was also of unique design, requiring only a forward pull of ¼" to release the cylinder. When the pin was released, a spring forced it back into place, thus there was no loose pin to keep track of when the cylinder was out of the gun. The cylinder pin housing was used as an ejector by forcing each chamber over the housing to push out the cartridge cases.

This gun was offered in cal. .32 short rimfire only, and with a five-shot cylinder. Barrel length is 3". Available with blue, nickel or gold-washed finish, and with grips of walnut, ivory or pearl. Engraving was available and is found on a very high percentage of surviving guns. Quality of engraving is quite good. Top of frame was marked: SMITH'S PATENT APRIL 15, 1873 in two lines. Marking is in script and must have been done before the gun was finished as most guns examined have very faint markings. Serial numbers are located under left grip. Made from 1873 to 1879. Production is estimated at 12,000.

Model 1873, Second Issue:

In 1875, Smith expanded his line to include cals. .22, .38, and .41 revolvers. Since these revolvers required different size parts than the cal. .32 revolver, he took the opportunity to simplify the lock design. Cylinder stop was moved from the top of the frame to the bottom. As a result, the total number of lock parts was reduced to 11, including only three springs. Manufacturing costs would have been significantly lower with this design. In all other respects, the design is the same as the First Issue. The Second Issue was offered in small frame and large frame versions. The small frame version was made in cal. .22 long rimfire only, and with a seven-shot cylinder. Barrel length is 2⅜". Available with blue or nickel finish and with grips of walnut, pearl, or ivory. Engraving was available but is seldom encountered on this model. Top of frame was marked in block letters: SMITH'S PATENT APR. 15, 1873 No 22, in two lines. Serial numbers are located under left grip. Made from 1875 to 1879. An estimated 3,000 were produced.

The large frame version was made in cals. .38 short or .41 short rimfire, both with five-shot cylinders. Barrel length is 2-11/16". Available with the same finish and grip options as the small frame version. A high percentage of these guns are found with high quality engraving. Depending on caliber, top of frame was marked in block letters: SMITH'S PATENT APR. 15, 1873 No 38 or SMITH'S PATENT APR. 15, 1873 No 41. Made from 1875 to 1879. Total production of both calibers is estimated at 2,500.

New Model Revolver:

This single-action, solid-frame revolver without ejector was obviously made with only one thought in mind; the lowest possible manufacturing costs. It was a complete turn-around from the 1873 models, sharing nothing in common. The lock was the simplest possible design and the cylinder pin was a simple pin held in place with a crossbolt release.

The biggest cost saving, however, was in the construction of the barrel and frame. They were made from a single brass casting, including front and rear sights. Once the barrel/frame casting was machined, only the cylinder, cylinder pin and its release, lock parts, and grips had to be assembled to have a complete revolver.

The cylinder pin release is of special interest since it was deliberately made to look like a hinge, even to the extent of having a screw in the center of the thumb piece. As a result, the New Model gives the appearance of a top break revolver.

It was offered only in cal. .32 short rimfire with a five-shot cylinder. Barrel length is 3". Available in nickel finish only and with black hard rubber or pearl grips. Low quality engraving is occasionally found but the great majority are plain guns. Top of frame is marked: SMITH'S NEW MODEL. Hard rubber grips bear the initials OAS in separate letters. Serial numbers are located under the left grip. Made from 1880 to 1900, production is estimated at 30,000.

Model 1887 Revolver:

On Dec. 20, 1881, Otis A. and John T. Smith received Patent No. 251,306 which included the feature of forcing a top-break revolver to half-cock position when the barrel catch was released. On March 11, 1884, John T. Smith received Patent No. 295,064 for a design of an automatic ejecting, top-break revolver. Both of these features are found on the Model 1887 revolver. This model is a double-action, top-break revolver, very similar in appearance to many others of the period. It was the only top-break revolver made by Smith and was offered in cal. .38 Smith & Wesson only, with a five-shot cylinder. Barrel length is 3". Available in nickel finish only and with black hard rubber grips with an OAS monogram at the top. Insufficient numbers of this model have been examined to estimate the number produced. Made from 1887 to 1910. ■

Eagle 3″ flask that accompanied a Sharps Six Shooter in the original box

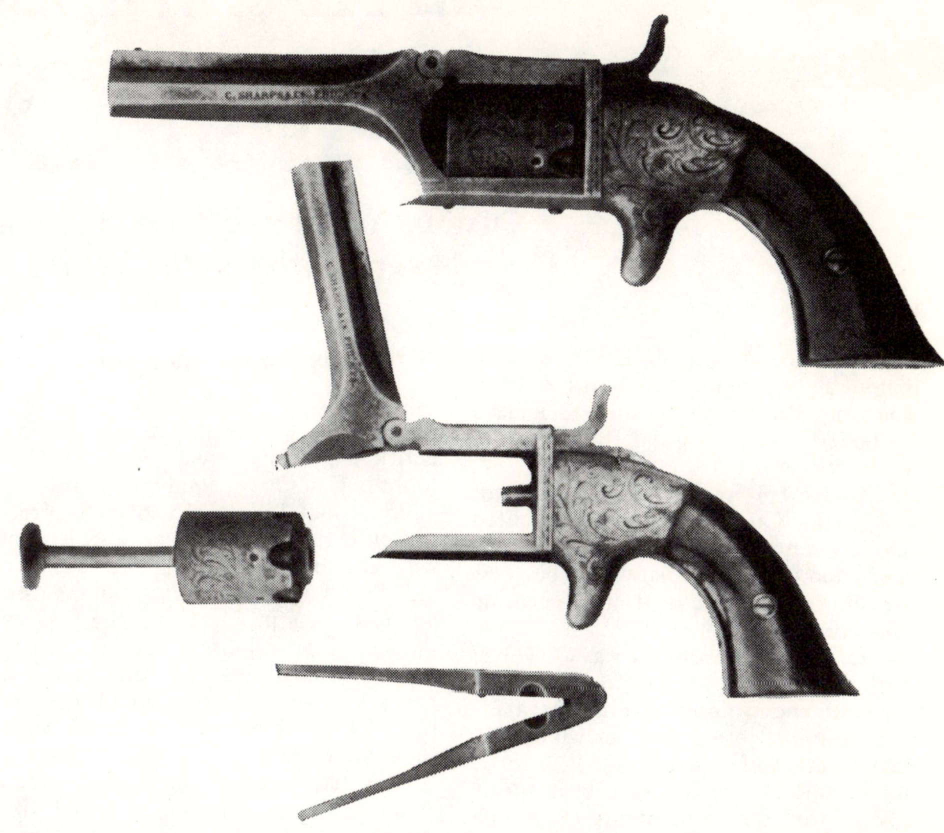

Sharps Six Shooter assembled, and broken for loading. Single-cavity brass bullet mold seen below guns was part of equipment in original box. Loading tool is shown partially inserted in cylinder

By HARRY C. KNODE

THE SHARPS SIX SHOOTER

POSSIBLY between 1857 and 1860, Christian Sharps of Sharps rifle fame made a percussion revolver that is little known beyond collectors of Sharps arms. This weapon was named "Sharps Six Shooter".

I have had the opportunity of examining and photographing a fine specimen of the Sharps Six Shooter. It was in the original brown cardboard box which bore no identifying label. Besides the revolver, the box holds an Eagle 3″ flask, single-cavity brass mold, and loading tool. "Directions For Use" were printed inside the box cover. This cal. .25 six-shot revolver bears serial No. 33. The frame and cylinder of this specimen are engraved and the frame was possibly at one time silver-plated. The barrel, barrel catch, cylinder, trigger, and hammer are blued.

Two specimens known are engraved and entirely silver-plated except the trigger and hammer which are blued. Early specimens were marked in tiny letters on top of the barrel rib "C. SHARPS & CO. PHILA. PA". Later guns have the same markings, but in larger letters on the left barrel flat. Two guns known do not carry the Sharps markings on the left barrel flat, but one has a dealer's stamp. Early guns have a slot milled out of the frame over the cylinder, apparently to give greater clearance for the hammer striker, and a second screw is present on the barrel catch. Both features were eliminated on later guns.

Colt Paterson similarity

The cylinder revolving mechanism is similar to that of the Colt Paterson revolver. It has a separate ratchet which revolves the cylinder by a guide pin. Since this feature is found on early Smith & Wesson revolvers also, and the Sharps Six Shooter bears some similarity to the First Model Smith & Wesson, a theory has been put forth that the Sharps was originally intended as a cartridge arm and was later made percussion to avoid an infringement suit by Smith & Wesson. This is disputed by others. They claim the Sharps revolver was made too early to be a copy of the Smith & Wesson in any way.

The "Directions for Use" are explicit.

Push down on the end of the Barrel Spring, and then raise the Barrel at right angles with its former position. Raise the hammer slightly, and with the other hand remove the cylinder. Then charge the chambers, using no wad or patch for the balls, which should be driven below the mouths of the chambers. Use percussion caps of such size as will fit closely to the cones when pressed down. Replace the cylinder, turning it to the left until it becomes locked; then return the barrel to its place, (being sure it is down) when the arm is ready for use.

The balls should be of the softest lead, and none but full and perfect ones should be used; to make which heat the mould before casting, and keep the lead hot. Also use the best quality of powder. While carrying the arm the hammer should rest between two of the caps to avoid accident.

TO CLEAN:

Take the cylinder from the frame, wash it in warm water, dry it thoroughly and then oil it: also wipe out the barrel and oil it.

The directions named F. G. Wheeler, 229 Broadway, New York, as agent.

Research shows that approximately 1900 to 2000 of these revolvers were made. Thirty-six specimens have been located by Frank Sellars, a Sharps collector. The serial numbers range from 5 to 1888. ■

SMITH & WESSON
EVASIONS

Part 1

Curious revolvers that successfully circumvented the Rollin White patent

By Lewis Winant

OF all the peculiar revolvers created to avoid infringement of the patent rights obtained by Smith & Wesson from Rollin White, none is as hard to believe as the original Rollin White revolver itself.

On April 3, 1855, Rollin White, of Hartford, Connecticut, was granted U. S. patents 12,648 and 12,649 for his invention of what he claimed to be "new and useful Improvements in Repeating Fire-Arms".

Mr. White's invention was a revolver with a magazine fitted in the frame back of the cylinder. This magazine was described as "a box, in which cartridges are laid side by side . . . to be forced one by one sidewise by a spring . . . into the charging-tube, which stands behind and in line with one of the chambers of the cylinder". The cartridges were merely paper-wrapped containers for charges of powder and ball. Percussion caps were to provide the external priming which was almost universally used at the time. The cartridges were to be moved from the charging-tube into the cylinder by means of a "charging-piston", actuated by the hammer. Mr. White did not explain what advantage there was in having this magazine. It is not apparent that it was other than an unnecessary complication which increased the danger of accidental explosions.

Had two safeguards

Men who fired the early percussion revolvers soon learned it was possible all charges would go off simultaneously, with results possibly disabling to both gun and user. Mr. White designed two safeguards for his revolver, one to prevent accidental multiple explosions, and the other to minimize the effects of any accidental explosions which took place anyway. The first of these safeguards was an attachment to the hammer "by which in the act of falling it may close the mouth of the magazine . . . before exploding the priming, and thus protect the charges within the magazine from ignition". This device was far from foolproof. The second safeguard was "a stout metal plate" to cover the front of all cylinder chambers not in line with the barrel. This guard was provided with a recess to catch bullets from any chambers in which the charges "exploded by lateral fire or any accident". Mr. White stated that this guard in front of the cylinder should best be placed a short distance from it, "so as to leave a space . . . for the escape of the exploded powder in front of the cylinder", but Mr. White added that the guard could be made to fit "close to the front of the cylinder if a free escape for the exploded powder is provided for by leaving suitable open space in the rear". It is clear that if this device were put to the test, the results would be unpleasant if it did not work, and perhaps more unpleasant if it did.

This Rollin White gun was never put in production. As far as I can discover only one model was built and tested. In the test the operator tied the gun to a tree, fastened a cord to the trigger, and went around a corner before pulling the cord. All shots went off in unison.

There was one other claim made by Mr. White. Had it not been for this, Smith & Wesson would have had not the slightest interest in Mr. White's incredible revolver. Mr. White stated, in patent 12,648, that his invention included "extending the chambers through the rear of the cylinder for the purpose of loading them at the breech from behind".

Smith & Wesson had invented a metallic self-primed cartridge, and they were about ready to market a revolver to shoot this new cartridge. The cartridge was to be loaded in a cylinder having its chambers bored through. Mr. White's claim to patent rights for such a cylinder was of vital importance. Previously, revolver cylinders were usually enclosed at the rear of the chambers by percussion nipples.

One course open to Smith & Wesson was to ignore the Rollin White patent, proceed to manufacture and market revolvers with cylinders bored through, and prepare to contest any action Mr. White might bring. They must have felt they would have some chance of showing the White invention was utterly useless, and they must have believed they would be on firm ground in showing that a bored-through cylinder was nothing new. Regarding the novelty of a bored-through cylinder, it may be said that a revolver with such a cylinder had been patented by Hertog & Devos in Belgium, June 16, 1853, and that a pepperbox revolver, using pinfire cartridges in barrels bored through, invented by Lefaucheux in France, in 1845, was well-known and had been exhibited in the London Exhibition of 1851. George Leonard, in his 1850 pepperbox patent, U. S. No. 7493, referred to barrels "drilled and bored entirely through".

However, Messrs. Smith and Wesson, being practical men, knew they could not be sure a court would decide in their favor, even though they felt they had convincing arguments to upset White's claims to novelty. *Further, they realized that if they did demolish the Rollin White claims, they would gain no exclusive rights, but would open the way for any competitor who wished to manufacture bored-through cylinders.*

An alternative for Smith & Wesson was to attempt to arrange with Mr. White to manufacture under his patent —and then hope against hope that its vital claim would be held valid if a test became necessary.

An agreement was made

White made an agreement with Smith & Wesson to let them manufacture under his patent on a royalty basis. Smith & Wesson shrewdly inserted the provision that Mr. White would defend his patent claims against any infringement.

Soon after Smith & Wesson brought out their revolvers, other manufacturers began marketing revolvers that were clearly infringements of the Rollin White patent. The more prominent of the manufacturers who by 1862 were producing revolvers with bored-through

---

LEWIS WINANT, *East Orange, New Jersey, a member of the New Jersey Arms Collectors' Club, has authored two books on collectors' arms.*

cylinders included Allen, Warner, Prescott, and Pond. Smith & Wesson resorted to court action, climaxed by the November 1863 verdict in favor of Smith & Wesson, in the Federal Circuit Court in the District of Massachusetts.

Rollin White testified he started tests on his invention as early as April 1849, and completed four tests within a year. The court held Mr. White had not abandoned his invention, though he had waited five years to apply for a patent, and that therefore the Belgian 1853 patent could not be relied upon to destroy the novelty of Mr. White's invention. The Lefaucheux 1845 invention was ruled not to apply inasmuch as the pepperbox revolver had only a cylinder, not a cylinder with a barrel attached. That last ruling explains why certain cartridge pepperboxes were manufactured without hindrance. The Rupertus pepperbox, with its eight chambers for .22 rimfire cartridges bored completely through its revolving cylinder, was not considered as infringing the patent. The makers of the Rupertus weapon, before producing it as a pepperbox, did for a short time manufacture it as a revolver with a single directing barrel — and that was declared by Smith & Wesson to be an infringement.*

Thousands of revolvers, ruled to be violations of the Rollin White patent, were turned over to Smith & Wesson. The widespread manufacture, except by Smith & Wesson, of revolvers with cylinders bored through was effectually halted until April 3, 1869, when the Rollin White patent ran out.

* Anyone who wishes to read all the evidence and to know the process of reasoning which resulted in a decision that "the thing which constituted the subject matter of the patent" did not exist before Rollin White made it, is referred to Case No. 17,535, Smith & Wesson vs. Allen, "Federal Cases Circuit & District Courts, 1789-1880".

Decision appealed and upheld

Ethan Allen appealed the Rollin White vs. Allen case to the United States Supreme Court, where it became the case of Ethan Allen, Appellant, vs. Rollin White, Horace Smith, and Samuel B. Wesson. Less than two months before the patent expired by limitation the Supreme Court gave its judgment. The minutes of the Court for February 8, 1869, state that the decree of the Massachusetts Circuit Court was affirmed, "the court being equally divided in opinion, upon the question of affirming or reversing the decree".

Perhaps more astonishing than the fact that Mr. White obtained a patent for his remarkable revolver, is the fact that when his 14-year rights expired, he came very close to getting a seven-year extension.

Some months before the patent expiration date Rollin White applied to the Commissioner of Patents for an extension, on the ground of insufficiency of compensation. The application was rejected.

Within a week after the patent expired a "Bill for the Relief of Rollin White" was passed by both Houses of Congress, without debate, authorizing the Commissioner of Patents to reconsider. President Grant returned the bill to the Senate without approval and accompanied it with a letter written by the Chief of Ordnance, A. B. Dyer, which gave reasons for the veto. The letter stated that ". . . justice to the government and to the public forbids this patent from being renewed." It stated:

"The validity of the patent has been questioned for many years, and it is understood that it was only affirmed by the Supreme Court by a tie vote, four of the justices voting affirmatively, and an equal number negatively.

"Its renewal is urged by Rollin White upon the ground that he has not been sufficiently compensated for his invention. Rollin White has received nearly seventy-one thousand dollars as royalty. Smith & Wesson, for the years 1862—'63—'64—'65—'66—'67 and '68, returned incomes amounting in the aggregate to about one million dollars. This was derived chiefly from the manufacture of fire-arms under Rollin White's patent, that firm holding the exclusive right to manufacture under it, and being engaged almost exclusively in their manufacture.

"It is believed that the government suffered inconvenience and embarrassment enough during the war in consequence of the inability of manufacturers to use this patent, and that its further extension will operate prejudicially to its interest by compelling it to pay, to parties already well paid, a large royalty for altering its revolvers to use metallic cartridges."

The Senate returned the bill, with the President's objections, to the House of Representatives, and on June 23, 1870, the House "resolved that the bill do not pass over the veto".

One more bill (H. R. 4056) for the relief of Rollin White was reported to the House of Representatives, on February 28, 1873. This was recommitted to the Committee on Patents—and that was the end of it.

Evasions made early

Even before the Circuit Court ruled the Rollin White patent valid, some inventors had been working to produce revolvers that would fire self-primed metallic cartridges from cylinders that were not bored entirely through. As

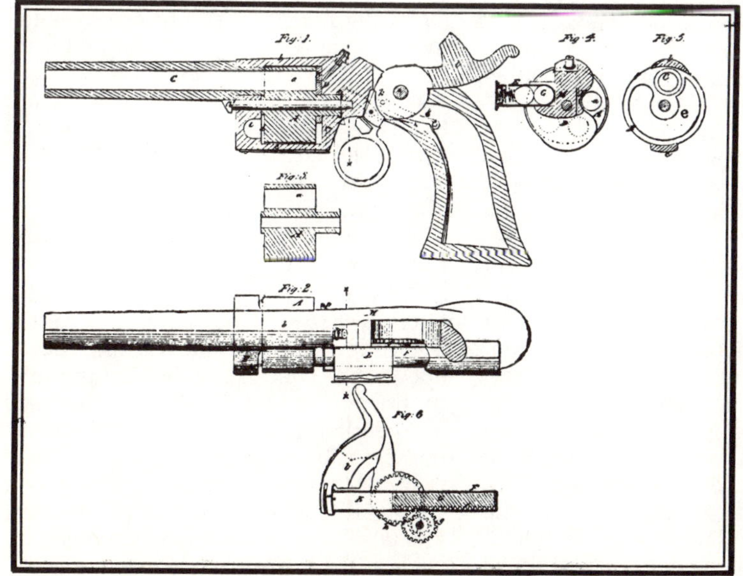

Rollin White repeating firearm, patent No. 12,648, issued April 3, 1855

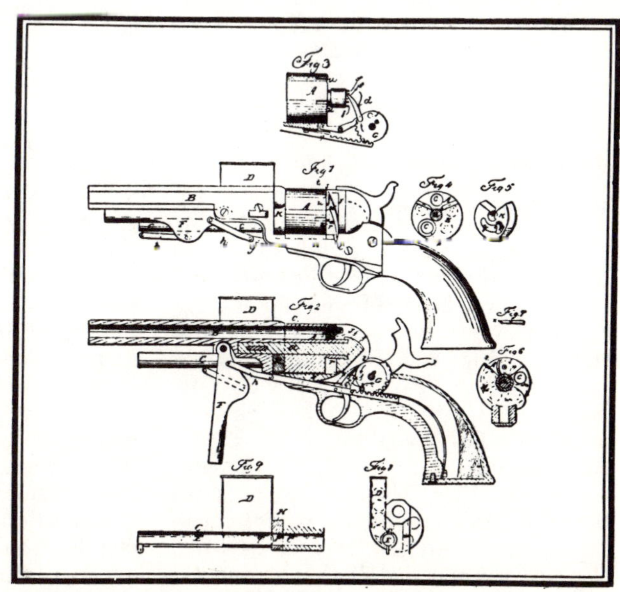

Rollin White revolver, patent No. 12,649, issued April 3, 1855

soon as the court's ruling was announced the problem of making such revolvers was attacked in earnest.

In the period from 1859 through 1866 there were 30 or more U. S. patents issued for revolvers designed to circumvent the White patent. All of these designs avoided infringement, but some did not get past the experimental stage. If there exist any revolvers made under the patents granted such inventors as M. F. Geraghty (No. 39,642), E. H. Graham (No. 40,687), R. H. Plass (No. 46,023), C. E. Sneider (No. 46,612), J. B. Doolittle (No. 54,065), those revolvers are probably models, not meant for sale.

We are concerned here only with the Smith & Wesson evasions that were manufactured for sale. Of these, some made use of the regular rimfire cartridges; others used cartridges of unconventional design, loaded from the front of the cylinder. None had a cylinder bored all the way through.

Some of the front-loading evasions were advertised as superior to revolvers with rear-loading cylinders. They were in fact superior to Smith & Wessons in their sturdy solid-frame construction, and certainly equal in accuracy and—caliber for caliber—hitting power. Further, they were free from the possibility their cylinders might be jammed by cartridge rims. With the early rear-loading revolvers it occasionally happened the hammer, when crushing the cartridge rim, would so distort it as to arrest cylinder movement.

The front-loaders were inferior to Smith & Wessons in ease and safety of reloading and their cartridges were more likely to cause injury to the shooter by exploding while being pushed into the chambers.

The Moore and the Plant front-loaders sold well. Men who carried pocket revolvers in those days, or who kept them in table drawers and under pillows, gave little thought to ease of reloading. They assumed no time would be granted for reloading if they ever stood in crucial need of a gun.

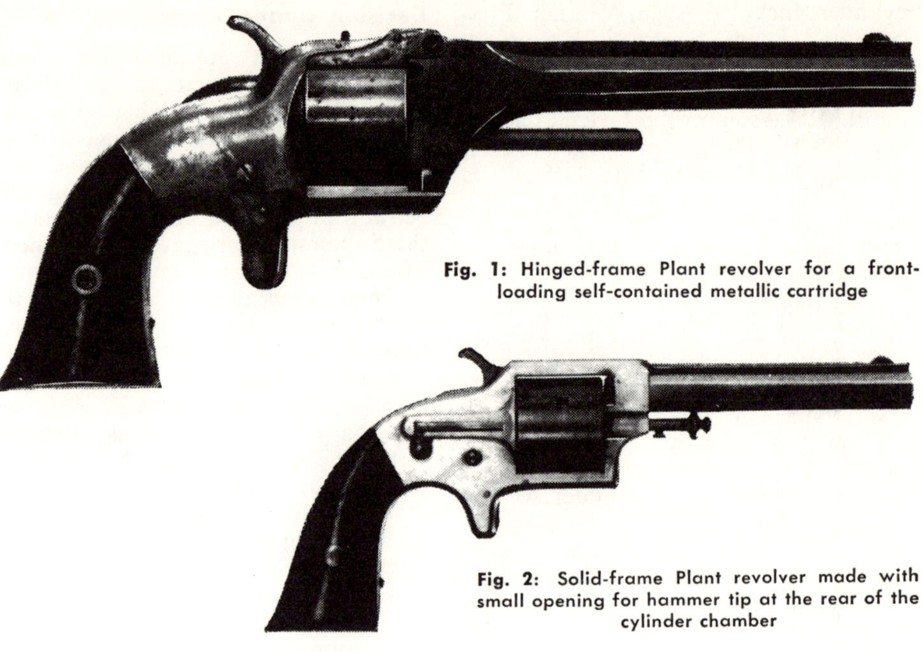

Fig. 1: Hinged-frame Plant revolver for a front-loading self-contained metallic cartridge

Fig. 2: Solid-frame Plant revolver made with small opening for hammer tip at the rear of the cylinder chamber

The Plant revolver

The first of the successful evasions to be put on the market was the scarce and little known hinged-frame Plant. An example which bears serial 102 is illustrated in Fig. 1. This gun is marked on the barrel "PLANT'S MFG. CO. NEW HAVEN CT." and on the cylinder "PATENTED JULY 12, 1859". As it has important features of the later solid-frame Plant revolvers but does not bear the 1863 date for the patent covering those features, it may be assumed the gun was made while that patent was pending. (A solid-frame 1863 Plant-type cup primer revolver which will be described later is shown in Fig 2.) The 1859 patent, 24,726, was the first patent issued for a revolver cylinder using front-loading self-contained metallic cartridges, and it was issued to Willard C. Ellis and John N. White, of Springfield, Massachusetts (John was not known to be related to Rollin). These two men were granted another patent on July 21, 1863, No. 39,318, which "simplified the construction of the cylinder", but which described the same sort of front-loading cartridges. To distinguish these cartridges from ordinary rimfires, the inventors stated, "They are made without the laterally projecting flanges commonly provided, but have flanges projecting in a rearward direction or parallel with the bores of the chambers to contain the fulminate priming". Nowadays collectors call them "hollow base" or "cup primer" cartridges.

These and other cartridges used in Smith & Wesson evasions are illustrated and described in Herschel Logan's book *Cartridges*.

The important feature of the 1859 patent was the peculiar cartridge. The important feature of the 1863 patent was the constructing of the cylinder chamber, without boring it entirely through, so that a small round opening was formed at the rear to permit the tip of the hammer to strike the interior of the hollowed base of the cartridge. This construction left at the rear of the chamber an annular ring, or shoulder, which served adequately as a recoil shield.

Ejecting rod added

A further use for this rear opening in the chamber was later discovered by Henry Reynolds, who invented an ejecting rod, U. S. patent 42,688 of May 10, 1864, which fastened to the frame back of the cylinder, and was pushed through the opening to force out fired cases.

The early cartridges had a narrow flange projecting outward at right angles at the bullet end. This flange was "simply to give a hold for removing the exploded shell" as explained in the 1859 patent. With the invention of the ejecting rod the flange on the front of the cartridge became unnecessary.

The 1863 patent taken out by Willard Ellis and John White was assigned to this same Henry Reynolds, and a reissue of this patent, No. 1528, dated August 25, 1863, was assigned to Henry Reynolds, Ebenezer H. Plant, Amzi H. Plant, and Alfred Hotchkiss. Ebenezer and Amzi were partners in Plant's Manufacturing Co., located first at Southington, Connecticut, and later in New Haven.

A detailed study will show many differences between the early .42 caliber hinged-frame Plant and the fully developed solid-frame .42 caliber Plant Army. In brief, both are six-shot, with blued octagon barrels and silver-plated bronze frames. The hinged-frame model has a rounded frame with an ejecting rod anchored under the barrel. Removing waste cases requires taking the cylinder out of the frame so the rod can be pushed through a chamber. The solid-frame model has a flat frame with the previously described Reynolds patent ejecting rod, which permits extraction of fired cases without the necessity of taking out the cylinder.

The hinged-frame Plant looks much like an outsize edition of the first Smith & Wesson .22, and it has mechanical features which will strongly remind the collector of early Smith & Wesson construction. The cylinder stop in the top of the frame, actuated by the hammer, is quite similar to the early Smith & Wesson design. So is the ratchet assembly, with the ratchet teeth on a stud projecting from the rear of the cylinder into a recess in the frame.

On the solid-frame revolver the stop and the rotating mechanisms for the cylinder have no similarity to the devices used to control the turning of the cylinder on the early model, and consequently do not resemble the Smith & Wesson construction. On this later solid-frame model the stop is located in the frame under the cylinder. The ratchet, instead of moving against teeth in a projecting stud, moves against pins inserted at the inner edge of a circular depression in the rear face of the cylinder. As the frame of the gun did not open to permit withdrawal of the cylinder, it was necessary to eliminate the protruding stud on the back of the cylinder, and thus permit removal sideways.

Only two calibers known

Solid-frame, front-loading revolvers manufactured under the patent owned by Plant's Mfg. Co. have been reported in calibers .28, .30, .36, and .42, but I am not sure they were made in other than two calibers, one about .28 and the other about .42. The guns are found with varied markings, including "PLANT'S MFG. CO." and "REYNOLDS, PLANT & HOTCHKISS" with New Haven addresses, as well as "MERWIN & BRAY" and "EAGLE ARMS CO." with New York addresses. Merwin & Bray were sales agents, rather than manufacturers. The Plant factory in New Haven burned December 8, 1866. Van Rensselaer and Satterlee both report that manufacture was probably continued after the fire by J. M. Marlin.

These various solid-frame revolvers differed in weight, caliber, barrel length, and overall dimensions, but otherwise they were alike in construction and appearance. The one in Fig. 2 will pass as a .42 Army in a photograph that does not show its size in relation to some other familiar object. Actually the gun is a .28 caliber made by Eagle Arms Co. under the Plant controlled patent. It bears both the 1859 and 1863 patent dates on the cylinder, and is marked on the barrel rib, "EAGLE ARMS CO., NEW YORK". It is 7½ inches overall. The hinged-frame Plant in Fig. 1 is 11 inches overall.

The Plants, like the later Thuer Colts, were sometimes furnished with two cylinders, one for front-loading metallic cartridges, the other for loose ammunition exploded by percussion cap ignition. The interchangeable cap-and-ball cylinders had the nipples set in a recess so the caps would be below the flat rear surface of the cylinder.

Another front-loading six-shot revolver that shoots cup primer cartridges is the Connecticut Arms Co. revolver. I believe this was made in .28 caliber only. One of these is pictured in Fig. 3. This gun, from the Herbert Green collection, is marked "CONN ARMS CO. NORFOLK CONN" on the barrel rib, and "PATENTED MAR 1st, 1864" and "PATENTED JAN 16, 1866" on the cylinder. This is sometimes called the Wood revolver. S. W. Wood, of Cornwall, New York, was the patentee.

Main feature missing

The main feature of the March 1, 1864, patent No. 41,803—and this feature constituted the only claim for patent protection asked by Mr. Wood—is missing in the actual revolver. This distinctive feature, though it probably never existed in any revolvers put on the market, was so unusual as to warrant a word of description here. The idea was to have a hammer with a nose so long it would reach almost to the front of the cylinder, and to use a metallic cartridge with its fulminate in a cannelure of the bullet, close to its base. The nose of the hammer was to drive through an aperture in the cylinder wall and strike the side of the cartridge just over the fulminate in the bullet groove. Small notches, or openings in the base of the bullet acted as vents to permit the fire from the detonated fulminate to explode the powder charge. In the actual gun, the hammer nose strikes through small openings well back in the cylinder.

The other patent, 52,105 of January 16, 1866, specifies that the mouth of each chamber have a shallow groove cut in its inner periphery, so that a cartridge with a very slightly flared front end, when pressed firmly in, will pass the extreme front edge of the cylinder and be retained by the groove. The difficulty of ejecting a cartridge so held is overcome by a "cartridge-extractor", which may be seen pivoted to the frame below the cylinder. This device acts as a lever to start expulsion of an exploded case from the mouth of the chamber.

The files of the Patent Office reveal other firearms patents granted to this same Mr. Wood, who evidently gave a lot of thought to front loading revolvers. One patent, 44,363, of September 20, 1864, covers a revolver with a barrel that could be turned aside to permit front loading of metallic cartridges, and also to permit expelling the empty cases, without removing the cylinder from the frame. The front-loading cartridges were to be tapered to the rear like the later Thuer cartridges, and to be ejected from the front of the cylinder by blows from the hammer. The circumventing of the Rollin White patent by the Thuer method also provided for driving empty cases from the chambers by hammer blows.

The Thuer Colt will be described in Part II in next month's issue. Other revolvers which were successful in circumventing the Rollin White patent, including the Moore, the National, the Slocum, the Pond, the Crispin, and the Polain, will also be described and pictured. ◆ ◆ ◆

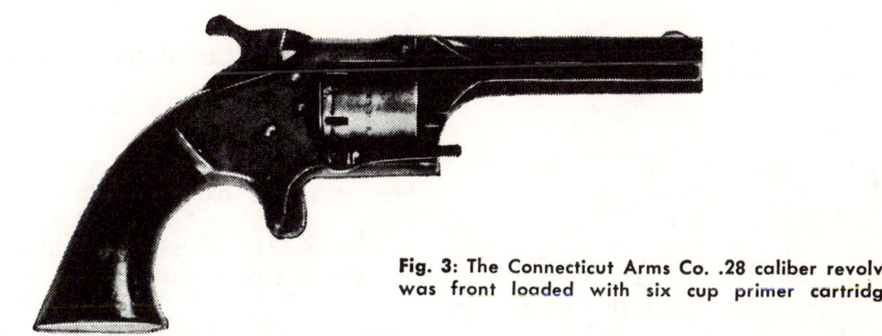

Fig. 3: The Connecticut Arms Co. .28 caliber revolver was front loaded with six cup primer cartridges

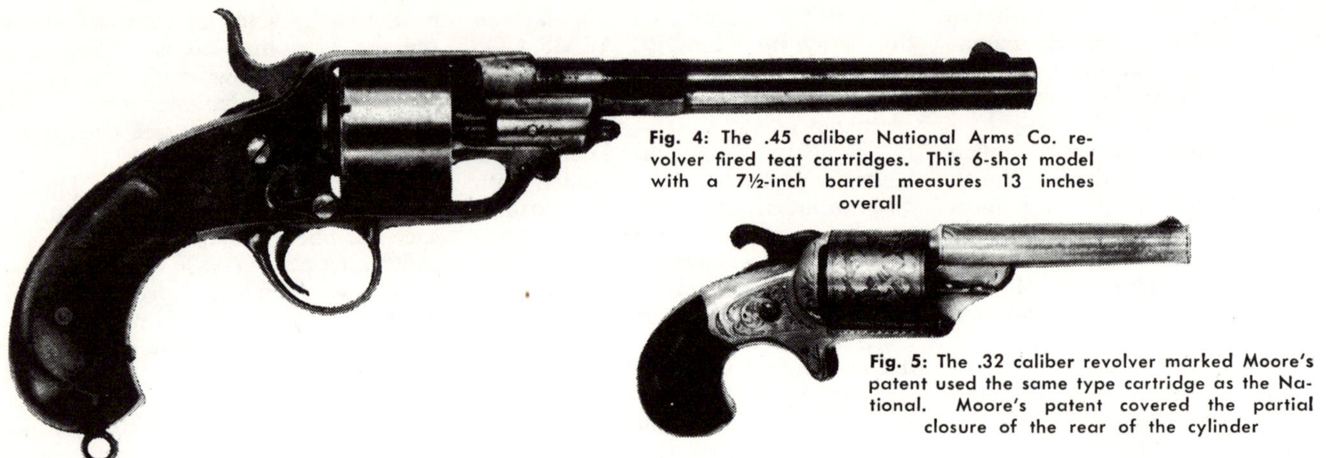

Fig. 4: The .45 caliber National Arms Co. revolver fired teat cartridges. This 6-shot model with a 7½-inch barrel measures 13 inches overall

Fig. 5: The .32 caliber revolver marked Moore's patent used the same type cartridge as the National. Moore's patent covered the partial closure of the rear of the cylinder

SMITH & WESSON EVASIONS

CONCLUSION **Curious revolvers that successfully circumvented the Rollin White Patent**

By Lewis Winant

THE front-loading revolvers that probably had the largest sales were the Moore and the National revolvers that used .32 caliber teat cartridges. The dealers in these revolvers persuaded many men not to buy the new-fangled Smith & Wesson revolvers that left the cartridge heads fully exposed at the rear. They argued speciously, but effectively, that the explosive force of the powder acted backward as well as forward, and that energy was wasted and bullet velocity reduced by having the chamber wide open at the rear, with only a weak recoil shield to back the cartridge and protect the shooter.

The teat-cartridge revolvers were made in .45 caliber as well as .32, but these large .45 caliber models are rarely found. A good example is shown in Fig. 4. This one from the Colt Museum is six-shot, 13 inches overall with a 7½-inch barrel. It is marked "NATIONAL ARMS CO., BROOKLYN, N.Y."

Two of the .32 caliber revolvers are shown in Figs. 5 and 6. The one with the elaborately chiselled cylinder is marked "MOORE'S PATENT F. A. CO., BROOKLYN, N. Y." The other, from the Arnott Millett collection, is marked like the .45 caliber model, "NATIONAL ARMS CO., BROOKLYN, N. Y".

Daniel Moore, who had previously manufactured a revolver which infringed the Smith & Wesson patent, was granted a patent for the teat-cartridge revolver on April 28, 1863, U. S. patent 38,321. This was manufactured by Moore Patent Fire Arms Co. until about 1867. Manufacture was then continued by National Arms Co. until about 1870.

Mr. Moore's 1863 patent covered the formation of the rear of the cylinder so as partially to close the chambers, preventing the use of a rear-loading cartridge but permitting the use of a front-loading cartridge having fulminate contained in a teat in the base. The patent claim included a swinging gate at the front of the cylinder. This gate, when closed, as in Fig. 5, keeps the cartridges in place in the cylinder. The later models had this gate fitted with an extension to the rear which served to start ejection of the cartridge. In Fig. 6 this combination of gate and ejector is shown open with a cartridge case partly ejected.

No patent for cartridge claimed

Mr. Moore seems to have felt that his teat cartridge was not patentable. In fact, he mentioned in his patent, "I do not claim a cartridge entered from the front into the chamber; neither do I claim a teat or projection on such case; neither do I claim a flange around the forward end of the case." On January 5, 1864, David Williamson obtained U. S. patent 41,183 which claimed the construction of a front-loading cartridge with a hemispherical rather than a flat base, and also the use of a flattened rather than a round teat. He also was granted patent 41,184, which covered a hemispherical or domed rear end for a cylinder chamber to take his new cartridge. Mr. Williamson assigned both patents to Moore's Patent Fire Arms Company. It would appear, both from the Moore patent drawing and from statements in Mr. Williamson's patent, that the earliest Moore teat-fire revolvers were chambered for flat-based front-loading cartridges with round teats. I have never seen such a gun. All the Moore and National teat-cartridge revolvers I have examined were made to use cartridges with hemispherical heads. Some of these revolvers chamber either the round or flat teat cartridges; some chamber the flat teat only.

The explosion of these cartridges resulted from the hammer's crushing the fulminate-filled teat against the anvil formed by the side of the opening through which the teat protruded. The revolvers that used flat teat cartridges only, required a little more care in loading, to be sure each cartridge was turned properly so it would be fully chambered.

Many of the Moore and National revolvers have "D. WILLIAMSON'S PATENT JAN. 5, 1864" stamped on the cylinder. Some will also have a Williamson patent date of May 17, 1864. This patent, No. 42,823, covers an improvement in the cylinder stop, whereby a round stop enters round slots between the ratchet teeth. The

---

LEWIS WINANT, *East Orange, N. J., is the author of* Pepperbox Firearms *and* Firearms Curiosa.

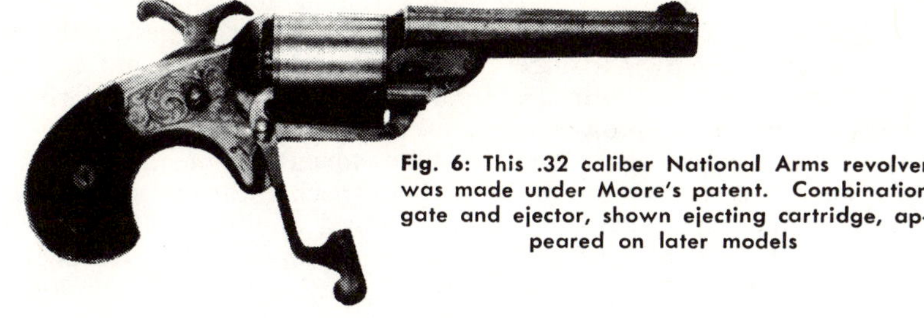

Fig. 6: This .32 caliber National Arms revolver was made under Moore's patent. Combination gate and ejector, shown ejecting cartridge, appeared on later models

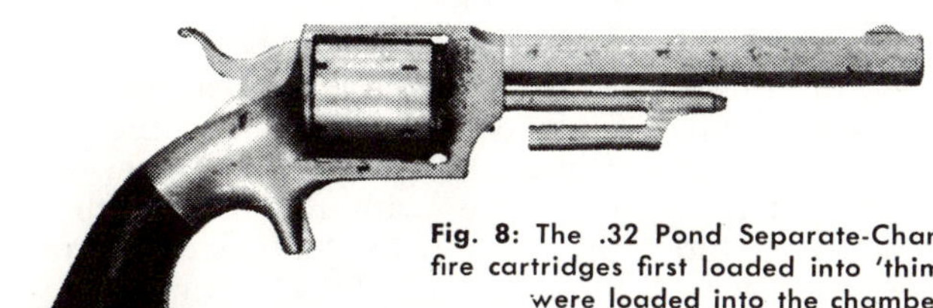

Fig. 8: The .32 Pond Separate-Chamber revolver fired rimfire cartridges first loaded into 'thimbles', then the thimbles were loaded into the chambers of the cylinder

stop on the early models was differently placed, was flat and engaged an oblong opening.

The stamping on the cylinder of the revolver shown in Fig. 6 is wholly clear, and reads, "D. WILLIAMSON'S PATENT JUNE 5—MAY 17, 1864." I wonder how many more are marked with that incorrect date. There was a January 5, but no June 5, Williamson patent.

Slocum used conventional rimfires

The first successful revolver designed to use a conventional rimfire cartridge without infringing the Smith & Wesson patent was the Slocum manufactured by Brooklyn Arms Co. One of these five-shot, .32 caliber revolvers is shown in Fig. 7. Its full name is "Slocum's Patent Side-Loading Revolver". It is marked "B. A. CO. PATENT APRIL 14TH, 1863".

The Slocum, once loaded, was a very good pocket revolver, safe, strong, and sure-fire. Testimonials of the period mentioned the "ease and certainty in loading, either in the dark or light" and the fact the gun did not require being taken apart for loading or unloading. A dexterous and practiced operator can load the gun very quickly, but a man who is "all thumbs" considers the procedure complicated.

Frank Slocum obtained his patent for this revolver April 14, 1863, U. S. patent 38,204. The invention permits the loading of rimfire cartridges sideways into a cylinder which is not open at its rear end, except for a slot for the hammer nose. Rounded troughs, open at the front only, are cut in the cylinder and fitted with sliding tubes which function as chambers for the cartridges. Loading requires the hammer be brought to half-cock, with a tube in line with a "stationary piston" which also serves as an ejecting rod. When a small catch at the rear of the cylinder is turned out of a groove in the tube, or chamber, the tube is pushed forward over the piston, a cartridge dropped sideways in the trough, and the tube drawn back. The operation can be completed in less time than it can be explained.

A discharged shell will fall out when the revolver is turned partly over with the tube pushed forward over the "piston".

Papers sent to me by John Hintlian tell of an early popularity contest, held at the Northwestern Fair of the Sanitary Commission and Soldiers Home in Chicago in 1865, which awarded the winner a gold-mounted, engraved, and inlaid Slocum revolver. That revolver, now in the collection of the Smithsonian Institution, is illustrated in Fig. 7.

The contest was to pick "the best General". The Chicago *Evening Journal* in the issue of May 22, 1865, after describing the two Slocums on exhibit as "probably the richest pistols ever made" went on to say, "The one in full gold will be in charge of a handsome young lady at the Fair to be given to the General having the greatest number of votes, each vote representing a sum of money". The Brooklyn *Daily Eagle*, on June 24, 1865, in telling about the contest at Chicago, said, "The voting was variable, Sherman being ahead until the eleventh hour, when Sheridan's friends made a sudden dash in imitation of their favorite's tactics, and carried off the prize. The final vote stood: Sherman 447; Sheridan 879". Years later in 1884 and 1885, General P. H. Sheridan served two terms as president of the National Rifle Association.

The Chicago *Merchants' Circular* of May 19, 1865, ended its account of these luxury Slocums with, "In these dangerous times, when so many have lately been assaulted in our streets after nightfall, it would be well if our citizens generally carry this efficient protection."

Times change. Beauty queens now dominate popularity contests. The papers no longer urge citizens to carry guns. And, of course, our streets are now free of violence?

Frank Slocum invented another Smith & Wesson evasion revolver, before the one shown here, but that earlier type was probably never put on the market. It was patented January 27, 1863, U. S. patent 37,551, and like the successful later model was designed to use regular rimfire cartridges, loaded sidewise in the cylinder. The chambers had hinged lids that were raised to permit loading. A solid sliding ring encircled the cylinder. This ring was used to secure the lids after the chambers were loaded.

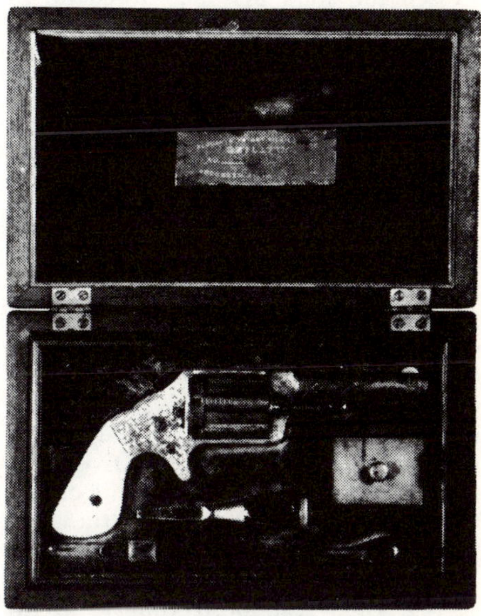

Fig. 7: The .32 caliber Slocum revolver fired rimfire cartridges loaded sideways into the cylinder. It was the first successful revolver using rimfire ammunition which did not infringe the Rollin White patent

The Slocum Patent Side-Loading Revolver was probably made in .32 caliber only.

A novel feature

Another evasion that also used regular rimfire cartridges, the Pond Separate-Chambers Revolver, was made in both .22 and .32 calibers, seven-shot and six-shot respectively. An example of a .32 is shown in Fig. 8. It is marked on the top flat of the octagon barrel "L. W. POND, WORCESTER, MASS. PAT'D SEPT 8, 1863" and on the flat next to the left "PAT'D NOV. 8, 1864". The 1863 U. S. patent, No. 39,869, was granted to John H. Vickers, and the 1864 U. S. patent, No. 44,953, to Freeman W. Hood. The 1863 patent pertains to a cylinder having chambers of sufficient diameter to enclose "lining-thimbles" which themselves held rim-fire cartridges. The thimbles were tubes "with a proper internal caliber to receive the cylindrical portions of the cartridges, and of an external circumference equal to that of the flanges of the cartridges". One of these hollow thimbles, with a cartridge pressed in up to its rim, is an easy fit in a chamber. The 1864 patent related to the ejector which was made integral with the center pin. This ejecting rod—it was called a stem —may be turned through 90 degrees. It is shown turned down, in shooting position, in Fig. 6 on page 51. In this position the chambers cannot be loaded or unloaded. When a spring-catch is pressed the stem may be turned up to the left and then, when it is lined up with a chamber, the cylindrical thimble may be drawn forward out of the chamber and over the stem. A cartridge may be dropped into the chamber and the thimble pushed back over it. If a fired case be in the thimble when drawn out of the chamber, it will be knocked out by the stem. The cylinder is, of course, not bored through, but its rear edge is pierced with notches through which the hammer nose gets through to strike a cartridge rim. There are other notches, so small they will hardly show in the photograph, located midway between the larger notches. It is only when the hammer nose rests in one of these very small notches that the stem will line up with a chamber and permit either loading or unloading.

The knob seen protruding from the butt is the end of a short screwdriver. Some Ponds have this; others haven't.

The man who had trouble loading a Slocum Side-Loading Revolver probably had more trouble loading a Pond Separate-Chambers Revolver.

A rare revolver

The scarcest of the Smith & Wesson evasions that got past the patent model stage are the Crispins. Probably very few were made. I have seen just two, both unmarked. Charles Edward Chapel's book, *The Gun Collector's Handbook of Values,* reports one marked "SMITH ARMS CO., NEW YORK CITY, CRISPIN'S PAT. OCT. 3, 1865".

An example of a Crispin, six-shot, 10½ inches overall, from the Smithsonian Institution collection, is shown in Fig. 9.

The Crispin revolver was designed to use a very odd cartridge. Silas Crispin, of New York City, received U. S. patent 50,224, on October 3, 1865, for the revolver. He received his patent for the cartridge, No. 49,237, on August 8, 1865. In this patent for the cartridge he claimed a "cartridge . . . with the fulminate placed within a projecting annular recess or rim, which is formed at a point between the ends of the cartridge". This peculiar metal cartridge, with its raised and fulminate-filled belt encircling its mid-section, is known to collectors in at least four sizes, and is found most often in a large caliber used in one late model of the Gilbert Smith carbine.

The Crispin revolver has a hinged frame and a two-part cylinder, both sections of which revolve. When the gun is opened with the barrel tipped down, the cylinder comes apart into two right-circular divisions, one being connected to the swinging barrel and the other to the frame. Each section has its own center pin. The rear section has chamber borings that match those in the front section, except that they are not bored through. When the gun is loaded, by inserting the ball ends of the cartridges in the front section of the cylinder and then closing the gun, the cartridges then have their bases seated in the rear section of the cylinder, and the cartridges then act as dowel pins. With the chambers so loaded, with the fulminate-filled rims at the junctions of the two cylinder sections, the front section of necessity turns with the rear section. The gun is single action, with the usual ratchet for revolving the cylinder. In the gun illustrated the hammer nose is long, to reach the hoop-like rim. Sometimes a firing pin, rather than a long hammer nose, was employed. Crispin suggested the use of such an "igniting rod" and Sawyer reported the existence of a Crispin revolver so equipped.

One advantage in the Crispin was that no mechanical ejector was needed for removal of fired cartridges. When the gun was opened the cartridges could easily be withdrawn with the fingers.

One major disadvantage was the danger of premature explosion when the gun was being closed if a cartridge was not properly seated.

Mr. Crispin remarked that the entirely closed rear end of the cylinder protected "the cartridges from coming in contact with the stock with which they have heretofore generally come in contact, and the objections to which are well known to all conversant with firearms". Mr. Crispin probably was thinking of cylinders jammed as a result of deformed cartridge heads.

A Belgian product

Probably the only revolver that used a pin-fire cartridge and was still able to avoid infringement of the Rollin White patent was the Polain. An example of one of two Polain revolvers in the Colt Museum at Hartford is shown in Fig. 10. This one, six-shot, 11¼ inch overall, using 12 mm. pin-fire cartridges, bears serial No. 24. It is marked "P. POLAIN BREVETE".

Prosper Polain, of Brussels, Belgium, patented his invention in the United States, March 27, 1866, patent No. 53,548. He obtained a patent in France too, and perhaps in other countries.

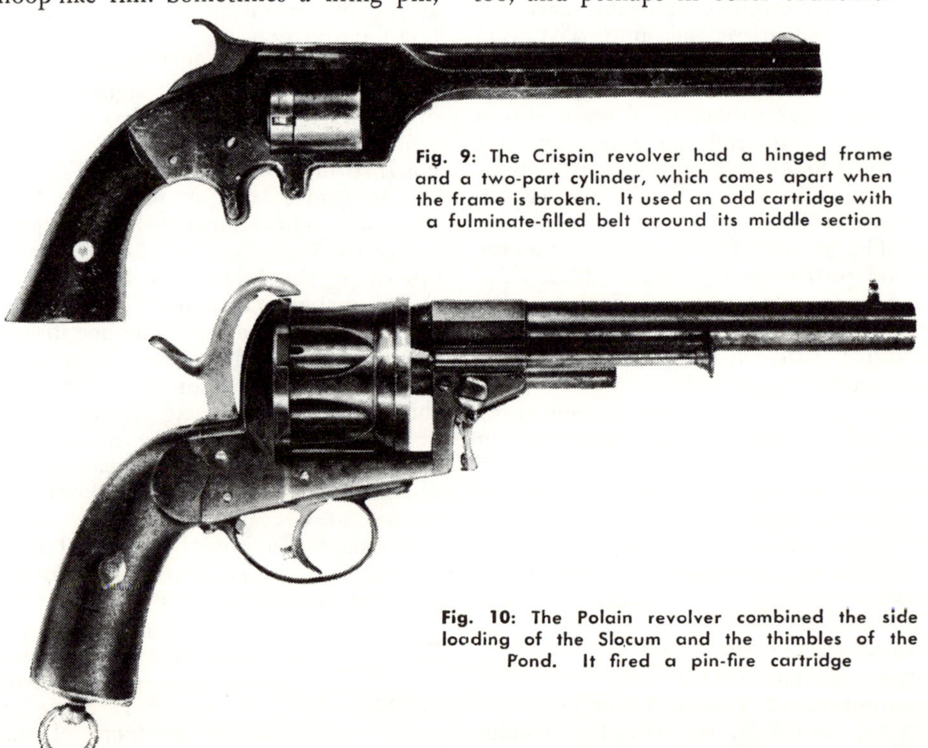

Fig. 9: The Crispin revolver had a hinged frame and a two-part cylinder, which comes apart when the frame is broken. It used an odd cartridge with a fulminate-filled belt around its middle section

Fig. 10: The Polain revolver combined the side loading of the Slocum and the thimbles of the Pond. It fired a pin-fire cartridge

The Polain invention combined the main feature of the Slocum revolver—side loading—with the main feature of the Pond—the "lining thimble". What Pond called "lining thimbles" were called "cartridge-tubes or small barrels" by Polain. In the Pond revolver these tubes are separate entities; in the Polain they are grouped in a circle and fastened at the front to a metal disc. In both guns these cylindrical, open-end tubes act as containers for conventional metallic cartridges and they are inserted into cylinder chambers, which are not bored through, by being pushed back into those chambers. The metal disc in the Polain revolver, to which these tubes are secured, is free to revolve with the cylinder, and it has holes in it corresponding to the front openings in the tubes.

Looking either at the actual gun, or at the photograph in Fig. 10, it is not at once apparent what is so unusual about the cylinder.

It will be noticed there are large grooves, shaped like pointed bullets, in the side of the cylinder. These grooves are not troughs; they are lengthwise openings cut right through the cylinder wall, wide enough to accept 12 mm. cartridges. The cartridge-tubes, with slots in their rear ends for the cartridge pins, are visible through these large cylinder openings. The raised disc to which these tubes are attached may be seen just in front of the cylinder itself.

By moving a lever, which may be seen turned down under the barrel breech, the entire barrel assembly may be drawn forward, along with the disc and the cartridge-tubes. When loading a cartridge through the side of the cylinder it is necessary to guide the cartridge pin forward into its slot in the cartridge-tube.

There is an ejecting rod under the barrel. Extraction of a fired case is made easier by the fact the cartridge pin is caught at the point of the long opening in the side of the chamber when the tubes are drawn forward.

The Polains were the last of the evasions, except for the Thuer Colts.

It has been often said, and I suppose it is true, that Samuel Colt was offered the original Rollin White invention and that he refused to have anything to do with it. It turned out that Colt made a mistake in failing to acquire the manufacturing rights, but he could hardly have been expected to back every long odds chance that paid off, "more by fortune than by merit".

A Thuer Colt is a Colt revolver that has been converted from a percussion cap weapon to a cartridge gun by the installation of a special cylinder, invented by F. Alexander Thuer and patented by him September 15, 1868, U. S. patent 82,258.

Used all-metal reloadable cartridges

The cartridge used is front-loading, tapering down slightly from the bullet to the primer end, and is loaded with the loading lever in the usual way. It is metallic, rimless, center-fire, and reloadable. The Thuer Colt revolver is not only the last of the Smith & Wesson evasions; it is the first Colt revolver to use metallic cartridges, and the first American revolver to use all-metal self-primed reloadable cartridges.

The Polain revolvers used self-primed metallic cartridges that were readily reloadable, but, though patented and sold in this country, it is believed none were manufactured here. The example shown bears Belgian proof marks.

A fine example of an 1861 Colt Navy equipped with a Thuer cylinder is shown in Fig. 11. This is from the collection of Henry Stewart.

The usual method of producing one of these patented cylinders was to turn down the rear of a percussion cylinder far enough to expose the ends of the chambers but not deep enough to interfere with normal operation of the ratchet, and fit an intricate ring, equipped with both a firing pin and an ejecting lever in place of the turned-off portion. This ring, or annular plate, is capable of lateral movement, independent of the cylinder. When it is turned to the right the firing pin will be driven by the hammer against the cartridge head in line with the barrel when the trigger is pulled. When the ring is turned to the left, snapping the hammer will cause the ejecting lever to give a sharp blow to a fired case in the chamber second to the right of the hammer. The striking end of this small ejecting lever is recessed in the center to prevent contact of the lever with the primer, so a loaded cartridge may be ejected safely.

Under the illustration of the Thuer Colt a complete set of Thuer cartridge reloading tools is shown. These are the subject of Mr. Thuer's U. S. patent 98,529, of January 4, 1870. The tool at the right is the shell holder. It has a saddle-shaped base so it may be placed partly around the center pin and back against the recoil shield when the cylinder is removed. It has a short mandrel and a longer socket, protruding from the base. Just to the left is a small threaded "capping-plug" that is screwed into the concave face of the plunger on the loading lever. Next to the left is the capping-guide. Farthest to the left is the ball-guide. Underneath is a punch, to be used for knocking out used primers, or for pushing out loaded cartridges from the socket of the shell holder. In use, with the shell holder in position (the short mandrel in line with the rammer and an empty shell placed on that short mandrel), a primer is placed in the head of the capping-guide, which has been inverted over the end of the shell. When the ramming lever is lowered the capping-plug seats the primer. After priming a supply of shells, the capping-plug is unscrewed. A shell, charged with powder, is placed in the socket of the shell holder, which has been turned so the socket will come in line with the rammer. The ball-guide is placed over the powder-loaded shell and a ball placed in it. The ball is rammed home when the loading lever is pulled down.

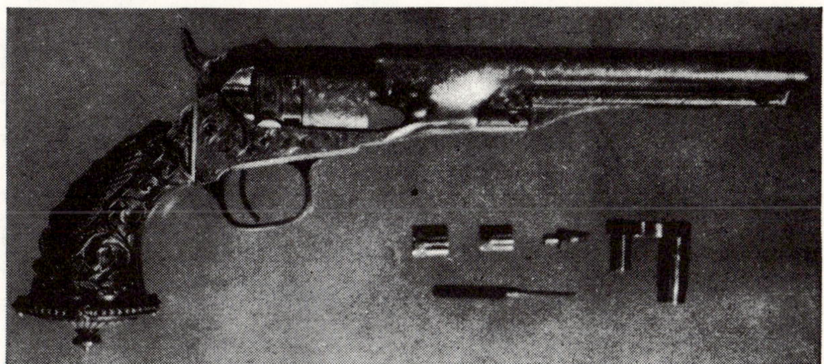

Fig. 11: Colt equipped his revolvers with Thuer cylinders, which were loaded from the front with a cartridge which tapered from the front to the rear. This is an 1861 Colt Navy so equipped

To permit proper use of the Thuer cartridge-loading apparatus, it was necessary to tap a small hole in the concave face of the rammer. James E. Serven in his book, *Colt Firearms*, mentions that it was the usual practice to deepen the groove on the right side of the barrel lug, to permit easy cartridge ejection, but no change whatever was required in a Colt percussion revolver to enable it to fire Thuer cartridges other than the removal of the percussion cap cylinder and the substitution of a proper Thuer cylinder. ◆ ◆ ◆

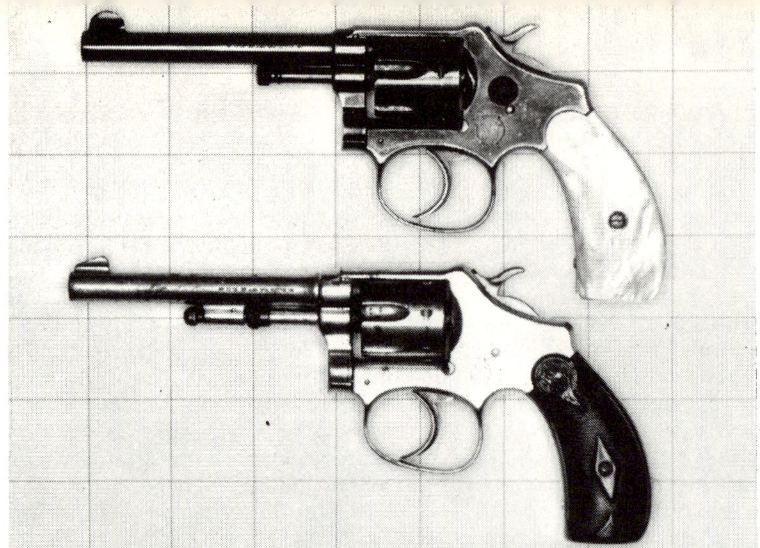

The first and second models of the S&W Ladysmith .22 revolver (from top, above)

The third model of the S&W Ladysmith

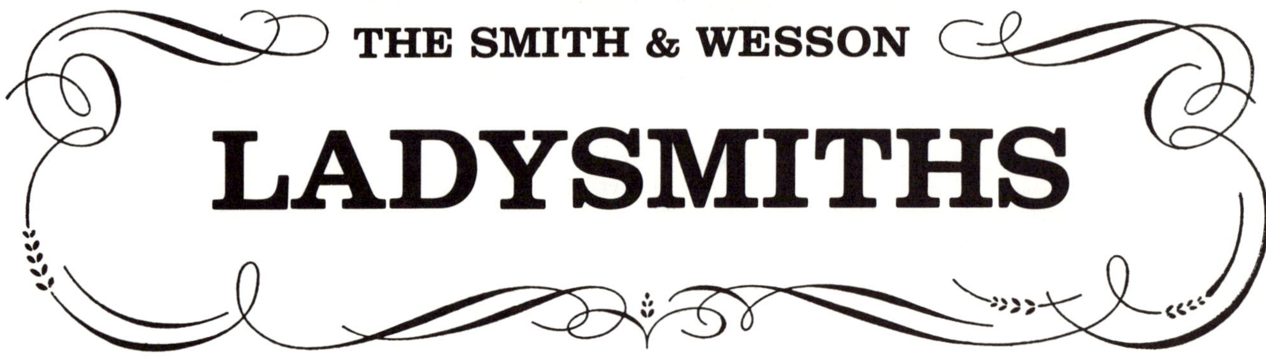

THE SMITH & WESSON LADYSMITHS

By Herschel C. Logan

Here's a little handgun that earned its name from its popularity with the fair sex

JUST what prompted Daniel Wesson, inventor of the Smith & Wesson, to design a .22 caliber revolver in 1902 is not altogether clear. Some twenty-three years had then elapsed since the firm had produced any .22 caliber multi-shot arms. Their attention during the interim had been devoted to the larger calibers.

We can but speculate at this distant date as to the reason for the production of the first model Ladysmith, a beautifully designed arm of diminutive size. Two reasons would appear to be logical. The first may have been due to an inward yearning of the aged inventor to produce a modern revolver in the same caliber with which his firm had pioneered in the field of firearms, using metallic ammunition, some forty-five years previously. The second reason could well have been a purely business one in which the firm would endeavor to win the approval of a large field of lady users. If this latter was their logic, it was to prove eminently correct.

Originally named the "Model M, .22 Hand Ejector" by the factory, this small revolver has been known for many years among collectors as the Ladysmith, mainly, we suspect, due to its popularity among the feminine sex. Some writers of the past have intimated that lady bicycle riders of the days when it was not thought unladylike to carry a pistol of some kind in their handbags, found in the new Model M an ideal weapon for their use.

Few variations

Three models of the Ladysmith were

produced in the comparatively short period of its manufacture. It is possible that slight variations may be found on the three distinct models, but any such variations are not enough to classify the arm as a separate model. Once in a long while an experimental model, upon which some custom gunsmithing has been done, does get away from the factory. If such a piece falls into the hands of a collector, he is unusual indeed if he does not immediately suspect that he has an unrecorded model when he discovers any minor variations.

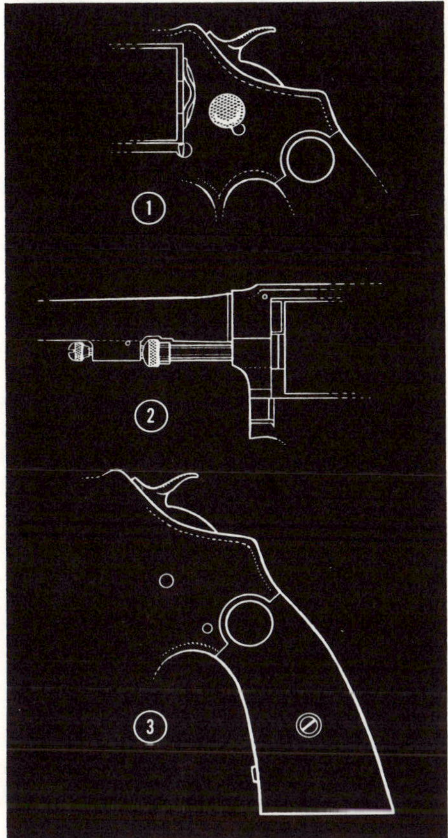

Characteristics of the three Ladysmith models. First model (1) has latch button on frame. Latch of second model (2) is at front of ejector rod lug. Third model (3) is identified by square butt

It is these slight variations in arms which cause the hair of a considerable number of collectors to turn gray, or to fall out entirely.

In order to keep this study factual, only the three models designated by the factory will be considered. Descriptions will be brief. All three models were 7-shot, double action, solid frame. Calibers were .22 short, .22 long, and .22 long rifle. In their 1912 catalog the factory recommends the use of the .22 S&W Long with 5 grains of blackpowder and a 40-grain bullet. It should be distinctly understood that the Ladysmith is not suitable for the modern long rifle cartridge and their continued use in it is most likely to bring unhappy results.

Major points of difference between the Ladysmith models may be summed up as follows:

First Model

Patent dates: Oct. 24, 1899; Aug. 14, 1900; Oct. 8, 1901.

Rear cylinder lock. Cylinder released for side swing by a round button-shaped thumbpiece located on the left side of the frame, to the rear of the cylinder shield.

Round butt, hard rubber grips.

Barrel lengths: 2¼ inches, 3 inches, and 3½ inches.

Serial numbers 1 to 4575.

Manufactured from Feb. 1902 to 1906.

Second Model

Front and rear cylinder lock. Locking bolt in lug on under side of barrel. To unlock cylinder, pull knurled knob forward; this releases bolt from extractor rod at front end and permits the inside spring to push forward the inside pin, thereby unlocking the rear of cylinder and permitting it to be swung out at left.

Barrel lengths: 3 inches and 3½ inches only.

Serial numbers 4576 to 13950.

Manufactured from Aug. 1906 to 1911.

Third Model

Patent dates: Aug. 4, 1898; Oct. 8, 1901; Nov. 10, 1903; Feb. 6, 1906; Sept. 4, 1909.

Square type butt with plain walnut grips in which is set the gold S&W monogram.

Barrel lengths: 3 inches, 3½ inches, and the special 6-inch barrel for target shooting. Equipped with regular or target sights.

Serial numbers 13951 to 26154.

Manufactured from May 1911 to 1921.

The inside mechanism of these unique little arms is as finely and as delicately made as that of many watches.

It should be remembered that these small revolvers were not designed for rough usage, but given proper care they could, and many have, lasted for the 50 and more years since they first made their bow to m'lady fair.

Take care of it

And now a word to the wise. Lest you are tempted to take your prized Ladysmith out and use it for 'plinking', or to let some visitor to your gunroom pick it up and dry snap it for the fun of it, let it be pointed out that old springs and delicate parts do break. Today such damaged parts can only be repaired by a custom gunsmith at considerable expense, because the factory no longer has available component parts for the Ladysmiths.

After all, the Ladysmiths and many of the older arms are now collectors' items and should be treated as such. They have earned their right to retire. Few men would think of driving a 1910 automobile with the same abandonment they would a present-day model; replacement parts are far too costly. The same applies to many of the older arms. Admire and enjoy them but go easy on the rough usage!

My good friend Lucian Cary, writing in *True* magazine some years ago, tells an interesting story in connection with the little Ladysmiths. Since he spent many days at the factory securing data and interviewing the older personnel, the story is regarded by Smith & Wesson authorities as quite authentic. It goes something like this. . . .

Surprising popularity

Even though the small revolver was designed with a weather eye out for feminine appeal, it came as a distinct shock to the respected management to learn that their pet arm was being used by ladies of the oldest profession in the world. In fact, it had become quite a favorite with the fair denizens of the sporting houses. It was light weight, carried a persuasive charge, and took up but little space in their handbags or muffs.

To Joseph Wesson, who had inherited many of the old virtues from his father, Daniel Wesson, this revelation presented a serious dilemma. At last, he reasoned, there could be but one answer to the problem—stop the manufacture of the little guns. And, rightly or not, that is exactly what happened.

Thus it was that on March 10, 1921, the last third model Ladysmith (#26154) was shipped from the factory, only a few more days beyond the nineteen years during which the popular Ladysmith had been produced.

Perhaps it is just as well, for certainly their short period of manufacture has made them a choice collectors' item among arms of the past half century.

My thanks to Fred Miller, Carl Kountz, and Harmon Remmel for their kind assistance in the preparation of this study.—H. C. L.

Cartridge Dates

Judging from the number of questions on the subject that the Dope Bag answers each year, we believe that the date of first availability of specific cartridges is of interest to many shooters and collectors. Accordingly, we present here, in numerical order, a table of rifle and pistol cartridges currently available from the major U.S. manufacturers: Federal, Remington-Peters or Winchester-Western.

The introduction dates are, in some cases, approximate, as such factors as wildcats preceding factory shells, "introduction without production" and vice versa, must be taken into consideration. In a few cases, only rough estimates of first use dates could be made. Factory loaded shotshells, in various gauges and lengths, have been available for over 100 years. The 3½″ 10-ga. Magnum was introduced in 1932; the 3″ .410 in 1934. The introduction dates of the more common shotshells are difficult to determine with certainty.

In order to keep the list short, synonyms, and there are hundreds of them, are not given.

These tables, then, are not meant to show the evolution of fixed ammunition or to show an exact time when a particular round may have surfaced in similar guise, but merely to be a convenient, quick reference to what is now being made here and its first appearance in Europe or the U.S.

Cartridge	Date
.17 Rem.	1971
.218 Bee	1938
.22 Short	1857
.22 Long	1871
.22 Long Rifle	1887
.22 WRF	1890
.22 Win. Mag.	1959
.22 Win. Auto	1903
.22 Rem. Jet	1960
.22 Hornet	1930
.221 Fireball	1963
.222 Rem.	1950
.222 Rem. Mag.	1958
.22-250	1965
.223 Rem.	1963
.225 Win.	1964
.243 Win.	1955
.25 ACP	1906
.25-06 Rem.	1969
.25-20 Win.	1894
.25-35 Win.	1895
.250 Sav.	1915
.256 Win. Mag.	1961
.257 Roberts	1934
.264 Win. Mag.	1958
.270 Win.	1925
.280 Rem.	1957
.284 Win.	1963
.30 Carbine	1941
.30 Luger	1900
.30 Rem.	1906
.300 H&H Mag.	1925
.300 Sav.	1920
.300 Win. Mag.	1963
.30-'06 Sprg.	1906
.30-30 Win.	1895
.303 Brit.	1888
.303 Sav.	1899
.30-40 Krag	1892
.308 Win.	1952
.308 Norma Mag.	1960
.32 ACP	1900
.32 Short Colt	1875
.32 Long Colt	1875
.32 S&W	1878
.32 S&W Long	1896
.32 Win. Spl.	1895
.32-20 Win.	1882
.338 Win. Mag.	1958
.35 Rem.	1908
.350 Rem. Mag.	1965
.351 Win. S-L	1907
.357 Mag.	1935
.358 Win.	1955
.358 Norma Mag.	1959
.375 Win.	1978
.375 H&H Mag.	1912
.38 ACP	1900
.38 Short Colt	1875
.38 Long Colt	1875
.38 S&W	1876
.38 Spl.	1902
.38 Super	1929
.380 ACP	1908
.38-40 Win.	1878
.41 Rem. Mag.	1964
.44 Spl.	1907
.44 Rem. Mag.	1955
.444 Marlin	1964
.44-40 Win.	1873
.45 ACP	1905
.45 Auto Rim	1920
.45 Colt	1873
.45 Win. Mag.	1978
.45-70	1873
.458 Win. Mag.	1956
5 mm Rem.	1968
6 mm Rem.	1963
6.5 mm Rem. Mag.	1966
7 mm (7x57)	1892
7 mm Exp. Rem.	1979
7 mm Rem. Mag.	1962
8 mm (8x57)	1905
8 mm Rem. Mag.	1978
9 mm Luger	1903
9 mm Win. Mag.	1978

"Walking Tall" Revolver

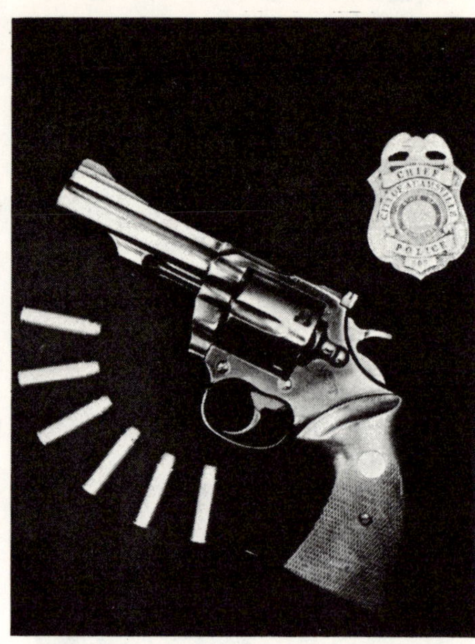

Lawman Buford Pusser's .357 Mag. revolver, a Colt Trooper Mark III, as carried while he served as sheriff of McNairy Co., Tenn.

There seems to be more data available on the guns of infamous criminals than those of famous lawmen. Surely this is not due to any lack of interest in the latter category. Could you comment on the guns of some of these latter day heroes such as Buford Pusser.

Answer: The guns of criminals are usually retained as evidence and many end up in permanent official collections where they can be viewed by the public (see *American Rifleman*, Oct. 1979, p. 26). This is not the case for the guns of retired lawmen, as these guns, unless privately owned, are usually kept within the department for continued use or, as in the case of the F.B.I., are destroyed when the agent who was issued the gun dies or retires.

While Sheriff of McNairy Co., Tenn., the celebrated Buford Pusser owned and carried a Colt Trooper Mark III with Serial No. J94734. This 4″ .357 Mag. revolver is shown together with the badge issued to Pusser in his earlier position as Chief of Police of his hometown of Adamsville, Tenn. The gun and badge are now in a private collection. — P.D.

S&W
POCKET AUTOMATIC PISTOLS

A brief history of the small pistols produced by Smith & Wesson 1913-1936

By DANIEL K. STERN

WHEN Smith & Wesson entered the pocket automatic pistol field in 1913, the future for that type of weapon looked bright. When they left it almost 24 years later, they had turned out the rarest production model pocket pistol of any major U. S. maker, the .32 S&W.

This cal. .32 ACP gun (ACP stands for Automatic Colt Pistol) and its forerunner, the cal. .35 S&W, are among the highest quality arms of their type ever built. And that was one reason why they failed to sell in quantity.

In 1909 S&W was the nation's ranking producer of top-break revolvers. They had made more than a million revolvers in pocket sizes alone but, unlike their competitors, did not offer a pocket automatic pistol. The decision was made to manufacture this type of pistol. After surveying the field S&W selected the Belgian Clement design.

Charles P. Clement's original 1907-model pistol used a small cal. 5 mm. bottlenecked cartridge with little stopping power. A revamped model of this pistol was offered in 1909 in cals. .25 and .32 ACP.

Patents assigned

By late 1910, Clement had his American patents and assigned them to Smith & Wesson. The 1909 model Clement became the basis for the new Smith & Wesson pistol.

Additional patents, redesign, and the development of the new cal. .35 S&W cartridge took nearly 3 years. It was early May 1913 before the new pistol was marketed.

The new S&W pistol had a non-removable barrel. By unlocking the trigger guard, the barrel could be lifted for breech-cleaning.

The slide did not have to be pulled back against strong spring resistance when chambering the first round. The light breechblock could be detached from the recoil spring by means of a crossbolt. This feature was a necessity because the recoil spring had to be made heavy to compensate for the light breechblock, and chambering a round against spring tension was difficult.

No magazine disconnector

The fixed rear sight, a groove in the frame, was independent of the breechblock. The grip safety on the front of the grip was meant to be operated by a single finger. A manual wheel safety in the rear of the grip replaced Clement's conventional side safety. There was no magazine disconnector mechanism.

S&W improved the over-all appearance of the Clement gun and added ½" to the barrel length. The clip held 7 rounds. They substituted steel-backed Circassian walnut panels for the rubber grips of the Clement.

Most major parts were made of nickel steel. The pistols were given S&W's lustrous blue-black finish, but nickel finish was optional. The result was a handsome pocket pistol of superior design and workmanship.

The bullet for the new cal. .35 S&W cartridge, usually called a 'half-mantle', had a cupro-nickel jacketed nose and an exposed lead bearing section with grease groove. It was thought that this design would lessen barrel wear. Except for 2 slits in the jacket which helped anchor the lead core, the nose portion is identical to that of any other round-nose automatic pistol bullet.

Remington later found that the jacket slots, apparently the patented feature of this bullet design, were unnecessary. Remington began manufacture of the new cartridge in 1912, and by August of that year had assembled the first lot. This was more than 9 months in advance of the marketing of the pistol. Winchester did not market its .35 S&W ammunition until 1914. Other headstamps found include Peters and U. S. Cartridge Co. Some ammunition was produced with soft-point bullets.

The new cartridge was not a true cal. .35. Standard bullet diameter was .320", compared with .312" for the .32 ACP. The .35 S&W cartridge will not chamber in cal. .32 ACP pistols, although the .32 cartridge will chamber in the .35.

The extractor groove of the .35 S&W cartridge is about twice the width of that on the .32 ACP. Both cases carried banding rings marking bullet seating depths of about ⅛". The .32 ACP cartridge is .003" longer than the .35 S&W. The cal. .35 bullet weighed 76 grs. as compared to 71 grs. for the .32 ACP. The label on my Remington ammunition says in part: "These Smokeless Cartridges . . . are made according to the specific directions of Smith & Wesson. . . ."

Cartridge was inferior

The new cartridge was ballistically inferior to the .32 ACP. Muzzle velocity was 809 feet per second (f.p.s.), or 155 f.p.s. less than the .32 ACP. Muzzle energy was 111 foot-pounds (ft.-lbs.), or 41 ft.-lbs. less than the .32 ACP.

This was the gun and ammunition which S&W introduced in the spring of 1913. An S&W price list for February 1915 gives the retail price of the gun as $16.50. The Colt and Savage cal. .32 pistols then sold for $15. This extra 10% cost over 2 established guns was the first strike against the S&W. The .35 S&W and .32 ACP cartridges were priced the same, $18.50 per 1000. In 1917 the price of both cartridges increased to $31.50 per 1000.

Most of the claimed points of superiority proved academic. The slight extra accuracy afforded by the fixed barrel and sights failed to impress knowledgeable shooters, and the ammunition was not readily available. Dealers found that the .32 ACP cartridge would chamber and shoot in the S&W pistol, so they sold this ammunition to their customers. The recoil spring of the pistol was too weak for the .32 ACP cartridge and allowed the light breechblock to slam back too hard, battering its contents. S&W redesigned the recoil spring tunnel to hold a stronger spring.

The safeties and magazine release latch were also criticized. The finger-operated grip safety required a slight sidewise wiggle to release it so that the gun could be fired. This built-in safety precaution was a liability under emergency conditions, so Smith & Wesson removed the wiggle.

Outward changes

These internal changes did not affect outward appearance of the pistol. First outward change was made in the clip-release latch. The small grooved latch required a left-to-right release motion across the main axis of the pistol. The release was awkward and worked stiffly, so the clip would not be released accidentally. This cross-axis latch was changed to one which was of conventional forward-back type.

This alteration, plus a few marking changes, constitute all the outward changes made during the gun's 7½-year history. Guns with the original magazine latch are known to collectors as Type I; the others as Type II. There were some 8350 of both types produced. I have never seen any breakdown which shows how many of each type exist, but I believe the change was made about, or shortly after, gun No. 2000. Type II is much easier to find than Type I.

All marking changes occurred in Type II, so this type can be subdivided again. Originally, all markings other than patent data were on the left side of the barrel and frame. Patent dates were stamped on the slide rib. The barrel was marked ".35 S&W AUTO CTG." The left rear frame flat and grips carried the S&W trademark.

At about gun No. 6000, the trademark does not appear on the frame. Guns between the end of Type I and the removal of the trademark comprise the original Type II pieces. This largest group includes 4000 pistols or nearly half of all those that were made. It is the commonest variety.

During the 7000-series, the legend ".35 S&W AUTO CTG." was moved to

1 S&W cal. .35 pocket automatic, Type II without frame monogram. Pistol has both finger-operated grip safety and wheel safety at rear of grip. Bolt release latch is operated by pressing from left to right. Barrel pivots upward on pin at rear end

2 S&W cal. .32 pocket automatic. Wheel safety at rear of grip has been eliminated. Major change is in counter-recoil assembly, which travels to rear with breechblock on rails projecting from top of barrel, as can be seen by comparing muzzle view with cal. .35 pistol above. A change in extractor exterior has also been made

3 Cals. .35 S&W cartridge (l.) and .32 ACP cartridge. Cal. .35 cartridge has wide extractor groove, and lead protrusion that anchors core in jacket is visible

the right side of the barrel, and the words "SMITH & WESSON" in slightly larger capital letters replaced it. I do not know how many guns were so marked. The piece referred to is in the mid-7700's, but another gun with a serial number that is less than 100 units higher carries the cartridge reference in the normal left side location without the firm name. Neither has the monogram.

In the meantime, World War I had begun and Smith & Wesson became involved in military production. With the return of peace, they decided to discontinue the cal. .35 pistol. The last pistol left the factory in mid-January 1921. Remington did not discontinue the cartridge until 1937.

Tips on reloading

For those who might like to reload for their .35 S&W's, here are a few suggestions. Use .32 ACP cases, preferably fired ones. Cast the bullets hard and size them to not more than .001" larger than barrel groove diameter. Linotype metal works well. Use Ideal #308252 or similar mold. Powder charge should start at 1.9 grs. of Bullseye, or possibly less, depending on the condition of the counter-recoil spring.

Most of these springs retain their full strength, but some are weak. If gun can be cocked without releasing block, spring strength is questionable. If the weak spring cannot be replaced, powder charges must be cut. Keep the powder charge as low as possible consistent with full slide operation and good accuracy. Expand the .32 ACP case mouth for the first firing of the oversize bullet. Chamfering is a must. The bullets should be seated tightly, but seated without a crimp.

The failure of the cal. .35 pistol did not stop S&W's interest in pocket automatics. A new gun was being designed before the last cal. .35 gun had left the factory. The new design eliminated objectionable features of the old.

The new gun fired the .32 ACP cartridge. The manual safety and pivoted barrel system were discarded. The barrel was made separate from the counter-recoil mechanism. Frame and trigger guard were made integral.

The new sights were of Patridge pattern with the rear sight formed from an extrusion. The front sight extended only 1/16" above its base. Both sights were attached to the counter-recoil unit, but did not remain stationary when the gun was fired.

The breechblock and recoil spring housing recoiled together. The breechblock could still be separated from its spring, but this was no longer necessary. The gun cocks fairly easily without blocking the recoil spring. The slide rides on rails machined above the barrel. The breechblock runs on another rail on the left side of the frame. The extractor and ejector were redesigned. The ejector was shifted from the left side to the top of the block.

Lines were refined

Externally, the lines of the original cal. .35 pistol were refined, giving the new model a sleek, solid look. The cal. .32 pistol was offered in blue finish only. The left side of the slide was stamped "SMITH & WESSON". The monogram was on the left rear frame flat. Patent information, in 2 lines, was stamped along the top of the sight rib. There were 5 patents listed, as before, but the 1912 dates on the old gun were replaced with a 1916 date and a 1921 date. The right side of the slide was marked "32 AUTO CTG". The inscription "MADE IN U.S.A." appeared below the port on the frame. The new piece weighed about 25½ ozs. unloaded, about 1½ ozs. more than the cal. .35 pistol.

A little more than 3 years after the demise of the old model, the new S&W .32 automatic was ready for the market. It was expensive to produce. The old model had some 50 parts, the new model pistol had 61.

Colt .32's and .380's during this period retailed for $20.50. Because of its quality and high production cost, S&W had to price their gun at $33.50.

Manufacture began on Feb. 29, 1924, with pistol No. 1. A total of 957 was manufactured. The last factory delivery of this model pistol was made in November 1936. ■

Author's Note: Much of the information in this article was obtained from Smith & Wesson and the Remington Arms Company.

American Arms Co. Revolver

My six-shot revolver, produced by The American Arms Co., Boston, Mass., is of top-break design and appears to be cal. .32. It is of hammerless type and has a safety lever on the upper rear of the frame. On the left side behind the cylinder is a pin in an elongated slot. What is the purpose of this pin? Where can I get ammunition for this revolver? I cannot find a caliber marking on it.

Pin (arrow) is selective-fire device which can be slid forward to set gun for precise shooting.

Answer: The American Arms Co. revolver you describe was produced in cal. .32 S&W Long and .38 S&W, and apparently your gun is chambered for the .32 S&W Long cartridge. It will also fire the .32 S&W cartridge which has a shorter case than the .32 S&W Long. These cartridges as well as the .38 S&W are still produced, and are available from gun dealers.

The pin in an elongated slot is a selective-fire device. By sliding it forward, the gun is set for precise shooting. The trigger is pulled to rotate the cylinder and cock the revolver. Pressure on the trigger is then relieved, and the trigger remains to the rear so that only a short pull is required to release the hammer. With the pin to the rear, a normal long pull of the trigger without an extra pull is required. This is designed for rapid-fire use where rough accuracy would suffice.

Another revolver similar in many respects to that offered by the American Arms Co. was introduced in 1887 by Smith & Wesson. Called the New Departure Safety Hammerless revolver, this Smith & Wesson top-break arm was fired by a long pull of the trigger. Just prior to release of the hammer, there was a hesitation or stopping point of the trigger. A slight additional pressure on the trigger released the hammer, and it was therefore possible to shoot with reasonable accuracy. An advantage of this revolver was that no selective-fire device had to be worked to obtain hesitation of the trigger for precise shooting. While this revolver had rather complex lockwork, it survived until 1940, several decades after the American Arms Co. revolver had been discontinued. —L.O.

Horace Smith and Daniel Wesson began making revolvers in 1857. By 1860, their business warranted the construction of this factory on Stockbridge Street in Springfield, Mass.

Smith & Wesson Tip-Up Revolvers

By ROBERT J. NEAL

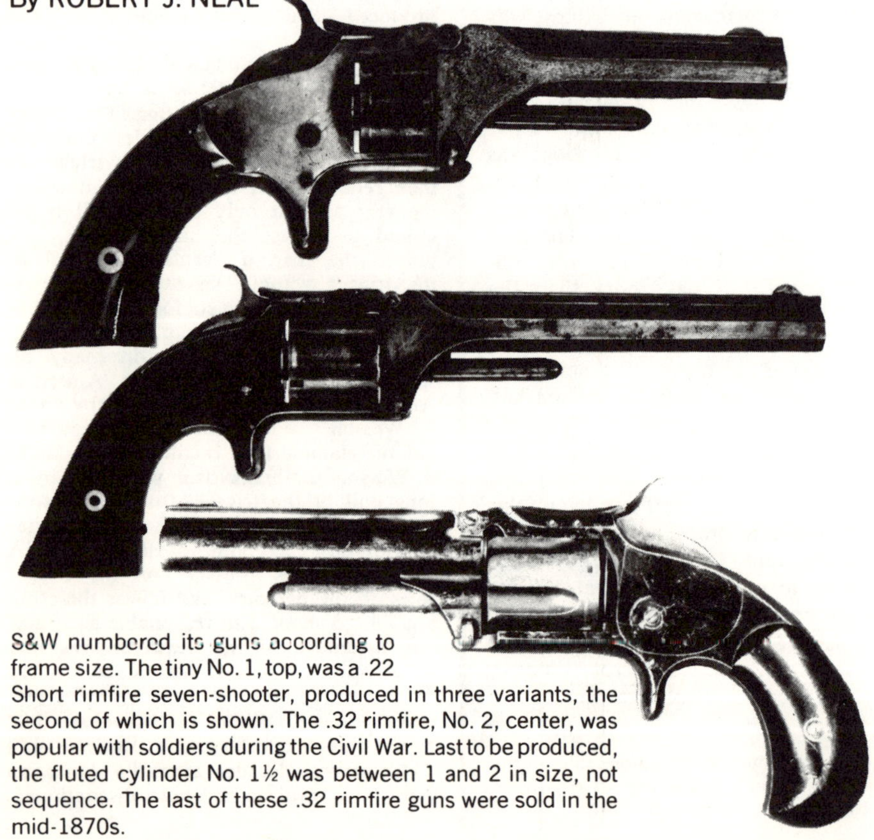

S&W numbered its guns according to frame size. The tiny No. 1, top, was a .22 Short rimfire seven-shooter, produced in three variants, the second of which is shown. The .32 rimfire, No. 2, center, was popular with soldiers during the Civil War. Last to be produced, the fluted cylinder No. 1½ was between 1 and 2 in size, not sequence. The last of these .32 rimfire guns were sold in the mid-1870s.

HORACE Smith and Daniel B. Wesson sold their first pistol on Oct. 19, 1857. It was a small brass-frame, seven-shot revolver made to fire cal. .22 rimfire cartridges. The gun's serial number was 2—its price, $12.

Though seemingly insignificant, this sale was in truth epochal, for it marked the commercial birth of a firm that remains among the foremost manufacturers of handguns in the world. It was also the first sale of a metallic cartridge-firing revolver in the form that we know today.

Smith & Wesson eventually sold thousands of these tip-up barrel No. 1-size revolvers. Following negotiations by D. B. Wesson, the company had purchased the rights to Rollin White's Patent No. 12648, of April 3, 1855, on a revolver cylinder, the chambers of which were bored completely through from end to end, allowing cartridges to be inserted into the rear. The combination of White's cylinder and the self-contained metallic cartridge developed by Wesson quickly proved superior to any of the various means devised for loading a cartridge into the front of a revolver cylinder. Protected by White's patent, S&W enjoyed a full decade during which it alone could manufacture and sell effective metallic cartridge-firing revolvers.

One problem plagued the early No. 1 S&W revolvers—bulging cartridge cases. The soft copper from which early cases were made allowed them to expand when fired and bind against the recoil plate, jamming the revolver cylinder. To resolve this difficulty, S&W made No. 1 revolvers with a total of five different recoil plates.

The earliest of these rotated with the cylinder. The last were changed to include a raised surface directly behind the base of the cartridge in firing position. The raised surface minimized bulging of case heads upon firing and permitted extra clearance for fired cases. Simultaneous improvements in case materials alleviated the problem.

A significant redesign of the No. 1 took place in May, 1860. The jointed hammer needed to properly operate the little gun's cylinder stop was replaced by a solid hammer that included a cam to unlock the cylinder as the hammer was cocked. Brass continued to be used for the frame of the Second Issue No. 1, but the cross-section was changed from oval to flat. The side plate was enlarged to provide better access to the internal mechanism.

By this time, 11,500 of the First Issue No. 1s had been built, and demand was growing. Other handgun manufacturers were limited to the production of percussion revolvers. The market now appeared for a larger, more powerful revolver that provided the clear advantages of rapid reloading and easy-to-carry ammunition.

In June, 1861, S&W introduced the No. 2 revolver, a belt-size, cal. .32 rimfire, six-shot pistol with an iron frame and barrel lengths of 4″, 5″ or 6″. The design of the No. 2 followed that of the Second Issue No. 1 very closely, and the pistol—especially the 6″ barrel version—proved extremely popular as a non-standard sidearm for military use. Spurred by the Civil War, production of both the No. 1 and No. 2 revolvers proceeded at full capacity.

Despite S&W's best efforts, by mid-1864 production was two years behind sales. Still, with high expectations for future capacity, the firm undertook the design of a smaller version of the No. 2 revolver. Production of the new model—termed No. 1½ because it fell between the No. 1 and No. 2 in size—was contracted. King & Smith of Middletown, Conn., provided 15,000 sets of parts for the No. 1½. Assembly, and finishing was done at the S&W plant in Springfield, Mass. The first No. 1½ revolvers reached the market in May, 1865.

Like the No. 2 revolvers, the No. 1½ was chambered for the .32 rimfire cartridge. When introduced, it was available only with 3½″ barrel. In April, 1866, a 4″ barrel also became available, though few were produced in this length. No. 1½ pistols had wrought-iron frames. The standard finish was blue with piano-finish rose-wood stocks. Optional nickel or half nickel-half blue, and silver or gold plate finishes were available, as were ivory or pearl stocks. Engraving could also be ordered, but is rarely encountered on this model. The barrels of No. 1½ revolvers were marked on the rib "SMITH & WESSON, SPRINGFIELD, MASS. Pat'd Apr. 3d 1855 & July 5th 1859." About serial number 15,500, the patent date "Nov. 21, 1865" was added.

A second contract to King & Smith, for some 10,000 sets of parts, was let in September, 1865, and another small order shortly thereafter. Then, when about 26,000 had been made, the No. 1½ was redesigned and a Second Issue of the pistol began.

The No. 1½, First Issue (also called the Old Model by collectors) had a design feature that made it unique among S&W tip-up revolvers. Other revolvers of this basic design have the cylinder stop mounted in the top strap and activated by the upward movement of the hammer nose upon cocking. On the Old Model 1½, the stop was mounted in the bottom of the frame and activated by a cam on the bottom of the hammer.

In 1868, the Model 1½ Second Issue (or New Model) was introduced. The New Model 1½ abandoned the bottom stop in favor of the old style. Cosmetic changes included the introduction of a fluted cylinder and change to a bird's-head grip. These same cosmetic alterations were applied to No. 1 pistols, giving a "Third Issue" of that model.

After switching to New Model production, some 1,500 Old Model barrels were found still on hand. This was too large an investment to be wasted, so a way was found to use them. The firm of Savage & Smith of Middletown was contracted to furnish 1,500 plain, non-fluted cylinders made with the stop notches over the chambers to be used in conjunction with the old barrels and New Model frames. This produced what collectors now call "Transition" Model 1½s.

Although early company correspondence indicates that there should have been enough parts to produce 1,500 of these revolvers, existing records only account for 650 being sold. All found so far fall in the serial range 27200 to 28800. Sales were recorded as follows: 50 to C.W. May on March, 27,1869, for sale in Japan; 200 to J.W. Storrs on April 19, 1869, for U.S. sales; and 400 to C.W. May on May 17, 1869, for French sales.

No. 1½ New Model pistols were produced with serial numbers starting at about 26301 and continuing to about 127,100. Standard barrel length was 3½″, with a 2½″ length becoming available in the early 1870's. The 2½″ version is by far the scarcer. The barrel rib was marked with the company name and address and the patent dates April 3, 1855, July 5, 1859, and November 21, 1865.

Standard finishes of the No. 1½ New Model were blue or nickel, with nickel the most popular. Stocks were piano-finish rosewood with ivory or pearl optional. This was one of the most popular models ever produced for engraving by both company and contract engravers. Most of those engraved were cased and a few were also gold-or silver-plated. Many were done by contract engravers, including L.D. Nimschke, doing business in New York City. Of the company engravers working during that period, Gustave Young was the best known, and many now consider him the master engraver of his time.

Between 1861 and 1868, S&W released about 4,400 No. 1, Second Issue revolvers that had minor flaws in the frame casting or in the finish. These guns were marked "2d Quality" on either barrel or frame and were sold at discount. Likewise a very few No. 1½ New Models with casting or finish flaws were marked "2d Quality" and sold. The quantity of 1½s, however, is much smaller—41 in 1870 and four in 1871—making this variant by far the rarest of all S&W tip-up revolvers.

At the beginning of the 1870s, S&W changed the direction of its effort. No longer protected by the Rollin White patents, the firm had to compete with companies long experienced in the manufacturing of large-caliber revolvers. Heavy-caliber, faster-loading guns were needed. The tip-up models could not compete.

The No. 3 revolver, a top break, auto-ejecting single-action in cal. .44 was introduced in 1870. That same year, the last No. 2 revolvers were made; most were exported for sale in France, and by 1871 the factory stocks were depleted. Savage & Smith continued to furnish parts for both No. 1 and No. 1½ pistols until mid-1874. By early 1875 remaining stocks of 1½s had all been shipped. The No. 1 lasted longest. Lots of as many as 20,000 guns were sold to jobbers in the years between 1872 and 1877. The final 1000 pistols were shipped in 1881. In 24 years, S&W made and sold just less than 350,000 of the tip-up pistols that ushered in the era of the modern cartridge revolver. ■

S&W Model 1½ Single Action

S&W Model 1½ revolver was available in wood box at 25¢ extra. Standard cardboard box was similar, having partitions and instruction label.

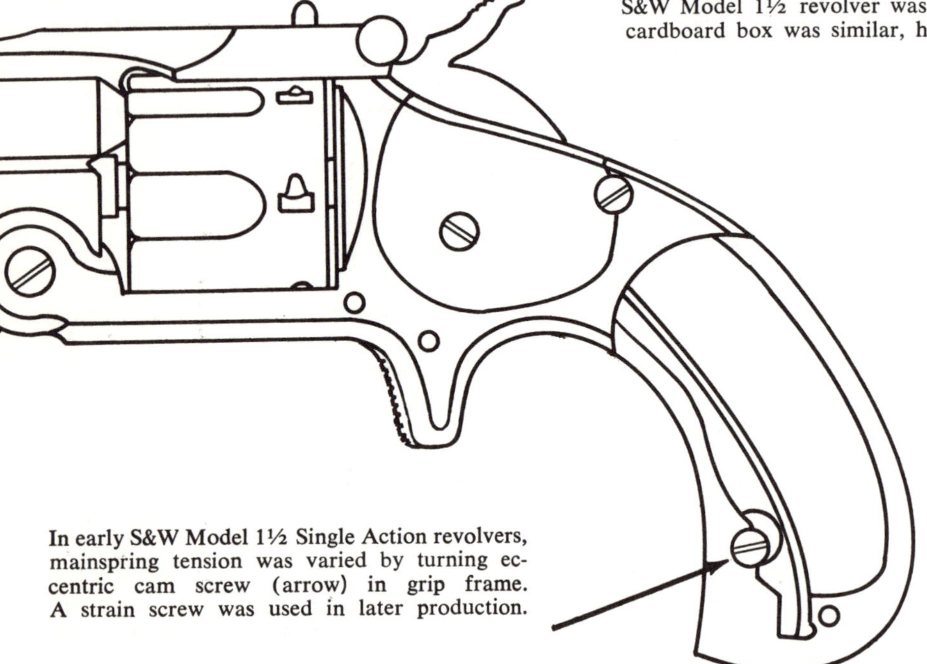

In early S&W Model 1½ Single Action revolvers, mainspring tension was varied by turning eccentric cam screw (arrow) in grip frame. A strain screw was used in later production.

A close look at the first revolver chambered for the .32 S&W cartridge

By ROY G. JINKS

INTRODUCED in March 1878, the Smith & Wesson Model 1½ Single Action revolver—originally called the New Model 32 No. 1½ Central Fire—was the first of a long line of revolvers to be chambered for the .32 S&W cartridge. A total of 97,540 were manufactured before production was discontinued in 1892.

The Model 1½ Single Action was changed very little during its period of manufacture. However, there are a few variations of interest to the collector of Smith & Wesson arms.

The most important variation occurred between serial numbers 6002 and 6786, when Smith & Wesson returned to the conventional strain screw to control tension of the mainspring. When first introduced, the Model 1½ Single Action incorporated a unique device for adjusting mainspring tension. It differed from the conventional strain screw in that it was a cam rotating in a recess in the grip frame. In making the tension adjustment, it is necessary to remove the left grip so that a screwdriver can be inserted in the slotted face of the cam. Mainspring tension is increased by turning the cam in a clockwise direction.

The second important variation is indicated by the instruction label on early boxes made for the Model 1½ Single Action revolver. Data on the label reveals that the first revolvers of this pattern were manufactured with a half-cock or safety notch on the hammer. However, I have examined many of the revolvers between serial numbers 100 and 500 and have yet to find one with this feature. It is possible that only the first 50 or 100 guns were made with the half-cock notch.

The third and least important in this series of variations is found between serial numbers 1216 and 1405 when the patent dates of Apr. 20, 1875, and Dec. 18, 1877, were added to the top strap over the cylinder. Patent No. 162,208, the one dated Apr. 20, 1875, was is-

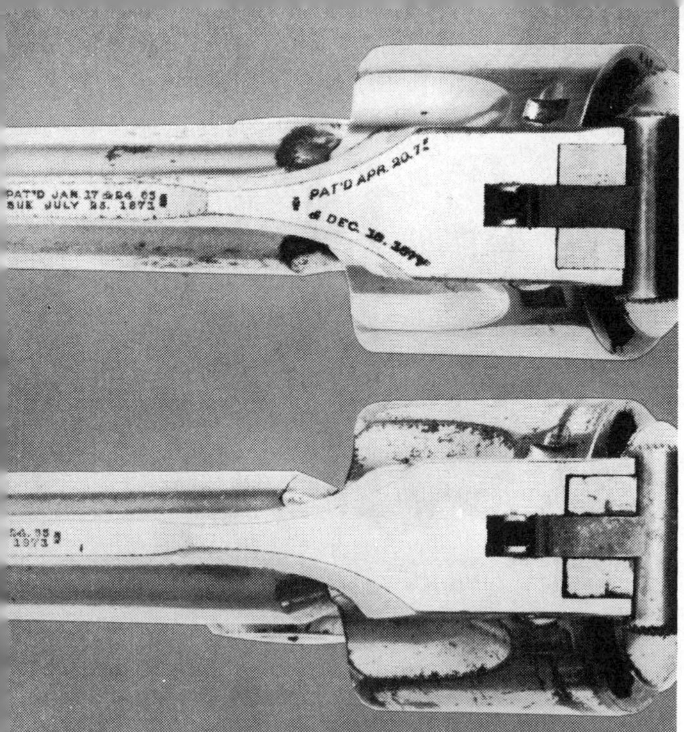

Between serial numbers 1216 and 1405, additional patent dates were stamped on top frame strap as in upper gun.

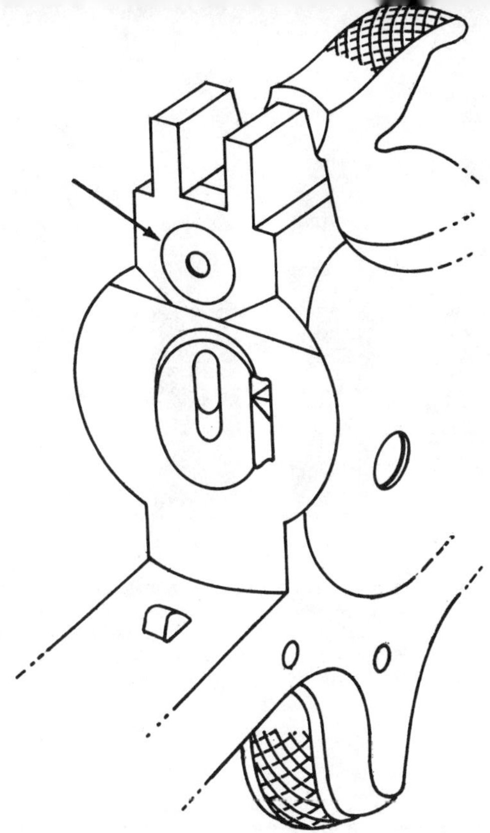

Coincident with change in extractor lifter, frame was reinforced by addition of recoil plate bushing (arrow) to back up cartridge head.

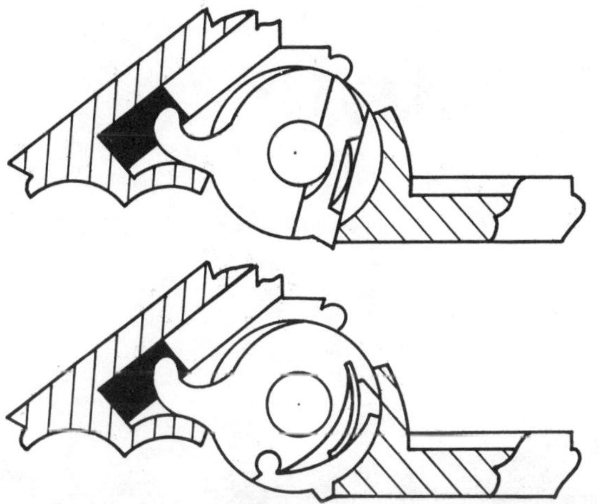

In 1880, between serial numbers 50,000 and 51,000, the extractor lifter was changed from spring-type (lower) to a more efficient sliding-bar construction.

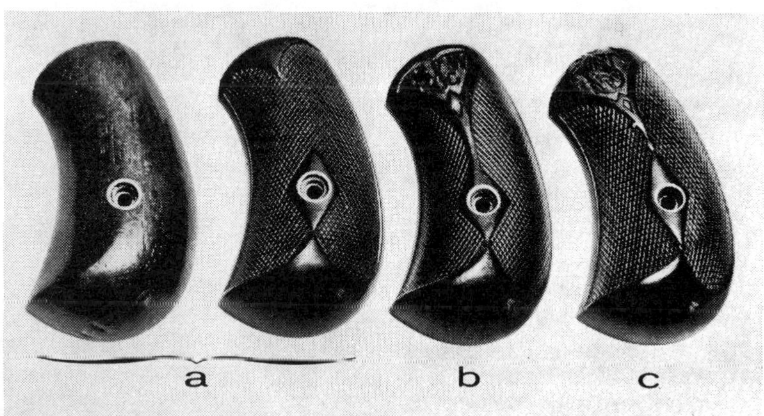

Model 1½ grip styles with approximate serial number ranges: **(a)** plain walnut and unmarked rubber (1-15,000); **(b)** marked black rubber (15,000-29,000); **(c)** monogrammed mottled red or black (29,000-97,540).

sued to Rollin White. It covered a simultaneous extraction system different from that incorporated in this revolver. The more important patent, No. 198,-228, was granted to D. B. Wesson and J. H. Bullard on Dec. 18, 1877. It covered the rebounding hammer introduced first on this model.

After changing from the cam to the conventional mainspring strain screw, Smith & Wesson made no additional improvements for 2 years. In 1880 the last changes were made in the Model 1½ Single Action. Between serial numbers 50,000 and 51,000, the extractor lifter was changed from a spring lever to a slide bar, the latter system being covered by Patent No. 227,481 issued to J. H. Bullard on May 11, 1880. These 2 types of extractor lifter are illustrated above. At this time, the frame was strengthened by addition of a steel bushing or recoil plate directly behind the cartridge to be exploded.

The grip design used on this model was covered by 2 patents, No. 10,421 and No. 10,423, issued to D. B. Wesson on Jan. 29, 1878. Although the grip design did not change throughout the course of manufacture, the styles of grip did (see illustration).

From 1878 until 1887, the Model 1½ Single Action was available in either blue or nickel finish, and with 3″ or 3½″ barrel. In 1887 Smith & Wesson's catalogs listed it as being available with 3″, 3½″, 6″, 8″, and 10″ barrels. The latter 2 barrel lengths are uncommon and it is not known how many were manufactured. In its Apr. 1, 1888, model circular and price list, Smith & Wesson listed the Model 1½ Single Action in blue or nickel finish with 3″ and 3½″ barrels for $10; 6″ barrel for $11; 8″ barrel for $11.50; and 10″ barrel for $12.

Long considered one of the least glamorous pocket revolvers, the Smith & Wesson Model 1½ Single Action is nevertheless a unique addition to a small-arms collection. ■

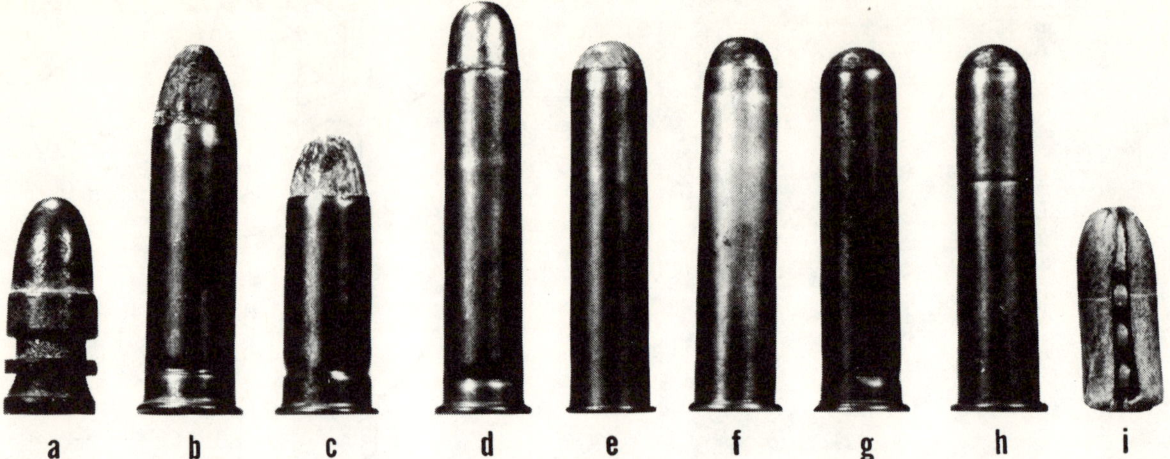

Fig. 1: a) Cal. .58 Shaler sectional bullet, as used in Civil War; b) .50-70 rifle cartridge, inside primed with iron cup, Frankford Arsenal 1868 (FA for Frankford Arsenal); c) .50-45 Cadet cartridge, also for Remington Navy Carbine and M1869 pistol. Inside primed, iron cup, FA1869; d) .45 carbine cartridge, inside (cup) primed, FA1878; e) .45 multiball cartridge, Phoenix Cartridge Co.; f) .45 Guard cartridge, FA1886; g) .45 multiball cartridge, FA1878; h) .45 multiball cartridge, Union Metallic Cartridge Co. contract; i) Paper-cased multiple projectile

Springfield Breech-Loading Pistol

By Col. B. R. Lewis, USA

During the early years of Springfield and Harpers Ferry Armories, several types of little-known, oddly-marked, or otherwise controversial arms were produced in small quantities. That there should be inadequate information or misunderstanding about arms of that period is not surprising. Entries in the shop records were made in quite broad terms, various items being lumped together. Although the records showed work done for the account of the War Department, many of these arms were distributed to the Navy, Indian Commissioners, and other agencies.

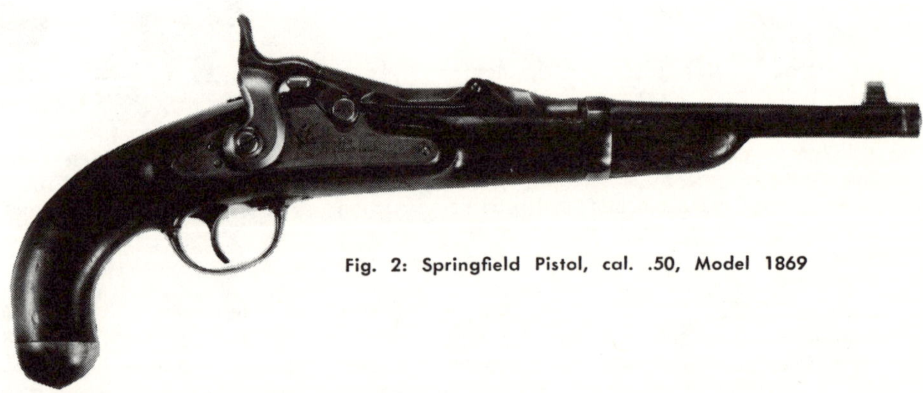

Fig. 2: Springfield Pistol, cal. .50, Model 1869

It seems strange, however, that there should be disagreement about the very existence of a Service arm made at Springfield Armory after the Civil War. The item is the single shot, breech-loading pistol made there in 1869. While this handgun never went beyond Service tests, it none the less was a legitimate U. S. martial pistol, made with Ordnance Board sanction. Thus it is at least as worthy of a place in the list as the so-called Model 1818 pistol, which

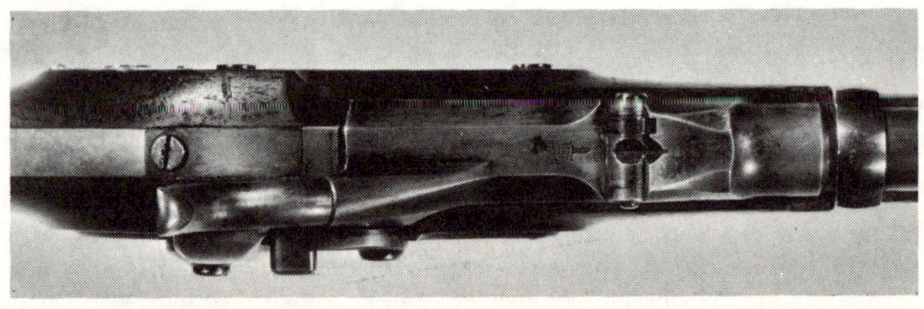

Fig. 3: Top view of Springfield Pistol, cal. .50, Model 1869

was made through a misunderstanding, never authorized by the Ordnance Office for use, never issued to troops, and eventually all sold unused as surplus. Certain recognized and usually reliable arms authorities have stated that the Model 1869 pistol never existed and that reported specimens are fakes. I would like to explain something about the background of the Springfield 1869 pistol and also what brought about the doubt in the minds of collectors.

While the old .69 caliber smoothbore musket was in use, the buck-and-ball cartridge was popular for use in wooded country or wherever the target was indefinite. In fact, buck-and-ball was considered the standard musket load at the time of the War of 1812, though both ball and buckshot cartridges were also provided. When the caliber was reduced to .58, that bore proved too small to contain a stack of three buckshot of effective size. During the Civil War, the Shaler sectional bullet was used to fill the need for a scatter load. (Fig. 1*a*)

After the war, interest continued in developing a practical multiball cartridge, particularly for Cavalry handguns. One element of the Ordnance Board felt that, as it was impossible to load more than one ball in the converted muzzle-loading revolvers then in use, it might be better to adapt the new Allin breech-loading system to a single-shot pistol, which could handle a longer cartridge of larger caliber. Accordingly, Springfield Armory was directed to design a .50 caliber pistol to use the .50-45-350 Cadet cartridge loaded with three or four pellets. It was believed the average trooper would have a better chance of hitting an Indian from horseback with such a load than with the conventional revolver bullet. Fig. 1*i* shows the sort of bullet used, though complete specimens of the cartridges tested are not known to me. This was very likely loaded into a cup-primed Cadet case like that illustrated.

The Armory produced some of these pistols in 1869, following the general style and hardware design of the percussion model of 1842. Just how many were made I cannot say, but a very reliable source, the late Major Jerome Clark, once told me he had talked with a lieutenant of Cavalry in whose troop the pistols were given their official Service test. The officer said that 25 were supplied for that purpose. Two of the pistols are still at Springfield, in the Armory Museum. One is shown in Fig. 2. It is dated 1869 on the breech (Fig. 3) and has a special lock, somewhat smaller than the usual rifle size. At any rate, the results of the tests were negative and no more of the pistols were made. I have found no hint as to what became of the others.

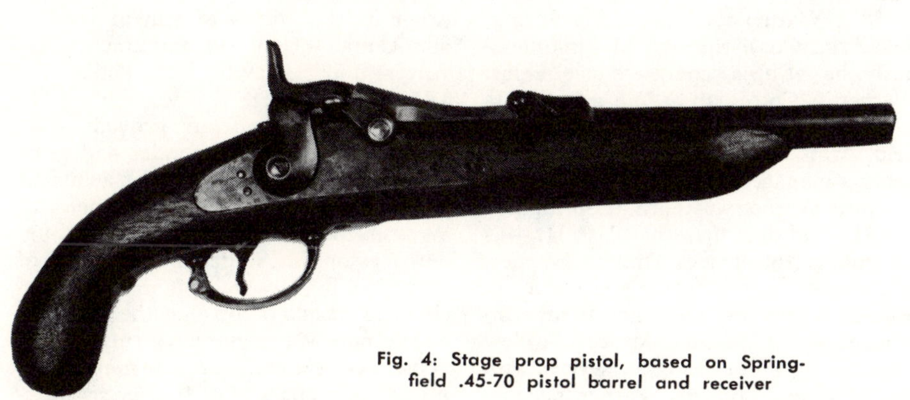

Fig. 4: Stage prop pistol, based on Springfield .45-70 pistol barrel and receiver

The idea of a multishot cartridge was not dead, however. A Lieutenant Wright was an enthusiast for a buck load or the equivalent for the Cavalry handgun. In the mid-1870's he started to promote the idea of such a cartridge for the Service revolver (then mostly Colt or S&W single-actions). He was finally authorized to make for test a special Colt revolver with an extra-long cylinder to take the .45-70 cartridge case. This case he planned to load with various multiball combinations for evaluation. In the tests he shot three-ball loads with various charges, and also tried a standard carbine cartridge for comparison. This cartridge (Fig. 1*d*) varied from the rifle load only in having 55 grains of powder instead of 70 grains, the bullet at that time being the 405-grain for both loads. As the heavier rifle load could be fired inadvertently in this revolver, it was tried and functioned satisfactorily, though it must have been a bit nasty to shoot. Someone started a persistent story to the effect that when Sergeant Donovan of Springfield Armory (who did most of the test firing) tried this load the gun was blown from his hand. I can find no mention of any such difficulty during these tests. On the contrary, in his final report in 1879, Wright, then a Captain at Frankford Arsenal, said, "The revolver has been fired over 575 times, mostly from the fixed rest, but many times from the hand . . . [the recoil] is however not enough to trouble one in firing."

Several multiball loads were tested. Frankford Arsenal made some with three slightly flattened round balls (Fig. 1*g*), a type which survived for many years as a guard cartridge (Figs. 1*f* and 1*h*). Phoenix Cartridge Company made another similar cartridge (Fig. 1*e*) which may have been tried by Wright —reference was made to "another cartridge". A second series of cartridges was developed at about the same time, having two or three slugs loaded in a special revolver cartridge with an overall length of 1.61 inches. These would go into the standard Colt cylinder suitably reamed out. After extensive tests of this last version, the whole idea was dropped as of limited advantage.

However, during the tests, which dragged on for several years, someone at Springfield became interested in a single-shot pistol all over again, and without any authorization started to make up a small lot of them, using .45-70 barrel sections and receivers. When the revolver project was terminated, the Ordnance Office heard about this unofficial work and ordered it stopped at once. Only barrels and receivers had been made. They were sold for scrap a few years later to W. Stokes Kirk of Philadelphia, a dealer in surplus Army materials, still in business in 1957.

The late W. S. Kirk, Jr., told me that in the early days of moving pictures his father received an order for some "pirate pistols". As he had these barrels and receivers, he took parts for .45-70 rifles which were on hand, and completed the pistols as stage props. One of them is shown in Fig. 4. Obviously, it is not a Springfield Armory product, except in its parts. There are probably more of these around the country than there are of the Model 1869 pistols, and they are the source of the turned-up noses of many collectors when single-shot Springfield pistols of the breech-loading type are mentioned. The two can be distinguished easily by the difference in caliber (.50 vs. .45) and the date 1869 on the legitimate article. The others have whatever dates might have been on the blocks that Mr. Kirk used —I have noted dates between 1873 and 1884.

Springfield Revolvers

James Warner's attempt to circumvent the Colt and S&W revolver patents

By MARIUS B. PELADEAU

Many firearms makers during the 1840's and 1850's sought ways to circumvent the patents of Samuel Colt and, later, of Rollin White, that gave the Colt Patent Firearms Mfg. Co. a practical monopoly on the initial manufacture of percussion revolvers, and allowed Smith & Wesson to corner the early market for rimfire cartridge revolvers.

One of the principal features of Colt's first patent, which most other manufacturers tried to evade, was the method of locking and unlocking the cylinder automatically by the action of the hammer. Inventors worked diligently to find other ways of turning a revolver cylinder without infringing on Colt's patent claims.

An enterprising inventor who sought to cash in on the market for revolvers opened up by the success of Colt's arms was James Warner of Springfield, Mass. In 1851 Warner established the Springfield Arms Co. in Springfield. Simultaneously, he set up a separate concern, Jas. Warner & Co., at the same address, as a promotional agency to sell Springfield Arms Co. products. Warner was general manager of both firms.

James Warner was born at Springfield in 1818 and died there in 1870. He was the younger brother of Thomas Warner, who served as Master Armorer at Springfield Armory and later as superintendent of the Whitney Armory in New Haven, Conn. Following his service with Eli Whitney, Thomas Warner became associated in 1849 with the Massachusetts Arms Co. of Chicopee Falls, Mass.

The Massachusetts Arms Co. had its origin in the efforts of Edwin Wesson and Daniel Leavitt to manufacture revolvers under Leavitt's U.S. Patent No. 182 of Apr. 29, 1837. These early Wesson & Leavitt revolvers proved to be impractical since the cylinder had to be turned by hand. The Massachusetts Arms Co. was formed by the heirs of Wesson to manufacture revolvers under Wesson's U.S. Patent No. 6669 of Aug. 28, 1849, which embodied a mechanical means of turning the cylinder.

The new Massachusetts Arms Co. revolvers were barely on the market before Colt brought suit. In a court judg-

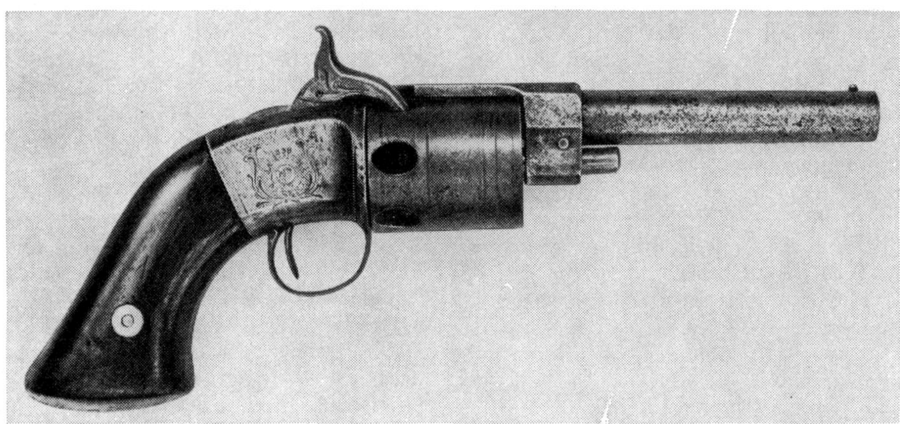

To compete with Samuel Colt's percussion revolvers, Warner established the Springfield Arms Co. in 1851. His first revolvers were made under Elijah Jaquith's patent which claimed a means of revolving the cylinder which Warner hoped would not infringe on Colt's claims. Backstrap is marked "SPRINGFIELD ARMS CO." and sideplate is stamped "1838/JAQUITH'S PATENT." This cal. .31 revolver originally had a blued finish. Rear sight is hidden behind the hammer.

Part of Colt's patent claim was the placing of partitions between the nipples to prevent accidental chain-firing. Jaquith placed the nipples in depressed cavities at the rear of the cylinder. Warner continued to use this feature on all his revolvers except the very last solid-frame models.

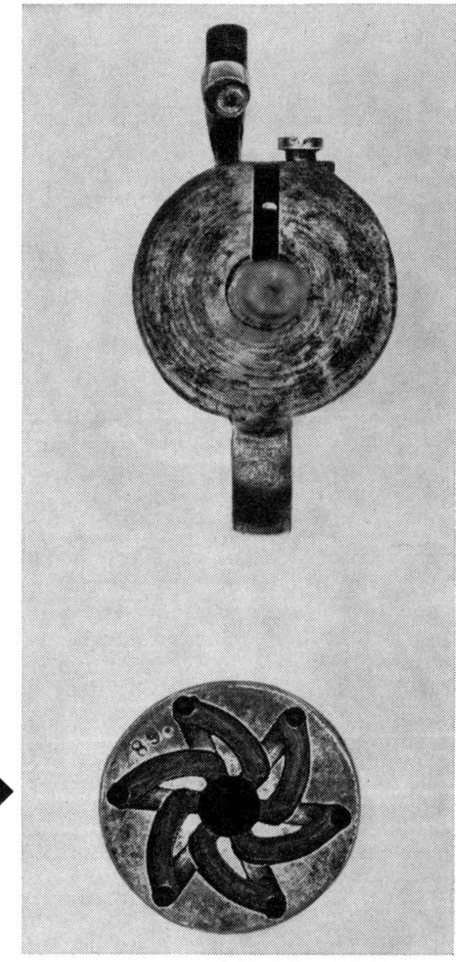

The reason that only a few Jaquith patent revolvers were made by Springfield Arms Co. was that the machining of the rear of the cylinder was too costly for the Warner factory facilities to accomplish. Machining of the curved and inclined planes had to be done precisely, especially since the hand which worked in the grooves served both to revolve the cylinder and lock it at the moment of firing. The hand worked in a direct up-and-down motion over the cylinder pin, rather than off to the side, as in Colt revolvers.

The first 2 types of Springfield Arms Co. revolvers made under Warner's patent of Jan. 7, 1851 (No. 7,894). Lower revolver was first type made by the company. It has 2 triggers, and although made in cal. .28, the barrel is unrifled. Small rear trigger fires the gun after the hammer has been cocked, but does not revolve the cylinder. This is accomplished by pulling the front trigger. Barrel and cylinder are etched with floral and scroll designs. There is no rear sight.

Upper revolver was the second type made by Warner. It employs the same frame and barrel assembly used on the earlier double-trigger model. However, the interior mechanism was improved and simplified so that the one trigger both revolves the cylinder and cocks and fires the revolver. The cal. .28 barrel is rifled and the cylinder is roll-engraved in geometric designs. This revolver also incorporates Warner's patent of July 15, 1851, which embodies the use of a stud on the top of the frame which fits into a notch in the backstrap to give better and stronger alignment between the two.

The single trigger revolvers employed a simplified method of revolving the cylinder to make them easier to manufacture than the earlier double trigger type. Tongue at the bottom of the frame acts as a cylinder stop but is unconnected with the action of the hammer and acts independently.

This shows the involved cylinder ratchets on the double trigger Springfield Arms Co. revolvers and explains why Warner found them as difficult to machine as the Jaquith revolvers. Warner stopped producing this model and switched to the simpler single trigger variation.

ment of Aug. 4, 1851, the company was enjoined from manufacturing further revolvers.

Despite the failure of the Massachusetts Arms Co. to compete with Colt, Warner felt that with a little thought an inventor could circumvent the Colt patents. To do this, in 1851 he set up his own company at the corner of Lyman and Gardner streets in Springfield.

Warner's first attempt to evade the Colt patent was by purchasing from Elijah Jaquith of Brattleboro, Vt., the right to make revolvers under Jaquith's U.S. Patent No. 832 issued on July 12, 1838. Jaquith's invention employed a method of revolving the cylinder by means of "motion (of the mainspring or hand) both endwise and vertical on grooves in the rear end of the cylinder for the purpose of producing . . . the revolution of the cylinder by the act of cocking."

The rear of the cylinder was machined with a series of involved inclined planes which resulted in the turning of the cylinder. Warner felt that the patent was sufficiently different from Colt's so that he could avoid infringement. However, the Jaquith revolver involved so much precision tooling on the rear face of the cylinder that Warner found it too expensive to manufacture, especially since he hoped to sell his arms at prices which would undercut those of Colt's more expensive revolvers.

The result is that the Springfield Arms Co. revolvers marked "Jaquith's Patent" are among the rarest of this company's products. No serial number over 3 digits has been observed.

Warner next turned to manufacturing a revolver made under his own U.S. Patent No. 7894 of Jan. 7, 1851. This covered a means of revolving a cylinder, again different from Colt's. The hand, rather than working in an up-and-down action as in the Colt arm, operated in an axis in line with the cylinder; that is, horizontal to the cylinder.

The first revolvers made under this patent have 2 triggers, as well as a separate hand and cylinder stop. The hammer can be pulled back separately and the small rear trigger will fire the gun, but does not revolve the cylinder. The front trigger will revolve the cylinder and fire the arm by tripping the rear trigger. The action is somewhat similar to that used later on Starr Arms Co. revolvers during the Civil War. The use of 2 triggers, however, proved to be impractical, and the cost of machining the rear of the cylinder was again nearly as expensive and complicated as on the Jaquith revolvers.

Warner then made the same revolver with only one trigger and embodying a simplified method of turning the cylin-

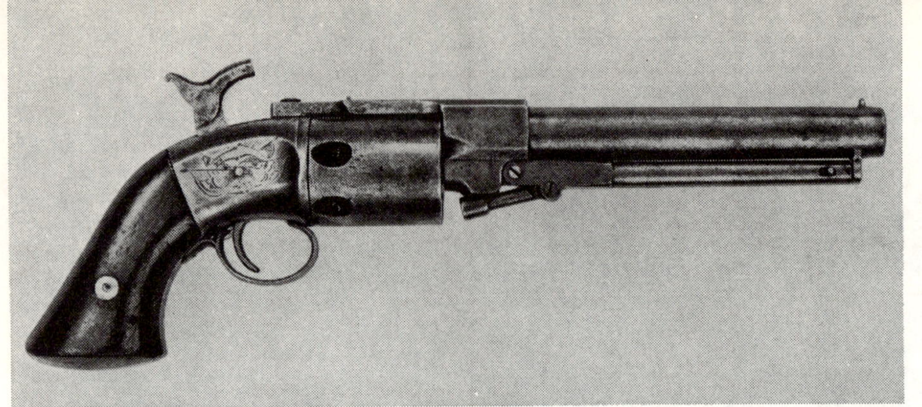

Military-sized Springfield Arms Co. revolver purchased by soldiers during the Civil War. It was available in both cal. .36 and cal. .44. The largest and strongest revolver made by the Springfield Arms Co. This one carries Serial No. 27. Caliber is .36 and it is rifled to the right with an extremely slow twist. Over-all length is 11-5/16"; barrel length is 5-15/16". Rear sight is visible on the top of the backstrap. Ribband above and below the trophy of arms design on the sideplate reads: "WARNER'S PATENT/ JAN. 1851." Backstrap is marked "SPRINGFIELD ARMS CO."

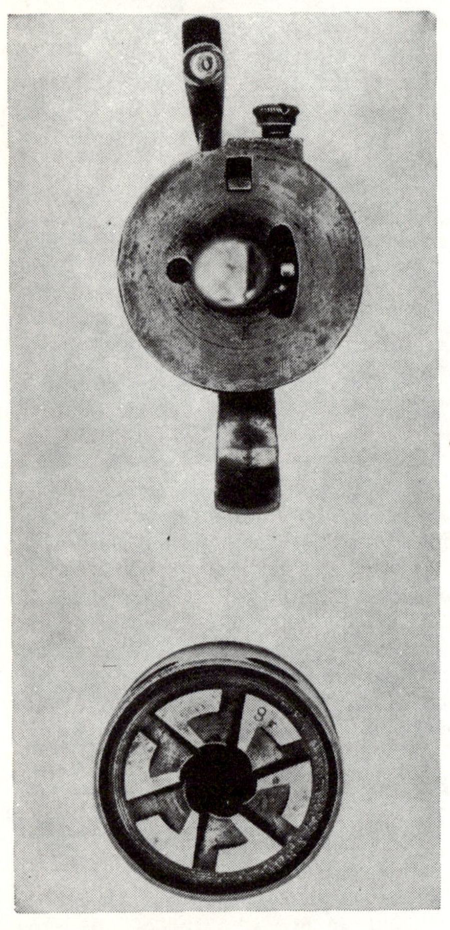

◀This illustration shows the ratchets in the rear of the Springfield Arms Co. military-size revolver cylinder. Also shown is the hand to the side of the cylinder and the cylinder stop at the top of the frame. The hand, which moves in an upward motion in the curved groove in the frame, turns the cylinder by sliding up the inclined plane in the ratchet. Cylinder is locked before firing by the action of the cylinder stop at the top of the frame falling into the rectangular slot not filled up by the hand. This was the best of Warner's attempts to find a method of revolving a cylinder without infringing on Colt's patent. Pin in the round hole in the recoil shield was provided to steady the hammer.

der. He changed the mechanism so that cocking the hammer revolved the cylinder. The revolver used the same frame as the earlier double-trigger model. However, there is a slight change in the backstrap of the barrel assembly which screws into the top of the frame.

This change was contained in Warner's U.S. patent of July 15, 1851, No. 8229. It covered an improvement in the mode of attaching the barrel to the frame. This consisted of a small stud on the top of the frame which engaged a slot in the bottom of the backstrap. This allowed for a more positive alignment of the barrel and the frame as well, and placed less stress on the retaining screw.

Both the small single- and double-trigger revolvers were made in cals. .28 and .31, but only in limited quantities since their action proved fragile and easily broken in normal use. They certainly did not have the strength to compete on the same level with the more rugged Colt revolvers.

Warner was persistent, however, and he must be given credit for continually attempting to improve his products. Probably his best arms were the so-called military models, in cal. .44 Army and cal. .36 Navy. These revolvers, which had loading levers, were strong, well made, and well balanced. Many enlisted men and officers during the Civil War purchased them, although the U.S. Government never bought any directly.

The military models were nicely finished with blue finish and casehardening, and the interior machining was of good quality. All in all, they were serviceable arms. On the military models Warner employed still another type of ratchet arrangement on the rear of the cylinder. The cylinder stop at the bottom of the frame is not directly attached to the hammer; although it operates in sequential conjunction with the hammer, it works independently via a spring action. The result was a crisp and positive locking action, the best of all the Springfield Arms Co. revolvers.

But Warner must have been aware that his weak method of attaching the barrel to the frame had serious drawbacks. The popularity and advantages of the solid-frame Remington, Whitney, and other military revolvers were apparent, and Warner started to turn out the first of a series of solid-frame revolvers just before the Civil War.

The solid-frame revolvers were constructed around his U.S. Patent No. 17904, issued on July 28, 1857, using a series of ratchet grooves on the rear of the cylinder and a lever which turned the cylinder by retreating and advancing horizontally through the cocking motion of the hammer. It was a sophistication of Warner's earlier Patent No. 8229. The cylinder stop was a simple flat spring with a right-angle bend at one end which was set into the top of the frame. The hook made by the bend fell into a cylinder stop in the cylinder as it came into line with the frame. The action of the spring and the locking of the cylinder was by spring tension only and not related to the cocking of the hammer and the turning of the cylinder.

On later solid-frame models this spring was placed at the bottom of the frame where it was less noticeable and interfered less with the act of sighting along the top of the frame. These solid-frame revolvers, generally found in cals. .28, .31, and .36, were available with either octagonal or round barrels, and with different grades of engraving and finish. Their evolution can be traced by the improvement in the cylinder spring mentioned above, as well as changes in the design of the hammer and the side from which several screws enter. The final revolvers of this model were manufactured with barrel and frame forged as one piece.

As much as Warner tried, he could not compete with the larger revolver makers. He had neither the large manufacturing facilities nor the promotional setup. Seeking a new field, Warner went into the manufacture of cartridge revolvers early in 1862. These revolvers were built on the solid frame used in the last of the percussion arms, and only the cylinder was different.

Springfield Arms Co. was barely able to gets its new cartridge revolvers on the market before Smith & Wesson slapped a patent infringement suit against the company. The case went to court and in 1863 the judgment was handed down which stipulated that Springfield Arms Co. was to turn over to Smith & Wesson 1513 cartridge arms which had not been sold. These were later stamped "Manufactured for Smith & Wesson" and sold through regular Smith & Wesson retail outlets. Those Warner revolvers which were sold before the court judgment are, of course, not so marked and carry only the usual "Springfield Arms Co." marking.

The unfavorable court judgment sounded the death knell to Warner's attempts to manufacture revolvers. Instead, he turned all his attention to interesting the U.S. Government in his breech-loading carbine (U.S. Patent No 41732). By the close of the Civil War the Ordnance Dept. had purchased a total of 4001 Warner carbines which were made at the Greene Rifle Works in Worcester, Mass.

At the end of the Civil War, Warner tried to cultivate a civilian market for his carbine but without success. With his death in 1870, the Springfield Arms Co. failed.

Although the total production of the Springfield Arms Co. was not large compared to that of other larger and better known revolver manufacturers, the variety and uniqueness of the company's products are of interest to modern day collectors as examples of great inventiveness and persistence in the face of even greater odds. ■

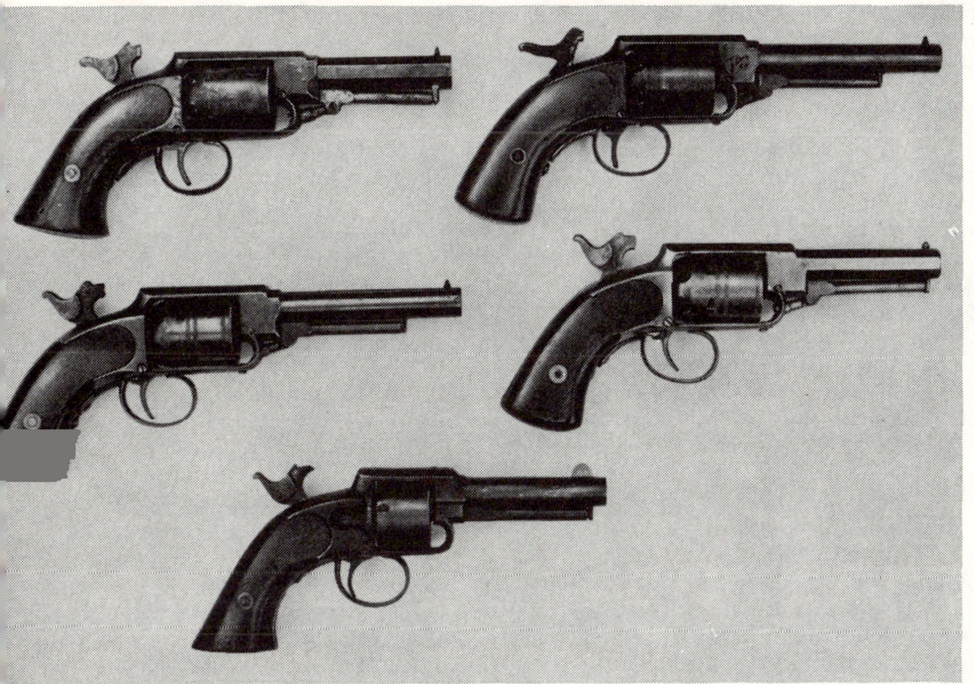

Minor variations in Springfield Arms Co. solid-frame percussion revolvers.

(1) First type followed Warner's patent drawing of July 28, 1857, and has the screw which retains the cylinder pin and loading lever enter from the right side of the frame. Cylinder stop spring is fastened to the top of the frame (not shown) and the hammer has a sharp edge at the top. Butt is flatter and more flared than in later versions. This revolver is Serial No. 45 and is blued but unengraved. Grips are oiled black walnut.

(2) Second variation saw a change in the shape of the butt, a rounding off of the top of the hammer and the entering of the cylinder pin screw from the left side. Barrel is round and the cylinder has a rolled decoration. It is finely blued and has varnished black walnut grips. Serial No. 175.

(3) Third variation reflects the elimination of the reinforcing webbing on the sides of the hammer. Hammer nose is round rather than oblong. This revolver is Serial No. 198 and is of better quality than most, with etched cylinder, engraved frame and varnished rosewood grips.

(4) Last Springfield Arms Co. percussion revolvers were made with barrel and frame forged from one piece of iron, rather than having the barrel screwed into the frame as is in earlier types. The webbed hammer returned, however. Serial No. is 527.

(5) Very few cartridge revolvers were made by Springfield Arms Co. before Smith & Wesson brought suit against the company for infringement of the Rollin White patent. Revolver was loaded from a hinged gate on the right side, but there was no ejector. This revolver, in cal. .22, is Serial No. 2415. Frame is a shortened version of the one used for the percussion revolvers.

Lead Bullets In Collections

Cartridges in my collection have acquired a whitish corrosion on lead bullets and on any lead exposed in jacketed bullets. This has happened on modern as well as old ammunition types. My collection was first kept in shallow drawers made of pine, later in redwood drawers in cabinets made of fir plywood treated with a wood sealer. I think most if not all the corrosion occurred before I changed the storage cabinet and drawers. Can you tell me how to prevent this?

Answer: This was experienced by collectors for many years without any cause or correction being found. Then Col. B. R. Lewis, who until his death was a contributing editor of *The American Rifleman*, obtained the answer by consulting the Research Laboratories of the National Lead Co.

The corrosion product is lead carbonate. It is the end product of corrosion of lead in an environment of air, moisture, and materials which give off acidic vapors. Oak, of which many storage cabinets and drawers are made, gives off tannic acid and appears to be worst, but your experience shows that pine also can have this effect. It takes place whether the lead is in contact with the wood or not.

Any wood cabinet which is to contain lead should have an interior finish to seal off the wood. This can be provided by a heavy sealer.—C.R.S.

Early High Standard Pistols

I have begun collecting early-model High Standard semi-automatic pistols as manufactured prior to World War II and am confused as to their order of introduction according to their alphabetical model designations. Can you give the years of introduction for the Models "A" through "E"?

Answer: The first pistol in this series was the Model "B" introduced in 1933 and chambered for the .22 long rifle cartridge. Offered initially with 6¾" barrel, it was available later with 4½" barrel.

The Model "C" pistol chambered for the .22 short cartridge and made with both 6¾" and 4½" barrels was introduced in 1937. In 1938 the Models "A", "D", and "E" were introduced, all with 6¾" barrel chambered for the .22 long rifle cartridge. Apparently the only difference between the three models was in the weights of their barrels which affected overall weights of the guns. The Model "A" pistol weighed 36 ozs., Model "D", 40 ozs.; and Model "E", 42 ozs.

In 1932, the High Standard Manufacturing Co., of New Haven, Conn., had taken over the Hartford Arms & Equipment Co., of Hartford, Conn., and prior to its bankruptcy that firm had manufactured both a semi-automatic and a single-shot pistol chambered for the .22 long rifle cartridge. There are indications that some of the Hartford pistols on hand at the time of the takeover were sold later by the High Standard firm, but it is not known if they carried the High Standard firm name.—M.D.W.

J. Stevens — And His Pistols

By Herschel C. Logan

AMERICAN shooters owe a debt of gratitude to A. C. Gould, the noted shooter and arms authority of his day. Gould did as much as any man to stimulate interest in guns and shooting, by founding the magazine known today as THE AMERICAN RIFLEMAN and by authoring two important books on firearms developments. He wrote in his book *Modern Pistols and Revolvers* (1888): "The Stevens pistols have made some of the most wonderful scores known. The barrels, upon which so much depends, seem to be perfect, and probably at the present time there are more Stevens pistols in the hands of famous marksmen throughout the world than any other make." This is enough to arouse an interest in these guns of other days and the man who made them.

Joshua Stevens was born in Chester, Hampden County, Massachusetts, on September 10, 1814. At the age of 20 he became an apprentice to a Chester toolmaker.

For some years following 1837 Stevens was engaged, with Edwin Wesson (an elder brother of Daniel Wesson) and S. C. Miller, in the manufacture of hand-turned-cylinder percussion revolvers. These arms were produced under patent No. 182 (April 29, 1837) issued to Daniel Leavitt. The business was located at Hartford, Connecticut.

Stevens was employed for a time by Cyrus B. Allen, a gunmaker of Springfield, Massachusetts, later known as the maker of Elgin cutlass pistols and Cochran turret revolvers.

HERSCHEL C. LOGAN, *Salina, Kans., has written and illustrated many articles on collector arms and ammunition. He is author-illustrator of books entitled* Cartridges *and* From Handcannon to Automatic.

Worked briefly for Colt

During the late 1840's Stevens is reported to have worked for Samuel Colt, and to have helped establish Colt's Hartford factory.

In 1850 upon establishment of the Massachusetts Arms Company at Chicopee Falls, to produce revolvers under the Edwin Wesson patent No. 6669 (August 28, 1849), young Stevens became associated with this new company. It was during this period that Stevens applied for, and received, four patents on percussion revolvers. They were:

(1) No. 7802 (November 26, 1850) —Six-shot hammerless tip-up revolver hinged in the rear of cylinder, double-action, powder and ball, no loading lever. (The .28 caliber Massachusetts Arms Company, Maynard primer revolver carries this patent date on the barrel release.)

(2) No. 8412 (October 7, 1851)—Side hammer tip-up revolver with frame hinged at rear of cylinder, powder and ball, loading lever.

(3) No. 9929 (August 9, 1853)—Hammer (side) and hammerless types of powder and ball revolvers, frame hinged at rear.

(4) No. 12189 (January 2, 1855)—Six-shot double-action, powder and ball, solid-frame, solid-top revolver with (right) side hammer and a single nipple which must be capped with each shot.

Even though the Massachusetts Arms Company was prevented by court action brought on by Colt from producing a revolver based on Edwin Wesson's patent, they did continue to produce a few small arms under other patents, including those of Joshua Stevens.

Formed own company

Late in 1864, following receipt of patent No. 44123 (September 6, 1864) for a single-shot pistol, Stevens made the decision to start out on his own. His first shop was in a small room adjoining a sawmill on the north side of the Chicopee River.

Organized on a modest scale, and not subjected to the rapid expansion as beset other companies of that war-time era, the firm of J. Stevens & Company was able to establish itself on a solid foundation. Stevens, being a resourceful individual, supplemented his armsmaking with other items.

From a reference source in Chicopee comes this bit of interesting data on the early firm:

"In 1867, 20 men were employed in

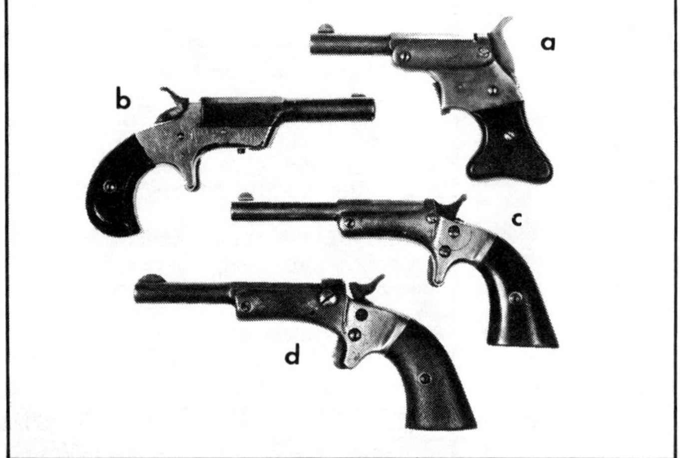

Fig. 1: Early Stevens pistols: a) Original tip-up model, .30 caliber; b) Gem side-swing-barrel pistol, .22 caliber; c) First model tip-up with split breech and circular side-plate; d) Model No. 41 tip-up pistol

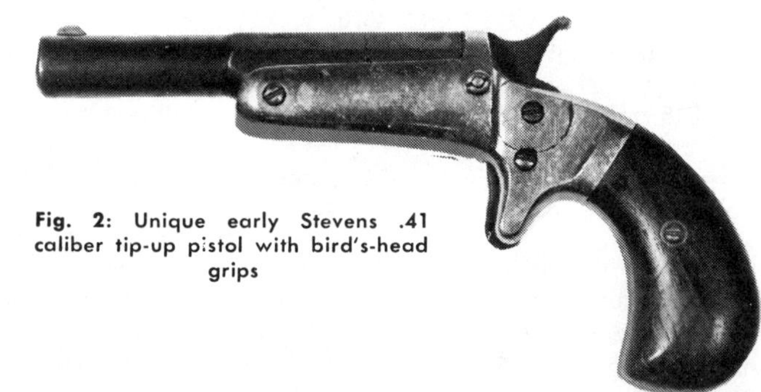

Fig. 2: Unique early Stevens .41 caliber tip-up pistol with bird's-head grips

From this building on the banks of the Chicopee River came the first Stevens pistols and rifles

the manufacture of pistols, calipers, dividers, and pruning shears. The half-time service of a traveling salesman was secured and in 1868 the plant was enlarged somewhat. In 1872 the plant started the manufacture of a breech-loading shotgun and 40 men found employment in the shop. This was just before the panic of 1873, but in 1877-78 orders were plentiful and it was necessary to start night work in order to keep up with the demand for sporting rifles. With the general improvement in business in 1880-81 it was planned to double the existing production capacity."

In 1885 the company was incorporated with a capital of $40,000 as the J. Stevens Arms & Tool Company. Joshua Stevens and W. B. Fay each subscribed 120 shares of stock in the new corporation. Fay had been a gunsmith. George S. Taylor took ten shares; his brother James subscribed 110 shares and was appointed treasurer. I. H. Page, the bookkeeper, took 40 shares.

In January 1896 Page bought the stock held by Stevens and Taylor and assumed entire control, acting as president and treasurer.

Stevens lived nearly 11 years more, even to seeing the firm he had organized engage in the manufacture of one of the country's early horseless carriages, the Stevens-Duryea automobile. He passed away in 1907 at the age of 92.

Now subsidiary of Savage

Savage Arms Corporation secured an interest in the firm in 1920, at which time the name was changed to J. Stevens Arms Company. Later, in 1936, Savage assumed full control of the company. Operating today as a subsidiary of Savage Arms Corporation, the Stevens firm still produces rifles and shotguns.

So much for the historical background of this American arms company. Let us now turn to the handguns produced by them. It should be pointed out that this study is not an effort to list every type and model produced by Stevens, if such were possible; rather, it is to present a general picture of the pistols produced by Stevens during their period of handgun production.

Generally conceded to be the first of the Stevens line is their Vest Pocket Pistol (Fig. 1a), a uniquely-shaped single-shot of .30 caliber. Even though it has the familiar barrel catch found on all Stevens tip-up pistols, it does not have the extractor, which was a part of his first patent on these arms. Since this model seldom shows up on dealer lists, it is logical to assume production was not large. It is a well-built, compact little piece and a worthy progenitor of the Stevens line.

Hardly had the little Vest Pocket been placed on the market than it was succeeded by a new single-shot. This new pistol, produced under Stevens' patent of September 6, 1864, provided these features as outlined in his patent application. "The nature of my invention consists in an arrangement and combination of a breech-elevating spring and a cartridge-shell discharger or starter in such a manner that the said spring, while performing its function of elevating the barrel at its breech, shall retract the cartridge-shell discharger or starter for the purpose of either wholly or partially expelling from the barrel the shell or case of the exploded cartridge."

Known at the time as a 'tip-up' pistol, due to the action of the spring in tipping up the breech of the barrel when pressure was exerted on the barrel release button, this pistol (Fig. 1c) was the first of the popular Stevens tip-up series. This early type is easily distinguished by its split breech and the distinctive circular side-plate on the left side of the frame. Made in both .22 and .30 calibers, they could be purchased with either brass frame and blued barrel or fully nickel-plated. The round-and-octagonal barrel was 3½ inches in length. This little pocket and target pistol must have been quite popular because it was still listed in firearms catalogs of the late 1880's, more than 20 years after its advent. Perhaps the price of $2.50 had something to do with it. For taxidermists' use the pistol could be supplied with an eight-inch smoothbore barrel, for dust shot, at a price of only $5. Before it was removed from the line, this first model with ejector was made for a time without the circular side-plate. In other respects it was the same.

Model with bird's-head grips

Unusual among the early Stevens products, and believed to be most unique, is the .41 caliber tip-up (Fig. 2) with bird's-head grips, which was a feature unknown to any other Stevens tip-up pistol. The one illustrated has all the features of the early model, including the split breech, the spring tip-up, and the circular side-plate. The four-inch round-and-octagonal barrel is rifled with five lands and grooves, left-hand twist. The serial number is 82. Could this have been a bid by Stevens to enter the derringer market, which at that time was so active? If so, despite its sturdy construction and its free-and-easy feel in the hand, it had two strikes against it in the competitive derringer field. Its overall length of 6½ inches, as compared with the mere 4½ to five inches of the usual pocket derringers then on the market, soon took it out of competition, and by so doing relegated it to

Joshua Stevens

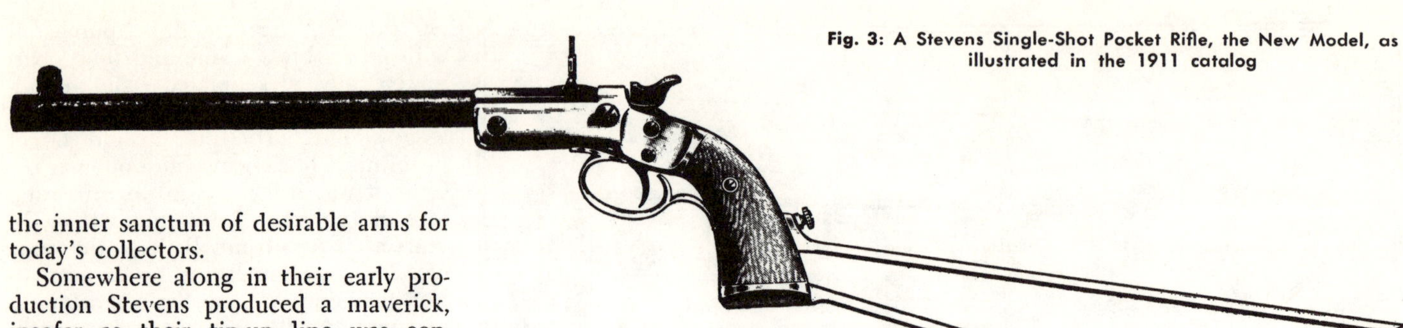

Fig. 3: A Stevens Single-Shot Pocket Rifle, the New Model, as illustrated in the 1911 catalog

the inner sanctum of desirable arms for today's collectors.

Somewhere along in their early production Stevens produced a maverick, insofar as their tip-up line was concerned. Listed in their catalogs of the 1880's was an inexpensive, single-shot, side-swing-barrel pistol without extractor (Fig. 1b). It could be supplied in either .22 or .30 caliber. Unmarked except for the serial number and the name 'Gem' stamped on the top of the three-inch round-and-octagonal barrel, it has often been erroneously ascribed to Marlin. True there is enough similarity—at first glance—between it and the Marlin 'OK' single-shot to warrant such an assumption. However, upon careful examination there are enough distinguishing features to place it in the Stevens camp, where it rightfully belongs. The slope of the frame away from the split breech; the placing of the trigger pin in the spur trigger housing; the inside projecting arm from the frame to hold the grip screws, and the fastening of each grip separately, all lend credence to its being a genuine Stevens even if its being in the Stevens catalog is not sufficient reason for designating it a Stevens 'Gem'.

Here the Stevens line of pistols widens and becomes quite prolific, and it is a bit difficult, in the absence of actual factory records, to place the proper sequence to this or that model.

Popularized pocket rifles

Even though other manufacturers had produced pistols with extension stocks, it remained for Stevens to popularize this combination with their line of 'Pocket Rifles'. It is regrettable that today, through an interpretation of the National Firearms Act of 1934, the combination is considered a 'firearm' as defined by the Act. The pistol without stock is legal, but with stock attached it is considered as a sawed-off shotgun or rifle which may be concealed upon the person and therefore illegal.

Charles Folsom of New York, an agent for 'J. Stevens & Co.'s Celebrated Arms', in the 1883 issue of his catalog has this to say: "Among the first small arms made by J. Stevens & Co. was what is called the 'Old Model Pocket Rifle' (circa 1869) with barrels from 6 to 10 inches long and very light in all its parts, the whole weight being 10 ounces only. These have a very large sale, and in the hands of skilled marksmen did some remarkable shooting at short ranges. There is a limited demand for them still, but they have mostly given way to the New Model which, while it occupies but little more space, is heavier and stronger in every part, and will throw a ball much farther with accuracy. The 15- or 18-inch will really shoot almost as well as a rifle."

One of the popular pistols, and one which enjoyed a lengthy sale, was the graceful Diamond Model No. 43 (Fig. 4a). Equipped with either open or peep sights, it was available in .22 long rifle caliber in either six- or ten-inch barrel length. (The .22 long rifle cartridge was introduced about 1889 in Stevens pistols. It was originated by Union Metallic Cartridge Company at the request of Stevens.) The Diamond was listed at $5 to $8.50 in the 1898 Stevens catalog. The split breech of the earlier types had given way to a solid breech with firing pin on this and subsequent models. Many men today have fond memories of using one of these light guns in their youth.

The Diamond Model with ten-inch barrel and extension stock was designated as the Reliable Pocket No. 42. It was chambered for the .22 long rifle and .22 Stevens-Pope Armory rimfires. Though it would shoot the short and long rimfires, the factory did not recommend them for accuracy.

Produced simultaneously with the Diamond Model was a single-shot pocket pistol known as the Tip-up No. 41 (Fig. 1d). It was identical with the Diamond Model but with shorter grips and a shorter barrel. Removal of grips from a Diamond pistol will show how relatively simple it was to adapt the frame to the Pocket Model. Made in both .22 rimfire short and .30 rimfire calibers, this popular pocket gun was in the line for many years.

Variety of models made

With the advent of the New Model Pocket or Bicycle No. 40 (Fig. 3) (circa 1872) barrel length and calibers were varied. Calibers listed in a later catalog were .22 long rifle, .22 Stevens-Pope Armory, .25 rimfire, and .32 long rimfire. Barrel lengths were ten, 12, 15, and 18 inches. An identical model equipped with special sights was called Stevens Vernier New Model No. 40½. The same guns were also produced with a smoothbore choked barrel to use .38-40 Everlasting shells. It was listed as Shotgun No. 39. The 1906 catalog contained a note that this model had been discontinued.

Not only were Stevens pistols made for target shooting but they were also designed for hunting. This is evident from the designation of Hunter's Pet No. 34 for another tip-up pocket rifle. In addition to the .22 rimfire, .32, .38, and .44 center-fire, barrels could be chambered for the .38 or .44 caliber Everlasting cases, and also for the 20-gauge shotshell. The octagonal barrel lengths were 18, 20, 22, and 24 inches. Prices ranged from $11 to $14.75, with a $1 increase for each two-inch addition to the barrel length. The 1898 catalog also listed the following calibers for the Hunter's Pet: .22 long rifle rimfire, .25 rimfire, and .32 long rimfire. A 'Vernier' Hunter's Pet was available at the same time. In addition to special sights, it was equipped with a round-and-octagonal barrel. Price in 1898 for this special model was $16. At least one specimen of this later model is known to have been made into a .38 caliber handgun with a much shorter barrel. It is believed to have been a factory job due to the shorter version of the octagonal part of the barrel. If such was the case then it may be expected that other specimens will show up in the future.

Produced outstanding target pistols

Comes now what are perhaps the most distinguished models of the Stevens line, certainly insofar as their target models are concerned. They are the noted Lord Model Gallery Pistol No. 36, Conlin Model No. 38, Gould Model No. 37 (Fig. 5 a, b, c), and the

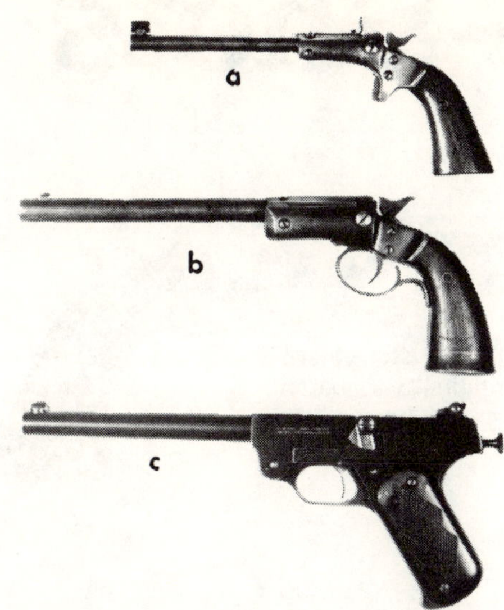

Fig. 4: Three popular Stevens target pistols of other days: a) Diamond Model No. 43, .22 caliber; b) Off-Hand Target No. 35, .22 caliber; c) The No. 10 Stevens Target, .22 caliber

Off-Hand Model No. 35 (Fig. 4b).

It was Frank Lord, a celebrated New York pistol shot, who suggested the model which bears his name. Physically large and endowed with large hands, he desired a heavy pistol with a long grip. The Lord Model, weighing three pounds in .22 caliber with ten-inch barrel, was the result. Ira Paine, one-time champion pistol shot of the world, commented thus on this addition to the Stevens line: "Your Lord Model is certainly a *wonderful* pistol. I have taken a life in my hands with it some thousands of times, and it has never failed me." Paine preferred, and used, this model in exhibitions throughout his distinguished career.

Named for James S. Conlin of Conlin's Shooting Gallery in New York City, the Conlin Model while retaining the spur on the trigger guard from the Lord Model was nevertheless the beginning of the popular Off-Hand Model. It was made in .22 long rifle and .25 rimfire, and upon special order could be supplied in .32 long, .38 long, .32-44 S&W, and .38 S&W at extra cost. Barrel lengths were ten and 12 inches; weight two to 2¼ pounds.

A. C. Gould, in an attempt to adapt a pistol more to his liking, reworked one of the Conlin Models and sent it to the factory. The result became the Gould Model. Fitted with an open wind-gauge rear sight and bead front sight, it was one of the truly great target pistols of its time. Lighter and smaller than the big Lord Model, the Gould Model appealed to noted shooters of that day. W. W. Bennett, famous holder of the 50-shot record at 50 yards on Standard American Targets, wrote, "I consider my Gould Model far superior to any other pistol or revolver made".

Popular over long period

Following its illustrious predecessors came the Stevens Off-Hand Target Pistol No. 35 (Fig. 4b), a model which was to enjoy many, many years of popularity in the Stevens line, and in fact only disappeared from their catalogs in recent years. First made with a heavy cast trigger guard, the later models employed a lighter strap iron guard. Otherwise the pistol still retained the features of the first adaptation from the Gould Model. It was made in both .22 and .25 calibers, and could be procured with either six-, eight-, ten-, or 12¼-inch barrel lengths.

The Off-Hand Model No. 35 Auto-shot could at one time be had in .410-bore for rodents, roadside hunting, and general shooting where a shotshell was desired, but under present interpretation of the National Firearms Act such arms are subject to registration.

Still employing their 'tip-up' action, Stevens early in this century brought out their Single-Shot Target Pistol No. 10 (Fig. 4c). Totally unlike any of its predecessors it is designed along the lines of an automatic. Sights were open at the front, while the rear had elevation and windage adjustments. It is said that many target pistol experts collaborated with the Stevens company in the designing of this latest model in their famous line. It seems to have been produced for only a short period of time, and although not particularly scarce, specimens in good condition are met with rather infrequently today.

Recent years have seen the disappearance from the market of all models of this once-illustrious line of Stevens single-shot pistols—a line which had its birth in 1864 in a small frame building on the banks of the Chicopee River.

My personal thanks to the Public Library of Chicopee, Mass., G. Robert Lawrence, Richard Short, Maj. Hugh Smiley, Frank Wheeler, Art Tucker, Col. L. C. Jackson, Charles T. Waller, Howard Scott, A. W. Rowe, Bob McReynolds, and others who so kindly assisted with this study.—H. C. L.

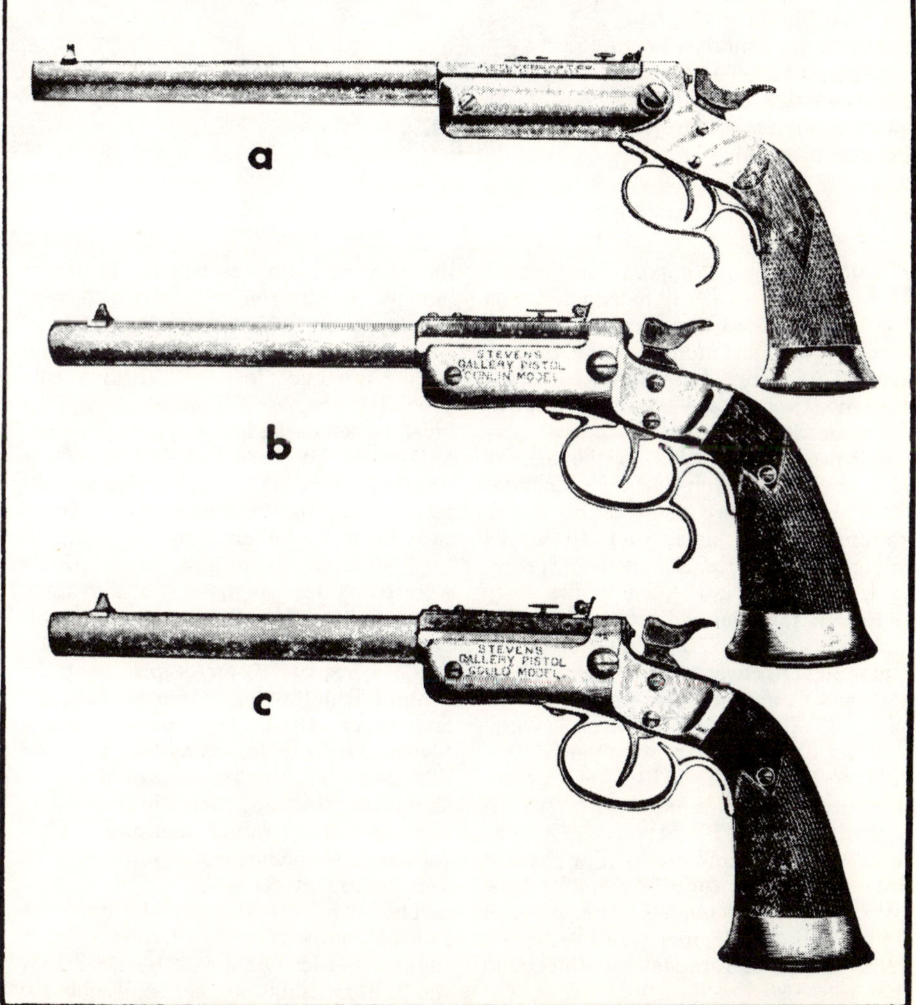

Fig. 5: The three noted Stevens target pistols: a) Lord Model No. 36; b) Conlin Model No. 38; c) Gould Model No. 37

Stevens Single-Shots

By KENNETH L. COPE

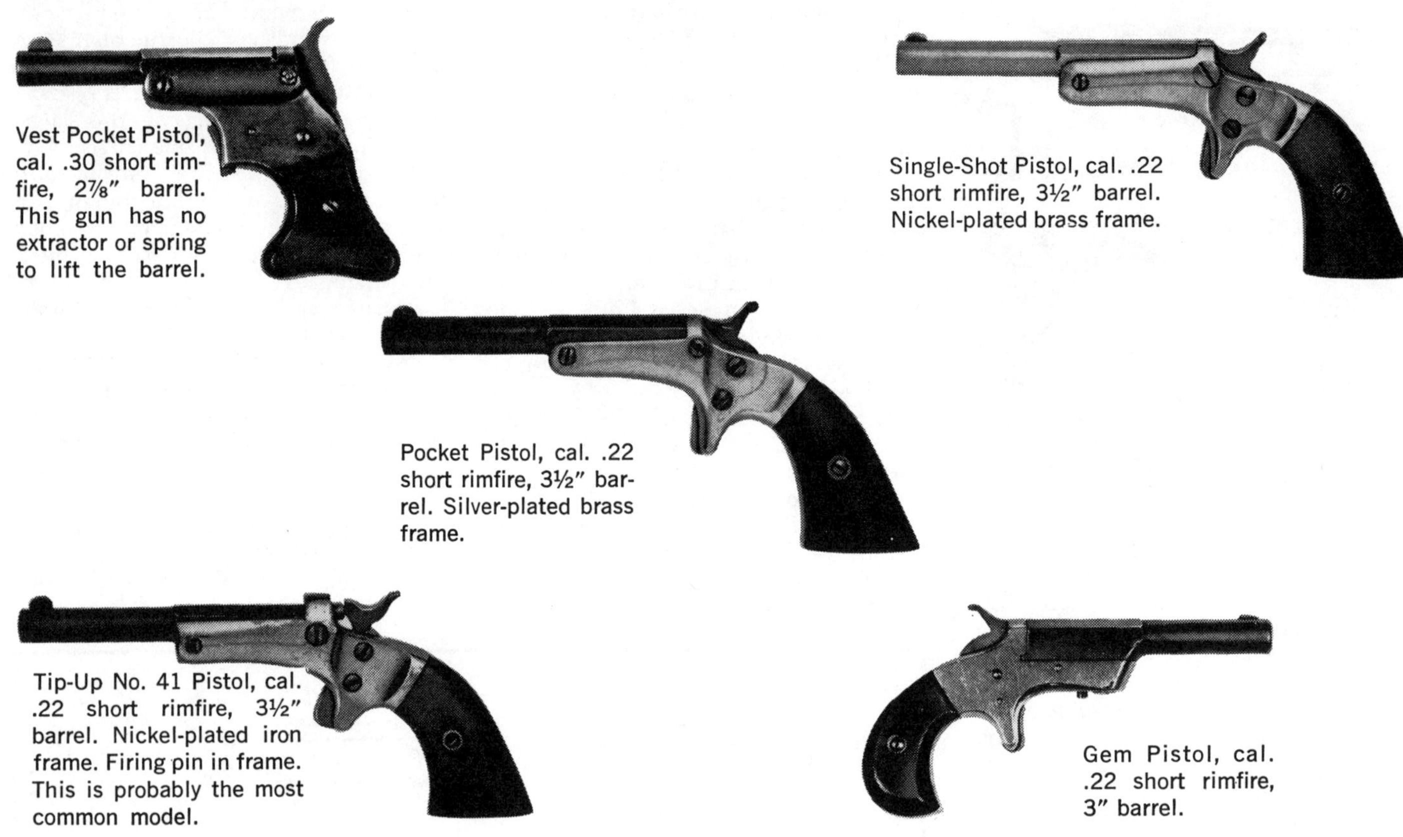

Vest Pocket Pistol, cal. .30 short rimfire, 2⅞" barrel. This gun has no extractor or spring to lift the barrel.

Single-Shot Pistol, cal. .22 short rimfire, 3½" barrel. Nickel-plated brass frame.

Pocket Pistol, cal. .22 short rimfire, 3½" barrel. Silver-plated brass frame.

Tip-Up No. 41 Pistol, cal. .22 short rimfire, 3½" barrel. Nickel-plated iron frame. Firing pin in frame. This is probably the most common model.

Gem Pistol, cal. .22 short rimfire, 3" barrel.

ONCE the most popular single-shot target pistols in America, Stevens pistols have faded into obscurity. There were 14 distinct models made over a span of 78 years, but except for common models they are now little known.

Joshua Stevens, founder of the Stevens firm, died in 1907 at the age of 92. He was born in 1814 at Chelsea, Mass., where he received his early training as a machinist. In 1838 he was employed by Cyrus B. Allen in Springfield, Mass. He left Allen in the early 1840's to join Samuel Colt.

After working for Colt for some years, Stevens invented a revolver which he began to manufacture under his own name. A patent infringement suit by Colt terminated its production.

U. S. Patent No. 44123 for a single-shot pistol was granted to Stevens on Sept. 6, 1864, and J. Stevens & Co. was founded that same year. This patent became the basis for all except 2 of the 14 Stevens pistol models. The identical tip-up action principle was used from 1869 to 1894 for Stevens rifles and shotguns also.

Early Stevens pocket pistols were only moderately successful. The rise of the Stevens pistol, especially the target models, began after 1886 when Stevens developed the .22 long rifle cartridge. First manufactured by the Union Metallic Cartridge Co., the .22 long rifle proved to be, as it remains today, an ideal target cartridge.

During the 1880's and 1890's, the single-shot target pistol achieved its peak of popularity, and was considered superior to the revolver for target shooting. Stevens single-shot target pistols were recognized as the best at that time.

A. C. Gould, author and firearms authority of the 1880's and 1890's, made a test of .22 target pistols at the Walnut Hill Range, Woburn, Mass., in September 1888. He found that a Stevens target pistol, using the then new .22 long rifle cartridge, would ". . . shoot finer than any target in use among pistol shooters would measure." During this particular test, Gould shot a 1⅝" group at 50 yds.

The year 1888 also saw the introduction of competitive 50-yd. pistol shooting in America. At a match held during the fall meeting of the Massachusetts Rifle Ass'n, Stevens pistols were used by the first prize winner, W. W. Bennett, and by J. B. Fellows, who shot a perfect score of 5 tens, the only perfect score made that year. This domination of the target pistol field was not to last, however. By 1904, the last year a Stevens pistol won the United States Revolver Association Championship, 2 of the 4 Stevens target models had been discontinued and full-adjustable sights were no longer supplied on the others. Introduced during the decline of the target models, the small-frame Tip-up No. 41 pocket pistol and the heavier frame Offhand No. 35 sporting pistol were produced in large quantities. These are the models most commonly encountered today.

In January 1920 the Savage Arms Corp. gained control of Stevens. Only the Offhand No. 35 model was continued. It was first made in pre-World War I form; later it was made in slightly modified form, and in the .410-bore Autoshot No. 35 model.

The only new model to be introduced after Savage assumed control was the Target No. 10, patented Apr. 17, 1920. Externally similar to an automatic pistol, it was the only departure from the 1864 styling since the discontinuance

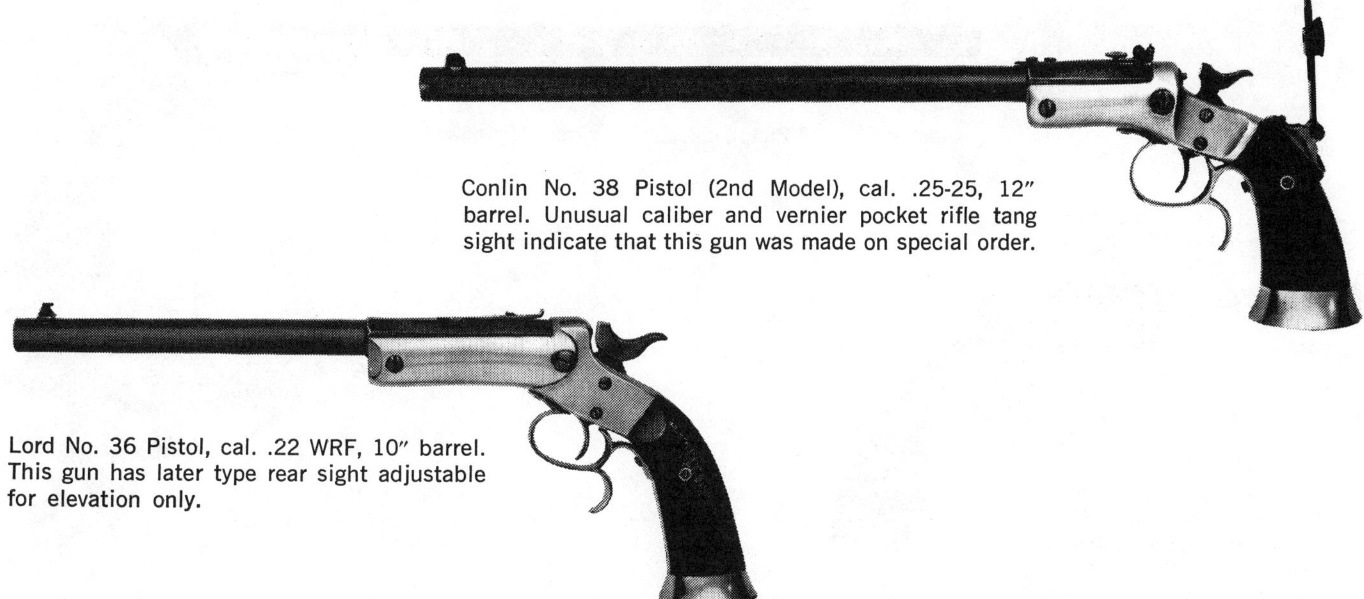

Conlin No. 38 Pistol (2nd Model), cal. .25-25, 12" barrel. Unusual caliber and vernier pocket rifle tang sight indicate that this gun was made on special order.

Lord No. 36 Pistol, cal. .22 WRF, 10" barrel. This gun has later type rear sight adjustable for elevation only.

of the Stevens derringer model in 1890.

Although the Target No. 10 never achieved the popularity of the earlier target models, this model is a very interesting one. It was the first production single-shot target pistol to use the better pointing automatic-style frame and to have the striker blow in direct line with the barrel.

Depending on date of manufacture, Stevens pistols were marked as follows:

1864-1888—"J. Stevens & Co.
Chicopee Falls, Mass."
1888-1919—"J. Stevens Arms & Tool Co. Chicopee Falls, Mass. USA"
or
"J. Stevens A&T Co.
Chicopee Falls, Mass. USA"
1919-1942—"J. Stevens Arms Co.
Chicopee Falls, Mass. USA"

The marking is on the barrel in 2 lines and, on early models, includes the patent date, Sept. 6, 1864. The serial number is usually found on the left side of the barrel and under the left grip. A star may precede the serial number, but its meaning is unknown to this author.

The caliber marking, if present, is stamped above the serial number or on the barrel flat. Most were not marked to indicate caliber. Even on those pistols so marked, often only the bore size is shown. A pistol marked .25, for example, can be a .25 rimfire, .25-20 center-fire, or chambered for some other cal. .25 cartridge. My 2nd Model Conlin pistol, marked only with a .25 under the serial number, is chambered for the .25-25 cartridge.

One model conforms to none of the usual rules for marking. The Target No. 10 model has the caliber plainly marked under the barrel with all other markings on the side of the frame.

Stevens pistols with English proof marks are known. Many were sold in England prior to World War I and some have come back to the United States. A Diamond model in my collection bears a Birmingham view mark in use prior to 1904 and proof marks used only after 1954. The proving of export firearms is required under the British Gun Barrel Proof Acts of 1868 and 1950. The later marks include the caliber (.22 long rifle) and the chamber length (.610").

The following list of standard models cites their features. The Stevens firm was accommodating to special orders. Thus deviations in barrel length, caliber, sights, and finish will be encountered.

Production records of all Stevens pistols have been lost and the quantities produced or the serial number ranges of the various models are not known.

Many Stevens target pistols offered for sale today are actually Hunter's Pet or Pocket Rifles with the detachable shoulder stock missing. These are recognizable by the dovetail cut in the butt and, in most models, by the folding rear sight. Now loosely classified as pistols, they were regarded by the manufacturer as light rifles. They are a separate class of firearm, and are not covered here.

Except as noted, all models listed are of the same basic design in which the rear of the barrel tips up when a release stud on the side of the frame is depressed.

THE POCKET MODELS

Vest Pocket Pistol—Flat-sided iron frame; fish-tail grip. Cals. .22 short and .30 short rimfire, 2⅞" barrel. Sheath trigger; no extractor on some specimens; hammer has integral firing pin. Marked "Stevens & Co. Vest Pocket Pistol, Chicopee Falls, Mass." Only Stevens pistol to be marked with model name. Externally similar to Remington vest pocket derringer, but has typical Stevens tip-up barrel. Usual finish is full nickel.

One of the original models introduced when company was founded in 1864, it was discontinued in 1875. Also known as "Kickup" model.

Pocket Pistol—Small, rounded brass frame; oval grip. Cals. .22 short and .30 short rimfire, 3½" barrel. Sheath trigger; small stud on barrel release. Hammer has integral firing pin. Notch in hammer is rear sight. The spring under the barrel forces the barrel up and operates the extractor when the release stud is depressed. Automatic extraction is sole feature claimed by Stevens in his 1864 patent. Listed in Stevens catalogs as Old Model Pocket Pistol following introduction of Gem Model. Usual finishes are full nickel or nickel frame with blue barrel.

This model was introduced in 1864 and shown in patent description. It was discontinued in 1888 when replaced by Single-Shot Pistol.

Single-Shot Pistol — Identical to Pocket Pistol model except that barrel spring was replaced by a linkage which operates extractor when the barrel is manually tipped up. Barrel elevating spring design patented by Stevens proved weak in use and few pistols are found with spring intact.

Introduced in 1888 as improved version of the Pocket Pistol, the Single-Shot Pistol was discontinued in 1898 when replaced by Tip-Up No. 41.

Tip-Up No. 41—The only tip-up model so designated by Stevens. Similar to Single-Shot Pistol model, but with firing pin mounted in frame; flat hammer nose; larger mushroom-shaped stud on the barrel release, and a frame groove for use as rear sight. This model was first made in cals. .22 short and .30 short rimfire. After 1903 it was avail-

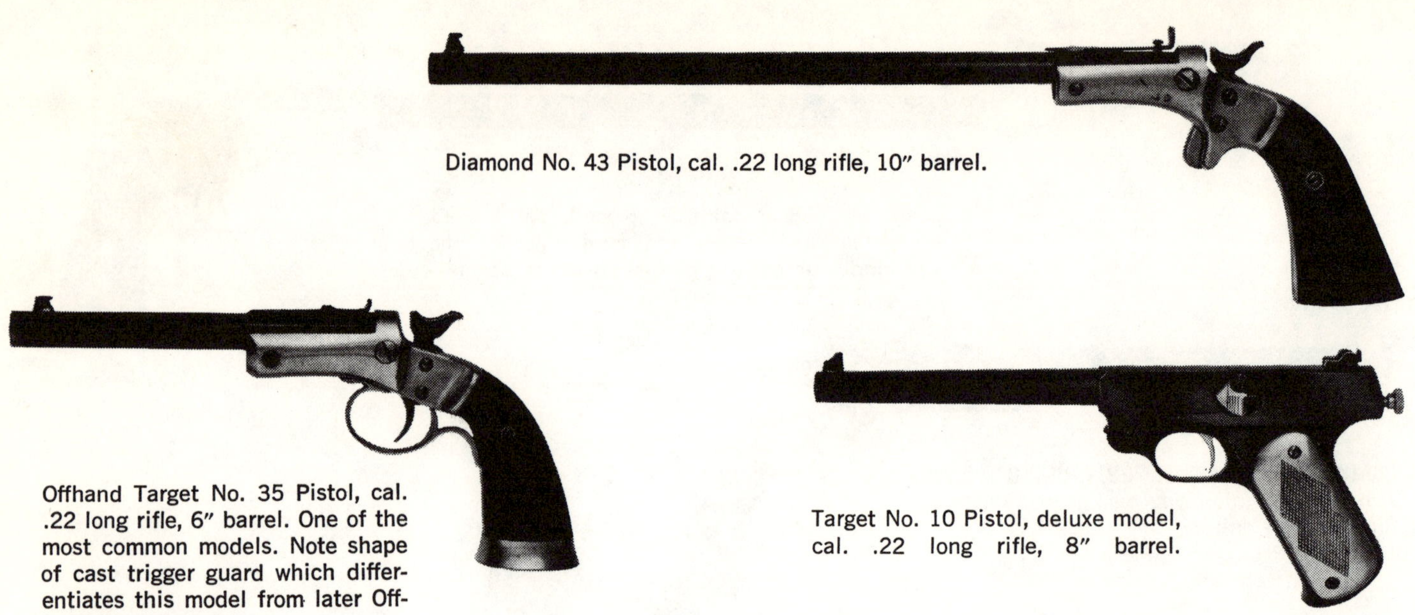
Diamond No. 43 Pistol, cal. .22 long rifle, 10" barrel.

Offhand Target No. 35 Pistol, cal. .22 long rifle, 6" barrel. One of the most common models. Note shape of cast trigger guard which differentiates this model from later Offhand No. 35 model.

Target No. 10 Pistol, deluxe model, cal. .22 long rifle, 8" barrel.

able in cal. .22 short only. The last Stevens pocket model, it was introduced in 1898 and discontinued in 1916.

Later production of the Single-Shot Pistol also had larger stud on the barrel release.

Gem Pistol—Small birdshead grip derringer similar to Marlin OK model. Cals. .22 short and .30 short rimfire. Three-inch barrel swings to side to load. Usual finish is full nickel.

Introduced about 1872, it was only model to depart from tip-up barrel design, and was discontinued in 1890.

THE TARGET MODELS

Lord No. 36—Only Stevens pistol made on heavy Hunter's Pet frame, it was first offered in cal. .22 short rimfire only, later in .22 long rifle, .22 Stevens-Pope Armory, .22 WRF, .25 Stevens, .32 long rimfire, and .38 long Colt center-fire. Ten or 12" barrel; spur on trigger guard for second finger; very long, heavy butt with checkered grips. Rear sight adjustable for windage and elevation until 1903, when replaced by sporting sight adjustable for elevation only. Also available with open, non-adjustable sights. Usual finish is nickel frame with blue barrel. Named for Frank Lord, who was a well-known pistol shot.

Introduced in 1880, Lord model was longest lived and most famous Stevens target pistol. Discontinued in 1911.

Conlin (1st Model)—Made on medium-weight pocket rifle frame. Cals. .22 short, .22 long, and .32 long rimfire. Spur trigger; checkered grips, 10" and 12" barrel lengths. Usually supplied with combination sights adjustable for elevation only, but also available with open, non-adjustable sights. Usual finish is nickel frame with blue barrel.

Introduced in 1872, this model was at first a pocket rifle, without provision for detachable shoulder stock. Later listed as a gallery pistol, it was named about 1885 for James S. Conlin, owner of a New York shooting gallery. Discontinued in 1888 when it was replaced by Conlin No. 38 (2nd Model).

Conlin No. 38 (2nd Model)—Similar to 1st Model, but has regular trigger and trigger guard with outside finger spur. Full-adjustable target sights. Made in cals. .22 long rifle, .22 Stevens-Pope Armory, .22 WRF, .25 Stevens, .32 long rimfire, and .38 long Colt center-fire. Usual finish is nickel frame and blue barrel. Introduced in 1888 to incorporate features suggested by A. C. Gould as improvements on 1st model, it was discontinued in 1903.

Gould No. 37—Identical to Conlin 2nd Model, but without trigger guard spur. Named for A. C. Gould, author of *Modern American Pistols and Revolvers* and editor of *The Rifle*, predecessor to THE AMERICAN RIFLEMAN.

Introduced in 1890 after Gould refused to allow Conlin 2nd Model to be named for him. He objected to trigger guard spur. Discontinued in 1903.

Diamond No. 43—Made on the light pocket pistol frame. Cals. .22 short, .22 Stevens-Pope Armory, and .22 long rifle rimfire. Sheath trigger; some have checkered grips; 6" or 10" barrels. Available with globe front and peep rear, open front and rear, or with both types of sights. Usual finish is nickel frame and blue barrel.

Introduced in 1888, Diamond model was only Stevens target pistol made on light frame. At first considered too light for accurate shooting, it proved to be an excellent target pistol, and was discontinued in 1916.

Offhand Target No. 35—Lower priced revival of Gould model, with rear sight adjustable for elevation only; plain unchecked grips; 6", 8", or 10" barrel. Cals. .22 short, .22 long rifle, .22 WRF, and .25 Stevens rimfire. Usual finish is nickel frame and blue barrel.

Introduced in 1907, this model was called a target pistol by Stevens, but was not meant for competitive target shooting. Discontinued in 1916.

A replica of this model has been imported in recent years.

Target No. 10—Made on a frame externally similar to an automatic pistol; 8" barrel tips up to load when released by catch on left side of frame; cocking knob on rear of frame; full-adjustable rear sight. Cal. .22 long rifle only. Deluxe model available with blued barrel, browned frame, nickel plated trigger and barrel catch, and checkered aluminum grips. The standard model had hard rubber grips, and trigger and barrel catch were blued.

Introduced in 1920, this attempt to reenter target pistol field was not overly successful. Discontinued in 1933.

THE SPORTING MODELS

Offhand No. 35—Identical to Offhand Target No. 35 pistol except for stamped, sheet metal trigger guard used after 1929, instead of earlier cast guard. Available with 6" or 8" barrel in cal. .22 long rifle and, from 1923 to 1929, in .410-bore smoothbore. Usual finish is full blue. Introduced in 1923, it was postwar revival of Offhand Target No. 35 model, without the claim to target pistol status. Discontinued in 1942, this was the last Stevens pistol.

Autoshot No. 35—Offhand No. 35 model .410-bore smoothbore. Available with 8" or 12¼" barrel; checkered grips; shotgun bead front sight, and a groove rear sight in top of frame. Usual finish is full blue.

Introduced in 1929, and discontinued in 1934 when passage of National Firearms Act imposed $5 transfer tax. ■

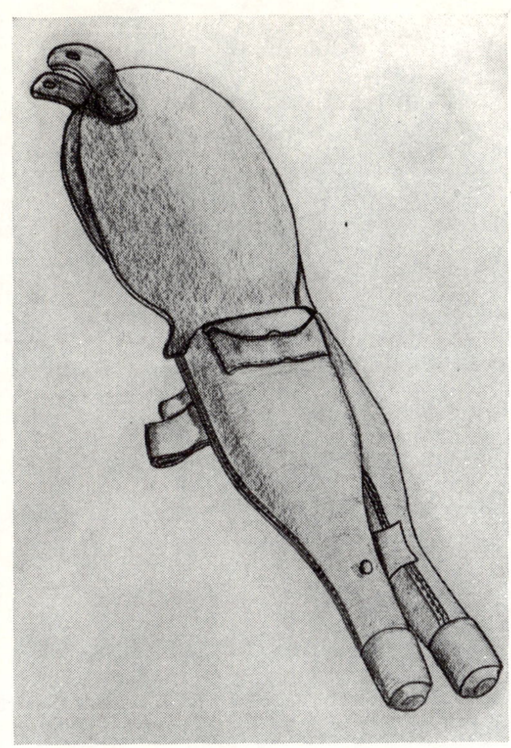
1

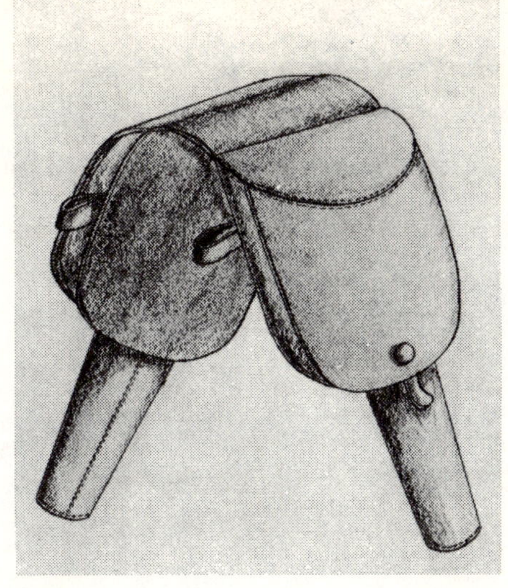
2

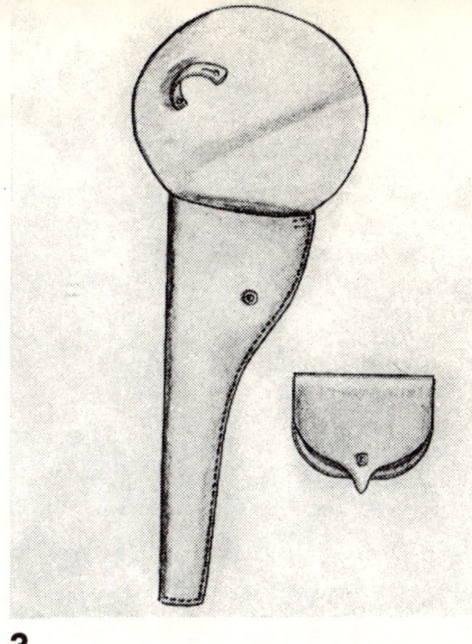
3

4

U.S. Military Holsters

By EARL J. ATHERHOLT, JR.

ISSUE holsters for U. S. military pistols and revolvers are only occasionally mentioned and illustrated in books and articles, and their existence is usually taken for granted.

The first official U. S. military pistols were single-shot flintlocks made by North & Cheney and adopted in 1799. Following these were various other models of flintlock pistols. Single-shot percussion pistols were adopted in 1842. These flintlock and percussion pistols as well as Colt Dragoon revolvers were issued in pairs to mounted officers. They were carried in twin saddle holsters (Figs. 1 & 2) fastened across the saddle pommel forward of the user's thighs.

The box-like saddle holsters are made of heavy black leather with brass studs to fasten the top flaps. Some of them are fitted with a brass covering around the bottom, and some with a pocket on the front under the flap for percussion caps, balls, and accessories. Such holsters were used until about the Civil War. Then as comparatively small and light percussion revolvers replaced the cumbersome single-shot pistols and Colt Dragoon revolvers, belt holsters were adopted by the military.

Cavalrymen of the Civil War period carried their percussion revolvers butt forward on the right side and a saber on the left. The horse was controlled with the reins in the left hand. Thus either the revolver or saber could be drawn with the right hand. On the holster (Fig. 3) of this period a large flap with a leather tab inside fastens over a brass stud to secure the revolver. The half-round leather pouch with the holster is for percussion caps.

In 1873, the U. S. Army adopted the Colt single-action cal. .45 revolver made for metallic cartridges. The holster (Fig. 4) for this revolver is generally similar in size and shape to holsters for percussion revolvers. Twelve cal. .45 revolver cartridges were carried in the leather pouch shown with the holster.

A black leather holster (Fig. 5) was used for the Colt cal. .38 double-action revolver adopted by the U. S. Navy in 1889. "USN" in an oval is stamped on the flap. The leather cartridge pouch matches the holster.

Officers of the U. S. Naval Academy used a web holster (Fig. 6) for the Colt cal. .38 double-action revolver. The toe cap, rivets, and flap snap of this holster are bronze, and "USN" is stamped on the snap. This holster as well as the Navy holster in Fig. 5 were worn on the officer's right side with revolver butt to the rear.

During the Spanish-American War, New York cavalrymen used a leather holster (Fig. 7) for the Colt cal. .38 double-action revolver. Stamped "N.Y." in an oval, the holster was carried on the right side with revolver butt forward. A matching 12-round leather car-

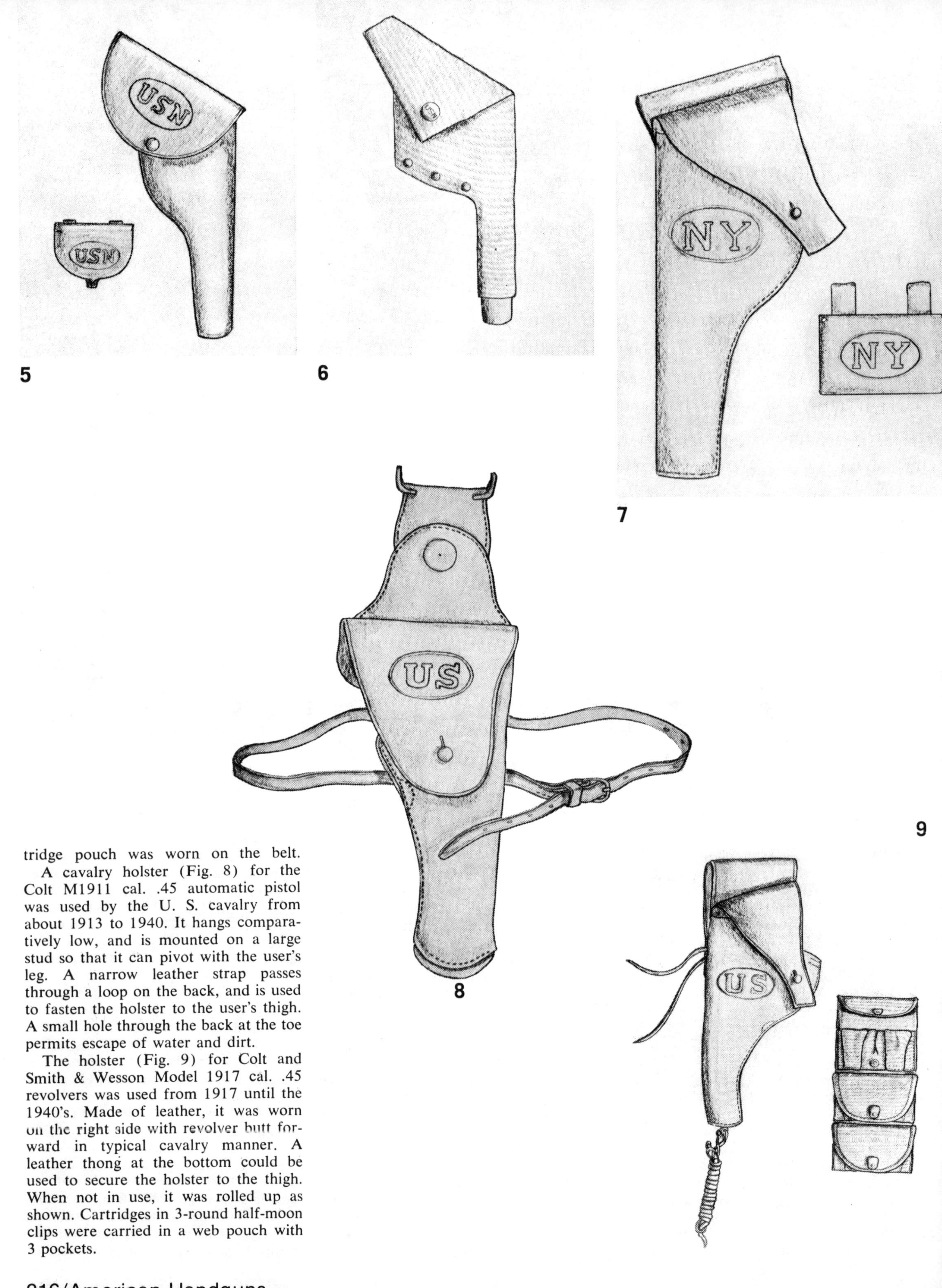

5

6

7

8

9

tridge pouch was worn on the belt.

A cavalry holster (Fig. 8) for the Colt M1911 cal. .45 automatic pistol was used by the U. S. cavalry from about 1913 to 1940. It hangs comparatively low, and is mounted on a large stud so that it can pivot with the user's leg. A narrow leather strap passes through a loop on the back, and is used to fasten the holster to the user's thigh. A small hole through the back at the toe permits escape of water and dirt.

The holster (Fig. 9) for Colt and Smith & Wesson Model 1917 cal. .45 revolvers was used from 1917 until the 1940's. Made of leather, it was worn on the right side with revolver butt forward in typical cavalry manner. A leather thong at the bottom could be used to secure the holster to the thigh. When not in use, it was rolled up as shown. Cartridges in 3-round half-moon clips were carried in a web pouch with 3 pockets.

10

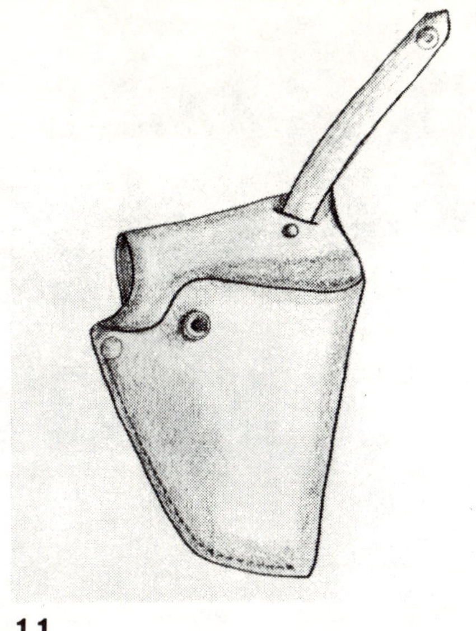
11

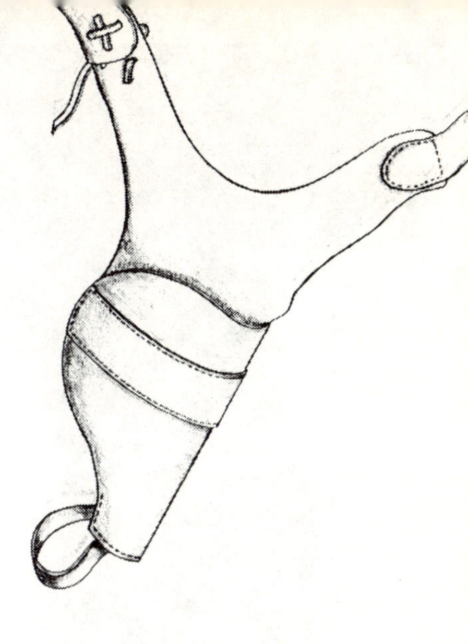
12

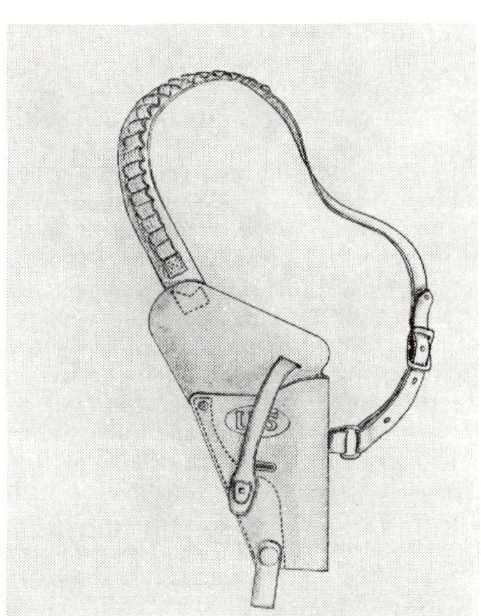
13

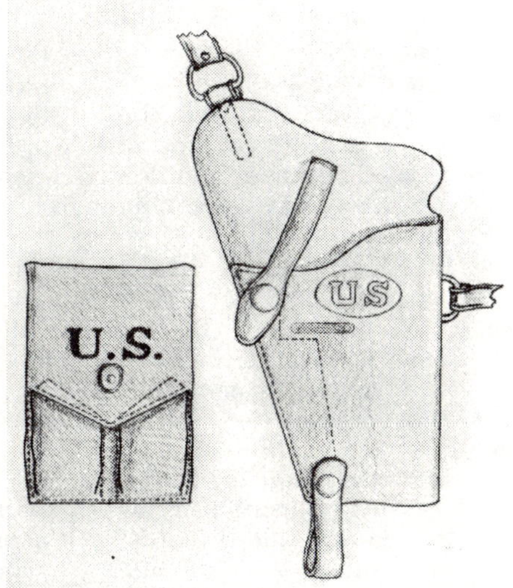

14

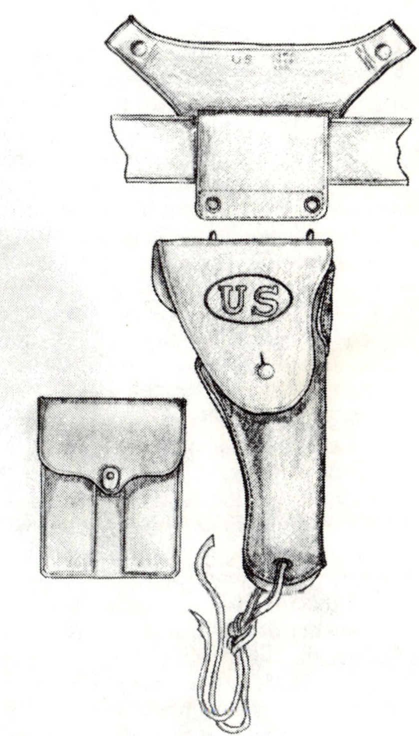

15

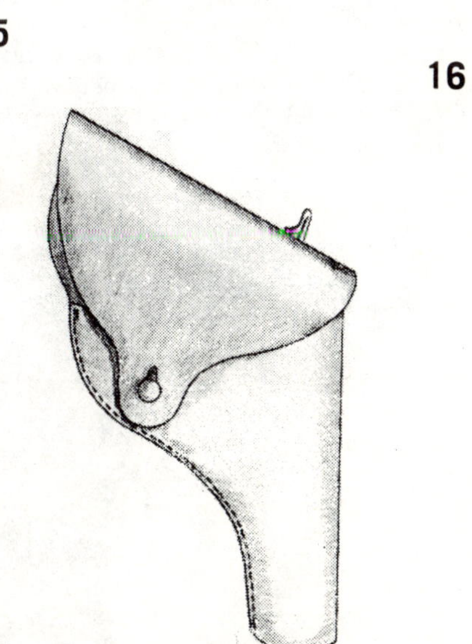
16

A green nylon survival vest with a holster (Fig. 10) for a Colt cal. .45 automatic pistol was used by U. S. Army fliers during World War II. The holster is made of heavy canvas, and is sewed on the lower left of the vest. A retaining strap holds the pistol in place.

Some Army and Air Force personnel are armed with cal. .38 Spl. revolvers. The hip holster (Fig. 11) is for the Colt Detective Special .38 Spl. revolver with 2" barrel. It is furnished with a retaining strap, and is fastened to the user's belt.

There is also an Army and Air Force shoulder holster (Fig. 12) for the Colt Detective Special revolver. A leather-covered spring clip holds the revolver in place without use of a retaining strap.

U. S. Navy and Marine Corps pilots in World War II and the Korean War used a leather shoulder holster (Fig. 13) to carry the Smith & Wesson Victory Model .38 Spl. revolver. A belt loop strap on the bottom secures the holster to the waist belt. Cartridges were carried in nylon loops on the leather shoulder strap.

Shoulder holsters are used by aircraft and tank crewmen since hip holsters interfere with activities of such personnel. The M7 shoulder holster (Fig. 14) is for the Colt cal. .45 automatic pistol. Spare magazines are carried in the 2-pocket web pouch on the waist belt.

The standard hip holster for the Colt cal. .45 automatic pistol is the Model 1916 (Fig. 15). For military police use, it is fastened to a Y-shaped leather drop loop, and the upper part of the drop loop is fastened to a chest strap known as a Sam Browne belt. For other use, this holster is fastened to a web waist belt. A leather thong through the toe can be used to secure the holster to the user's thigh. Spare magazines are carried in a 2-pocket pouch.

Smith & Wesson Military & Police cal. .38 revolvers used by Navy shore patrols are carried in a leather belt holster (Fig. 16) with top flap. The toe of the holster is open. ■

Warner's Infallible Auto

BY KENNETH L. COPE

IN 1915, semi-automatic pocket pistols were still fighting for acceptance by an American public that had grown up with the idea that revolvers were the ultimate in handguns. The major objection to semi-automatic pistols, often expressed in the sporting magazines of the day, was their reputed lack of reliability. It is understandable, therefore, that the Warner Arms Corp. chose a name for its new .32 cal. semi-automatic pistol designed to assure the buyer of the gun's reliability. They called it "Infallible."

The man responsible for the design of the Warner Infallible was no novice. Andrew Fyrberg of Worcester, Mass., was a 30-year veteran of firearms design. He obtained his first patent in 1886 and by 1914 had been granted over a dozen more. Most of these earlier patents were for revolvers and single barrel shotguns.

In 1914 and 1915, Fyrberg was granted two patents which formed the basis for the Warner Infallible pistol. The first, issued July 28, 1914, (#1,105,416), covered the manner in which a breechbolt and twin recoil rods were mounted in the solid frame of the pistol; and the manner in which the rods limited the recoil of the breechbolt. The other was issued March 9, 1915, (#1,131,360) and covered a device by which the breechbolt could be quickly disconnected from the recoil rods, thus allowing the breechbolt to be pulled back with very little effort. Fyrberg also claimed a novel breechbolt stop which could be disengaged and locked when the breechbolt was to be removed from the frame.

Fyrberg assigned his patents to the Warner Arms Corp., of New York City, N.Y. Warner Arms, the creation of Franklin B. Warner, made Infallible pistols — or had them made — for a period of about six years. Infallibles come in one of four major variations, produced in one of two locations.

Regardless of particular variation, all Infallibles were made in .32 ACP. All were supplied with two 7-shot, single column magazines. Overall length of the Infallible is 6½", with a barrel length of 3¼". Most guns are found with an all blue finish, but a number have been noted with a case hardened frame and blued barrel.

Black, hard rubber grips were standard. No guns have been observed with fancy grips or with any sort of embellishment such as engraving or nickel plating.

The front sight is integral with the barrel rib. The rear sight is a V notch cut into the top of the breechbolt. A shallow groove is machined along the top of the frame to allow clearance for sighting.

The serial number appears on the bottom of the grip frame, behind the magazine well.

The safety is located forward and just above the left grip. When applied, the letter S is visible on the frame. In operation, the safety prevents movement of the sear and, through the linkage, blocks full travel of the trigger.

Takedown is accomplished by rotating or removing the breechbolt disconnect pin (depending on the model), depressing the breechbolt stop release, and pulling down the breechbolt stop with the hook provided. The breechbolt can then be withdrawn from the frame.

Further disassembly requires removal of the pin or pins which secure the barrel to the frame. With the barrel removed, the recoil rods and springs can be pushed out through the front of the frame.

Reassembly is in reverse order except that care must be taken when inserting the breechbolt in the frame. The trigger must be pulled so that the breechbolt can override the sear or damage to the delicate sear mechanism will result.

The first Infallible pistols, and they comprise the first production variation, were made for Warner Arms Corp., by subcontractors around Norwich, Conn., in 1915 and 1916. The First Model is easily

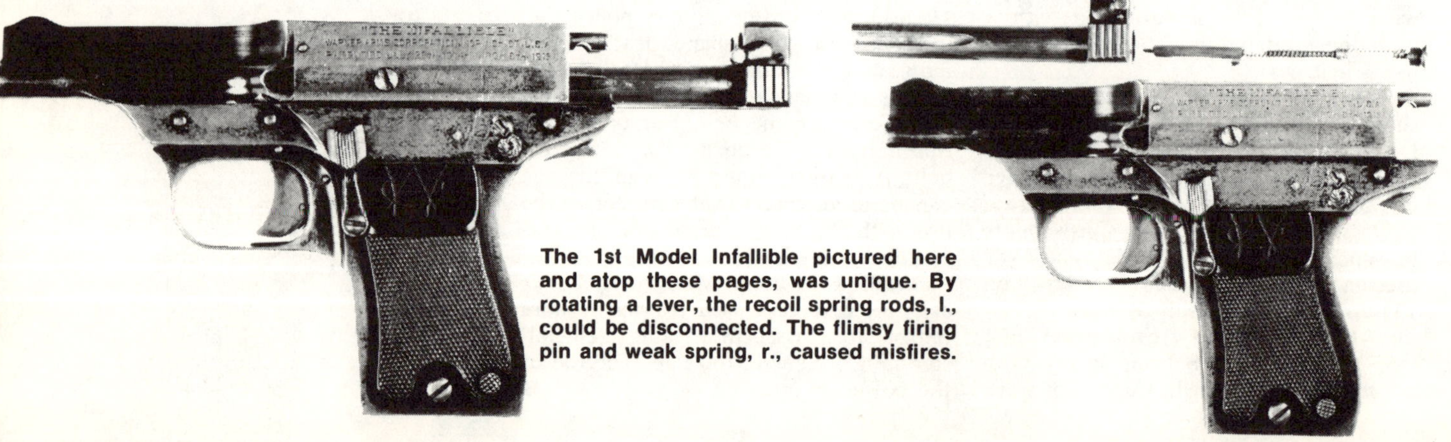

The 1st Model Infallible pictured here and atop these pages, was unique. By rotating a lever, the recoil spring rods, l., could be disconnected. The flimsy firing pin and weak spring, r., caused misfires.

was an attempt to produce a low-cost, reliable pistol. Low-cost it was; infallible it was not!

identified by its straight barrel rib, two pins to hold the barrel to the frame, grooves milled into each side of the frame, and a distinctive, curved backstrap. These major manufacturing differences clearly show that the First Model guns were made with different fixtures, tooling, and casting patterns than were the later models.

Other points of identification are: the rotating breechbolt release, the magazine release button located on the left side of the grip, and a large WAC monogram on both grips. First Models are marked on the left side of the frame:

"THE INFALLIBLE"
WARNER ARMS CORPORATION,
NORWICH, CT, U.S.A. PATENTED
JULY 28th, 1914-MARCH 9th, 1915

With a production of between 500 and 1500, the First Model is among the rarest of all American-made, regular production, semi-automatic pistols. Factory records are not available, but a study of serial numbers indicates a production of not more than 1,500 guns. Production could be as low as 500 if Warner started serial numbering at 1,000; a common practice in those days. The lower figure is supported by the extreme scarcity of this model today. The .32 cal. Smith & Wesson semi-automatic pistol, with a known production of 957, is encountered more often than is the First Model Infallible.

In 1917, Warner, in conjunction with N. R. Davis & Sons of Assonet, Mass., formed the Davis-Warner Arms Corp., with its manufacturing facilities in the N. R. Davis & Sons factory on Waters St. in Assonet and the office and salesrooms at 96 Chambers St., in New York City. Pistols made from 1917 until April, 1919, are marked with the Assonet address, and comprise the second production variation.

The connection with N. R. Davis & Sons allowed the new corporation to claim 1853 as the date of its establishment and give the appearance of an old, well established, firm. The year 1853 is when Nathan R. Davis began manufacture of percussion firearms in Assonet, later forming N. R. Davis & Sons which was well known for the manufacture of single- and double-barrel shotguns.

Production of the Second Model began in early 1917 following establishment of manufacturing facilities at the N. R. Davis Co. plant. With this new start, the gun was considerably simplified although it retained all of Fyrberg's patent features. The barrel rib was changed to a contoured form; the backstrap was made in a straight line; only one pin was used to secure the barrel to the frame; and the milling of the frame was simplified.

The redesigned grips carry a smaller WAC monogram contained within a circle and surrounded by the words "BLOCKS THE SEAR."

The only functional design change was to move the magazine release to the front of the grip frame, allowing easier operation with either hand.

Approximately 2,000 of the Second Model were made before the introduction of the Third Model in early 1918. Second Models are marked on the left side of the frame:

—INFALLIBLE—
DAVIS-WARNER
ARMS CORPORATION,
ASSONET, MASS, U.S.A.
PAT. JULY 28, 1914-MARCH 9, 1915

By 1918 it must have become apparent to Warner that his Infallible pistol was an inherently dangerous design. In early 1918, therefore, the rotating breechbolt release used in both First and Second Model guns was changed to a solid pin that was designed to be pushed out with the magazine floorplate for disassembly.

Simultaneously, the four coarse serrations on the back of the breechbolt were changed to 10 finer serrations. This allowed a slightly better grip when operating the breechbolt.

In all other respects the Third Model is the same as the Second. Approximately 2,500 Third Model guns were made between early 1918 and April, 1919.

Continued on page 224

Second Model Infallibles were made in Assonet, Mass. by Davis-Warner. Changes in barrel contour and grip shape show use of new tools.

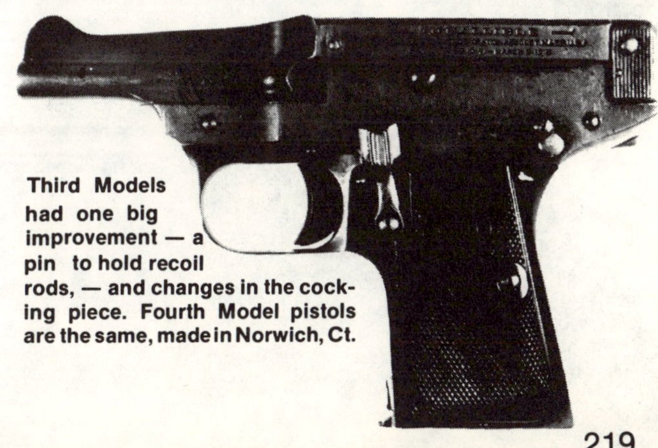

Third Models had one big improvement — a pin to hold recoil rods, — and changes in the cocking piece. Fourth Model pistols are the same, made in Norwich, Ct.

The Winchester-Mason single action 6-shot revolver. c. 1883. No markings; .44-40 caliber. Finished in the white.

Revolvers By WINCHESTER

This well-known firm was a pioneer in revolver development

By R. L. WILSON

THAT the Winchester firm, of New Haven, Conn., manufactures rifles, shotguns, and ammunition is common knowledge, and that they have been active as an arms manufacturer for over a century is also well known. But that Winchester ever made a handgun might be disputed by many. Even some active arms collectors are unaware of the Winchester design work in the development of cartridge handguns.

A total of 11 pistols in the Winchester Gun Museum and one in a private collection offer significant proof of this little known aspect of arms history. The story these rare guns tell involves such diverse parties as Colt's, U.S. Navy Ordnance, Russian Army Ordnance, and 2 of the leading designers in 19th Century gunmaking; Hugo Borchardt and William Mason.

Thirteen Winchester revolvers were made: 12 in 1876, and one c. 1883. Twelve have been accounted for, and the thirteenth is assumed to be in Russia, though it may have been lost or destroyed. The Model 1876 revolvers are attributed to designer Hugo Borchardt, while the 1883 Model is attributed to William Mason.

Two major designs were developed in Borchardt's experiments. The first had a fixed cylinder and a thumb extractor; the second had a swing-out cylinder with cylinder pin extraction. Only one fully finished thumb-extractor model was made, and this is revolver #1783 in the Winchester Museum. Four swing-out cylinder models were fully completed—a test gun for the U.S. Navy, a sample for Russian Ordnance tests, and Winchester Museum guns Nos. 647 and 649.

All the thumb-extractor revolvers have unusually long cylinders, and their precise chambering has yet to be identified. Three of these are of an experimental .44 caliber. The fourth is of an experimental .38 caliber. It is believed that Winchester considered introducing a companion handgun to the Model 1876 rifle. If so, this would explain their choice of a long cylinder; the Model 1876 rifle was chambered for the .45-75, and later the .45-60, .50-95 Express and .40-60 cartridges.

The swing-out cylinder revolvers are all in .44-40 caliber, excepting one pistol in an unidentified experimental .44 chambering. Undoubtedly these guns, had they gone into production, would have been promoted as companion sidearms to the Model 1873 rifle. The common caliber for that gun was .44-40.

Factory records

Precise data on the Winchester-Borchardt revolvers come from miscellaneous references in an original contract book from the 1870's. This rare volume lists various special orders of an experimental nature, including all 12 Winchester-Borchardt pistols.

The making of these revolvers began as early as Mar. 2, 1876, with an order to contractor R. H. Brown to make "1 Frame for Self cocking model pistol." This gun is No. 644 in the Win-

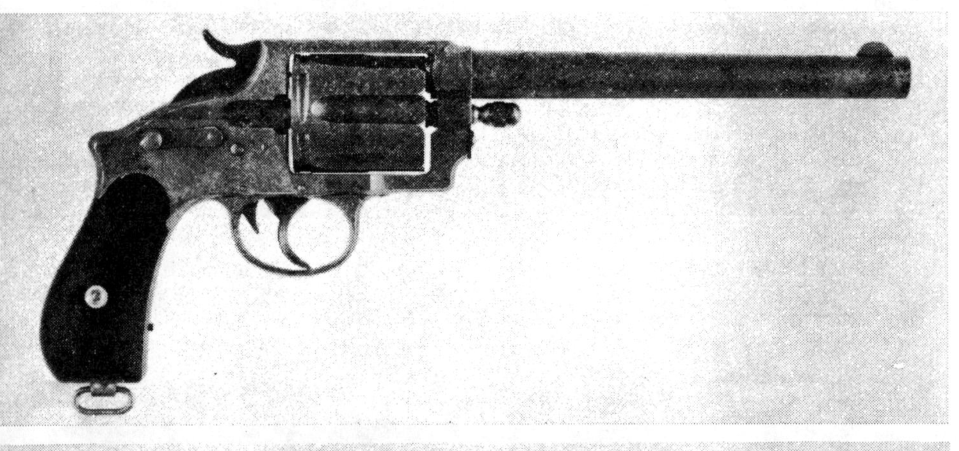

Probably the first Winchester-Borchardt revolver made was double action 6-shot cal. .44 revolver with thumb-extractor. Note length of cylinder, stop grooves in periphery.

The only completely finished thumb-extractor model of the Borchardt design is of cal. .44 and has long cylinder. Finish is nickel plating, the grips are checkered walnut. Thumb catch holds cylinder in place.

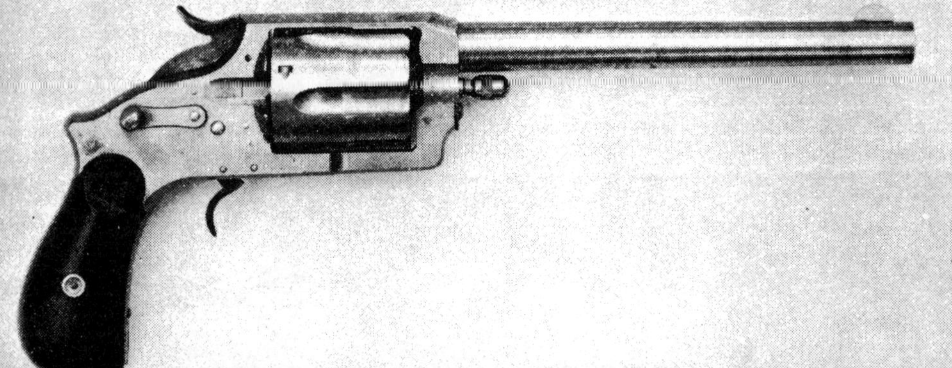

Single-action 6-shot thumb-extractor revolver is of cal. .44 and has long fluted cylinder. Note wide-spur hammer and small cylinder stop notches. Finished in the white; no trigger guard.

Single-action 6-shot thumb-extractor revolver chambered for cal. .38 experimental cartridge. Note spur in trigger guard, and unusual extractor on frame. Finished in the white, with walnut grips.

chester Museum. Notes for Apr. 25 include references to "Counterboring Recess for head of extractor." As the swing-out cylinder revolvers were fitted with ejectors, it is probable that the various notes for Apr. 25 refer to the thumb-lever extractor types. References to "Pistol Frame Drill jigs" are assumed to be for the thumb-extractor types, mainly due to their closeness in date to the Apr. 25 references.

Some months later, the factory contractor records noted: "New Model #44 Pistol Frame" and "#44. pistol Frame". These are the swing-out cylinder types. They total 6 revolvers, one of them the privately owned specimen and another the missing Russian test gun. The other 4 are Nos. 647, 649, 1779, and 1781 in the Winchester Museum.

The final date for revolvers in the contractor notes is Oct. 20, 1876. March through October gives the known design period a total of only 8 months. How much time of preparation preceded that earliest known date, of Mar. 2 is currently unknown.

According to George R. Watrous' *The History of Winchester Firearms 1866-1966,* pages 23-24:

> On Dec. 5, 1876, Amory Edwards, representing the Winchester Repeating Arms Company, submitted to the Ordnance Bureau of the United States Navy a sample of the revolver with a quantity of cartridges and copies of the instructions covering the method of operating the firearm. . . .

Winchester obviously settled on the swing-out cylinder type as a superior design, since that is the gun submitted to the Navy Ordnance. Further studying Watrous' quotation, in which instructions for operations are reviewed, it is apparent that the submitted revolver was the privately owned specimen illustrated.

This pistol is complete in every detail, and fits the operational description quoted as accompanying the submitted revolver:

> To open: Take the pistol in the left hand, draw the rod on the under side toward the muzzle with the right hand and press it toward you. The revolving chamber opens toward you. The extractor is pressing down on the end of the rod, and it closes with a twist of the left wrist.

Since the Army and Navy both had a preference for case-hardened frame colors—as witness the Single Action Army Colt revolver which had been bought by Army Ordnance since 1873—it is understandable why this Navy test gun is similarly finished. Other noteworthy similarities with the already tried and true Single Action Colt are the barrel lengths (Winchester 7", Colt 7½"), the solid frame, open sights, single action mechanism, 6 shot half-fluted cylinder, and the caliber (Winchester: 44-40; Colt: .45).

The history of the "Navy Test Gun" has been traced in ownership to the original Washington Navy Yard Museum, which had originated in the 1830's as a depository of test and experimental arms submitted for consideration by Navy Ordnance. Many guns from that collection are now in the Smithsonian Institution, Washington, D.C. and the Marine Corps Museum, Quantico, Va.

The Watrous study also states: "The revolver was . . . submitted to (Col. Ordinetz) of the Ordnance Department of the Russian Army." Precisely when such action took place is unknown, but it was probably early in 1877. Kasavery Ordinetz was a Russian inspector and contract agent for the purchase of firearms. He was prominently involved in the purchase of handguns from Smith & Wesson during the 1870's, holding the rank of Captain, and later Colonel. Russian preference was for a large handgun firing .44 caliber cartridges. Ordinetz himself is credited with some of the prominent design features on the S&W "Russian Model" revolvers, including the distinctive spur on the trigger guard. Many features on these pistols were close to what Borchardt developed for Winchester: .44 caliber, 6 shots, 7" barrel, large frame, saw-handle type grip with hump at top, wide spur hammer, and fluted cylinder. There is a striking similarity in profile between the S&W Russian models and the Winchester Borchardt swing-out cylinder revolvers.

Over 100,000 "Russian Model" revolvers were purchased by Russia. Most of these were on contracts signed before the Winchester-Borchardt designs of 1876 were fabricated. The last Russian contracts with S&W were in 1876-77, and totalled 41,248 revolvers. These were sizeable amounts of guns, and well worth pursuit by Winchester, Colt's, and other gunmakers.

The present whereabouts of the Russian test gun—the only missing Winchester revolver—is unknown. Should it ever be discovered it will likely have as part of its design the spurred trigger-guard as had the S&W Russian Model.

A lack of markings is common to all but 6 of the Winchester-Borchardt revolvers. Four of these have W.R.A. Co. engraved in script on the top of each barrel, a marking added several years after production to show factory ownership. The 2 other marked guns are of special interest. Gun No. 1781 is a swing-out cylinder design, in the white, with case-hardened hammer, trigger, and trigger guard. This revolver is marked with an M (denoting Model) on the cylinder, the crane, the extractor, and on the barrel. The date 1877 is marked on the cylinder. The other marked revolver is No. 1779. This pis-

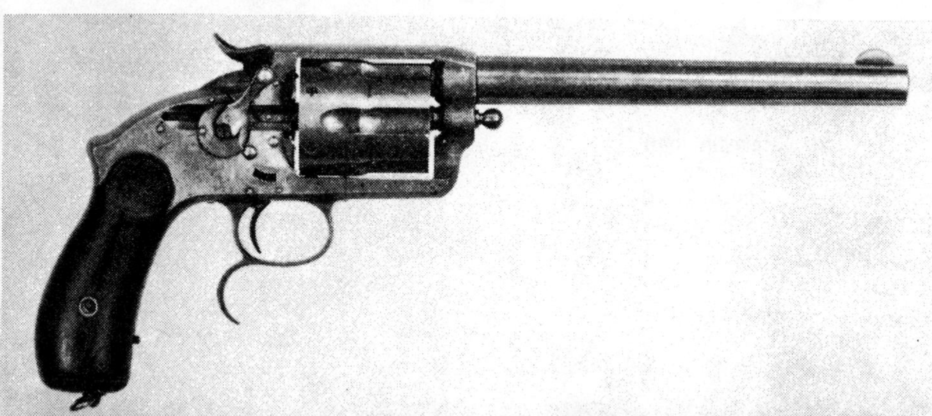

tol is incomplete, lacking a cylinder, grips, and several minor parts. On the barrel is marked the tiny number "1". This gun is closely similar to the Model 1877 pistol and to the "Navy Test Gun," and shows some thought on the part of Winchester toward entering into production.

No documentary evidence exists to prove or disprove any part played by Hugo Borchardt in the design of the Winchester revolvers of 1876. Tradition credits him as their designer, and both George R. Watrous and Edwin Pugsley (long-term Winchester officials) were told by company personnel that these guns were Borchardt's creation. Further evidence is from the company memoir written by former Winchester Director D. H. Veader and Secretary-Treasurer A. W. Earle. These men had joined Winchester in 1869 and 1883 respectively, and Earle was involved in patent work in addition to his other duties. Their study was put into typed form in 1918, and the reliability of their attributions to Borchardt has the endorsement of Winchester Museum Curator T. E. Hall.

Winchester, Sharps, and Colt's employed the talented Borchardt as a mechanic and designer during various periods of his career. He is credited with playing an important role in the development of the Luger automatic pistol and the Sharps Borchardt single shot rifle. He also designed many features used on early Colt automatic pistols. Borchardt is regarded as a man of vision whose ideas were often well in advance of his contemporaries in the arms field. Certainly the Model 1876 and 1877 revolvers reflect the approach of such an individual.

Records show his period of employment with Winchester as including the years 1875, 1876, and 1877. His interest in and knowledge of handguns are well known. It has been said, and probably accurately, that the lack of any production by Winchester on his new revolvers was a factor in Borchardt's decision to leave their employ. Recent research reveals that an S. W. Wood was involved in much of the design work on the "Navy Test Gun", though nothing but an obscure reference in a Winchester letter of December 5, 1876 suggests this. No data are presently known about Wood.

William Mason, a talented inventor and engineer, joined the Winchester Repeating Arms Company in 1882.

One of his first projects was the design of a single action revolver. This pistol is illustrated, and includes the following features: .44-40 six shot fluted cylinder, 7½" barrel with integral ejector tube, and solid frame with fixed cylinder.

Only one revolver of the Mason design was produced, and it is now in the Winchester Museum. It bears no markings and there is no evidence it was ever patented. Finish is in the white, as was common with experimental arms of the period. A close comparison of this pistol with the Colt Single Action Army shows many points of similarity. The most obvious are overall symmetry, caliber, barrel length, and the single action mechanism. It is not surprising to note that Mason's employer previous to Winchester was the Colt firm, and that he had been the chief designer and patentee of the Colt Single Action Army revolver.

William Mason is well known to collectors, as he had many patents on hand and long arms with the Colt firm, for whom he worked as a designer and engineer in the period 1870 through 1882. However, it is not widely known that Mason was also an employee of the Remington Arms Company (prior to joining Colt's), and of the Winchester Repeating Arms Company (after resigning from Colt's). With Winchester, where he remained until his death in 1913, one of Mason's best known achievements was in the design of the single action revolver described above.

Mason is known to have had some 125 patents through the course of his long career. The majority were in the arms and ammunition field, but they also included inventions in the areas of steam engines, textiles, and bridge con-

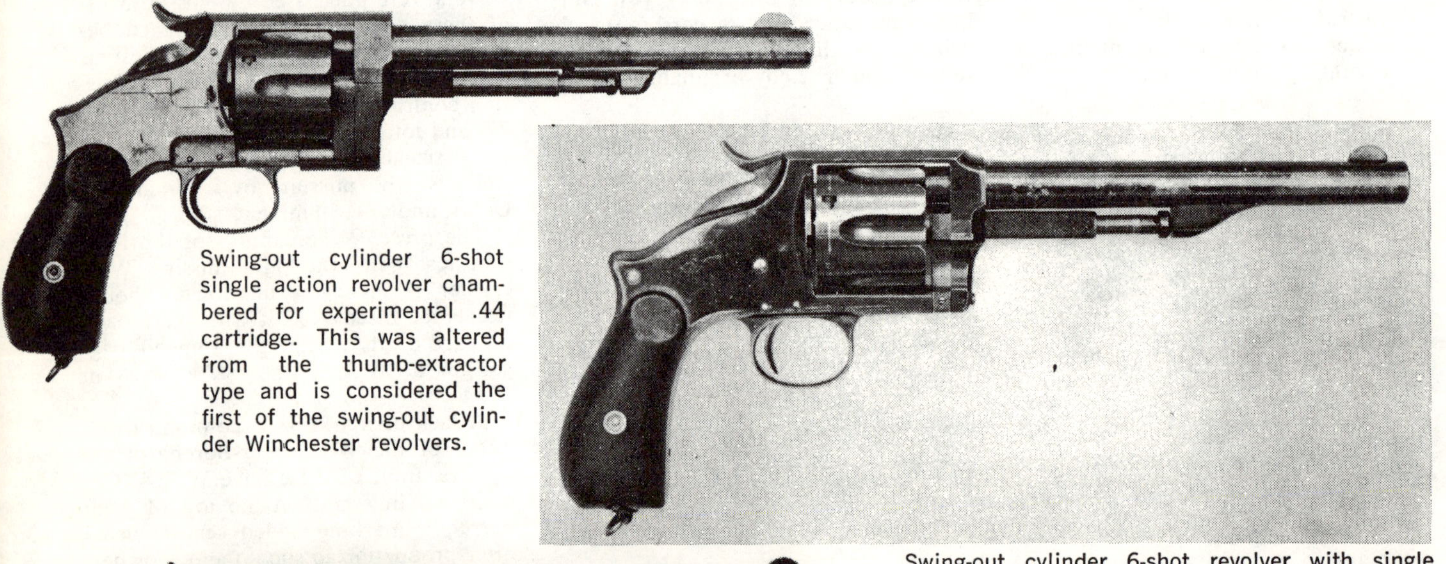

Swing-out cylinder 6-shot single action revolver chambered for experimental .44 cartridge. This was altered from the thumb-extractor type and is considered the first of the swing-out cylinder Winchester revolvers.

Swing-out cylinder 6-shot revolver with single action mechanism in cal. .44-40. Blued finish, with walnut grips; lanyard ring in butt. The cylinder locks in place at the front section of frame.

One of the 3 known completely finished specimens of the Borchardt swing-out cylinder design pistols in cal. .44-40 with 6-15/16" barrel. Cylinder locked in place at front section of frame.

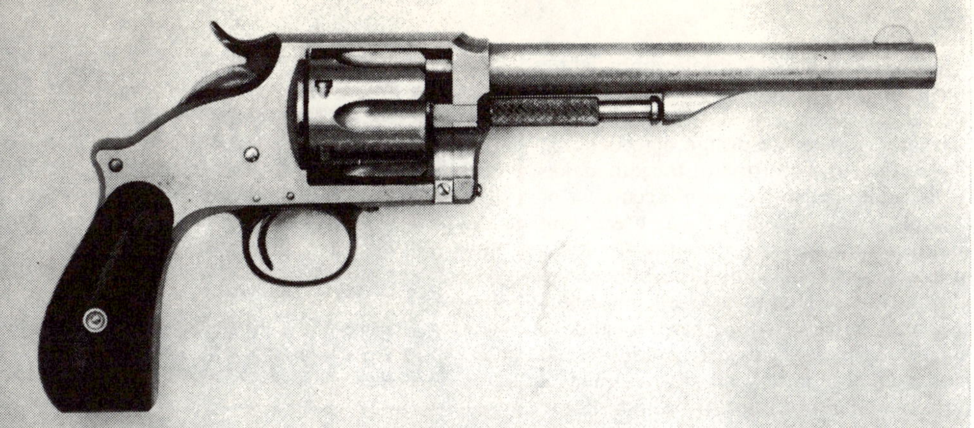

In-white Borchardt design Winchester revolver, marked M and dated 1877 made in 1876.

struction. It was unusual that a design of such merit as the single action .44-40 Winchester revolver was not patented for possible future manufacture, when the prolific Mason had it seems patented everything else he had developed.

For some unknown reason Winchester never patented the revolver designs of either Borchardt or Mason. This perhaps can be interpreted as evidence the firm did not intend to enter the highly competitive handgun field, excepting for a United States or Russian government order. The advanced designs of both the Model 1876-77 and Model 1883 revolvers demonstrate Winchester's capability to enter the handgun market had they wished to do so.

In the 1870's the sizeable purchases of handguns by the United States and Russian governments, from Colt's and Smith & Wesson respectively, did not go unnoticed by the Winchester firm. It appears that since Winchester went so far as to make samples of revolvers for test by both the U.S. Navy Ordnance and the Russian Army Ordnance, they intended to enter into production to satisfy any ensuing contracts.

The Mason Model of 1883 probably was prompted by 2 circumstances: (1) Mason's availability as a newly hired Winchester designer with proven aptitude for handgun design, and (2) the threat from Colt's Burgess lever action rifle as competition to the Model 1873 Winchester. It is a tradition at both Colt's and Winchester that officials of each agreed that Colt's would leave the lever action rifle business if Winchester would not enter into handgun manufacture.

One might assume that if Winchester were seriously considering entering the handgun field, more than one revolver of the Mason design would have been produced. The date proximity—1883 for both the Burgess rifle and the Winchester-Mason revolver—helps to suggest a 'gentleman's agreement.' Having 10 Borchardt revolvers in their engineering department gave Winchester more than just the Mason revolver as tools for any bargaining with Colt's.

Colt's suddenly dropped the Burgess after production of approximately one year. The threat of Winchester competition plus a possible weak sales showing of the Colt-Burgess probably were responsible for this halt in production.

It may also be that the credited source of the gentleman's agreement story, T. G. Bennett, was much too reliable to have been responsible for a tall tale. Bennett, a son-in-law of Oliver Winchester, was Company Secretary, then Vice President, and later President. He told Edwin Pugsley about the historic meeting not long after Pugsley joined the firm in 1911, not too many years after the event allegedly took place.

Though no one can prove it one way or the other, the 'gentleman's agreement' story seems to be true. But true or not, it is certainly one of the more colorful traditions from the histories of the Winchester and Colt firms.

The first swing-out cylinder and cylinder-pin-ejection revolver mass produced in America was the Colt Double Action Model 1889. As a world leader in handgun manufacture, Colt's initial patent for this new type handgun was the Ehbets design of 1884 (Patent No. 303827, Aug. 19, 1884). It is of great interest to note that Winchester, which never entered into revolver manufacture, made the first known swing-out cylinder and cylinder-pin-ejection revolver in the United States, or for that matter, in the world. Their Model 1876-77 Borchardt predates the Ehbets-Colt pistols by no less than 8 years and the Model 1889 Colt by 13.

The Borchardt and Mason revolvers are the only handguns made under the Winchester name, and with a total production of only 13 are among the great rarities in gun history.

These pistols are also very early specimens of .44-40, .44 and .38 cartridge chamberings. It was not until 1878 that Colt's brought out the Single Action Army in .44-40 caliber. As far as known at present, the unidentified .38 and .44 cartridges of the Borchardt Winchesters were experimental.

The Winchester revolvers are proof of the progressive and aggressive approach the Winchester firm has traditionally assumed in the arms field. As one of the world's foremost gun and cartridge makers they have retained a position of leadership into our modern era. Their expansion into related arms fields, including the promotion of skeet and trap ranges, is in the tradition of leadership traceable to their beginnings in the 1860's, and such pioneer accomplishments as the Borchardt and Mason revolvers. ■

The author wishes to express his appreciation to Messrs. T. E. Hall, John J. Malloy, and Alan S. Kelley for their assistance in completing this study. Illustrations courtesy Winchester-Western and Messrs. Kelley-Malloy.

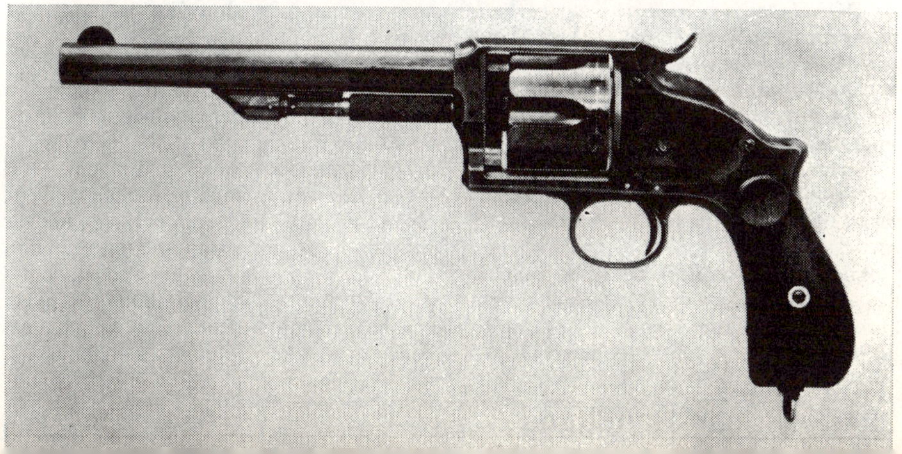

This is the "Navy Test Gun" of the Winchester revolver series. Considered the most sophisticated of the Borchardt designs done for Winchester in 1876. Caliber is .44-40, 6-shot, swing-out cylinder, barrel length 7". The only Winchester-Borchardt revolver in private hands.

Warner Infallible

Continued from page 219

The Davis-Warner Corp. was short lived. On April 19, 1919, Franklin Warner assumed full control, changed the name of the company back to The Warner Arms Corp. and returned to Norwich, Conn., taking with him the manufacturing equipment for the gun. Thus, the Fourth Model is mechanically identical to the Third. Only the marking was changed, to read:

"THE INFALLIBLE"
WARNER ARMS CORPORATION,
NORWICH, CT, U.S.A.

Approximately 2,000 of this model were made from April, 1919, until all production ceased in 1920 or 1921.

It is unfortunate irony that the gun called "Infallible" was actually a very unreliable piece. The paradox is furthered by the fact that the same mechanical features that made it unique, made the Infallible dangerous.

As the gun was made, the breechbolt disconnect took the form of a lever on the left side of the bolt. Rotating the disconnect 180° frees the bolt from the recoil springs. This feature might have appealed to some who had trouble in pulling back the slide of a conventional semi-automatic pistol, but its fatal weakness was that the gun could be fired with the recoil rods disconnected. In that event only the bolt stop kept the breechbolt from recoiling clear of the gun and possibly striking the shooter. To further compound this hazard, the bolt stop could be disengaged — as though for disassembly — and the gun could still be fired.

The Warner Arms Corp. must have recognized these problems at some time prior to the introduction of the Third Model. An instruction sheet, packed with one of the guns, lays stress on making certain that the breechbolt is connected to the recoil rods before firing the gun. In addition, as previously noted, the rotating disconnect lever of the First and Second Models was replaced in the Third Model guns by a pin that had to be pushed out with the magazine floorplate before the recoil rods could be disconnected.

Other serious weaknesses are apparent from the following *"DON'TS"* included in the instruction sheet:

"DON'T try to cock the pistol with safety on; you will break or bend your sear."

"DON'T pull with over 10 pounds to fire the pistol without looking to see if the safety is on or you will bend your sear."

I can vouch for the validity of the first "don't." I have a broken Infallible, the result of cocking the pistol with the safety on.

Another mechanical defect is quickly noted. The firing pin is unusually light and, although the firing pin spring is quite long, it is of small diameter. Due to this, the Infallible has a noticeably lighter firing pin blow than other semi-automatic pistols.

In addition to the design defects noted above, the configuration of the gun makes it difficult to shoot with accuracy or comfort. The design of a breechbolt sliding within the frame and the mounting of the recoil rods above the bolt places most of the weight high, directly above the shooter's hand. This makes the gun so muzzle light that it will stand erect if placed on the butt. Warner attempted to turn this feature into a selling point, claiming that: "The gun is so scientifically balanced that it will stand upright alone on an even surface, a very valuable quality to ensure accuracy under rapid fire." This statement ignored accepted principles of handgun balance, but at least it was something that could be said about the Infallible that could not be said about any other semi-automatic pistol.

With all the recoiling mass high above the shooter's hand, the Infallible gives more felt recoil than other .32 cal. semi-automatic pistols. This problem is aggravated by the short grip needed to keep the overall height within a reasonable limit. Thus, a man with an average size hand will be able to place only two fingers around the front of the grip.

Having pointed out all the bad features, it is time to look at some of the good ones. First, the very features that made the Infallible dangerous — it being top heavy and muzzle light — made it cheap and easy to manufacture. Rather than a complex and expensive slide, the Infallible had a simple, lathe-turned bolt which slid within a hole drilled in the frame. The recoil rods and springs also were mounted in drilled holes in the frame. This meant little or no fitting and very little milling, both expensive operations. The barrel was solidly attached to the frame with two pins (one pin on later models) and required only a minimum of fitting.

At first glance, the barrel looks like a machinist's nightmare, but the milling required could have been done in a single operation with form cutters. In short, the design which had so many flaws was a deliberate attempt to minimize the manufacturing costs of the gun. The attempt was successful. A Warner Infallible, complete with two magazines, a leather holster, and six shooting lessons, was priced at $18.50, about $7.00 less than most semi-automatics.

Despite its low cost, the Infallible was a failure. With its inherent shortcomings, it stood no chance against the many well-designed products of Colt, Savage, Remington and the various European makers. However, the unique features of the Infallible, coupled with a short life span of only five to six years and a total production of less than 10,000 guns make it a much sought-after piece for the arms collector of today. ■

Questions & Answers

Walman Pistol

Pre-World War I pistol might appear to be American made from the name stamped on the slide but is actually of Spanish origin.

I have a Walman Patent. 32 ACP pistol marked **American.** *I am told that it is actually not American made but is of Spanish origin. Can you confirm this and tell me when my gun was made and if parts are available for it?*

Answer: Your information is correct. The firm of Arizmendi y Goenaga was founded in Eibar, Spain in 1886 and devoted its early years to the manufacture of revolvers. Around 1908, their first autoloading pistols were introduced — among them those bearing the Walman Patent marking. Some of these pocket pistols were also marked *American Automatic Pistol,* apparently for the export market.

Your pistol bears Arizmendi y Goenaga's half-moon/AG/crown mark which indicates manufacture before 1914, when the firm name was changed to Francisco Arizmendi Cia. As the Spanish Civil War saw the end of the Arizmendi products, which also included such pistols as the Ydeal and Singer, replacement parts have long been unobtainable except by chance.
— P.D.

IDENTIFICATION & DESCRIPTION

Handgun Grip Styles

A graphic survey of the variety of handgun grips that have been used down through the centuries

By HERSCHEL C. LOGAN

HANDGUN grips down through the centuries have been as varied as the arms upon which they were placed.

It is the purpose of this article to present the basic types to be found. More than one of some types are shown, to illustrate the variety achieved. Simple pen and ink sketches have been employed to best convey at a glance the various basic contours.

The shape of some of the grips is understandable in view of the use of the guns upon which they are found. On other arms one wonders why such a form was employed. Some grips fit the hand remarkably well. Others seem to leave much to be desired, if accuracy was to be any factor.

Grips were designed to afford a means for grasping the gun, but now and then grips having a dual purpose are encountered. An example is the pistol sword, where the grip is used for both pistol and sword. Or the Arabian rat-tail, called by some the original commando arm. Its grip afforded a hold on the gun and served as a very effective gouge for hand-to-hand combat. In cartridge arms one finds the 'knuck' derringers and knuckledusters, arms which could be used to fire a cartridge or as 'knucks' in a personal encounter.

Receptacles are found in the grips of many percussion arms. These were used for holding caps, patches, grease, or nipples. Grips in self-loading arms often hold the cartridge magazine.

Materials used in making grips have included everything from a small forked limb of a tree to ivory or pearl, to say nothing of steel and precious metals. Inlays of wire, ivory, or precious stones are not uncommon.

Through the years designations have been given by collectors to various types of grips, but these by no means cover the field. There are grips which more or less defy any set classification. This treatise recognizes the present names given to some grip contours, and suggests a few new ones. Most familiar of grip shapes are these:

Ball—Grip ending in a large ball, or semi-ball shape. Found on early wheel lock dags (short pistols).

Bird's head — Curved grip usually ending in a rather pointed tip that turns forward.

Bulbous—Grip with butt end formed in exaggerated bulb-like shape.

Combination—Grip having a secondary use as applied to the gun itself. May contain a receptacle for powder, balls, caps, grease, patches, etc. Also includes arms holding a cartridge magazine within the grip. Grips with built-in safety device fall into this category.

Compact—Grip of small square, rectangular, or irregular shape that is economical of space. Found, for the most part, on small pocket arms.

Decorative—Grip having an ornamental butt cap of a face, or of an entire head of a human or animal. May be of wood, ivory, ebony, or metal.

Dual purpose—Grip which has 2 distinct functions, as a handle for the gun and an alternate use. Best typified by those guns commonly known as 'knuck' derringers and knuckledusters. The grip becomes a pair of knucks in the hand of its owner, in combat.

Fishtail, heart, lemon, ram's-horn—Grips of distinctive shapes to be found on early Scottish pistols.

Flared—Grip with butt spreading quite noticeably to both the front and rear rather than to the sides.

Fluted—Grip resembles shape of western grips, but identified by grooves or flutes running up curved vertical part of grips.

Rat-tail—Long pointed finale, ideally suited for personal combat.

Rounded—Butt has rounded corners, rather than the severe edges of the western type.

Saw handle—Grip which bears a similarity to a hand saw handle. Generally set at a right angle to the frame and barrel, and has a slight, or pronounced, projection extending back over the hand.

Shotgun—Grip bearing a resemblance to the stock of a long arm, rather than the customary pistol grip.

Squeezer—Moveable grip which activates the firing mechanism.

Sword, dagger, knife—Straight grips found on edged weapons, rather than on guns.

Western—Grip with wide flat butt sloping up to a smaller neck as it joins the frame. Peculiar to some early American percussion and, later, cartridge arms. Style has been referred to as 'square butt.'

Note: The term "modified" has been used to indicate slight variations in designations. ■

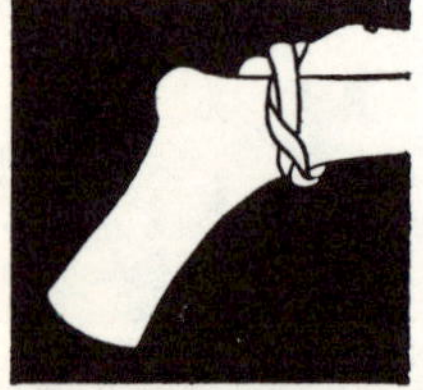
HAND CANNON
Tree limb

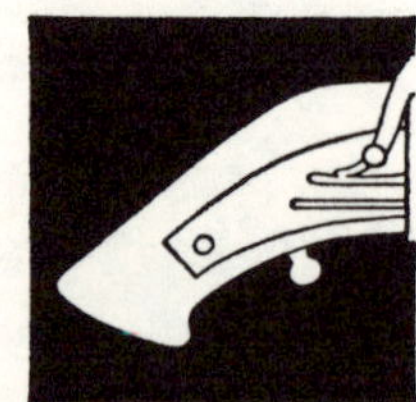
MATCHLOCK
Typical

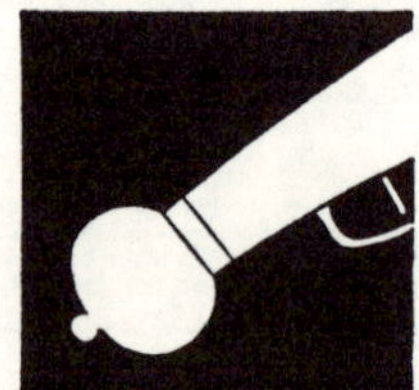
WHEEL LOCK
Ball

WHEEL LOCK
Fishtail, modified

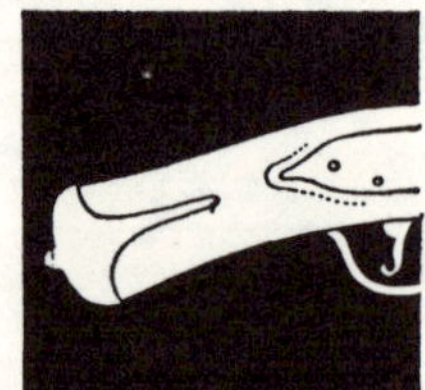
SNAPHAUNCE
Straight, modified

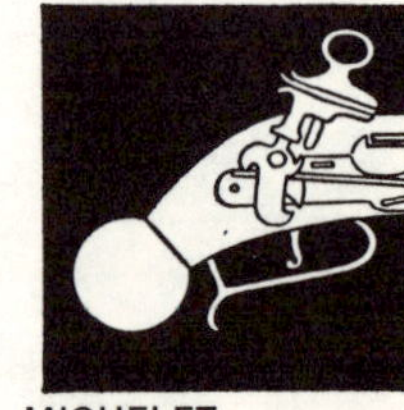
MIQUELET
Ball

MIQUELET
Ball (Cossack)

MIQUELET
Rat-tail

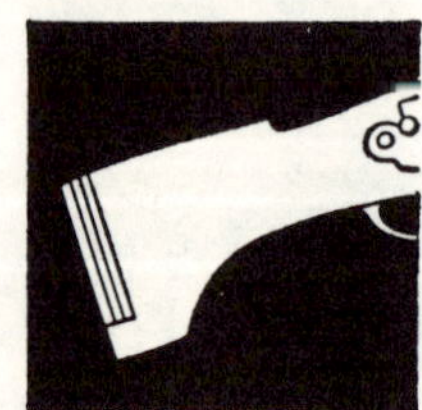
MIQUELET
Shotgun

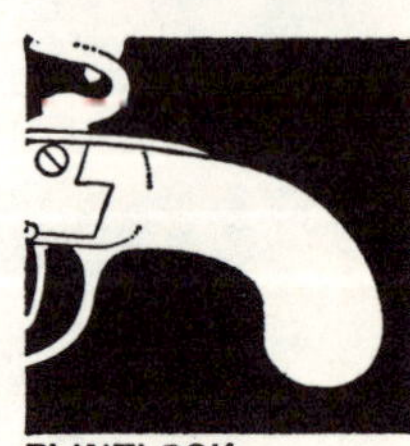
FLINTLOCK
Bag, modified

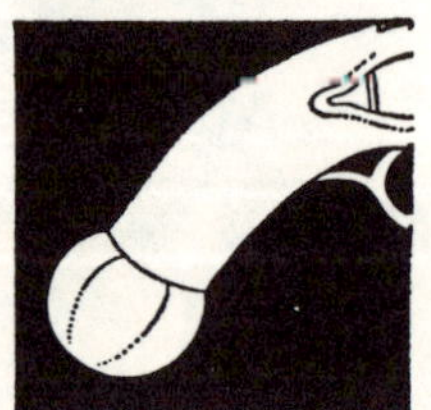
FLINTLOCK
Bulbous, hexagonal

FLINTLOCK
Decorative, ivory

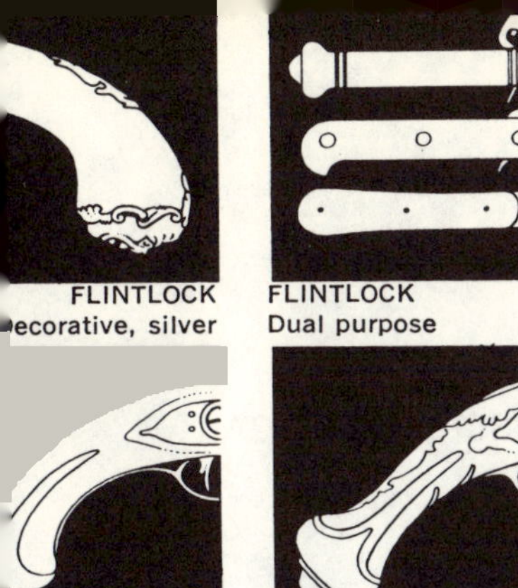

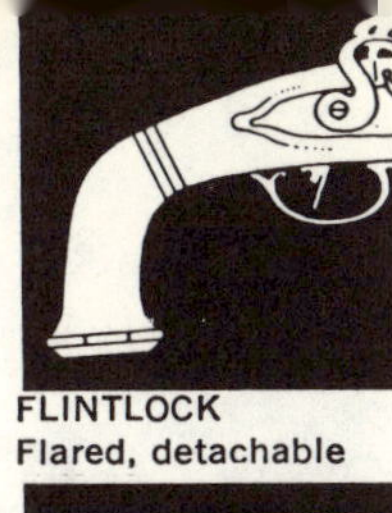
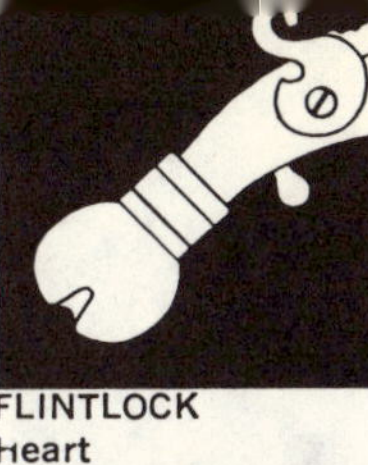
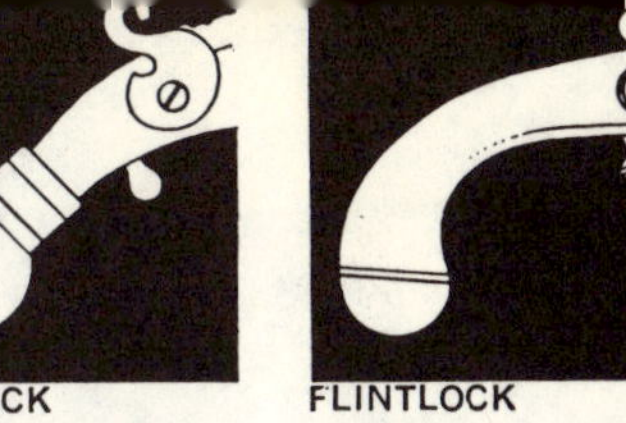

FLINTLOCK
ecorative, silver

FLINTLOCK
Dual purpose

FLINTLOCK
Dual purpose

FLINTLOCK
Fishtail

FLINTLOCK
Flared, detachable

FLINTLOCK
Heart

FLINTLOCK
Lemon

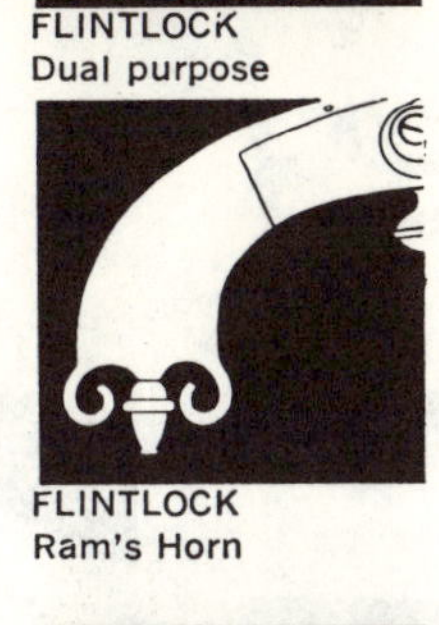

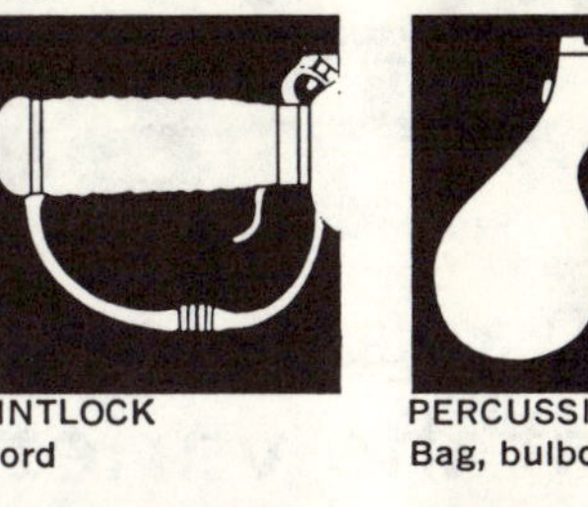

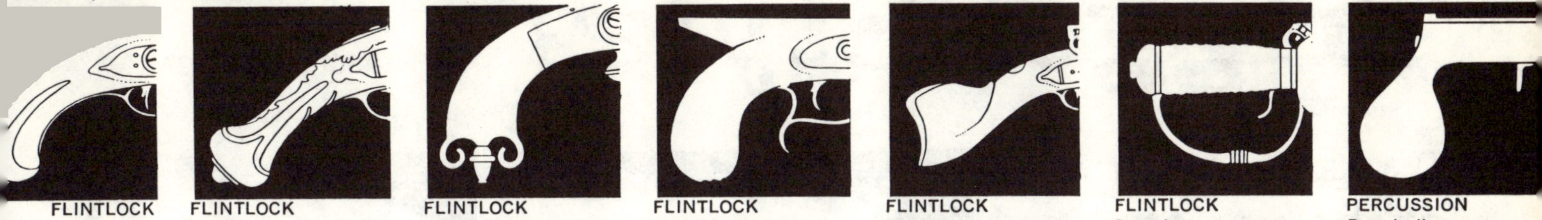

FLINTLOCK
Martial, American

FLINTLOCK
Oriental

FLINTLOCK
Ram's Horn

FLINTLOCK
Saw handle

FLINTLOCK
Shotgun

FLINTLOCK
Sword

PERCUSSION
Bag, bulbous

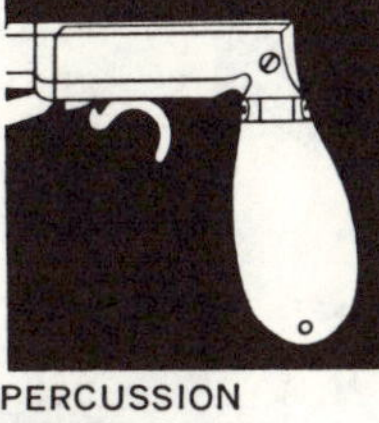
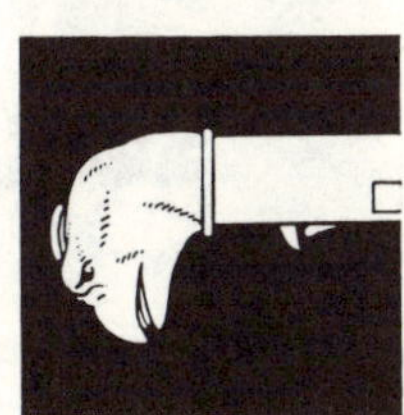
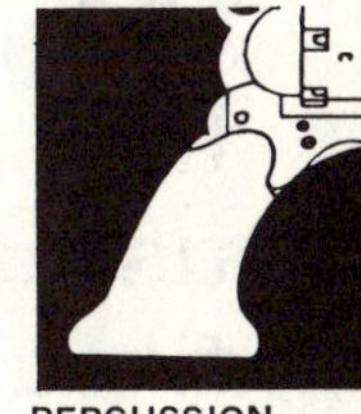

PERCUSSION
Bird's head

PERCUSSION
Combination, container

PERCUSSION
Combination, container

PERCUSSION
Decorative, wooden

PERCUSSION
Decorative, metal

PERCUSSION
Dual purpose, cutlass

PERCUSSION
Flared, Western

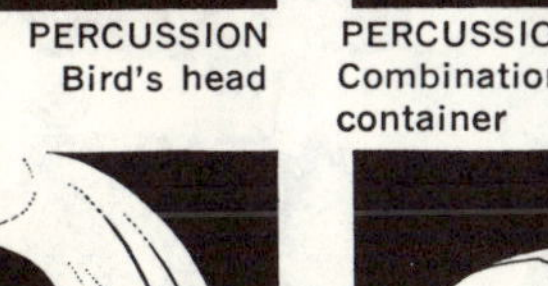
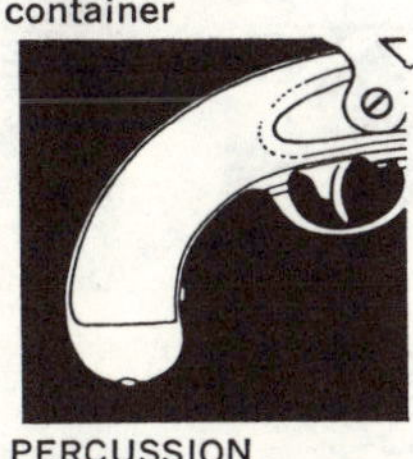

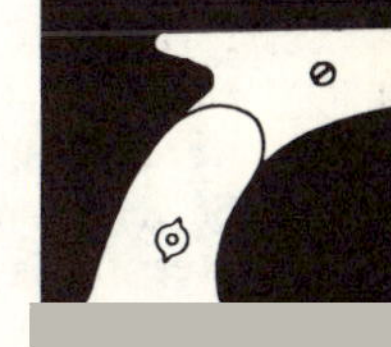

PERCUSSION
Fluted

PERCUSSION
Japanese

PERCUSSION
Martial

PERCUSSION
New England underhammer

PERCUSSION
Saw handle

PERCUSSION
Saw handle

PERCUSSION
Saw handle, modified

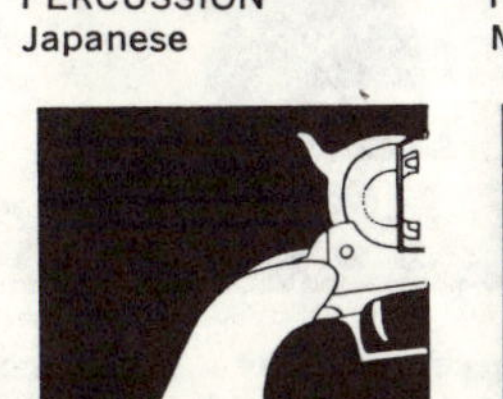
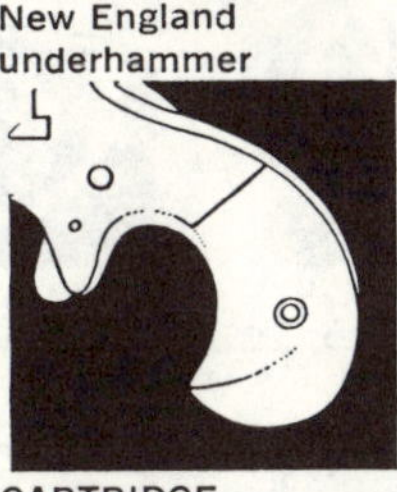
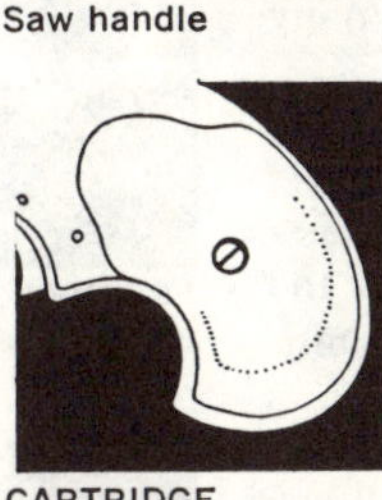
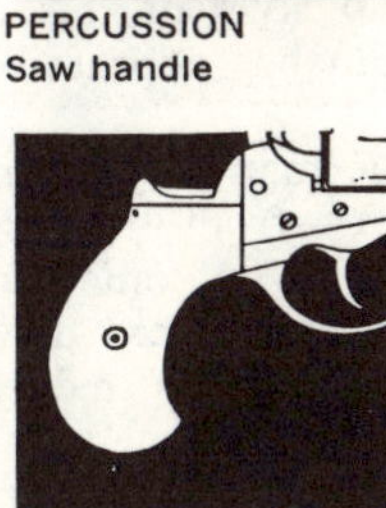
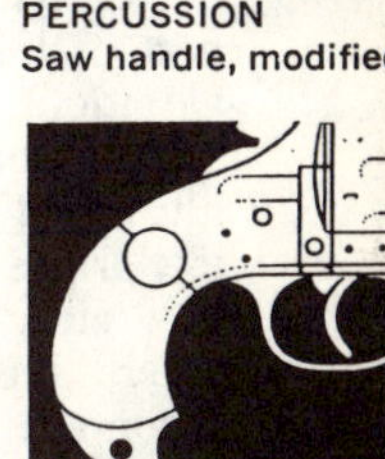
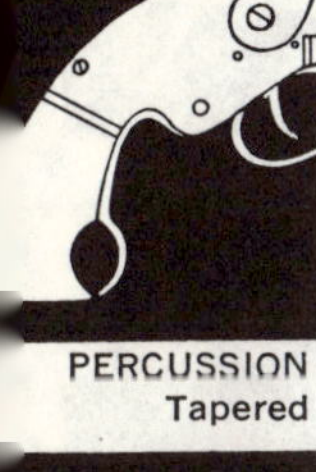

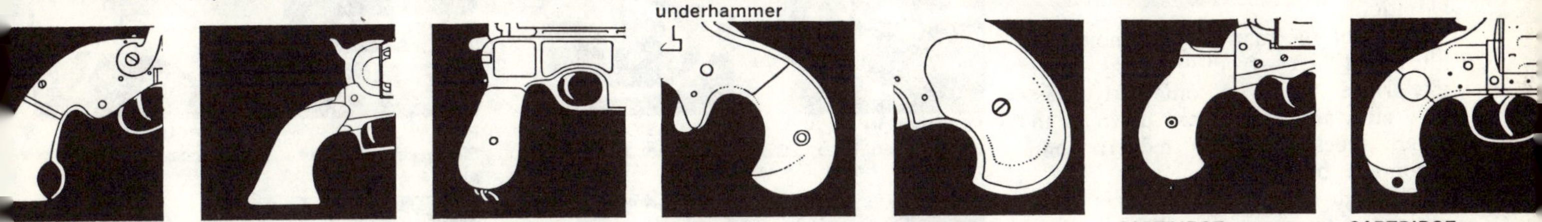

PERCUSSION
Tapered

PERCUSSION
Western

CARTRIDGE
Bag, autoloading

CARTRIDGE
Bird's head, typical

CARTRIDGE
Bird's head, modified

CARTRIDGE
Bird's head, hump

CARTRIDGE
Bird's head, crested

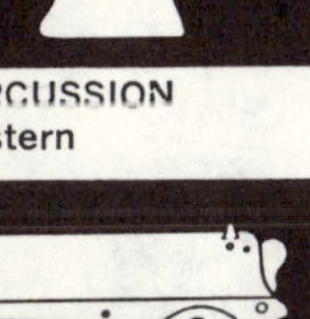
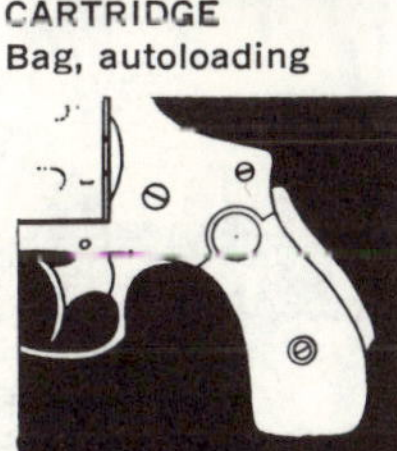
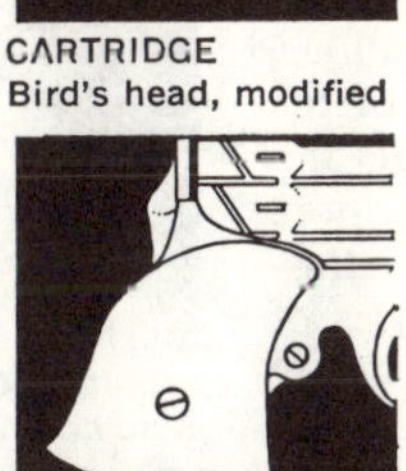
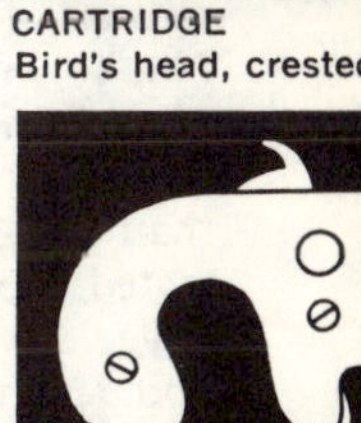
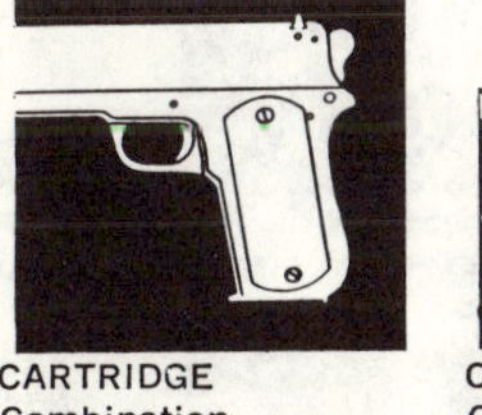

CARTRIDGE
Bird's head, extreme

CARTRIDGE
Combination

CARTRIDGE
Combination, grip safety

CARTRIDGE
Compact, single-shot

CARTRIDGE
Compact, irregular

CARTRIDGE
Compact

CARTRIDGE
Dual purpose, "knuck"

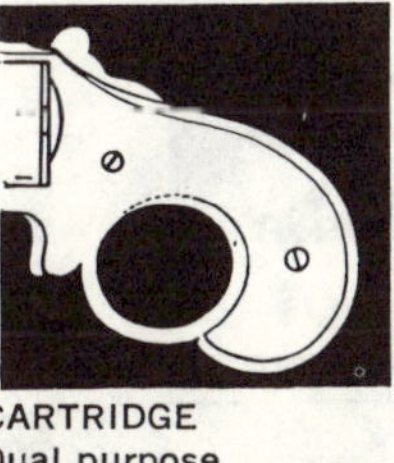
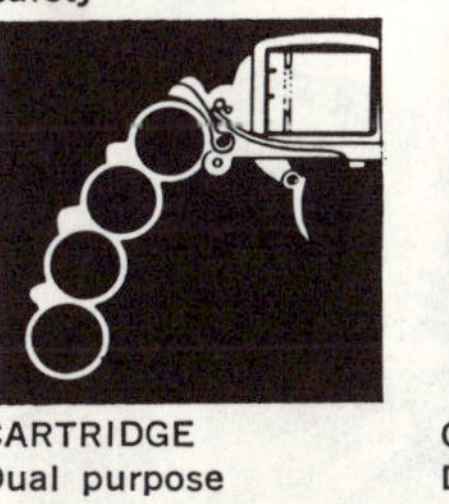
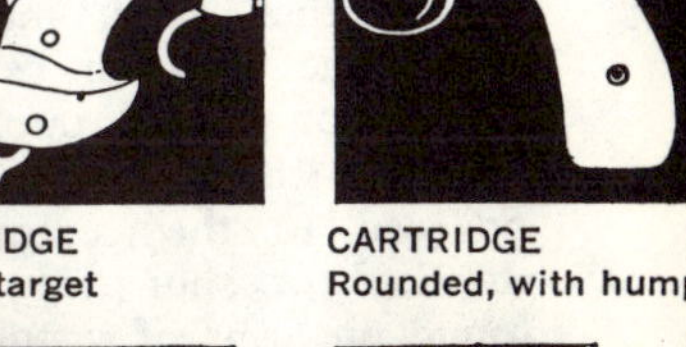

CARTRIDGE
Dual purpose "knuckleduster"

CARTRIDGE
Dual purpose

CARTRIDGE
Dual purpose

CARTRIDGE
Dual purpose, knife

CARTRIDGE
Fishtail

CARTRIDGE
Fitted, target

CARTRIDGE
Rounded, with hump

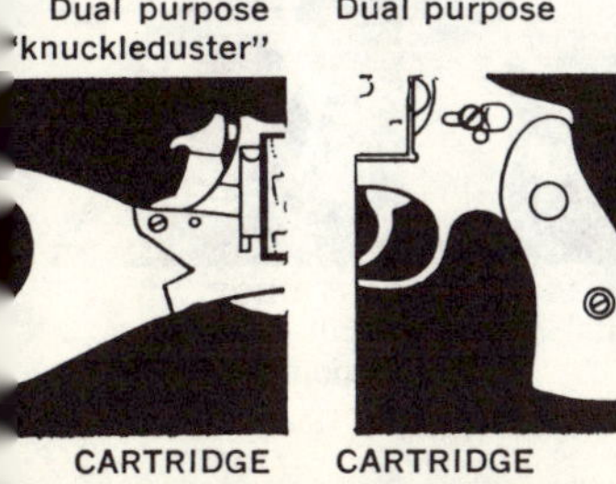
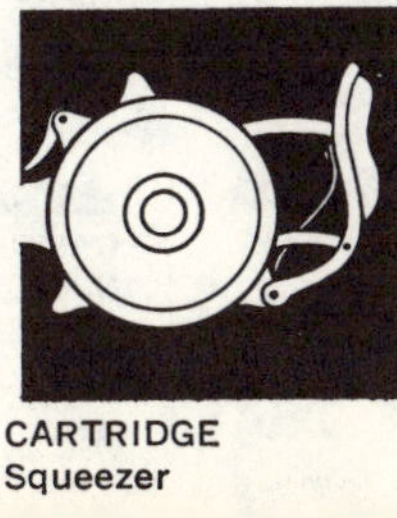
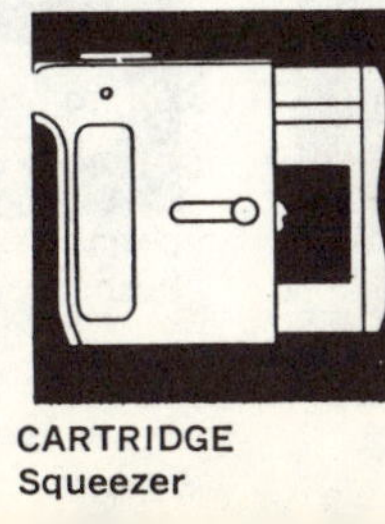
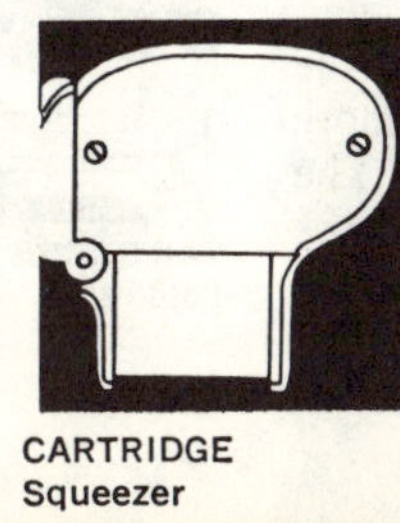
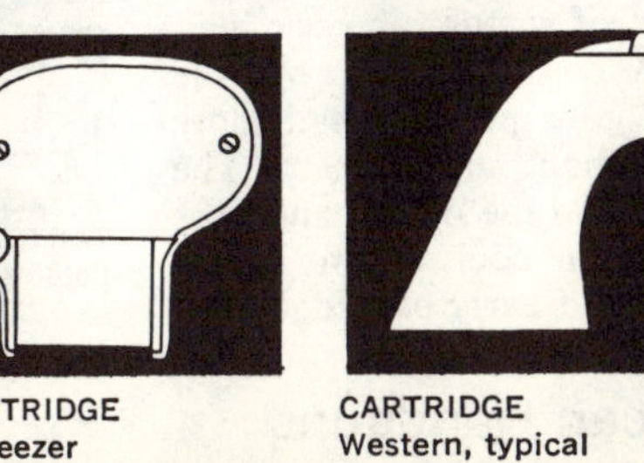

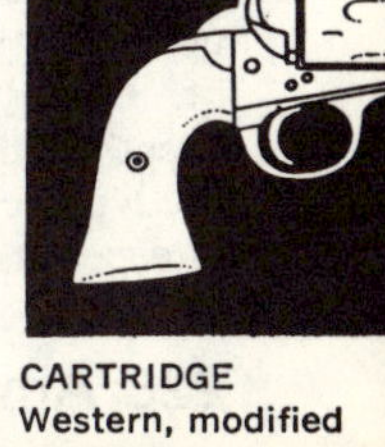

CARTRIDGE
otgun, modified

CARTRIDGE
Square butt

CARTRIDGE
Squeezer

CARTRIDGE
Squeezer

CARTRIDGE
Squeezer

CARTRIDGE
Western, typical

CARTRIDGE
Western, modified

Trigger Styles

By HERSCHEL C. LOGAN

A graphic survey of the variety of triggers that have been used on firearms

THE trigger is a most important part of any gun. Its function is that of activating the lock mechanism when pressure is applied, thereby discharging the firearm. Down through the centuries the design and style of this necessary part of the gun has appeared in many variations.

Some of the many styles known are illustrated here—from the large lever-like trigger found on some early cross-bow guns and matchlocks down to the severe types found on modern semi-automatic handguns.

Through common usage most designations of trigger styles will be familiar. Not so well known may be some of the type names given to other usual and unusual triggers. In some instances more than one variation of a type is illustrated. To attempt to show all styles of triggers would be impossible. They are about as varied as the guns themselves. However, this cross-section will cover most of the basic styles.

Some triggers fall into more than one classification. The folding trigger may be concealed or open. The stud trigger may be but a projection, or it may have a button-like head. A ring trigger may be just that, or it may perform an extra function such as revolving the cylinder or barrel group.

Open triggers without guards, as opposed to the commonly accepted sheathed or spur triggers, are to be found on arms of virtually every ignition period. As a class of arms the under-hammer guns possibly had more of this type than any other. The sheathed trigger, on the other hand, was used principally on pocket arms of the late percussion and early cartridge eras.

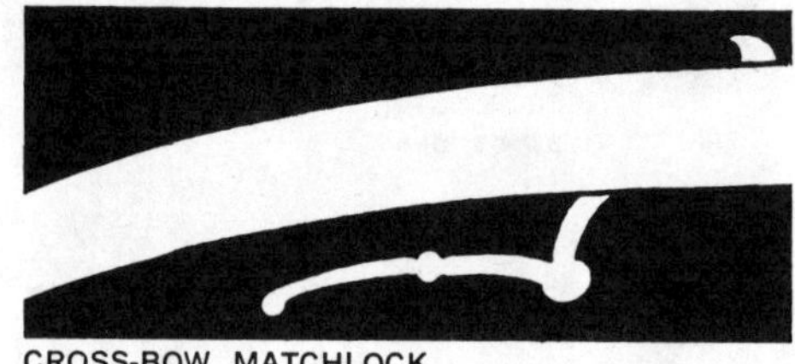
CROSS-BOW, MATCHLOCK
Lever

MATCHLOCK
Ball

MATCHLOCK
Semi-stud

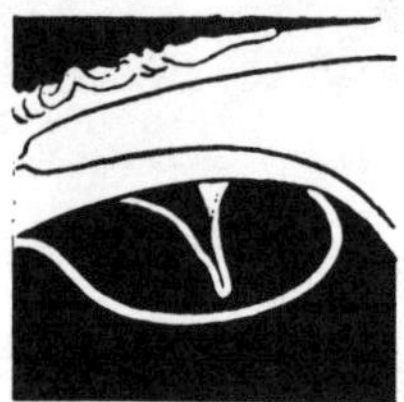
WHEEL LOCK
Skeleton

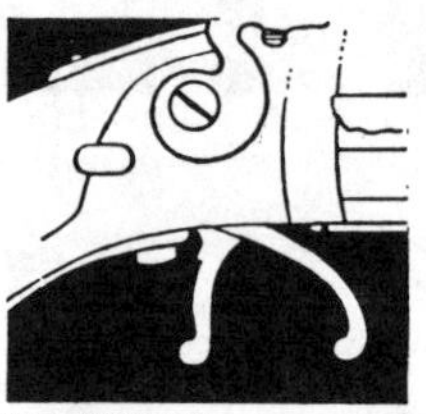
FLINTLOCK
Double open

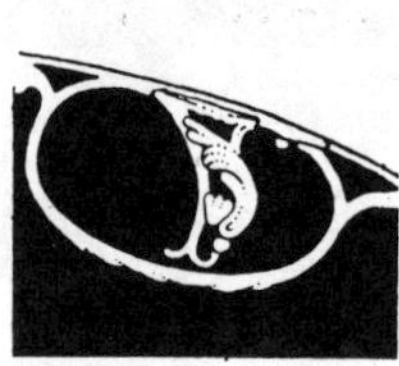
FLINTLOCK
Ornamental

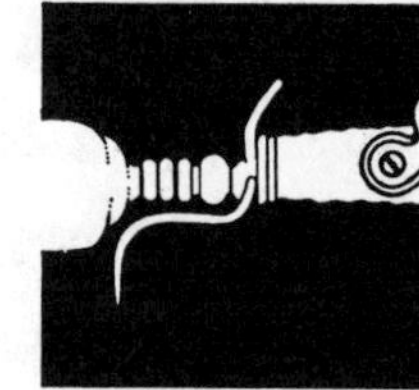
FLINTLOCK
Combination trigger-guard

PERCUSSION
Combination, lower cocks, upper fires

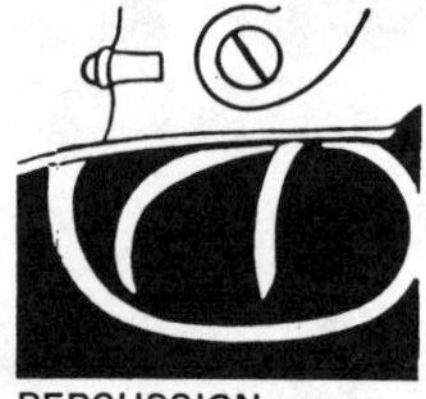
PERCUSSION
Double for 2-shot guns

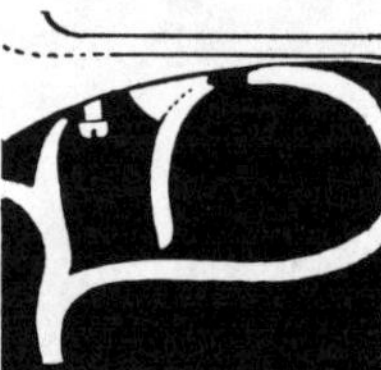
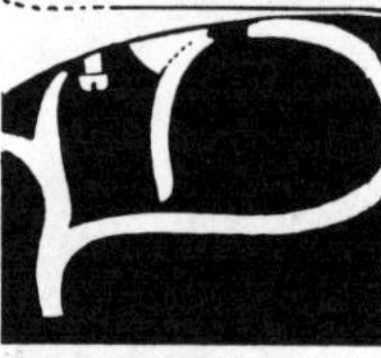
PERCUSSION
Single-set for target pistols

PERCUSSION
Concealed, folding

PERCUSSION
Stud on grip

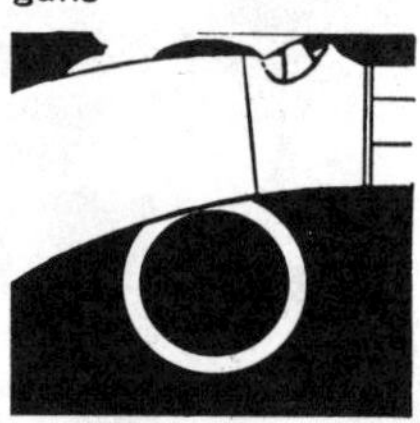
PERCUSSION
Ring

PERCUSSION
Double-set for target pistols

CARTRIDGE
Squeezer, ring-type

CARTRIDGE
Folding with lanyard

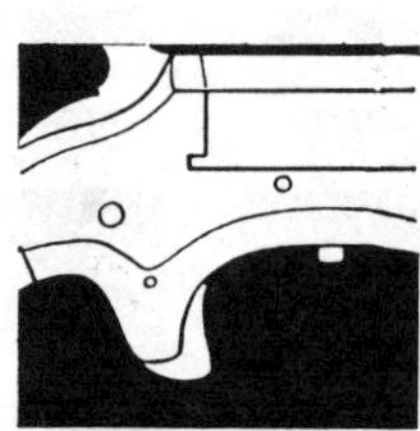
CARTRIDGE
Spur, sheathed

CARTRIDGE
Button, or stud

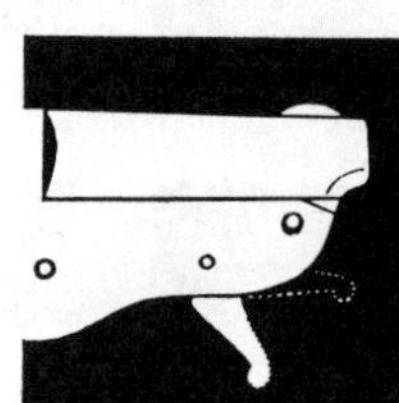
CARTRIDGE
Folding

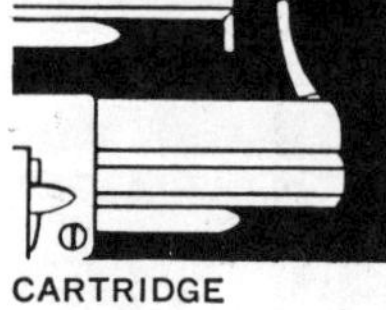

CARTRIDGE
Folding

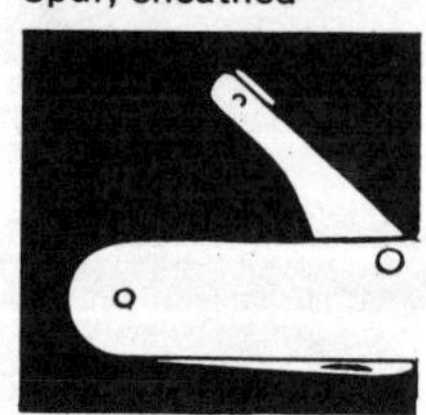
CARTRIDGE
Push, concealed

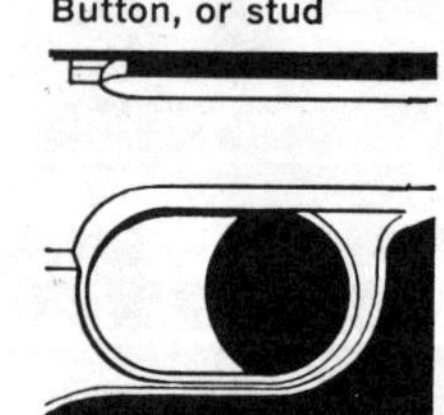
CARTRIDGE
Sliding, horizontal

CARTRIDGE
Circular, on semi-automatic

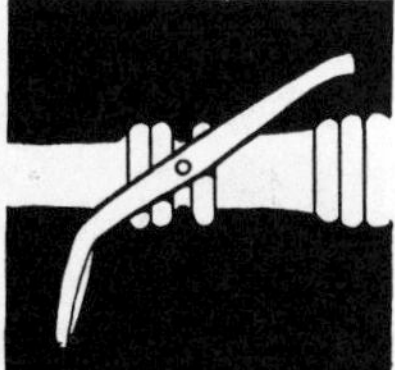
MATCHLOCK
Combination trigger-cock

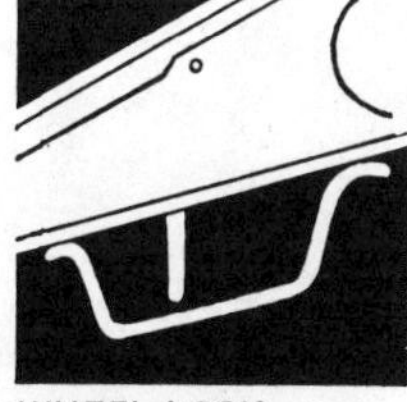
WHEEL LOCK
Straight

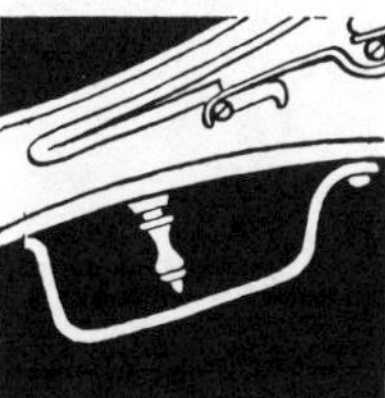
WHEEL LOCK
Decorative

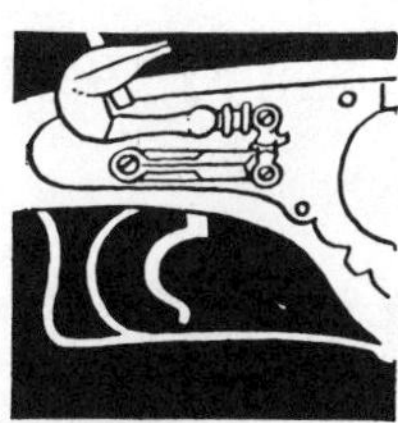
WHEEL LOCK
Half circle

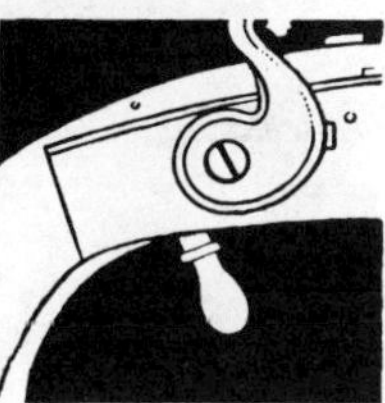
FLINTLOCK
Lemon or tear drop

FLINTLOCK
Semi-ball or spheroid

FLINTLOCK
Reverse or S-curve

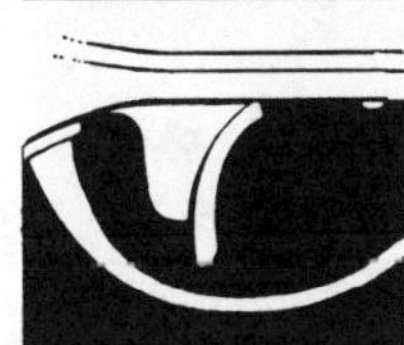
FLINTLOCK
Heavy martial

PERCUSSION
Corkscrew, folding

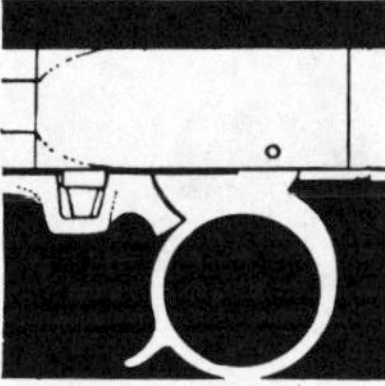
PERCUSSION
Ring

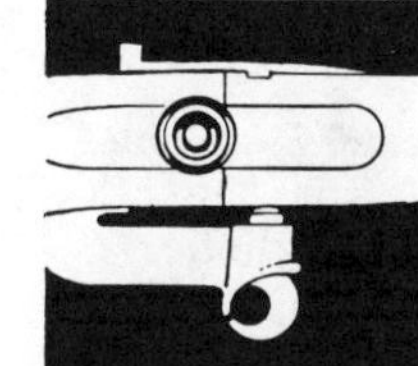
PERCUSSION
Side button

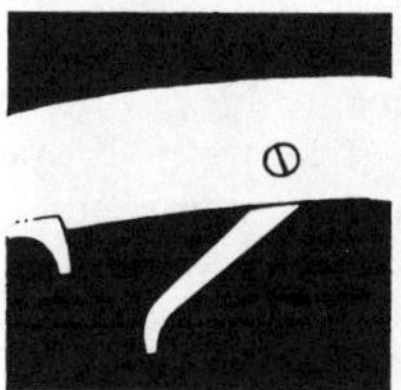
PERCUSSION
Concealed, folding

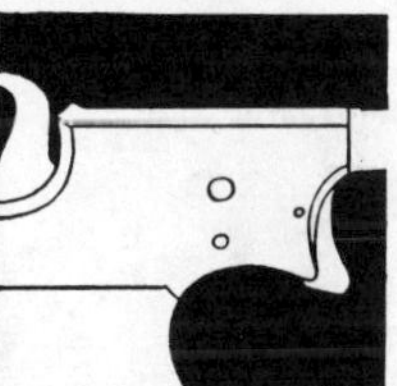
CARTRIDGE
Sheathed

CARTRIDGE
Ring, combination to revolve barrel group

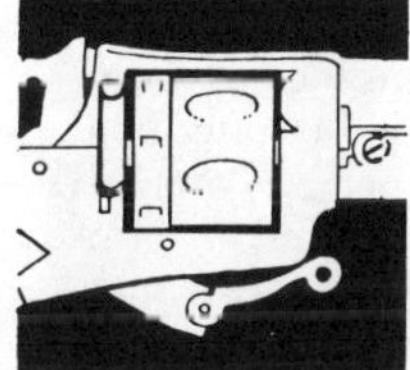
CARTRIDGE
Folding

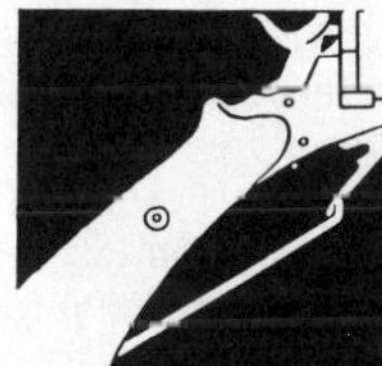
CARTRIDGE
Special, for fingerless person

CARTRIDGE
Button

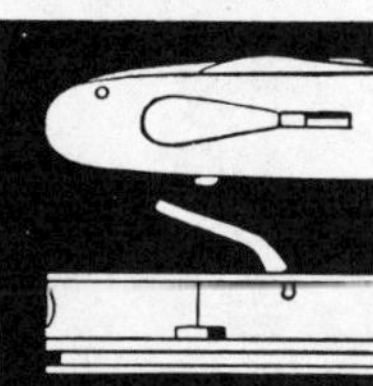
CARTRIDGE
Push, folding

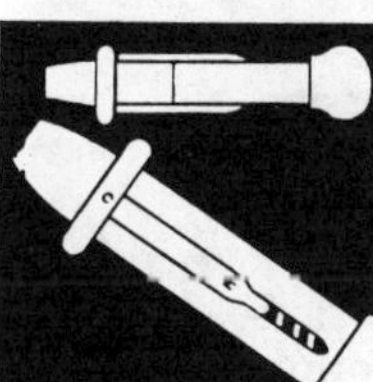
CARTRIDGE
Squeezer

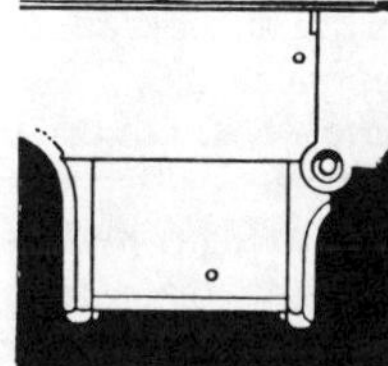
CARTRIDGE
Squeezer

PERCUSSION
Typical styles—underhammer guns

Antique Gun Safety

San Jose, Calif.

Editor:

Most users of antique muzzle-loading firearms are aware of the need for a solidly-fitting breech plug. Most are also aware of the peril from pits in damascus or twist steel shotgun barrels.

But few realize that pitted musket or pistol barrels can hold the same threat, especially those of twist or damascus type. This was recently brought home to me in testing a fine British carbine-bored 16-ga. flintlock pistol made about 1810.

This firearm is far above the quality of Tower-marked pistols of the same type. It has a smooth, beautifully polished lock and a heavy twist steel barrel with walls ⅛" thick at the muzzle. The gun retains most of its finish, indicating it had not seen great use. Except for a few scattered light pits, the bore was smooth and bright, the breech plug checked out tight, and a bore light used in a darkened room disclosed no obvious holes.

Determining safety

However, to determine if this gun was really safe and could be fired without damage or danger, it was fitted snugly with a patched ball and a relatively light charge of powder—in this case 25 grs. or less than a half charge. This is contrary to normal practice in proving, which requires an overload. But I was not interested in proving as such, for 2 reasons. First, if the gun blew up I would have lost a valuable collector piece. Second, even if it did hold, the heavy charge could have imposed undue strain on the old gun to the extent that any further shooting might be dangerous.

Note that even with the light loads, test firing should be done from a rest, not from a hand hold.

After test firing, the barrel should be examined closely for tell-tale smudges of black powder fouling, not forgetting the area concealed beneath the stock. The explosion will drive gas through any weak points, leaving smudges where none should be. In most cases where such pin-point holes exist, tests with light loads will not harm the gun. If the pits look bad, obviously no attempt should be made to fire.

Firing test of this pistol revealed 2 tiny leaks, one a couple of inches from the muzzle and the other about the same distance from the breech plug. Neither lined up exactly with the small pits in the barrel bore. Of the 2 holes, the one at the rear was the more dangerous since it was near the point of maximum pressure.

Daniel K. Stern

Gun Hammers

By HERSCHEL C. LOGAN

Basic types of gun hammers used from matchlock era to modern times

SERPENTINE, cock, striker, mule-ear, or whatever called, the hammer is one of the most important parts of a gun. It has but one primary function—that of serving as an agent in the ignition of the powder charge.

The study of hammers is in reality a story of the various ignition systems in arms. Those illustrated here, it is believed, portray most of the basic types employed from the matchlock era to the present day.

Matchlock—Some may question the classifying of the matchlock serpentine as a hammer. True, it was rarely activated by a spring, but it was man's first attempt to utilize a piece of metal to hold the igniting agent—in this instance, a slow-burning 'match' of specially prepared cord.

Most serpentines are plain and unornamented. With a simple holder for the burning cord provided, both of the shooter's hands could be used to grasp the weapon. On most European types, the serpentine was ahead of the pan and faced to the rear. A few were made with forward-moving serpentines, but these were early.

Wheel lock—With the advent of wheel lock ignition, gunmakers more often embellished their work with engraving and other forms of ornamentation. The lock mechanisms were often objects of art with beautiful designs, including hunting scenes, animals, figures, or elaborate scroll patterns.

The principle of wheel lock ignition is similar to that of the modern cigarette lighter. In the wheel lock, a piece of pyrite, clamped in the jaws of the cock, is pressed against a rapidly rotating wheel. The friction between wheel and pyrite creates sparks which ignite the priming charge in the pan to set off the main charge in the gun bore.

Flintlock—In the flintlock, a flake of flint is clamped in the jaws of the spring-driven cock. When the trigger is pulled, releasing the cock, the flint strikes a glancing blow against a hard steel surface on the battery, or frizzen. This causes a shower of sparks to fall into the priming charge in the pan. The flash of the priming charge then sets off the main charge of powder in the gun bore.

The flintlock period saw 3 notable lock systems emerge—the snaphaunce, the miquelet, and the true flintlock. Flintlock cocks can be roughly divided into the following groups: side lock, center lock, gooseneck cock, double-necked or reinforced-cock, doglock cock, and reversible head cock.

Percussion lock—The percussion era saw an ever-increasing number of innovations in hammers, both in functional use and design. This period marked the development of several new hammer forms, including the bar hammer, ring hammer, mule-ear hammer, and spurless hammer.

Another type, the one-piece combination hammer, made its appearance during the percussion era. It was in the early years of the percussion era that some of the finest metal work was done on firearms.

Cartridge period—Gun hammers in this category are of functional design. Gone is the beauty of form associated with earlier hammers. Some semi-modern hammers assumed a dual purpose. The movable tip on the hammer of one early cartridge revolver raised a catch, permitting the cylinder to revolve. Another had a slot across the face to lock the barrel securely when the gun was fired. There are double hammers, chisel-nose hammers, hammers with revolving firing pins, and flat-faced hammers designed to strike an independent firing pin in the gun frame.

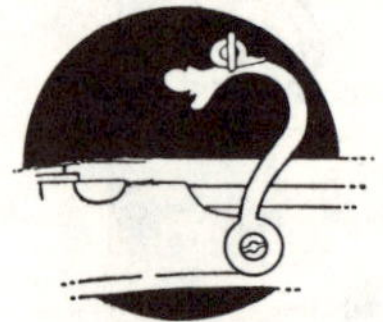

MATCHLOCK
European,
rear facing

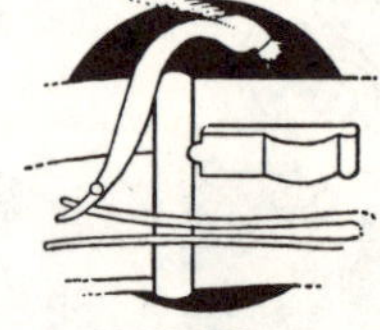

SNAPPING
MATCHLOCK
Japanese,
forward facing

WHEEL LOCK
Combination
matchlock-wheel lock

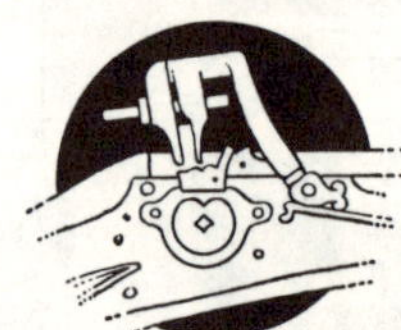

WHEEL LOCK
German, c. 1560

WHEEL LOCK
Spur dog
German, late
16th Century

FLINTLOCK
Combination
Wheel-lock-flintlock
German, mid-
17th Century

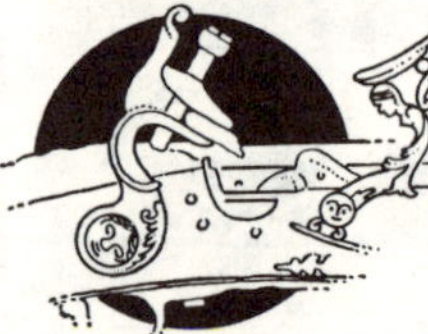

SNAPHAUNCE
Italian

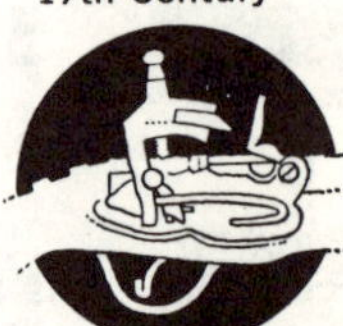

FLINTLOCK
Near Eastern
miquelet

FLINTLOCK
Spanish miquelet

FLINT COCK
Dutch or English
Early 1600's

FLINTLOCK
Dog-lock

FLINTLOCK
Left-hand

FLINTLOCK
Underhammer

FLINTLOCK
Center gooseneck

FLINTLOCK
Side gooseneck

FLINTLOCK
Reinforced

FLINTLOCK
Scottish

FLINTLOCK
Reversible double head

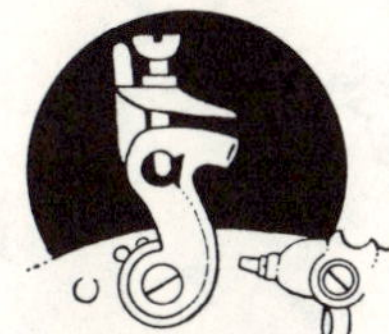
PERCUSSION
Combination flintlock-percussion

PERCUSSION
Forsyth, 1st model

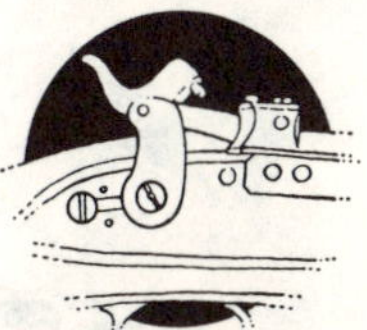
PERCUSSION
Forsyth, 2nd model

PERCUSSION
Pill lock double

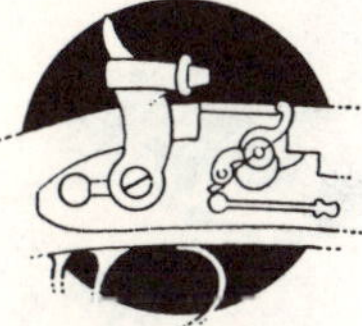
PERCUSSION
Tube lock

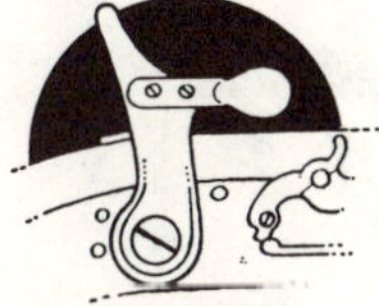
PERCUSSION
Tube lock

PERCUSSION
Tape primer

PERCUSSION
Disk primer

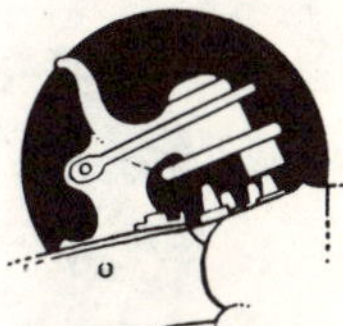
PERCUSSION
Revolving head

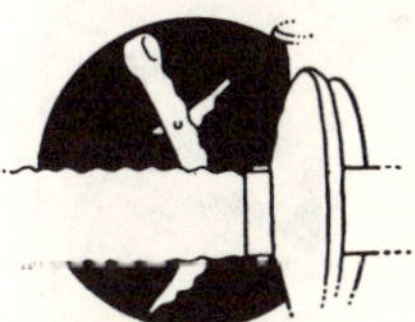
PERCUSSION
Folding

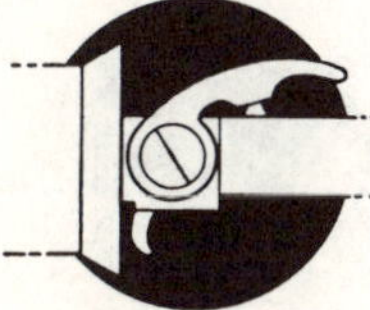
PERCUSSION
Japanese

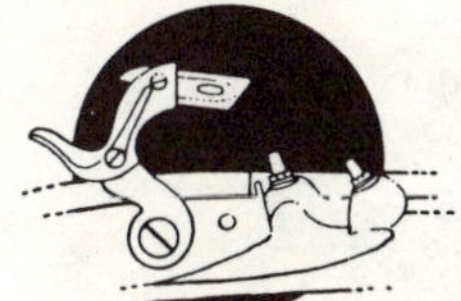
PERCUSSION
Movable head

PERCUSSION
One-piece hammer-trigger

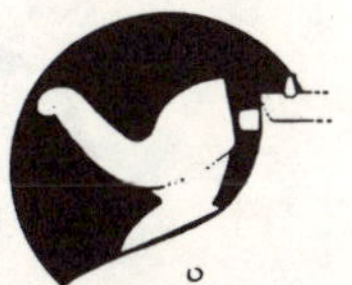
PERCUSSION
Flat nose

PERCUSSION
Shotgun

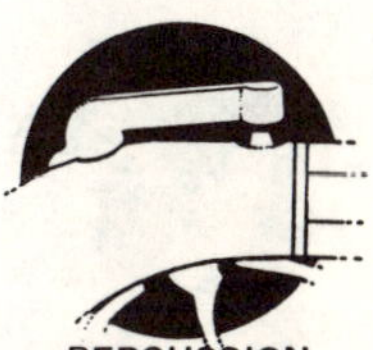
PERCUSSION
Bar

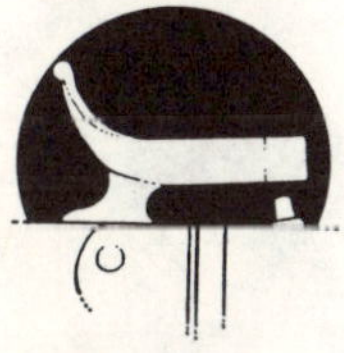
PERCUSSION
Bar

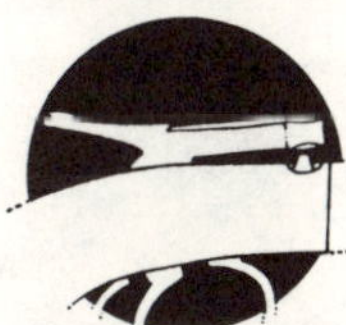
PERCUSSION
Bar

PERCUSSION
Combination

PERCUSSION
Cocking, guard mainspring

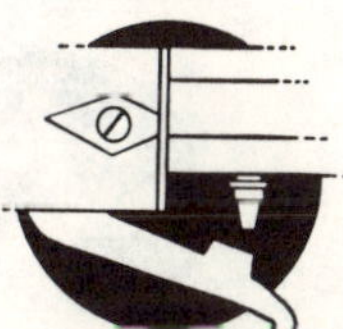
PERCUSSION
Underhammer

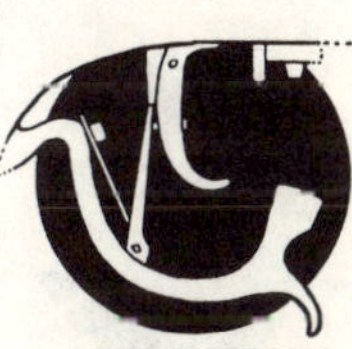
PERCUSSION
Combination

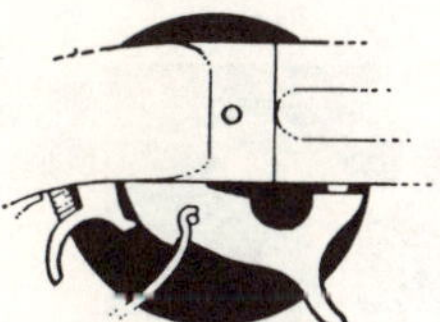
PERCUSSION
Underhammer

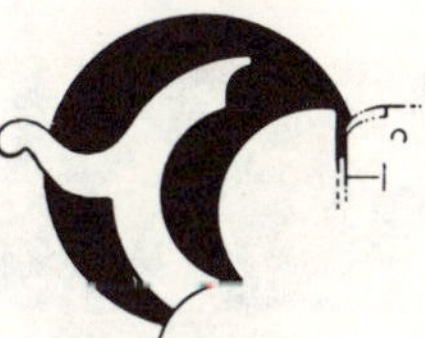
PERCUSSION
Circular

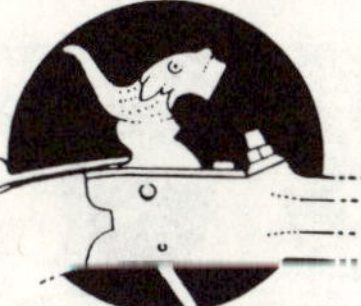
PERCUSSION
Central

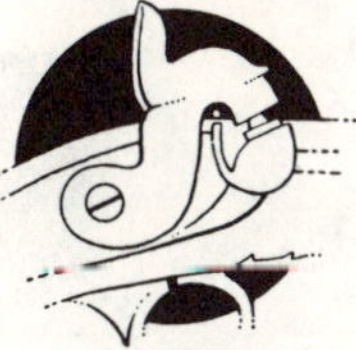
PERCUSSION
Deringer

PERCUSSION
Horsehead

PERCUSSION
Box-lock

PERCUSSION
Double

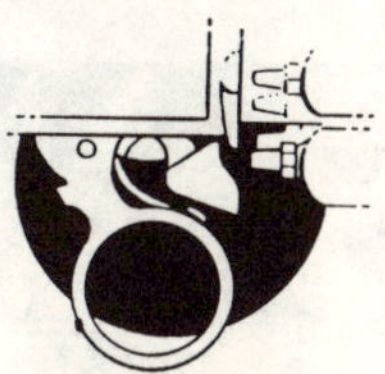
PERCUSSION
Underhammer

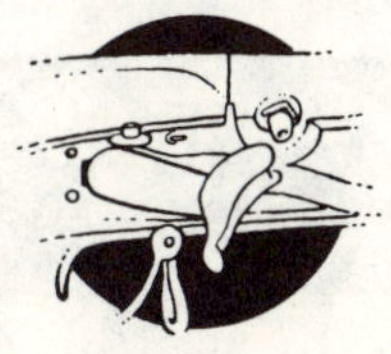
PERCUSSION
Side

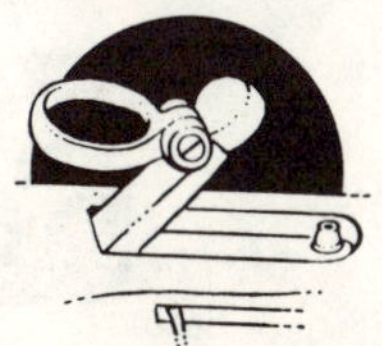
PERCUSSION
Folding

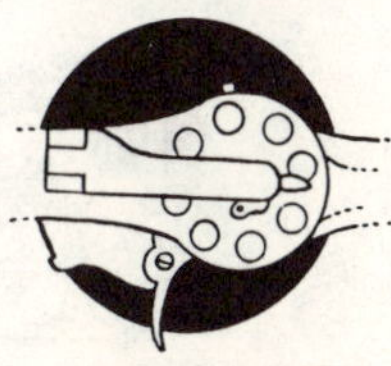
PERCUSSION
Side

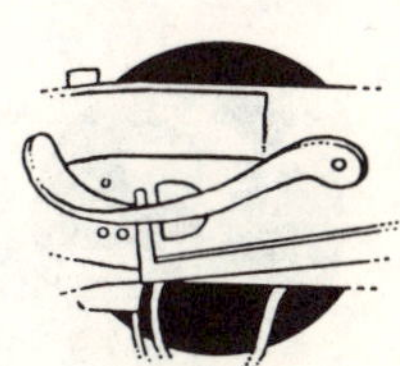
PERCUSSION
Side

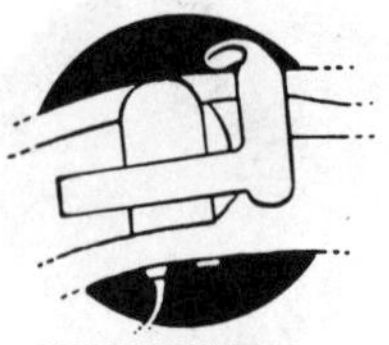
PERCUSSION
Side

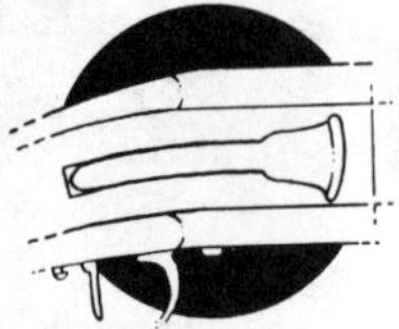
PERCUSSION
Side

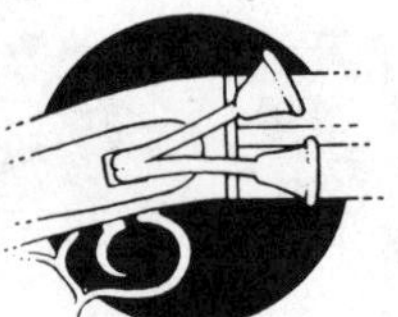
PERCUSSION
Double

PERCUSSION
Side

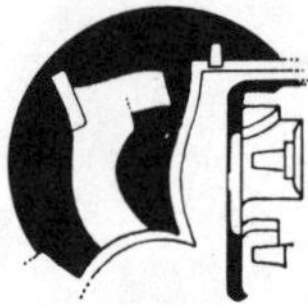
PERCUSSION
Spurless

PERCUSSION
Movable head

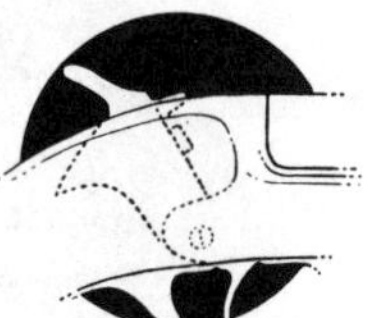
CARTRIDGE
Combination
percussion-rimfire

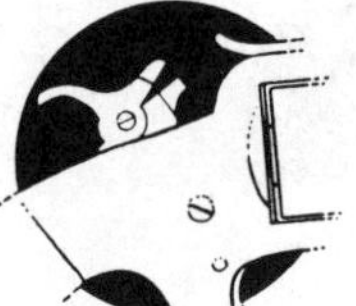
CARTRIDGE
Dual purpose

CARTRIDGE
Pinfire

CARTRIDGE
Chisel point

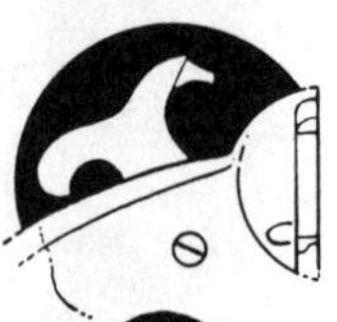
CARTRIDGE
Teatfire

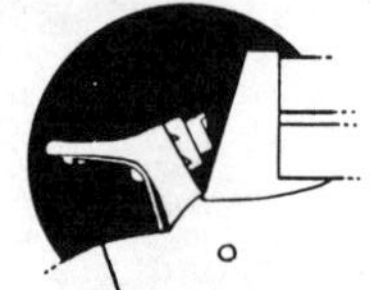
CARTRIDGE
Revolving firing pin

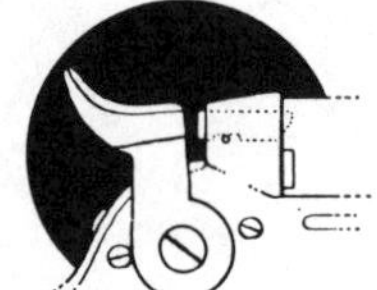
CARTRIDGE
Side

CARTRIDGE
Extension firing pin

CARTRIDGE
Combination
hammer-breechblock

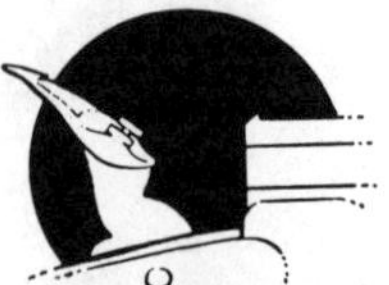
CARTRIDGE
Combination
hammer-breechblock

CARTRIDGE
Ring

CARTRIDGE
Knob

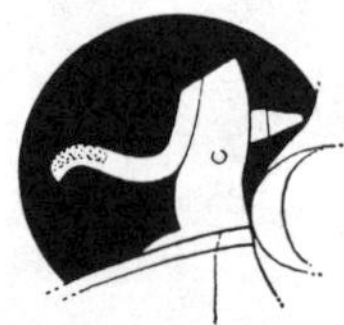
CARTRIDGE
Bisley

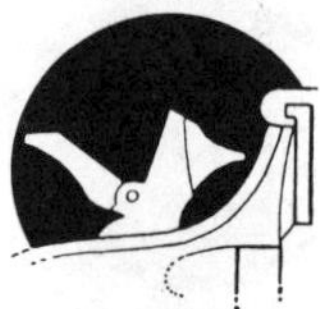
CARTRIDGE
Folding

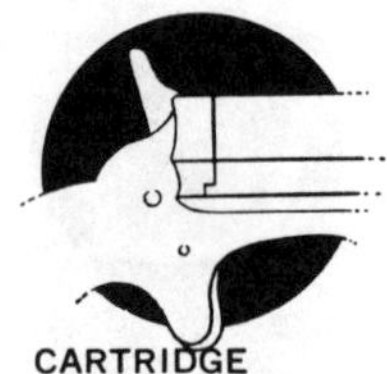
CARTRIDGE
Straight

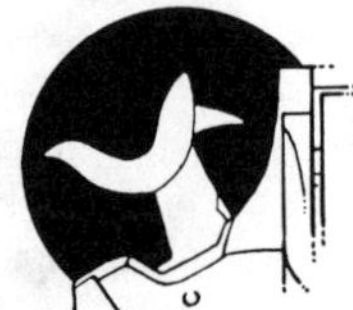
CARTRIDGE
Bull-dog revolver

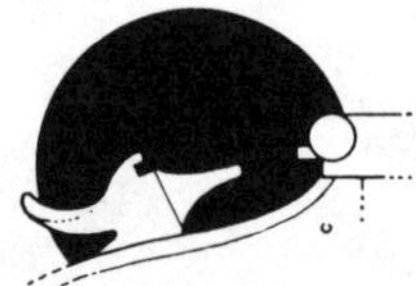
CARTRIDGE
Dual purpose

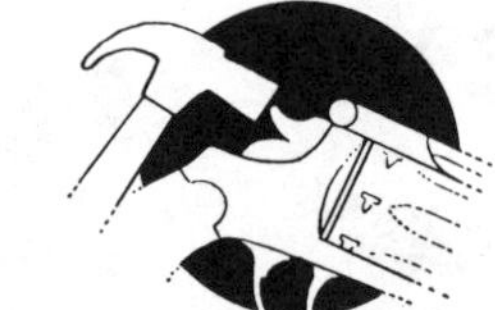
CARTRIDGE
Trademark

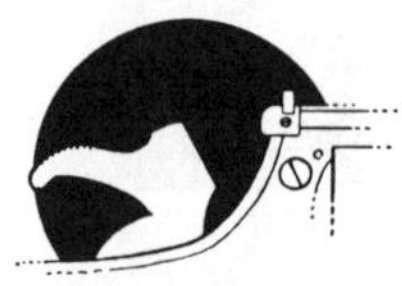
CARTRIDGE
Flat faced

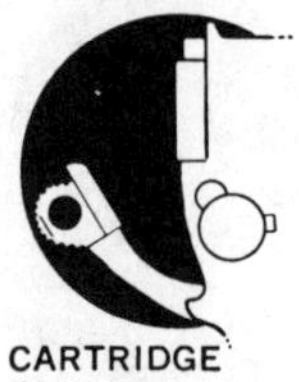
CARTRIDGE
Ring

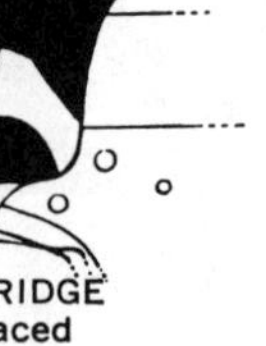
CARTRIDGE
Flat faced

DECORATIVE. Animal

DECORATIVE
Humorous figure

DECORATIVE
Animal

DECORATIVE. Animal

Grip Marks On AMERICAN HANDGUNS

By HERSCHEL C. LOGAN

IDENTIFYING marks on obsolete as well as current American handgun grips can be placed in 3 general classifications: initials or monograms, geometrical designs, and animate subjects. These designs are most often found on hard rubber or composition grips. Occasionally they will be of metal set into the grips. Or they may be etched or stamped on the gun frame.

The idea of using an identifying mark on the grip of the gun seems to have had its beginning here in the middle 1870's. An important innovation at that time was the introduction of molded hard rubber grips which permitted use of more elaborate designs than could be achieved with wood. These decorative grips reached their heyday between the 1870's and the early 1900's.

The designs are usually found at the top of the grip on either side. In a few instances, however, they will be positioned around the central grip-plate screw. In addition to these identifying marks, a few arms carry a second design—usually at the base of the grips. Typical would be a bas-relief of Lincoln or Washington, an eagle, policeman and thug, and various geometrical designs.

The grip designs are representative. Some Colt markings have been omitted since they are so well known.

INITIALS OR MONOGRAMS

American Arms Co., Boston, Mass.; 1870—1893. Milwaukee, Wis.; 1893—1904. Revolvers

Colt's Patent Firearms Mfg. Co., Hartford, Conn. 1836 to date. Automatic arms

Davis - Warner Arms Corp., Assonet, Mass. Cal. .32 Infallible automatic pistol

Forehand & Wadsworth. Worcester, Mass. 1871—1890. Also found on some arms produced by Forehand Arms Co.

Forehand Arms Co. Worcester, Mass. 1890—1900. Grips are believed to have been left over from the preceding firm, Forehand & Wadsworth. Used on both exposed hammer and hammerless revolvers. Sold out to Hopkins & Allen

Andrew Fyrberg & Co. Hopkinton, Mass. Revolvers made by Meriden Firearms Co. of Meriden, Conn.

Harrington & Richardson. Worcester, Mass. 1871 to date. Revolvers

J. C. Higgins. Model 88 9-shot revolver

High Standard Mfg. Co. New Haven, Conn. Hi-Standard Model "B" automatic pistol marked "Property of U.S."

Hopkins & Allen. Norwich, Conn. 1868—1915. Pistols and revolvers

Hopkins & Allen. Norwich, Conn. 1868—1915. Safety Police Cal. .32 revolvers

Henry M. Kolb. Philadelphia, Pa. Circa 1897—1911. Baby Hammerless revolvers

Iver Johnson Arms & Cycle Works. Worcester, Mass.; 1871—1891. Fitchburg, Mass. 1891 to date. Revolvers stamped "U.S. Revolver Co."

Maltby-Curtis Co. New York, N.Y. Exact dates unknown

Maltby - Henley. New York, N.Y. Circa 1878—1890. Agents for guns produced under the John T. Smith patents. Spencer Safety Hammerless

J. M. Marlin. New Haven, Conn. 1870—1881. Early J. M. Marlin arms and some Marlin Fire Arms Co. arms

Marlin Fire Arms Co. New Haven, Conn. 1881 to date. Revolvers

Marlin Fire Arms Co. New Haven, Conn. 1881 to date. Arms carrying above marking and also J. M. Marlin arms. #32 Standard 1878 revolvers

E. Remington & Sons. Ilion, N.Y. 1844—1886. No. 3 New Line revolvers

Remington Arms Co. Ilion, N. Y. 1886—1902. Model 1890 .44-40 revolver

Remington-UMC Ilion, N.Y. Automatic pistols

T. E. Ryan. Norwich, Conn. 1890—1893. Marquis of Lorne, Napoleon, and Retriever revolvers

Sears-Roebuck Co. Chicago, Ill. Revolvers

R. F. Sedgley, Inc. Philadelphia, Pa. Circa 1910—1938. Successors to Henry M. Kolb. Baby Hammerless revolvers

C. S. Shattuck Arms Co. Hatfield, Mass. 1875—1918. Cal. .32 revolvers made under Shattuck patent of Nov. 4, 1879

C. S. Shattuck Arms Co. Hatfield, Mass. 1875—1918 Revolver

Sheridan Products, Inc. Racine, Wis.

Otis A. Smith. Rock Falls, Conn. 1873—1884. Smith's New Model revolver

Smith & Wesson. Springfield, Mass. 1857 to date. Standard trademark

Smith & Wesson. Springfield, Mass. Baby Russian revolvers

Turner & Ross. Boston, Mass. 1873—1885. Agents for arms made by Whitney at Whitneyville, Conn., and by Hopkins & Allen at Norwich, Conn. Czar revolvers

Warner Arms Corp. Norwich, Conn. Cal. .32 automatic pistol The Infallible

Unknown. Pioneer brass-frame revolver, maker unknown

GEOMETRICAL DESIGNS

Bliss & Goodyear. New Haven, Conn. 1866—1887. Hartford Arms was a trade name used by Bliss & Goodyear. Royal, Liberty. Gypsy and Bull's Eye revolvers

Bliss & Goodyear. New Haven, Conn. Revolvers

Dead Shot. Maker unknown

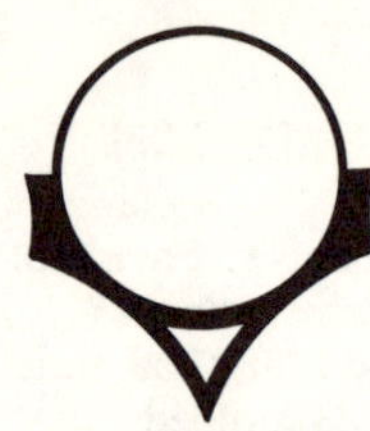

Eastern Arms Co. Chicopee Falls, Mass. Trade name for some guns made by Stevens Arms Co.

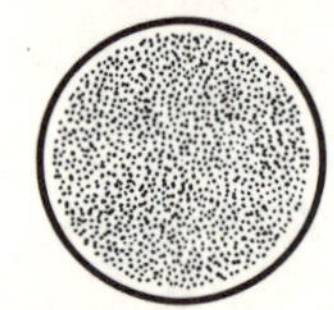

Forehand & Wadsworth. Hopkins & Allen. Norwich, Conn. Revolvers bearing either name

Harrington & Richardson. Worcester, Mass. 1871 to date. Aetna 2½ revolver and White Star revolver

Harrington & Richardson. Worcester, Mass.

Harrington & Richardson. Worcester, Mass. 7-shot cal. .32 revolver with patent date of May 28, 1876

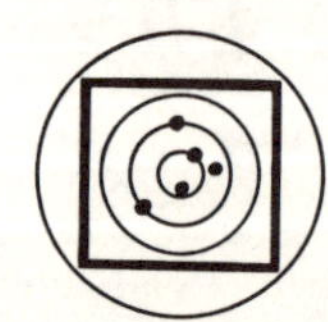

Harrington & Richardson. Worcester, Mass.

Hood Firearms Co. Norwich, Conn. 1875—1880. F. W. Hood's Victoria Revolver

Hopkins & Allen. Norwich, Conn. 1868—1915. Cal. .32 Dictator revolver

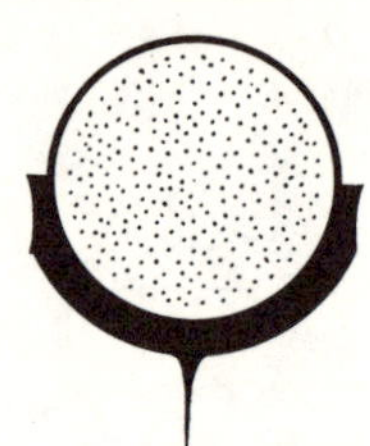

Hopkins & Allen. Norwich, Conn. Arms made for Merwin, Hulbert & Co., agents

Hopkins & Allen. Norwich, Conn. Revolvers made for Merwin, Hulbert & Co., agents

Kaiser. Maker unknown

Maltby-Henley. New York, N. Y. Revolvers

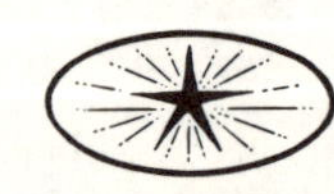

J. M. Marlin. New Haven, Conn. XX Standard revolvers

Osgood Gun Works. Norwich, Conn. Circa 1880. Osgood Duplex revolver

Pioneer. Maker unknown. Distributed through Kruse Hardware Co. of Cincinnati, Ohio

ANIMATE SUBJECTS

Cody Mfg. Corp. Springfield, Mass. Cody Thunderbird cal. .22 revolver

Colt's Patent Firearms Mfg. Co. Hartford, Conn. 1836—to date

Iver Johnson Co., model 1879 American Bulldog and Swift side-swing cylinder revolvers.

High Standard Mfg. Corp. New Haven, Conn.

Hopkins & Allen. Norwich, Conn. 1868—1915. Czar, Blue Jacket 1½, and other revolvers

Iver Johnson Arms & Cycle Works. Worcester, Mass.; 1871—1891. Fitchburg, Mass.; 1891 to date

Reising Mfg. Corp. New York, N.Y. Reising automatic pistol

Savage Repeating Arms Corp. Utica, N.Y.; 1895—1899. Savage Arms Co.; 1899—1917. Savage Arms Corp.; 1917 to date. Cal. .32 and .380 automatics

Savage Arms Corp. Chicopee Falls, Mass. Model 101 single-shot pistol

Sturm, Ruger & Co. Southport, Conn. Revolvers and automatic pistols ■

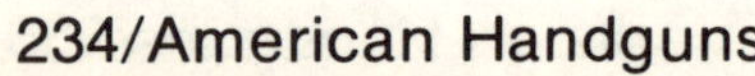

Grip Marks On American Handguns

THE identifying marks on American handguns shown here supplement those given in THE AMERICAN RIFLEMAN, October 1962, pages 55-56. These grip designs can be placed in 3 classifications: initials or monograms, geometrical designs, and animate subjects.

Marks in left and middle columns appear on various revolvers made by Iver Johnson Arms & Cycle Works, Worcester, Mass. (1871 to 1891), and Fitchburg, Mass. (1891 to date).—HERSCHEL C. LOGAN

Iver Johnson Co., model 1879 American Bulldog and Swift side-swing cylinder revolvers.

Iver Johnson Co., variation of bulldog design on American Bulldog, Boston Bulldog, and British Bulldog revolvers.

Iver Johnson Co., American Bulldog revolver with large eagle covering most of grip.

Iver Johnson monogram around grip screw. Found on grips with owl or bulldog head.

Iver Johnson Co. monogram around grip screw. Found on early grips with bulldog head facing forward.

Iver Johnson Co., variation of eagle design covering most of grip.

Iver Johnson Co., Defender 89 birdshead grip revolver.

Iver Johnson Co., Secret Service Special revolver. Jobbed by a firm in Chicago.

Meriden Firearms Co., Meriden, Conn.; 1907-1909.

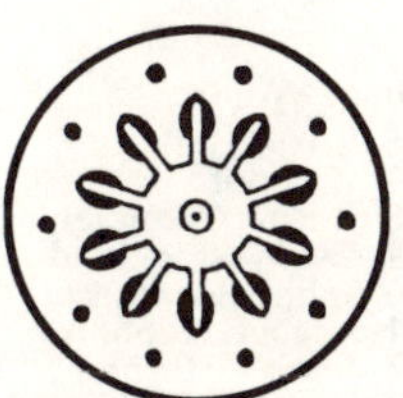

Meriden Firearms Co., Meriden, Conn.

Forehand & Wadsworth. Worcester, Mass.; 1871-1890.

American Arms Co., Boston, Mass.; early 1870's to 1904.

Maker unknown. Inexpensive pocket revolvers; 1880-1890 period. ■

Cleaning Muzzle-Loading Arms

Littleton, Colo.

Editor:

There is much satisfaction, not to mention economy, in shooting blackpowder firearms; however, this is diminished by visions of the messy cleaning to follow. Much fouling is easily removed by soapy water or even saliva on a cleaning patch. But, unless the bore is dried and oiled, danger of corrosion remains. By use of a product called Vapor Phase Inhibiter (VPI) marketed by Shell Oil, a quick clean up and preservation is possible—and under field conditions.

For the last three years I have used the following method to clean and preserve my muzzle-loading Kentucky rifle with a minimum of effort and without a trace of corrosion. While still in the field or at the range, the caked fouling in the nipple is loosened with a small piano wire pick and a cap or two snapped to clear. Then, several saliva moistened patches are run through the bore to remove the fouling, followed by a couple of dry patches to absorb most of the moisture. Likewise, the nipple and lock exterior are wiped with a wet and then dry patch. The dry patch is followed by a lightly oiled patch both through the bore and around the lock. A small leather cap is placed over the nipple and held snug by lowering the hammer. VPI crystals are then shaken down the bore; no more than the salt on your breakfast egg. The muzzle is then stoppered to prevent the loss of the protective vapor. This vapor renders water non-corrosive to iron and steel. A cork cut to fit the bore and glued to a black cap which matches the barrel exterior works well and is unobtrusive when the rifle is hung on the wall. So long as the seal is not broken, the bore is safe. The VPI does not develop pressure, so absolute sealing is not critical. If left unsealed, however, the vapor gradually dissipates and protection is lost. For the next shooting session, run a dry patch through the bore, snap a cap to ensure a clear nipple and then load.

The above method is *not* a substitute for a thorough cleaning and oiling. My rifle gets the full treatment about twice a year when the wife is away. The longest I have left it unattended was six months after a late hunt. No corrosion occurred.

Two ounces of VPI crystals have lasted more than three years. I always carry it in my hunting bag. A few grains in the bore and inside the gun case after a hunt in bad weather ensure getting home without a rusty gun inside or out.

If the foregoing seems impossible you can make the same test I did. A common nail was cleaned in alcohol to remove any oil which might protect it. The bottom half of the nail was then rolled between the fingers to simulate handling and placed in a small jar of the kind containing olives. The nail was then half covered with water and VPI added (no more than a paper match head). The cover was tightly sealed and the jar placed in a warm spot. The jar has been moved around from time to time but never opened. To this day, no rusting is visible.

DON YALE

U. S. Small Arms Inspectors

A listing of names giving identification, area of operation, and years active

By Lt. Col. R. C. Kuhn, USAFR (Ret'd)

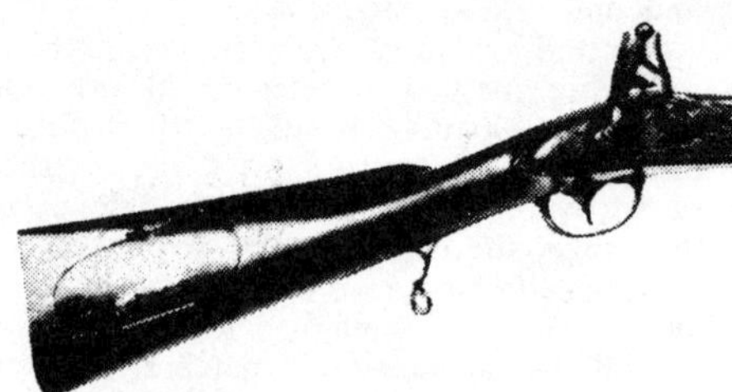

U. S. Model 1819 flintlock rifle manufactured by Nathan Starr, Middletown, Conn.

GUN collectors often wonder about an initial or initials on a military small arm. Why is it so marked? What is the significance of the letters? If the letters are a person's initials, what was his name?

In a letter dated Nov. 20, 1861, Capt. George T. Balch said, "All that work which having been submitted, is rejected, is marked **c** (condemned)," and again, "All these pistols can be detected by the following marks. A small **o** or center punch mark under or over the number of the pistol, on the barrel, guard, strap and frame."

The inspection for Government acceptance of small arms was always covered by regulations. Some arms have one or more inspector's initial or initials. The barrel was inspected before the balance of the arm was manufactured. So we see one inspector's mark on the barrel and another on the rest of the parts. Inspectors were always assisted by an Armory foreman or master armorer as a sub-inspector.

Both the Navy and Army purchased arms commercially and also contracted directly with manufacturers. The Navy also purchased some arms from the Army. The Army owned many more cal. .36 revolvers than the Navy. The Navy also used many cal. .44 Army revolvers. All this in spite of .44 Army and .36 Navy.

The names, lacking any model or make of arm inspected, were found in orders, letters, payrolls, etc., of the Ordnance Dept., where they were titled "Inspectors". From early days to 1831, most small arms contract inspectors were civilians or Springfield Armory employees. Their official titles on the payrolls were master armorer or assistant. A Springfield Armory payroll shows some inspectors.

The following is an abstract of the payrolls at Springfield Armory, for the year ending Aug. 31, 1841.

Entry	*Name*	*Occupation*	*Amount of Yr.'s Pay*
6	Elizur Bates	Inspector	$169.24
7	C. Foot	Inspector	800.00
8	Rufus Chandler	Inspector	800.00
9	Cyrus Buckland	Inspector	775.31
10	John Hawkins	Inspector	191.59
11	Asabel Hubbard	Inspector	800.00
12	Joseph Harniss	Inspector	168.47
13	John B. Kirkham	Inspector	800.00
14	Joseph Lombard	Inspector	800.00
15	Nahum W. Patch	Inspector	50.00
16	Justice Murphy	Inspector	800.00
17	John C. Stebbins	Inspector	800.00
18	William Smith	Inspector	781.01
19	Luther Luge	Inspector	74.70
20	Oliver Sexton	Inspector	800.00
21	John C. Bragg	Inspector	230.58
178	Luther Sage	Lock Filer	255.23

These men all had regular Armory jobs and small-arms inspection was in addition to their regular duties. The title sub-inspector appears in the Springfield Armory Special Orders which detailed the Ordnance officer and a civilian Armory employee assistant to the contract manufacturer. Prior to 1909 these were titled Post Orders but after were Special Orders.

Post Order No. 1 of Jan. 17, 1880, detailed Lt. D. A. Lyle and Mr. David F. Clark to inspect revolvers at the Colt factory. Their initials can be seen on the Colt .45 S. A. Army revolvers. The duties of inspector and sub-inspector were additional duties for officers concerned, and upon completion these officers returned to their regular stations. As small-arms contracts and production rates increased, more inspectors became necessary. Most added inspectors were Armory foremen. Army or Navy inspectors had control over all sub-inspectors. A sample record of inspection and delivery follows.

Berlin Connecticut, 2 Jany 1813

Callender Irvine, Esqr Commissary Genl

To Simeon North, D^r

To 42 pair of pistols at $11—seven eighths per pair $498.75

To two boxes $1 . . . . 2.00

$500.75

I certify that I have proved, Inspected, and passed the above 42 forty two pr. pistols for which I have signed triplicates.

Charles Williams, Inspector

Rec'd New Haven 1813 Jan 6th of Sim^n North for acct. for the United States two boxes containing Forty two pair pistols inspected by Charles Williams as per his certificate of the 2nd inst. for which I have signed triplicates

William Lyon
Military Storekeeper

Initials of John Newbury appear on barrel of U. S. Model 1819 rifle

Initials of Joseph Weatherhead are stamped on the stock of U. S. Model 1819 rifle

U. S. Navy Model 1870 cal. .50 rifle with Remington rolling-block action manufactured at Springfield Armory. Converted to cal. .22 short rimfire for gallery practice

In the following list of inspectors military personnel are from the Bureau of Ordnance if Navy, or from the Ordnance Dept. if Army. Unidentified inspectors can be determined by date of arm involved. The maker, government delivery date, etc., should be checked against the same initials on the following list, to determine name, rank, and active inspecting years.

A

Initials	*Name, Title*	*Period*
DA	Daniel Ammen, Lt., USN	1836-78
EA	Epaphroditus Allis, Armory S-I* 1815 and 1818 Springfield pistol	1818-41
ESA	E. S. Allin, Armory S-I Civil War rifle-muskets	1850-65
FBA	Francis B. Austin, Armory S-I Colt Model 1911 cal. .45 semi-automatic pistol	1917
FJA	Frank J. Atwood, Lt. Col., USA Model 1911A1 cal. .45 semi-automatic pistol by Ithaca, Union Switch and Signal, and Remington Rand	1943-45
FWA	F. W. Adams, Armory S-I	1904-06
GBA	G. B. Allen, Armory S-I	1894-1902
GTA	G. T. Allen, Armory S-I	1898-1902
JA	J. Arnold, Jr., Armory S-I	1869-71
JA	Joel Abbot, Lt., USN	1812
JCA	J. C. Ayers, Armory S-I	1881
JWA	J. W. Alden, Armory S-I	1905-06
LCA	Lucius C. Allin, Armory S-I Colt Dragoon, Massachusetts Arms Co.—Adams, Starr revolvers	1859-79
OA	Oliver Allen, Armory S-I North Model 1816 pistol	1816-18
OWA	O. W. Ainsworth, Armory S-I Smith & Wesson American 1869, Remingtons, Colt percussion and conversion revolvers	1831-74
TA	Thomas Annely, Armory S-I Musket and pistol barrels	1797

B

Initials	*Name, Title*	*Period*
ABB	A. B. Blackington, Armory S-I Starr and Colt Model 1860 revolvers	1860-62
AJB	Aldeige J. Bessette, Armory S-I Colt	1940
CAB	Charles A. Brand, Lt., USN Smith & Wesson cal. .38 revolvers	1899-1900
CB	Cyrus Buckland, Armory S-I	1841
CB	Charles Boarman, Capt., USN	1847
CLB	C. L. Bartlett, Armory S-I	1904-10
CMB	C. M. Boyington, Armory S-I	1901-10
CRB	C. R. Bunker, Armory S-I	1875
CWB	C. W. Bacon, Armory S-I	1875
EB	Edmund Byrne, Lt., USN	1837
EB	Elizur Bates, Armory S-I Waters Model 1836 pistol	1841-46
EB	Edward Barrett, Cdr., USN	1837
EBB	E. B. Boutwell, Cdr., USN	1828-50
ELB	E. L. Bolles, Armory S-I	1902
EWB	E. W. Blake, Armory S-I	1818
EWB	E. W. Bruce, Armory S-I	1875
FB	Frank Baker, Maj., USA Colt Model 1909 cal. .45 revolver	1909-17
GTB	George T. Balch, Capt., USA Colt and Savage revolvers	1861-62
HMB	H. M. Brooks, Armory S-I Colt revolvers	1902-06
HRB	Howard R. Booth, Armory S-I Colts	1940
IB	Isack Bartlett, Armory S-I Forged lockplates	1808
JAB	John A. Bell, Lt., USN Colt Model 1895 and Model 1902, and Smith & Wesson Model 1902 revolvers	1902-03
JAB	John A. Brooks, Jr., Lt. Col., USA Colts	1940
JAJB	James A. J. Bradford, Capt., USA Hall carbines	1833-35
JB	James Bell, Armory S-I	1827
JCB	John C. Beaumont, Lt., USN I. N. Johnson pistol	1852-55
JCB	Joseph C. Bragg, Armory S-I R. Johnson, Waters, Ames, pistols, Colt Dragoon revolvers	1841-42 1846-49
JGB	J. G. Benton, Lt. Col., USA	1866-81
JGB	John G. Butler, Capt., USA Colts	1886
JJB	John J. Breen, Capt., USA Colts	1936-37
JKB	J. K. Burbank, Armory S-I	1901-10
JNB	J. N. Boyer, Armory S-I	1905-06
JOB	J. O. Bush, Armory S-I Barrel inspector	1864
JSB	J. S. Burns, Armory S-I	1898-1910
JTB	James T. Baden, Lt., USA Remington, Starr, Whitney, and Savage revolvers	1862-64
LAB	Lester A. Beardslee, LCdr., USN Starr revolvers	1860
MPB	M. P. Benjamin, Armory S-I	1899-1910
NB	Nehemiah Baden, Lt., USA North Model 1816 pistol	1813-20
NLB	N. L. Benoit, Armory S-I	1900-04
PB	Peter Barrett, USN gunner Colt Model 1860 and 1861 revolvers	1861-68
PHMB	P. H. M. Brooks, Armory S-I	1885-1910
PMB	Paul M. Buzby, Lt., USA Remington Model 1911 cal. .45 semi-automatic pistol	1917
RB	Robert Beals, Armory S-I Colts	1862
RB	Rogers Birnie, Jr., Lt., USA	1879-80
RB	Robert Blanchard, Armory S-I North, Hall carbines	1831
RLB	Rufus L. Baker, Capt., USA	1818-20
RPB	Robert P. Barry, Capt., USA Remington, Starr, and Rogers & Spencer revolvers	1860-65
SB	Samuel Barron, Lt., USN	1827-45
SEB	Stanhope English Blunt, Capt., USA Colt revolvers	1889-90
SEB	S. E. Bugbee, Armory S-I	1901-10
SHB	S. H. Broughton, Armory S-I	1899-1910
SPB	Samuel P. Baird, Lt., USN Starr, Whitney revolvers	1861-73
STB	Samuel T. Bugbee, Armory S-I Starr revolvers	1862-85
TWB	T. W. Booth, Armory S-I Sharps	1861-65
VLB	V. L. Bennett, Armory S-I	1875
WB	William Blanchard, Armory S-I	1831
WB	Waldemar Broberg, Col., USA Colts	1941
WAB	W. A. Benjamin, Armory S-I	1898
WAB	William A. Borden, Lt. Col., USA Colts	1936-39
WAB	W. A. Bennet, Armory S-I	1898
WEB	W. E. Benjamin, Armory S-I	1898
WEB	W. E. Boynton, Armory S-I	1902-10
WFB	W. F. Bradbury, Armory S-I	1898-1902
WHB	W. H. Brundrett, Armory S-I	1898-1900
WJB	William J. Bowers, Armory S-I Colts	1938
WLB	William L. Bell, Lt., USA Colts	1937
WLB	William L. Borden, Armory S-I	1844-54
WWB	W. W. Bartlett, Armory S-I	1899-1904

* Sub-Inspector

C

Initials	*Name, Title*	*Period*
—C	— Cloue, Armory S-I	1844-54
AC	Alexander Cameron, Armory S-I Colts	1940

W. W. Kimball, Lt. USN probably inspected and approved U. S. Model 1870 rifle shown following conversion to cal. .22

Initials	*Name, Title*	*Period*
AFC	A. F. Cameron, Armory S-I	1875
AMC	A. M. Cooley, Armory S-I	1901-10
APC	A. P. Casey, Armory S-I Smith & Wesson Schofield cal. .45 revolvers	1875-77
CGC	C. G. Chandler, Armory S-I Remington Beals .36 and .44, Remington Model 1861 .36 and .44, Pettengill, and Colt Dragoon revolvers	1861-63
DC	Daniel Cotton, Armory S-I Lockmaker	1798
DFC	David F. Clark, Armory S-I Hotchkiss rifle, Colt, Starr, Remington, and Savage revolvers	1861-86
EEC	E. E. Chapman, Maj., USA Remington Model 1911 cal. .45 semi-automatic pistol	1918-19
EMC	E. M. Camp, Armory S-I Colt Model 1860 cal. .44 percussion revolver	1860-63
EWC	E. W. Clarke, Armory S-I	1875
FC	F. Chillingworth, Armory S-I	1875
FMC	F. M. Chapin, Armory S-I	1898
FTC	Frank T. Cleveland, Armory S-I Colt Model 1873 S. A. cal. .45 revolver	1875
GKC	George K. Charter, Armory S-I Starr Navy revolvers	1861-63
GMC	George M. Colvocoresses, Cdr., USN Whitney revolvers	1860-67
GWC	George W. Chapin, Armory S-I Starr revolvers	1862
HKC	Henry Knox Craig, Maj., USA Waters Model 1836 pistols	1837-38
JBC	J. B. Craig, Armory S-I	1896-1902
JBC	J. B. Cooley, Armory S-I	1898
JC	J. Clancy, Armory S-I	1905-07
JC	James Carrington, Armory S-I Whitney, Blake, and Starr muskets	1803-30
JEC	J. E. Craig, Armory S-I	1898-1906
JEC	Joseph Edgar Craig, Lt., USN	1861-69
JEC	J. E. Connolly, Armory S-I	1902
JFC	J. F. Coyle, Armory S-I	1907-13
JFEC	J. F. E. Chamberlain, Armory S-I Smith & Wesson Schofield cal. .45 revolvers	1875
JJC	John J. Cornwell, Cdr., USN	1847-67
JJC	John J. Callahan, Armory S-I Colts	1940
JKC	John K. Christmas, Lt. Col., USA Singer Model 1911A1 cal. .45 semi-automatic pistol	1942

JMC J. M. Crighton, Armory S-I 1894-1910

JMBC J. M. B. Clitz, Capt., USN 1867 Remington barrels

JPC James P. Chapman, Armory S-I 1848 Ames Model 1843 pistols

JSC J. S. Cooley, Armory S-I 1898

JSC J. S. Chauncey, Cdr., USN 1812

JTC John T. Cleveland, Armory S-I 1856-77 Colt Model 1873 S. A. cal. .45 Smith & Wesson, and Savage revolvers

LBC Luke B. Chase, USN 1860

LC Lyman Converse, Armory S-I 1863 Spencer rifles

MMC M. M. Custer, Armory S-I 1906-10

PC P. Chapman, Civilian USN 1844

PC Pierce Crosby, Cdr., USN 1870 Norfolk Navy Yard brass trigger guards on Remington Model 1866 cal. .50 pistol

RAC Rinaldo A. Carr, Armory S-I 1875-1909 Colt cal. .38 and .45 revolvers and semi-automatic pistols

RBC R. B. Chamberlain, Armory S-I 1906

RC Rufus Chandler, Armory S-I 1831-50 Ames Model 1843 pistol in 1845

RC Robert Corbit, Armory S-I 1798 Lock filer

RC Russel Curtis, Armory S-I 1818 1815 and 1818 Springfield pistol stocks

RWC R. W. Chandler, Armory S-I 1917 Smith & Wesson and Colts revolvers

RZC R. Z. Crane, Capt., USA 1935 Colts

SC Silas Crispin, Capt., USA 1862 Remington Model 1861 revolvers

TLC T. L. Childs, Armory S-I 1917 Colt Model 1911 cal. .45 semi-automatic pistol

WC William Cadwell, Armory S-I 1860-61 Remington Beals cal. .44 percussion revolver

WHC W. H. Clayton, Armory S-I 1898-1901 Colts

WJC W. J. Clark, Armory S-I 1898

WLC W. L. Crowl, Armory S-I 1898-1902

D

CD C. Davis, Armory S-I 1905-06

CD C. Drommer, Armory S-I 1898-1910

DD Daniel Dunsmore, USN gunner 1861-68 Remingtons

CFD Charles F. Dupee, Armory S-I 1937-38 Colts

DJD D. J. Davis, Armory S-I 1904-06

EFD E. F. Dunbar, Armory S-I 1875

EHD Elbert H. Dewey, Armory S-I 1917 Colt Model 1911 cal. .45 semi-automatic pistol

GD G. Dillingham, Armory S-I 1875

GD G. During, Armory S-I 1898-1910

GHD Guy H. Drewry, Lt. Col., USA 1930-57 Smith & Wesson cal. .38 revolvers and Colt cal. .45, .38, and .22 revolvers and semi-autos.

HHD H. H. Denny, Armory S-I 1898

JD Joseph Dale, Armory S-I 1815-1818 1815 and 1818 Springfield pistol lock maker

JD J. Dowlar, Armory S-I 1811 Stocks and barrels

JHD J. H. Doyle, Armory S-I 1894

JLD J. L. Doppman, Jr., Armory S-I 1936 Colts

JRD J. R. Dearborn, Armory S-I 1894 and 1901-06

JSD James S. Dudley, Lt., USA 1861-70 Colt Model 1860 cal. .44 revolvers and Starr cal. .44 revolvers

JSD John S. Dexter, Armory S-I 1798

KMD K. M. Dennon, Armory S-I 1896

LD Lewis Draper, Armory S-I 1876 Colts

LPD L. P. Dustin, Armory S-I 1894

MD Mario D'Ippolito, Armory S-I 1939 Colts

MD Maurice Distel, Armory S-I 1939 Colts

OD Otis Dudley, Armory S-I 1830 North, Hall rifles

PJD Peter J. Diffley, Lt., USA 1941 Colts

RCD R. C. Downie, Lt. Col., USA 1943 Union Switch and Signal Co. Model 1911A1 cal. .45 semi-automatic pistols

RDD R. D. Draper, Armory S-I 1905-06

RMD R. M. Dennon, Armory S-I 1895-1902

SD Samuel Dale, Armory S-I 1817

TD Thomas Dale, Armory S-I 1796 Lock maker

WD William Dickinson, Armory S-I 1849-1850

E

AWE Arthur W. Evans, Lt., USA 1917-18 Remington-U. M. C. Model 1911 cal. .45 semi-automatic pistols

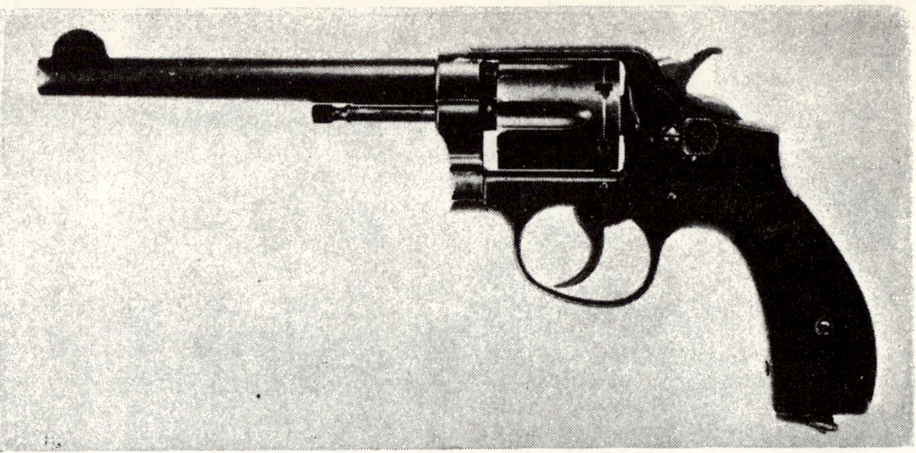

S&W Model .38 Hand Ejector Military & Police First Model, cal. .38 Long Colt. U. S. purchased 1000 of this model

CEE C. E. Evans, Armory S-I 1905-06

EAE E. A. Elliott, Armory S-I 1894-1910

FHE F. H. Elwell, Armory S-I 1894-1910

HE Henry Erven, Cdr., USN 1867 Remington Model 1867 pistol barrels

JHE J. H. Ewig, Armory S-I 1898

JRE John R. Edie, Capt., USA 1874 Colts

JWE J. W. Ewig, Armory S-I 1898-1910

RE R. Ellis, Armory S-I 1818

WE W. Easley, Armory S-I 1902

F

AF Abonijad Foot, Armory S-I 1818-22

ABF Archibald B. Fairfax, Lt., USN 1823-43

AHF Andrew H. Forsythe, Armory S-I 1917 Colt Model 1911 cal. .45 semi-automatic pistols

CF C. Foot, Armory S-I 1829-41 Locks

EF E. Farrar, Armory S-I 1860-82 Starr cal. .44 revolvers

EF Edgar Freeman, Lt., USN 1817-28

EJF E. J. Frost, Armory S-I 1864 Barrels

ELF Elbert L. Ford, Lt. Col., USA 1938-41 Colts

FGF F. G. Fisher, Armory S-I 1899-1902

GF George Flegel, Armory S-I 1812-23 Waters muskets and Deringer rifles

GF George Flyn, Armory S-I 1824 Locks

GDF G. D. Fisk, Armory S-I 1875

JGF J. G. Flagg, Armory S-I 1859-1900

JHF J. H. Fletcher, Armory S-I 1909

JPF J. P. Farley, Capt., USA 1874-76 Smith & Wesson and Colt revolvers

LF Lewis Foster, Jr., Armory S-I 1837 Waters Model 1836 pistols

LBF Leon B. Fanning, Armory S-I 1938 Colts

LMF Lewis M. Ferry, Armory S-I 1863

NF Noah Foot, Armory S-I 1824

NF Nathan Forbes, Armory S-I 1798-1801

RJF Russell J. Fournier, Armory S-I 1937 Colts

TJF T. J. Fitzpatrick, Armory S-I 1898

WCF W. C. Fielding, Armory S-I 1898-1907

WFF W. F. Fennyery, Armory S-I 1904-06

WMF William M. Folger, Lt. Cdr., USN 1873-75 Hotchkiss rifles

G

EAG E. A. Gowrie, Armory S-I 1902-09

EAG E. A. Graves, Armory S-I 1894-1902

CG Calvin Gay, Armory S-I 1818-31 Evans and J. J. Henry, Boulton pistols

GFG G. F. Gray, Armory S-I 1904-06

GG Guert Gansevoort, Cdr., USN 1850-61 Remington New Model percussion revolvers, Colt and Whitney converted revolvers, and Dahlgren bayonets

GRG G. R. Goring, Armory S-I 1908-10

HGG H. G. Gould, Armory S-I 1898

JAG James A. Greer, Lt., USN 1848

JEG John E. Greer, Capt., USA 1876-83 Colt and Whitney revolvers

JG John Garvin, Lt., USN 1875

JHG John H. Griffith, Civilian USN 1862 Whitney

JMG J. M. Gibert, Lt. Col., USA 1917-18 Colt revolvers and Model 1911 cal. .45 semi-automatic pistols

JRG J. R. Graham, Armory S-I 1875

JRG John R. Goldsborough, Capt., USN 1864 Whitney

LG Lewis Ghriskey, Armory S-I 1811 Stocks and barrels

LGG L. G. Gilmore, Armory S-I 1896-1904

OBG O. B. Graham, Armory S-I 1875

PG Peter Getz, Armory S-I 1803 and 1806-08

SGG Samuel G. Green, Lt. Col., USA 1939 Colts

SLG Sidney L. Gibson, Lt., USA 1941 Hi-Standard cal. .22 semi-automatic pistols

WG W. Ganeard, Armory S-I 1901-02 Colt cal. .38 revolvers

WFG William F. Gallagher, Capt., USA 1940 Colts

WHG W. H. Greene, Armory S-I 1901-02

WTG Walter T. Gorton, Maj., USA 1924-26 and 1938 Colts

H

AH Asabel Hubbard, Armory S-I 1813-47 Barrels and stocks, Whitney and Starr muskets, and North and Johnson pistols

AAH Andrew A. Harwood, Cdr., USN 1818-46

AJH A. J. Hall, Armory S-I 1904

ALH A. L. Hallstrom, Armory S-I 1916-17 Colt Model 1911 cal. .45 semi-automatic pistols and Smith & Wesson revolvers

AWH A. W. Hatch, Armory S-I 1903

BH Benjamin Hannis, Armory S-I 1861 Allen & Wheelock, Colt Model 1860, Remington, Savage "Figure 8", and Starr revolvers

BH Benjamin Huger, Maj., USA 1854-58

CCH C. C. Hubbard, Armory S-I 1906

CHH C. H. Hunt, Armory S-I 1864

CGH Charles G. Howe, Lt., USA 1917 Colts

CWH C. W. Hartwell, Armory S-I 1831-1860

EH Ethan Hancock, Armory S-I 1918

EH Edward Hooker, Lt. Cdr., USN 1867 Remington Model 1867 pistol barrels

EAH E. A. Hendrick, Armory S-I 1894

FH Frank Heath, Capt., USA 1883-84 Colts

FDH Filser D. Hoppert, Armory S-I 1940 Colts

FFH F. F. Hull, Armory S-I 1905-06

FLH F. L. Hosmer, Armory S-I 1898-1923 Colt Model 1911 cal. .45 semi-automatic pistols and Colt revolvers

GH George Haines, Armory S-I 1860

GPH George P. Howland, Armory S-I 1939 Colts

GRH George R. Harrington, Armory S-I 1901

GWH George W. Hagner, Armory S-I 1845-46

GWH George W. Hamlin, Armory S-I 1846-52 Colt Model 1851 revolvers

HBH H. B. Hart, Armory S-I 1875

HKH Henry K. Hoff, Com., USN 1865 Whitney revolvers

HSH H. S. Hill, Armory S-I 1862-75 Springfield

HWH Harry W. Hunt, Armory S-I 1899-1902

JBH Joseph B. Hayes, Armory S-I 1940 Colts

JEH Jay E. Hoffer, Maj., USA 1903 Colt cal. .38 revolvers

JH James Harris, Armory S-I 1837-51 R. Johnson, I. N. Johnson pistols, and Colt Model 1851 revolvers

JH James Hawkins, Armory S-I 1848 Colt Second Model Dragoon revolvers

JH John Hawkins, Armory S-I 1838-52 Starr Model 1817 rifles

JH John Hill, Armory S-I 1813-35

JH Joseph Harniss, Armory S-I 1841-44 Starr Model 1817 rifles, Waters Model 1836 pistols

Initials of John T. Thompson are on left grip of S&W M&P revolver shown. Also note initials of Sub-Inspector Kelly S. Morse stamped on side of frame above grip

Initials of Sub-Inspector Kelly S. Morse are on right grip of S&W M&P revolver shown

JHH	J. H. Howarth, Armory S-I	1899-1910
JLH	James L. Hatcher, Maj., USA Colts	1938
JLH	James L. Henderson, Cdr., USN Colt Model 1851 and 1861 cal. .36 revolvers	1858-61
JNH	J. N. Hemenway, Armory S-I	1907
LOH	L. O. Hale, Armory S-I	1902-06
MEH	M. E. Hawkins, Armory S-I	1898
MH	Michael Hayes, Armory S-I Colt revolvers	1860
ORH	Orvin R. Hayden, Armory S-I Colts	1938
PBBH	P. B. B. Havens, Armory S-I	1875
RMH	R. M. Hill, Maj., USA	1875-76
TMH	Thomas M. Hervey, Maj., USA Colts	1938
TTH	Thomas T. Holme, Lt., USA Colts	1941-42
TWH	Thomas W. Hafer, Armory S-I Colts	1941
TWH	T. W. Holmes, Capt., USA Colts	1926
WEH	W. E. Hosmer, Armory S-I Springfield Model 1903 cal. .30 rifles and Colt Model 1911 cal. .45 semi-automatic pistols	1905-15
WEH	William E. House, Capt., USA Colts	1938
WHH	W. H. Hayden, Armory S-I	1901-06
WJH	W. J. Hines, Armory S-I	1904-10

J

CJ	Catesby Jones, Capt., USN, Evans pistol barrels	1831-32
BFJ	B. F. James, Armory S-I	1904-06
GKJ	G. K. Jacobs, Armory S-I	1862-75
HBJ	H. B. Johnson, Armory S-I Remington Beals Navy revolver	1859-63
JDJ	J. D. Johnson, Armory S-I U. S. Model 1819 North pistol barrels	1819-22
JNJ	John N. Jordan, Lt., USN Lee 6 mm. Navy rifles	1891-95
RJ	Robert Johnson, Armory S-I	1822-26
RSJ	Robert S. Johnson, Armory S-I Colts	1940
SJ	Seth Janes, Armory S-I Pomeroy muskets	1818-24
TMJ	Thomas M. Jervey, Maj., USA Colts	1937-38

K

ADK	A. D. King, Armory S-I Colt Third Model Dragoon, Colt Model 1851, and Colt Model 1861 revolvers and Starr revolvers	1850-65
ALK	Albert L. Koones, USN	1862-65
DMK	David M. King, Lt., USA Colts	1898-1905
EAK	E. A. Kingsbury, Armory S-I	1904-06
EJK	E. J. Kernan, Armory S-I	1909-10
FK	Frank Krack, Rock Island Insp. Renumbered, mutilated Colt Model 1911 and 1911A1 cal. .45 semi-automatic pistols	1940
FMK	F. M. Kelsey, Armory S-I	1904-06
HK	H. Kane, Armory S-I	1902
HWK	Herbert W. Kerr, Armory S-I Colts	1940
JK	J. Kimball, Armory S-I	1875-79
JBK	John B. Kirkham, Armory S-I Locks	1823-41
JWK	John W. Kelly, Lt., USN Remington cal. .44 and Starr cal. .44 revolvers	1853-64
LLK	L. L. Kuralt, Armory S-I	1905-10
PK	P. Keller, Armory S-I	1904-06
PJK	P. J. Kiley, Armory S-I	1901-06
SK	S. Knows, Armory S-I Aston pistols and Colt Dragoons	1846-52
SK	Samuel Keeler, Armory S-I Colt First Model Dragoon	1848
WWK	W. W. Kimball, Lt., USN Remington Lee rifles and Colt cal. .38 revolvers	1879-89

L

—L	T. K Laley, Armory S-I	1844-58
AL	A. Lavigne, Armory S-I	1894-1909
AHGL	A. H. G. Lewis, Armory S-I	1906
BL	Benjamin Lamphear, Armory S-I Filed Locks	1798
BL	B. Lyon, Armory S-I	1875
BBL	B. B. Lombard, Armory S-I	1898
BFL	B. F. Lougharan, Armory S-I	1906
CPL	C. P. Lynn, Armory S-I	1906
CSL	Charles S. Lowell, Maj., USA Starr D. A. cal. .44 revolver and Colt Model 1860 cal. .44 revolver	1858-61
CSL	C. S. Leonard, Armory S-I	1862-75
DL	D. LeGro, Armory S-I	1826-31
DAL	David A. Lyle, Lt., USA Colt Model 1873 S. A. cal. .45 revolvers, Whitney revolvers, and Smith & Wesson Schofield revolvers	1876-1917
EML	E. M. Lovering, Armory S-I	1909
FSL	F. S. Leonard, Armory S-I	1899-1902
GDL	George D. Little, Ens., USN Colt Model 1860 cal. .44 revolvers	1862-65
HFL	Harry F. Lynch, Armory S-I Colts	1939-40
HJL	Harold J. LaBonte, Armory S-I Colts	1939
HLL	H. L. Lathrop, Armory S-I Colt Model 1860 cal. .44 revolvers	1862
JHL	J. H. Lyons, Armory S-I	1898
JL	Joseph Lanman, Lt., USN Ames pistols	1837-45
JL	J. Lippold, Armory S-I	1875
JL	Joseph Lombard, Armory S-I Barrels and bayonets and in 1836 ramrods	1819-41
JL	Joseph Lumbard, Armory S-I Swords	1818
JJL	John J. Lynch, Armory S-I Colts	1940
JJL	J. J. Lee, Armory S-I	1898
LL	Luther Luge, Armory S-I	1841
MPL	Mann Paige Lomax, Maj., USA Waters and R. Johnson pistols and Hall carbines	1837-1843
NL	N. LeClair, Armory S-I	1905-06
RL	Roswell Lee, Armory S-I	1818-19
RSL	Robert S. LaMotte, Capt., USA Sharps	1861-69
SL	Samuel Leonard, Armory S-I Colt and Savage revolvers	1862-75
SBL	Samuel B. Lathrop, Armory S-I	1818
TJL	T. J. Lovett, Armory S-I	1904-06
TTSL	Theodore T. S. Laidley, Maj., USA	1864-66
VAL	Viotto A. Luukkonen, Armory S-I Colts	1940
WML	W. M. Lyndon, Armory S-I Colts	1898

M

BM	Benjamin Moore, Armory S-I North pistols	1810-1815
CCM	Charles C. Morrison, Lt., USA Colts	1879-82
DWM	D. W. Massey, Armory S-I	1909
EAM	E. A. May, Armory S-I	1819-31
FAM	F. A. Massey, Armory S-I	1905-06
FWM	F. W. Macher, Armory S-I	1906
GAM	George A. Magruder, Capt., USN	1855
GEM	G. E. Miller, Armory S-I	1905-06
GFM	George F. Morrison, Lt., USN Starr S. A. cal. .44 revolvers	1864
GHM	G. H. Munroe, Armory S-I	1899-1900
GJM	G. J. McCallin, Armory S-I	1902
GSM	G. S. Morse, Armory S-I Starr revolvers	1862
GWM	George W. McKee, Capt., USA	1874-78
HM	Henry Metcalfe, Lt., USA Smith & Wesson American revolvers	1869-75
HM	H. Murdock, Armory S-I	1875
HEM	H. E. Madden, Armory S-I	1902
HJM	H. J. Meldrun, Armory S-I Colts	1898
JM	Julian McAllister, Maj., USA	1865
JM	J. Mills, Armory S-I	1862-75
JM	Joseph Morgan, Armory S-I North & Cheney pistols	1798-1802
JM	Justice Murphy, Armory S-I	1841
JM	Justin Murphy, Armory S-I Jenning, Pomeroy, Starr, Springfield Mfg. Co., Waters, North, and R. Johnson	1813-33
JDM	J. D. McIntyre, Capt., USA Colts	1926
JJM	J. J. Murphy, Armory S-I	1898
JPM	J. P. McGuinness, Lt., USN Smith & Wesson and Colt revolvers	1905
JRM	John R. McGinness, Capt., USA	1868-69
JWM	James W. McCoy, Armory S-I Colt cal. .38 revolvers	1927-29 and 1938
KM	Kenneth Morton, Maj., USA Colt Model 1906 cal. .45 semi-automatic pistol	1907-08
KSM	Kelly S. Morse, Armory S-I Winchester Model 1895 rifles, Smith & Wesson Model 1899 cal. .38 revolvers, and Colt Model 1911 cal. .45 semi-automatic pistols	1875-1915
LJM	L. J. Megette, Armory S-I	1898
LM	L. Menz, Armory S-I	1907
MM	M. Moulton, Armory S-I Savage and Colt Model 1851 cal. .36 revolvers	1861-63
MLM	Moses L. Morse, Armory S-I	1822-24
MRM	M. R. Marsh, Armory S-I Colt cal. .38 revolvers	1898
RM	R. Matthews, Armory S-I	1906
RWM	Robert W. McNeely, Armory S-I	1890
RWM	Richard W. Meade, Cdr., USN Colt Model 1851 and Model 1861 converted revolvers	1860-67
SM	Samuel Marcy, Lt., USN	1852-62
SM	Stillman Moore, Armory S-I Aston pistols	1846-52
TPM	T. P. Maroney, Armory S-I	1898
WM	William Maynadier, Lt. Col., USA	1838-63
WHM	W. H. Morley, Armory S-I	1898-1902
WMM	W. M. Mills, Armory S-I	1894

N

HN	Henry Nettleton, Armory S-I Lee, Hotchkiss rifles, and Remington, Smith & Wesson, and Colt Model 1873 cal. .45 revolvers	1874-82
JN	John Newbury, Armory S-I R. Johnson, Starr, North, Springfield, and Pomeroy	1818-26
JN	John Nicholson, Sr., Armory S-I Musket barrels	1797-98
JN	John Nicholson, Jr., Armory S-I	1799-1807
JN	John Norman, Armory S-I	1830
UN	Urban Niblo, Lt., USA Colt cal. .38 revolvers	1928
WN	Walter North, Armory S-I Aston pistols and Colt Model 1851 cal. .36 revolvers	1831-52
WDN	William D. Nicholson, USN Remington Model 1866 pistols	1866

O

HO	Herbert O'Leary, Maj., USA Colts	1926-29
JO	J. O'Malley, Armory S-I	1896-1902
JPO	James P. Oeller, Lt., USN J. J. Henry, Boulton pistols	1809-48
JPO	J. P. O'Neil, Armory S-I	1904-10
NO	Noble Orr, Armory S-I North & Cheney pistols and Whitney muskets	1798-1802

U. S. Cal. .45 ACP M1911 Service Pistol

Initials of Gilbert H. Stewart are stamped on left side of M1911 Service pistol shown

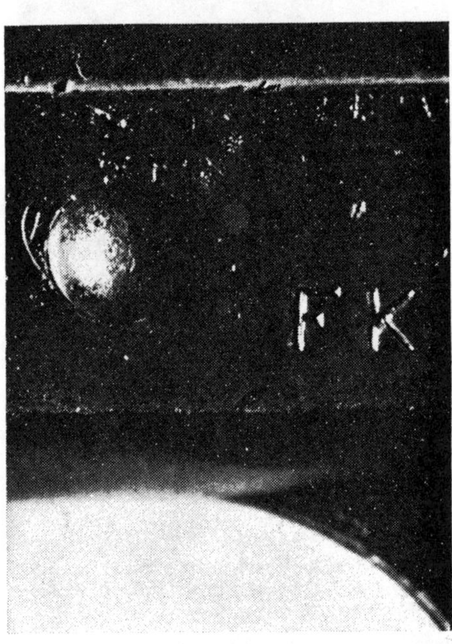

Initials of Frank Krack are on right side of M1911A1 Service pistol rebuilt at Rock Island Arsenal

RO Robert Orr, Armory S-I 1798-1808
North & Cheney pistols and Whitney muskets

WCO Warren C. Odell, Armory S-I 1939
Colts

WJO W. J. Ober, Armory S-I 1904-06

P

ACP A. C. Perrin, Capt., USA 1935
Colts

CP Charles Packard, Armory S-I 1818
1818 Springfield pistols

CHP C. H. Parker, Armory S-I 1902

DP Daniel Pettibone, Armory S-I 1808-09
Evans, Henry, and Miles muskets, Henry, Fry, and Shuler pistols, Henry rifles, and Rose & Sons swords

EBP E. B. Peck, Armory S-I 1898-1902 and 1909-13
Colts

ECP Edward C. Perry, Armory S-I 1937-40
Colts

EHP E. H. Pearson, Armory S-I 1898

GP Giles Porter, Armory S-I 1862-75
Remington New Model revolvers and Pettengill revolvers

GLP G. L. Prentice, Armory S-I 1875

GWP G. W. Patch, Armory S-I 1846-58
Colt Third Model Dragoon revolver

HHP Henry H. Perkin, Armory S-I 1810-1816
North pistols and Starr swords

JP James Perkin, Armory S-I 1815

JP Joseph Perkin, Armory S-I 1798

JP Jacob Perkins, Armory S-I 1819-21
Waters muskets

JP John Pope, Lt., USA 1843

JCP J. C. Parker, Armory S-I 1905-06

JSP James S. Palmer, Lt., USN 1836-46

LP L. Papanti, Armory S-I 1898

LJP Laurance J. Phelan, Armory S-I 1939-40
Colts

NWP Nahum W. Patch, Armory S-I 1831-49
Colt Walker and First Model Dragoon revolvers, Ames and R. Johnson pistols, Starr rifles, and North-Hall carbines

OHP Oliver H. Perry, Lt., USN 1829-45

ONP O. N. Perkins, Armory S-I 1898

RP Richard Parker, Lt., USA 1838-47

RP Richard Paine, Civilian, USN 1843-48
Ames pistols, and Jenks carbines by Ames and Remington

RAP Ray A. Pillivant, Lt., USA 1938-41
Colts and Harrington & Richardson semi-automatic pistols

RPP Robert P. Parrott, Capt., USA 1836

SP S. Priestley, Armory S-I 1904-06

TP Thomas Palmer, Armory S-I 1808-09
Henry, Fry, Henry, Guest, and Brong, Cook, and Shuler pistols

WP William Prince, Capt., USA 1875-77
Whitney

WGP Walter G. Penfield, Maj., USA 1909-14
Colt Model 1911 cal. .45 semi-automatic pistols for Army and Navy

WPP W. P. Pulcifer, Armory S-I 1883 1896

R

AR Adam Rhulman, Armory S-I 1835-54
Harpers Ferry muskets and rifles

CR Cadwalader Ringgold, Capt., USN 1828-62

CFR Charles F. Rogers, Armory S-I 1917
Colts

CSR Charles S. Reed, Maj., USA 1938-40
Colts

DR Daniel Reynolds, Civilian, USN 1863

DR David Rice, Armory S-I 1835-63
Stocks

FR Frank Richard, Armory S-I 1871
1871 Springfield

FR Frederick Rodgers, Cdr., USN 1873
Remington cal. .44 cartridge revolvers

FER F. E. Randall, Armory S-I 1906

FMR Francis M. Ramsay, Cdr., USN 1870
Remington Model 1866 pistol pattern brass trigger guards

GDR G. D. Ramsay, Jr., Capt., USA 1863-65

GMR George M. Ransom, Capt., USN 1854-77
Colt Model 1851 converted revolvers

GTR Garland T. Rowland, Capt., USA 1932-34
Colts

GWR George W. Rodgers, Cdr., USN 1839-59
Colt Model 1851 cal. .36 revolvers

HR Harold Richards, Armory S-I 1940
Colts

IR I. Randall, Armory S-I 1904-06

JR J. Reid, Armory S-I 1904-10

JRjr James Rockwell, Jr., Lt., USA 1874-76
Smith & Wesson Schofield revolvers

JFR J. F. Riley, Armory S-I 1898-1910

JWR James W. Reilly, Maj., USA 1859-95
Remington cal. .44 cartridge revolvers

JWR James W. Ripley, Gen., USA 1832-60

MER Mark E. Reynolds, Armory S-I 1937
Colts

SCR S. C. Rowan, Cdr., USN 1850-60
Colt 1851 conversions

THR T. H. Rodgers Armory S-I 1881-1904

WR William Richardson, Armory S-I 1808

WR William Russell, Armory S-I 1808

WHR William H. Roberts, Armory S-I 1863
Colt Model 1860 cal. .44 revolvers

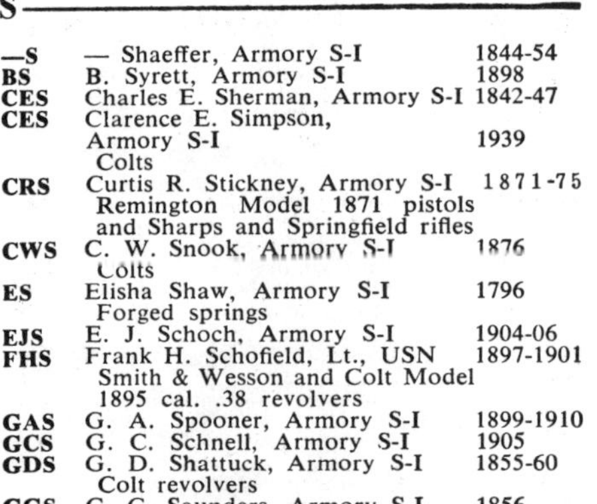

S

—S — Shaeffer, Armory S-I 1844-54

BS B. Syrett, Armory S-I 1898

CES Charles E. Sherman, Armory S-I 1842-47

CES Clarence E. Simpson, Armory S-I 1939
Colts

CRS Curtis R. Stickney, Armory S-I 1871-75
Remington Model 1871 pistols and Sharps and Springfield rifles

CWS C. W. Snook, Armory S-I 1876
Colts

ES Elisha Shaw, Armory S-I 1796
Forged springs

EJS E. J. Schoch, Armory S-I 1904-06

FHS Frank H. Schofield, Lt., USN 1897-1901
Smith & Wesson and Colt Model 1895 cal. .38 revolvers

GAS G. A. Spooner, Armory S-I 1899-1910

GCS G. C. Schnell, Armory S-I 1905

GDS G. D. Shattuck, Armory S-I 1855-60
Colt revolvers

GGS G. G. Saunders, Armory S-I 1856
Colt Dragoon revolvers

GHS Gustavus H. Scott, Cdr., USN 1828-73
Colt Model 1860 cal. .44 revolvers

GHS Gilbert H. Stewart, Col., USA 1915-19 and
Smith & Wesson and Colt revolvers and Model 1911A1 cal. .45 semi-automatic pistols

GWS G. W. Sword, Armory S-I 1856-59
Colt Dragoon revolvers

GWS G. W. Smith, Armory S-I 1857
Colt Dragoon revolvers

GWS G. W. Sherman, Armory S-I 1858-60
Colt Dragoon revolvers

GWS G. W. Schuman, Armory S-I 1858-60
Colt Dragoon revolvers

HS H. Saunders, Armory S-I 1875

HS Harrison Shaler, Lt. Col., USA 1945
Remington Rand cal. .45 Model 1911A1 semi-automatic pistols

HS H. Stephens, Lt., USA 1816
Starr swords

HS Howard Stockton, Lt., USA 1868

HS H. Syrett, Armory S-I 1904-06

Initials	Name, Title	Period
JCS	John C. Sharpe, Lt., USN	1837
JCS	John C. Stebbins, Armory S-I North-Hall carbines, Waters pistols, and Deringer rifles for Navy	1834-41
JCS	John C. Symmes, Capt., USA	1847-61
JS	Jacob Shough, Armory S-I Henry, Fry, and Guest pistols, and Henry rifles and pistols	1809-11
JS	Josiah Snell, Armory S-I North & Cheney pistols	1800-01
JS	Joseph Smith, Capt., USN	1809-37
JS	John Stebbins, Armory S-I	1819-35
JS	James Stillman, Armory S-I	1831-60
JS	James Stubblefield, Armory S-I Harpers Ferry pistols of 1807 and 1808, and Harpers Ferry rifles and muskets	1807-21
JS	John Symington, Col., USA Model 1855 Springfield rifle-muskets	1832-63
JFS	J. F. Sullivan, Armory S-I	1898-1908
JLS	J. L. Sticht, Lt., USN Smith & Wesson and Colt Model 1895 cal. .38 revolvers	1895-1904
JLS	J. L. Strong, Armory S-I	1896-1902
JNS	J. N. Sollace, Armory S-I	1831-60
LAS	Laurence A. Stone, Lt., USA Colts	1940
LS	Luther Sage, Armory S-I North Model 1813, 1816, and 1819 pistols, R. Johnson, Waters, Whitney, Pomeroy, and Starr muskets, and 1815 and 1818 Springfield pistols	1813-37
MS	Maurice Sherman, Armory S-I Colts	1940
OS	Oliver Sexton, Armory S-I	1841
RS	Robert Sears, Col., USA Colt Model 1911A1 cal. .45 semi-automatic pistols and Colt Ace cal. .22 Service Model semi-automatic pistols	1940-45
RS	Richard Smith, Lt. Col., USMC	1806-30
RNS	R. N. Stannard, Armory S-I	1906
SPS	Sidney P. Spaulding, Lt. Col., USA Colts	1940
TS	Thomas Stuart, Capt., USA	1813
TS	Thomas Sangster, Capt., USA	1812
TS	Thomas Stockton, Capt., USA	1812-25
TS	Townsend Stith, Capt., USA	1810
THS	Thomas H. Stevens, Lt., USN Starr cutlasses	1816
TJS	T. J. Smith, Col., USA Colts	1935-37
WS	William Smith, Armory S-I Evans barrels and bayonets	1828-60
WS	W. Syrett, Armory S-I	1904-06
WBS	William B. Shubrick, Capt., USN	1806
WES	W. E. Strong, Armory S-I Colt Model 1911 cal. .45 semi-automatic pistols	1916
WHS	W. H. Soderholm, Maj., USA Colts	1936
WRS	W. R. Shipley, Armory S-I	1898

T

Initials	Name, Title	Period
ACT	A. C. Trego, Capt., USA Smith & Wesson cal. .45 revolvers and clips	1918
DAT	D. A. Turner, Armory S-I Colt Model 1911 cal. .45 semi-automatic pistols	1914-15
DMT	Daniel M. Taylor, Capt., USA Colt cal. .38 revolvers	1892
DT	Daniel Tyler, Lt., USA Starr muskets	1831-50
EMT	E. M. Tinkham, Armory S-I	1898-1906
ET	Elisha Tobey, Armory S-I North Model 1816 Navy, 1819, and 1826 Navy pistols, 1818 Springfield pistols, and R. Johnson, Starr, and Waters muskets	1816-21, 1823-30
ET	Edwin Tyler, Armory S-I	1813-19
FHT	Feno H. Traux, Lt., USA Hi-Standard cal. .22 semi-automatic pistols	1941-42
GT	George Talcott, Lt., USA	1836-38
HT	H. Tracy, Armory S-I	1831-50
JBT	J. B. Tyler, Armory S-I	1894 and 1899-1910
JT	Joseph Tarbell, Capt., USN	1798-1815
JT	Josiah Tatnal, Capt., USA Massachusetts Arms Co., Adams revolvers	1858
JT	John Taylor, Armory S-I Colt Model 1860 cal. .44 revolvers, and Starr cal. .36 revolvers, and Savage cal. .36 revolvers	1861-62
JTT	John T. Thompson, Capt., USA Colt Model 1900 cal. .38 semi-automatic pistols, Colt Model cal. .45 revolvers, and Smith & Wesson cal. .38 Army revolvers	1896-1902
NCT	Nathan C. Twining, Lt., USN Colt Model 1895 cal. .38 Navy revolver	1885-95
OAT	O. A. Thornton, Armory S-I	1907-10
PAT	P. A. Teahan, Armory S-I	1907-10
SLT	S. L. Tuttle, Armory S-I	1894
WAT	William Anderson Thornton, Capt., USA Nippes Model 1840 musket, Ames, Aston R. Johnson, and Waters pistols, and Massachusetts Arms—Adams, Remington Beals, Savage, Colt Paterson, Walker, and Dragoon revolvers	1840-61
WT	William Taggart, Civilian, USN	1843-49
WT	William Turnbull, Armory S-I	1843-51

U

Initials	Name, Title	Period
CFU	C. F. Ulrich, USN gunner Colt and Smith & Wesson revolvers	1905

V

Initials	Name, Title	Period
CJV	C. J. Van Amburgh, Armory S-I Colt machine guns	1912
CV	C. Valentine, Armory S-I	1898-1905

W

Initials	Name, Title	Period
AAW	A. A. White, Armory S-I	1905-06
ALW	A. L. Woodworth, Armory S-I Colt cal. .38 revolvers	1905-28
ARW	Abraham R. Woolley, Capt., USA Muskets	1813
BRW	B. R. Whitcomb, Armory S-I	1899
CAW	C. A. White, Armory S-I	1904-05
CHW	C. H. Wicker, Armory S-I	1904
CW	Charles Woodman, Armory S-I Smith & Wesson Schofield cal. .45 revolvers	1859-77
CW	Charles Williams, Armory S-I Harpers Ferry and North pistols, Starr swords, and contract muskets	1807-14
DW	Decius Wadsworth, Col., USA	1802-21
EAW	E. A. Williams, Armory S-I Spencers	1875
ELW	E. L. Wunder, USN Colts	1903
ELW	Edson L. Wood, Armory S-I Colts	1940
FCW	Frank C. Warner, Civilian, USN Remington Model 1866 pistols	1867-69
FEW	F. E. Willson, Armory S-I	1901-06
FEW	F. E. Wyman, Armory S-I Colts	1909
GAW	George A. Woody, Lt. Col., USA Colts	1929-32 and 1941-42
GAW	George A. White, Armory S-I	1875
GEW	G. E. Worden, Armory S-I	1905-06
GLW	G. L. Wotykns, Capt., USA Colts	1926
GTW	G. T. Weaver, Armory S-I	1882-99
GW	George Wells, Lt., USN	1845-62
GW	George Wright, Armory S-I Aston pistols	1850-52
GWW	George W. Wassmer, Armory S-I Colts	1939
HCW	H. C. Washburn, Armory S-I	1904-06
HDW	H. D. White, Armory S-I	1899
HEW	H. E. Wallenberg, Armory S-I	1906
HW	Henry Walke, Com., USN Remington Model 1866 pistols	1866-68
JAW	J. A. Wood, Armory S-I	1875
JAW	J. A. Woodward, Armory S-I	1906
JGW	J. G. Woodbury, Armory S-I	1904
JHW	J. H. Wowarth, Armory S-I	1898
JW	Joseph Weatherhead, Armory S-I North Model 1819 pistols, and Starr, Waters, R. Johnson, and Pomeroy muskets and rifles	1821-22, 1825-26
JW	John Williamson, Capt., USA	1838-49
LW	Leicester Wheeler, Armory S-I	1818
MTW	Marine T. Wickham, Armory S-I Evans muskets and North pistols	1811-15
MW	M. Witkop, Armory S-I	1909
RCW	Russel C. Wilson, Armory S-I Hi-Standard cal. .22 semi-automatic pistols	1941
RHKW	Robert Henry Kirkwood Whiteley, Capt., USA Aston Navy pistols, Colt Dragoon and Model 1851 revolvers, Starr, and Savage revolvers, and Sharps carbines	1838-75
TW	Thomas Warner, Armory S-I R. Johnson pistols	1833-37
WAW	W. A. Walker, Jr., Armory S-I	1905-06
WDW	Wm. D. Whiting, Cmdr. USN Remington pistol barrels	1867-68
WFW	W. F. Wilbur, Armory S-I	1905-06
WW	William Walters, Armory S-I Remington Model 1861 cal. .44 revolvers and Pettengill cal. .44 revolvers	1862-64

Y

Initials	Name, Title	Period
—Y	— Young, Armory S-I	1844-54

Z

Initials	Name, Title	Period
GZ	G. Zauche, Armory S-I	1905-06 ■

Arms Production

Detailed information on firearms that is of interest to the serious student of firearms history. The material is generally limited to arms that are no longer manufactured.

Inspectors Marks

Small arms of the U. S. Army and Navy bear an initial or initials which are called inspectors marks. These marks appear on stocks, grips, or metal parts. Some arms, especially older ones, have more than one inspector's initial or initials. The barrel was inspected before the rest of the arm was produced, and thus there may be one inspector's mark on the barrel and another on the rest of the parts.

The Army and Navy purchased arms from commercial outlets and also contracted directly with the manufacturers. The Navy also purchased some arms from the Army.

From early days to 1831, most small arms contract inspectors were civilians or Springfield Armory employees. Officers who served as inspectors were from the Army Ordnance Dept. or the Navy Bureau of Ordnance. There were also sub-inspectors who had regular jobs at Springfield Armory, and small arms inspection was in addition to their regular duties. Army or Navy inspectors had control over all sub-inspectors.

Supplemental List of Inspectors' Marks

A

Initials	Name, Title	Period
JA	John Avis, ASI[1], Waters flintlock pistols	1837-38
RKA	Remick K. Arnold, ASI	1862-77
SA	S. Adams, ASI	1860

B

Initials	Name, Title	Period
AB	A. Buckminster, ASI, Sample carbines	1860
AGB	A. G. Bennett, ASI, Rem. Navy revolvers, Ward-Burton rifles	1868-79
AJB	A. J. Bristol, ASI, Rem. Navy revolvers, Sharps trial carbines	1870-79
CEB	C. E. Buckland, ASI	1859
EBB	Edgar B. Boyd, ASI	1862
ECB	Edmund C. Bailey, ASI	1862
FRB	F. R. Bull, ASI, Sample arms	1860
GFB	Geo. F. Bowen, ASI	1878
GGB	Geo. G. Bowe, ASI, Stocks	1862-63
HBB	Hanson B. Bullock, ASI	1862
LCB	L. C. Brown, ASI	1874
PB	Pomeroy Booth, ASI	1862
RHB	R. H. Bailey, ASI, Cadet M1869 Rem. rifles, Sharps trial carbines	1870-85
RLB	R. L. Buckland, ASI, Sample arms	1860
RPB	Robert P. Beales, ASI	1862-79
TAB	Theodore A. Belknap, ASI	1862
WB	Wm. Bradbury, ASI	1860
WB	Wm. Brown, ASI	1862
WLB	Wm. L. Bates, ASI, Rem. Navy Revolvers	1870-79

WHB	Wm. H. Barber, ASI	1862
WHB	Wm. H. Bulkley, ASI	1862
ZB	Zadock Butt, ASI	1862

C		
AHC	Archibald H. Ceiley, ASI	1862-63
AHC	A. H. Clark, ASI, FI[2], Springfield M1868 rifles	1859-79
APC	A. P. Casey, ASI, Army & Navy perc. double-action revolvers	1859-61
APC	A. P. Cobb, ASI	1874
CBC	Calvin B. Cross, ASI	1862-63
CGC	Chas. G. Curtis, ASI	1862-63
CSC	Chas. S. Cotton, Lt. USN	1863-64
EKC	E. K. Colton, ASI	1860-64
EWC	E. W. Clark, ASI	1870-79
FC	Francis Camp, ASI	1859-61
GC	Geo. Curtis, ASI	1861
GBC	G. B. Cruzen, ASI, Rem. 1861 New Model revolver	1861
GEC	Geo. E. Chamberlain, ASI	1862-79
HBC	H. B. Cooley, ASI, FinSI[3]	1862-63
JC	Jas. Chattaway, ASI, Sample arms	1862-63
JEC	J. E. Cummings, ASI, MI[4]	1862-63

[1] *Armory Sub-Inspector*
[2] *Filing Inspector*
[3] *Finishing Shop Inspector*
[4] *Milling Inspector*

JHC	J. H. Cooper, ASI, Rem. M1868, Cadet M1869 rifles, Rem. Navy revolvers	1870-79
JLC	Jos. L. Cottle, ASI, Colt .45 M1873 revolvers	1863-75
MWC	M. W. Carr, ASI	1862-63
PTC	Patrick Thos. Cunningham, Lt., USN	1863-64
WC	Wm. Chapman, ASI, Purchased arms and parts	1860-64
WGC	W. G. Chamberlain, ASI	1859-75
WHC	Wm. H. Carver, ASI	1862-63
WHC	Wm. H. Chandler, ASI	1862-63

D		
EMD	Edward M. Dustin, ASI, Burnside carbines	1862-63
GHD	Geo. H. Dupee, ASI	1862-63
HD	H. Dana, ASI, MI	1862-63
JSD	John S. Duston, ASI	1862-63
LD	L. Dustin, ASI, Purchased arms and parts	1863
SD	Stephen Danks, ASI, SI[5]	1863
SAD	S. A. Dinsmore, ASI	1862-63

E		
JRE	John R. Esleek, ASI, Parts of arms	1863
WDE	W. D. Earl, ASI, Parts of arms	1863

F		
EF	Edward Flather, ASI	1862-63
ESF	Edward S. Frost, ASI, Stocks	1862-63
GBF	Geo. B. Foote, ASI	1862-63
HGF	H. G. Firmin, ASI, Rem. M1868 and M1869 rifles, Rem. Navy revolvers, Sharps, Spencer, Enfield rifles	1868-82
WF	Wm. Foster, ASI, Parts of arms	1863

G		
ASG	Albert S. Granger, ASI, FSI[6]	1862
CNG	Chas. N. Goodrich, ASI, FSI	1862-63
GDG	Gilbert D. Greason, ASI	1862
GHG	Geo. H. Graham, ASI	1862

H		
CPH	Chas P. Hill, ASI	1874
FH	Fred Harvey, ASI	1862
GH	Geo. Hosmer, ASI, FSI, Rem. M1870 rifles, Ward-Burton rifles, Spencer rifles	1862-89
GHH	Geo. H. Hubbard, ASI, FSI	1862-63
HDH	Henry D. Hastings, ASI	1862
HEH	H. E. Hollister, ASI, FSI	1862-63
HHH	H. H. Hamilton, Sharps rifles	
HHH	H. H. Hartzell	
JH	John Hannis, ASI	1862
JH	Jos. Hannis, ASI, 1838 Waters pistols	1838-62
JEH	J. E. Hitchcock, ASI, FSI	1862-63
JHH	Jos. H. Hubbard, ASI	1862
SH	Samuel Hawkins, ASI	1862
TBH	Thos. B. Hawks, ASI, FSI	1862-63

J		
CTJ	C. T. Judd, ASI, MI	1863
HDJ	Henry D. Jennings, ASI	1862-63
MMJ	Martin M. Johnson, ASI	1862-63

K		
AHK	Albert H. Kirkham, ASI	1862-63
HK	Henry Kirk, ASI	1862-63
JWK	John W. Keene, ASI	1862-63
MTK	Marian T. Krepps, ASI	1862-63

L		
CFL	C. F. Lewis, ASI, MI	1863
GAL	Geo. A. Lawrence, ASI, Stocks	1862-63
HSL	Homer S. Lathe, ASI	1862

Stock Inspector
Filing Section Inspector

N		
AHN	A. H. North, ASI	1862
FSN	F. S. North, ASI	1862-63
LN	L. Newell, ASI, Sharps rifles Springfield rifles, bayonets, swords	1876-85
WN	Walter North, ASI	1859-63

M		
ACM	Alfred C. Manning, ASI	1863
DFM	Dexter F. Mosman, ASI	1862
EM	Edwin Martin, ASI	1862
EM	Edward McCue, ASI	1862
JM	John Maggs, ASI	1862
JHM	Jas. H. McGuire, ASI	1862
MWM	M. W. Morley, ASI, Purchased arms	1862

P		
AGP	Anson G. Perkins, ASI, FI[2]	1859-62-63
DAP	Dwight A. Perkins, ASI	1862
EHP	Edwin H. Perry, ASI	1862
GP	Geo. Palmer, ASI	1862
JWP	J. W. Porter	
SWP	S. W. Porter, ASI, FI[2]	1859-60-62
WP	Wm. Page, ASI	1863

Q		
BFQ	B. F. Quimby, ASI	1863

R		
AR	Alexander Reuben, ASI, FSI	1862-63
FR	Franklin Root, ASI	1862-63
GBR	Geo. B. Russell, ASI, CEI[7], cavalry equipment	1862-63
TWR	Thos. W. Russell, ASI	1862
WHR	Wm. H. Russell, ASI	1862-63

S		
CS	Clark Swallow, ASI	1862
DPS	Daniel P. Strong, ASI	1862
FSS	Frederic S. Strong, ASI	1862
FWS	F. W. Sanderson, ASI, Stocks, Rem. trial arms	1862-79
GES	Geo. E. Saunders, ASI	1862
HS	Horace Scott, ASI	1878-85
HS	Harris Smith, ASI, FShI[8]	1862-79
JS	John Stahl, ASI, PI[9]	1868
PTS	P. T. Safford, ASI	1874
RTS	R. T. Safford, ASI	1862-85
TJS	T. J. Stevenson, ASI, Enfield rifles	1870-79
UPS	Urial P. Strong, ASI	1862
WWS	W. W. Street, ASI	1874-75

T		
AHT	Albert H. Thompson, ASI	1862
DWT	D. Waldo Tyler, ASI	1862
GFT	Geo. F. Tucker, ASI	1862
JT	Jerome Towne, ASI	1862-63
WPT	Wm. P. Taylor, ASI, SI	1862-64

V		
HEV	Henry E. Valentine, ASI	1862
PV	P. Valentine, ASI, Purchased arms	1862
TV	Thos. Valentine, ASI	1863

W		
CEW	Chas. E. Wilson, ASI	1862
ECW	E. C. Wheeler, ASI, FSI, Springfield rifles, Rem. Navy revolvers, Ward-Burton rifles, Spencer rifles	1862-82
HWW	Henry W. Wilcox, ASI	1862
JW	John Wilder, ASI, PI, Enfield, Sharps, Spencer rifles	1868
JPW	Jos. P. Wells, ASI, MI	1863
NW	Nathaniel Whiting, ASI	1862
SLW	Samuel L. Worsley, ASI, FSI	1862-63
WSW	Wm. S. Wood, ASI, FSI	1862-63

[7] *Cavalry Equipment Inspector*
[8] *Filing Shop Inspector*
[9] *Parts Inspector*

—LT. COL. R. C. KUHN, USAFR (Ret'd)

Fakery in Antique Arms Revealed by Acid Test

Etching solutions reliable means to detect gun forgeries

By ELLIOTT L. MINOR

In altering old firearms to resemble much more valuable specimens of other makes, fakers often remove original die-produced markings, lengthen barrels, or make other changes by welding operations. Sometimes new markings are substituted for old. Fortunately, experienced gun collectors can detect many transformed pieces by careful examination. Where this fails, however, there is a more positive method of detection. An attempt can be made to "revive" the original markings or to detect welded barrel extensions or welded joints by means of etching solutions.

Their uses are based on the fact that most metals consist of a mass of microscopic crystals arranged in one of several patterns. When a hardened stamping die such as commonly used in marking and numbering firearms is forced into the metal, the normal crystal pattern around and beneath each of the resulting markings is disturbed. When the marking is filed off, crystal disturbance or strain hardening often remains in the metal. By treating the metal with a suitable etching solution, the hardened areas etch at a different rate than the softer surrounding area. For this reason obliterated markings may appear, quite legibly, after treatment. If, however, the metal was ground too deeply, the markings cannot be restored because the areas of strain have been removed. Similarly, engraved markings cannot be restored through use of an etchant as the normal crystal patterns around the inscriptions are not affected by action of the graver.

(The collector is cautioned that the etching solutions contain harsh chemicals that remove finishes. Their uses on fine specimens with much original finish could be disastrous for this reason.)

Scientists have long used a number of etching solutions in preparing metal surfaces for microscopic examination. More recently law-enforcement agencies have used successfully such solutions as a method of restoring obliterated markings on typewriters, firearms, automobile engines, and other items. Because satisfactory results can be obtained with a minimum of experience and without elaborate equipment, this method also is well suited for use by gun collectors.

Techniques for restoring obliterated markings are quite simple. Locate a likely area where markings may have been removed, such as the barrel top. The surface may require some polishing with fine abrasive cloth or paper to remove rust or minor pits. Next, degrease this area, using an effective solvent such as acetone. The etching solution can now be applied to the metal. Since it may require several days for markings to appear, it is recommended that a wax or modeling clay dam be formed around the area to contain the fluid. Fresh solution can be added at intervals with an eyedropper. The etching process can be speeded up by swabbing the surface with a heated solution, but care must be taken that the markings do not appear and then vanish forever due to too-fast etching.

Etching can be speeded up with an electrical current. This usually causes the markings to appear in several minutes, depending on how deeply the metal was removed. Required additional equipment includes a supply of cotton swabs, a source of low voltage direct current, such as a six volt heavy-duty lantern battery, and two lengths of small-diameter insulated wire with small alligator clips attached on the ends.

Surface preparation and degreasing are similar to the method described. By means of the alligator clips and wires, the positive battery pole is connected to the work, and the negative pole to a cotton swab dipped in etching solution. Attach the clip so as not to interfere with the swabbing area of cotton, but so that there is a flow of electricity through the solution. The area then is swabbed gently until markings appear, care being taken not to proceed too fast and risk losing the marking altogether.

Etching solutions can either be mixed by the individual or purchased ready mixed from a commercial source. In NRA Museum tests, adequate results were obtained on steel using a solution of 12 cc. of concentrated hydrochloric acid ($HC1$), 12 cc. water (H_2O), and 1 gram cupric ammonium chloride ($CuNH_4C1_2$). This and many other etching solution formulas specifically suited for use on various types of metals can be found in Vol. 1, of J. Howard Mathew's book, *Firearms Identification.* Etching solutions may be purchased from Faurot, Inc., 299 Broadway, N. Y., or Sirche Fingerprint Laboratory, P. O. Box 269, Moorestown, N. J. Local distributors of police equipment are likely to stock fluids made by these firms.

The "electrolytic" method was used with good results on four known counterfeit handguns in the NRA Museum collection. One was a fake Rigdon & Ansley revolver made from a Colt M1851 Navy by removing all Colt markings and turning the barrel partly round to dragoon shape. Additional locking notches were milled in the cylinder, bringing the number of notches to 12. The marking "CSA" was stamped on top of the flat portion of the barrel.

The second revolver had the remains of the markings "Haiman" and "Columbus, Ga." and presumably was made from a Manhattan .36 caliber percussion revolver. The third "Confederate" handgun tested was supposed to be a Dance revolver made in Texas. It had a round European-appearing brass trigger guard, part-round barrel, and, typically, no recoil shields.

For the fourth test, a fake Palmetto Armory single-shot percussion pistol was selected. Several dozens of these pistols are said to have been faked in the midwest from U. S. M1842 percussion pistols, both makes being identical.

Etching solution was applied to both the "Rigdon & Ansley" and "Dance" handguns on the flat barrel top where Colt M1851 revolvers are marked. Enough of the original markings reappeared to prove conclusively that the barrel portions were made by Sam Colt, the man who appropriately advised, "Beware of counterfeits." An attempt was made to restore the serial numbers near the lower front of the frame. No success was achieved on the "Dance" revolver, but the numbers of the "Rigdon & Ansley" fairly jumped out with only about three strokes of the electrically-connected swab. The barrel top of the "Haiman" revolver yielded the following letters: "K, N.J.", undoubtedly the remains of the "Newark, New Jersey" address of the Manhattan firm.

Solution was applied on the lock plate of the Palmetto pistol. The marking "H. Aston" appeared almost exactly within the area of the phony Palmetto Armory marking. Markings on the tail of the lock were illegible.

After obliterated markings appeared, the etched parts were washed thoroughly to remove remaining traces of solution, and then dried and oiled. In the absence of any original finish, the experiment did no physical harm to these old pieces—but it would have come as a severe shock to any unwary buyer who had purchased them at top prices as very rare specimens of the arms they were faked to represent. ■

Let the Gun Collector Beware

Guide for separating replicas and fakes from the real McCoy

By E. DIXON LARSON

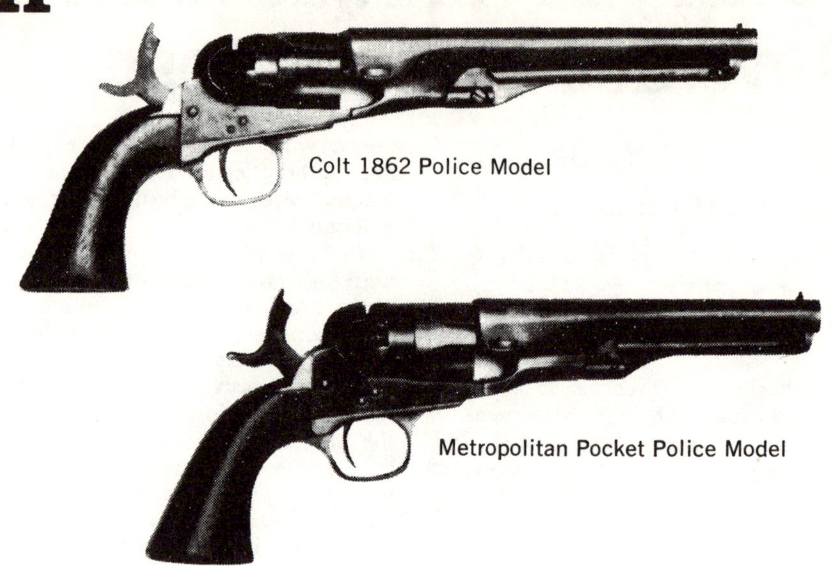

Colt 1862 Police Model

Metropolitan Pocket Police Model

Original or copy?

EVERY collector and enthusiast is plagued with the thought of being tempted by a scarce piece and trying to remember the specific differences that make it a rarity. Ever present is the possibility that it may be a forgery, and it is difficult to recall the basic facts that are so necessary when purchasing antique arms. Although many enthusiasts own and continually build onto a voluminous library, most cannot recall all the facts from each book, and certainly it is not convenient to carry one's library with him.

Usually, an enthusiast progresses into being a semi-advanced collector without realizing it. A change in values seems to occur also. A couple of hundred dollars for a scarce arm doesn't seem as much as when the hobby started. The collector can watch himself pursue specific arms he never considered in the beginning. A desire for the scarcer arms seems to increase directly proportionate to the years of interest.

Unfortunately, there is little to compare with the disappointment one experiences from purchasing an arm that is out of character and could have been avoided with just a little clue or two. A current example is that of the Colt fluted cylinder Army Model 1860. It is doubtful that the total production equaled the number of re-worked plain Army models that have emerged from basements into the hands of disappointed buyers. This is also true of many other models that approach each other in similarity.

Barrel lengths in Winchester arms are critical. Many have been observed short ⅛" to ¼" of their original length. Such a shortening was practiced by old gunsmiths when the muzzle became "belled" from cleaning and use. This can greatly affect the value of the arm.

Even reputable dealers have been known to be in error due to lack of knowledge. A common dealer-seller error is the offering of Colt single-action models with "eagle grips" that are not compatible with the serial number range in which the grips were offered by the Colt Company. In other words, the year the arm was manufactured fails to match the years the grips were available. This can be a costly oversight to the purchaser. But most differences can be ferreted out with a little knowledge and an inherent right to be on guard.

In an effort to provide a comprehensive handy reference, most of the leading books and articles published in the last 15 years have been studied and computerized on a frequency basis, so that the following salient points could be provided. It is believed these will keep many from entering into a costly transaction, by providing a ready reference into the information that an enthusiast may not have time or perseverance enough to obtain. Some of the information presented is found only in expensive books, in factory records, or by consultation with arms collectors.

Remember, these are basic points, and there are exceptions. The notations that follow are directed to rare, specific models of each group or type or arm or model that are very desirable, generally expensive if original, and usually not readily available for comparison. However, exotic or extremely expensive models have been omitted because it is assumed that a prospective buyer of such items would be knowledgeable, consult an arms expert, or purchase from a reputable dealer.

COLTS

Colt 2nd Model Dragoon

Rarest of 2nd Models between serials 800-10000. Has "V" hammer spring and no hammer bearing wheel.

Colt 3rd Model Dragoon

8" barrel models, usually in 19000 serial range.

7½" barrel models cut for a stock, serial numbers between 16620 and 17940, IRON backstrap.

Colt 1851 Navy Model, cut for stock

Usually 4-screw frame, IRON backstrap (few transition models with brass backstrap observed between 164000 and 166000). Standard serial ranges: 67000-79000, 90000-93000, and 128000's.

Note: The IRON backstrap is on all models for Colts cut for a stock.

Colt Percussion 1851 Square Back Navy Model

Under Serial Number 3000, small cut-out lug, lever screw enters from right side.

Colt 1849 Pocket Model

Scarce variation has the Hartford address with iron backstrap and trigger guard.

Colt "Wells Fargo" Rammerless Model

Either big or small trigger guard with two-line address (out of charac-

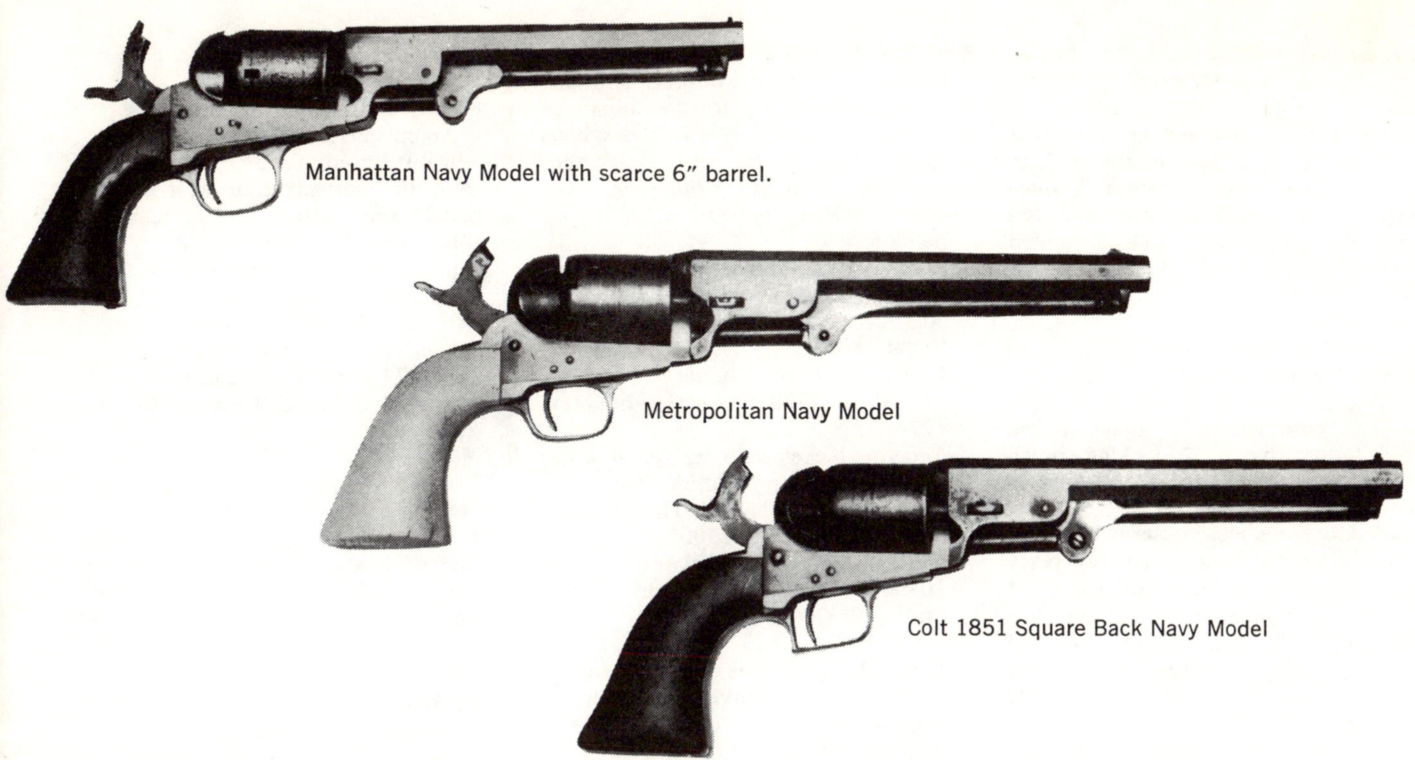
Manhattan Navy Model with scarce 6″ barrel.
Metropolitan Navy Model
Colt 1851 Square Back Navy Model

The informed collector spots that slight difference.

ter with one-line address). This model should be verified by a gammagram, X-ray, or written guarantee by a reputable seller.

Colt Percussion 1860 Fluted Cylinder Army Model

Serial number under 6000. Left-twist rifling, opposite to the right twist of the standard 1860 Army Model.

Colt Single-Action Army Models

Possible Custer guns—between 11500 and 14500. Eagle grips—1882 to 1896 or serial numbers 73000 to 168001.

Long fluted cylinders—1915 or serial numbers 330000 to 331380.

Smokeless powder models—1896 or serial numbers after 165000. Wells Fargo & Company factory marked—1906 or serial numbers 287000 to 311525.

.357 Magnum caliber—1935—serial number 356000 to present.

Script barrel markings—before 15000.

Round ejector heads—serial number 85000.

Flat top target models—1888 or after serial numbers 125000.

Factory change to stamping number on frame only and under the grip (right side)—1920 or after serial number 338000.

Bisley Model

Serial numbers between 159000 and 325000.

Original barrels will be stamped "Bisley Model" on left side of barrel. 7½″ barrel length is scarcest and most desirable.

Colt Marked Copies

All licensed Colt copies of percussion models, primarily .36 caliber arms, will have W. G. Ormsby's naval scene on the cylinder and two-line barrel markings: "Colt Brevete" or "Colt Patent." Beware of many types of misleading marking on these models.

Colt Cartridge Conversions

Rarest of the Colt factory conversion is the Richards-Mason type WITHOUT loading cut out and standard Mason ejector.

Smith & Wesson Revolvers

Variations exist in the Smith & Wesson arms, but so minor that only an advanced collector would be concerned. However, 3 specific identification points that might concern a neophyte S&W collector are:

Model No. 1, .22 R.F. cal., serial numbers 844 to 3242.

"WF&Co. Ex" stamped on UNDER side of ejector housing on Schofield Models Type 1.

Japanese Model No. 3 has Navy anchor on underside ahead of trigger guard.

Remington Big Frame Percussion Models

Army 1861 Models—6494 to 10446.

Navy 1861 Models—2044 to 21533.

New Model Navy—24246 to 44944.

These serial ranges are for the early type Remingtons, listed to protect the buyer from being confused with the later type.

Remington Big Frame Cartridge Models

1875 Single Action, 7½″ barrel—serial numbers 1 to 25000. 1890 Single Action, 5½″ and 7½″ barrel - serial numbers 1 to 2000.

Metropolitan Navy Percussion Revolver

Rolled-on cylinder scene after serial 1800. Revolvers marked for distribution by "H.E. DIMICK - ST. LOUIS" were in the serial range 1100 to 1800.

Metropolitan Pocket Police Model

In appearance almost an exact copy of the 1862 Colt Police Model, except loading lever is held by a small visible screw and no ratchet as is characteristic with the Colt. 50% of the total 3000 were UNMARKED; therefore a premium price is usually attached to marked specimens.

Manhattan Navy Percussion Revolver

Easy recognized. 6″ barrel is considered scarcer than the 6½″ and usually commands a premium price; therefore careful examination should be made of 6″ models.

Nepperhan 31 Cal. Percussion Revolver

Non-integral trigger guard of brass differs from other makes such as Bacon and Manhattan.

The following are scarce, but because of similarity to replica models currently available, specific differences are noted:

Columbus Percussion Revolver

Highly prized model, serials under 100. Marked in two lines "Columbus Firearms Manufacturing Co., Columbus Ga." on barrel and cylinder.

Griswold "Marked" Percussion Revolver

7-3/16″ to 7½″ barrel lengths, serial

numbers under 4000, last 5" plus turned round. A cryptic letter proof on frame, cylinder, and barrel. Brass frame.

Several replica percussions are presently being aged and represented as the "Griswold and Gunnison." Inasmuch as the originals were both red and yellow brass and had unmarked barrels, this is a simple "fake."

Leech & Rigdon Percussion Revolver

Scarce variation of Navy type revolver, marked atop barrel "Leech & Rigdon Novelty Works, C.S.A." Pin & ball loading lever catch common on this model, also on those marked "Augusta, Ga. C.S.A." that have 12 locking notch cylinder, termed "Rigdon & Ansley" revolvers.

Spiller & Burr Percussion Revolver

A very close kin to the Whitney Navy revolver, known by most collectors and not rare or difficult to recognize. The problem results from a worn or abused Whitney minus marking being passed as a "Spiller & Burr." Remember—the FRAME IS BRASS.

Dance Brothers Percussion Revolver

Caution on this big frame .44 caliber that resembles a Colt Dragoon, because some clever "fakes" from England have turned up at U.S. gunshows. An obvious distinguishing feature of the Dance revolver is absence of recoil shields, making a FLAT FRAME.

Tucker, Sherrard & Company Percussion Revolver

Tucker & Sherrard revolvers come in the image of Colt Dragoon 44's and 1851 Navy Models with either round or square guards, the most obvious difference being NO CUT OUT lug for loading. Beware of acid etched, CRUDE barrel markings "L.E. Tucker & Sons."

LeMat "Grapeshot" Percussion Revolver

Very few enthusiasts can recognize the three basic types of this rare and desirable Civil War Arm.

1st Type - Serial 1 to 450. Barrel part octagon and part round, trigger spur, swivel lanyard ring, loading lever on RIGHT side.

2nd Type—Serial 450 to 951. Lever changed to LEFT side, octagon barrel, trigger spur, swivel lanyard ring.

3rd Type—Serial 951 to highest number 8448 reported by a reputable dealer. Octagon barrel, solid lanyard ring with hole, no trigger spur, lever on LEFT side.

Original barrel length was 7.3".

Bacon, Cooper Tranter, Wesson & Leavitt, Allen & Wheelock, Savage Navy, Adams, Deane, Starr, Rogers & Spencer, Whitney, and other miscellaneous manufacturers are relatively easy to recognize and identify. Further, there are few exceptions in these makes.

WINCHESTER LEVER ACTION RIFLES

Excluding minor variations and differences that appeal to the advanced Winchester student, an effort has been made to catalog the more important points the average Winchester fan would do well to remember.

Henry Rifles

Purchased by the U.S. Army, marked C.G.C on barrel and frame; serials 3000 to 4200.

Model 1866

Round barrel rifles made after 1876 - over serial 130000. Total production 1779.

Octagon barrel carbines—*over* serial 150000. Total production 791.

Transition models with Henry markings—*under* serial 23000.

Turkish models - between serials 104000 to 118000, and 81000 through 96000.

Model 1873

Barrel lengths over 24" are scarce. Also scarce are heavier barrels measuring over 23/32" across the flats at muzzle.

Model 1876

Saddle ring carbines—standard barrel length 22", with a rapid taper.

—North West Mounted Police generally marked N.W.M.P. on right side of stock in a semi half moon pattern. Serials below 12000, 23801 to 33000, and 43900 to 66000.

Muskets—32" round barrels with a rapid taper.

High Wall Single Shot

Serials under 600 can be considered scarce and rare, and must have FLAT SIDE receivers.

Model 1886

Octagon barrels—found both tapered and untapered. Tapered octagon barrel with lightweight stock is scarcer.

Saddle ring carbines—very scarce in this model. Barrel length 22".

Barrels over 28"—should have TWO magazine bands.

Musket—the 1886 is rarest of lever action muskets. Barrel length 30".

Model 71 (1886-type actions)

Made in 2 barrel lengths, 24" and 20".

Model 1892

Muskets—barrel length 30".

Model 53

Extremely scarce. 22" barrel, button magazine, shotgun butt plate. Marked "Model 53" on left side of barrel.

Watch for rebuilt Model 92's with Model 53 marked barrels.

Model 65 (1892 action)

Extremely scarce. 22" and 24" rapid taper barrels. Marked "Model 65" on right side of barrel.

Watch for rebuilt Model 92's with Model 65 marked barrels.

Model 1895

FLAT SIDE—can be considered rare and desirable; also has one-piece lever instead of two-piece as on later rifles. A further premium could be expected from an 1895 FLAT SIDE with one-piece lever and a PISTOL GRIP original stock. Saddle ring carbines —scarcest WITH receiver sight in place of the conventional ring. ■

LeMat 1st Model (at top), with loading lever on right, is characterized by half-round half-octagonal barrel, trigger spur, and lanyard swivel. (Below) LeMat 3rd type, with loading lever on left, lacks trigger spur. Lanyard loop is integral with frame.

Counterfeit Arms

By Harry C. Knode

A matter of primary concern to arms collectors is the commerce in counterfeit arms and accessories presented as genuine, with fraudulent intent. This practice has been brought to the fore in recent years by the great increase in number of arms collectors, plus inflated valuations placed on more desirable items.

The answer to all this is caution. Be suspicious of one-of-a-kind types, and don't be rushed into buying. An honest seller will give you time to obtain other opinions. An appraisal from a reliable dealer costs relatively little, and is a form of cheap insurance.

Comparison only method

The only safe way to authenticate a rare and valuable item is to compare it with a similar item that is known to be genuine.

If there is the slightest suspicion that a gun has been welded or brazed, that a trigger guard has been altered, that a barrel has been lengthened or shortened, a serial number changed, or a hole welded up, by all means arrange for an X ray or gammagram.

The best protection is a bill of sale incorporating a complete description of the arm or accessory. No honest dealer or other individual will object to its use, and it affords redress at law if the item is later proved spurious.

The accompanying photographs illustrate some of the ways in which faking is done. Note that they vary from clever to palpable.

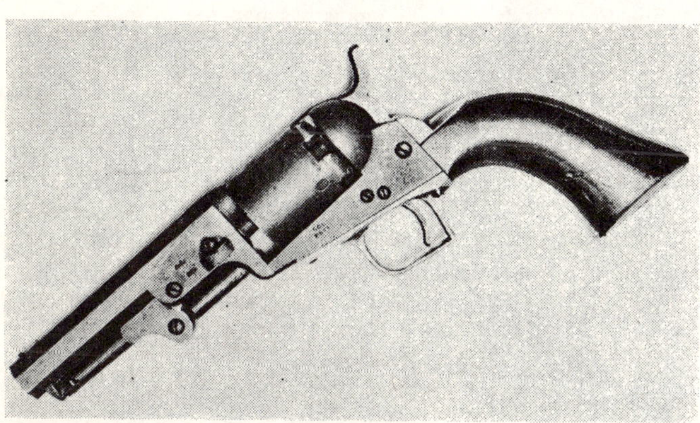

This Colt fake was made in England from parts of 2 different guns. Trigger guard and some other parts were from a Baby Dragoon; balance from the later Pocket Model. Serial numbers on some parts were engraved

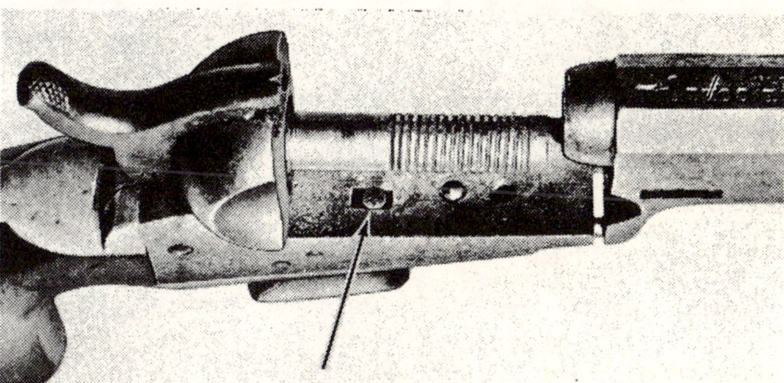

Note round cylinder locking bolt in rectangular frame slot on English-made Colt fake

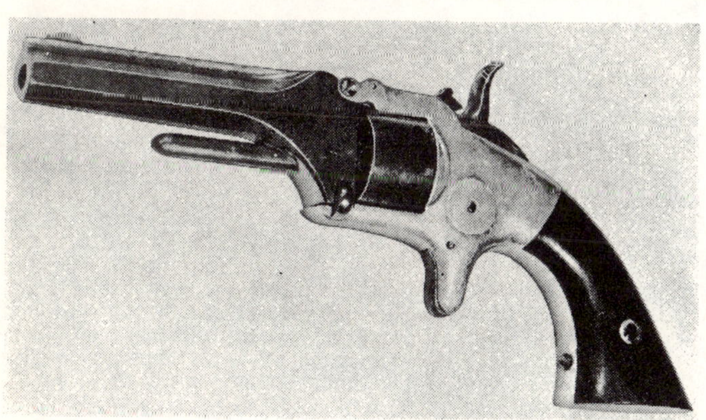

This composite fake incorporates Manhattan frame with Smith & Wesson First Model, First Issue barrel assembly

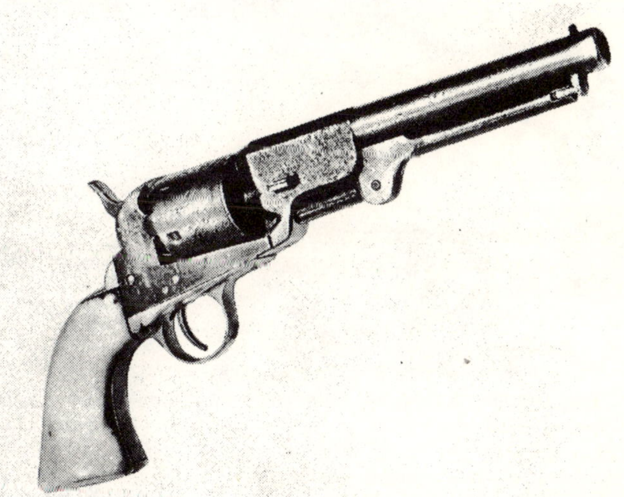

A rather fine job of faking a Dance Brothers Confederate revolver

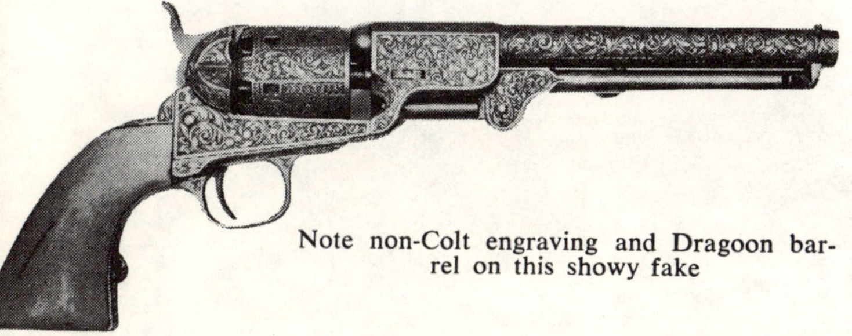

Note non-Colt engraving and Dragoon barrel on this showy fake

Crudely stamped spurious barrel signature on 1851 Colt Navy

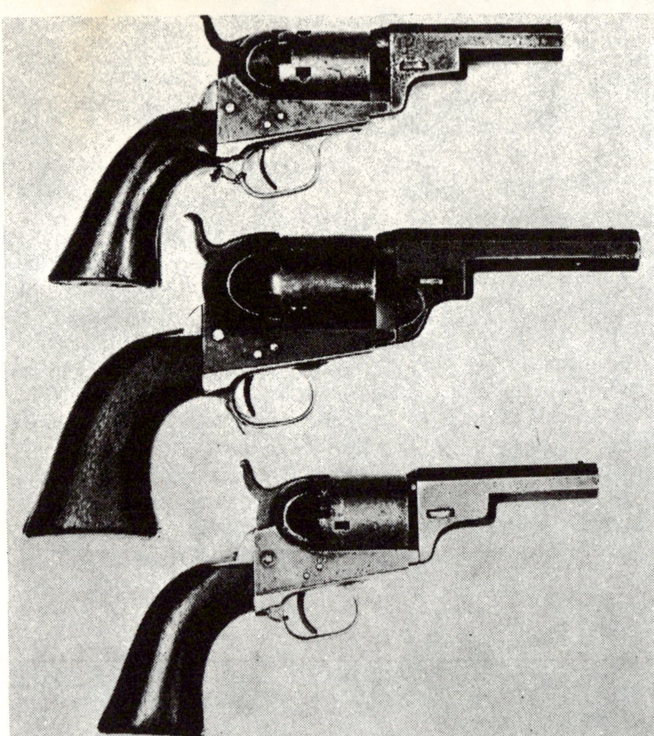

Top and bottom guns are genuine cal. .31 Wells Fargo Pocket Models made without loading slots, as barrels were removed to load the cylinders. Cal. .36 fake gun in center was attempt to make a "Wells Fargo" Navy from an 1851 Navy. Authentic Wells Fargo Navy revolvers are unknown. On another specimen seen, loading slot had been welded up, a type of alteration that shows up clearly in a gammagram

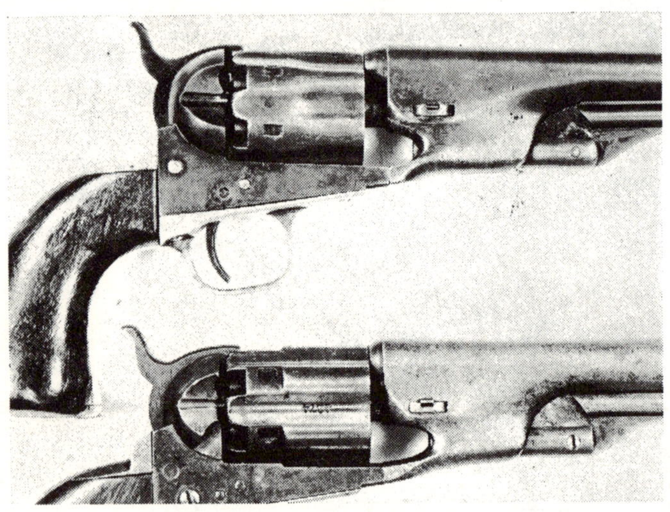

Comparison between fake cylinder on full fluted 1860 Army revolver (top) and an honest specimen. Very poor workmanship

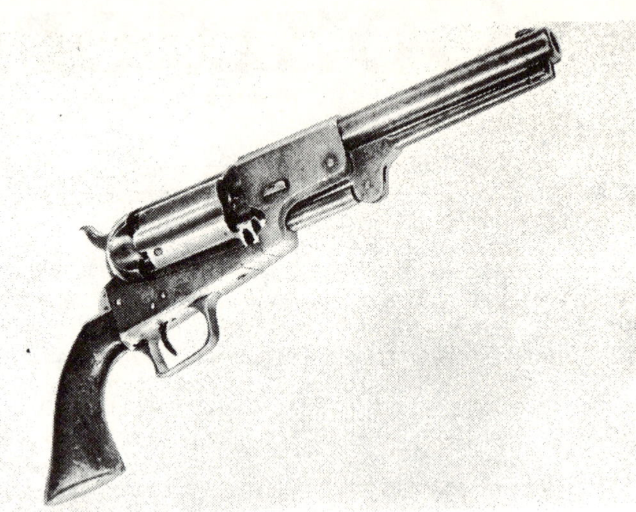

A fine First Model Colt Dragoon has had the cylinder worked over to fake a rare fluted Dragoon

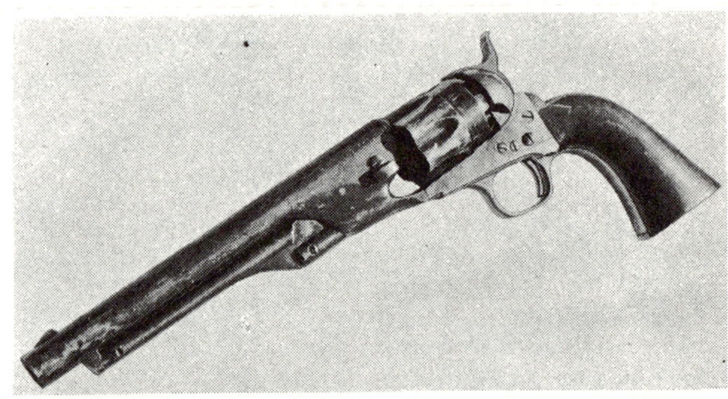

An attempt to make a gun that was never produced by Colt's—a semi-fluted-cylinder Model 1860 Army. The faker even went so far as to make a stamp to put the patent date on the cylinder

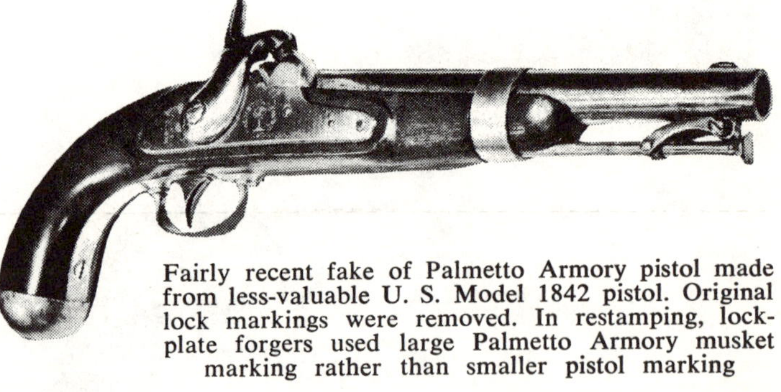

Fairly recent fake of Palmetto Armory pistol made from less-valuable U. S. Model 1842 pistol. Original lock markings were removed. In restamping, lockplate forgers used large Palmetto Armory musket marking rather than smaller pistol marking

Fake semi-fluted cylinder from Model 1860 Army. Note that stamp was made too long

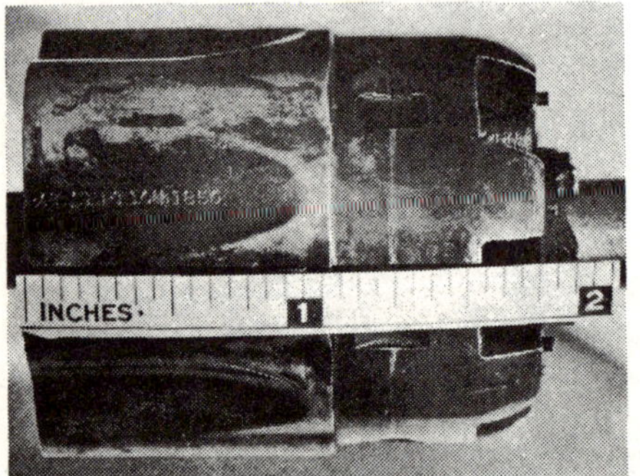

Note difference between genuine (left) and fake (right) Palmetto Pistol markings. Markings on fake pistol are too clean and sharp, and effect of aging is noticeably absent from surface of lockplate ■

NRA Membership

Be sure to check your desired Membership Status, and print clearly so that your membership will be entered correctly. Thank you.

Name ______________________ Birthdate ____/____/____

Street ______________________ Apt. ______

City ____________ State ______ Zip ______ Phone No. ______

☐ Check enclosed ☐ Bill me (NOT FOR LIFE MEMBERSHIP)

Check magazine you wish to receive (choose one)

☐ **The American Hunter** ☐ **The American Rifleman**

NRA
- ☐ 1 Year .... $ 15
- ☐ 3 Years ...... $ 40
- ☐ 5 Years ...... $ 60
- ☐ Life $300

NRA SENIOR
(65 and over)
- ☐ 1 Year .... $ 10
- ☐ Life $150

NRA ASSOCIATE
(spouse)
(without magazine)
- ☐ 1 Year .... $ 10
- ☐ Life $100

NRA JUNIOR
(Under 18)
- ☐ 1 Year $10
- ☐ 1 Year .... $ 3 (without magazine)
- ☐ Life $150

FOREIGN: add $2.00 postage per year

NRA Membership

Be sure to check your desired Membership Status, and print clearly so that your membership will be entered correctly. Thank you.

Name ______________________ Birthdate ____/____/____

Street ______________________ Apt. ______

City ____________ State ______ Zip ______ Phone No. ______

☐ Check enclosed ☐ Bill me (NOT FOR LIFE MEMBERSHIP)

Check magazine you wish to receive (choose one)

☐ **The American Hunter** ☐ **The American Rifleman**

NRA
- ☐ 1 Year .... $ 15
- ☐ 3 Years ...... $ 40
- ☐ 5 Years ...... $ 60
- ☐ Life $300

NRA SENIOR
(65 and over)
- ☐ 1 Year .... $ 10
- ☐ Life $150

NRA ASSOCIATE
(spouse)
(without magazine)
- ☐ 1 Year .... $ 10
- ☐ Life $100

NRA JUNIOR
(Under 18)
- ☐ 1 Year $10
- ☐ 1 Year .... $ 3 (without magazine)
- ☐ Life $150

FOREIGN: add $2.00 postage per year

NRA Membership

Be sure to check your desired Membership Status, and print clearly so that your membership will be entered correctly. Thank you.

Name ______________________ Birthdate ____/____/____

Street ______________________ Apt. ______

City ____________ State ______ Zip ______ Phone No. ______

☐ Check enclosed ☐ Bill me (NOT FOR LIFE MEMBERSHIP)

Check magazine you wish to receive (choose one)

☐ **The American Hunter** ☐ **The American Rifleman**

NRA
- ☐ 1 Year .... $ 15
- ☐ 3 Years ...... $ 40
- ☐ 5 Years ...... $ 60
- ☐ Life $300

NRA SENIOR
(65 and over)
- ☐ 1 Year .... $ 10
- ☐ Life $150

NRA ASSOCIATE
(spouse)
(without magazine)
- ☐ 1 Year .... $ 10
- ☐ Life $100

NRA JUNIOR
(Under 18)
- ☐ 1 Year $10
- ☐ 1 Year .... $ 3 (without magazine)
- ☐ Life $150

FOREIGN: add $2.00 postage per year

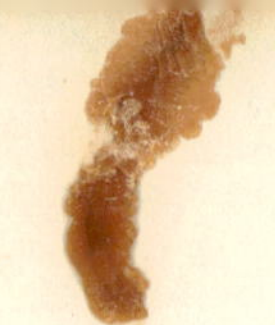

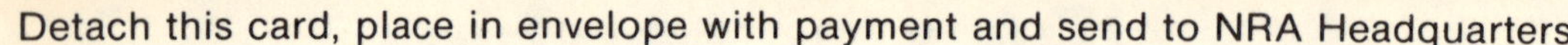

Detach this card, place in envelope with payment and send to NRA Headquarters.

NRA Pledge

I hereby apply for membership in the **National Rifle Association.** I certify that I am a citizen of the United States; that I am not a member of any organization which has as any part of its program the attempt to overthrow the government of the United States by force or violence; that I have never been convicted of a crime of violence; and that, if admitted to membership, I will fulfill the obligations of good sportsmanship and good citizenship.

National Rifle Association
1600 Rhode Island Avenue, N.W., Washington, D.C. 20036

Signature ______________________________

Detach this card, place in envelope with payment and send to NRA Headquarters.

NRA Pledge

I hereby apply for membership in the **National Rifle Association.** I certify that I am a citizen of the United States; that I am not a member of any organization which has as any part of its program the attempt to overthrow the government of the United States by force or violence; that I have never been convicted of a crime of violence; and that, if admitted to membership, I will fulfill the obligations of good sportsmanship and good citizenship.

National Rifle Association
1600 Rhode Island Avenue, N.W., Washington, D.C. 20036

Signature ______________________________

Detach this card, place in envelope with payment and send to NRA Headquarters.

NRA Pledge

I hereby apply for membership in the **National Rifle Association.** I certify that I am a citizen of the United States; that I am not a member of any organization which has as any part of its program the attempt to overthrow the government of the United States by force or violence; that I have never been convicted of a crime of violence; and that, if admitted to membership, I will fulfill the obligations of good sportsmanship and good citizenship.

National Rifle Association
1600 Rhode Island Avenue, N.W., Washington, D.C. 20036

Signature ______________________________